BRITISH SOCIAL TRENDS SINCE 1900

Also by A. H. Halsey

CHANGE IN BRITISH SOCIETY
ORIGINS AND DESTINATIONS
HEREDITY AND ENVIRONMENT
POWER AND IDEOLOGY IN EDUCATION (*with J. Karabel*)
THE BRITISH ACADEMICS (*with M. Trow*)
EDUCATION, ECONOMY AND SOCIETY (*with Jean Floud*)
ENGLISH ETHICAL SOCIALISM (*with Norman Dennis*)

British Social Trends
since 1900

A Guide to the Changing Social Structure of Britain

Edited by
A. H. Halsey

Fellow of Nuffield College
Professor of Social and Administrative Studies
University of Oxford

First edition (*Trends in British Society since 1900*) 1972
Second (completely revised) edition (*British Social Trends since 1900*) 1988

Published by
THE MACMILLAN PRESS LTD
Houndmills, Basingstoke, Hampshire RG21 2XS
and London
Companies and representatives
throughout the world

Typeset by Latimer Trend & Company Ltd
Plymouth

Printed in Hong Kong

British Library Cataloguing in Publication Data
British social trends since 1900: a guide
to the changing social structure of Britain.
1. Great Britain—Social conditions—
20th century
I. Halsey, A. H.
941.082   HN385
ISBN 0–333–34521–5 (hardcover)
ISBN 0–333–34522–3 (paperback)

Contents

Contents

List of Tables

List of Figures

xxiv

List of Figures

Notes on the Contributors

George Sayers Bain, Professor of Industrial Relations, School of Industrial and Business Studies, University of Warwick.

Peter Brierley, European Director, Missions Advanced Research and Communications Centre, Bromley, Kent.

David Butler, Fellow of Nuffield College, Oxford.

Judith Chance, Graduate student, Nuffield College, Oxford.

David Coleman, University Lecturer in Demography, Department of Social and Administrative Studies, University of Oxford.

Andrew Dilnot, Senior Research Officer, Institute for Fiscal Studies.

A. H. Halsey, Professor of Social and Administrative Studies, University of Oxford, and Fellow of Nuffield College.

Kenneth Macdonald, Lecturer in Applied Social Studies, Department of Social and Administrative Studies, University of Oxford, and Fellow of Nuffield College.

Klim McPherson, University Lecturer in Medical Statistics, Department of Community Medicine and General Practice, University of Oxford, and Fellow of Nuffield College.

Julia Maxted, graduate student, Nuffield College, Oxford.

Catriona Mirrlees, graduate student, University College, London.

Julia Parker, University Lecturer in Social Administration, Department of Social and Administrative Studies, University of Oxford.

Ceri Peach, Faculty Lecturer in Geography, School of Geography, University of Oxford, and Fellow of St Catherine's College.

Robert Price, Lecturer, School of Industrial and Business Studies, University of Warwick.

John Ridge, University Lecturer in Sociology, Department of Social and Administrative Studies, University of Oxford.

Vaughan Robinson, Lecturer in Geography, University of Swansea.

Nigel Walker, Wolfson Professor of Criminology (Emeritus), University of Cambridge.

Bruce Wood, Senior Lecturer in Government, University of Manchester.

Preface

The first edition of this book was intended as a guide to the changing social structure of twentieth-century Britain. It covered the period from 1900 to the end of the 1960s. By the mid-1980s the time came to bring this compilation of British social facts up-to-date. Hence this second edition, which perhaps is better described as a sequel in that both the country and the sources of numerical information about it have changed significantly.

As to sources, *Social Trends* was introduced in 1970 by the then Head of the Government Statistical Services, Claus Moser (now Warden of Wadham College, Oxford). From the outset it included trend statistics from official sources reaching back to the 1951 census and even further back towards the beginning of the century on some demographic topics. This government publication also included some attempt to compare Britain with other countries, especially the 'first world' states, with membership of OECD. By 1987, therefore, an arithmetic post-war history of a large number of facets of British social structure had been compiled with at least some comparative international reference. The contents of the present book are rather wider and they draw on unofficial as well as official statistics. However, *Social Trends* has been a significant addition to the array of relevant government publications and has greatly aided us in bringing the book up-to-date. Moreover, I am indebted to Miss Jackie Morris of the Central Statistical Office (CSO) for her patient courtesy in securing access to recent official statistics. In particular I am grateful for the opportunity of incorporating into Chapter 1 a modified version of my contribution to *Social Trends* (no. 17) under the title 'Social Trends Since World War II'.

The structure of this sequel to *Trends in British Society since 1900* remains as it was with the exception of the omission of the previous chapter on leisure. There has, however, been some change of authorship. Most of the contributors to the first edition have remained. These and the new contributors gratefully acknowledge the work put into the first edition by Constance Rollett, Robert Bacon, John Pimlott, John Sheehan, John Vaizey, Kathleen Jones, Robert Currie, Alan Gilbert and Juliet Cheetman. We also had valuable labour on the statistics from Lisa Halsey, Catriona Mirrlees, Jane Parker and Monica Dowley. I would also like to acknowledge the superbly efficient wordprocessing provided by my secretary Miss Sally Wright.

I remarked in the first Preface that readers would inevitably find errors, omissions and dispensable inclusions. They did, and this new work has profited from their advice. It is reasonable to suppose that a third edition will complete the story of the twentieth century in Britain as a whole. I should therefore be glad to hear of any new corrections and suggestions.

A. H. HALSEY

Acknowledgements

The authors and the publishers wish to thank the following who have kindly given permission for the use of copyright material:

Gower Publishing Company for the tables from *British Social Attitudes Survey 1986* edited by R. Jowell and C. Airey; Her Majesty's Stationery Office and their Departments – Office of Population Censuses and Surveys and Central Statistical Office – for permission to reproduce Crown Copyright material acknowledged in various places in the book; Population Investigation Committee for the table from *British Control Practice and Marital Fertility in Great Britain* by C. M. Langford; Unwin Hyman for the table from *Statistics of Education*, by J. Vaizey and J. Sheehan; Carfax Publishing Company for the tables and the quotation from *Oxford Review of Education*, by Maurice Scott; Oxford University Press for permission to use the tables from *Origins and Destinations* by A. H. Halsey, A. F. Heath and J. M. Ridge, 1980, and the table from *World Christian Encyclopaedia*, © Oxford University Press 1982; Cambridge University Press for the tables from *Government and the Universities in Britain* by J. Carswell; The Universities Central Council on Admissions for the table derived from Statistical Supplements; R. A. Pinker for renewed permission to use tables from *English Hospital Statistics 1861–1938*; *The Lancet* for the table from 'Mortality Decline in Widening Social Inequalities', by M. G. Marmot and M. E. McDowall, 1986; Anglican Consultative Council for the table 'Age Structure of Church of England Clergy' from *Preparatory Information, The Lambeth Conference 1978*; Church House Publishing for the figures drawn from various editions of *The Church of England Year Book* and *Church Statistics*; Macmillan for material from *British Political Facts 1900–1985* by David Butler and Gareth Butler.

Every effort has been made to trace the copyright-holders, but if any have been inadvertently overlooked, the publishers will be pleased to make the necessary arrangement at the first opportunity.

1 Introduction: Statistics and Social Trends in Britain

A. H. Halsey

Within a few years of our work for the first edition of this book the post-war period came to an end. Dates are somewhat arbitrary but perhaps the winter of 1973–4 can be taken as the turning point of a 30-year economic boom into a period of recession and readjustment affecting the whole of the 'first world' and not least the United Kingdom. For this reason alone a new book of statistical tables indicating trends and shifts in social structure needs no apology. British society in any case has experienced many changes throughout the twentieth century. The task and the interest is therefore to put the new developments of the most recent decade into the perspective of the experience of the three previous generations. Our method is numerical: the result is a series of statistical trends with comments on their sources, guidance against their misuse and suggestions for their interpretation.

FACTS AND STATISTICS

The facts, it is sometimes held, especially in the form of numbers, speak for themselves. But neither life nor sociology are so happily simple as that. The very concept of a trend may generate unintended distortion. Trends are absurdly easy to find. If a series of observations between two points of time yields neither random fluctuation nor absolute stability there must be a trend. But what follows? Stability may be equally significant. A zero rate of population growth would have momentous social implications in most countries in our time. Facts are given significance or meaning only in the context of some prior theory or interpretation, whether explicit or implicit. Bias may come in subtle forms from contentious, unproven or false theories of history. There are no established laws of historical development or decline. The view that social institutions evolved and culminated in Victorian liberal society – the so-called Whig version of British history – could be said to be an extravagant preference for graphs moving upwards to the right. It is now regarded with scepticism. The underlying theory is a belief in progress and in the superiority of European civilisation, especially the activities of British men. Similarly the Marxist theory of history, at least for 'capitalist' societies, looks for downward trends, for example in the rate of profit or the income of proletarians, towards a revolutionary crisis.

1

The statistics about trends in British society in the twentieth century which are collected together in this book are vulnerable in the same way – a theory of social structure and social change must underlie them. To describe is also, however imperfectly, to explain. Statistical compilations of the kind made here can all too easily inform the student only to deceive. They may appear, or even purport, to 'speak for themselves': but this is never completely so, and often very far from so, for two broad reasons. There may be difficulties about the meaning of the numbers which arise from the manner of their collection and classification. Or, more fundamentally, the chosen collection may reflect a partial or distorted view of what is significant in social structure and change.

The first type of difficulty is the lesser: it can, admittedly laboriously, be avoided by careful description of the sources and of the method of collection and definition of the data. Thus one aim of each of the following chapters is to guide students in the use of the statistical sources and to point out the dangers in interpreting statistics which are typically collected for administrative purposes rather than to answer questions in the social sciences. Illustrations of this kind of difficulty recur in every chapter. Classifications may change, as for example in the occupational classifications used by the Registrar-General in successive censuses. Or the administrative basis of data collection may change, as for example in the statistical series on unemployment, the basis of which has shifted during the century with the extension of unemployment legislation.[1]

The second type of difficulty, which merges into the first, is more intractable. It arises if we reverse the logical procedure implied by a table of bare social statistics (that is, to infer a conception of change from the facts), and start instead from a conception of social structure and deduce what facts should be collected.

At the outset, therefore, the student must expect disappointment. Sociologists must rely to a considerable degree on data collected by other people for other purposes. A recurring problem is one which arises particularly in interpreting data relevant to social policy and the provision of welfare services. This is the difficulty of gaining from the statistics any idea of quality or adequacy. Obviously any analysis of health, or welfare services, or of housing, should include some statement about how far the standard or amount of the service supplied meets the need for it. Unfortunately, for the most part, the figures are concerned only with supply; independent measures of need which would be required to judge adequacy are sparse and controversial. In Chapters 10, 11 and 12 we look at the growth or decline of various public services but for the most part we are not able to relate them to the needs they are designed to meet.

In the face of theoretically inadequate statistics, the social scientist may, of course, resort to the academic sociological survey which can be designed in explicit relation to theory.[2] The direct sociological investigation is a powerful tool,[3] and 'panel' or longitudinal studies in which a cohort of respondents is followed over a long period of time[4] can yield information on trends: but such studies do not constitute more than a tiny fraction of the numerical data available, the bulk of which is collected and published by governmental agencies. The measurement of social mobility is a case in point which is dealt with in Chapter 5. To answer questions concerning the rate of mobility, reliance has to be placed on the results of direct sociological inquiry with the resulting difficulty that trends are difficult to establish without exact replication of a given study at later points in time. Theoretically informed statistical studies are rarely repeated by sociologists, partly for reasons of academic organisation (systematic storage of survey data only began in the 1960s), and partly because theoretical interest in the social sciences and definitions of concepts are influenced as much by fashion as by cumulation.

In practice, therefore, the problem remains largely that of adapting to social science ends statistics which, from the point of view of the sociologist, are a by-product of administrative and organisational activity. The authors of this book have had to wrestle with this problem in every chapter. One example is Bruce Wood's attempt (in Chapter 9) to use a sociological definition of urbanism in addition to the legal definition in terms of local government boundaries. Thus, in order to bring into focus the increasing interdependence of town and country he has to use such indicators as the journey to work, shops, and centres of entertainment. Another example recurs frequently in the analysis of stratification. When the sociologist attempts to use the census for analysis of any aspect of the British system of stratification, he finds a host of tables using 'social class' or 'socioeconomic group' as a variable. But frequently he wants to ask questions which pre-suppose distinction between class, status and power and between the 'subjective' and 'objective' character of stratified social relationships. The Registrar-General's tables may not yield answers. Thus, in a review of one of the best known earlier books of British political arithmetic,[5] and referring to three tables on 'industrial status', 'type of income', and 'social class' derived from the census, John Rex made the plaintive comment that:

> It is figures like this which drive the theoretically oriented sociologist to something like despair. Is the classification of the population into status groups meant solely as a statistical exercise, or are these classifications meant to refer to groups who might act as groups, or who might be thought of by their fellows as sharing a common way of life and meriting a characteristic degree of esteem? Clearly there does seem to be some claim that these represent real groups rather than statistical classifications. The ... table ... is said to be a classification according to 'social class'. But the implications of this term are left open to be filled in by the reader according to his own ideological preconceptions. Surely it would be more valuable if statisticians, who continually claim to be using sociological concepts, were

to find out what groupings were of real sociological importance and then seek to describe these, rather than the groupings which are of little importance, but which happen to be easily measurable.[6]

What is a society?

But what groups are of sociological importance? What notion of structure and change would be adequate to prescribe the scope and character of statistics to be collected, either officially or academically? This question is the first to confront anyone who tries to devise a book like this one but there is little agreement amongst sociologists about the definition of their own subject. What T. B. Bottomore wrote in 1962 is still true, 'The fundamental conception, or directing idea, in sociology is that of *social structure*'[7] but 'while many useful distinctions have been made, an adequate classification of societies, social groups and social relationships has still not appeared'.[8] This immediately raises the problem of what *is* a society? What are the limits in time and space which are in practice to be used meaningfully in order to specify British society as a more or less circumscribed network of social relationships.

The time span must be arbitrary since neither evolution nor revolution ever totally transform all the institutions of a society, its language, its kinship structure, its economy. We have chosen to confine our attention to the twentieth century, but for particular reasons we might just as reasonably have begun with, say, the first census in 1801, or the Education Act of 1870, or the beginning of the First World War in 1914. Though there would be general agreement that Britain in 1700 was a different society in respect of its fundamental institutions and culture from Britain in 1986 – the former being classified as pre-industrial or agricultural and the latter as industrially advanced or even post-industrial – there could be no agreement as to a unique date for any transition. Again, the partial social integration of England, Scotland, Wales and Northern Ireland as well as the regions within them raises the same question in relation to population. The main focus of this book is on England and Wales, each author having decided whether it would make more sense to use Great Britain or the United Kingdom as the aggregate unit for analysis in the light of knowledge of national variations in the structure of the social relationships with which he or she is concerned, and in the light of the availability of statistics. Already then, though we may begin with the intention of defining the data collection in terms of sociological concepts, there will be ambiguities in theory and obstacles in practice which result in more or less unsatisfactory compromise.

These problems of delimiting a society in both time and space might well be held to distort the picture induced from the statistics in this book. The period in question is one in which the relations between Britain and the rest of the world have changed radically; and the consequences are not only external but ramify throughout the indigenous structure of British life. During the century Britain has lost a vast empire which once:

> meant that India and Africa and parts of the Middle and Far East were also in a sense the lower strata of British society, the peak of which was the destined inheritance of the successful survivors of institutional discipline . . . The dissolution of the Empire and increasing real independence of the English-speaking dominions have contracted the size of the society over which the British elite – and British society as a whole – were superordinated.[9]

The Leninist thesis concerning export of exploitation by imperial countries cannot be tested merely by trend statistics on the material conditions of British manual workers. Neither the pattern of migration nor the course of immigration nor the statistical trends reported in the chapters on housing, health and welfare can more than partially and incompletely express the changes in class structure which have accompanied the transition of British society to its post-imperial position.

There is another severe limitation of the currently available statistics from which we have drawn. It is related both to the protest by John Rex referred to earlier – that statisticians do not use sociological concepts – and also to Edmund Leach's comment on the position taken by Meyer Fortes:

> The anthropologist's focus of interest is not in the [social structure] as such but in 'the way it works' – that is in the perception of the way in which living human beings, who are all the time being born, growing older, and dying, *pass through* an ordered system of offices.[10]

Official statistics, quite apart from their deficiencies as a record of objective experience, also seldom offer data on the subjective experience of actors in social systems. The census, and most surveys undertaken for Royal Commissions, eschew 'opinion'.[11]

Replicated surveys (or panel studies) yield trends. But again the theorist may be thwarted in that the surveys may not bear directly on the questions he wishes to put. In this sense the survey is never more than historical evidence, albeit precise and quantified, to be used like any other historical evidence as a servant which may not be adequate to its theoretical master.[12]

The central term 'social structure' has no single usage. It derives from biology as an organismic analogy. Among British anthropologists the term was defined by Radcliffe-Brown, in a way synonymous with the term social organisation, to include the whole network of social relationships in a society. Other anthropologists and sociologists have also used the term with empirical reference but more narrowly. If a society is a bounded network of social relationships, social structure is the relatively enduring and sanctioned set of relations within the network.[13] This definition again has the problem of time buried within it. It excludes the more ephemeral and fleeting of social interactions and emphasises the complex of *institutions* which constitute the more or less permanent structure of a society. Institutions are enduring, organised and sanctioned structures of relationships between individuals and groups, for example, marriage or property.[14] But the definition of enduring is ambiguous. It may refer to regularities in the life cycle in which individual members of the population move through sequences of positions or it may refer to stability in the pattern of behaviour and sanctioning involved in the institution.

It is, moreover, useful in defining social structure to include reference to the group formations as well as to the patterns of relationship involved, because the approach to institutions is often to define them as made up of social roles, and thereby to focus attention on individual actions. Though the difference is largely one of emphasis, many sociologists take the view that to concentrate on the roles which make up institutions (which in turn and in interaction make up social structure) is to distract attention from larger groups or collectivities such as social classes or religious denominations, which may occupy a significant place in a society, characterising and changing it in ways which are not fully appreciable if social behaviour is reduced to the acts or sum of the acts of individuals.

It should be added that those, particularly anthropologists, who work in the Radcliffe-Brown tradition link structure closely to function, and are interested as much in the working of institutions as in their form: but in either case 'a full description of the social structure would entail an analysis of all of the offices and corporations in the system – a task which would be plainly impossible but which can be carried out piecemeal in a partial way'.[15] The statistical series which comprise this book cannot be expected to achieve the impossible: they are indeed piecemeal and partial. In the context of the whole field of analysis of social structure and change they offer no more than a useful addition to other kinds of sociological, anthropological and historical evidence. They have, as we have pointed out, limitations derived from the non-sociological purposes for which the bulk of them were initially assembled, they have shortcomings of reliability, validity and consistency and, above all, they may defy, or at least resist, adaptation as indicators or measures of sociological concepts.

What then can be expected of them? It would seem reasonable to expect them to cover the essential institutional framework of the society for the chosen period. The functional prerequisites of society are such that certain institutions and groups are easily identifiable in all societies. We may list these minimum requirements as five institutional systems:[16]

A system of *production*
A system of *reproduction*

A system of *power and authority*
A system of *ritual*
A system of *communication*

All societies must produce goods and services and reproduce appropriate social personalities in order to maintain themselves. Hence the necessity for a division of labour, work organisations and familial and educational institutions. These two systems of production and reproduction together form the basis of social arrangements for the distribution of life chances which 'work' through a system of power and authority. At least in societies with a complex division of labour, life chances are distributed unequally and the society is composed of groups which are stratified by class, status and power. Social cohesion is then further reinforced through ritual institutions serving to assert and reassert values and to offer social recognition to personal events such as birth or marriage. Finally, society presupposes communication and hence requires institutions of language and organisations for storing and transmitting information.

Each of these elements has to be covered in the following chapters, but according to the special form of social structure which has emerged in modern Britain. It is at this point that our own emphases and interpretations have entered. We have paid little attention to the institutions of language.[17] The British population is almost universally literate in a common language, though in earlier centuries dialects and illiteracy would have to be taken into account, and in any case it is open to debate how far the existence of the Welsh language, of class-linked linguistic structure and usages, and of non-English-speaking communities among the ethnic minorities can be disregarded. Chapter 2 is concerned with those aspects of social structure which determine the reproductive character of the society. The productive system is dealt with in Chapters 3 and 4. Having thus outlined the twin bases of stratification we go on to examine social mobility in Chapter 5. Chapters 6 and 7 on schools and higher education are concerned with the formation of social personalities. Chapter 8 on the electorate and the House of Commons, as well as Chapter 9 on urbanisation and local government, may be seen as statistics on the distribution of power and authority. We then look at three aspects of the distribution of life chances – housing (Chapter 10), health (Chapter 11), and welfare (Chapter 12) in the context of the so-called welfare state. Chapter 13 on religion deals in part with the system of ritual, but Chapter 14 on immigration and ethnicity and Chapter 15 on crime may also be thought of as concerned with those institutions which maintain social cohesion. However, this classification of the content of chapters is somewhat arbitrary since all groupings and institutions tend to have multiple functions; for example, churches and chapels are also part of the system of communication, the economy, the socialisation process and the distribution of authority and power.

The trends shown in these chapters may now be briefly summarised in terms of the fundamental elements of social structure to which we have referred.

THE PRODUCTIVE SYSTEM

Though we have already characterised twentieth-century Britain as a contracting society because of its transition from the position of a dominant imperial power it is, none the less, important to note the expansion of its productive system. The Gross National Product (GNP) has risen since 1900 from £1926 million to £277 877 million in 1984. This increase in available goods and services has, of course, to be discounted in terms of inflation and population increase and cannot, in any case, be wholly satisfactory to the sociologist because of the methods used in calculating it. It excludes a wide range of social exchanges (for example, between friends and spouses) which are not defined as 'economic' and it includes economic exchanges such that, for example, the employment of more warders to guard more prisoners would count as economic progress and a reduction in the staff of tuberculosis clinics would count as economic regression. None the less, the amelioration of material conditions must be taken as a central fact of this century and especially of the period since the Second World War in Britain, as in other advanced industrial countries, which account for roughly a third of the world's population. Between 1900 and 1984 Gross Domestic Product (GDP) multiplied 4.5 times, consumers' expenditure 3.5 times and central government expenditure 6.5 times. Hence the interest of trends shown in Chapter 3 concerning the distribution of national income and wealth which gives us an indication of changes in the structure of classes and status groups. Again there are difficulties in interpreting the data, for example, the probability that tax avoidance is positively correlated with income and therefore inequality may be underestimated. Inequality remains the outstanding feature of both income and, especially, wealth distributions. As may be seen from Table 3.18, there has been a marked fall in the share of wealth held by the richest 1 per cent and richest 5 per cent of the population since 1900. Since 1966 this has also been true for the richest 10 per cent but the bottom 50 per cent have yet to show signs of benefiting. Taking occupational and state pension rights into account (Table 3.19) reduces the measure of inequality in wealth distribution. In 1983 the share of the richest 1 per cent was 12 per cent.

The changing class structure appears from another point of view in Chapter 4, where the development of the division of labour is traced. Income distribution statistics in Chapter 3 show a steady rise throughout the century in the share going to the salariat and this now can be seen as a growth of 287 per cent in the white-collar labour force between 1911 and 1981. White-collar workers are now in a majority, and within their ranks the growing number of managers and professionals, especially in the most recent decades, reflects the development of an increasingly complex division of labour on the basis of an increasingly scientific and capital-intensive technology. The productive life of the working class has been gradually transformed in the process. As a proportion of the labour force, manual workers fell from three-quarters to under one-half between 1911 and 1981. Figure 1.1 shows the trend. Hours of work have been reduced and paid holidays dramatically increased. Moreover, a sombre aspect of the same phenomenon, unemployment in the late 1970s and 1980s, returned to, or exceeded, the levels of the 1930s. The working man also figures less prominently on the work scene for the double reason of extended education and increased longevity.

Meanwhile corporate organisation of working men in occupational or industrial unions has increased sevenfold since the beginning of the century – increasing the proportion of actual to potential male union membership (or density) from 16.7 per cent to 54.4 per cent in 1979. Trade union membership and density fell with the rise of unemployment from 1980, but retained its grip on the employed population. The interests of groups included in the productive process have thus become highly organised. This should not, however, be interpreted as evidence for growing proletarian solidarity. The most dramatic

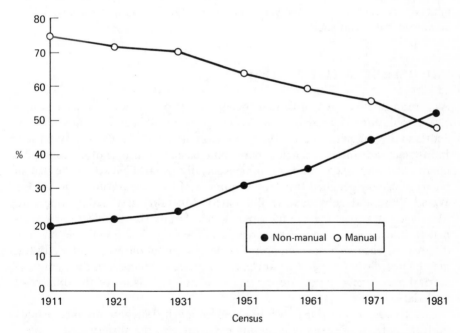

Figure 1.1   Percentage of occupied population in manual and non-manual occupational groups, 1911–81, Great Britain

Source: Table 4.1.

recent rises of unionisation have been among white-collar workers and in the 1970s among women. The interests of 'the proletariat' have become divided by a complex of competing occupational groups within the broad stratum of manual workers. Perhaps the most telling reflection of advancing material affluence in statistics concerning working-class living standards is that of the progressive shift of the definition of a 'cost of living' from its narrow and normative focus on the 'necessities of life' towards a retail price index reflecting the consumption patterns of the general population. These patterns have changed, especially since the war, towards greater emphasis on the purchase of leisure, private transport and consumer durables.

The upward trends in women's participation in paid employment are the opposite of those of men. By 1981 women formed 39 per cent of the total occupational population. Women have contributed especially to the growth of white-collar, especially clerical and sales, employment. This is all the more remarkable in the light of developments in the institution of marriage and of increased longevity which might have been expected to produce reverse results. Indeed, especially since 1951, the increasing participation of married women is the most outstanding factor in the changing balance between employment and non-employment – a fact which raises many questions about the changing structure of family life, and particularly for the Parsonian analysis of the relation between marriage, kinship and economy in an advanced industrial society.[18]

THE REPRODUCTIVE SYSTEM

As a reproductive system, British society has also expanded in this century. The population of England and Wales grew by 45 per cent and that of Scotland by 16 per cent to 1970 but from the late 1970s has stabilised. Industrially-advanced countries share some basic similarities of demographic history and there seems to be nothing especially remarkable about the British record. Fertility declined from the beginning of the century until the Second World War, and subsequently fluctuated. Mortality declined throughout. Marriage rates rose: the age of marriage fell: family size has decreased, one-person households have much increased among the young and the old, and divorce has become more common. The details are set out in Chapter 2 but, it may be noted, they are just as unclear as a guide to changes in the quality of marital and family life as are income statistics a measure of the quality of material existence.

The trends in marriage, fertility and longevity suggest an increasingly uniform pattern of sexual and family experience in the society as a whole – spinsterhood, membership of a large family or early death or bereavement have become increasingly rare. Nevertheless, it should be noted that differential experience in those respects continues to mark off the social classes from each other. Later marriage remains more common among the better off. The earlier inverse relation between family size and social class turned to a J shape by 1961. But the subsequent trends, within a further trend towards low fertility, have become complicated as is explained in Chapter 2.

Another aspect of the demographic trends, which appears again later in the discussion of urbanisation in Chapter 9, is the emergence of families and households which are not only smaller, but more mobile. The net result of internal migration during the century has been a faster rate of population growth in the South-East, South-West and Midlands, compared with the North of England, Scotland and Wales. Throughout the century Scotland has exported part of its natural increase, that is has 'reproduced' Englishmen, Americans, Canadians and Australians. At the same time, it emerges from Chapter 9, while nineteenth-century industrialisation had urbanised the society, there has been a more recent trend to 'reproduce' a more mobile and suburban style of life, which adds another facet to the attenuation of working-class life from its earlier attachment to the workplace. The working-class community as a dormitory annexe to the industrial factory has become less visible and more fluid in this century. This loosening of local occupationally homogeneous and single-class communities by increased mobility is also indicated by the trends in the issue of motor-car licences.[19] Before the Second World War the development of urbanisation was mainly an outcome of market forces. Since that time state planning has superimposed itself on the earlier pattern: a million and a quarter people have been moved to new towns or other planned 'overspill' developments outside the conurbations. In the same process the seven great conurbations (Table 9.6) lost 1.8 million between 1961 and 1981. And the inner city became recognised from the late 1960s as a locus of economic decline, physical deterioration and social disintegration.

Mobility is not restricted to movement within regions and localities. Part of the imperial legacy was a net loss of population overseas up to about 1931, a continuous interchange throughout the century, and a large influx of immigrants, especially between the end of the war and 1962 when the Commonwealth Immigration Act put severe restriction on entry. The more recent immigrations must certainly be regarded as working against the trend towards a more homogeneous society. At the same time the new ethnic communities have contributed disproportionately to the lower-paid manual strata and have hence introduced a new complication into the changing structure of class, status, and mobility.

Mobility has yet another dimension – what sociologists call social mobility normally refers to either intragenerational or intergenerational movement between occupational classes or strata carrying different degrees of prestige. The transformation of the occupational structure which we have noted has led to increased absolute rates of mobility especially upwards into the expanding middle classes. But in Chapter 5 the question of relative as distinct from absolute rates is also addressed, that is, the odds of moving to an occupational destination are compared for people starting from different occupational-class origins. Broadly, the evidence on relative mobility favours the view that there has been 'constant social fluidity' over the course of the century. But the detailed picture is more complicated and evidence for a trend towards polarisation of society since the mid-1970s is considered below. What is perhaps most remarkable is that the strong emphasis on egalitarian policies in education, which has developed during the twentieth century, has not led to unequivocal evidence of greater movement between the classes.

This is not to deny that the educational system has become more important as the agency of selection for different places in the hierarchy. But it re-emphasises the crucial influence of family background over the educational performance of children. The basic strategy for the equalisation of educational opportunity has been educational expansion. Children from all social origins have taken advantage of the developing opportunities for secondary and, more recently, for higher education. But despite this raising of the general standard, class differences in relative educational attainment have remained fairly constant.

The state has increasingly intervened in the distribution of life chances in this century, not only through taxation and education, but also in other fields of social policy which are dealt with below in the chapters on housing, health and welfare. Exchequer subsidies to housing rose from £1 million in 1919–20 to over £1500 million between 1983 and 1984. Expenditure on the health and welfare services rose from 3.9 to 6.2 per cent of GDP between 1960 and 1983. In consequence, just as there is more education, so there is more health, housing and welfare. But the impact of these expansions in state activity on the pattern of class differences in life chances is similarly unclear. Certainly infant mortality has dropped to a tenth of what it was at the beginning of the century. But the Registrar-General's Class V (of unskilled workers) has had consistently higher death rates than the other classes throughout, as well as higher rates of morbidity (measured by the consultation rate).

Housing standards have improved markedly during the twentieth century and there has been a wholesale shift into owner-occupation. There has been a diminution in the amount of overcrowding: 16 per cent of householders were living at a density of more than one and a half persons per room in 1921, but only 0.1 per cent in 1981. Amenities have also improved: 37 per cent of households lacked baths in 1951 and only 1 or 2 per cent in 1981.

Yet poverty, albeit relatively defined by the official recognition of rights to supplementary benefit, has not disappeared with a growing national income. Indeed, since the early 1970s there has been an upward trend, especially of the poorest who live at or below the supplementary benefit standard. In 1983 there were 19 million people (36 per cent of the population) living at or around the supplementary benefit level. Nor has rising prosperity meant more generous treatment of the poor. While assistance rates doubled in real terms between 1946 and 1984, their relation to average earnings remained the same.

POWER AND AUTHORITY

The great institutional centres of power in Britain, as in most advanced industrial societies, are in politics and the economy. We have already commented on the slow reduction of economic inequality shown by the trends in Chapters 3 and 4. Two aspects of the distribution of political power are dealt with in Chapter 8 – the electorate and its voting behaviour in Parliamentary elections and the social composition of Parliament.

This century has seen the completion of universal enfranchisement which started with the 1832 Reform Bill. By 1900 the electoral roll included 58 per cent of adult males. By 1950 plural voting had gone and some 95 per cent of adult men and women were on the roll. In 1969 the franchise was extended to 18-year-olds. But the enfranchisement of the whole population has not created enormous discontinuities in the political power structure. The number of women MPs never reached 40 until 1987. The pattern of party support is, of course, class related; but the Conservative Party has continued to attract a quarter of the votes of the unskilled and one-third of the skilled workers down to the present day. Meanwhile Conservative MPs, and even more, the members of Conservative cabinets, remain dominantly upper and middle class. They are recruited overwhelmingly from independent schools (70 per cent in 1983). The rise of the Labour Party permitted working-class leaders and trade unionists to enter government. But it, too, has recruited increasingly from the professional classes, and about a fifth of its post-war MPs were educated in the independent schools. Since 1966 more than one-half of the Labour MPs have been university graduates.

In the final section of Chapter 9, Bruce Wood discusses a further aspect of the distribution of political power, by focusing attention on the structure of local government. The traditional principle of separate government for town and country has been subject to a large amount of modification. The 1963 London Government Act, by creating the vast Greater London Council and 32 new London Boroughs, probably offers the clearest example. But, *in toto*, earlier changes were at least as dramatic. After all, no fewer than 350 county districts 'disappeared' in one decade (the 1930s), and from 1888 to 1970 the creation of 25 new county boroughs, coupled with more than 300 boundary extentions, meant the transfer of over 750 000 acres and 4.5 million people from the county to the county borough system of government.

Large though it may be, this rate of change would probably have been far higher but for two restrictive factors. First, there was the principle of an urban-rural dichotomy in local government. Secondly, successive governments were not prepared to legislate for anything which could be termed 'radical' change (London, possibly, apart). Modification there was, but most of it was directed at keeping up with the trends in urbanisation, discussed earlier in this chapter. As the 'bricks-and-mortar' approach to urbanisation was superseded by the 'sociogeographic' concept so, too, the principle of an urban-rural dichotomy in local administration was increasingly questioned, for example, in the Redcliffe-Maud Report. But the issue remains unresolved despite the creation of the metropolitan authorities in 1974 and their abolition in 1986.

RITUAL AND COMMUNICATION SYSTEMS

Arrangements for the maintenance of order and cohesiveness in society are part and parcel of all of the major institutions. But we can single out the chapters on crime, on religion and on ethnicity in order to throw light on particular trends and problems. The sociologist will examine the statistics on crime and punishment to seek a measure of the level of adherence to or respect for the legitimacy of the social order. The statistics, as Nigel Walker shows, are difficult to interpret. An increasingly complex society generates, on the one hand, a more elaborate code of formal rules and therefore raises the potential of the population to offend against them, and, on the other hand, also generates a more complex system of social control and crime detection. Thus Walker quotes Lady Wootton's comment that 'the internal combustion engine has revolutionalised the business of our criminal courts'. On the other hand, although the number of men and women employed by the police forces have more than doubled since 1900, the actual man hours worked per thousand of the population has remained more or less the same throughout the century.

As a general measure of trends in criminality, Table 15.8 records the history of recorded indictable offences. The frequency of murder has changed very little while the frequency of attempts at burglaries and other 'breaking and entering' crimes has increased 42-fold.

On the side of punishment there are again difficulties in interpreting the statistics. There is a discernible tendency towards longer sentences for crimes which do serious personal harm and greater leniency, including non-custodial dispositions, for crimes which do not. The daily average prison population rose from 17 435 in 1901 to 43 760 in 1980, a long high increase despite the development of non-custodial forms of treatment such as community service and the introduction and expansion of parole from 1967. Prison has become used less readily as punishment. Even in the Higher Courts the percentage of offenders imprisoned has fallen from over 90 per cent to 51 per cent. The validity of calculations of clear-up rates is always suspect. But it seems that the clear-up rate for property offences is low and getting lower while for offences against the person it is high but also declining.

The trends in religion assembled in Chapter 13 throw light on social cohesion from another point of view. In general there has been a decline in organised religion in both absolute and relative terms as indicated by the rise of civil marriages, and the reduction in membership of religious organisations. Only the Roman Catholics and the Church of Scotland among Christian churches have increased their numbers. In 1900 there were 1 945 000 Church of England communicants on Easter Day, and by 1985 this total had fallen to 1 468 000. The Presbyterian churches have resisted decline rather better than the Church of England. Robert Currie and Alan Gilbert suggest that the relative success of the Church of Scotland may be due to its nationalist appeal.[20] Yet the appeal to a national community has not greatly helped the Presbyterian Church of Wales (the Calvinist Methodists), whose membership has been in continuous decline since 1960.

Even over the last 15 years British church membership has declined by 1.5 million to 7 million, and the number of full-time ministers by 4000. On the other hand, 11 per cent of the adult population go to church at least once a month. A minority of slightly more than one-quarter have no religious adherence of any kind.

In general it is difficult to assess the course of participation in national and community rituals. The rise of television to near saturation point in access has undoubtedly introduced a new element into popular consciousness. It should also be noted that while participation in sports has undoubtedly increased, attendance at sporting events which, at least in part, serve community ritual functions, has declined.

Finally, we may glance at another aspect of national integration which has become an important preoccupation in recent years – the ethnic minorities. The British Isles, as is well known, are thought of as having had a somewhat isolated and homogeneous ethnic and cultural character. While the UK population grew from 38 million at the beginning of the century to 58 million by 1986 there was a *net* migration loss of 2.3 million. Nevertheless there were also migration gains, particularly of refugee Jews, and much larger labour inflows from Ireland. Then in the second half of the century a 5 per cent minority has emerged from international labour migration to incorporate a million South Asians and half a million West Indians. There was in addition a 'mixed' population of a quarter of a million. The influx of immigrants from the so-called 'new Commonwealth' led to a political backlash which, in turn, caused a restrictive definition of British citizenship through the control legislation of the Immigration Acts of 1962–71. Some legislative attempts have been made to combat racial or ethnic discrimination. But social division remains, and the ethnic minorities tend to be concentrated in the inner cities, in unskilled labour and in poor housing.

Policy-makers are now forced to recognise that the older assimilationist approach ended with the restrictions introduced by the 1962 Act which had the paradoxical consequence of increasing the flow of Indian and Pakistani families to settle permanently in place of the groups of male temporary workers intending to return to their homelands. Subsequent developments have underlined the assumption of the older assimilative theory that the coloured population was a homogeneous collection of individuals. This was never a fact. Distinctions have to be drawn not only between different nationalities and ethnic groups but also within these between castes, classes and occupations and between individuals, families and types of community group. The pattern of group formation among the British coloureds is changing rapidly, and in different directions among West Indians, Pakistanis and Cypriots, as well as between the first and second generation of immigrants.

At the same time the terms of assimilation have been transformed. The assimilative readiness of Britain as a host society is no longer that of a homogeneous culture. At root the coloured communities raise in a relatively dramatic form the basic problem of social inequality and social integration. There is overwhelming evidence that the coloured population suffers discrimination on grounds of colour in employment, housing, leisure activities and over the whole range of social relationships. Differences in power and advantage, whether based on colour or on any other socially-evaluated attribute, tend to be generalised and to be transmitted between generations. They therefore form systems of social stratification which are highly resistant to change. The citizenship status of the coloured Briton underlies and emphasises the continuing problem of maintaining the legitimacy of a conservative and stratified society.

SOCIAL TRENDS SINCE THE SECOND WORLD WAR

We have pointed to some of the major social trends from the beginning of the century which are illustrated in later chapters, and we end this introduction by emphasising two further changes occurring since the end of the Second World War. The choice of these more recent trends is vulnerable to the charges of bias and subjectivity that we have already discussed. But movements identified as significant by one observer can at least serve to invite others to specify or sharpen their own interpretations. We would like to select for special notice first, the comprehensive shifting of the division of labour over the past 40 years and, secondly, a new form of polarisation in British society, developing after the middle of the 1970s when the years of prosperity after the war came to an end.

The context

Britain's position in the world is the anxious subject of popular debate at the present time. The United Kingdom is still a major international figure. It has a GDP of over £300 billion (about 6.3 per cent of the GDP of the Organization for Economic Co-operation and Development (OECD) countries). The first quarter century of the reign of Elizabeth II was one of mounting prosperity. Between 1951 and 1976 real disposable income per capita at 1980 prices rose from £1375 to £2536. The average weekly earnings of male manual workers aged 21 or over rose from £60 in April 1951 to £109 and further to £111 in April 1983.[21] Basic paid holidays for manual workers increased from one and three quarter weeks to three and a half weeks; ownership of cars rose from about 14 per cent of households to 56 per cent (62 per cent in 1985) and, in general, post-war Britain has been an increasingly prosperous society.[22] However, its relative economic position has been weakening for many years. In the decade 1975–84 the GDP of the OECD block grew by 12 per cent more than in the UK.[23]

The relations between men and women are also in process of fundamental change in our time. In April 1986 the newspapers were carrying comment on the possibility of new rules concerning the retirement of women from employment and their entitlement to pensions. This single news item is sufficient to dramatise how much British society has changed in the period since the end of the Second World War. Today the underlying assumptions are that men and women should be treated equally with respect to employment and that laws with respect to gender and employment relations could originate in Europe and have a claim to adherence in Britain. Both assumptions would have seemed strange to British citizens under the post-war Attlee government. Women at that time were thought of as belonging primarily and essentially to the domestic economy, social equality was thought to be about class rather than gender and the idea of any kind of primacy for European over British law would have been swamped by the shared conception of Britain as an imperial world power, of London as the centre of the world through which the Greenwich meridian appropriately ran, and by awareness that a quarter of the world's population as well as a quarter of the land surface were under British control. Popular self-caricature could still depict the British male as one who:

in spite of all temptations
to belong to other nations
[he] remains an Englishman.

In 1945 the island society, on this perspective, comprised the upper echelons of a wold-wide commonwealth. In the 40 subsequent years the size of the UK population, though 16 per cent larger in absolute numbers, has declined from one-fiftieth to one-hundredth of the population of the world. For better or worse, the first industrial and the greatest imperial nation has been displaced within the memory of those aged 50 or more from the centre of the economic, military and political stage, if not to a marginal off-shore station of Western Europe, at least to a relatively minor position among the world's major powers.

So much then for context, and as a safeguard against the interpretation of British statistics as representing the inevitable historical pathway of all industrial societies. Every country has its peculiar genius: Britain's post-war record is not a reliable proxy for the recent history of western, European, industrial, capitalist, 'first world', 'post-industrial', democratic or any other postulated type of society. It is within the context of British experience that our two theses concerning the renegotiation of the division of labour and the passing of the post-war period into a new phase of polarisation must be discussed.

The division of labour

Behind its virtue and its victory, Britain emerged from the Second World War as a classical industrial economy, a centralised democratic polity with a familistic social structure. It was a society with historical roots in a social order in which there had been minimal government, and in which welfare had been dominated by the relation between the family and the workplace through the market for labour. The institutional division of labour of prototypic industrialism was an essential triangle joining the family, the economy and the state. Families raised children: men worked: women ran households. The economy produced, the family reproduced and consumed, and the state protected and redistributed.

All this was to change. In political terms there was a national consensus built during the war on the need for a welfare state which, in an earlier political language, constituted 'interference' in the exchanges between the family and the economy. The rise of the welfare state required an elaboration of the collection of taxes (partly from households, partly from enterprises and partly from the labour market transactions between them) to be used as redistributive resources for the education of children, the relief of men temporarily out of work, the maintenance of women without men to connect them to the economy, the sustenance of the old, and the protection of the health and safety of the population as a whole.

In the following generation a different and more elaborate pattern of relationships developed. Thus the family produces as well as consumes. People take recreation or 'live', as well as work, in factories, and work, as well as live, in houses. The family has fewer children and breaks up, as well as reforms, more frequently. Women have increasingly entered the formal economy and men have been drawn back more into the household and the informal economy. Adults as well as children learn. More children than in the past labour competitively for qualifications during their compulsory years at school. The state, especially in the early part of the period, had invaded the productive system, partly through the taxation and regulation of firms but also in the direct production of goods and of an increasingly complicated array of social services. In short all of the words used to describe the classical triangle now have modified meanings because the functions of the major institutions have mingled. Leisure in the family includes do-it-yourself work.

Business enterprises and trade unions have taken on some of the regulatory functions of government, and the state, through its employment of policemen, doctors, nurses, teachers and social workers, has encroached on the traditional role of the parent. All of these shifts, institutional and individual, together add up to a renegotiated division of labour in the Britain of the 1980s compared with that of the 1940s.

Accordingly it should be possible to identify statistical trends reflecting the movements in the division of labour which I have sketched. Comparing the beginning and the end of the period we should find that the following changes have occurred:

In the family (Table 1.1)
1.   More women, especially married women, in employment.
2.   Less childbirth, but more illegitimate childbirth.
3.   More divorce and remarriage, and more one-person households.
4.   More men economically inactive, whether as unemployed, retired, or drawn into the domestic economy.
5.   More men and women in adult education.
6.   More children in extended schooling.
7.   A population with higher formal qualifications.

Statistics taken from the various editions of *Social Trends* confirm these expectations. Between the end of the war and the mid-1980s the proportion of economically-active women has risen from just over a third to nearly half, and the proportion of economically-active married women, albeit mainly in part-time jobs, has more than doubled. In the same period fertility, though reaching a peak in 1964, has fallen below replacement levels and the proportion of illegitimate births has multiplied by four. Moreover, not only has reproduction moved marginally but significantly outside the traditional family but the family itself is less stable with a more than fivefold increase in the divorce rate between 1961 and 1985. Remarriages now account for over a third of all marriages.

The reciprocal movement of men into domesticity is also revealed by the evidence in Table 1.1. But again the reduction in the percentage of men who are economically active is mainly caused by the retirement of increasing numbers of men over 65. There are no firm statistics concerning the involvement of men in the domestic economy. What we do know from Table 1.2 is that tradition is persistent: women still bear the main burden of domestic management in practice, equal sharing is more of an ideal than a reality and honoured by men more in the breach than in the observance.

Figures for enrolments of adults aged 21 or over on both leisure and vocational courses illustrate the rising tendency for older people to learn while Figure 1.2 shows the trend towards extended schooling among children. The tendency to stay on voluntarily has continued into the recent difficult years on

Table 1.1   Trends in the family, United Kingdom

Categories	1931	1951	1961	1966	1971	1976	1981	1985
1. Percentage of all women aged 16 or over economically active[1]	34[6]	35[7]	37[7]	42[7]	43[7]	47	48	48
Percentage of married women aged 16 or over economically active[1]	10[6]	22[7]	30[7]	38[7]	42[7]	49	49	52
2. Total period fertility rate[2]	—	2.16	2.78	2.78	2.40	1.72	1.79	1.78
Illegitimate births as a percentage of all births	5	5	6	8	8	9	13	19
Persons divorcing per 1000 married population[3]	—	3	2	3	6	10	12	13
3. Remarriages as a percentage of all marriages	11[1]	18[1]	15[1]	16[1]	20	31	34	35
One-person households as a percentage of all households	7	11	12	15	18	21	22	24
4. Percentage of all men aged 16 or over economically active[1]	91[6]	88[7]	86[7]	84[7]	81[7]	79	76	74
Men in the domestic economy					(See Table 1.2)			
5. Thousands of students,[4] in part-time								

higher education[5]:								
Men	—	—	107	115	142	168	207	212
Women	—	—	6	8	23	50	87	107
Aged 21 or over in:								
Non-advanced further education	—	—	—	—	1987	2260[8]	1986[9]	2200
(of which adult education)	—	—	—	—	—	—	1169[9]	1349
Part-time higher education[5]	—	—	—	—	216	201[8]	236	269
Full-time higher education[5]	—	—	—	—		266[8]	235	252
6. Children in extended schooling					(See Figure 1.2)			
7. Formal qualifications					(See Figure 1.3)			

Notes:

1. Great Britain only.
2. The average number of children which would be born per woman if women experienced the age specific fertility rates of the period in question throughout their child-bearing life-span.
3. England and Wales only.
4. Data are for academic years ending in the year shown.
5. Includes universities, Open University, and advanced courses in major establishments of further education.
6. Aged 14 or over.
7. Aged 15 or over.
8. 1976/77.
9. 1981/82.

Source: Social Trends, 17 (Table A1). Reproduced with the permission of the Controller of Her Majesty's Stationery Office.

Table 1.2   Household division of labour: by marital status, 1984, Great Britain (percentages)

| | Married people[1] | | | | | | Never-married people[2] | | |
| | Actual allocation of tasks | | | Tasks should be allocated to | | | Tasks should be allocated to | | |
	Mainly men	Mainly women	Shared equally	Mainly men	Mainly women	Shared equally	Mainly men	Mainly women	Shared equally
Household tasks (percentage[2] allocation)									
Washing and ironing	1	88	9	—	77	21	—	68	30
Preparation of evening meal	5	77	16	1	61	35	1	49	49
Household cleaning	3	72	23	—	51	45	1	42	56
Household shopping	6	54	39	—	35	62	—	31	68
Evening dishes	18	37	41	12	21	64	13	15	71
Organisation of household money and bills	32	38	28	23	15	58	19	16	63
Repairs of household equipment	83	6	8	79	2	17	74	—	24
Child-rearing (percentage[3] allocation)									
Looks after the children when they are sick	1	63	35	—	49	47	—	48	50
Teaches the children discipline	10	12	77	12	5	80	16	4	80

Notes:
1. 1120 married respondents, except for the questions on actual allocation of child-rearing tasks which were answered by 479 respondents with children under 16.
2. 283 never-married respondents. The table excludes results of the formerly married (widowed, divorced, or separated) respondents.
3. 'Don't knows' and non-response to the question mean that some categories do not sum to 100 per cent.
Sources: British Social Attitudes Survey, 1984; Social and Community Planning Research, Gower, 1984).

Figure 1.2 Pupils staying on at school for at least one[1] extra year, and at least two[2] extra years: by sex, England and Wales, and Scotland

Notes:
1. To 1st year sixth in England and Wales and S5 in Scotland.
2. To 2nd year sixth in England and Wales and S6 in Scotland.

Source: *Social Trends* 17 (Jan 1987) p. 14. Reproduced with the permission of the Controller of Her Majesty's Stationery Office.

top of the raising of the school-leaving age from 15 to 16 in 1972. And Figure 1.3 illustrates the marked rise during the past 30 years in the possession of qualifications. This particular form of illustration also brings out the strata of age cohorts in the population at a given point of time. In 1985 72 per cent of the population in the 25 to 29 age group held an educational qualification, whereas only 40 per cent of those aged 50 to 59 did so.

In the economy (Table 1.3)
The expected correlative changes in the economy include:

8. A higher GDP per capita.
9. Fewer manual workers.
10. Shorter hours of work.
11. Longer holidays.

These changes are illustrated in Table 1.3. The national income continued to rise. At 1980 prices GDP grew from 1961 (£148 billion) to 1973 (£215 billion) at about 3 per cent per year. Growth from 1973 to 1980 slowed to about 1 per cent per year. Between 1973 and 1984 the increase in GDP per capita was 1 per cent compared with 1.5 per cent for all the OECD countries.

Table 1.3   Trends in the economy, United Kingdom

	1931	1951	1961	1966	1971	1976	1981	1985
8. Gross domestic product at market prices at 1980								
prices (£ billion)	—	112	148	171	195	220	228	253
Index (1980=100)	—	49	64	74	85	96	99	110
Per head (£)	—	2226	2811	3138	3495	3918	4037	4465
9. Percentage of men in manual occupations[1]	77	72	—	—	62	—	58	—
Percentage of women in manual occupations[1]	76	64	—	—	53	—	44	—
Percentage of total in manual occupations[1]	77	70	—	—	59	—	52	—
10. Average weekly hours of work[1,2] for full-time male manual employees	48[4]	48	48	46	46	45	44[2]	44[2]
11. Percentage of manual employees[3] with basic holiday entitlement of over 3 weeks	—	—	—	—	4	81	98	100

Notes:
1. Great Britain only.
2. At April. Prior to 1983 data cover males aged 21 or over; since then they cover males on adult rates.
3. Employees covered by national collective agreements or Wages Council Orders.
4. October 1938.

Sources: Guy Routh (1965) *Occupation and Pay in Great Britain* (Cambridge University Press); *British Labour Statistics Historical Abstract*, Central Statistical Office; *Social Trends* Reproduced with the permission of the Controller of Her Majesty's Stationery Office.

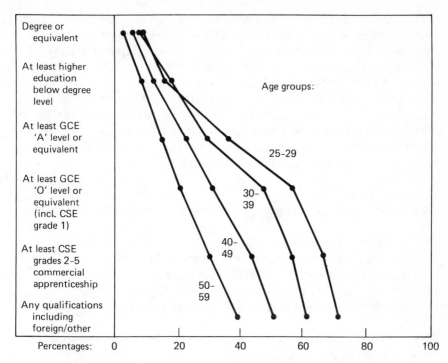

Figure 1.3   Highest qualification level of the population: by age, 1985, Great Britain.

Source: *Social Trends* 17 (Jan 1987) p. 15. Reproduced with the permission of the Controller of Her Majesty's Stationery Office.

Table 1.4   Self-rated social class, 1986, Great Britain (percentages and numbers)

Social class	Self	Parents
	(percentages)	
Upper middle	1	2
Middle	24	17
Upper working	21	12
Working	48	59
Poor	3	8
Don't know/no response	3	2
Sample size (= 100%) (numbers)	3066	3066

Source: British Social Attitudes Survey, 1986, *Social and Community Planning Research* (Gower, 1986).

The proportion of both men and women in manual occupations declined. This gradual transformation of what was, at the beginning of the century, the most proletarian country in the world (that is, composed mainly of the industrial working class), appears in a different guise in Table 1.4. In 1986 29 per cent of a national sample of adults thought of themselves as having moved into a higher social class and only 9 per cent thought of themselves as having come down in the world compared with their parents. Between the two generations hours of work diminished and holidays increased. Whereas at the end of the Second World War no manual workers were entitled to four weeks paid holiday, now virtually all have that right.

In the state (Table 1.5)
With respect to statistics concerning government we would expect to find:

12.   Higher expenditure on education.
13.   Increased numbers of parent surrogates in the employment of the state (police, teachers, doctors, social workers, etc.).
14.   Increased nursery provision for the under-fives.
15.   A higher proportion of the GDP spent by the state.

These incursions into the traditional realm of the family are illustrated in Table 1.5. Expenditure and manpower in education, health and the social services are higher today than they were at the end of the 1940s. The state spends more than it did then out of a much bigger national purse. There are, in fact, more policemen, doctors, nurses and social workers and there are more children in school or otherwise in the care of the public authorities. A detailed account of the rise of employment in the social services up to 1970 can be found in *Social Trends*, (1971).[24] Between 1976 and 1983 the total of those employed in the health and personal social services increased by nearly 13 per cent. It is true that the numbers working in the NHS in England fell by about 2 per cent between 31 March 1983 and 31 March 1985.[25] But this is an element in the second of our theses to which we can now turn.

Economic transformation and social polarisation

Before the post-war period came to an end with the oil crisis of 1973–4, there had been 30 years of economic prosperity with high rates of economic growth, full employment and burgeoning public sector activity. The more recent period has been one of declining employment, economic activity shifting out of classical towards 'high tec' or service industry, struggles with inflation, determination to move decision-making out of Westminster and Whitehall into the market and the locality and policies designed to cut back the public and strengthen the private sector. The question is not so much whether this

Table 1.5 Trends in the United Kindom (percentages and thousands)

	1931	1951	1961	1966	1971	1976	1981	1985
Government expenditure on education as a percentage of gross domestic product[1]	—	—	—	—	5.2	6.3	5.4	—
Manpower in social services[2] (000s)	769	1188	1725	2088	1978[5]	—	—	—
Regional and district health authorities staff (000)	—	—	—	—	—	926	1026	—
Family practitioner professionals (000s)	—	—	—	—	—	49	54	—
Personal social services (000s)	—	—	—	—	—	228	251	273[7]
Under fives in education as a percentage of all 3 and 4 year olds	—	—	—	15	20	34	44	—
Day-care places for under-fives (000s)[3] at end March	—	51[4]	54[4]	128[4]	409[6]	511	540	—
General government expenditure as a percentage of gross domestic product	—	—	35	—	—	46	46	—

Notes:
1. Financial years ending in the year shown.
2. Education, health, welfare, and social security (includes part-time).
3. England and Wales only.
4. At end of December.
5. Estimated full-time equivalent total for 1970.
6. 1972.
7. 1984.

Source: Social Trends (various); Central Statistical Office.

historical watershed is a reality: that is not in serious dispute. It is rather how it
is reflected in the statistics pertaining to the changing division of labour.
Clearly the post-war boom and the current period of transition are fairly
sharply distinguished by their rates of unemployment and their shifts out of
manufacturing industry[26] into the service sector. And the increasing proportion of GDP absorbed into, and spent by, the government, reaching 48 per
cent in 1975, has since been reduced. But most of the trends in the reorganisation of family and economic life are the result of forces distinct from those
affecting relations between government and the governed. The changing
structure of relations between classes, sexes and age groups may or may not be
modified by political activity but, at least in the case of Britain since the
Second World War, have not fundamentally changed the direction of their
development.

There remains, however, the question of whether the distribution of life
chances – and the modern national state is, after all, the principal redistributive agent in society – has been crucially altered since the mid-1970s, and

Table 1.6   Distribution of original, disposable, and final household income, United
Kingdom (percentages)

	Bottom fifth	Next fifth	Middle fifth	Next fifth	Top fifth	Total
Original income[1]						
1976	0.8	9.4	18.8	26.6	44.4	100.0
1981	0.6	8.1	18.0	26.9	46.4	100.0
1983	0.3	6.7	17.7	27.2	48.0	100.0
1984	0.3	6.1	17.5	27.5	48.6	100.0
Disposable income[2]						
1976	7.0	12.6	18.2	24.1	38.1	100.0
1981	6.7	12.1	17.7	24.1	39.4	100.0
1983	6.9	11.9	17.6	24.0	39.6	100.0
1984	6.7	11.7	17.5	24.4	39.7	100.0
Final income[3]						
1976	7.4	12.7	18.0	24.0	37.9	100.0
1981	7.1	12.4	17.9	24.0	38.6	100.0
1983	6.9	12.2	17.6	24.0	39.3	100.0
1984	7.1	12.1	17.5	24.3	39.0	100.0

Notes:
1.   Households ranked by original income.
2.   Households ranked by disposable income.
3.   Households ranked by final income.
Source: *Social Trends*, 17 (Table A8). Reproduced with the permission of the
Controller of Her Majesty's Stationery Office. But see also Chapter 3, Table
3.11 and page 152 for comparision of the two tables.

particularly since the new administration which came in in 1979. This brings us to the hypothesised new trend towards polarisation – a widening gap between two components of the population as a whole.

A hundred years ago discussion of Disraeli's 'two nations' was the stock-in-trade of political arithmeticians. In the 1880s most social observers in Britain agreed that the Marxist polarisation thesis of the 1840s, with its prophesy of mass pauperisation, of exploited labour, and the accumulation of surplus value into fewer and fewer capitalist hands, had been tested and found wanting in the natural laboratory of Victorian history. By and large the social trends ran in the opposite direction and, however slowly and haltingly, continued to do so through the first three-quarters of the twentieth century. But now the question arises whether a new version of the two nations has appeared in the last decade in the form of a widening division between a prosperous majority in secure and increasingly well-paid employment, and a depressed minority of people who are unemployed, sick, old or belong to the unsuccessful ethnic minorities.

Evidence is available on three aspects of this thesis. First there are the trends in the distribution of income and wealth between the better and the worse off families, shown in Table 1.6. Between 1976 and 1984 the movement of original or market incomes was towards greater inequality. The bottom fifth of households dropped their share from 0.8 to 0.3 per cent and the top fifth moved up from 44.4 to 48.6 per cent. The redistributive activity of the state modified this inequality but did not change the direction of movement. The bottom group had final household incomes amounting to 7.4 per cent of the whole in 1976 reduced to 7.1 per cent in 1984, while the top fifth raised their share from 37.9 to 39.0 per cent.

On the side of wealth the story shown in Table 1.7 is less clear. In 1984 the richest 1 per cent and 10 per cent of the adult population owned 21 and 52 per cent respectively of marketable wealth. With the addition of pension rights these shares declined to 12 and 35 per cent. In the early 1970s the share of marketable wealth owned by the richest groups was reduced by a marked fall in the prices of stocks and shares. The late 1970s and early 1980s brought very little change in the pattern of ownership. For marketable wealth plus occupational and state pension rights there was also a movement towards less inequality in the early and mid-1970s, but since 1977 there has been little change.

With respect to social mobility John Goldthorpe and Clive Payne have concluded unequivocally from their analysis of the 1983 general election study that:

the stability of relative rates or chances of inter-generational class mobility, which our analyses of the 1972 data suggested went back to the 1920s, has *not* been disturbed to any appreciable degree in the first decade after the ending of the post-war era.[27]

Table 1.7   Distribution of wealth, United Kingdom (percentages and £s billion)

	1971	1976	1981	1984
Marketable wealth				
Percentage of wealth owned by:				
Most wealthy 1%	31	24	21	21
Most wealthy 5%	52	45	40	39
Most wealthy 10%	65	60	54	52
Most wealthy 25%	86	84	77	75
Most wealthy 50%	97	95	94	93
Total marketable wealth (£s billion)	140	263	546	762
(*Marketable wealth plus occupational and state pension rights*)				
Percentage of wealth owned by:				
Most wealthy 1%	21	14	12	12
Most wealthy 5%	37	27	24	25
Most wealthy 10%	49	37	34	35
Most wealthy 25%	69–72	58–61	55–58	56–59
Most wealthy 50%	85–89	80–85	78–82	79–83

Note: See also Chapter 3, especially Tables 3.18 to 3.20.
Source: *Social Trends*, 17 (Table A9). Reproduced with the permission of the Controller of Her Majesty's Stationery Office.

But these authors then go on to consider whether absolute rates have been affected by the new period of transition, and particularly whether there has been a freezing of mobility and especially the upward mobility of working-class and lower-middle-class sons into the middle-class professions, salariat or 'service class'. The evidence is that absolute rates of upward and of total mobility have continued to rise. A comparison of the 1972 and 1983 samples of these national enquiries is given in Table 1.8. In 1972, 16 per cent of the men of working-class origin had found their way into the middle class: by 1983 the percentage had risen to 23.6. Again in 1972, 61.2 per cent of those of working-class parentage were themselves in working-class jobs: by 1983 the percentage had fallen to 52.6. Thus there is considerable support for the optimistic liberal theory of an expansion of middle-class opportunities. But the picture is modified by unemployment.

In 1972 the unemployment rate was virtually negligible. In 1983 it was in double figures at over 12 per cent and more than a million had been out of work for at least a year. The unemployed could reasonably be viewed as an additional depressed class which needed to be included as a 'destination status' in mobility tables. So, while the expansion of the professional and technical middle class remains a feature of late twentieth-century Britain, as it was in the prosperous years after 1950, unemployment has emerged as a possible outcome, especially for those who begin in the working class, which tends to make the chances of mobility more unequal.

Table 1.8   Class distribution by class of father, 1972 and 1983,
England and Wales (percentages)

	Respondent's class			
Father's class	*Middle class*	*Lower-middle*	*Working class*	*All*
1972				
Middle class	57.7	23.2	19.1	100.0
Lower-middle	31.2	31.9	37.0	100.0
Working class	16.0	22.7	61.2	100.0
1983				
Middle class	62.0	22.2	15.8	100.0
Lower-middle	34.2	34.3	31.5	100.0
Working class	23.6	23.8	52.6	100.0

Note: 1972 figures based on national sample of men in England and Wales (N = 9434).
1983 figures from the British General Election Study (N = 1173).
For details see Goldthorpe and Payne (1986) 5.

Sources: John Goldthorpe and Clive Payne (1986) 'Trends in Intergenerational Class Mobility in England and Wales', *Sociology*, 20(1): 1–24; *Social Trends*, 17, Table A10. Reproduced with the permission of the Controller of Her Majesty's Stationery Office.

   A similar process of social division has also been observed in housing. The dominant trend in the twentieth century has been towards owner-occupation, much encouraged in recent years. From his study of trends in housing tenure, Hamnett concludes that, as between owner-occupation and local authority renting, there has been 'an increasing degree of social polarisation.[28] Between 1961 and 1981, as the privately-rented sector continued to decline, the higher socioeconomic groups became more concentrated in owner-occupied dwellings, and the unskilled and semi-skilled families were more heavily represented among council tenants. The trend will be exacerbated if under recent legislation giving tenants the right to buy their dwellings more better-off families become owner-occupiers, leaving the poorer in the less attractive council property. This movement represents a drawing apart of the social classes in terms of their tenure position. It should be remembered, however, that in terms of actual standards of accommodation local authority dwellings remain marginally the best equipped with amenities, though owner-occupied dwellings are now similar (Table 10.21). In so far as there has been a shift out of the notoriously poor quality private sector into the better quality council accommodation, there has been an improvement in the housing standards of the worst off.

Finally we may consider the evidence of spatial polarisation assembled in the Archbishop of Canterbury's report on Urban Priority Areas, *Faith in the City* (1985).[29]

Using the most recent studies of the Economic and Social Research Council,[30] the Archbishop's Commission assembled a comparison of types of area in Britain in terms of a composite measure of advantage and deprivation.[31] The measures include such indicators as the proportion of people unemployed (negative), in professional jobs (positive), the infant mortality rate, the proportion of owner-occupiers and of car owners and many other manifestations of prosperity or poverty. Column 1 of Table 1.9 shows that there is a gradient of advantage ascending from the inner city districts and the peripheral council estates to the fringe areas outside classical industrial Britain. The second column of Table 1.9 shows the shifts in population between 1971 and 1981. Column 1 shows the clear gradient of multiple inequality from the urban priority areas to the fringe areas. Column 2 shows that the urban priority areas are losing population. The process is one of deprived people being left in the urban priority areas as the successful move out to middle Britain. The former have decreasing wealth, health services,

Table 1.9   Inner city polarisation by type/area, 1971 and 1981 (numbers and percentages)

	Advantage and deprivation (1981 index)[1]	Population change (%) (1971–81)
Metropolitan inner cities:		
Inner Birmingham	− 2.37	− 19.3
Inner Manchester	− 1.77	− 25.5
Peripheral council estates:		
Knowsley	− 1.36	− 15.3
Other old city centres:		
Inner Derby	− 1.97	− 20.1
Other old industrial urban areas:		
Outer Derby	0.58	+ 7.4
Rest of Greater Manchester	0.67	+ 0.37
Rest of Outer London	1.42	− 9.0
Fringe areas:		
West Midlands south fringe	1.43	+ 16.6
Mersey north fringe	1.22	+ 17.1
Manchester south fringe	1.29	+ 5.3
London south fringe	2.32	− 3.8

Note:
1.   See note 31 of text.
Source: *Faith in the City*, Report of the Archbishop of Canterbury's Commission on Urban Priority Areas, 1985.

income, investment, and amenity: the latter have rising affluence, opportunity, power and advantage: in one ugly word – polarisation.

Of course the poor are not confined to the urban priority areas. As the Archbishop's Commissioners put it, 'The city remains part magnet to the disadvantaged newcomer, part prison to the unskilled, the disabled and the dispirited, part spring-board for the ambitious and vigorous who find escape to suburbia, and part protection for enclaves of affluence'.[32]

SUMMARY CONCLUSION

The search for trends necessarily involves selection and interpretation. It is, moreover, a procedure which intrinsically emphasises change rather than continuity. The perspective adopted here focuses on changes in the relations between family, economy and government – what I have called the institutional division of labour – and shows a shifting pattern of responsibility between them. Government has taken on more familial and more economic functions; industry has absorbed more regulatory duties; family stability has weakened and fertility declined. The traditional meanings and experiences attached to masculinity, femininity, adulthood, childhood, work, leisure and learning have all changed as the division of labour has altered.

The post-war period to the mid-1970s was one of economic growth, full employment, and prosperity against an international background of rapid dismantling of imperial power and relative decline of economic productivity. The managerial, professional and technical classes waxed and the industrial working class waned. Women, particularly married women, moved increasingly into paid employment.

Then, after the oil crisis of the mid-1970s a new phase of economic and social transformation appeared. The shift away from nineteenth-century urban industrial manufacture was accelerated; unemployment rose; people moved away from the inner cities towards suburbia, the South-East and New Towns. And in the process a pattern has emerged of a more unequal society with a majority securely attached to a still prosperous country and a minority in a marginal economic and social position, the former moving into the suburbs of the newer economy of a 'green and pleasant land', the latter tending to be trapped in the old provincial industrial cities and their displaced fragments of peripheral council housing estates. In short a still recognisable Britain is facing new challenges in the late twentieth century in the ancient struggle to accommodate both freedom and equality in a United Kingdom.

Notes

1. See Chapter 4, pp. 173–7.
2. A classic example is J. H. Goldthorpe, D. Lockwood, F. Bechhofer, and J. Platt (1969) *The Affluent Worker*, 3 vols (Cambridge University Press). This interview survey was designed to test the theory of embourgeoisement.
3. For an exposition of survey methods see C. A. Moser and G. Kalton (1971) *Survey Methods in Social Investigation* (Heinemann).
4. See, for example, the follow-up investigations carried out under the auspices of the Population Investigation Committee and directed by Dr J. W. B. Douglas, and the follow-up study undertaken by the Scottish Council for Research in Education into the trend of intelligence. See especially the introduction by D. V. Glass to J. W. B. Douglas (1964) *The Home and the School* (MacGibbon & Kee). An excellent recent example of follow-up study (of the Rowntree survey of poverty in York in 1951) is A. B. Atkinson, A. K. Maynard and C. G. Trinder (1983) *Parents and Children: Income in Two Generations* (Heinemann).
5. A. M. Carr Saunders, D. Caradog Jones and C. A. Moser (1958) *A Survey of Social Conditions in England and Wales* (Oxford University Press).
6. In E. Butterworth and D. Weir (eds) (1970) *The Sociology of Modern Britain* (Collins: Fontana) 203–4.
7. T. B. Bottomore (1962) *Sociology – A Guide to Problems and Literature* (Allen & Unwin) p. 20.
8. Ibid., p. 36.
9. Edward Shils (1964) Background to Policies: Britain Awake, in Hall, P. (ed.) *Labour's New Frontiers* (Andre Deutsch).
10. E. R. Leach, 'Social Structure', in *International Encyclopaedia of Social Sciences* (Free Press: The Macmillan Co., NY) 14: 485. In this article Leach gives a succinct account of the history and current usage of the term social structure.
11. It is noteworthy and welcome that systematic survey of opinion is now attempted annually by Roger Jowell and his associates. See Roger Jowell and Colin Airey (1984) *British Social Attitudes: the 1984 Report* and Roger Jowel and Sharon Witherspoon (1985) *British Social Attitudes: the 1985 Report*, Social and Community Planning Research (Gower).
12. In his attempt to answer the question of what had been the relation between institutionalised inequalities and awareness or resentment of them in twentieth-century Britain, W. G. Runciman (1966) used the results of a national sample survey in 1962 in combination with non-survey evidence from the social history of England since 1918. Use of the two types of material, as he argues, 'should be seen as the connected parts of a single argument; the difference between them is one of style, not of kind', *Relative Deprivation and Social Justice* (Routledge) 8.
13. Some writers, for example, Lévi-Strauss, have a quite different usage, referring to general models of social structure rather than directly to actual social relationships.
14. Thus Weber defined the institution of property as made up of relations of exclusion between individuals and groups in respect of objects having exchangeable value in society.
15. E. R. Leach (1960) 'Social Structure', in *International Encyclopaedia of Social Sciences* (Free Press: The Macmillan Co., NY) 14: 404.
16. Cf. T. B. Bottomore (1962) *Sociology – A Guide to Problems and Literature* (Allen & Unwin) 111.
17. Though we are, of course, aware that English has emerged as a world language, spoken by a billion people, of whom the inhabitants of the United Kingdom form a small minority.

18. Parsons denies evidence for a trend to homogeneity of sex roles and stresses the complementality or non-competing character of women's employment compared with men – 'The American Family' in T. Parsons and R. Bales (1955) *Family Socialisation and Interaction Processes* (Free Press: The Macmillan Co., NY). But see also Norman Dennis's (1962) 'Secondary Group Relations and the Pre-eminence of the Family', *Int. J. Comp. Social.*, 3(3): 80–90. See also Susan McRae (1986) *Cross-Class Families: A study of wives' occupational superiority* (Oxford: Clarendon Press).
19. See Table 9.9, p. 526.
20. See A. H. Halsey (ed.) *Trends in British Society Since 1900* (1st edn), Chapter 13.
21. *British Labour Statistics Historical Abstract*, Tables 42, 90 and 94 and various editions of the *Employment Gazette*.
22. Cf. Daniel Bell (1978) 'Report on England: the Future that Never Was', *The Public Interest*, 51: 35–73. For statistics on basic holiday entitlement see Table A5. The figures for car ownership are unofficial estimates for 1951 and from the General Household Survey for 1976 and 1984.
23. Cf. David Mayes (1986) 'Britain's Position in the World', *Catalyst*, 2(1): 1–19.
24. See the article by S. Rosenbaum.
25. *Social Trends* 16: p. 130.
26. The number of employees in manufacturing industry reached its highest point in 1956 (see *British Labour Statistics Historical Abstract*, Table 135).
27. John Goldthorpe and Clive Payne (1986) 'Trends in Intergenerational Class Mobility in England and Wales 1972–83', *Sociology*, 20(1): 9.
28. C. Hamnett (1984) Housing the Two Nations: Socio-Tenurial Polarisation in England and Wales 1961–81, *Urban Studies*, 43: 384–405.
29. *Faith in the City: a call for action by Church and Nation*, (Church House Publishing, 1985).
30. See especially Victor A. Hausner (ed.) (1987) *Critical Issues in Urban Economic Development*, vol. 1 (Oxford University Press).
31. The analysis was supplied by David Eversley and Ian Begg. Essentially, the method was to collect data at ward level of over 70 indicators of advantage and disadvantage and to standardise them as Z scores. By this means an average Z score was produced for every territorial grouping over a range of favourable and adverse social indicators. It is a robust and stable score which provides a refined map of inequality. See Eversley, D. E. C. and Begg, I. (1987) 'Deprivation in the Inner City: Social Indicators from the 1981 Census', in Victor A. Hausner (ed.), ibid.
32. *Faith in the City* (1985)25.

2 Population

D. A. Coleman

INTRODUCTION

One of the most startling trends about demography today, compared to 1972 when this book first appeared, is the frequency with which the word demography now appears in public. Debates about unemployment, pensions, inner cities, the frailty of the family, health and immigration all invoke demographic data, trends or concepts. The demographic scene is indeed quite different from what it was. Demographic dimensions to problems are nowadays much better known. Techniques have advanced greatly and a new breadth of data, particularly from surveys, has made demographic data more flexible than ever before.

This chapter is intended to sketch the main demographic events and trends since 1900 to the present day, to assess their significance and their likely future development, and to be a guide to the sources available for their study. Only key figures will be given, in tables and graphs, to guide the eye to the points that really matter. Rather than pretend to an impossible degree of completeness, the reader is encouraged to seek out the basic data for himself, which are more abundant, more attractively presented, and more accessible than in 1972.

SOURCES OF DATA

It helps to know something about primary sources. The quality of data defines the scope and accuracy of analysis. And it is important to know where to look for more, or to check on secondary sources like this one. Fortunately British demographic data are among the most complete and comprehensive in the world. Especially since the reorganisation of the General Register Office as the Office of Population Censuses and Surveys (OPCS) in 1973, analysis and presentation have been among the best too.

The bases of demographic data are the complete population data from the census, collected compulsorily from every household every ten years since 1801 (except 1941) and the records of vital events (births, marriages and deaths) recorded compulsorily as they occur since 1837. The former provide the denominator, the latter the numerator, for the calculation of the rates at which demographic processes occur. They are not, of course, collected solely for demographic purposes, but for legal, health, welfare and planning reasons (Glass, 1973).

Census returns for each household are confidential to the OPCS and are not available for study (or to other government departments) for 100 years (see Bulmer, 1976). Aggregate data are published in great detail on a county basis (local authorities are the biggest consumers of census data) and also in national summaries and analysis of age structure, marital status, occupation, migration and birthplace, journey to work, Welsh language and other topics (see OPCS, 1977). Up to 1951 a written report drew attention to the salient points of the census with further analysis, and in earlier years was lavishly illustrated. This has since diminished to a mere analysis of purely statistical housekeeping questions. Small area statistics are available to order down to enumeration district level (about 200 households) but no public-use tapes (containing anonymous individual records) are available on the US model. Topics, questions and analysis change from census to census; that of 1981 was particularly thin, omitting questions on fertility and an expected question on ethnicity. The 1911 Census was a particular landmark, with the first questions on fertility and child survival, and the beginning of social-class analysis.

Vital registration not only records the fact of birth, marriage and death, but enables these events to be analysed according to age, occupation, geographical region and birthplace. Least information is collected about marriage (no birthplace) and that collected is often sketchy. Cause of death is recorded in detail for important legal and medical reasons. Most epidemiological research depends on their accuracy, but only a third of deaths are certified by autopsy which sometimes reveals important discrepancies in diagnosis (Royal College of Physicians, 1982). Divorces as legal proceedings are the responsibility of the Lord Chancellor's Department, but like adoptions, notifiable diseases and the migration records of the National Health Service (NHS) Central Register, the figures are published through OPCS.

The old Registrar-General's *Statistical Review* ceased in 1973, when the General Register was reorganised as the Office of Population Censuses and Surveys. Its tables and analysis continued and are developed through a regular series of annual OPCS publications (now with commentary) on fertility, marriage, mortality and migration and other topics. The most up-to-date information is presented through OPCS *Monitors* in the same series. Commentary (to which volume III of the *Statistical Review* used to be devoted), further analysis, and quarterly demographic summary comes in the OPCS house journal *Population Trends* as well as other more detailed occasional publications. Separate series of data on international migration come from OPCS and the Home Office. Neither are demographically very satisfactory. There is no direct record at all of internal migration as it happens, unlike some Continental countries which maintain population registers. Surrogate data from changing doctors' registration from the NHS Central Register are used instead, together with census and survey questions. They are discussed in the migration section.

The biggest change has come from regular official surveys and longitudinal studies. The General Household Survey (GHS), instituted 1971, analyses with commentary the results of an annual survey of 13 000 households, including data available nowhere else; on colour, income and household size, or remarriage and occasionally on family intentions, cohabitation, contraception, perceived illness, and smoking and drinking habits. The biennial (annual since 1983) Labour Force Survey (LFS) is big enough (original sample size 90 000 households) to be called a microcensus. It provides the only population denominators for ethnicity, and intercensal ones for occupation and marital status. Researchers can conduct their own analysis on tapes of these surveys, available from the Economic and Social Research Council (ESRC) Data Archive.

Although the theoretical and practical advantages of cohort studies can be exaggerated (Brass, 1974), enormous strides have been made in analysing the cumulative effect of life experiences and age upon the demographic behaviour of individuals. Four major cohort studies, all still extant, have been started since the Second World War and provide information not available from any other source (for example, Fogelman, 1983). The biggest of all is the record linkage study from the 1971 Census. Unlike the three surveys, which require contact to be kept with an inevitably diminishing proportion of the original sample, this 4:365 (530 000 people) sample from the 1971 Census of persons born on four selected dates is kept in play through computer linkage of records of subsequent births of offspring, cancer registration, death, etc. – linked by date of birth (which thereby excludes marriages which lack this information) (see Fox and Grundy, 1985).

One major drawback with UK population statistics is their division between no less than three Registrars-General: for England and Wales, Scotland and Northern Ireland. Data are usually published separately and at different levels of detail although the position is now improving. The census schedules differ slightly, as do the resources available for analysis and publication. Data for England and Wales are by far the most abundant and most comprehensively analysed and commented upon. Data for Great Britain (England, Wales and Scotland) can quite easily be found; those for the UK (Great Britain plus Northern Ireland) tend to be more rudimentary (although it is, of course, the normal level of analysis for international migration). Northern Ireland does in fact have some rather distinctive characteristics of fertility and mortality which deserve special attention. Unfortunately, there is insufficient space here to do other than note them in a few of the tables. A comprehensive analysis is given by Compton (1981).

DEMOGRAPHIC REGIMES

Western countries have for the most part closely similar demographic trends, and especially in fertility the similarity has been growing in the post-war period (see Hiorns, 1980). British population in the earlier twentieth century is dominated by the latter phases of the 'demographic transition' from high to low birth- and death-rates. Most developed societies are now emerging from the far end of this transition (see Lesthaeghe 1983; Bourgeois-Pichat, 1980). Later in the century – from the interwar period onward – the population of Britain is characterised by the beginning of a new and unprecedented 'post-transitional' demographic regime of low birth-rates, low death-rates and low or negative growth, whose final form is still unclear. 1900 is but an arbitrary marker in these processes. The *ancien* demographic *régime* had been destabilised since around 1750 with a slow decline in the death-rate and in the severity and frequency of mortality crises, and by a rise in fertility around the turn of that century, following a reduction in the average age of marriage. Together these initiated a prolonged period of population growth; first to half a per cent per year, then to a peak of one and a half per cent per year by the 1830s. Although rates of population growth of this magnitude had probably been reached before, in the thirteenth century and in the sixteenth, never before had they been sustained for so long, for 200 years of uninterrupted growth; never before had the British population managed to break decisively through the barrier of a population size of about five million.

FERTILITY

Population, birth- and death-rates all move together, but it makes sense to describe the course of life events first. They determine the size and the age structure in the total population. Fertility will be described here; mortality is considered in Chapter 11.

By 1900 a hitherto unprecedented decline in family size within marriage, first clearly apparent in Britain in the marriages of the 1870s, was well established (Tables 2.1 to 2.3, Figure 2.1). In this new development Britain was somewhat ahead of most of the rest of Europe and the English-speaking world, but well behind France, where married couples had begun to limit their children, especially third and subsequent births, from the 1780s onwards. By the 1900s contraception had been firmly established on most British families' agenda (see Banks, 1954; Fryer, 1964; McClaren, 1978; Leathard, 1980). Most middle-class families (except farmers) practised it, including the professional pioneers whose own professional bodies still continued to condemn the practice for its supposed spiritually and physically debilitating effects. The General Medical Council succeeded in preventing it being taught in medical schools until 1928. By then many 'patients' knew more than their own doctors

British Social Trends since 1900

Table 2.1(a)   Birth- and death-rates and natural increase, 1901–85, England and Wales, and Scotland (per 1000 population)

| | England and Wales | | | Scotland | | |
Period or year	Births	Deaths	Natural increase	Births	Deaths	Natural increase
1901–05	28.2	16.0	12.2	29.2	17.0	12.2
1906–10	26.3	14.7	11.6	27.6	16.1	11.4
1911–15	23.6	14.3	9.3	25.4	15.7	9.7
1916–20	20.0	14.4	5.6	22.8	15.0	7.8
1921–5	19.9	12.1	7.8	23.0	13.9	9.1
1926–30	16.7	12.1	4.6	20.0	13.6	6.4
1931–5	15.0	12.0	3.0	18.2	13.2	5.0
1936–40	14.7	12.2	2.5	17.6	13.6	4.0
1941–5	15.9	12.8	3.1	17.8	14.1	3.7
1946–50	18.0	11.8	6.2	20.0	12.6	7.4
1951–5	15.3	11.7	3.6	17.9	12.1	5.8
1956–60	16.4	11.6	4.8	19.2	12.2	7.0
1960–5	18.1	11.8	6.3	19.7	12.3	7.4
1966–70	16.9	11.7	5.2	17.9	12.1	5.8
1971–5	14.0	11.9	2.1	14.5	12.2	2.3
1976	11.9	12.2	−0.3	12.5	12.5	−0.1
1977	11.6	11.7	−0.1	12.0	12.0	0.0
1978	12.1	11.9	0.2	12.4	12.6	−0.2
1979	12.9	12.0	0.9	13.2	12.7	0.5
1980	13.2	11.7	1.5	13.4	12.3	1.1
1981	12.8	11.6	1.1	13.3	12.3	1.0
1982	12.6	11.7	0.9	12.8	12.6	0.2
1983	12.7	11.7	1.0	12.6	12.3	0.3
1984	12.8	11.4	1.4	12.7	12.1	0.5
1985	13.1	11.8	1.3	13.0	12.4	0.5

Sources: Registrar-General's *Statistical Review of England and Wales*, Part I: *Medical*, and II: *Population*, 1968;
Annual Reports of the Registrar-General, Scotland, Table A1.2.
OPCS, *Birth Statistics*, Series FMI no. 5, (1978) no. 12 (1985) Table 1.3.

about it, thanks in part to the tireless efforts of early enthusiasts such as Marie Stopes. There were working-class pioneers in contraception too, especially those in service jobs working close to middle-class people, also women working in textiles with one of the most pressing reasons (preserving their incomes) for limiting their fertility. Miners and agricultural workers in their isolated communities, with little opportunity for women to work, retained high fertility until later.

From an average Victorian family size of about six children ever-born (about one would die in infancy, another before maturity), fertility since 1900 had declined considerably and was then in a state of rapid change. The actual average family size of all ages of women at all durations of marriage at the

Table 2.1(b)   Birth- and death-rates and natural
increases, 1901–85, Northern Ireland (per 1000
population)

Period or year	Births	Deaths	Natural increase
1911–15	24.0	17.7	6.3
1916–20	22.5	18.0	4.5
1921–5	23.1	15.6	7.5
1926–30	21.2	14.8	6.4
1931–5	20.0	14.3	5.7
1936–40	19.8	14.3	5.5
1941–5	22.7	13.4[1]	9.3
1946–50	22.0	11.9[1]	10.1
1951–5	20.8	11.3	9.5
1956–60	21.7	10.8	10.9
1961–5	23.0	10.8	12.2
1966–70	21.0	10.6	10.4
1971–5	18.7	11.0	7.7
1976	17.1	11.1	6.0
1977	16.5	11.1	5.4
1978	17.1	10.5	6.6
1979	18.3	10.9	7.4
1980	18.5	10.9	7.6
1981	17.5	10.4	7.1
1982	17.2	10.2	7.0
1983	17.3	10.2	7.1
1984	17.9	10.1	7.8

Note:
1.   Civilian population only.
Source: *Annual Report* of the Registrar-General
Northern Ireland, Table A1.

time of the census of 1911 was 3.5 children. The rate of child-bearing in 1901 among all ages of women, measured as if all women experienced it as they themselves went through life, was equivalent to a completed family size of 3.5 (Table 2.3). This is the 'total fertility rate' (TFR), calculated by summing the age-specific rates. By the end of their child-bearing career, women married in 1900–1909 had had on average 3.4 children (surviving or otherwise) (Table 2.4). Subsequent marriage cohorts continued the plunge into low fertility for a further 20 years, an almost linear decline except for the disruption of the Great War. The low fertility of 1914–18 represents a birth deficit of about 600 000, not entirely restored by the short but massive baby boom which followed. This short boom was, however, bigger than the much better known one which followed the end of the Second World War in 1946–8. 1933 ended the trend begun in 1870. That year saw a nadir of fertility unmatched for a further 45 years, total fertility rate (TFR) equalling 1.72.

Table 2.2   General fertility rate: live births per 1000 women aged 15–44, 1901–85, England and Wales, Scotland, and Northern Ireland

Year	England and Wales	Scotland	Year	Northern Ireland
1901–05	113.0	120.2[1]	1900–1902	99.7[2]
1906–10	105.3	112.1[3]	—	—
1911–15	95.4	105.6	1910–12	101.8[2]
1916–20	80.2	95.3	—	—
1921–5	80.3	94.5	1920–2	104.8
1926–30	67.8	83.1	1925–7	93.9
1931–5	61.7	76.8	1930–2	87.7
1936–40	60.9	73.3		84.5
1941–5	67.2	75.9		93.2
1946–50	80.6	87.6		95.1
1951–5	72.5	81.7		96.7
1956–60	81.8	92.5		106.1
1961–5	91.3	97.6		113.9
1966–70	87.5	91.5		111.8
1971–5	72.8	74.2		97.2
1976–80	61.9	62.0		86.4
1981	61.3	63.8		84.3
1982	59.9	59.8		82.6
1983	59.7	58.9		82.0
1984	59.8	58.4		—
1985	61.0	59.5		—

Notes:
1. Figure for 1900–1905.
2. Estimated from Eire figures to be comparable with later years.
3. Excludes 1908.
Sources: OPCS, *Birth Statistics*, Series FM1, no. 1, Table 1.16 1974;
OPCS, *Birth Statistics*, Series FM1, no. 7, Table 1.16 1980;
OPCS, *Birth Statistics*, Series FM1, no. 12, Table 1.16 1985;
Registrar-General, Scotland, *Annual Reports* for relevant years up to 1930; no. 114 (1968) Part II (*Population and Vital Statistics*) Table S1.6; no. 117 (1971) Part II (*Population and Vital Statistics*) Table S1.5; no. 126 (1980) Table S1.5; Table S2.1 in *Annual Reports* no. 127 (1981), no. 128 (1982), no. 129 (1983), no. 130 (1984) and no. 131 (1985);
CSO, *Annual Abstract of Statistics*, no. 84 (1935–46) to date;
Registrar-General Northern Ireland, *Annual Reports*, no. 59, Table C1 and E; no. 60, Table C1 and E; no. 61, Table C1; no. 62 Table C1 and E1.

Although the total fertility rate had fallen to about 1.8, the completed family size of women at peak child-bearing age at this time was eventually about 2.0 – about replacement level (Figure 2.1). It is typical of 'period' measures of fertility like the TFR that they exaggerate the current fertility trend – because changes in tempo (timing of fertility) usually accompany a decline in the quantum (the final achieved family size) and cumulative period measures can conflate the two, exaggerating (or underestimating) the outcome

Table 2.3   Fertility trends, 1901–85, England and Wales, and Scotland
(live births)

Period	Average annual number of legitimate births per 1000 married women aged 15–44	Illegitimate births per 1000 unmarried women 15–44	Net reproduction rate	Total period fertility rate
England and Wales				
1901–05	230.5	8.4	1.2	3.5
1911–15	190.7	7.9	1.1	2.8
1921–5	156.7	6.7	1.0	2.4
1931–5	115.2	5.5	0.8	1.8
1941–5	105.4	11.4	0.9	2.0
1951–5	105.0	10.1	1.0	2.2
1961–5	125.9	19.1	1.3	2.8
1971–5	97.8	19.7	1.0	2.1
1976–80	86.0	18.1	0.9	1.8
1981	88.8	19.7	0.85	1.80
1982	87.0	21.0	0.84	1.76
1983	86.8	22.3	0.84	1.76
1984	86.7	24.1	0.84	1.75
1985	87.8	26.7	0.86	1.78
Scotland				
1900–02	271.8	13.1[1]	—	—
1910–12	233.2	13.7[2]	—	—
1921–5	205.2	11.2	—	—
1931–5	159.3	9.6	—	—
1941–5	136.4	11.8	1.0	2.4
1951–5	110.2	8.3	1.1	2.5
1961–5	122.2	12.7	1.4	3.0
1971–5	86.8	17.1	1.0	2.2
1976–80	75.9	15.2	0.8	1.8
1981	77.9	18.1	0.88	1.84
1982	74.2	19.5	0.83	1.74
1983	73.9	19.0	0.81	1.70
1984	73.2	20.4	0.81	1.68
1985	74.0	23.1	0.82	1.71

Notes:
1. Figure for 1902.
2. Figure for 1912.
Sources: *Annual Reports* of Registrar-General for Scotland for relevant years up to no. 92 (1946); Scottish data from 1951: Registrar-General, Scotland, *Annual Report*, no. 131 (1985) Tables S1.2, S1.7 and S1.8;
OPCS, *Birth Statistics*, Series FMI, no. 4 (1977) Tables 1.1b and 1.4;
OPCS, *Birth Statistics*, no. 12 (1985) Tables 1.1b and 1.4.

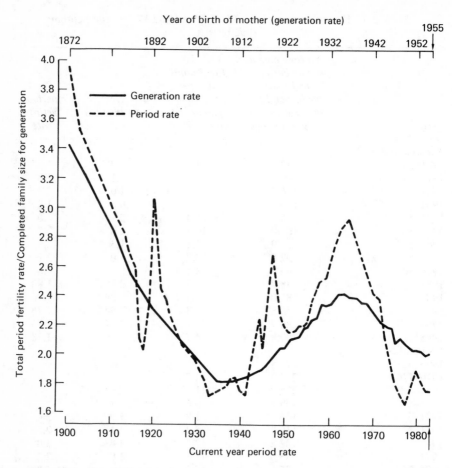

Figure 2.1   Trends in period and generation fertility rates, England and Wales

Source: OPCS (1986) *Variant Population Projections*, 1983–2023, Series PP2 no. 14,
            Fig. 1.

as measured by cohort rates. Fertility at this level is below the level needed for
its long-term replacement. In the 1930s fears of the 'twlight of parenthood'
(Charles, 1936) future underpopulation and of 'race suicide' became lively
topics (Keynes, 1937) in academic and some political circles in Britain and
elsewhere. The fertility decline was given added bite by the earlier decline of
middle-class fertility, compared to working-class (Table 2.5), and of European
compared to other nations (Hogben, 1938). The spur it gave to demographic
analysis included the widespread use of such calculations as the 'net reproduction rate' (NRR). This shorthand projection, not much used nowadays, shows
how far the current fertility as measured by the total fertility rate, discounted

Table 2.4 Live births per woman, 1889–1965 (first
marriage, woman under 45 years of age)

Period of marriage	At 25 years duration of marriage	At census date
Up to 1889	5.06	5.14
1890–99	4.30	4.34
1900–09	3.51	3.53
1910	3.10	3.11
1915	2.61	2.61
1916–20	–	2.46
1920–4	2.32	1921–5 2.18
1926	2.14	1926–30 2.04
1931	2.08	1.99
1936–40	2.02	1.97
1941–5	2.13	2.15
1946–50	2.21	2.20
1951–5	2.28	2.29
1956–60	2.35	2.27
1961–5	(2.23)[1]	(1.89)

Note:
1. At duration 20 years.
Sources: Up to 1915: Glass, D. V. and E. Grebenik 1954;
1946 Great Britain *Family Census*, Volume 1, Table
9 (London: HMSO); 1916–20 onwards: 1971 *Census Fertility Report*, Series DS No. 5, Table 1
(England and Wales) (London: HMSO); Birth Statistics 1980 (Series FM 1, No. 7) Table 10.4 (London: HMSO); recent unpublished figures from Fertility Statistics Unit, OPCS.

by the mortality of children up to the age of their mother and referring to one sex only, will enable the present generation of mothers to replace themselves – or not – and by extension the whole population. Thus a net reproduction rate of 1 implies long-term population replacement (other things being equal); 0.9 a reduction by 10 per cent per generation (about 27 years), 1.1 an increase of 10 per cent per generation (see Table 2.3).

Elsewhere in Europe fear of this population decline with its economic and military connotations, unleashed population policies designed to prevent abortion (which in the late 1920s exceeded live births in Germany) and the dissemination of contraceptive knowledge, particularly in France (Glass, 1942). In Britain the more decorous response was to appoint a Royal Commission on Population. Its report (1949) was a pioneering work in demography, and it conducted the first official enquiry on family planning, in 1946. The Population (Statistics) Act 1938 enabled voluntary questions to be asked at the registration of births, on the date of marriage, and the number

Table 2.5(a)   Comparative fertility 1911. Number of children ever born to married women, 1911, by social class of husband (at 20–25 years duration of marriage, age in 1911 less than 45). Standardised.

Class	Rate per woman	Nature of class
I	4.24	Upper and middle
II	5.02	Occupations intermediate between I and III
III	5.86	Skilled occupations
IV	5.99	Occupations intermediate between III and V
V	6.54	Unskilled occupations
VI	5.37	Textile workers
VII	7.25	Miners
VIII	6.50	Agricultural workers

NB: Classes VI to VIII do not form part of a series in that they are not ranked in descending order of social position. These occupations were thought sufficiently important to warrant separate identification. Classes I to V are not unlike the present Registrar-General's Social Class scale, but the categories here do not distinguish employers from employees.

Source: 1911 Census volume XIII Fertility of Marriage Pt II, Table 25.

Table 2.5(b)   Comparative fertility 1931. Number of infants under age 1 enumerated with fathers in 1931.

Class	No. of infants, average = 100
I	64.5
II	66.5
III	97.2
IV	114.8
V	132.2

Source: Registrar-General's Decennial Supplement 1931 Part IIb Occupational Fertility. Table E (p. 42) (HMSO). Reproduced with the permission of the Controller of Her Majesty's Stationery Office.

NB: In 1931 male clerks were transferred from Social Class II to Social Class III – about ½ million people.

Table 2.5(c)   Mean family size at 1971 Census[1] of
married women[2] by period of marriage and husband's
social group

Date of marriage	Social Group		
	Manual workers	*Non-manual workers*	*All persons*
1931–5[3]	2.69	2.19	2.56
1936–40[3]	2.22	1.96	2.13
1941–5[3]	2.23	1.96	2.13
1946–50	2.29	2.00	2.18
1951–5	2.37	2.13	2.28
1956–60	2.32	2.11	2.24
1961–5	1.92	1.74	1.85
1966–70	0.89	0.63	0.79

Notes:
1. Based on 10 per cent sample.
2. Married women married once only at ages under 45 and enumerated with husband at census.
3. Women married in these years are under-represented in census of 1971 because the questions on fertility were confined to women aged under 60 at census date.

Source: OPCS, Series DS no. 5, *Fertility Report from the 1971 Census – Decennial Supplement*, Table 5.4 (HMSO) (p. 43). Reproduced with the permission of the Controller of Her Majesty's Stationery Office.

and age of previous children. This enabled fertility to be analysed in a more sophisticated way than was previously possible, and has helped us to avoid repeating some of the errors of demographic judgement of the 1930s. Private concerns had set up the National Birth Rate Commission in 1916; while the Eugenics Society set up the Population Investigation Committee in 1935 (now incorporated in the London School of Economics) which recently celebrated its 50th birthday (Hobcraft and Murphy, in press).

   This reduction in fertility – reached by most industrial countries at about the same time – had no historical precedent. The transition was not over in the 1930s – there were still many large families, and their decline continues slowly up to the present day – but a new fertility regime was about to begin, which has lasted up to the present. This is characterised, in almost all developed societies, by a wholly unprecedented volatility in fertility, especially in its timing, made possible by the new power enjoyed by parents to adjust the pace of their child-bearing to their perceived circumstances and personal wants, with a precision hitherto impossible. This has generated much bigger swings in fertility over a short time than had previously been possible through the old

Malthusian regulator of the delay or avoidance of marriage. One child more or less in a family size of six is a change of 17 per cent, but with an average family size of 2 it is 50 per cent. The erratic course taken by fertility since the 1930s has dominated the demography of the industrial world for the rest of the twentieth century and will dominate it well into the next through its effects on the age-structure (Figure 2.2).

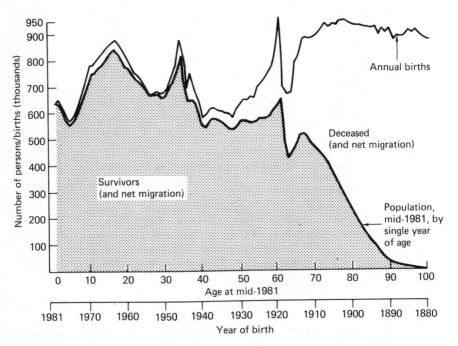

Figure 2.2 Mid-1981 age distribution compared with past births, England and Wales

Source: J. Craig (1983) 'The Growth of the Elderly Population'; *Population Trends*, 32:29 (Fig. 1). Reproduced with the permission of the Controller of Her Majesty's Stationery Office.

The course of fertility gently rose up to the Second World War – a predictable Malthusian response, through the relaxation of preventive checks on births including earlier marriage, to gently rising prosperity at a time when men's wage-packets still dominated household income. The war itself first depressed fertility, the return of defeated armies in 1940 may have helped to restore it. Wartime output of births peaked in 1944 (751 000); fertility fell again in 1945 and rose to a sharp peak after the end of the war in 1946) (TFR 2.69 in 1947). Most European countries had a short post-war baby boom – even the vanquished and the neutrals.

Not surprisingly we are rather short of data to document this decade. The war stopped the 1941 Census. There are no really adequate population denominators available for the calculation of vital rates as a result; in any case the population was distorted internally by evacuation and the absences abroad of many men in the armed forces. A National Register, compiled in record time in September 1939 for National Registration, provides some information, but already distorted by wartime conditions. Unfortunately this followed the mean and restricted census of 1931, which had only a relatively short series of questions. It was then assumed that the census would thereafter be held every five years as provided for in the 1920 Census Order. In fact these powers have only ever been made use of in 1966 (and abortively for the cancelled censuses of 1976 and 1986).

After the war the late 1940s seemed like the 1930s revisited, with fertility apparently drifting down again towards replacement rate (TFR in 1951, 2.14; NRR (Net Reproduction Rate) 1.00). Official projections made even in the early 1950s assumed continuing low fertility and consequent slow population growth (Figure 2.3). Fluctuations in fertility have been subverting official projections ever since. The most interesting feature of the post-war fertility in the developed world was the great boom in births from the early 1950s until the late 1960s, peaking in 1964 in the UK with a TFR of 2.94 (see Glass, 1968). This baby boom added about 2 million births to the number that would have occurred had fertility remained at its 1955 level through to the 1970s. As a later section discusses, it put heavy pressure on the primary schools, secondary schools, higher education and the employment system in turn (in 1986 its effect on the housing system is at its height). It caught demographers quite by surprise (Holmans, 1987) and even now the boom and its subsequent decline are hard to account for. Projections made at the height of the boom looked forward to a UK population of 60 million in 1980 and 70 million in 2000 (1986 population 56 million). These projections (Figure 2.3) were an important reason why so much high-density local authority building, which now causes so much trouble, was put up – to avoid the countryside becoming covered with houses. These great expectations also gave added impetus to regional policy, to divert population away from the already crowded South-East. Until 1972 fertility was well above the level required for replacement, and generated population growth (with intermittent help from immigration) up to 0.6 per cent. This was modest by third-world or even nineteenth-century standards, but enough in the growing environmental consciousness of the day to provide a rash of public warnings against the harmful effects of continuing UK population growth on city size, rural environment, economy and infrastructure, which continued even after fertility had already slowed down in the early 1970s (for example, Taylor, 1970; Select Committee on Science and Technology, 1971).

The final phase of fertility change has lasted from the early 1970s to the present. The fall in fertility from 1964 levelled out by the mid-1970s. But while no longer declining, fertility as measured by the TFR has remained stubbornly

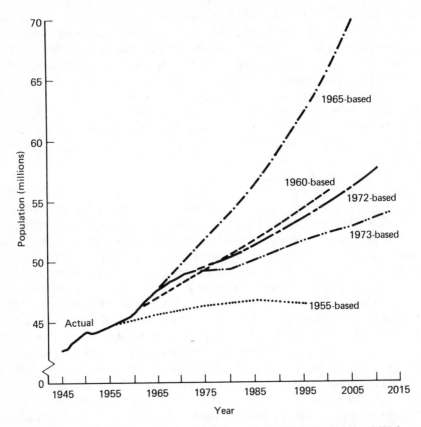

Figure 2.3   Actual and projected population, 1945–2010, England and Wales

Source: Registrar-General's *Quarterly Return*, no. 501, 1st Quarter 1974, Chart 2, p. 50. Reproduced with the permission of the Controller of Her Majesty's Stationery Office.

below replacement rate ever since 1972, not varying much between the nadir of 1.66 in 1977 and 1.78 in 1985 (Figure 2.4). As usual, cohort rates have not yet shown the same volatility (Table 2.6). This also stimulated further interest in the problems of an ageing or even declining population, although in a more demographically and economically informed context where zero population growth is no longer automatically regarded as a problem (Central Policy Review Staff, 1973). But within this sub-replacement level now maintained for over a decade, much change is taking place in the pattern of child-bearing.

Components of fertility trends

Thanks to the data collected under the Population (Statistics) Act 1938, the fertility inquiry in successive censuses and more recent surveys, we can make

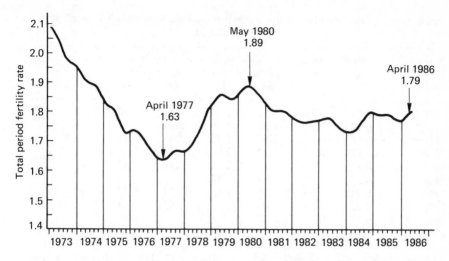

Figure 2.4   Trend in total period fertility rate, January 1973 to April 1986

Source: Live births during the first half of 1986, OPCS *Monitor* FM1 86/6, Figure 1.

more precise statements about the components of these fertility changes (by age of mother, duration of marriage, number of previous children) and their proximate determinants, such as marriage and contraception: the immediate behavioural influences on the chances of child-bearing. In general, these show that changes in the rate of fertility depends more on changes in the timing of child-bearing (the 'tempo') than in the final achieved family size (the 'quantum').

Table 2.6(a)   Total number of live births per woman by woman's year of birth and age, England and Wales

Woman's year of birth	Mean number of children per woman achieved by successive ages reached before the end of 1985					
	20	25	30	35	40	45
1921	0.08	0.58	1.33	1.76	1.98	2.05
1926	0.08	0.72	1.41	1.87	2.12	2.18
1931	0.11	0.77	1.57	2.10	2.30	2.34
1936	0.12	0.90	1.80	2.25	2.38	2.40
1941	0.17	1.08	1.89	2.22	2.32	2.34
1946	0.22	1.04	1.74	2.05	2.16	
1951	0.24	0.89	1.51	1.87		
1956	0.20	0.76	1.40			
1961	0.16	0.65				
1966	0.14					

Table 2.6(b)   Total number of live births per woman by woman's year of birth and age, Scotland

Woman's year of birth	Mean number of children per woman achieved by successive ages reached before the end of 1985						
	20	25	30	35	40	45	
1921	0.10	0.78	1.67	2.20	2.47	2.56	
1926	0.09	0.74	1.51	2.06	2.34	2.41	
1931	0.11	0.81	1.67	2.25	2.48	2.51	
1936	0.11	0.97	1.92	2.39	2.54	2.56	
1941	0.16	1.09	1.96	2.32	2.41	2.43	
1946	0.21	1.11	1.84	2.14			
1951	0.24	0.93	1.56	1.89	2.25	2.27	} projections
1956	0.22	0.78	1.40		1.99	2.01	
1961	0.17	0.68					
1966	0.14						

Sources: OPCS, *Birth Statistics*, Series FMI, no. 12 (1985) Table S13; Registrar-General's, Scotland *Annual Report* (1985) Table S1.10.

Changes in average age at marriage and in its popularity have had an important effect, especially since the Second World War. Up to the late nineteenth century, as Wrigley and Schofield (1981) have shown, trends in marriage – in its timing and its avoidance – were the main determinant of fertility trends. Although this primacy has yielded to contraception within marriage, marriage patterns – which have changed radically in the twentieth century – still have a significant effect on births. In brief, from the 1930s until the 1970s marriage became much more popular and occurred earlier in life than ever before, especially among women. This general advance of marriage from the 1930s is a broad social change requiring a general explanation, and is discussed later.

But it had an important effect on the pattern of age-specific fertility (Table 2.7), so that women in the 1950s and 1960s had their babies earlier in life than had previously been normal. Particularly striking increases were evident in birth-rates of women in their early twenties and among teenagers – initially at least because a much higher proportion were married (Glass, 1967; see also Glass, 1976). These rates doubled, or more than doubled, from 1938 to 1964. The rise of family planning allowed couples to enjoy the consolations of married life without the need to acquire its burdens in the form of children straight away. From 1900–1909 to 1930–34 the median interval from marriage to first born (in 2-child families) only increased modestly from 18 months to 19 months. But rather surprisingly, this interval remained relatively constant from the 1930s to the 1970s: it was 20 months in 1971. But since then it has lengthened considerably, reaching 29 months in 1980 (Britton, 1980) and 28 months in 1985. On top of this, since the 1930s women have increasingly

Table 2.7 Age specific fertility rates, general fertility rate and total fertility rate all live births to married and unmarried women, 1938–85 (England and Wales)

Period	Age of woman								TFR
	15–44	15–19	20–4	25–9	30–4	35–9	40–4	45–9	
1938	62.2	14.7	92.3	113.2	82.9	47.3	16.1	1.5	1.83
1940	58.7	15.3	90.7	108.4	75.2	43.0	14.8	1.4	1.74
1945	68.8	17.2	102.9	117.6	93.6	57.7	18.5	1.4	2.04
1950	73.0	22.2	126.3	136.2	89.4	48.3	14.2	1.1	2.18
1955	72.8	23.5	137.0	141.7	84.3	44.2	12.4	0.8	2.22
1960	86.8	34.0	165.5	171.9	100.8	46.4	13.8	0.8	2.66
1965	92.1	45.4	179.5	180.8	102.6	48.1	12.6	0.9	2.86
1970	84.3	49.4	156.1	154.7	80.1	34.7	8.6	0.6	2.41
1975	63.0	36.5	114.7	123.2	58.5	20.0	4.8	0.4	1.79
1976	60.4	32.2	110.2	119.8	57.9	18.7	4.4	0.3	1.72
1977	58.1	29.8	104.7	119.0	59.1	18.3	4.1	0.3	1.66
1978	60.1	29.9	107.9	123.9	63.9	19.7	4.2	0.4	1.73
1979	63.3	30.7	112.2	132.7	70.0	21.5	4.3	0.4	1.84
1980	64.2	30.9	114.1	135.7	71.3	22.6	4.3	0.5	1.88
1981	61.3	28.1	105.3	129.1	68.6	21.7	4.4	0.5	1.80
1982	59.9	27.4	101.6	126.4	69.1	22.8	4.2	0.5	1.76
1983	59.7	26.9	98.5	126.4	71.5	23.1	4.4	0.5	1.76
1984	59.8	27.6	95.5	126.2	73.6	23.6	4.5	0.4	1.75
1985	61.0	29.5	94.5	127.6	76.4	24.1	4.6	0.4	1.78
Index figures of age specific fertility									
1950 with 1938 set at 100		151	137	120	108	102	88	73	
1964 with 1950 set at 100		191	144	138	121	103	89	91	
1977 with 1964 set at 100		69	57	63	54	37	32	30	
1980 with 1977 set at 100		104	109	114	121	123	105	167	
1985 with 1980 set at 100		95	83	94	107	107	107	80	

Sources: OPCS, *Birth Statistics*, Series FM1, no. 12 ( ) Table 3.1b; *Population Trends*, Table 10; Registrar-General's *Statistical Review*, vol. II, *Population*, Table EE(b).

Table 2.8   Legitimate live births by duration of marriage, England and Wales (thousands). Women married once only

| | Completed months | | | | | Completed years | | | | |
Period	0–7	8–11	0	1	2	3	4	5–9	10–14	15+
1938	38.7	48.9	87.6	79.4	63.1	53.8	45.3	139.4	65.2	40.0
1941	32.0	40.6	72.6	94.7	56.6	43.9	38.4	121.3	62.6	39.8
1946	32.3	49.6	81.9	84.5	53.0	52.9	62.5	259.0	98.4	46.1
1951	42.1	39.4	81.5	85.7	70.0	65.9	57.5	153.3	78.6	31.3
1956	46.9	43.5	90.4	80.7	68.6	63.9	58.5	186.6	65.4	34.0
1961	59.1	43.6	102.7	88.1	81.2	76.1	67.7	208.4	86.6	35.7
1966	71.6	43.3	114.9	94.7	87.8	81.3	70.3	203.8	76.7	34.5
1971	67.3	32.8	100.1	87.2	89.4	86.2	73.0	182.3	56.8	23.1
1976	35.4	17.1	54.5	53.5	60.5	66.5	62.7	165.8	31.4	10.9
1977	32.9	15.9	48.8	50.9	57.0	60.2	60.0	166.7	32.0	9.8
1978	34.5	16.9	51.5	51.7	57.9	61.0	58.5	177.1	36.5	10.0
1979	37.4	18.8	56.2	55.7	58.7	60.6	59.1	191.4	42.7	10.4
1980	39.8	19.8	59.6	59.5	59.7	59.3	57.8	186.6	46.9	11.0
1981	36.2	18.1	54.3	58.2	60.3	55.0	52.2	175.4	48.1	11.3
1982	34.0	17.2	51.1	54.0	60.0	56.6	50.4	164.2	49.0	11.8
1983	33.3	17.5	50.8	52.6	57.9	58.3	51.2	158.0	49.1	12.2

Source: OPCS Birth Statistics, Historical Series, Series FM1 No. 13. Table 5.5a London, HMSO. Reproduced with the permission of the Controller of Her Majesty's Stationery Office.

completed their families within the first ten years of marriage (Table 2.8). Irrespective of family size, the interval between marriage and last birth, and between first and last birth has been getting shorter, especially since the marriages of 1951 (Table 2.9). This trend also raises birth-rates of women in their twenties and made child-bearing among women over age 30 relatively rare, until recently.

These measures have a particular bearing on the rate at which babies are being born at any given time. In the longer run population growth or decline depends particularly on how many women have a second birth, or (especially) a third birth, and so on – the 'parity' of births (Table 2.10). This naturally affects the distribution of family size (Table 2.11). As far as the final family size is concerned, one-child families became relatively common for the first time in the marriages of the 1920s and 1930s. This is evident in the numbers of families going on to have another child from any given existing family size (the 'parity progression ratio') which have changed in a most interesting way. 84 per cent of women married in 1900–1909 with at least one birth had gone on to have a second within 15 years of marriage; only 68 per cent of women married 1925–9 did so. But childlessness and one-child families became markedly less popular in the 1950s and 1960s and women were more likely to go on to a second. 19 per cent of women married in 1926–30 were childless in 1961; only

Table 2.9   Interval between marriage and last birth, and first and last birth.
Marriages 1931–60 England and Wales, women married once only under 45 years

Year of marriage	2 children born by 1971		3 children born by 1971	
	Marriage/ last birth	First birth/ last birth	Marriage/ last birth	First birth/ last birth
1931–5	8.6	6.0	11.5	9.8
1936–40	8.1	5.0	10.9	8.7
1941–5	7.5	4.6	10.6	8.4
1946–50	7.1	4.5	10.2	8.2
1951–5	7.0	4.0	9.5	7.4
1956–60	6.1	3.4	7.8	6.0

Source: 1971 Census, *Fertility Report*, Table 7.3 (HMSO). Reproduced with the permission of the Controller of Her Majesty's Stationery Office.

Table 2.10   England and Wales, legitimate live births by previous liveborn children.
All married women. 1938–1985

Period	Total	No. of previous liveborn children					
		0	1	2	3	4	5 or more
1938	594 825	250 552	152 133	77 884	42 086	25 033	47 127
1941	548 033	243 752	129 709	72 059	39 478	22 730	40 305
1946	766 800	325 301	230 195	105 283	47 309	24 105	34 607
1951	644 758	243 830	202 058	103 366	46 298	22 058	27 148
1956	666 801	264 193	197 342	101 266	50 029	25 198	28 773
1961	762 791	280 478	232 717	124 827	60 376	29 895	35 575
1966	782 767	287 368	246 310	129 718	60 335	28 662	30 374
1971	717 477	283 615	240 784	111 651	45 859	18 844	16 724
1976	530 504	217 211	203 576	70 967	23 569	8 425	6 756
1977	513 880	214 573	195 035	68 796	21 935	7 521	6 020
1978	535 781	226 566	198 088	74 173	23 358	7 684	5 892
1979	568 561	238 890	206 667	82 742	25 963	8 182	6 117
1980	578 862	240 975	209 164	86 336	27 537	8 651	6 199
1981	553 509	224 290	205 690	82 400	26 160	8 940	6 040
1982	536 074	211 862	200 681	81 431	27 123	8 861	6 116
1983	529 923	211 753	195 630	80 728	26 646	8 956	6 210
1984	526 353	210 421	193 093	80 643	26 860	15 336	6 368
1985	530 167	212 017	193 058	82 403	26 865	15 824	6 569

Source: OPCS Birth Statistics, Series FM1 Table 4.1 OPCS Birth Statistics, Series FM1 No. 13, Historical Series, Table 4.1. Reproduced with the permission of the Controller of Her Majesty's Stationery Office.
(NB. Figures differ slightly from Registrar General's Statistical Review Table HH.)

Table 2.11   Women with uninterrupted first marriage: distribution of family size by selected years of marriage, 1911–65, England and Wales, up to 1971

Year of marriage	Number of children								Total
	0	*1*	*2*	*3*	*4*	*5*	*6*	*7 or more*	*Total*
1911–15	139	193	224	159	102	64	42	77	1000
1921–5	178	252	245	139	76	43	26	41	1000
1931–5	175	270	266	143	70	35	18	23	1000
1941–5	97	258	331	167	77	34	18	18	1000
1951–5	112	179	334	197	100	42	20	16	1000
1961–5	113	205	444	175	48	11	3	1	1000

Note: Family size of some women married 1961–5 would not be completed by 1971.
Source: OPCS, Series DS no. 5, *Fertility Report from the 1971 Census – Decennial Supplement*, Table 4.7 (HMSO) (p. 36). Reproduced with the permission of the Controller of Her Majesty's Stationery Office.

10 per cent of those married in the late 1940s and late 1950s were childless in 1971. Involuntary childlessness afflicts about 5 per cent of married couples. A similar but more variable proportion choose not to have children. The priorities behind voluntary childlessness have been studied seriously only recently (Campbell, 1985; Baum and Cope, 1980).

The fall in the number of people with large families with over three children continued from the previous century (Table 2.11). This may be regarded as a longer-term trend whereby knowledge of family planning and the ideal of a small family have become familiar even to many of the poorest and least-educated families. Thus family size has become more concentrated around two children than previously. But even though two-child families resulted from only 22 per cent of the marriages of 1911–15 and are now 44 per cent of the marriages of 1961–5, they are still not quite the majority of families. Almost a quarter (24 per cent) are larger; almost a third comprise one or no children. But this post-war pattern has itself been shaken up since the 1970s.

The components of the latest sub-replacement phase of fertility are rather different from the previous one. The age pattern of fertility has shifted back again. Teenage births are less common, women are having children later in life, more often into their thirties. More women than before are having a third or even further babies, while first births decline and second births remain about constant. And a much higher proportion of children are illegitimate. In so far as there was a revival in fertility after the low point of 1977, it was older women and women who had already had at least two babies who provided most of the increase – including remarried women, who only produce 1 in 13 of all babies but who were responsible for 41 864 births in 1985 compared to 25 119 in 1975 and 16 794 in 1966. So consolidation of the small nuclear family continues with a further reduction in the number of very large families. A growing proportion of such families are now born to immigrant mothers – their fertility will be discussed under a separate heading.

CONTRACEPTION AND ABORTION

It would not be right to attribute the general decline in fertility since the 1960s to the improved contraception (the pill) of that decade or the Abortion Act of 1967. Total abortions only account for about one-third of the birth deficit of the present day compared to 1964; in any case, most are to unmarried women or to older or high-parity married women. And, of course, legal abortion must to a great degree replace the level of illegal abortion before the 1967 Act – variously estimated at between 30 000 and 100 000 per year. Better contraception merely allows family intentions to be translated more accurately into reality; it doesn't change these ideals or intentions and has no particular tendency of itself to reduce them – that only happens to the unwanted component of fertility. The birth famine of the 1930s was achieved with decidedly old-fashioned means of contraception – withdrawal and the condom – while the baby boom of the 1950s occurred at a time of progressively wider use of family planning. The first major family planning enquiry of 1946 by Lewis-Faning, in conjunction with the 1946 Family Census, covers couples married in the first half of the century. Knowledge of family planning in the nineteenth century comes from other sources, including statistical inference from the results of the 1911 Census (Matras, 1965; Banks, 1954). Since the Family Census of 1946 there have been a large number of surveys of contraceptive knowledge, attitude and practice (for example, Langford, 1976; Cartwright, 1978; Dunnell 1979). Some of the results are summarised in Table 2.12.

Contraception has become almost universal, with over 80 per cent of women aged 16–40 currently using some form of family planning, and over 90 per cent ever having done so. Older methods of contraception such as withdrawal and the sheath have become less popular, and the pill and, to a lesser extent, the IUD more so. The most spectacular increase is in sterilisation; with a sixfold increase in the proportion of women protected by

Table 2.12(a)   Family planning and contraception (Women married 1941–65. Ever-use of family planning, by social group), Great Britain

Year of marriage	Manual (%)	Non-manual (%)	All (%)
1941–5	76.8	88.7	82.1
1946–50	86.4	88.2	86.7
1951–5	86.3	95.8	89.7
1956–60	89.3	93.3	90.6
1961–5	91.3	92.7	91.4

Source: Glass, D.V., 'The Components of Natural Increase in England and Wales', Memorandum Submitted to the First Report of the Select Committee on Science and Technology. 1971 London, Table 3, (HMSO).

Table 2.12(b)   Trends in *ever*-use by marriage cohort

Year of marriage	% ever use	Pill	IUD	Condom	Cap	With-drawal	Safe period	Sperm-icide	Other
				Method used by ever-users					
1941–50	84.6	6	<1	59	15	47	9	27	5
1951–60	90.2	22	2	65	22	47	12	29	4
1961–65	91.4	31	4	60	17	36	13	22	3
All	88.2	18	2	61	18	45	11	27	4

Source: Langford (1976), Table 4.1.

sterilisation from 1970 (4 per cent) to 1983 (24 per cent). This is becoming the predominant form of contraception for women over age 30. Among the 28 per cent of cohabiting or married women protected by sterilisation in 1983, only 9 per cent of women aged 25–29 were protected in this way, but 31 per cent of women aged 30–34 and 44 per cent of women aged 35–39. Finally, social class differences have narrowed; in 1967–8 32 per cent of professional mothers used the pill, and 13 per cent of mothers in unskilled manual workers' households. By 1975, these percentages were 32 per cent and 41 per cent respectively. And in 1983 the proportion of manual workers' wives protected by sterilisation exceeded that of non-manual workers' wives (29 per cent against 26 per cent).

There seems to be little further room for any expansion of the use of family planning within marriage, with 90 per cent of women using some form of contraception at some time. But among certain groups (unmarried adolescents, some categories of immigrant women) contraceptive use is still at late nineteenth-century levels, if that. And repeated scares about the safety of oral contraception, by no means all justified, are persuading older and more educated women to move to less effective forms of contraception (for example, the sheath) or to be sterilised. There are likely to be contraceptive consequences, too, from the growing pressure to use condoms as a protection against AIDS, especially in the context of extracurricular sexual activity.

Abortion is not a front line method of contraception in Britain. Since the 1967 Abortion Act its impact has been concentrated on pregnancies outside marriage (72 per cent in 1983) or pregnancies of married women aged over 35. The abortion ratio in Britain remains low (the ratio of abortions to live births) and has not exceeded 214: but it has been increasing since the late 1970s (Table 2.13). During the 1970s abortions on resident women increased slowly from 95 000 (12 per cent of all conceptions) to 121 000 (16 per cent of all conceptions). Since 1980 there has been a more rapid increase to 136 000 in 1984, which represents 17 per cent of all known conceptions. It should be pointed out that these figures omit conceptions terminated by spontaneous abortion and illegal abortion, but they include stillbirths which have declined from 40 per 1000 all births in 1928, when they were first registered, to 5.5 in 1985. Most conceptions (perhaps 75 per cent) abort spontaneously, mostly

Table 2.12(c) Ever–married women aged 16–39/40 (trends in *current* use of different forms of contraception), 1970–83

Form of contraception	1970 England and Wales Family Planning Services Survey (%)	1975 England and Wales Family Planning Services Survey (%)	1976 Great Britain Family Formation Survey (%)	1983 General Household Survey (%)
Pill	19	30	32	29
IUD	4	6	8	9
Condom	28	18	16	15
Cap	4	2	2	2
Withdrawal	14	5	5	4
Safe period	5	1	1	1
Abstinence	3	1	0	1
Other	—	3	1	1
At least 1 non-surgical	71	63	61	58
Female sterilisation	} 4	} 13	8	12
Male sterilisation			8	12
Total at least one	75	76	77	81
Not using any	25	24	23	19
Sample base	2520	2344	3378	2850

Note: Figures for ever-use are higher than for current use, and these are congruent with Table 2.12(a).
Source: General Household Survey, 1983, Table 5.5. Reproduced with the permission of the Controller of Her Majesty's Stationery Office.

Table 2.13 Legal abortions on women resident in England and Wales, 1968–85 (thousands)

Year	Total	Under 16	16–19	20–34	Single women	Married women	Widowed, divorced etc.	Total live births	Ratio of abortions to 1000 live births
1968[1]	22.1	0.2	3.6	13.5	10.1	10.1	1.9	819 272	27
1969	49.8	1.2	8.1	29.9	22.3	23.0	4.6	797 538	62
1970	75.4	1.7	13.5	45.5	34.1	34.3	7.0	784 486	96
1971	94.6	2.3	18.2	56.0	44.3	41.5	8.7	783 155	121
1972	108.6	2.8	21.8	63.8	51.1	46.9	10.6	725 440	150
1973	110.6	3.1	23.5	64.1	52.9	46.8	10.9	675 953	164
1974	109.4	3.3	24.2	63.0	53.3	45.1	11.0	639 885	171
1975	106.2	3.6	24.1	60.4	52.3	43.1	10.8	603 445	176
1976	101.9	3.4	24.0	57.5	50.9	40.3	10.7	584 270	174
1977	102.7	3.6	24.6	57.5	51.8	39.6	11.2	569 259	150
1978	111.9	3.3	26.4	63.8	56.4	42.2	13.3	596 418	188
1979	120.6	3.5	29.2	68.6	62.6	43.3	14.7	638 028	189
1980	128.9	3.7	31.9	74.5	68.8	44.3	15.9	656 234	196
1981	128.6	3.5	31.4	74.9	70.0	42.4	16.1	634 492	203
1982	128.6	3.9	31.3	74.8	71.8	40.5	16.2	625 931	205
1983	127.4	4.1	31.2	74.1	73.3	38.4	15.7	629 134	202
1984	136.4	4.2	33.4	80.6	81.1	38.7	16.6	636 815	214
1985	141.1	4.0	34.2	85.1	87.2	37.7	14.6	656 417	215

Notes:
1. 8 months only.
Source: OPCS, Population Trends, 45: Table 23, p. 64;
OPCS, Birth Statistics, Series FMI Table 1.1;
Registrar-General's Statistical Review of England and Wales, Supplement on Abortion, Table 2A.

Table 2.14 Proportion of pregnancies outside and inside marriage terminated by abortion, 1969–83, England and Wales

Year	Under 16	Under 20	*Conceptions outside marriage* 20–4	25–9	30–4	35–9	40 and over
1969	26	14	19	22	21	24	27
1971	37	26	33	34	34	38	40
1973	45	33	40	40	39	45	51
1975	52	38	41	40	41	44	54
1977	53	39	39	38	40	47	59
1979	55	40	39	37	39	49	64
1981	57	41	39	37	39	48	62
1983	57	40	37	34	36	45	59
1984	56	40	36	34	35	43	59

Year	Under 20	*Conceptions within marriage* 20–4	25–9	30–4	35–9	40 and over
1969	1	1	3	7	13	23
1971	2	3	5	12	23	38
1973	2	3	6	15	29	47
1975	3	4	6	14	31	51
1977	3	4	5	12	30	52
1979	4	4	5	11	28	51
1981	4	4	5	11	27	48
1983	3	4	5	10	23	44
1984	4	4	5	9	22	43

Sources: OPCS *Monitor*, FMI 85/8, 'Trends in Conception in England and Wales During 1983', Tables 4, 5; OPCS, *Birth Statistics*, Series FMI no. 12 (1985) Tables 12.3, 12.5.

because of genetical defects, in most cases without the mother being aware of it. The most striking changes in the proportion of pregnancies terminated by abortion has been in unmarried teenagers, where the proportion almost doubled from 1971 to 1981. The 1980s has seen no further tendency for extramarital pregnancies to end in abortion, in fact the tendency is downwards, in association with the higher proportion of births to relatively stable unions outside marriage. A similar trend in married women aged over 35 cannot be explained in such terms (Table 2.14). A high proportion of such abortions are carried out on medical grounds.

BIRTHS INSIDE AND OUTSIDE MARRIAGE

Marriage continues to be the usual framework for child-bearing, although one of the major trends of the twentieth century has been a reduction of its importance as a determinant of fertility. This has happened because birth control has displaced a major part of the fertility regulation function of marriage, and because of the rise of illegitimate births. Much of the recent increase in illegitimacy has been to cohabiting couples who see no need for marriage formalities. While the timing of marriage continues to be related to the timing of births, there is no doubt that there has been some disconnection between fertility and marriage, especially since the 1950s. This is apparent in the reduced emphasis on marriage in the analysis of fertility recently.

Illegitimacy

Until the 1950s, illegitimacy accounted for less than 5 per cent of births. Its frequency had declined throughout most of the nineteenth century in western Europe (Shorter, Knodel and Van de Walle, 1971). After the inevitable wartime increases (Figure 2.5) it was particularly low in the 1930s and the 1950s (Pearce and Farid, 1977). From the 1960s illegitimacy has been resolutely increasing (Table 2.15), as it has generally in Europe; the UK is now top of the European league outside Scandinavia. About one child in five is now born illegitimate. In 1985 there were 126 000 illegitimate births in England and Wales; 37 000 to teenagers, 48 000 to women aged 20–24, 24 000 to women aged 25–29. A proportion – a great part of the increase – of these births can be regarded as a replacement for marital fertility; many are born to couples living together in some form of relatively stable union (Table 2.16). This can be inferred from the joint registration on birth certificates of illegitimate births (65 per cent in 1985) and the identity of addresses of such parents (72 per cent in 1985). These proportions are both considerably higher among older single women. 'Traditional' mostly unwanted, illegitimate births still occur in large numbers to teenage girls, many of whom are still living at home: there were 36 900 such births in 1985 compared to 20 500 in 1975. But 34 per cent were jointly registered in 1975 and 57 per cent in 1985, so the number of teenage illegitimate births which are singly registered have only increased by about 2000 over the decade. The trend suggests that but for the 1967 Abortion Act the number would be greater still.

Recent trends have been quite complex because of abrupt changes in the popularity of teenage marriage, changes in teenage sexual activity and in the availability of contraception and abortion (Table 2.17). In 1938 there were 25 000 teenage births, of which 81 per cent were legitimate and 3 per cent were premaritally conceived. The number of teenage births doubled up to 1960, primarily because of the novel popularity of teenage marriage – the proportion illegitimate scarcely changed at all. But after the 1960s the position reversed. Teenage births peaked in 1966 at 87 000 and declined to 58 000 in 1976, at which level it has remained relatively constant ever since, as has the underlying ratio per 1000 teenagers. But the number of legitimate births has

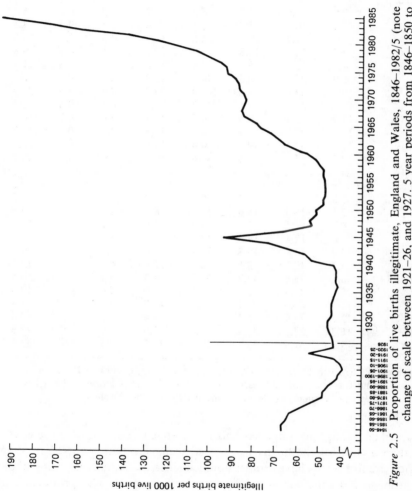

Figure 2.5   Proportion of live births illegitimate, England and Wales, 1846–1982/5 (note change of scale between 1921–26, and 1927. 5 year periods from 1846–1850 to 1921–1926; single years from 1927.)

Source: OPCS, *Birth Statistics*, Series FMI, London, HMSO.

Table 2.15   Birth-rates by age of mother: illegitimate live births per 1000 unmarried
women, 1939–85, England and Wales, and Scotland

Year	15–19	20–4	25–9	30–4	35–9	40–4	45+	Total 15–49
England and Wales								
1939	2.9	7.6	9.1	8.2	6.7	2.7	0.2	5.2
1941	3.4	10.5	13.8	11.1	7.6	3.3	0.2	7.4
1946	4.9	19.3	28.2	25.0	13.9	4.5	0.3	13.8
1951	3.7	12.2	20.5	20.7	12.6	4.1	0.3	9.8
1956	4.8	15.7	25.1	24.6	15.4	4.9	0.3	11.4
1961	8.0	25.2	40.2	34.6	20.2	6.8	0.4	16.5
1966	12.3	32.4	53.2	44.4	25.3	7.6	0.5	21.7
1971	14.6	29.6	47.1	41.2	21.7	6.1	0.3	22.3
1976	11.9	23.4	29.5	24.6	13.7	3.6	0.2	16.7
1981	13.7	27.8	33.7	26.0	11.9	4.1	0.1	19.7
1984	17.4	32.1	39.1	30.4	15.4	3.8	0.2	24.1
1985	19.7	35.2	41.8	32.6	16.2	4.0	0.2	26.7
Scotland								
1939	5.3	12.0	11.5	10.6	7.7	2.8	—	8.2
1941	5.1	14.4	15.0	13.3	8.5	2.6	—	9.6
1947	4.7	17.5	26.5	19.5	12.6	4.1	—	12.3
1951	3.7	12.4	18.6	18.9	12.5	3.0	—	9.6
1956	4.2	13.3	18.8	18.4	11.6	3.4	—	9.6
1961	5.7	17.2	29.5	23.8	15.0	4.8	—	12.4
1966	8.8	25.2	43.7	34.3	19.0	5.9	—	16.5
1971	12.1	29.3	42.7	38.1	20.6	4.6	—	19.4
1976	11.2	23.0	25.1	24.7	13.7	3.3	—	15.8
1981	12.5	27.9	35.7	26.4	13.4	3.3	—	19.6
1984	16.3	27.5	32.4	26.6	12.6	2.9	—	22.6
1985	19.1	31.6	33.1	27.8	13.7	2.5	—	23.1

Sources: OPCS, *Birth Statistics*, Series FMI no. 12 (1985), Table 3.1b.
Registrar-General's *Statistical Review*, vol. II, *Population*, Table EE(G).
Registrar-General Scotland, Annual Report 1985 Table s1.8

collapsed as teenage marriage has become relatively rare – in 1985 there were less than a third of the births to married teenagers that occurred in 1966. Illegitimate live births have almost doubled since then and from being about one teenage birth in four are now about two in three. The proportion of legitimate live births which were conceived before marriage increased to 60 per cent in 1968 but then declined to a steady 50 per cent since 1975 – a consequence of more widely available contraception and abortion, as well as a greater tolerance of illegitimate birth, as Figure 2.6 makes clear. There is no doubt that sexual activity before marriage has become much more popular and has started earlier as time has gone on. Recently there has been a rash of

Table 2.16(a)   Illegitimate live births according to registration by mother or by both parents, 1975–85, England and Wales

Year		All ages No. (000s)	*Age of mother at birth*					
			All ages	Under 20	20–4	25–9	30–4	35 and over
			Percentage sole/joint in each age-group					
1975	Total	54.9						
	Sole	28.0	51.0	65.8	50.7	35.6	31.8	32.5
	Joint	26.9	49.0	34.2	49.3	64.4	68.2	67.5
1976	Total	53.8						
	Sole	26.4	49.0	63.7	48.0	35.2	29.9	31.8
	Joint	27.4	51.0	36.3	52.0	64.8	70.1	68.2
1977	Total	55.4						
	Sole	26.1	47.1	60.8	46.4	34.2	29.5	31.1
	Joint	29.3	52.9	39.2	53.6	65.8	70.5	68.9
1978	Total	60.6						
	Sole	27.8	45.9	59.0	44.9	34.1	29.2	31.4
	Joint	32.8	54.1	41.0	55.1	65.9	70.8	68.6
1979	Total	69.5						
	Sole	31.1	44.8	57.1	44.3	33.9	29.4	31.8
	Joint	38.3	55.2	42.9	55.7	66.1	70.6	68.2
1980	Total	77.4						
	Sole	33.2	42.9	54.3	42.6	33.5	28.7	29.6
	Joint	44.2	57.1	45.7	57.4	66.5	71.3	70.4
1981	Total	81.0						
	Sole	33.8	41.8	51.7	41.6	33.4	29.7	29.9
	Joint	47.1	58.2	48.3	58.4	66.6	70.3	70.1
1982	Total	89.9						
	Sole	36.5	40.6	50.3	40.1	33.5	28.3	29.5
	Joint	53.4	59.4	49.7	59.9	66.5	71.7	70.5
1983	Total	99.2						
	Sole	38.4	38.7	47.2	38.5	32.5	28.6	30.3
	Joint	60.8	61.3	52.8	61.5	67.5	71.4	69.7
1984	Total	110.5						
	Sole	40.6	36.7	45.1	36.2	30.9	27.9	28.8
	Joint	69.9	63.3	54.9	63.8	69.1	72.1	71.2
1985	Total	126.2						
	Sole	44.5	35.2	43.0	34.5	30.4	27.8	26.7
	Joint	81.8	64.8	57.0	65.5	69.6	72.2	73.3

Table 2.16(b) Jointly registered illegitimate births according to whether parents gave same or different addresses of usual residence at registration: age of mother, 1983–85, England and Wales

Year	Addresses of mother and father	All ages[2]	Age of mother				
			Under 20	20–24	25–9	30–4	35 and over
			Percentage same/different addresses in each age-group				
1983	Total						
	Same	73.1	56.5	76.2	83.1	82.2	80.0
	Different	26.9	43.5	23.8	16.9	17.8	20.0
1984	Total						
	Same	72.4	55.9	73.0	81.1	85.0	83.2
	Different	27.6	44.1	27.0	18.9	15.0	16.8
1985	Total						
	Same	72.2	57.2	73.8	79.3	84.3	82.5
	Different	27.8	42.8	26.2	20.7	15.7	17.5

Notes:
1. Births registered in July and November of each year.
2. Includes a few cases with mother's age not stated.
Source: OPCS, *Birth Statistics*, Table 3.9, FMI no. 12 (1985), p. 46; Table 3.10, FMI no. 12 (1985), p. 47. Reproduced with the permission of the Controller of Her Majesty's Stationery Office.

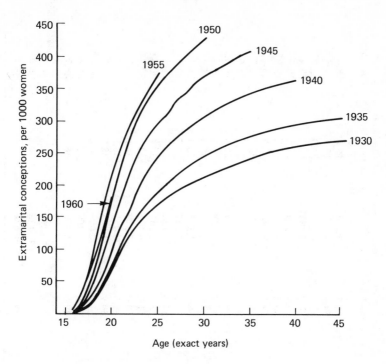

Figure 2.6   Extramarital conceptions achieved by exact ages per 1000 women born in selected years, England and Wales.

Source: Werner (1982). Reproduced with the permission of the Controller of Her Majesty's Stationery Office.

media interest in the 'new chastity', even before the threat of AIDS. But so far there is no statistical evidence from surveys that sex is losing its popularity with the young, although the rapid increase of sexually transmitted diseases such as gonorrhoea has abated. In 1974–5 42 per cent of single girls aged 16–19 had experienced sexual intercourse compared with 17 per cent in Scotland in 1976. Scots girls were still more reticent in 1982 than the English in the 1970s; 26 per cent of teenagers had experienced intercourse (Bone, 1986).[41] Other things being equal, this would lead to an enormous increase in premarital conceptions. There has been an increase, but contraception has made it less than expected. Every 1000 women born in 1930 produced about 270 conceptions outside marriage, compared with 360 per 1000 women born in 1940 and 430 to women born in 1950. This had already been exceeded (up to age 25) by women born in 1955, but women born in 1960 had reduced the rate (Figure 2.6). Extramarital conceptions in 1970 were likely to lead to marriage. By 1980 most either ended in abortion or an illegitimate birth (Figure 2.7) – see Werner, 1982.

The highest age specific rates of illegitimate fertility are to unmarried

Table 2.17 Teenage births and illegitimacy, 1938–85, England and Wales (all data refer to women under aged 20)

Year	Total live births	Rate 1000 women	Legitimate live births	Rate 1000 women	Pre-maritally conceived[1]	% of legitimate live births	Illegitimate live births	Proportion Illegitimate of all live births to woman under 20	Rate/1000 unmarried women under 20
1938	25 410	14.7	20 680	519.6	13 768	66.6	4 730	18.6	18.6
1940	26 270	15.3	21 683	330.5	12 782	58.9	4 587	17.5	17.5
1945	25 437	17.2	16 779	289.8	8 031	47.9	8 658	34.0	34.0
1950	30 847	22.2	25 492	455.2	13 995	54.9	5 355	17.4	17.4
1955	32 947	23.5	27 407	402.7	15 456	56.4	5 540	16.8	16.8
1960	51 645	34.0	41 957	442.6	23 567	56.2	9 688	18.8	18.8
1965	81 611	45.4	62 325	523.3	35 610	57.1	19 286	23.6	23.6
1966	86 746	47.9	66 164	489.4	36 745	55.5	20 582	23.7	23.7
1967	84 542	49.1	62 900	502.0	35 793	56.9	21 642	25.6	25.6
1968	82 075	49.2	60 266	490.0	35 675	59.2	21 809	26.6	26.6
1969	81 659	49.9	60 033	491.7	35 256	58.7	21 626	26.5	26.5
1970	80 975	49.4	60 112	464.5	34 815	57.9	20 863	25.8	25.8
1971	82 641	51.0	61 086	434.5	34 598	56.6	21 555	26.1	26.1
1972	79 087	48.1	57 350	403.9	31 936	55.7	21 737	27.5	27.5
1973	73 270	43.9	52 547	355.5	28 503	54.2	20 723	28.3	28.3
1974	68 724	40.4	47 863	359.6	25 272	52.8	20 861	30.4	30.4
1975	63 507	36.4	43 015	307.9	21 940	51.0	20 492	32.3	32.3
1976	57 943	32.2	38 124	294.6	19 044	50.0	19 819	34.2	34.2
1977	54 477	29.4	34 426	293.5	17 402	50.5	20 051	36.8	36.8
1978	55 984	29.4	34 341	315.3	17 417	50.7	21 643	38.7	38.7
1979	59 143	30.3	35 138	332.4	17 936	51.0	24 005	40.6	40.6
1980	60 754	30.4	34 894	340.4	17 768	50.9	25 860	42.6	42.6
1981	56 570	28.1	30 140	324.8	14 950	49.6	26 430	46.7	46.7
1982	55 435	27.4	26 696	331.2	13 377	50.1	28 739	51.8	51.8
1983	54 059	26.9	23 636	329.7	12 031	50.9	30 423	56.3	56.3
1984	54 508	27.6	21 373	338.7	10 711	50.1	33 135	60.8	60.8
1985	56 929	29.5	20 057	358.8	10 010	49.9	36 872	64.8	64.8

Note:
1. Born within 0–7 months of marriage.
Sources: OPCS, *Birth Statistics*, Series FMI no. 12 (1985) Table 3.1; FMI no. 3 (1976) Tables 3.1, 5.1, no. 13 (1987) Table 5.4.

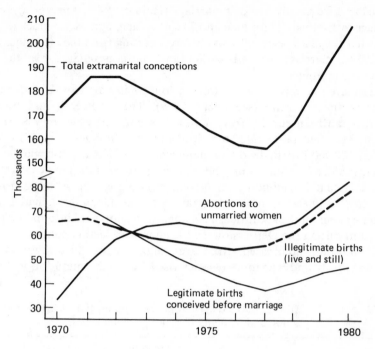

Figure 2.7 Extramarital conceptions by outcome, 1970–80, England and Wales.

Source: Werner (1982). Reproduced with the permission of the Controller of Her Majesty's Stationery Office.

women aged 25–29. Some of these unmarried women are divorcees living with new partners, some of them still awaiting divorce. (Most couples living together include at least one partner who was formerly married to someone else, or still is). Statistics are silent on the number of illegitimate children born to continuing marriages: they have more social than demographic consequence. Reports on blood group matching some time ago suggested that up to 30 per cent of births within marriage might be illegitimate (that is, the father was not the husband) but geneticists' gossip – about the only source – suggests that only 10 per cent at most of births fall into this category.

MARRIAGE, DIVORCE AND REMARRIAGE

Marriage

From the sixteenth until well into the twentieth century, marriage in Britain conformed to the long-established West European marriage pattern of delayed and frequently avoided marriage (Hajnal, 1965). Average age at first marriage in 1931 was 27 for men and 25 for women; figures not much different from what they had been 100 years before. Starting from the marriages of the late 1930s, marriage became earlier and more popular for both sexes, especially for women.

The differential advantage of women follows in part from a shift in their favour in the sex ratio (see Leete, 1979). The nineteenth and twentieth centuries had been cursed (from a woman's point of view) by an excess of women. Male mortality rates remained higher in infancy. The First World War left 600 000 British dead and many women unmarried and widowed (see Winter, 1985). More important, the great emigration of the nineteenth century which had sent 2.5 million men permanently across the Atlantic from the 1840s to the 1900s, as well as migration to the Dominions, had a corresponding effect on the sex ratios. This migration continued into the 1900s and 1920s. But during the Depression, as the migration section considers further, return migration dominated; afterwards migration was at a lower intensity than previously and was more characterised by family migration to the Old

Table 2.18   Sex ratios at selected ages from census data, 1901–81, England and Wales, and Scotland (females per 1000 males)

Year	All ages	At birth	Age groups 5–9	20–4	30–4	60–4	80–4
England and Wales							
1901	1068	964	1005	1119	1100	1171	1481
1911	1068	962	1001	1113	1091	1138	1556
1921	1096	950	992	1176	1186	1132	1685
1931	1088	953	980	1057	1132	1130	1690
1951	1082	944	957	1051	1034	1282	1703
1961	1067	942	953	1007	987	1243	1956
1971	1058	942	950	989	966	1136	2258
1981	1059	948	947	975	993	1118	2310
Scotland							
1901	1057	956	976	1059	1088	1261	1737
1911	1062	958	992	1079	1089	1163	1763
1921	1080	953	988	1113	1180	1125	1816
1931	1082	963	986	1049	1154	1092	1704
1951	1094	940	964	1112	1076	1295	1573
1961	1086	946	956	1090	1042	1293	1668
1971	1079	950	951	986	1029	1191	2200
1981	1080	957	953	974	988	1196	2480

Sources: CSO, *Statistical Abstract of the United Kingdom*, 1924–38.
CSO, *Annual Abstract of Statistics* no. *89* (1952), no. *122* (1986).
OPCS, *Birth Statistics*, Series FMI no. *1* (1974), no. *11* (1984).
Registrar-General, Scotland, *Annual Report*, no. *131* (1985).

Commonwealth which had much less impact on the age structure and the sex ratio (Table 2.18).

The popularity of marriage increased for more than 30 years, reaching its peak in 1972, some years after fertility had begun to decline (for a general account see Leete, 1979; Coleman, 1980). First marriage rates for teenage bachelors changed little before the Second World War, then increased sixfold to the peak in the early 1970s. Marriage rates of men in their early twenties doubled; those of young women almost trebled. These rates greatly increased the proportions of men and women ever married in their twenties, to levels not seen for centuries (Table 2.19). In the peak year of 1971, 37 per cent of men aged 20–24 had been married, twice the previous level and 31 per cent of those aged 25–29. By the same year 60 per cent of women in their early twenties had been married, compared to about a quarter before the war, and 87 per cent by their late twenties. These cohorts have broken all records for nuptiality as they age (Table 2.20). 'Nuptiality' is an index, based on life-table techniques, which shows the proportion of bachelors and spinsters who would have been married by a given age if current risks of marriage remain constant. For the first time the proportions of women ever marrying by age 50 are exceeding those of men. Before the 1940s about 15 per cent of women would be lifetime single, and about 8 per cent of men (Table 2.21). But the cohorts marrying in the seventies will only have about 5 per cent spinsters and 7 per cent bachelors. These records are likely to stand for a long time, because since 1972 the statistics suggest a return to the earlier pattern of later and less popular marriage. But in fact the pattern is a new one.

Later marriage is now often preceded by cohabitation (Brown and Kiernan, 1981) and extramarital child-bearing, and of course many cohabit without any intention to marry (Table 2.22). 24 per cent of first married couples in 1979–82 lived together before their marriage, and 65 per cent of remarrying couples. The majority of currently cohabiting women (64.1 per cent) were currently married (that is, living with someone other than their husband), 27 per cent were single. What proportion live together but never marry is uncertain, but according to the General Household Survey in 1983, 12 per cent of non-married women aged 18–49, and 7 per cent of all women aged 20–24 were cohabiting (Table 2.23). This can account for a substantial fraction of the delay and the avoidance of marriage, but it has not replaced marriage as a stated expectation of most young people (Kiernan, 1983), whereas this is happening elsewhere, particularly in Sweden and Denmark.

It is widely supposed that this change in marriage behaviour is not just due to the broad demographic trend of the sex ratio but more specifically to the socioeconomic changes arising out of the enhanced opportunity for women to follow careers and for married women to continue to work. Marriage is a better deal for men than for women; especially from the viewpoint of financial support and security. The widely perceived impermanence of marriage shown by the startling increase in divorce figures makes it a less certain lifetime

72

Table 2.19 First marriage rates by sex and age, 1901–84, England and Wales (per 1000 population)

Period	16–19	20–4	25–9	30–4	35–9	40–4	45–9	50–4	55 and over	First marriage rate per 1000 population over 16
Bachelors										
1901–05	3.0	82.8	128.0		44.3		14.8		3.4	59.6
1906–10	2.7	78.2	124.7		44.1		14.6		3.5	58.0
1911–15	3.1	81.0	144.0	102.7	62.7	36.7	21.8	12.5	4.5	61.8
1916–20	4.2	82.3	153.1	121.6	80.2	52.1	32.7	17.8	5.8	64.7
1921–5	3.6	89.0	165.8	122.1	67.7	37.0	21.2	12.6	5.3	63.5
1926–30	3.7	79.4	160.8	108.5	62.3	34.9	20.8	13.1	5.9	61.1
1931–5	3.9	72.3	162.9	129.5	65.8	34.1	19.5	11.7	5.2	62.6
1936–40	4.9	94.4	210.6	156.3	83.8	38.8	22.5	13.5	5.3	78.7
1941–5	9.5	109.9	148.8	114.4	76.0	44.4	26.5	15.4	4.9	71.2
1946–50	7.1	110.2	180.3	132.1	73.8	39.6	23.6	15.6	5.2	75.6
1951–5	8.4	131.8	174.4	107.3	60.7	35.6	21.7	14.1	5.1	75.9
1956–60	14.0	152.8	184.9	100.9	52.8	31.0	20.6	11.7	4.8	78.7
1961–5	17.5	159.6	187.3	92.1	47.7	27.3	17.6	11.2	4.6	75.6
1966–70	23.5	170.0	179.4	91.0	43.7	24.7	15.8	10.3	4.1	82.1
1971–5	24.1	154.1	161.9	87.4	45.0	24.9	16.4	11.3	4.5	76.6
1976–80	16.0	112.8	136.5	84.7	42.6	22.2	13.0	8.9	3.6	60.0
1981	11.1	94.1	120.8	70.3	39.1	20.1	11.5	7.4	3.1	51.7
1982	9.6	85.4	116.6	70.3	37.5	18.7	11.0	7.1	2.8	48.7
1983	8.5	79.4	115.1	70.9	37.4	19.5	11.5	6.9	2.7	47.5
1984	7.6	74.0	113.4	72.8	38.8	19.9	11.4	6.6	2.8	47.1
1985	7.1	67.8	109.0	72.4	36.8	19.3	11.5	6.8	2.6	45.6

Spinsters

Period									
1901–05	15.4	103.4	90.5			25.1		8.9	1.4	57.4
1906–10	14.2	100.8	91.1			24.5		8.7	1.6	55.8
1911–15	16.0	104.7	116.4	65.3	34.0	18.7	11.6	6.6	1.9	58.7
1916–20	15.8	107.0	113.6	66.0	37.1	21.4	13.4	7.1	2.1	57.4
1921–5	16.7	108.6	116.7	60.3	29.1	15.7	10.1	6.0	2.0	55.2
1926–30	18.6	107.2	117.7	57.8	27.6	14.9	9.9	6.2	2.4	54.8
1931–5	21.0	109.7	127.6	62.3	27.8	15.1	9.6	5.8	2.3	57.3
1936–40	33.1	154.4	171.3	78.7	34.7	18.2	11.0	6.4	2.1	73.3
1941–5	45.6	171.6	132.2	62.6	32.0	19.1	12.1	6.9	1.9	67.6
1946–50	47.6	205.2	153.5	81.4	41.4	22.0	13.5	8.3	2.2	75.7
1951–5	55.5	231.9	157.2	75.1	38.6	21.2	12.8	7.9	2.1	76.8
1956–60	72.7	261.6	164.4	75.9	36.1	22.0	12.7	7.9	2.1	82.6
1961–5	76.4	260.2	161.3	73.8	38.0	21.8	13.5	8.2	2.2	83.6
1966–70	85.0	260.9	159.4	72.7	37.2	20.4	13.6	8.5	2.1	94.2
1971–5	86.2	228.2	167.8	83.4	42.2	23.7	16.3	11.6	2.6	91.9
1976–80	58.3	177.3	139.3	83.7	42.4	21.8	13.4	8.7	1.9	74.7
1981	41.5	140.8	120.2	67.0	36.1	19.2	10.9	7.2	1.5	64.0
1982	36.6	129.0	115.6	63.4	35.3	18.4	10.0	6.2	1.5	60.4
1983	32.9	122.0	115.6	64.3	33.8	18.5	11.2	6.3	1.4	59.1
1984	30.4	115.4	117.8	67.2	34.5	18.3	10.8	6.6	1.4	58.9
1985	27.7	107.9	112.4	66.1	34.3	18.6	10.5	7.0	1.3	57.1

Note: Rates from 1981 are not exactly comparable with those for earlier years due to a new definition and population base.

Sources: OPCS, *Marriage and Divorce Statistics* FM2 no. 2 (1975), Table 3.3a (p. 14);
OPCS, *Marriage and Divorce Statistics*, FM2 no. 12 (1984), Table 3.3a (p. 17).

Table 2.20   Gross nuptiality to age 49,
England and Wales, 1900–1985

Year	Bachelors	Spinsters
1900–02	880	816
1911–15	898	843
1921–5	932	832
1931–5	925	844
1941–5	934	915
1948–50	949	949
1951–5	935	946
1956–60	941	960
1961–5	938	958
1966	939	957
1970	936	961
1971	930	960
1972	936	967
1973	924	958
1974	914	951
1975	907	949
1976	858	917
1977	882	930
1978	883	927
1979	877	924
1980	873	920
1981	831	873
1982	814	853
1983	818	857
1984	814	855
1985	800	843

Note: These numbers represent the proportion per thousand bachelors and spinsters at age 16 who would have been married by age 49 given the continuation of current rates of marriage in each given year. The calculation of 'gross' nuptiality takes no account of the risks of mortality from age 16 to 49.

Sources: Up to 1974, Coleman (1980) Table 3;
OPCS, *Marriage and Divorce Statistics*, FM2 each individual year since 1974 Table 3.8.

option; cohabitation may be regarded therefore as a cautious compromise (Ermisch, 1981).

Professional women have always been least likely to get married; women with fathers in unskilled manual occupations are the most likely (the reverse is true of men). (Haskey, 1983). However, there does not seem to be a marked social gradient in cohabitation (Haskey and Coleman, 1986).

Divorce

Divorce is orders of magnitude more frequent in the twentieth century than in any previous century. Before 1858 a civil divorce was impossible without a private Act of Parliament at a total cost of about £1000 (Macfarlane 1986). Successive legislation has broadened its availability in terms of grounds and access; equalising the grounds (1938) granting Legal Aid (1948), changing the cases for divorce from 'facts proven' to 'irretrievable breakdown' and introducing divorce by mutual consent (1969, effective in 1971) and shortening even further the minimum duration of marriage before divorce (1985). Each measure has stimulated at least a temporary upward movement in frequency (Leete, 1979), but in general the figures show that the increase in divorce has not depended on these steps but has preceded them, and has occurred within most of them (see Schoen and Baj, 1984), especially in the unsettled conditions during and after both world wars (Table 2.24). There were,in fact, declines in divorce in the 1930s and 1950s (after peaks following each world war), which can be regarded both in respect of family stability and the level of illegitimate births, as 'golden ages'. Only 2 per cent of the marriages of 1926 had ended in divorce after 20 years, only 6 per cent of the marriages of 1936, only 7 per cent of the marriages of 1951 (Figure 2.8). In the previous century, marriages had been broken by death of one or other partner almost as often as they break through divorce in the 1980s – that is to say, about a third by 25 years duration (Coleman, 1980; Haskey 1982). But in the 1930s and 1950s, because of the much reduced chances of dissolution by death, and the scarcely-awakened threat from divorce, marriages enjoyed a stability without precedent in history – and one which is unlikely ever to be restored (Anderson, 1983). Since then, rates of divorce have increased rapidly, accelerated, but not caused, by law reform in 1969 and 1984. 19 per cent of the marriages of 1974 ended after just ten years and 11 per cent of those of 1978 after just five years.

One of the most important advances since the first edition of this book has been in the volume of data available for the study of marriage and divorce and the techniques adopted to analyse them. Although it is quite helpful to relate divorce to existing marriages to compute a rate, the numerical values of the rates are not intuitively very meaningful. It is better to use the more detailed data now available to make some estimate of the likely impact of the continuation of current divorce rates upon the chances of survival of the

Table 2.21 Persons ever married as a percentage of the total population by sex and age, 1901–81, England and Wales, and Scotland (numbers per 1000 or relevant age-group)

	16–19	20–4	25–9	30–4	35–9	40–4	45–9	50–4	55–9	60–4	65–9	70–4	75–9	80–4	85–9	90–4	95+
								Men									
England and Wales																	
1901	4	174	550	746	826	860	884	896	913	910	920	925	933	937	—	938	
1921	5	178	555	769	837	863	876	885	894	900	906	914	925	933	933	915	908
1951	6	237	651	810	867	892	902	913	923	921	917	915	917	926	934	938	924
1961	13	309	706	826	868	892	904	912	915	920	927	924	921	923	926	931	920
1971	26	364	739	861	889	892	900	913	918	922	923	930	—	—	937	—	—
1981	12	251	654	830	886	906	910	906	909	920	924	928	—	—	930	—	—
1984	7	188	599	805	878	904	914	911	910	918	924	928	—	—	929	—	—
1985	7	173	577	798	875	903	914	914	910	916	925	928	—	—	929	—	—
Scotland																	
1901	3	126	450	666	768	813	848	861	880	878	893	893	897	902	907	901	871
1921	6	146	463	684	767	806	824	840	853	864	877	886	902	907	918	913	929
1951	5	203	583	758	828	855	864	873	883	878	867	865	876	886	901	899	891
1961	15	295	692	811	847	868	876	879	879	881	888	883	876	878	888	884	880
1971	23	384	749	858	884	883	883	890	891	890	886	891	899	894	—	892	—
1981	20	298	694	845	887	902	904	897	893	897	892	889	884	887	893	891	879

Women

	16–19	20–24	25–29	30–34	35–39	40–44	45–49	50–54	55–59	60–64	65–69	70–74	75–79	80–84	85–89	90–94	95+
England and Wales																	
1901	17	274	590	743	800	832	857	871	878	889	888	888	890	889	—	—	—
1921	22	273	590	740	796	821	833	841	845	848	860	860	867	869	872	882	849
1951	55	482	783	854	867	858	849	850	844	844	846	842	837	834	830	870	827
1961	82	580	844	890	902	903	895	877	862	857	848	846	844	839	832	823	796
1971	109	601	867	922	930	929	922	917	904	885	868	861	—	—	846	817	—
1981	57	455	802	911	940	947	943	935	927	921	908	889	—	—	864	—	—
1984	40	378	756	890	936	948	948	941	933	927	915	902	—	—	872	—	—
1985	36	354	737	883	933	948	950	944	935	928	920	906	—	—	875	—	—
Scotland																	
1901	21	236	525	682	744	781	803	814	821	817	816	803	800	796	798	776	788
1921	26	246	521	678	741	774	789	797	794	797	802	800	806	805	815	793	836
1951	44	397	708	809	823	813	796	795	791	786	781	777	775	770	768	766	765
1961	72	518	810	834	864	869	858	833	808	797	787	780	773	767	767	753	778
1971	79	580	854	908	912	899	886	882	865	837	809	795	780	773	—	761	—
1981	63	477	815	911	931	935	926	908	892	886	864	835	805	793	773	773	746

Sources: Census tables, England and Wales, 1901–81;
Census tables, Scotland, 1901–81;
OPCS, *Marriage and Divorce Statistics*, Series FM2 no. 11 (1984) Table 1.1.

Table 2.22　Proportion of women who had lived with their husband before their current or most recent marriage, by whether first or subsequent marriage, age of woman at marriage and year of marriage, Great Britain, 1960–83

Age of woman at marriage	Women aged 16–49, who were under 35 at time of this marriage Year of marriage[1]				
	1960–64	1965–69	1970–74	1975–78	1979–82
	(percentage who cohabited before marriage)				
First marriage for both partners					
Under 25	2	2	7	14	21
25–34[2]	—	—	10	21	40
Total[2]	—	—	8	15	24
Second or subsequent marriage for one or both partners					
Under 25	17	28	39	54	58
25–34[2]	—	—	45	59	69
Total[2]	—	—	42	57	65
TOTAL	—	—	12	24	35

Notes:
1. Data for the 1960–78 marriage cohorts are taken from the 1979, 1981, 1982 and 1983 surveys combined. Data for the 1979–1982 cohort are from the 1983 survey only.
2. Table excludes women married at ages 25–34 in the 1960s as some of them would have been aged over 50 when interviewed and so not asked the Family Information section.
Source:　General Household Survey (1983) Table 4.9. Reproduced with the permission of the Controller of Her Majesty's Stationery Office.

Table 2.23(a)　Recent trends in cohabitation, Great Britain: women aged 18–49

Legal marital status	Year									
	1979		1980		1981		1982		1983	
Married	—		—		—		—		—	
Single	8		8		9		10		10	
Widowed	nil	10.6	6	10.8	6	11.6	3	12.6	2	12.1
Divorced	20		20		20		21		21	
Separated	17		17		19		18		9	
Total	2.7		2.9		3.3		3.8		3.6	

Source:　General Household Survey (1983) Table 4.5. Reproduced with the permission of the Controller of Her Majesty's Stationery Office.

Table 2.23(b)   Percentage cohabiting by legal marital status and
age 1982, 1983, Great Britain: women aged 18–49

Legal marital status	18–24		25–39		35–49		Total	
Married	—		—		—		—	
Single	8		20		8		10	
Widowed	nil	8	(1)	21	2	12	2	12
Divorced	(5)		25		18		21	
Separated	20		15		11		14	
Total	6		5		2		4	

Note: Figures in brackets are based on sample numbers less than
10.
Source: General Household Survey (1983) Table 4.7. Reproduced
with the permission of the Controller of Her Majesty's
Stationery Office.

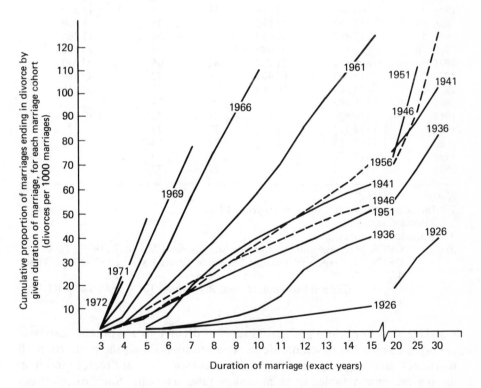

Figure 2.8   Marriage cohorts, 1926–72: cumulative divorce rates per 1000 (all ages at
marriage)0, England and Wales

Source: Coleman (1980)

British Social Trends since 1900

Table 2.24   Petitions for divorce, 1901–85, England and Wales, and decrees granted, 1901–85, Scotland

Period	Number of petitions filed[1] during period	Average per year	Percentage by husbands[2] (%)	wives[2] (%)	Number[3] of decrees of divorce dissolution and nullity of marriage
England and Wales					*Scotland*
1901–5	4 062	812	53	47	905
1906–10	4 043	809	48	52	975
1911–15	5 167	1 033	45	55	1 320
1916–20	14 768	2 954	67	33	2 655
1921–5	14 240	2 848	41	59	2 135
1926–30	20 260	4 052	41	59	2 390
1931–5	23 921	4 784	45	55	2 535
1936–40	37 674	7 535	47	53	3 750
1941–5	80 373	16 075	56	44	7 065
1946–50	194 503	38 901	55	45	12 175
1951–5	160 841	32 168	44	56	11 370
1956–60	137 392	27 478	45	55	8 960
1961–5	188 283	37 657	42	58	11 265
1966–70	285 449	57 089	37	63	20 280
1971–5	608 861	121 772	34	66	33 020
1976–80	812 403	162 481	28	72	45 340
1981–5	884 845	176 969	27	73	59 710
1980	171 992	—	29	71	
1981	170 126	—	27	73	
1982	174 373	—	27	73	
1983	169 315	—	27	73	
1984	179 976	—	27	73	
1985	191 055	—	27	73	

Notes:
1. Includes petitions for annulments from 1976.
2. Rounded estimates.
3. Rounded to nearest five.

Sources: OPCS, Marriage and Divorce Statistics, Series FM2 no. 2 (1975), Table 4.8.
OPCS, Marriage and Divorce Statistics, Series FM2 no. 12 (1984), Table 4.7.
Registrar-General Scotland, *Annual Report*, no. 131 (1985), Table R1.1 (p. 120).

marriage. The application of period rates of divorce to a synthetic marriage cohort, a calculation based on life table techniques, shows the proportion of marriages surviving to given ages of life at current risks of divorce (and in a double decrement table, from mortality rates as well). Such calculations showed that 8 per cent of marriages would have ended by husband's age 50 at the divorce rates of 1951, 13 per cent in 1966, 22 per cent in 1971 and 35 per cent in 1975 (Coleman, 1980). It is more useful to relate the risk of duration of marriage; the divorce rates of 1979 would end 33 per cent of marriages by 25 years duration, 56 per cent of teenage marriages, and 38 per cent of divorced men remarrying at age 30–34 (compared to 23 per cent of bachelors married at the same age) (Haskey, 1983, Table 2.25). The acceleration of the divorce rate has slackened off in the 1980s, primarily it is thought because age at marriage increased in the 1970s and therefore made the average recent marriage less divorce prone, other things being equal. Mortality still ends two-thirds of marriages at current risks, but in most cases well beyond the age of child-bearing or much chance of remarriage.

Table 2.25   Divorce by marital status before marriage, selected marriage cohorts, 1950–75, males age at marriage 25–29. Cumulative proportions divorcing per 1000 marriages

Marriage cohort	*Duration of marriage (years)*					
	5	*10*	*15*	*20*	*25*	*30*
Bachelors						
1950	4	20	36	51	73	92
1955	4	25	45	75	105	
1960	5	35	79	124		
1965	8	66	124			
1970	23	103				
1975	40					
Divorced men						
1950	14	53	81	106	139	164
1955	13	67	118	172	221	
1960	13	88	184	262		
1965	17	148	253			
1870	46	198				
1975	68					

Source: Haskey, 1983, Table 6; *Population Trends*, 32. Reproduced with the permission of the Controller of Her Majesty's Stationery Office.

Most marriages which are going to break up, break up fast, and the 1984 Act permitting divorce after one year's marriage (not three as before) has precipitated a new tide of petitions. The most important determinant of divorce rates, even more than social class (Haskey, 1984), length of previous acquaintance, and civil versus religious ceremony, is the age at marriage – the younger, the worse (Murphy, 1984; Kiernan, 1986).

The best way to study marriage breakdown is to link the data on divorce to the data of each individual marriage, such as facts claimed, and the custody granted to dependent children. Unfortunately the date of birth is given neither on marriage certificates nor on divorce decrees, so the linkage of individual divorces to individual marriages cannot be done by the routine processes used in the Longitudinal Study. Instead a more old-fashioned and laborious process is required which limits research to smaller-scale studies and short durations of marriage (Leete and Anthony, 1979).

Remarriage

Remarriage of the divorced and widowed is an increasingly important social phenomenon. In 1985 more than one wedding in three involved at least one formerly married person, and in 12 per cent two divorced persons (Table 2.26). As recently as the late 1960s 83 per cent of marriages were first marriages, compared to 88 per cent in 1901–05. Because high levels of divorce are relatively recent, the proportion of divorced and remarried people in the population has not yet caught up with current rates of divorce and remarriage – only about one in ten couples are currently remarried (one or both partners) (Coleman, 1987).

The late twentieth century is revisiting a pattern typical of previous centuries when almost one wedding in three was a remarriage for one or both partners (Anderson, 1983). But then, the opportunity for remarriage arose through premature mortality, not from divorce. And although the frequency of remarriage has greatly increased, remarriage rates themselves have changed little over the years, indeed for men they have declined slightly (Figure 2.9). The huge rise in remarriage is a function of the much greater number of people available to be remarried. And it must not be forgotten that remarriage to

Table 2.26   Proportion of marriages of different types (per 1000), England and Wales, 1901–85

Category of marriage	1901 –05	1906 –10	1911 –15	1916 –20	1921 –5	1926 –30	1931 –5	1936 –40	1941 –5
Bachelors/Spinsters	876	882	884	835	864	882	893	898	865
Bachelors/Widows	33	32	34	64	41	26	21	19	30
Bachelors/ Divorced women	<1	1	1	1	3	4	5	7	10
Widowers/Spinsters	56	54	49	57	53	50	47	41	43
Widowers/Widows	33	30	29	41	32	29	24	22	28
Widowers/ Divorced women	<1	<1	<1	<1	1	1	2	2	3
Divorced men/ Spinsters	1	1	1	2	4	6	7	9	16
Divorced men/ Widows	<1	<1	<1	<1	1	1	1	1	3
Divorced men/ Divorced women	<1	<1	<1	<1	<1	1	1	1	2

Source: OPCS, *Marriage and Divorce Statistics*, Series FM2, Table 3.2.

some extent drives divorce, in the sense that many partners divorce in order to marry or to live with another person. Cohabitation before remarriage is now normal. Many separated spouses move in with someone else but cannot, of course, remarry immediately. Younger divorced or widowed people remarry with little delay; age specific remarriage rates are higher than those of single people at almost all ages (Table 2.27). Remarriage rates for divorced persons are much higher than for widowed persons at all ages, no doubt because in many cases an alternative partner has already been lined up. Rates for men in either category are considerably higher than rates for women, especially after age 35, and a much higher proportion of formerly married men eventually remarry compared to women, competing with bachelors for younger women.

No natural limit to the increase in divorce is yet in sight except that determined by ability to afford the costs of such serial polygamy. Although the UK divorce rates are almost the highest in Europe, in the USA they are higher still. There, about 54 per cent of marriages are likely to end in divorce after 25 years duration at current rates, much more among teenagers, blacks, the remarried, and other groups. It is unlikely that divorce will become less frequent. It is a universally common phenomenon in modern industrial society, although individual countries do show interesting differences, only partly for legal reasons. While family size remains small, while women remain able and willing to go out to work when married, while traditional religious observance declines or remains relatively weak, high divorce rates are here to stay (Kunzel, 1974).

1946 –50	1951 –5	1956 –60	1961 –5	1966 –70	1971 –5	1976 –80	1981	1982	1983	1984	1985
792	816	843	842	827	730	661	647	644	642	642	641
33	20	16	13	11	10	8	7	6	6	6	5
37	35	30	32	37	63	81	83	83	84	84	85
36	29	23	19	14	10	8	7	7	6	6	6
26	26	25	25	24	24	21	19	18	18	17	16
8	9	9	9	9	13	13	13	13	13	13	13
46	40	33	35	43	70	88	94	95	96	98	99
9	8	7	7	8	13	14	13	12	12	12	12
14	16	15	18	26	66	106	117	121	123	123	125

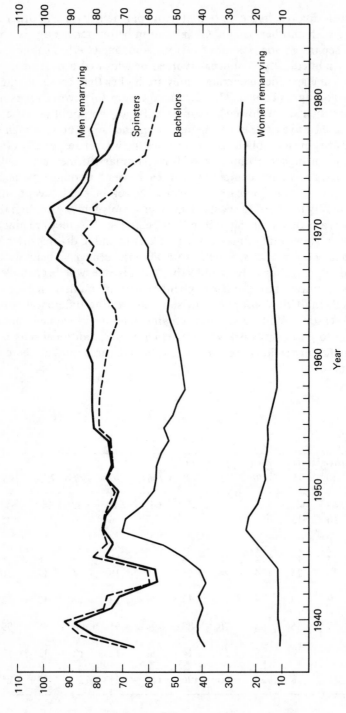

Figure 2.9   Marriage rates by previous marital status by sex, England and Wales, 1938–80. Bachelors/spinsters: first marriage rates per 1000 single, widowed and divorced: remarriage rates per 1000 widowed and divorced

Sources: Registrar-General's *Statistical Review*, vol. II, (1969), Table H1. OPCS, *Marriage and Divorce Statistics*, Series FM2 Table 2.1.

Table 2.27 Age-specific marriage rates. Rates per 100 persons in each category, England and Wales, 1980

	Men				Women				
Age	Bachelors	Widowed	Divorced	All formerly married	Spinsters	Widowed	Divorced	All formerly married	Age
16–19	14	–	–	–	49	–	–	–	16–19
20–4	104	147	310	304	164	132	375	359	20–4
25–9	132	257	282	282	143	147	271	265	25–9
30–4	85	158	227	225	80	110	169	166	30–4
35–9	44	172	176	176	44	72	122	117	35–9
40–4	22	116	142	140	21	49	91	82	40–4
45–9	13	91	117	113	13	33	69	55	45–9
50–4	8	68	90	83	8	19	46	29	50–4
55–9	} 3	48	68	57	} 2	10	24	13	55–9
60–4		34	51	40		8	14	9	60–4
65–9		23	39	26		4	8	4	65–9

Source: OPCS, *Marriage and Divorce Statistics*, Series FM2 1980, no. 7, Table 3.3, and calculated from Table 1.1 and Tables 3.6(a), 3.6(b).

CAUSES OF FERTILITY TRENDS AND THEIR IMPLICATIONS
FOR FUTURE FERTILITY

The best general explanation so far provided for the remarkable changes in post-war fertility is that the economics of child-bearing have been upset by substantial increases in the direct costs of children, including the extension of school-leaving age, and particularly by rises in their indirect cost caused by the greater propensity for married women to go out to work. The opportunity cost of raising children has rocketed to about £100 000 per child on average, while careful estimates in the United States suggest an all-in figure of about $250 000 to raise a child up to age 18. And while raising the average family may keep a woman away from work for about seven years, in terms of lost opportunities for promotion and career advancement a more realistic estimate of earnings lost is about 13 years (Joshi, 1986).

The married woman at work is a particular feature of the late twentieth century. In 1931 only 11 per cent of married women worked. Spinsters and widows have always mostly worked and show little trend in work force participation this century – see Table (4.4) in Chapter (4). Law and regulation had some effect – before the Second World War, women teachers and civil servants who married had to resign their jobs. But the new norm of family planning, only established shortly before the Second World War, meant that for the first time married women did not necessarily see most of their adult life committed to child-bearing and child-rearing. Instead there was a new opportunity of two or three decades of work and higher income for the family, especially to middle-class incomes progressively flattened by an increasing tax burden. And, unlike in France and other continental countries, there were no substantial compensating attractions of child welfare payments. But it took a generation – until the mid-1960s – for women to make use of the opportunity presented to them – a puzzle still unresolved (Hatton, 1986).

The rapid increase of married women in the work force really accelerated after the 1950s. Women's wages relative to men's improved rather later, from 1975, assisted by legal changes requiring women to be paid the same as men performing the same job, and in 1983 even for performing work alleged to be of 'equal value'.

Mathematical modelling rescues these notions from the merely anecdotal. For example, John Ermisch (1983) has tested the course of fertility against a linear model of women's work force participation and relative wages. It fits the pattern of past fertility well up to the early 1980s. It performs better than a rival model derived from Richard Easterlin's (1968) hypothesis which relates – with some success with US data – family size to relative income compared across generations and to the size of the birth cohort, which is deemed to have substantial effect upon chances and opportunities in later life (Easterlin, 1980).

If most families with two incomes want to keep them, and if women will not willingly give up the opportunity to broaden their lives, incomes and independence which work brings, then married women will remain important in the work force. That being so, family size is likely to remain small, and it should not show the volatility so evident in the half century since the consolidation of birth control. In other words, there are likely to be no more baby booms. The unprecedented fluctuations in fertility which followed the new ability to control the timing and number of births since the twentieth century discovered

Table 2.28   Expected family size, by year of birth of women.
Women aged 18–48, Great Britain, 1981, 1982, 1983

Year of birth of women	Age at interview	Children born so far None	At least one
1935–9	42–48	0.00	2.72
1940–4	37–43	0.07	2.59
1945–9	32–38	0.34	2.39
1950–4	27–33	1.21	2.37
1955–9	22–28	1.92	2.37
1960–4	18–23	2.28	2.37

Source: General Household Survey, (1983) Table 4.26a.

Average number of children expected in all in present marriage, by year of interview

Year of interview	Year of present marriage 1960–4	1965–9	1970–4	1975–9
1971	2.3	2.1	—	—
1972	2.4	2.1	—	—
1973	2.3	2.1	—	—
1974	2.4	2.1	—	—
1975	2.3	2.1	1.9	—
1976	2.3	2.1	1.9	—
1977	2.4	2.0	1.9	—
1978	2.4	2.1	1.9	—
1979	2.4	2.2	2.0	—
1980	2.4	2.1	2.0	2.0
1981	—	2.2	2.0	2.0
1982	2.4	2.2	2.0	2.0
1983	2.5	2.2	2.1	2.0

Average number of children expected in all, including children born by previous marriage or outside marriage

1982	2.4	2.3	2.2	2.2
1983	2.5	2.3	2.2	2.2

Source: General Household Survey (1983), Table 4.27. Reproduced with the permission of the Controller of Her Majesty's Stationery Office.

family planning, in the initial absence of high levels of married women's work force participation, should settle down to a new, more constant demographic regime.

But the level at which fertility will settle is a much more difficult question to answer. It is possible to speak of a 'natural' fertility level typical (say) of the demographic regimes of nomadic hunters and gatherers (between four and five), of tropical African cultivators (about eight), or pre-industrial European cultivators (between five and six); a number related to the prevailing (usually unchanging) ecology and economics of the society, the prevailing mortality rate, the mobility of the population and its needs for child spacing, and the need for children as contributors to labour, lineage and to the broader extended family role of risk insurance. Few of these considerations apply to modern Europe: the economic utility of children to their individual parents is usually zero. There seems so far to be no sure foundation – certainly not a microeconomic one – for specifying on *a priori* grounds a 'natural' family size for post-transitional populations.

No-child families and one-child families remain consistently unpopular in attitude surveys as ideal or intended family sizes (General Household Survey 1986). For most people, two is both the minimum and the maximum family size. These surveys also consistently point to an average expected family size somewhat above that currently being achieved (Table 2.28), both in the United Kingdom and in most other countries of the West where this question has been asked (Simons, 1986). At present, the total fertility rate implies a substantial number of childless couples or one-child families. It may therefore be appropriate to expect a slight increase in fertility, although it is not easy to specify what conditions are required to bring this about.

SOCIAL AND GEOGRAPHICAL DIFFERENCES IN FERTILITY

So far these comments on fertility and marriage have been generalised over the whole country, as though it were socially and geographically homogeneous.

Fertility and social class

The class relation with fertility is complex and has changed with time. Professionals were among the first to adopt family limitation within marriage. It generated notable occupational differences in family size and corresponding concern in some circles during the interwar period about the social origins of future generations. The 1911 Census was especially expanded to enquire into the important new phenomenon of family limitation, and the social class classification had its modern origins in the need to generalise about the social and occupational differences in family size then becoming apparent, and social

Table 2.29 Great Britain: number of live births per woman in separate social status categories. Ten-year and five-year averages. (Marriages under 45 years of age only)

Date of marriage	Social status categories									All status groups
	1 Professional	*2* Employers	*3* Own account	*4* Salaried employees	*5* Non-manual wage-earners	*6* Manual wage-earners	*7* Farmers and farm managers	*8* Agricultural workers	*9* Labourers	
Absolute values										
1890–9	2.80	3.28	3.70	3.04	3.53	4.85	4.30	4.71	5.11	4.34
1900–9	2.33	2.64	2.96	2.37	2.89	3.96	3.50	3.88	4.45	3.53
1910–14	2.07	2.27	2.42	2.03	2.44	3.35	2.88	3.22	4.01	2.98
1915–19	1.85	1.97	2.11	1.80	2.17	2.92	2.55	2.79	3.56	2.61
1920–4	1.75	1.84	1.95	1.65	1.97	2.70	2.31	2.71	3.35	2.42
Ratios: All status groups = 100 (for each cohort)										
1890–9	65	76	85	70	81	112	99	109	118	100
1900–9	66	75	84	67	82	112	99	110	126	100
1910–14	69	76	81	68	82	112	97	108	135	100
1915–19	71	75	81	69	83	112	98	107	136	100
1920–4	72	76	81	68	81	112	95	112	138	100
Ratios: 1900–9 cohort for each status group = 100										
1890–9	120	124	125	128	122	122	123	121	115	123
1900–9	100	100	100	100	100	100	100	100	100	100
1910–14	89	86	82	86	84	85	82	83	90	84
1915–19	79	75	71	76	75	74	73	72	80	74
1920–4	75	70	66	70	68	68	66	70	75	69

Source: Report on the Family Census of 1946, part I, Table 41. Reproduced with the permission of the Controller of Her Majesty's Stationery Office.

aspects of the infant mortality which still remained stubbornly high. Until 1970 we have had to rely on the census for this information, which does not always ask questions on fertility (for example, those of 1921, 1931 and 1981 did not). Since 1970 the occupational data on the birth certificate has been routinely analysed, although census data is required for the population data needed for the calculation of rates.

In general, in the earlier part of the century, the higher the class, the smaller the family size. Table 2.29(c) shows that this pattern held reasonably constant for the fertility of the marriages of the first quarter of this century, although the relationship was far from linear in detailed occupational terms; fathers in social class 2 delaying fertility change and some skilled operatives in social class 3N (non-manual) (especially where women were an important component of labour) anticipating their colleagues. But since then the relationship has become more complex. On the whole, fertility in manual working-class families, especially unskilled workers, has continued to decline. By 1961 the fertility questions of the census revealed that the relationship between family size and social class was becoming J-shaped, with the lowest fertility most apparent among families of social class 3N (routine non-manual workers). At the 1971 Census, the excess of fertility of women married to manual workers in 1931–5 was 23 per cent; in the marriages of 1961–5 this excess had declined to 10 per cent. Professionals (social class I) were starting to show higher fertility than other middle-class people in social class II (Tables 2.30, 2.31). The great reduction of fertility in the 1970s has been much more concentrated in the manual than in the non-manual groups (Table 2.32) (see Pearce and Britton, 1977). For a brief time in 1977 fertility in classes I and II was higher than class III (Figure 2.10). Now the older differentials have reasserted themselves – except that class IIIM (manual) fertility since 1977 has been lower than class IIIN. But social classes I and II have (together with class 3N) the highest

Table 2.30   Fertility trends by social class, England and Wales. Women married at age 25–9 years. Average family size at time of census

| | Social class of husband | | | | | |
	I	II	III	IV	V	All
1951	1.57	1.48	1.73	2.00	2.16	—
1961	1.66	1.63	1.68	1.72	1.93	—
1971	1.76	1.69	1.49 1.66	1.70	1.90	1.68
Change						
1951–61	+ 5.7%	+ 10.1%	− 2.9%	− 14.0%	− 10.6%	—
1961–71	+ 6.0%	+ 3.7%	− 6.3%	− 1.2%	− 1.6%	—

Note: There were no census fertility enquiries in 1921, 1931 or 1981.
Sources: Census, 1961, *Fertility Report 1951*, Census 1971, vol. II, Table 24, *Fertility Tables*.

Table 2.31   Married women married once only at ages under 45 and enumerated with husband. Mean family size at 1971 Census by social class of husband and year of marriage (10 per cent sample), England and Wales

Period of marriage	I	II	IIIN	IIIM	IV	V	Total
			Husband's social class				
1941–5	2.04	1.99	1.86	2.20	2.24	2.47	2.14
1946–50	2.11	2.02	1.90	2.24	2.29	2.57	2.19
1951–5	2.25	2.17	2.00	2.34	2.36	2.66	2.29
1956–60	2.23	2.12	2.00	2.29	2.31	2.58	2.25
1961–5	1.80	1.76	1.66	1.89	1.93	2.14	1.85
1966–70	0.60	0.66	0.62	0.85	0.92	1.05	0.79
All periods	1.75	1.81	1.62	1.95	2.03	2.26	1.68
All periods, by woman's class	1.45	1.61	1.35	1.65	1.95	2.39	1.70

Broadly speaking the social class categories are:

I	Professional occupations
II	Intermediate occupations
IIIN	Skilled occupations (non-manual)
IIIM	Skilled occupations (manual)
IV	Partly-skilled occupations
V	Unskilled occupations
'Other'	Includes armed forces and students

Note: Fertility of recent marriage cohort, especially 1966–70, is incomplete at 1971. 'Inadequately described' and 'others' omitted from table.
Sources: OPCS, Series DS no. 5, *Fertility Report* from the 1971 Census, Tables 5.7, 5.30.
Census 1971, *Fertility Tables*, vol. II, Table 24.

fertility of women aged 25–29, and more decisively among the smaller but growing numbers of births to women aged over 30 (Figure 2.11). In 1971 the census showed, however, that married women who were professional in their own right had smaller family sizes than women whose husbands were in social class I (Table 2.31).

A substantial part of this increase is due to a general upward shift in the occupational distribution (see Chapter 4). There are more middle-class parents nowadays (Werner, 1985). One consequence of all this has been a shift in the distribution of births, and therefore social origins of future generations, by social class. The trend is already sufficiently significant to become part of the controversy over future provisions for university places, for example, critics of the government's forecasts insisting that future student numbers have been underestimates because they have ignored this change in the social composition of births (Royal Society, 1983).

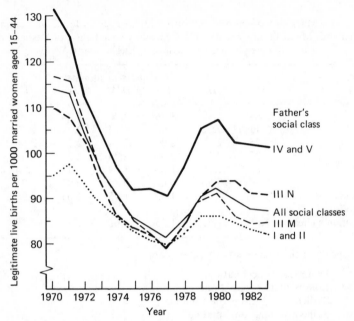

Figure 2.10   Legitimate live birth-rates by social class of father, 1970–83, England and
Wales.
Source: Werner (1985) Figure 2, p. 9. Reproduced with the permission of the
Controller of Her Majesty's Stationery Office.

Table 2.32   Estimated legitimate live births by social class of father, 1971–84,
England and Wales

Year	I & II	IIIN	IIIM	IV & V	Other	All
1971	154.7	75.3	297.9	160.1	29.5	717.5
1976	140.8	55.5	204.6	110.2	19.4	530.5
1981	163.3	60.4	198.2	111.4	20.1	553.5
1985	158.4	56.2	184.3	105.9	25.4	530.2

Figures expressed as a percent of all births in each year (omitting 'other')

Year	I & II	IIIN	IIIM	IV & V	All
1971	22	11	43	23	100
1976	28	11	40	22	100
1981	31	11	37	21	100
1985	31	11	37	21	100

Note: Percentages may not cast to 100 because of rounding.

Note: The 1981 and 1985 figures are based on different occupation definitions and
thus are not strictly comparable with the earlier figures.
Sources: OPCS, *Birth Statistics*, Series FM1 no. 4 (1977), Table 11.1;
OPCS, *Birth Statistics*, Series FM1 no. 12 (1985), Table 11.1.

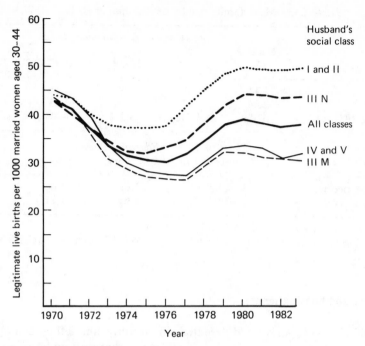

Figure 2.11 Legitimate fertility rates for married women aged 30 and over by social class of husband, 1970–83, England Wales.

Source: Werner (1985) Figure 3, p. 9. Reproduced with the permission of the Controller of Her Majesty's Stationery Office.

Some theorists, notably Gary Becker (1981), insist that the underlying relation of fertility with income (which is roughly related to social class) is positive, not negative; and that the U-shaped distribution therefore arises from unwanted fertility because of poor contraceptive motivation or practice among the poorest families. There is evidence for this from the USA and from West Germany.

Fertility and educational level

Fertility varies with education in a pattern similar to that for social class. In general, the least educated have the most children and the most educated the least. But a finer sub-division yields a more complex U-shaped distribution (Table 2.33) and the balance has shifted since the Second World War. Such information used to be obtained only from the census (which has not always asked the same educational question in successive censuses). But the General Household Survey, the Longitudinal Study, and the maturing of the 1946 and 1958 Cohort Studies have provided much more detailed information recently (see, for example, Kiernan and Diamond, 1982).

Table 2.33   Mean family size by educational level, 1951–1971

Census	Under 15	15–16	17–19	20+	Total
			Age at which education completed		
1951	2.11	1.48	1.44	1.58	2.01
1961	2.04	1.41	1.56	1.65	1.86
Change 1951–61	−3.3%	−4.7%	+8.3%	+4.4%	−7.5%

Census	'O' level or less	'A' level	Degree	Total
		Educational level		
1971 married women	1.93	1.66	1.66	1.91
1971 married men	1.95	1.65	1.72	1.91

Sources: *Fertility Report* of 1951 and 1961 Census.
OPCS, Series DS no. 5, *Fertility Report* on 1971 Census, Tables 5.38, 5.41.

Fertility and housing tenure

One of the most striking differentials in fertility and other demographic measures to have come to light in recent years is that relating to differences in housing tenure. The difference in average fertility between women living in owner-occupied houses and women living in homes rented from the local authority (2.11 to 2.95 in 1977) exceeds all but the extreme differences by social class (Murphy and Sullivan, 1985). Women in local authority rented tenure are also more than three times as likely to have four or more children, and have a markedly different pattern of child spacing; the average interval from marriage to first legitimate birth being 17 months compared to 27 for women in owner-occupation (Werner, 1986). The last differential is likely to be created by the encouragement to early child-bearing given by the points system for the allocation of council housing (Murphy and Sullivan, 1983) in contrast to the need of owner-occupier couples with mortgages to retain two incomes for as long as possible. Much of the rest may be due to selective process tendency to concentrate manual workers, single parents, low income groups and the less educated into council tenure. But some tenure differentials (in mortality) are partly independent of social class (Fox and Goldblatt, 1982). It may be that there are sub-cultural differences generated by the social circumstances on some of the larger estates, associated with relative social uniformity, isolation and labelling, and dependence, which affect behaviour. The current movement of tenure from council renting to owner-occupation may provide opportunities to test such ideas. So far there are no trend data, as interest in this variable is so recent.

Table 2.34 Fertility and housing tenure, Great Britain, 1977
(a) Average number of live births in current marriage to married women aged 40–44 in 1977

	Owner-occupied	Local authority	Housing tenure Private furnished	Private unfurnished	All
Women in first marriage	2.11	2.95	(1.67)	2.26	2.37
Remarried women	0.75	0.78	(0.50)	(0.13)	0.67
All married women	2.02	2.71	(1.20)	1.95	2.22

Note: ( ) = sample size less than 10.

(b) Family size distribution of married women aged 40–44

Live births	Owner-occupied (%)	Local authority (%)	Private rented (%)
0	13	10	22
1	17	13	22
2	38	26	20
3	23	22	25
4 or more	9	29	12

(c) Birth interval ever-married women aged 40–49

Interval marriage – first birth (months)	27	17	24
Average no. of live births	2.29	2.89	2.51
Average age at marriage	23.4	21.7	22.2

Source: Murphy and Sullivan (1985), Table 2.3.

Fertility and ethnicity

12 per cent of births in England and Wales are born to mothers born outside the UK. Two-thirds of those births are to mothers born in the New Commonwealth and Pakistan (Table 2.35). Immigration from the New Commonwealth has created a new plurality of demographic regimes in Britain. Completed family size in the countries of origin of the migrants, especially in the rural areas from which most have come, is between five and eight children. Marriage patterns are different too, with no tradition of the Western European marriage pattern of late and often avoided marriage.

Table 2.35 Live births by birthplace of mother, 1971–85

Birthplace	1971	1973	1975	1977	1979	1981	1983	1985
UK (Total)	689 697	596 893	530 481	494 470	554 212	551 432	549 435	575 220
(%)	88.1	88.3	87.9	86.9	86.9	86.9	87.3	87.6%
Outside UK	88 813	77 504	72 056	74 197	83 332	82 829	79 536	81 063
	11.3	11.5	11.9	13.0	13.1	13.1	12.6	12.3%
Irish Republic	21 583	16 383	12 823	10 373	9 658	8 262	6 711	6 311
	2.8	2.4	2.1	1.8	1.5	1.3	1.1	1.0%
New Commonwealth and Pakistan	53 363	40 968	39 965	44 349	52 181	53 165	52 010	52 733
	6.8	5.1	6.7	7.8	8.2	8.4	8.3	8.0%
Bangladesh	—	932	974	1 592	2 153	3 079	3 896	4 238
	—	0.1	0.2	0.3	0.3	0.5	0.6	0.6%
India	13 389	12 705	11 990	12 317	13 119	12 402	11 502	11 110
	1.7	1.9	2.0	2.2	2.1	2.0	1.8	1.7%
Africa	4 990	5 545	6 220	7 544	9 328	10 129	10 070	10 703
	0.6	0.8	1.0	1.3	1.5	1.5	1.6	1.7%
Caribbean	12 544	9 088	7 725	6 905	7 278	6 247	5 307	4 851
	1.6	1.3	1.3	1.2	1.1	1.0	0.8	0.7%
Pakistan	8 200	6 830	6 958	9 521	12 515	13 349	13 423	13 643
	1.0	1.0	1.2	1.7	2.0	2.1	2.1	2.1%
Total	783 155	675 953	603 445	569 259	638 028	634 492	629 134	656 417
	100	100	100	100	100	100	100	100%

Source: OPCS, *Birth Statistics*, Series FMI no. 12 (1985) Table 9.1; no. 5, Table 9.1.

Instead marriage is typically early and universal, and among Asians usually arranged; illegitimate fertility is typically very low. Neither, in many of these cultures, is there a tradition of nuclear families living in separate households after marriage – various kinds of extended family connections usually prevail (see, for example, Hajnal, 1982), creating large household sizes. All are different, but West Indians break most of these generalisations. One-parent families and visiting relationships are normal. Illegitimacy, as among US blacks, is correspondingly high. Trends in fertility and marriage among migrants to the UK ae a record of partial and limited transition from these patterns in the country of origin to those more characteristic of the UK. Most previous migrants had acculturated completely to British norms by the twentieth century or even become 'super normal' – notably Jews (Kosmin, 1982). The fertility of Irish-born people is still somewhat higher than the UK-born (Table 2.36) but the fertility, and contraceptive usage of Roman Catholics, who are mostly of Irish origin in the UK, is now scarcely distinguishable from the average (Coleman, 1983).

Table 2.36   Average family size by birthplace of mother, 1971, England and Wales, women married once only

Birthplace of mother	Duration of marriage		
	up to 9 years	15–19 years	All durations
Total	2.1	2.31	1.93
Irish Republic	2.42	2.81	2.38
Old Commonwealth	2.00	2.32	1.70
Africa	2.38	3.27	1.95
Caribbean	2.80	3.40	2.63
Cyprus, Gibraltar, Malta	2.33	2.89	2.30
India	2.48	3.38	2.55
Pakistan	2.76	3.98	2.76
Rest of New Commonwealth	2.11	2.77	1.87
Europe (not USSR)	1.87	2.06	1.77

Source: Census 1971, *Fertility Tables*, vol. I, Tables 2, 4.

Among the New Commonwealth immigrant groups, birth-rates to West Indian-born women are now at about the British average, while those of Asian women, particularly Pakistanis and Bangladeshis, remain much higher, although declining. The number of births in these populations is further inflated by their youthful age structure (see Table 14.10). The number of births to women born in the New Commonwealth and Pakistan was 53 000 in 1971 (data were not collected before 1969) – 6.8 per cent of all births. The trend has followed the ups and downs of British fertility in general, but at a higher level, falling to 40 000 births in 1975 (6.7 per cent) and rising again to 53 000 in 1985 – 8.0 per cent of births. Birthplace of mother is becoming obsolete as a measure of recruitment to the new ethnic minority populations, as an increasing proportion of births are to women of New Commonwealth and Pakistani ethnic origin but who were born in the UK. Births to these women are not distinguishable statistically from births to women of British (white) ethnic origin.

The population estimates by ethnicity derived from the Labour Force Survey since 1979 show that high proportions of potential younger mothers were born in the UK, especially among West Indians who were the earliest migrants. We know nothing directly of their fertility. But an estimate of the extra contribution they are making to births can be made from the Labour Force Survey data on the birthplace of mothers of non-white children born in the UK. At the 1984 LFS, 22 per cent of West Indian children aged 0–14 born in the UK had UK-born mothers (32 per cent of 0–4 year olds), compared to 3 per cent of Pakistani and Bangladeshi children and 63 per cent of children of mixed origin (OPCS, *Monitor*, LFS 85/1). The Labour Force Survey since 1979 has enabled estimates to be made of the population by birthplace which is not of British ethnic origin, and, therefore, to calculate total fertility rates. Because of the interrupted child-bearing of immigrant women, and rapid tempo changes, the fertility patterns are not stable (Thompson, 1982) but none the less show declines for most, but not all, categories (Table 2.37). The highly

Table 2.37   Total fertility rate by birthplace of mother, 1971–85, England and Wales

	Year				
Birthplace	*1971*[1]	*1979*[2]	*1981*	*1983*	*1985*
Total	2.38	1.84	1.80	1.76	1.78
UK	2.3	n.a.	1.7	1.7	1.7
Total outside UK	—	n.a.	2.5	2.4	2.5
New Commonwealth and Pakistan	4.0	3.5	2.9	2.8	2.9
India	4.3	3.9	3.1	2.8	2.9
Pakistan and Bangladesh	9.3	7.1	6.5	6.1	5.6
East Africa	2.7	n.a.	2.1	2.0	2.1
Rest of Africa	4.2	n.a.	3.4	3.1	3.0
West Indies	3.4	2.5	2.0	1.8	1.8
Malta, Gibraltar, Cyprus		n.a.	2.1	2.1	2.2
Hong Kong, Malaysia, Singapore, Brunei	2.7	n.a.	1.7	1.9	2.0
Rest of New Commonwealth		n.a.	2.3	2.4	2.3
Rest of world	n.a.	n.a.	2.0	1.9	2.0

Notes:
1.   OPCS, *Monitor*, Series FMI 84/9.
2.   Thompson (1982) Table IV (data refer to Great Britain).
Sources: OPCS, *Birth Statistics*, Series FMI no. 12 (1985) Table 9.5.

segregated nature of Asian society in particular, its multiple differences from British society, the frequent illiteracy of women, may retard the otherwise expected process of acculturation to low fertility norms, especially if a high proportion of spouses continue to come from the Indian subcontinent. Certainly the rather fragile statistics available show no clear trend towards more inter-ethnic marriage between Asians and whites, although they do show this for West Indians and whites (Coleman, 1985).

MIGRATION

Migration is the weak sister of the three major demographic processes. UK gross migration flows are a third or a quarter of the total number of births or deaths in a year; net migration an order of magnitude less (Table 2.38). None the less migration matters. It can introduce new kinds of people into the country who may then set up new ethnic minority communities which previously did not exist. It can selectively remove certain kinds of people, affecting the sex ratio, or threatening a brain-drain, and can affect overall population change at the margin, especially when natural increase is negligible, as at present.

It is also a weak sister in the statistical sense. In the UK there was no direct measurement of international migration of any consequence before the 1905 Aliens Act and effective series of immigration data on foreign citizens (not British or Commonwealth subjects) dates only from the Aliens Order of 1920. Commonwealth immigrants did not come under immigration control until the Commonwealth Immigrants Act of 1962 and reliable statistical series for them only date from 1964. Migrants from the Irish Republic are subject neither to control nor to counting, so no information at all is available directly on their migration flows. Statistics derived from the Home Office control of immigration apply in detail only to inward-bound persons granted leave to settle (either on arrival or afterwards) and follow non-demographic definitions derived from immigration law (see Home Office, 1986). The other major source, the International Passenger Survey, a voluntary sample survey of all arriving and departing passengers (except to and from the Republic of Ireland) provides more demographically useful information of less certain accuracy (see OPCS, 1986). There are no routine statistics available at all on migration to or from the Republic of Ireland (see Garvey, 1985). The decennial census also provides information on birthplace and, up to 1961, on nationality, while microcensuses such as the annual Labour Force Survey provide information on both, although only for a sample of the population (Coleman, 1983). Both censuses and surveys have undercounted coloured immigrant and ethnic minority populations to varying degrees (Peach and Winchester, 1974). The most systematic deficiency is in young West Indian males. Internal evidence suggests substantial omissions from the 1977 Natio-

British Social Trends since 1900

Table 2.38   Natural increase and net gain or loss by migration 1901–83, England
and Wales, Scotland, and Northern Ireland (000s)

Years	Population at beginning of period	Births	Deaths	Excess of births over deaths	Net gain (+) or loss (−) by migration	Actual increase or decrease (−)
England and Wales						
1901–11	32 528	9 290	5 246	4044	− 501	3543
1911–21	36 070	8 281	5 845[1]	2436	− 620	1816
1921–31	37 887	6 928	4 692	2236	− 170	2060
1931–51	39 952	13 297	10 249[1]	3048	+ 758	3806
1951–61	43 758	7 138	5 181	1957	+ 387	2347
1951–61	43 815	7 140	5 160	1970	+ 400	2380
1961–71	46 196	8 320	5 600	2720	+ 230	2960
1971–81	49 152	6 380	5 850	530	− 50	480
1981–83	49 634	1 257	1 167	90	− 70	20
Scotland						
1901–11	4 472	1 306	763	543	− 254	289
1911–21	4 761	1 185	824[1]	360	− 239	122
1921–31	4 882	1 005	652	352	− 392	− 40
1931–51	4 843	1 849	1 347[1]	502	− 220	253
1951–61	5 096	959	619	339	− 282	83
1951–61	5 102	950	620	330	− 260	83
1961–71	5 184	970	630	340	− 300	30
1971–81	5 217	700	640	60	− 120	− 40
1981–83	5 180	133	130	3	− 33	− 30

Northern Ireland Period	Population at beginning of period	Natural increase	Net loss by migration
1901–11	1237	79	65
1911–26	1251	114	108
1926–37	1257	81	58
1937–51	1280	158	67
1951–61	1371	146	92
1961–6	1425	97	38
1966–71	1485	76	32
1971–81	1536	108	82

Note:
1. Includes deaths of non-civilians and merchant seamen who died
   outside the country.
Sources: England, Wales and Scotland: CSO *Annual Abstract of
Statistics*, no. 106 (1969), no. 121 (1985). Registrar-
General Northern Ireland, Report 1983, Table W1.

nal Dwelling and Housing Survey (Hollis, 1982) and from the 1981 Labour Force Survey (Coleman, 1985).

The social changes brought by immigration can be highly salient. Immigration from the 1870s to the first decade of this century created the British Jewish community in its modern form. Immigration from Ireland peaked in the 1950s. Immigration from the New Commonwealth after the Second World War created the first substantial communities in the United Kingdom of people who were non-white and in the case of Asians, non-Christians who did not have English as their first language. Their arrival has enormously expanded the variety of demographic patterns in the UK – indeed it has created a plurality of demographic regimes where previously there was only one. Chapter 14 deals with the process of immigration and the settlement and employment patterns of the new communities in detail (see also Salt and Clout, 1978; Jones, 1977; Coleman, 1982). Comments here will be limited to trends in the numbers of emigrants and immigrants, the quality of data, and sources of future immigration.

The twentieth century began with a continuation of two existing contrary trends. Traditionally the UK was an exporter of people, particularly in the nineteenth century with young men leaving for North America, the Antipodes and the colonies. Family migration was less common. In all about 3 million people were lost from the UK to North America in the nineteenth century (more left, but like all migration streams, some came back). Over time the old pattern, which peaked in the decade before the First World War, had made an impact on the sex ratio sufficient to effect adversely the marriage chances of women. It was even encouraged as a means of strengthening the colonies and their ties with the UK, and for this reason continued to attract government sponsorship and interest until the 1960s. It had earlier been seen as one solution to rural poverty, although most of the migrants in fact came from towns.

The old pattern of migration of single men was lost after the 1920s. The war changed much, liberal attitudes to migration in the USA ended, the Depression was easier to weather at home. Immigration dried up, many migrants returned, to create the first net gain from migration recorded this century. The new pattern of family migration, more to Australia, New Zealand, Canada and South Africa, often under arranged passages, was less likely to have an impact on the sex ratio or age structure. It still continues on a smaller scale. Migration to South Africa has gone into reverse. But the Dominions' immigration policies no longer give preference to people of British origin or nationality; their populations are much more nationally heterogeneous than they were, and their links with Britain weaker. Qualifications are at a premium with the rapid growth of labour demand now much less than it was. At present, return migration of British citizens is at an all-time high.

British Social Trends since 1900

Immigration from the New Commonwealth

New Commonwealth immigration (Table 2.39) has given a net gain of about 1.3 million New Commonwealth immigrants into the UK, and in addition their 1 million UK-born descendants. But only in early 1962 in the rush to beat the 1962 Bill, in 1973 (Ugandan Asian refugees), and from 1983 to the present,

Table 2.39   Immigration from the New Commonwealth and Pakistan, 1963–85

Year	Total intended immigrants	Net balance immigrants	Total accepted for settlement	On arrival	On removal of time limit
1963	86	40	—	—	—
1964	84	43	—	—	—
1965	82	38	—	—	—
1966	76	35	—	—	—
1967	86 } 405	46 } 195	61	58	3
1968	88	48	61	56	4
1969	73	28	45	40	4
1970	70	25	38	33	4
1971	66	27	44	35	9
1972	84 } 336	39 } 139	69 } 226	60	9
1973	59	24	32	26	7
1974	57	24	43	25	17
1975	66	35	53	35	19
1976	67	36	55	37	19
1977	54 } 332	18 } 178	44 } 232	28	16
1978	69	41	43	25	18
1979	76	48	37	22	15
1980	60	24	34	19	15
1981	57	27	31	19	13
1982	58 } 300	18 } 125	30 } 148	17	14
1983	65	32	28	15	12
1984	60	24	25	14	11
1985	57	23	27	14	13

Notes:
1. 'Intended immigrants' are persons resident away from UK for at least 12 months intending to stay in UK, for at least 12 months, data from International Passenger Survey. Defined by *country of last residence*.
2. 'Acceptances for settlement' are defined by *citizenship*, data from Home Office.

Sources: Immigration: OPCS, *International Migration*, Series MN.

Registrar-General's *Statistical Review*, vol. II, Table S(c) (data from voluntary International Passenger Survey.

Acceptance for settlement from New Commonwealth and Pakistan: Home Office, *Control of Immigration Statistics*, Tables 14, 8, 15 (data from immigration control).

has total immigration exceeded emigration. At the moment emigration is particularly low, and immigration, particularly return migration of UK citizens (Devis, 1985), unusually high.

Estimates of future immigration are difficult. In theory almost all primary immigration from the New Commonwealth has been stopped. There are a few work permit migrants – about 2000 per year. The queue of dependants entitled to enter is theoretically limited, but it shows little signs of declining. Previous estimates have been long overtaken and the problem is exacerbated by large and complex families, lack of vital registration and different attitudes towards the state and its officials characteristic of New Commonwealth countries. The great majority of applications from some of the most important sending countries such as Bangladesh (95 per cent) include some element of deception (Home Affairs Committee, 1986). A third of all applications are turned down first time around. Despite more than two decades of immigration control, the decline in the number of entrants has been slight; the figures in the early 1980s are not much less than those ten years previously (Table 2.39).

Marriage is a source of immigration likely to grow in importance as time goes on. The practice of arranged marriages for women from the Indian subcontinent has proved quite resilient in Britain. Spouses from the area of origin at home are preferred; in addition right of entry conferred on a fiancée or spouse to join a partner already settled in the UK makes such partners very attractive on the Indian marriage market, where these advantages are widely advertised. The number of persons entering for purposes of marriage has been increasing constantly and will increase still further as the youthful age structure of the Asian population develops (Jones, 1982; Coleman, 1987) despite various attemps to curtail it by HM Government. And the recent (1985) equalisation of the right of residents of either sex to bring in fiancés is likely to increase the number of immigrants for purposes of marriage.

TOTAL POPULATION AND AGE-STRUCTURE

What does all this add up to in terms of effects on the population and its age structure? Fertility decline has pulled the rug from under British population growth in the twentieth century. Mortality improvement has made a modest contribution to population increase. Low fertility also creates an older population. Mortality reduction typically makes people younger, and has had this countervailing effect for most of this century. But as there is now more relative improvement in older ages, it, too, is helping to make the population older on average. On aggregate, international migration has had a negative effect on British population size for most of the century.

Table 2.40 shows how the population growth inherited from the previous century continued into this one, but at a declining rate until in 1977 the

Table 2.40   Population growth, 1901–85, England and Wales, Scotland, and
Northern Ireland

Year	Population	Increase since previous census	Intercensal increase (%)
England and Wales			
1901	32 527 843	+ 3 525 318	12.2
1911	36 070 492	+ 3 542 649	10.9
1921	37 886 699	+ 1 816 207	5.0
1931	39 952 377	+ 2 065 678	5.5
1939	41 552 000	+ 1 765 000	4.7[4]
1951	43 757 888	+ 2 297 888	5.3
1961	46 104 548	+ 2 346 660	8.9
1971	48 749 600	+ 2 645 052	5.7
1981	49 154 687	+ 405 087	0.8
1985[1]	49 923 500	+ 289 000	0.2
Scotland			
1901	4 472 103	+ 446 456	11.1
1911	4 760 904	+ 288 801	6.5
1921	4 882 497	+ 121 593	2.5
1931	4 842 980	− 39 517	− 0.8
1939	5 008 000	+ 165 000	4.4[4]
1951	5 096 415	+ 253 435	0.2
1961	5 178 490	+ 82 075	0.2
1971	5 228 963	+ 50 423	1.0
1981	5 131 735	− 97 228	− 1.9
1985[1]	5 136 509	+ 4 774	0.1
Northern Ireland			
1901	1 236 952	+ 896	0.1
1911	1 250 531	+ 13 579	1.1
1921[2]	1 258 000[2]	+ 7 469[2]	0.6[2]
1931[2]	1 242 600[2]	− 15 400[2]	− 1.2[2]
1951	1 370 921	+ 128 321	10.3
1961	1 425 042	+ 54 121	3.9
1971	1 536 065	+ 111 023	7.8
1981	1 509 892[3]	− 26 173	− 1.7
1984[1]	1 578 500[1]	+ 68 608	4.5

Notes:
1. Registrar-General's estimates of resident population, June 1985; OPCS, *Monitor*, PP1 86/1.
2. Estimates as no census was taken in Northern Ireland in these years.
3. Includes 19 664 non-enumerated persons.
4. Estimated percent increase to 1941.
Sources: Census 1981, *Historical Tables 1801–1981*, England and Wales;
Census 1981, Scotland: *Scottish Summary*, vol. 1;
The Northern Ireland Census 1981, *Preliminary Report*;
OPCS, *Monitor* PP1 86/1, *mid-1985 Population Estimates for England and Wales*;
National Register (1939) *Report and Tables* Table A;
Registrar-General, Scotland, (1985) *Population Estimates Scotland*;
Northern Ireland Annual Abstract of Statistics, no. 4 (1985).

population declined in peace-time for the first time since the middle of the eighteenth century. The decennial increase from 1971 to 1981 was the smallest since the census began in 1801. It looks as though the population is reaching the asymptote long predicted by devotees of the logistic curve. In this we follow most Western European countries. Some, for example, West Germany, have had declining populations for the last few years (Eversley and Köllmann, 1982). But replacement fertility does not bring an immediate end to growth. Because people live a long time populations have enormous inertia. Reproduction and high mortality rates are concentrated in particular different age groups. All potential mothers for the next 15 years or so have already been born, for example. So population growth rates do not just reflect todays vital rates. They also depend on those of the previous hundred years, which created the present age structure.

The age structure

In 1901 the age structure (Table 2.41) reflected the previous century of slow declining mortality and (until 1870) relatively even and high fertility. Neither nineteenth century mortality, nor fertility before 1870, had showed any great

Table 2.41 Age distribution of the enumerated population at 1901 and 1981 Census by sex, England and Wales, and Scotland (thousands)

| | England and Wales | | | | Scotland | | | |
| | 1901 | | 1981 | | 1901 | | 1981 | |
	Male	*Female*	*Male*	*Female*	*Male*	*Female*	*Male*	*Female*
0–4	1 855	1 861	1 492	1 418	268	265	158	150
5–9	1 739	1 748	1 647	1 560	249	243	176	168
10–14	1 671	1 671	1 972	1 875	238	231	218	207
15–19	1 608	1 639	2 054	1 966	230	226	228	219
20–24	1 473	1 648	1 805	1 760	210	223	200	195
25–29	1 328	1 496	1 648	1 627	181	198	172	170
30–34	1 158	1 274	1 835	1 822	151	164	181	178
35–39	1 034	1 111	1 554	1 538	133	145	150	151
40–44	897	953	1 405	1 387	119	127	141	147
45–49	760	813	1 351	1 338	100	108	140	146
50–54	636	693	1 381	1 404	84	93	140	146
55–59	497	555	1 403	1 474	66	77	138	151
60–64	410	480	1 196	1 337	56	70	114	137
65–69	282	347	1 100	1 326	37	50	106	135
70–74	195	251	871	1 191	26	38	83	120
75–79	113	151	544	914	15	22	51	92
80–84	52	77	248	573	7	13	23	56
85 and over	18	31	119	388	3	6	11	35
All ages	15 729	16 799	23 625	24 897	2 174	2 298	2 429	2 607

Source: Census 1901, 1981.

British Social Trends since 1900

fluctuations. The day of the mortality crisis had gone and the period of fertility fluctuations of the later twentieth century was still to come. The 1921 age structure (Table 2.42) shows more clearly the effects of falling fertility and the direct mortality effects of the First World War, the birth deficit during the war and baby boom afterwards. The 1961 figure is more mature: 40 years of low fertility had aged the population to create a more parallel-sided shape. But it is also more uneven: the demographic damage of two world wars shows up in excess male mortality, the deficit of births of both sexes and the baby boom after. It also shows the effects of new mid-twentieth century peace-time fertility fluctuations, arising from the new control of fertility – in the birth deficits of the 1930s, 1950s, and the beginning of the 1960s baby boom. The age structure of the 1980s (Figure 2.12) shows the maturing of that boom and the low births since. It is apparent why today's low fertility does not

Table 2.42   Broad age-groups as a percentage of the total population 1901–81, England and Wales, and Scotland   (%)

Year	The young (0–14)	Persons of working age (15–64)	The elderly (65 and over)	All ages	Dependency[2] ratio
England and Wales					
1901	32.4	62.9	4.7	100	59.0
1911	30.6	64.2	5.2	100	55.8
1921	27.7	66.2	6.0	100	50.9
1931	23.8	68.8	7.4	100	45.3
1939	20.6	70.2	9.2	100	42.5
1951	22.1	66.8	11.0	100	49.6
1961	23.0	65.1	11.9	100	53.6
1971	23.7	62.9	13.3	100	58.8
1981[1]	20.5	64.5	15.0	100	55.0
Scotland					
1901	33.4	61.7	4.8	100	61.9
1911	32.3	62.3	5.4	100	60.5
1921	29.5	64.5	6.0	100	55.0
1931	26.9	65.8	7.3	100	52.0
1939	24.1	67.2	8.7	100	48.8
1951	24.6	65.4	10.0	100	52.9
1961	25.9	63.5	10.6	100	57.5
1971	25.9	61.8	12.3	100	61.8
1981[1]	21.4	64.5	14.1	100	55.0

Notes:
1.   'Usually resident' population (0–14) + (65 and over) divided by (15–64).
2.   The 1939 estimate includes an allowance for non-enumerated servicemen.
Sources: *Statistical Abstract of the United Kingdom* for relevant years up to 1931;
          CSO Annual Abstract of Statistics for relevant years from 1951;
          National Register 1939.

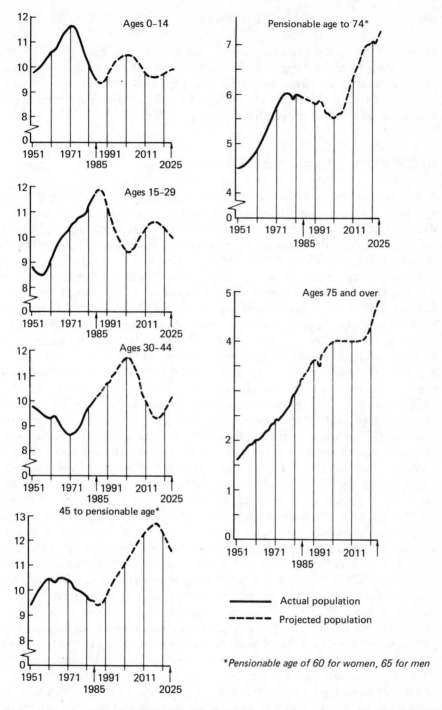

Figure 2.12   Acutal and projected home population by age-group, England and Wales
1951–2025, in millions.

Source: OPCS Monitor PP2 86/1. Population projections: mid-1985 based. Fig. 1
(London: OPCS).

immediately reverse population growth. Today's mothers, born 20 to 30 years ago, belong to older, larger birth cohorts. Figure 2.2 showed the contrast between the track of births since 1890 and their survivors in the present age-structure, left after the effects of mortality and of net migration (including of course the addition of people not born in the UK).

REGIONAL POPULATIONS

The sections above describe new trends in fertility mortality and migration and their impact on the population. Regional populations matter too. The dynamics of their populations are different from total populations. Many of the details are usefully summarised in the annual publication *Regional Trends* (Central Statistical Office, 1986) published since 1965.

There are regional differences in fertility and mortality. Regional fertility differences in the UK are modest outside Northern Ireland, which has (in its Roman Catholic population) the highest fertility in Western Europe (see Compton, 1985). Fertility levels (especially illegitimate fertility) tend to be higher in the Northern regions and the West Midlands (Armitage, 1987). Mortality differences are particularly interesting as they appear to relate to regional differences in life-style, or to risk defined by the national environment, somewhat independently of social class (Shaper, *et al.*, 1981). They are of long standing, having much the same form now as in the first Registrar-General's Decennial Supplement on Regional Mortality of 1851 (Registrar-General, 1978, 1986) even though the causes of death are now quite different. Migration dominates change in local overall numbers and age-structure, the more so the smaller the area being considered. Table 2.43 shows how much net migration exceeds natural change (the balance between births and deaths) even at the regional level. Because internal migration is not recorded in the UK (unlike some continental countries which have permanent population registers), most official data on migration come from the decennial census which asks questions on previous residence one and five years ago as well as birthplace (Table 2.44). These, of course, rapidly become obsolete. The National Health Service Central Register, now computerised, which records changes of doctors registrations is now used to make annual estimates of net migration flows (Table 2.45) down to regional level (Devis, 1984; OPCS, 1986). But its use necessarily involves a number of assumptions and only provides population estimates without social or demographic details. Most academic surveys concern labour migration or sometime marital migration. (But see Friedlander and Roshier, 1966, for a census-based historical analysis, and a contemporary survey of the 1960s). The Labour Force Survey allows an annual tab to be kept on regional population totals and their age-structure. Longitudinal surveys can trace migration very effectively but they have insufficient sample size to make generalisations at a geographically subdivided

Table 2.43 Components of population change mid-1983 to mid-1984 (000s)

Area	Population at start of period	Changes during period					Population at end of period
		Live births	Deaths	Net Natural change	Net civilian migration and other adjustments	Overall change	
United Kingdom	56 376.8	718.2	654.2	65.8	45.2	111.0	56 487.8
North	3 100.1	39.0	38.4	0.6	−7.6	−7.0	3 093.1
Tyne & Wear	1 145.3	14.3	14.6	−0.3	−2.6	−2.9	1 142.4
Remainder of region	1 954.8	24.7	23.8	0.9	−5.0	−4.1	1 950.7
Yorkshire & Humberside	4 908.5	62.5	59.4	3.1	−7.3	−4.2	4 904.3
South Yorkshire	1 310.5	16.1	15.5	0.6	−5.7	−5.1	1 305.4
West Yorkshire	2 059.3	28.0	25.4	2.6	−5.7	−3.1	2 056.2
Remainder of region	1 538.7	18.4	18.5	−0.1	4.1	4.0	1 542.7
East Midlands	3 859.8	48.1	42.7	5.4	9.1	14.5	3 874.3
East Anglia	1 925.2	23.1	21.4	1.7	12.7	14.4	1 939.6
South-East	17 041.8	216.5	186.7	29.8	40.8	70.6	17 112.4
Greater London	6 754.5	91.5	75.1	16.4	−14.9	1.5	6 756.0
Remainder of region	10 287.3	125.0	111.6	13.4	55.7	69.1	10 356.4
South-West	4 424.1	50.5	54.2	−3.7	40.8	37.1	4 461.2
West Midlands	5 176.3	67.4	57.2	10.2	−10.5	−0.3	5 176.0
West Midlands	2 657.6	36.4	29.9	6.5	−17.1	−10.6	2 647.0
Remainder of region	2 518.7	31.0	27.3	3.7	6.6	10.3	2 529.0
North-West	6 410.1	84.3	79.7	4.6	−19.2	−14.6	6 395.5
Greater Manchester	2 598.5	35.2	32.2	3.0	−13.2	−10.2	2 588.3
Merseyside	1 500.8	19.7	18.5	1.2	−11.3	−10.1	1 490.7
Remainder of region	2 310.8	29.4	29.0	0.4	5.3	5.7	2 316.5
England	46 845.9	591.4	539.5	51.9	58.6	110.5	46 956.4
Wales	2 807.8	35.2	34.1	1.0	−1.6	−0.6	2 807.2
Scotland	5 150.4	64.3	62.9	1.4	−6.1	−4.7	5 145.7
Central Clydeside Conurbation	1 705.7	21.9	21.0	0.8	−10.9	−10.0	1 695.7
Remainder of Scotland	3 444.7	42.4	41.9	0.6	4.8	5.3	3 450.0
Northern Ireland	1 572.7	27.3	15.8	11.5	−5.7	5.8	1 578.5

Source: Regional Trends, 21 (1986), Table 2.4. Reproduced with the permission of the Controller of Her Majesty's Stationery Office.

Table 2.44 Migration within one year before census date, 1961–81, England and Wales, and Scotland

	Resident population at census	Migrants within a district	Migrants between districts	Total migrants	Immigrants from all areas including abroad	Immigrants from elsewhere in GB only	Emigrants to areas in GB only
England and Wales							
1961	46 104 548	2 345 500	2 168 470	4 513 970	342 750	51 630	27 460
1971	48 749 600	2 650 010	2 567 860	5 217 870	417 050	60 000	45 740
1981	49 154 687	2 584 422	1 646 080	4 230 502	287 789	41 363	36 955
Scotland							
1961	5 178 490	336 510	143 030	479 540	47 070	27 460	51 630
1971	5 228 963	360 470	185 580	546 050	73 900	45 740	60 000
1981	5 131 735	335 602	100 513	436 115	55 659	36 955	41 363

Note: 1961 and 1971 figures are estimates based on a 10 per cent sample.

Sources: Census 1961, England and Wales, *Migration Tables*.
Census 1961, Scotland, *Internal Migration*.
Census 1971, Great Britain, *Migration Tables*, part 1 (10 per cent sample).
Census 1981, Great Britain, *National Migration Tables*, part 1 (100 per cent sample).

Table 2.45 Recorded movements between areas, by area of origin and area of destination, 1985, United Kingdom, Wales, Scotland, Northern Ireland and standard regions of England

(000s)

Area of origin

Area of destination	United Kingdom	North	Yorkshire & Humberside	East Midlands	East Anglia	South-East Total	Greater London	Remainder	South-West	West Midlands	North-West	Wales	Scotland	Northern Ireland
United Kingdom	–	49	83	78	45	244	201	228	89	87	99	45	54	11
North	40	–	8	3	1	10	4	6	2	3	7	1	5	1
Yorks & Humberside	71	9	–	11	3	18	6	12	4	6	12	2	5	1
East Midlands	84	3	14	–	6	29	9	20	5	11	9	2	4	1
East Anglia	64	2	4	7	–	36	12	24	4	3	4	1	3	–
South-East	228	14	23	25	23	–	–	–	45	28	30	15	20	4
Greater London	145	6	9	8	7	–	–	64	13	11	12	5	8	2
Remainder	267	9	14	17	16	–	120	–	32	18	18	9	12	2
South-West	130	3	7	7	4	71	20	50	–	15	10	8	5	1
West Midlands	78	3	7	11	3	25	8	17	10	–	10	7	3	1
North West	83	7	13	8	2	22	9	14	6	10	–	7	6	1
Wales	50	1	3	3	1	16	5	10	7	8	10	–	2	–
Scotland	46	5	5	3	2	16	6	10	4	3	6	1	–	2
Northern Ireland	8	–	1	–	2	3	1	2	–	1	1	–	1	–

Note: The totals for United Kingdom exclude movements within each area.
Source: OPCS, *Monitor*, MN 86/3, Table 4 (From National Health Service Central Register.)

Table 2.46   Regional population changes, 1911–81, England and Wales, and
Scotland (000s)

	1911–21		1931–9		1951–61		1971–81	
	No.	(%)	No.	(%)	No.	(%)	No.	(%)
England and Wales	1817	5.0	1492	3.7	2314	5.3	405	0.8
South-East	488	4.2	1893	7.3	565	4.2	−135	−0.8
North	677	5.6	162	1.0	559	3.3	−217	−1.5
West Midlands	108	5.1	146	7.6	107	4.8	38	0.7
South-West	−23	−1.2	63	2.3	179	5.5	268	6.6
East Midlands	296	7.4	98	5.4	225	10.3	186	5.1
East	32	1.8	258	10.6	638	20.6	203	12.2
Wales	237	9.8	−128	−4.9	42	1.6	61	2.2
Scotland	122	2.6	164	3.4	82	1.6	−98	−1.9

Note: Calculated from population present on census night 1911 to 1931, and 1951 to
1981.
Sources: Census of England and Wales 1931, *Preliminary Report*;
Census 1961, England and Wales, *Preliminary Report*;
Census 1981, *Historical Tables*, England and Wales;
Census 1981, Scotland, *Scottish Summary*, vol. 1.

level. The Longitudinal Study itself, with a very large sample size, can't record
migration directly as it is not recorded as a vital event. These deficiencies are
one reason why local authorities (the biggest consumers of demographic
information) often press for five-yearly rather than ten-yearly censuses. These
have been considered since the 1930s, but only implemented once in 1966
(abortive attempts were made to hold censuses in 1976 and 1986; both were
cancelled for financial reasons).

In migration at the regional level, the first half of this century was
dominated by the 'drift to the South', with consequent effects on relative
population sizes of the regions (Table 2.46). People moved away from the old
industries of coal, shipbuilding, and steel in the North and Wales to the light
industries and services of the more attractive South and Midlands. These
migration trends continue to the present day in a more modest way (Table
2.47). Scotland, the North, and South Wales, continue to lose population, the
South-East and particularly East Anglia and the South-West, are gainers. But
it is important to remember that most migration is within counties or regions,
and if outside them, to the adjacent county or region, as the 1981 Census and
the NHS Register data make clear (Brant, 1984). At the same time city centre
populations, which peaked early in the century (1901 in Inner London), have
declined since then in a move to the suburbs and as their traditional industries
have declined (Goddard and Champion, 1983; Martin and Rowthorn, 1986),
with only partial replacement since the 1960s by New Commonwealth
immigrant populations (whose high fertility has in some areas, notably

Table 2.47 Regional population changes, 1951–84, United Kingdom

| | Mid-year estimated population | | | | | | Annual growth rate (per cent) | | |
| | (based on 1966 boundaries) | | (based on 1981 boundaries) | | | | (using 1981 boundaries) | | |
	1951	1961	1961	1971	1981	1984	1961–71 (%)	1971–81 (%)	1983–84 (%)
United Kingdom	50 289	52 807	52 807	55 907	56 379	56 489	0.6	0.1	0.2
North	3 130	3 249	3 113	3 152	3 118	3 093	0.1	-0.1	-0.2
Yorks & Humber	4 488	4 586	4 677	4 902	4 918	4 904	0.5	–	-0.1
East Midlands	2 913	3 139	3 330	3 652	3 853	3 874	0.9	0.5	0.4
East Anglia	1 388	1 489	1 489	1 688	1 895	1 940	1.3	1.2	0.7
South-East									
(excl. Gr. London)	7 008	8 376	8 094	9 596	10 205	10 356	1.7	0.6	0.7
Greater London	8 209	7 980	7 977	7 529	6 806	6 756	-0.6	-1.0	–
South-West	3 247	3 436	3 712	4 112	4 381	4 461	1.0	0.6	0.8
West Midlands	4 426	4 761	4 762	5 146	5 186	5 176	0.8	0.1	–
North-West	6 417	6 545	6 407	6 634	6 460	6 396	0.3	-0.3	-0.2
England	41 226	43 561	43 561	46 412	46 821	46 956	0.6	0.1	0.2
Wales	2 589	2 635	2 635	2 740	2 814	2 807	0.4	0.3	–
Scotland	5 103	5 184	5 184	5 217	5 180	5 162	0.1	-0.1	-0.1
N. Ireland	1 371	1 427	1 427	1 538	1 564	1 579	0.8	0.2	0.4

Sources: CSO, *Abstract of Regional Statistics no. 5* (1969);
Regional Trends, 20 (1985), Table 2.1;
Regional Trends, 21 (1986), Table 2.1.

114   *British Social Trends since 1900*

Bradford, reversed the trend of inner city population decline), and a relatively few 'gentrifiers'. Greater London's population peaked in 1961 at almost 8 million. Since then, Glasgow, Merseyside and the Newcastle Conurbation (Tyne and Wear) followed Greater London into decline in the 1960s; in the 1970s all the conurbations lost population and they continue to do so today.

Young people (for example, aged 18–21) continue as always to be attracted to large cities, especially London. The decline of urban populations still continues, although at a slightly reduced rate. In Greater London the rate of decline is much reduced and is now the lowest of any of the former metropolitan counties (Table 2.48). Inner London's population decline, about 20 per 1000 population in 1971–4, is now about 5 per 1000, about the same as the central conurbation metropolitan districts of Leeds, Newcastle, Birmingham, and so on. Outer London boroughs are now hardly declining in population at all (Britton, 1986). As with the regions, migration greatly exceeds the effects of national change. Rates of national change have been positive and growing in all Metropolitan Counties since the late 1970s, except for Tyne and Wear, while the effects of migration, consistently negative in all areas since the early 1970s, have greatly exceeded their effect. Many of these areas, except Tyne and Wear, have substantial ethnic minority populations, where high fertility has made a substantial and growing contribution to their fertility (Table 2.49).

Unlike fertility, migration trends can be to some extent influenced by government policy. The Barlow Report before the Second World War recommended the dispersal of industry both for environmental and for strategic reasons. The Abercrombie Plan of 1944 proposed further decentralisation of population from London into New Towns, a policy further encouraged until the 1970s by such agencies as the Location of Offices Bureau, until the nature of the 'inner city problem' changed. Then the damaging effects of the selective migration of population out of inner urban areas, leaving too high a concentration of the unskilled and the elderly, became apparent.

Table 2.48   Conurbations (former metropolitan counties), average annual growth rate per thousand population

	1961–71	*1971–81*	*1979–84*	*1983–84*
Greater London	−0.6	−1.0	−0.4	—
West Yorkshire	0.4	−0.1	−0.2	−0.2
South Yorkshire	0.3	−0.1	−0.2	−0.4
West Midlands	0.8	−0.5	−0.4	−0.4
Tyne and Wear	−0.2	−0.5	−0.4	−0.3
Greater Manchester	0.1	−0.5	−0.4	−0.4
Merseyside	−0.3	−0.9	−0.7	−0.7
Clydeside	−0.5	−0.9	−0.7	−0.6

Sources: CSO, *Regional Trends*, 21 (1986), Table 2.1.
Britton, 1986, Table 3.

Table 2.49   Proportion of births to mothers born in the
New Commonwealth and Pakistan,
metropolitan counties   (%)

Area of mothers usual residence	Year 1971	1976	1981	1985
Greater London	17	21	22	21
Inner London	24	27	27	25
Tower Hamlets	18	31	41	45
Outer London	12	17	19	19
Brent	34	42	46	45
Greater Manchester	5	7	9	9
Bolton	8	13	16	16
Merseyside	1	1	1	1
South Yorkshire	3	3	4	4
Tyne and Wear	1	2	2	2
West Midlands	15	19	21	18
Birmingham	20	24	28	25
West Yorkshire	9	12	15	14
Bradford	17	21	27	27
Other urban districts with over 20% in 1985				
Luton	13	17	25	24
Slough	27	31	38	37
Blackburn	15	27	31	28
Leicester	20	30	32	32
England and Wales	6	7	8	8

Source: OPCS, *Monitor*, FMI 86/4, FMI 83/3, FMI 77/2.
FMI *Birth Statistics*, 1974 and unpublished data.

Perhaps one of the most important influences, although difficult to quantify and not intended to have a demographic effect, was the town and country planning legislation developed from the 1930s to the present day. The planning structure it created restricted the freedom of individuals to move around by limiting the areas where houses could be built and employment created. It thereby created distortions in the price structure, particularly in the South-East. Higher costs in the South-East had always deterred movement. The limited Green Belt set in place around London in 1938, expanded under the stringent provisions of the 1947 Town and Country Planning Act, and copied by other major urban areas from 1955, inhibits development beyond the suburbs and prevents the ribbon development which characterised 1930s urban sprawl. Green Belt now occupies, in all, an area greater than Wales. Planning restrictions in the South-East region cover the greater part of its land surface. Land for house-building or for new employment is correspondingly expensive. Land, house prices and market rents now suffer the steepest north/south gradient (twofold between the Northern Region and Greater London) of any variable or commodity, much more so than real wages or rates, for example.

Movement into the South-East has declined. In the 1960s it was the fastest growing region (excepting Greater London). In the 1970s the most rapidly growing regions were East Anglia and the South-West (Table 2.47) and at present these three, all growing at about the same rate, are by far the fastest growing regions. Present and likely future migration patterns suggest that the non-metropolitan areas in a belt from East Anglia to the South-West will grow fastest for the rest of the century. In the past, population decline in Scotland and Northern Ireland has been normal. But as fertility levels have ebbed, whole regions in England have started to lose population too, as migration continues. This started in the 1970s, with the North and North-West losing population between 1971 and 1981, as well as Scotland and Greater London. In the even lower fertility of the 1980s Yorkshire and Humberside is also losing population.

Rural populations declined throughout the nineteenth and early twentieth century. The agricultural depression of the 1930s drove even more off the land. Paradoxically, this occupational and geographical shift was accentuated by the higher productivity encouraged by the government after the war to improve British agricultural self-sufficiency. This made agriculture much more efficient and profitable by increasing productivity of labour and land (although not capital) so much that numbers in agricultural work have fallen to just 2 per cent of the work force, and 14 per cent of the working population even of rural areas. Rural population, especially away from towns, has correspondingly tended to decline further. The surprise of the 1981 Census (also found in the USA and elsewhere) was the revival of population in the rural areas for the first time since the census began (Champion, 1981). Population growth in the 1980s has been concentrated in districts which are not adjacent to a metropolitan district, falling from 8.3 per thousand per year on average in 1971–4 to 4.6 in 1981–5, while growth in non-metropolitan districts which are adjacent to such areas (that is, outer suburbs and commuter areas) has fallen from 6.6 per thousand in 1971–4 to −0.2 in 1981–5 (Britton, 1986). Small country towns are now a favourite location for new, small, high-technology industries, and attractive to their work forces. Retirement, resort and port areas in the South show particularly fast growth rates in 1981–5. But the growth of population in some of the more remote rural areas is relatively new. Almost none of this growth is in the agricultural sector.

HOUSEHOLD AND FAMILY STRUCTURE

Some of the most interesting developments have been taking place in the family and household. Average household size has declined from 4.6 in 1901 to 3.1 in 1961 to 2.6 in 1985 (Table 2.50). This is not just due to the modern

Table 2.50   Average household size, 1901–85, England and Wales

Year	Average household size	No. of private households (000s)
1901	4.6	7 037[1]
1911	4.6	7 943
1921	4.5	8 739
1931	4.1	10 233
1939	3.5	12 000[2]
1951	3.4	13 118
1961	3.1	16 189
1971	2.9	18 317
1981	2.7	19 493
1985	2.6	—

Note:
1. Modern household definition from 1911.
2. 'Potential' households.
Sources: Census 1911, *Preliminary Report*, Table A;
Census 1951, *Housing Report*, Table A;
Census 1981, *National Report*, Tables G and 4;
OPCS, *Monitor: General Household Survey 1985* no.
GHS 86/1, Table 1.
Holmans (1987) Table IV.4 (1939 only).
Social Trends, 15.

decline in fertility and the rarity of very large families. It is also due to the departure of domestic servants. 14 per cent of households had at least one residential domestic servant in 1861, just 1 per cent in 1951. Only 2192 persons were recorded as domestic servants in 1981 (1981 Census) – including nannies and au pairs. This must be a substantial underestimate. In 1985, 9190 au pairs alone were given leave to enter the UK, excluding any from the EEC). It has certainly not been due to any great change in the residential pattern of different generations of the same family. Contrary to popular myth, there never was any time in recorded history when 'extended' families were at all common in Britain, either vertically extended (3 or more generations) or horizontally (relatives outside the nuclear family). And Laslett has shown that average household size was about 4.6 for several centuries before the present (Laslett, 1983). 47 per cent of Victorian households in 1861 consisted of one or both parents with their children but no other relatives, exactly the same size as in 1961 and 1966 (Hole and Pountney, 1971). In 1861, 15 per cent of households contained relatives of the household head, the same as in 1951, although this fell to 10 per cent in 1966.

The distribution of household sizes is first available for England and Wales in 1911, when 5.3 per cent of households were one-person households (Table 2.51). There has been an enormous growth in single-person households at both ends of the age range – young people leaving home, and elderly people.

Table 2.51 Size of private households, 1911–81, England and Wales, and Scotland (percentages)

Year	Proportion of households of different sizes										Proportion of persons in households of different sizes									
	1	2	3	4	5	6	7	8–9	10+	Total	1	2	3	4	5	6	7	8–9	10+	Total
England and Wales																				
1911	5.3	16.2	19.3	18.1	14.4	10.4	6.9	6.9	2.5	100	1.2	7.4	13.3	16.6	16.6	14.3	11.2	13.2	6.3	100
1921	6.0	17.7	20.8	18.6	13.9	9.4	6.0	5.7	1.9	100	1.5	8.6	15.1	17.9	16.7	13.6	10.1	11.5	5.0	100
1931	6.7	21.9	24.1	19.4	12.4	7.3	4.1	3.2	0.9	100	1.8	11.8	19.4	20.8	16.7	11.8	7.8	7.2	2.7	100
1951	10.7	27.7	25.3	19.0	9.6	4.3	1.9	1.2	0.3	100	3.4	17.3	23.7	23.8	15.0	8.1	4.3	3.1	1.2	100
1961	11.9	30.2	23.4	19.1	9.1	3.8	1.5	0.9	0.1	100	3.9	19.6	22.9	24.8	14.7	7.5	3.4	2.4	0.8	100
1971	18.1	31.8	18.9	17.2	8.2	3.5	1.3	0.8	0.2	100	6.3	22.2	19.7	24.0	14.2	7.2	3.2	2.4	0.7	100
1981	21.7	32.1	17.0	18.1	7.3	2.5	0.7	0.4	0.1	100	8.1	23.8	18.9	26.9	13.5	5.6	1.9	1.1	0.3	100
Scotland																				
1951	11.1	24.1	23.7	18.9	10.8	5.6	2.9	2.1	0.7	100	3.3	14.2	21.0	22.3	15.9	10.0	6.0	5.1	2.2	100
1961	11.8	26.5	22.8	19.7	10.5	5.0	2.1	1.4	0.3	100	3.6	16.4	21.1	24.3	16.1	9.3	4.5	3.5	1.2	100
1971	18.4	28.3	18.7	17.1	9.4	4.6	1.9	1.3	0.3	100	6.1	18.8	18.6	22.6	15.6	9.2	4.5	3.5	1.1	100
1981	21.9	29.4	17.5	18.3	8.2	3.2	1.0	0.5	0.1	100	7.9	21.2	18.9	26.4	14.8	6.8	2.4	1.3	0.3	100

Note: 1901–31 census volumes for Scotland give analyses of number of persons by house, not distinguishing separate households sharing a house.

Sources: Census 1911, *Summary Tables, England and Wales*;
Census 1951, vol. III, *Scotland*;
Census 1961, *Household Composition Tables, England and Wales*;
Census 1961, Scotland, *Housing and Household Tables*;
Census 1971, England and Wales, *Household Composition Tables*, part 1 (10 per cent sample);
Census 1971, Scotland, *Household Composition Tables* (10 per cent sample);
Census 1981, *Household and Family Composition, England and Wales* (10 per cent sample);
Census 1981, *Household and Family Composition, Scotland* (10 per cent sample).

Table 2.52   Household type, 1983, Great Britain(%)

Type of household	Households	People
One person	23	9
Lone parent with dependent children	5	5
Married couple with non-dependent children only	8	11
Married couple with no children	27	21
Married couple with dependent children	30	47
Other	8	8
Total	100	100

Source: General Household Survey (1983), Figure 3A. Reproduced with the permission of the Controller of Her Majesty's Stationery Office.

The composition of single-person households has changed. There were many more unmarried adult men and (particularly) women in 1911 than today, who now predominate in the elderly population. There were more widows and almost no divorced persons. Many lived alone, others with their siblings. Old people commonly lived alone then as they do now. All this has greatly reduced average household size.

In 1983 almost a quarter of households (23 per cent) were single-person households (17 per cent in 1971), almost as many as married couples with no children (27 per cent) and married couples with dependent children (30 per

Table 2.53   Families with dependent children[1] by type and for lone mothers, by marital status, 1971–83, Great Britain (%)

Family type	1971–3	1973–5	1975–7	1977–9	1979–81	1981–3
Married couple[2]	92	91	90	89	88	87
Lone mother	7	8	9	10	10	12
single	1	1	2	2	2	3
widowed	2	2	2	2	2	2
divorced	2	3	3	4	4	5
separated	2	2	2	2	2	2
Lone father	1	1	1	1	2	1
All lone parents	8	9	10	11	12	13
Base = 100%	14 105	13 655	13 972	13 178	12 984	11 540

Notes:
1. Persons aged under 16, or aged 16–18 and in full-time education, in the family unit and living in the household.
2. Including married women whose husbands were not defined as resident in the household:
Source: General Household Survey (1983) Table 3.15. Reproduced with the permission of the Controller of Her Majesty's Stationery Office.

Table 2.54   Distribution of household type, 1971–83, Great Britain

Household	Percentage of households of each type							
	1971	*1973*	*1975*	*1977*	*1979*	*1980*	*1981*	*1982*
1 adult aged 16–59	5	5	6	6	7	8	7	7
2 adults aged 16–59	14	14	14	14	14	13	13	14
Youngest person aged 0–4	18	38	15	14	13	13	13	12
Youngest person aged 5–15	21		22	22	22	22	22	20
3 or more adults	13	12	11	11	11	12	13	13
2 adults, 1 or both aged 60 or over	17	17	17	18	17	18	17	18
1 adult aged 60 or over	12	13	15	15	16	15	15	16
Base = 100%	11 934	11 642	12 090	11 957	11 490	11 720	12 006	10 306

Source: General Household Survey (1983), Table 3.2. Reproduced with the permission of the Controller of Her Majesty's Stationery Office.

Table 2.55   Private households, 1981, England and Wales, 10 per cent sample

Type	Distribution of household type			
	Number of households	*(%)*	Number of persons	*(%)*
All households	1 770 699	100.0	4 780 807	100.0
No. in family	469 086	26.5	570 382	11.9
1 person	384 913	21.7	384 913	8.1
2 or more persons	84 173	4.8	185 469	3.9
Households with one family	1 286 158	72.6	4 120 295	86.2
Married couple, no children	485 363	27.4	945 265	19.8
without others	432 608	24.4	865 216	18.1
with others	25 755	1.5	80 049	1.7
Married couple with children	680 867	38.5	2 743 777	57.4
without others				
with dependent children	413 265	23.3	1 631 728	34.1
some children dependent	98 157	5.5	480 438	10.0
no children dependent	133 027	7.5	447 122	9.4
with others				
all children dependent	19 848	1.1	100 126	2.1
some children dependent	6 656	0.4	40 474	0.8
no children dependent	9 914	0.6	43 889	0.9
One-parent family	146 928	8.3	431 253	9.0
without others				
all children dependent	43 042	2.4	119 005	2.5
some children dependent	14 628	0.8	57 309	1.2
no children dependent	58 080	3.1	123 293	2.6
with others				
all children dependent	21 430	1.2	81 663	1.7
some children dependent	3 991	0.2	20 327	0.4
no children dependent	8 757	0.5	29 656	0.6

1983			Percentage of persons in each type of household						
	1971	*1973*	*1975*	*1977*	*1979*	*1980*	*1981*	*1982*	*1983*
7	2	2	2	2	3	3	3	3	3
13	10	10	10	11	11	10	10	10	10
14	27 ⎫	57	23	21	20	19	21	20	21
19	31 ⎭		34	33	34	34	33	31	30
13	15	14	13	14	14	15	16	17	17
18	11	12	12	13	12	13	12	14	13
16	4	5	5	5	6	6	6	6	6
10 068	34 720	32 993	33 561	32 387	30 716	31 443	32 410	27 160	26 587

Households with two or more families	15 455	0.9	90 130	1.9
all children dependent	7 458	0.4	43 301	0.9
some children dependent	4 691	0.3	31 715	0.7
no children dependent	1 591	0.1	7 959	0.2
no children	1 715	0.1	7 155	0.1

Source: Census 1981, *Household and Family Composition, England and Wales, 1984*, Table 1, Reproduced with the permission of the Controller of Her Majesty's Stationery Office.

cent) (Table 2.52). At the other end of the scale, only 3 per cent of households included six or more people in 1983 (comprising 7 per cent of people); a decline from 6 and 13 per cent respectively in 1971. It's important, though, to remember that the picture looks different when analysed by people, not households (Tables 2.52, 2.54, 2.55). Almost half the population – 47 per cent – lives in households of a married couple with dependent children, only 9 per cent of people live by themselves (although another 5 per cent are single-parent families with dependent children) (Table 2.52). (These families comprised 13 per cent of all families with dependent children, compared to 8 per cent in 1971–3 (Table 2.53).) Average household size is still going down, from 2.91 in 1971 to 2.64 in 1982 and 1983.

Some categories of household have remained roughly constant (for example, those consisting of two adults aged 16–59) where at least one is over 60 years old. Others have increased – single older people during the 1970s and of three or more adults, which declined up to the mid-1970s and then increased, the latter increase due to the growth of larger complex ethnic minority households (Table 2.54). The great increase in single-parent families is due to

Table 2.56　One-parent families by sex and marital status of head of family, 1972–84, Great Britain (%)

Family type	1972–4	1978–0	1980–2	1982–4	Change 1972/4 –82/4
Lone mothers					
Single	15	16	19	21	+6
Separated	26	21	19	18	−8
Divorced	25	34	37	40	+15
Widowed	21	16	14	12	−9
Lone fathers					
Single	1	—	—	—	−1
Separated	4	4	4	3	−1
Divorced	3	4	5	4	+1
Widowed	6	4	3	2	−4
All lone mothers	86	89	89	91	+5
All lone fathers	14	11	11	9	−5
All lone parents	100	100	100	100	−5
Sample number[1]	1162	1484	1484	1391	

Note:
1.　Forms base of 100 per cent.
Source:　J. Haskey (1986). Reproduced with the permission of the Controller of Her Majesty's Stationery Office.

the effects of divorce, not illegitimacy as is sometimes supposed. Table 2.56 shows that of all one-parent families with dependent children in 1982–4 39 per cent were headed by divorced women – a category almost non-existent in 1901 – and 15 per cent by separated women, while 23 per cent were headed by single women.

Within families the pace of change since the decline of fertility was established is much less dramatic and the distribution of sizes has changed relatively little from 1961 to 1981 (Tables 2.57, 2.58), as has the composition,except through divorce. The apparent changes that have occurred recently have largely arisen because conjugal links in their broad sense have become more varied and vulnerable (cohabitation, divorce) than in the past, as Kiernan (1983)[117] points out. These changes have meant that since 1931 growth in the number of households has been faster than the growth in population of household-forming age.

CONSEQUENCES OF POPULATION TRENDS

These changes suggest a number of ways in which population trends matter. Changes over time in the relative size of groups relying on transfer payments

Table 2.57   Families by size and number of persons, 1961, 1971, England and
Wales, and Scotland (%)

			Size of family					
	2	3	4	5	6–7	8–9	10 or more	All
England and Wales								
Families								
1961	39.1	26.9	20.6	8.3	4.3	0.7	0.2	100
								(1 259 062 × 10)
1971	41.4	22.9	20.8	9.0	4.9		1.0	100
								(1 317 920 × 10)
Persons								
1961	24.6	25.5	26.0	13.0	8.5	1.8	0.6	100
								(3 992 170 × 10)
1971	26.0	21.5	26.0	14.2	9.6		2.6	100
								(4 203 068 × 10)
Scotland								
Families								
1961	33.0	26.5	22.2	10.5	6.4	1.2	0.3	100
								(133 333 × 10)
1971	36.5	23.1	21.1	10.8	6.9		1.6	100
								(133 841 × 10)
Persons								
1961	19.4	23.4	26.1	15.5	11.9	2.8	0.9	100
								(452 772 × 10)
1971	21.6	20.5	25.0	16.0	12.9		4.2	100
								(452 766 × 10)

Sources: Census 1961, England and Wales, and Scotland, *Household Composition Tables*.
Census 1971, England and Wales, *Household Composition Tables*, part III (10 per cent sample), Table 33 (p. 23);
Census 1971, Scotland, *Household Composition Tables* (10 per cent sample) Table 35 (p. 202).

are particularly important. Figure 2.12 shows the sizes of the age-groups in the past and projected into the future. The projections are reasonably secure as far as they relate to people already born (OPCS, 1985). The mid-twentieth-century pattern of unstable fertility has brought this sharply into focus. It has meant rapid increases and decreases – up to 30 per cent in ten years – of cohort size of births, who then need medical care, education and employment. Policies on teacher recruitment, school building or – more recently – closure, and the like, need to anticipate these changes, but it is only recently that detailed attention has been paid to demographic trends in planning their provision (see Central Policy Review Staff, 1978). Some changes in the school-age population are shown in Table 2.59. Since the early 1970s primary school enrolment has been falling – the 5 to 9 age-group was 74% of its peak 1971

British Social Trends since 1900

Table 2.58   Families by type of head and number of persons, 1961 and 1971,
England and Wales, and Scotland   (%)

	Married couple with husband aged:				Married spouse absent	Single, widowed or divorced man aged:			
	under 45	45–64	65+	all ages		under 45	45–64	65+	all ages
England and Wales									
Families									
1961	41.5	38.5	11.0	91.1	1.9	0.2	0.6	0.6	1.4
1971	41.0	36.4	13.3	90.7	—	0.5	0.7	0.5	1.7
Persons									
1961	47.1	37.8	7.9	92.8	1.7	0.2	0.5	0.4	1.1
1971	48.4	34.8	9.2	92.3	—	0.4	0.6	0.4	1.4
Scotland									
Families									
1961	42.1	37.0	9.4	88.5	2.1	0.2	0.9	0.9	2.0
1971	42.0	35.0	11.7	88.8	—	0.4	0.8	0.7	2.0
Persons									
1961	47.1	37.0	6.8	90.9	1.7	0.2	0.7	0.7	1.6
1971	49.2	33.9	8.0	91.1	—	0.4	0.7	0.5	1.6

Sources: Census 1961, England and Wales, *Household Composition Tables*, Table 30 (p. 290), 10 per cent sample;
Census 1961, Scotland, *Housing & Households*, part II, *Household Composition Tables*, Table 30 (p. 185), 10 per cent sample;

figure in 1986. But it will increase temporarily in the 1990s. The secondary school population experienced a similar decline from the late 1970s and the enormous drop in potential candidates for tertiary education (and work force entry) will not affect 15 to 19 year olds until the early 1990s. In the early 1980s the whole school-age population was still dropping at the rate of a quarter of a million per year. The social composition of births mentioned in an earlier section matters here; because children from middle-class households are more likely to go on to tertiary education, it has been argued that the relative increase in the proportion of such births since 1971 will make for a greater demand for such places than the simple age-structure projections would suggest (Royal Society, 1983). At the school level of the catchment area, local migration is very important, emptying inner city schools even faster than the falling birth-rate by itself, and in some areas creating demand for new schools. Of course demography does not dictate the policy, as the discussions in the 1970s about how to deal with the bulge of student numbers in the 1980s showed.

Single, widowed or divorced woman aged:				Families with one parent as % of all familes	Total families	Total persons in families
under 45	45–59¹	60+	all ages			
						—
0.9	1.9	2.8	5.6	8.9	100 (1 259 062) × 10	
2.7	2.1	2.8	7.6	9.3	100 (1 317 920) × 10	—
0.8	1.6	2.0	4.4	7.2	—	100 (3 992 170) × 10
2.6	1.8	1.8	6.3	7.7	—	100 (4 203 068) × 10
1.1	2.7	3.7	7.5	11.5	100 (1 333 330)	—
2.8	2.7	3.7	9.2	11.2	100 (1 338 265)	
0.9	2.2	2.6	5.8	9.1	—	100 (4 527 720)
2.6	2.2	2.5	7.3	8.9	—	100 (4 519 480)

Census 1971, England and Wales, *Household Composition Tables*, part III Table 38 (p. 56); 10 per cent in sample;
Census 1971, Scotland, *Household Composition Tables*, Table 5 (p. 27) (100 per cent).

Further up the age-structure the ability of the British economy to 'create' jobs is easily exceeded by the ability of the British people to create babies. Whatever its economic cause, UK unemployment in the 1980s has certainly been worsened by the increase of 30 per cent in the annual supply of young people seeking jobs each year compared with the 1960s. It will be eased to a similar extent from the mid-1980s onwards, when the numbers entering the work force will be dominated, not by the rising cohorts of the early 1960s, but by the declining ones of the 1970s. Correspondingly small birth cohorts may not meet later demands for labour – the babies cancelled or postponed by mothers in the 1930s were to some extent replaced in the work force by West Indian and Asian immigrants in the 1950s, and even more, by married women.

One of the most important long-term problems concerns old-age pensions, particularly the relation of the numbers of pensioners to those in the working-age groups. This matters particularly because state pensions do not operate in the UK (and most other places) on a funded basis as private pensions schemes do, (whereby individual's contributions plus profits, are used to pay his

Table 2.59   Some changes in the school-age population, England and Wales (000s)

	5–9		Ages 10–14		15–19	
Year	No.	% change	No.	% change	No.	% change
1901	3487	—	3342	—	3246	—
1911	3697	+ 6.0%	3500	+ 4.7%	3337	+ 2.8%
1921	3519	− 4.8%	3660	+ 4.6%	3503	+ 5.0%
1931	3323	− 5.6%	3207	− 14.1%	3435	− 1.4%
1951	3162	− 4.8%	2812	− 14.0%	2705	− 21.3%
1961	3262	+ 3.2%	3725	+ 32.5%	3200	+ 18.3%
1971	4044	+ 24.0%	3627	− 2.6%	3314	+ 3.6%
1981	3200	− 26.4%	3102	− 14.5%	4071	+ 22.8%
1986	2986	− 6.7%	3196	+ 3.0%	3882	− 4.6%
1991	3165	+ 6.0%	2988	− 6.5%	3220	− 17.1%
1996	3558	+ 12.4%	3167	+ 6.0%	3014	− 6.4%

Sources: OPCS, *Monitor*, PP2 83/1, Table 2.52 Recent changes in selected age groups 1981–1985.
OPCS, *Monitor*, PP1 86/1, Table B.
1931 Census, *General Report* Table XLI.
1951 Census, *General Tables*, Table 18A.
1961 Census, *Age, Marital Condition, and General Tables*, Table 8.
1971 Census, *Age, Marital Condition, and General Tables*, Table 9.

subsequent pension). Instead, a pay-as-you-go scheme operates where tax payments by tax-payers are transferred directly to pensioners. Such a scheme depends particularly on population growth preserving a relatively helpful ratio between tax-payers and dependents, and on the absence of fluctuations in this ratio (funded schemes are not invulnerable to this either, as a more adverse dependency ratio will effect the productivity of the whole economy and thus the yield from invested funds). But state schemes are also vulnerable in all countries to the tendency of governments to buy geriatric votes today which the tax-payer must pay for tomorrow.

One of the most powerful demographic consequences of a declining birth-rate is the ageing of the population. Correspondingly, twentieth-century Britain – and most industrial countries – has seen a marked worsening of the ratio between tax-payers and pensioners (Table 2.60a). In 1931 the ratio stood at 9.7 to 1 of population 15–64 to 65 and over. Falling fertility and the consequent ageing of the population, together with modest improvements in survival at old age, brought it to 4.2 to 1 in 1981, corresponding to a ratio to persons of pensionable age of 3.3:1. There it will stay for the rest of this century. Now is the good time for pensioners and indeed the dependency ratio is becoming generally more favourable for a while. The work force is inflated by the baby boom and by the high work force participation of women, while

Table 2.60(a)   Ratios of elderly population to population of working age, 1911–85, England and Wales (000s)

Year	15–64 (A)	65+ (B)	Working age[1] (C)	Pensionable age[2] (D)	A:B	C:D
1911	23200.6	1883.0	23200.6	1883.0	12.3	12.3
1921	24897.8	2185.1	24268.2	2814.7	11.4	8.6
1931	27594.2	2856.3	26699.9	3750.6	9.7	7.1
1939	28788.2	3731.9	27724.5	4795.6	7.7	5.8
1951	29249.0	4813.0	28042.0	6020.0	6.1	4.7
1961	30076.8	5513.0	28720.8	6869.0	5.5	4.2
1971	30903.7	6591.8	29387.4	8108.1	4.7	3.6
1981	31995.5	7548.3	29795.9	8928.2	4.2	3.3
1985	32791.0	7633.7	30571.5	9098.7	4.3	3.4

1.   15–64 in 1911.
     15–64/59 from 1921–1971.
     16–64/59 for 1981 and 1985.
2.   65 and over in 1911.
     65/60 and over for remaining years.

Table 2.60(b)   Ratio of elderly population to population of working age, and of National Insurance contributors to pensioners, 1984–5 to 2025–6.

Year	Ratio of persons of working age to persons of pensionable age	Number of National Insurance Contributions per pensioner
1984–5	3.3	2.3
1995–6	3.3	2.2
2005–6	3.4	2.2
2015–16	3.1	2.0
2025–6	2.7	1.8

Sources: OPCS, *Monitor*, PP2 83/1;
DHSS (1982) *Population, Pension Costs and Pensioners' Income*, Table 1, Table 2.37., and unpublished OPCS data.

pensioner recruitment is low. The birth-rate in 1921 was low and declining (see Figure 2.2) so there will be a reduction in the number of new pensioners for the next decade or so, even though the numbers of the elderly over 75, and especially 85, will increase – they were born in the higher fertility years at the beginning of the century.

Problems start next century when the baby boom starts to age. Then pensioner numbers will sharply increase and their needs will have to be met by a reduced working population based on the depleted birth cohorts of the 1970s

Table 2.61(a)   Projections of future households and population, England and
Wales, 1981–2001   (000s)

Year	No. of households	% increase	Population in households	% increase	Average household size
1981	18 195	—	48 945	—	2.69
1986	18 922	4.0	49 042	0.2	2.59
1991	19 741	4.3	49 412	0.8	2.50
1996	20 311	2.9	49 935	1.1	2.46
2001	20 596	1.4	50 348	0.8	2.44

Table 2.61(b)   Projection of future households by type,
England only, 1983–2001 (000s)

Year	Married couples	Single parent	One person	Total[1]
1983	10 725	1470	4134	17 423
1986	10 641	1587	4473	17 879
1991	10 689	1728	4971	18 661
1996	10 767	1802	5355	19 205
2001	10 746	1832	5653	19 481

Note:
1.   Total includes some household types not listed separately.
Source: Department of the Environment (1986)
            1983—based estimates of numbers of households in
            England; 1983–2001, Table 2 (London: Department
            of the Environment).

and 1980s and – as far as we can see – of the 1990s too. As all the future
pensioners for the next 60 years are already born and death-rates are not
volatile, this problem can be predicted with confidence. The ratio of persons of
working age to pensions will fall below 3, that of National Insurance
contributions to pensions recipients below 2 (Table 2.60b). This has been an
important part of the controversy about the proposed State Earnings Related
Pensions Scheme (Kay, 1987; DHSS, 1984) and similar problems abroad.
Finally, it is worth mentioning that the change in the composition of numbers
of households will exert a different demand on housing provision from that
expected from the stagnant trend in population. From now until the end of the
century population will only increase 3 per cent or so. But households are
likely to increase by 9 per cent over the same period; a consequence of home-
building and family formation by the baby boom cohorts and high divorce

rates (see Holmans, 1987). But most of this increase will take place by the early 1990s; this can be expected to be the last demographically inspired housing boom for the foreseeable future (Table 2.61)

ACKNOWLEDGEMENTS

I am most grateful to Miss Catriona Mirrlees for help with the tables, to Mr Alan Holmans, of the Department of the Environment, and Mr John Haskey, of the Office of Population Censuses and Surveys, for helpful comments and corrections. All errors and omissions remain my own.

REFERENCES

ANDERSON, M. (1983) 'What is New About the Modern Family: An Historical Perspective', in British Society for Population Studies Conference Proceedings (1983) 'The Family', pp. 1–16, *OPCS Occasional Paper no. 31*, (London: OPCS).

ARMITAGE, R. I. (1987) 'English Regional Fertility and Mortality Patterns, 1975–1985', *Population Trends, 47*: 16–23.

BAINES, D. (1986) *Migration in a Mature Economy: Emigration and Internal Migration in England and Wales 1861–1900* (Cambridge: Cambridge University Press).

BANKS, J. A. (1954) *Prosperity and Parenthood* (London: Routledge & Kegan Paul).

BAUM, F, and COPE, D. R. (1980) 'Some Characteristics of Intentionally Childless Wives in Britain', *Journal of Biosocial Science, 12*: 287–99.

BECKER, G. S. (1981) *A Treatise on the Family* (Cambridge, Mass.: Harvard University Press).

BONE, M. (1986) 'Trends in Single Women's Sexual Behaviour in Scotland', *Population Trends, 43*: 7–14.

BOURGEOIS-PICHAT, J. (1980) 'Recent demographic change in Europe: an assessment.' *Population and Development review 7*, 1: 19–42.

BRANT, J. (1984) 'Patterns of Migration from the 1981 Census', *Population Trends, 35*: 23–30.

BRASS, W. (1974) 'Perspectives in Population Prediction, illustrated by the statistics of England and Wales', *Journal of the Royal Statistical Society, 137*: 532–83.

BRITTON, M. (1980) 'Recent Trends in Births', *Population Trends, 20*: 4–8.

BRITTON, M. (1986) 'Recent Population Changes in Perspective', *Population Trends, 44*: 33–41.

BROWN, A., and KIERNAN, K. (1981) 'Cohabitation in Great Britain: Evidence from the General Household Survey', *Population Trends, 25*: 4–10.

BULMER, M. (ed.) (1979) *Censuses, Surveys and Privacy* (London: Macmillan).

CAMPBELL, E. (1985) *The Childless Marriage* (London: Tavistock).

CARTWRIGHT A. (1978) 'Recent Trends in Family Building and Contraception', *OPCS Studies in Medical and Population Subjects, no. 34* (London: HMSO).

CENSUS 1981 (1984) *Household and Family Composition*, (London: HMSO).

CENTRAL POLICY REVIEW STAFF (Population Panel) (1973) *Report of the Population Panel*, Cmnd 5258 (London: HMSO).

CENTRAL POLICY REVIEW STAFF (1978) *Population and the Social Services* (London: HMSO).

CENTRAL STATISTICAL OFFICE (1986) *Regional Trends*, 21 (London: HMSO).

CHAMPION, A. G. (1981) 'Population Trends in Rural Britain', *Population Trends,* *26*: 20–23.

CHARLES, E. (1936) *The Menace of Under-Population: a Biological Study of the* *Decline of Population Growth* (London: Watts & Co).

COLEMAN, D. A. (1980) 'Recent trends in marriage and divorce in Britain and Europe', in Hiorns, R. W. (ed.) *Demographic Patterns in Developed Societies,* pp. 83–125 (London: Taylor & Francis).

COLEMAN, D. A. (ed.) (1982) *The Demography of Immigrants and Minority Groups in* *the United Kingdom* (London: Academic Press).

COLEMAN, D. A. (1983) 'The Demography of Ethnic Minorities', in Kirkwood, K., Herbertson, M. A. and Parkes, A. S. (eds) *Journal of Biosocial Science Supplement* *no. 8,* 'Biosocial Aspects of Ethnic Minorities' (Cambridge: Galton Foundation) pp. 43–90.

COLEMAN, D. A. (1983) 'Some Problems of Data for the Study of Immigration and Ethnic Minorities in the U.K.', *Ethnic and Racial Studies,* 6: 103–10.

COLEMAN, D. A. (1985) 'Ethnic Intermarriage in Great Britain', *Population Trends,* *40*: 4–9.

COLEMAN, D. A. (1987) 'UK Statistics on Immigration: Development and Limitations', *International Migration Review* 21 (to be published December 1987).

COLEMAN, D. A. (in press) 'UK Statistics on Immigration: Development and limitations', *International Migration Review.* (to be published by Oxford University Press).

COMPTON, P. A. (ed.) (1981) *The Contemporary Population of Northern Ireland and* *Population-related Issues* (Queen's University, Belfast: Institute of Irish Studies).

CRAIG, J. (1983) 'The Growth of the Elderly Population', *Population Trends, 32*: 29 (Fig. 1).

DEPARTMENT OF HEALTH AND SOCIAL SECURITY (DHSS) (1984) *Popula-* *tion, Pension Costs, and Pensioners' Income* (London: HMSO).

DEVIS, T. (1984) 'Population Movements Measured by the NHS Central Register', *Population Trends, 36*: 18–24.

DEVIS, T. (1985) 'International Migration: Return Migrant and Re-migrant flows', *Population Trends, 41*: 13–20.

DUNNELL, K. (1979) *Family Formation 1976* (London: HMSO).

EASTERLIN, R. (1980) *Birth and Fortune: the Impact of Numbers on Personal Welfare* (London: Grant McIntyre).

ERMISCH, J. (1981) 'Economic Opportunities, Marriage Squeezes and the Propensity to Marry', *Population Studies, 35*: 347–56.

ERMISCH, J. (1983) *The Political Economy of Demographic Change* (London: Heinemann Educational Books).

EVERSLY, D. E. C. and KÖLLMANN, W. (eds) (1982) *Population Change and Social* *Planning* (London: Edward Arnold).

FOGELMAN, K. (ed.) (1983) *Growing up in Great Britain* (London: Macmillan)

FOX, A. J. and GOLDBLATT, P. O. (1982) 'Socio-demographic Mortality Differentials', *OPCS Longitudinal Study 1971–75, Series LS no. 1* (London: HMSO).

FOX, J. and GRUNDY, E. (1985) 'A Longitudinal Perspective on Recent Socio-demographic Change', in British Society for Population Studies Conference (1985) *Measuring Socio-demographic Change,* pp. 10–25. *OPCS Occasional Paper, no. 34* (London: OPCS).

FRIEDLANDER, D. and ROSHIER, R. J. (1966) 'Internal Migration in England and Wales 1851–1951', *Population Studies,* 19(3): 239–280; 'A Study of Internal Migration in England and Wales, part II', *Population Studies,* 20(1): 45–59.

FRYER, P. (1964) *The Birth Controllers* (London: Secker & Warburg).

GENERAL HOUSEHOLD SURVEY (1986) (London: HMSO).

GARVEY, D. (1985) 'The History of Migration Flows in the Republic of Ireland', *Population Trends, 39*: 22–30.

GLASS, D. V. (1942) *Population Trends and Policies* (Oxford: Oxford University Press).

GLASS, D. V. and GREBENIK,E. (1954) *1946 Great Britain Family Census Vol. 1* (London: HMSO).

GLASS, D. V. (1967) 'The Components of Natural Increase in England and Wales', *Population Studies* (Supplement) 'Towards a Population Policy for Britain', also reprinted in *First Report of the Select Committee on Science and Technology* (1971).

GLASS, D. V. (1968) 'Fertility Trends in Europe since the Second World War', *Population Studies XXII*, (1): 103–46.

GLASS, D. V. (1973) *Numbering the People* (Farnborough: Saxon House).

GLASS, D. V. (1976) 'Recent and Prospective Trends in Fertility in Developed Countries', *Philosophical Transactions of the Royal Society (B)*, 274: 1–52.

GODDARD, J. B. and CHAMPION, A. G. (eds) (1983) *The Urban and Regional Transformation of Britain* (London: Methuen).

HAJNAL, J. (1965) 'European Marriage Patterns in Perspective', in Glass, D. V. and Eversley, D. E. C. (eds) *Population in History* (London: Edward Arnold).

HAJNAL, J. (1982) 'Two Kinds of Preindustrial Household Formation System', *Population and Development Review*, 8(3): 449–94.

HASKEY, J. (1982) 'The Proportion of Marriages Ending in Divorce', *Population Trends, 27*: 4–8.

HASKEY, J. (1983a) 'Marital Status Before Marriage and Age at Marriage: Their Influence on the Chances of Divorce', *Population Trends, 32*: 4–14.

HASKEY, J. (1983b) 'Social Class patterns of marriage', *Population Trends 34*: 12–19.

HASKEY, J. (1984) 'Social Class and socio-economic differentials in divorce in England and Wales Population Studies 38, 419.

HASKEY, J. and COLEMAN, D. A. (1986) 'Cohabitation Before Marriage: a Comparison of Information from Marriage Registration and the General Household Survey', *Population Trends, 43*: 15–17.

HASKEY, J. (1986) 'One-parent Families in Great Britain', *Population Trends 45*: 5–13.

HATTON, T. J. (1986) 'Female Labour Force Participation: The Enigma of the Interwar Period', *Centre for Economic Policy Research Discussion Paper No. 113* (London: Centre for Economic Policy Research).

HIORNS, R. W. (1980) *Demographic Patterns in Developed Societies. Symposia of the Society for the Study of Human Biology XIX* (London: Taylor and Francis).

HOBCRAFT, J. and MURPHY, M. (eds) *Population Research in Britain* (Oxford: Oxford University Press) (to be published).

HOGBEN, L. (ed.) (1938) *Political Arithmetic* (London: Allen & Unwin).

HOLE, W. V. and POUNTNEY, M. T. (1971) *Trends in Population, Housing and Occupancy Rates 1861–1961*, Department of the Environment (Building Research Station) (London: HMSO).

HOLLIS, J. (1982) 'New Commonwealth Ethnic Group Populations in Greater London', in Coleman, D. A. (ed.) *Demography of Immigrants and Minority Groups in the United Kingdom* (London: Academic Press).

HOLMANS, A. E. (1963) 'Current Population Trends in Britain', *Scottish Journal of Political Economy, XI*: 31–56.

HOLMANS, A. E. (1987) *Housing Policy in Britain. A History* (London: Croom Helm).

HOME AFFAIRS COMMITTEE (1986) *Immigration from the Indian sub-Continent*, Second Report, vol. 1, Session 1985/86 (London: HMSO).

HOME OFFICE (1986) *Control of Immigration Statistics 1985*, Cmmd 9863 (London: HMSO).

JONES, C. (1977) *Immigration and Social Policy in Britain* (London: Tavistock).

JONES, P. R. (1982) 'Some Sources of Current Immigration', in Coleman, D. A. (ed.) *The Demography of Immigrants and Minority Groups in the United Kingdom* (London: Academic Press).

JOSHI, H. (1987) 'The Cost of Caring', in Glendinning, C. and Millar, J. (eds) *Women and Poverty in Britain* (Wheatsheaf Books).

KAY, J. (in press) 'The Welfare Crisis in an Ageing Population', in Keynes, M., Coleman, D. A. and Dimsdale, N. H. (eds) *The Political Economy of Health and Welfare* (London: Macmillan).

KEYNES, J. M. (1937) 'The Economic Consequences of a Declining Population', *Eugenics Review, 29*: 13–17.

KIERNAN, K. E. and DIAMOND, I. (1982) 'Family of Origin and Educational Influences on Age at First Birth: The Experiences of the British Birth Cohort', *Centre for Population Studies Research Paper* no. 82–1. (London: London School of Hygiene and Tropical Medicine).

KIERNAN K. E. (1983) 'The Structure of Families Today: Continuity or Change?' in British Society for Population Studies Conference Proceedings (1983), 'The Family', *OPCS Occasional Paper 31* (London: OPCS).

KIERNAN, K. E. (1986) 'Teenage Marriage and Marital Breakdown: A Longitudinal Study', *Population Studies*, 40(1): 35–54.

KOSMIN, B. A. (1982) 'Nuptiality and Fertility Patterns of British Jewry 1850–1980: An Immigrant Transition?', in Coleman, D. A. (ed.) *Demography of Immigrant and Minority Groups in the UK* (London: Academic Press) pp. 245–61.

KUNZEL, R. (1974) 'The Connection Between the Family Cycle and Divorce Rates. An Analysis Based on European Data', *Journal of Marriage and the Family*, 36(2): 379–88.

LANGFORD, C. M. (1976) *Birth Control Practice and Marital Fertility in Great Britain* (London: London School of Economics, Population Investigation Committee).

LASLETT, P. (1983) *The World We Have Lost*, 3rd edn (London: Methuen).

LEATHARD, A. (1980) *The Fight for Family Planning*. (London: Macmillan)

LEETE, R. and ANTHONY, S. (1979) 'Divorce and Remarriage – A Record Linkage Study', *Population Trends*, (16): 5–11.

LEETE, R. (1979) 'Changing patterns of family formation and dissolution in England and Wales 1964–76', *OPCS Studies in Medical and Population Subjects, No. 39* (London: HMSO).

LESTHAEGHE, R. (1983) 'A Century of Demographic and Cultural Change in Western Europe: An Exploration of Underlying Dimensions', *Population and Development Review 9*: 411–36.

McCLAREN, A. (1978) *Birth Control in Nineteenth-Century England* (London: Croom Helm).

MACFARLANE, A. (1986) *Marriage and Love in England 1300–1840* (Oxford: Basil Blackwell).

MARTIN, R. and ROWTHORN, B. (eds) (1986) *The Geography of De-industrialisation* (London: Macmillan).

MATRAS, J. (1965) 'Social Strategies of Family Formation: Data for British Female Cohorts Born 1831–1906', *Population Studies*, XIX(2): 167–82.

MURPHY, M. (1984) 'The Association Between Socio-economic and related Factors on Family Formation and Breakdown: Some Evidence from a British National Survey', *Centre for Population Studies Research Paper* no. 84–2 (London: London School of Hygiene and Tropical Medicine).

MURPHY, M. J. and SULLIVAN, O. (1983) 'Housing Tenure and Fertility in Post-War Britain', *Centre for Population Studies Research Paper no. 83–2* (London: London School of Hygiene and Tropical Medicine).

MURPHY, M. J. and SULLIVAN, O. (1985) 'Housing Tenure and Family Formation in Contemporary Britain', *European Sociological Review* 1 (3): 1–14.

NATIONAL REGISTER (1939) *Statistics of Population on 29 September 1939. Report and Tables* (London: HMSO).

OPCS (1977) *Guide to Census Reports, Great Britain 1801–1966* (London: HMSO).

OPCS (1979) *Fertility Report from the 1971 Census.* Decennial Supplement Series DS no. 5 (London: HMSO).

OPCS, *Monitor Labour Force Survey 1984: Country of Birth, Ethnic Group, Year of Entry and Nationality* LFS 85/1 (London: OPCS).

OPCS (1985) *Population Projections 1983*, Series PP2, no. 13 (London: HMSO).

OPCS (1986a) *International Migration 1984*, Series MN, no. 11 (London: HMSO).

OPCS (1986b) 'Recorded Internal Population Movements in the United Kingdom, 1985', *OPCS Monitor MN 86/3* (London: OPCS).

PEACH, G. C. K. and WINCHESTER, S. W. C. (1974) 'Birthplace, Ethnicity and the Under-enumeration of West Indians, Indians and Pakistanis in the Census of 1966 and 1971', *New Community,* 3: 386.

PEARCE, D. and BRITTON, M. (1977) 'The Decline in Births: Some Socio-economic Aspects', *Population Trends, 7:* 9–14.

PEARCE, D. and FARID, S. (1977) 'Illegitimate Births – Changing Patterns', *Population Trends, 9:* 20–23.

REGISTRAR-GENERAL (1978) *Occupational Mortality 1969–1973*, Series DS no. 1 (London: HMSO).

REGISTRAR-GENERAL (1986) *Occupational Mortality 1979–1980, 1982–83.* Series DS no. 6. (London: HMSO).

ROYAL COLLEGE OF PHYSICIANS/ROYAL COLLEGE OF PATHOLOGISTS (1982) 'Medical Aspects of Death Certification', *Journal of the Royal College of Physicians of London 16*, (4).

ROYAL COMMISSION ON POPULATION (1949) *Report*, Cmnd 7695 (London: HMSO).

ROYAL SOCIETY (1983) *Demographic Trends and Future University Admissions.* Working Paper of the *ad hoc* Committee on University Funding (London: Royal Society).

SALT, J. and CLOUT, H. (1978) *Migration in Post-War Europe* (London: Oxford University Press).

SCHOEN, R. and BAJ, J. (1984) 'Twentieth Century Cohort Marriage and Divorce in England and Wales', *Population Studies* 38(3): 439–50.

SELECT COMMITTEE ON SCIENCE AND TECHNOLOGY (1971) *First Report: the Population of the United Kingdom* (London: HMSO).

SHAPER, A. G., POCOCK, S. J. *et al* (1981) 'British Regional Heart Study: Cardiovascular Risk Factors in Middle Aged Men in 24 Towns', *British Medical Journal* 283: 179–86.

SHORTER, E., Knodel, J. and van de WALLE, E. (1971) 'The Decline of Non-marital Fertility in Europe 1880–1940', *Population Studies XXV*, (3): 375–93.

SIMONS, J. (1986) 'Culture, Economy and Reproduction in Contemporary Europe', in Coleman, D. A. and Schofield, R. S. (eds) *The State of Population Theory: Forward from Malthus* (Oxford: Basil Blackwell) pp. 256–78.

TAYLOR, L. R. (1970) *The Optimum Population for Britain* (London: Academic Press).
THOMPSON, J. H. (1982) 'Differential Fertility Among Ethnic Minorities', in Coleman, D. A. (ed) *Demography of Immigrant and Minority Groups in the U.K.* (London: Academic Press) pp. 71–81.
WERNER, B. (1982) 'Recent Trends in Illegitimate Births and Extra-marital Conceptions', *Population Trends, 30*: 9–15.
WERNER, B. (1985) 'Fertility Trends in Different Social Classes, 1970 to 1983', *Population Trends, 41*: 5–13.
WERNER, B. (1986) 'Fertility and Family Background: Some illustrations from the OPCS Longitudinal Study', *Population Trends 35*: 5–10.
WINTER, J. M. (1985) *The Great War and the British People* (London: Macmillan).
WRIGLEY, E. A. and SCHOFIELD, R. S. (1981) *The Population of England 1541–1871. A Reconstructon* (London: Edward Arnold).

3 The Economic Environment[1]

Andrew Dilnot

Statistics on the level of income and wealth in the United Kingdom aim to present an overall picture of the economy in terms of frequently used concepts. The precise meaning of these concepts is not always clear; in Section 1 of this chapter the various statistics and concepts used later are therefore defined. Section 2 describes the sources of the statistics presented and some of the problems which may prevent straightforward interpretation. Section 3 summarises the main trends in the statistics.

SECTION 1 DEFINITION AND EXPLANATION

It is neither possible nor sensible in a book of this nature to give a full explanation of national income accounting: for this the reader should consult other texts.[2] Nevertheless, some knowledge of the concepts used by economists, and acquaintance with the basic framework of national accounts will aid understanding of the series presented in this chapter.

The income of a country

The central concept used in statistics relating to the economy is that of the level of national income. This can be defined in three ways, perhaps the most obvious of which is as the sum of all individual incomes received in return for currently supplying some good or service – the so-called 'income approach'. More exact definitions of the three approaches are given below.

Income approach
One measure of national income is the sum of all incomes created in the current production of goods and services. These are 'factor' incomes, accruing to the factors of production which enable the production of goods and services. Pensions, child benefits, unemployment benefits, private gifts etc., are not included because they do not correspond to any productive activity: such incomes are 'transfer' incomes. We should note that not all goods and services produced in an economy correspond to a payment. Such goods and services, of which the best example is perhaps those produced by housewives, are generally not included in any measure of national income.[3]

135

Expenditure approach

An alternative measure of national income is the sum of all expenditures on final goods and services. It is important to stress that expenditure on goods used to produce some other good is not included. For example: expenditure on a meat pie is included while the expenditure on the flour to make the pastry for the pie is not. The reason for this is that the price of the pie will include the cost of the flour to make the pastry, the meat to make the filling, the wages of the cook etc. To include expenditures on these 'intermediate' goods would imply double-counting.

The total spent on final goods and services is the source of the income of all those involved in their production, and thus should be identical to the sum of incomes. One important adjustment must be made. Some goods produced in any one year will not be sold in the same period. Since incomes will have been paid for this production, expenditure must be adjusted by the value of any changes to stocks and work in progress.

Output approach

Rather than measure expenditure, the value of final output can be calculated. Since final output is the goods and services which will be sold and counted as expenditure, total final output is identically equal to total expenditure on final goods and services and to total income.

The distinction between valuation at 'market prices' and valuation at 'factor cost'

The expenditure approach to measuring national income naturally values goods and services at the prices paid by their customers. These prices include all taxes on expenditure, and any subsidies. Such valuation is said to be 'at market prices'. If we wished to value the same goods and services as the sum of the factor incomes which had produced them, the taxes and subsidies would be excluded. Such a valuation would be described as being 'at factor cost.'

The distinction between valuation at 'constant' and 'current' prices

Thus far the discussion of measures of income has been in terms of 'current' prices. Goods sold in any year would be valued at the prices which were obtained for them in that year. However, one of the principal aims of this book is to examine changes over time. If we compare national income in current prices in 1900 with that in 1984, we find that in 1984 national income is very much higher. However, much of the increase is the result of rises in the level of prices and wages rather than any 'real' change. We can attempt to alleviate this problem by compiling series of figures at 'constant' prices, which value goods in each year at the prices which obtained for them in a given year. It is important to note that the year chosen for the prices (the 'base year') can make a substantial difference. It is desirable in constructing a constant price series to use only one base year, but this is not always possible. Where this is the case the sections of the series are not strictly compatible.[4]

National income identities

In the following sections, the measures of national income are split into component parts, made up as follows:

Income approach

　Income from employment:
　+ Gross trading profits of companies
　+ Gross trading profits of public corporations and other public enterprises
　+ Income from self-employment
　+ Rent
　+ Stock appreciation
　= Gross Domestic Product (GDP) (income approach) at factor cost
　+ Net property income from abroad
　= Gross National Product (GNP) (income approach) at factor cost

It should be noted that the figures for GDP and GNP derived by the income approach will in practice differ from those derived from the expenditure approach, as a result of measurement errors. In official publications the difference (the 'residual error') is added to the income series so that the final figures match. In the tables in this chapter this adjustment has not been made, so the two approaches give different results.

Expenditure approach

　Consumers' expenditure:
　+ Public authorities expenditure on goods and services
　+ Gross domestic fixed capital formation
　+ Stock appreciation
　+ Exports and property income from abroad
　− Imports and property income paid abroad
　− Taxes on expenditure
　+ Subsidies
　= Gross National Product (expenditure approach) at factor cost.

Statistics: General description

Historical period
Whenever possible, series are given from 1900 to 1983 or 1984. Some series are incomplete: data on the distribution of income and wealth for the pre-1948 period are particularly problematic.

Geographical coverage
Series are given for the United Kingdom unless otherwise specified. Prior to 1920 the data usually include Southern Ireland (Eire). This must obviously be taken into account when comparing periods before and after the First World War.

Sources of the economic statistics
Although the government published an annual *Statistical Abstract* from 1840, little material on the series presented in this chapter was given in official publications until 1946. We have therefore relied heavily on the work of a number of individual scholars in presenting data for the period before 1900. The greatest single debt is to C. H. Feinstein's *Statistical Tables of National Income. Expenditure and Output of the U.K. 1855–1965* (1976). For the period after 1965 the principal source of national income and expenditure information is the annual government publication *National Income and Expenditure*, the so-called 'Blue Book'. Precise definitions and discussion of problems associated with National Income Accounting are given in the government publication *United Kingdom National Accounts* (HMSO, 1985), and an earlier edition, *National Accounts Statistics: Sources and Methods*, edited by Rita Maurice and published by HMSO (1968).

SECTION 2   SOURCES OF STATISTICS AND POTENTIAL PROBLEMS

The series given in Tables 3.1 to 3.8 are taken from Feinstein[5] until 1965 and the annual 'Blue Books' thereafter. In all cases care must be taken in interpreting the statistics for two reasons:

(a) The data for the period before 1920 include Southern Ireland (Eire) but exclude it for 1920 and the following years.
(b) There is a break after 1965 with the figures up to and including 1965 derived from Feinstein and the figures thereafter derived from the annual 'Blue Books'.

The deflators used in Table 3.4 to derive constant price estimates are available for the components of national income reported in both Feinstein and the annual 'Blue Books'. The series are linked together in 1965, giving rise to the problem discussed above; the estimates should therefore be interpreted with care. The deflators used in Table 3.7 are given in Feinstein to 1965 and in the *Annual Supplement to Economic Trends* (HMSO) thereafter. As for components of national income, they are linked in 1965, and the table should therefore be interpreted with care.

Statistics relating to the distribution of income

Our focus here is on the size distribution of incomes, which can give us some ideas of the degree of equality or inequality in incomes received.

One way of examining this issue is to look at the proportions of all income received which goes to the richest 1 per cent, or 10 per cent, and compare this with the share of the poorest 10 per cent. This is done for incomes before and after tax in Tables 3.9 and 3.10. The source for these two tables is, for the period 1949–1974–5, 'Trends in the Distribution of Income' in *Economic Trends* (HMSO, May 1978), for 1976–7 *Social Trends 1980* (HMSO, 1980, for 1978–9 *Social Trends 1982* (HMSO, 1982), and for 1981–2 *Social Trends 1985* (HMSO, 1985). The figures on income before tax are given for three intermediate years between 1949 and 1968–9, but this is not possible for the figures on after tax income. This is because the number of ranges of income into which the post-tax income distribution was split was too few to allow any detailed breakdown.

Tables 3.9 and 3.10 allow an assessment of the change in the base distribution and the changing effect of the income tax system. However, they ignore all other taxes, and all government expenditures, both on direct payments such as social security benefits, and benefits in kind such as health and education services. Table 3.11 attempts to rectify this for a recent ten-year period. The share of total income received by each tenth of the population, ranked by their original income, is shown on the basis of this original income, and on the basis of final income, which is the sum of original income, cash benefits, and benefits in kind, less direct and indirect taxes. The table thus aims to describe the redistributive impact of government.

The information required for this table is derived from several of the annual articles published in *Economic Trends*, entitled 'The Effect of Taxes and Benefits on Household Income', the most recent of which was published in the December 1985 issue of *Economic Trends* (HMSO, 1985). Articles in the series have been published covering the years 1957–84, but the information presented in Table 3.11 is available only since 1974. The work is based on the government's annual *Family Expenditure Survey* (FES), a survey of around 7000 households per year, the principal purpose of which is to yield information on household expenditure patterns which is used to produce the weights required to compile the retail price index. Although the survey aims to be

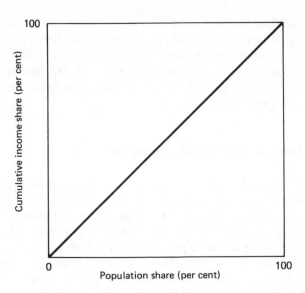

Figure 3.1   Complete income equality

Source: 'The effect of taxes and benefits in household income 1983; *Economic Trends*, December 1984 (London: HMSO). Reproduced with the permission of the Controller of Her Majesty's Stationery Office.

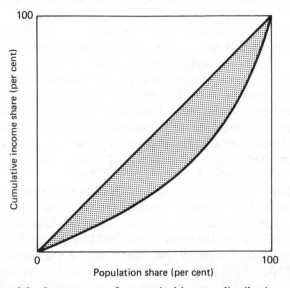

Figure 3.2   Lorenz curve for a typical income distribution.

Source: as for Fig. 3.1. Reproduced with the permission of the Controller of Her Majesty's Stationery Office.

representative there are some problems of low response, especially for those at high income levels.[6] Table 3.12 presents more detailed results for a single year. Table 3.13 presents Gini coefficients of original and final income for years from 1961 to 1984. The Gini coefficient is the most widely used summary measure of inequality in an income distribution. It can most easily be understood by considering a Lorenz curve, which is a graph of the cumulative share of income against the cumulative share of population. If all households had equal incomes, the poorest 10 per cent of the population would receive 10 per cent of total income. If the distribution of income were less equal, the poorest 10 per cent might receive only 5 per cent of total income. The curve representing complete equality of incomes is thus a straight diagonal line, as in Figure 3.1. A more typical Lorenz curve is illustrated in Figure 3.2. The shaded area between the Lorenz curve and the line of absolute equality is divided by the whole of the area beneath the line of complete equality, to give the Gini coefficient. A perfectly equal income distribution has a Gini coefficient of zero. As inequality increases, the size of the shaded area increases, and the Gini coefficient increases. If all income was received by only one individual, the Gini coefficient would be one. Gini coefficients must be interpreted with some care, but in general we can say that a smaller Gini coefficient implies less inequality.[7]

Statistics relating to the composition and distribution of wealth

Tables 3.14 and 3.15 present information on the composition of the wealth, both in physical and financial assets, of the personal sector for the period 1957–84. For 1957 and 1961 the source is 'National Balance Sheets and National Accounting. A Progress Report' in *Economic Trends* (HMSO, May 1971), for 1966 and 1970, 'Personal Sector Balance Sheets' in *Economic Trends* (HMSO, January 1978), for 1975 Table S12 in *Financial Statistics* (HMSO, February 1982), and for 1980 and 1984 Table S2 in *Financial Statistics* (HMSO, February 1986). The figures for 1957 and 1961 are derived from work done by J. Revell and A. R. Roe at the Department of Applied Economics in Cambridge. Those for 1966 and following years are the work of the Central Statistical Office (CSO). Some care must therefore be taken when comparing results from the two periods.

Tables 3.16 and 3.17 present estimates for the period 1900–1975 of the stock of physical assets held in the UK as a whole. The estimates for the period 1900–1948 are derived from the work of J. Revell[8] and are particularly tentative. For 1957 the source is the work of the Department of Applied Economics at Cambridge, and for 1966 and 1975 the CSO.[9]

Tables 3.18 to 3.20 present estimates of the share of total wealth, defined in different ways, held by various groups of the population. For the period 1923 to 1960 the figures in Table 3.18 are based on the work of Atkinson and

Harrison (1978).[10] For 1966 to 1983 in all three tables the data are derived from *Inland Revenue Statistics 1985* (HMSO, 1986). Care must therefore be taken when comparing results from the two periods. Table 3.19 includes occupational pension rights in its definition of wealth. Table 3.20 includes both occupational and state pension rights. The defence for including pension rights is that we are interested in wealth because it confers the ability to consume without working, which is precisely what pension rights do. In principal, pension rights could be traded for a lump sum of 'traditional' wealth. It is this calculation which is necessary to include them in the distribution.

SECTION 3   MAIN TRENDS IN THE ECONOMIC
ENVIRONMENT

Tables 3.1 and 3.2

The series for GDP at factor cost decomposed into types of income is only available at current prices, which makes interpretation of the changes in level over time problematic. This caveat is less true for the information on shares presented in Table 3.2. The share of income from employment, which rose rapidly from 1900 to 1920 has been relatively steady since 1925, falling since its peak in 1975 perhaps as a result of higher unemployment. Gross trading profits of private companies were relatively steady both pre- and post-1940, although at a higher level in the second period. The fall to 1975 in the period of high inflation after the oil shock is very noticeable. The share of profits of public corporations jumps in the post-war period with the onset of mass nationalisation under the Attlee government, and is relatively stable thereafter. The share of rental and self-employment income declined steadily to the 1960s, but has been stable for the last 15 years.

Tables 3.3 to 3.5

Series at constant prices are presented in Table 3.4. These are the most straightforward to interpret. GDP is some 4.5 times larger in real terms than it was in 1900. Consumers expenditure some 3.5 times larger, central government expenditure 6.5 times larger, and gross domestic fixed capital formation 6.25 times as great. The advent of both world wars led to substantial increases in GDP in 1915 and 1940, which were followed by a fall after the first war and very small increases after the second. The wars also caused large jumps in government expenditure, which returned to roughly its pre-war level by 1925, but fell back by much less after the second war.

Table 3.1 Gross Domestic Product and factor incomes at current prices, 1900–1984, United Kindom (£ million)

| Year | Income from employment | Gross Trading Profits of | | | Income from self-employment and rent | Total domestic income | Stock appreciation | Grosss Domestic Product at factor cost |
		Private companies	Public corporations	Other government bodies				
1900	909	230	0	8	532	1 679	0	1 679
1905	913	228	0	13	537	1 691	0	1 691
1910	1 027	261	0	17	568	1 873	0	1 873
1920	3 449	621	0	21	976	5 066	200	5 266
1925	2 419	468	0	42	942	3 871	139	4 010
1930	2 485	411	0	54	978	3 928	213	4 141
1935	2 597	514	8	60	1 042	4 221	−26	4 195
1940	3 843	1 109	0	77	1 276	6 305	−500	5 805
1945	5 889	1 350	0	119	1 479	8 837	−50	8 787
1950	7 627	2 126	196	139	1 923	12 016	−650	11 366
1955	11 244	2 886	315	112	2 452	17 009	−196	16 813
1960	15 164	3 739	539	179	3 248	22 869	−135	22 734
1965	21 218	4 820	995	96	4 349	31 478	−354	31 124
1970	30 553	6 105	1447	180	7 317	45 602	−1061	44 541
1975	68 494	11 762	3095	115	16 575	100 041	−5521	94 520
1980	137 353	29 024	6161	132	33 445	206 115	−6732	199 383
1984	180 342	47 900	8732	−250	48 348	285 072	−5163	279 909

Sources: C. H. Feinstein (1976) *Statistical Tables of National Income, Expenditure and Output of the U.K. 1855–1965* (Macmillan); for years to 1965 – *National Income and Expenditure* from Central Statistical Office (CSO); thereafter annual 'Blue Books'.

Table 3.2   Percentage shares of factor incomes in Gross Domestic Product,
1900–1984, United Kingdom

| Year | Income from employment | Gross Trading Profits of | | Rental and self-employment income |
		Private companies	Public corporations and other government bodies	
1900	54.1	13.7	0.5	31.7
1905	54.0	13.5	0.8	31.8
1910	54.8	13.9	0.9	30.3
1920	68.1	12.3	0.4	19.3
1925	62.5	12.1	1.1	24.3
1930	63.3	10.5	1.4	24.9
1935	61.5	12.2	1.6	24.7
1940	61.0	17.6	1.2	20.2
1945	66.6	15.3	1.3	16.7
1950	63.5	17.7	2.8	16.0
1955	66.1	17.0	2.5	14.4
1960	66.3	16.3	3.1	14.2
1965	67.4	15.3	3.5	13.8
1970	67.0	13.4	3.6	16.0
1975	68.5	11.8	3.2	16.6
1980	66.6	14.1	3.1	16.2
1984	63.3	16.8	3.0	17.0

Sources: C. H. Feinstein (1976) *Statistical Tables of National Income, Expenditure and Output of the U.K. 1855–1965* (Macmillan);
for years to 1965 – *National Income and Expenditure* from Central Statistical Office (CSO);
thereafter annual 'Blue Books'.

Table 3.3   National income and items of expenditure at current prices, 1900–1984, United Kindom (£ million)

Year	Gross National Product at factor cost	Consumers' expenditure	Central government current expenditure	Local government current expenditure	Gross domestic fixed capital formation	Gross Domestic Product at factor cost
1900	1 926	1 637	123	59	199	1 822
1905	2 030	1 736	80	83	177	1 907
1910	2 239	1 877	38	94	136	2 069
1915	3 096	2 384	939	106	130	2 931
1920	5 858	5 020	277	211	482	5 612
1925	4 447	3 878	186	226	420	4 215
1930	4 443	3 932	180	263	435	4 228
1935	4 380	3 935	209	274	456	4 199
1940	6 878	4 799	2 557	395	520	6 718
1945	8 754	6 391	3 758	432	350	8 674
1950	11 737	9 461	1 491	571	1 700	11 341
1955	16 794	13 110	2 324	846	2 829	16 800
1960	22 790	16 990	2 864	1 299	4 120	22 559
1965	31 953	22 956	3 828	2 091	6 331	30 840
1970	44 592	31 932	5 476	3 557	9 376	43 997
1975	96 543	65 211	13 527	9 592	21 035	95 653
1980	199 027	136 995	29 940	18 966	41 588	199 246
1984	277 877	194 673	42 892	26 763	55 319	274 573

Sources: C. H. Feinstein (1976) *Statistical Tables of National Income, Expenditure and Output of the U.K. 1855–1965* (Macmillan);
for years to 1965 – *National Income and Expenditure* from Central Statistical Office (CSO);
thereafter annual 'Blue Books'.

Table 3.4   National income and items of expenditure at constant 1984 prices,
1900–1984, United Kingdom (£ million)

Year	Consumers' expenditure	Central government current expenditure	Local government current expenditure	Gross domestic fixed capital formation	Gross Domestic Product at factor cost
1900	56 875	8 350	4 005	8 840	61 728
1905	59 740	5 460	5 665	8 969	66 143
1910	62 669	5 768	6 162	6 578	70 023
1915	69 036	49 276	5 562	4 694	84 352
1920	63 472	8 720	6 642	7 342	66 560
1925	66 655	6 499	7 897	10 598	73 176
1930	72 570	6 371	9 309	11 960	77 685
1935	79 089	7 692	10 085	13 382	82 992
1940	73 510	37 099	11 910	11 803	109 194
1945	75 466	32 434	9 476	N.A.	105 687
1950	90 731	26 205	10 035	17 844	111 836
1955	100 693	31 285	11 388	22 866	129 832
1960	115 782	29 291	13 285	29 986	145 990
1965	134 291	31 611	17 267	40 480	173 531
1970	148 537	32 117	20 862	47 028	204 677
1975	167 165	37 657	26 702	50 623	231 356
1980	183 336	41 142	26 062	50 682	254 742
1984	194 673	42 892	26 762	55 319	274 573

Sources: C. H. Feinstein (1976) *Statistical Tables of National Income, Expenditure and Output of the U.K. 1855–1965* (Macmillan);
for years to 1965 – *National Income and Expenditure* from Central Statistical Office (CSO);
thereafter annual 'Blue Books'.

Tables 3.6 to 3.8

Table 3.8, which presents the shares of various goods in total expenditure is perhaps the most straightforward of these tables.

The share of food in total expenditure rose very slightly from 1900 to 1925, but has fallen fairly steadily since then. This is the pattern we would expect to observe since real income has increased substantially, and food is in some sense a necessary item, similar amounts of which will be consumed irrespective of income. The share of drink has remained very constant, with the increase in 1945 the result of very high tax rates. The share of tobacco rose steadily to peak just after the Second World War. Peak real expenditure, as shown in Table 3.7, was in 1975. It appears that tobacco consumption may be responding to the publicity on health risks. The share of housing was fairly steady from 1915 to 1960, but has increased since then in response to increased

Table 3.5   Shares of expenditure items in Gross National Product (current prices), 1900–1984, United Kingdom

Year	Consumers' expenditure	Central government current expenditure	Local government current expenditure	Gross domestic fixed capital formation
1900	85.0	6.4	3.1	10.3
1905	85.5	3.9	4.1	8.7
1910	83.8	3.9	4.2	6.1
1915	77.0	30.3	3.4	4.2
1920	85.7	4.7	3.6	8.2
1925	87.2	4.2	5.1	9.4
1930	88.5	4.1	5.9	9.8
1935	89.8	4.8	6.3	10.4
1940	69.8	37.2	5.7	7.6
1945	73.0	42.9	4.9	4.0
1950	80.6	12.7	4.9	14.5
1955	78.1	13.8	5.0	16.8
1960	74.6	12.6	5.7	18.1
1965	71.8	12.0	6.5	19.8
1970	71.6	12.3	8.0	21.3
1975	67.5	14.0	9.9	22.0
1980	68.8	15.0	9.5	20.9
1984	70.1	15.4	9.6	20.1

Sources: C. H. Feinstein (1976) *Statistical Tables of National Income, Expenditure and Output of the U.K. 1855–1965* (Macmillan);
for years to 1965 – *National Income and Expenditure* (CSO);
thereafter annual 'Blue Books'.

owner-occupation. The share of fuel and light has been very stable. The share of clothing, steady at around 10 per cent until 1960 has fallen since, although the level of real expenditure has increased. This effect is largely the result of falling real clothing prices. The share of durables has increased as real incomes have risen and the availability of durables improved. The share of travel and communication has been very stable, that of running cars has grown steadily.

Tables 3.9 and 3.10

Perhaps the most striking feature of Table 3.9 is the reduction in the share of the top 1 per cent in pre-tax incomes, from 11.2 per cent in 1949 to only 5.7 per cent in 1981–2. Apart from this change, the distribution of pre-tax income seems remarkably similar in 1978–9 and 1949. Comparison of Tables 3.9 and 3.10 shows that post-tax income is more equally distributed than pre-tax

Table 3.6 Selected items of consumers' expenditure at current prices, 1900–1984, United Kingdom (£ million)

Year	Food	Drink	Tobacco	Housing	Fuel + light	Clothing	Durables	Travel + communication	Running cars	Total
1900	464	187	27	167	75	153	63	64	16	1 637
1905	502	172	31	194	63	157	67	72	15	1 736
1910	534	163	37	211	67	178	71	82	16	1 877
1915	724	179	49	227	83	193	88	94	20	2 384
1920	1 547	450	120	272	174	795	183	200	42	5 020
1925	1 241	338	116	325	158	432	164	197	42	3 878
1930	1 163	301	140	375	162	418	167	196	59	3 932
1935	1 054	273	153	416	164	388	204	185	73	3 935
1940	1 244	378	260	528	222	501	556	190	82	4 539
1945	1 398	705	562	616	259	535	600	323	41	6 391
1950	2 371	734	766	841	356	1 063	488	423	111	9 461
1955	3 615	832	880	1 122	528	1 297	934	549	244	13 110
1960	4 255	954	1 140	1 660	751	1 647	1 420	711	451	16 990
1965	5 105	1 415	1 428	2 546	1 087	2 059	1 892	940	928	22 956
1970	6 365	2 311	1 720	4 140	1 495	2 666	2 322	1 357	1 696	31 387
1975	12 059	4 856	2 748	9 237	2 916	5 296	4 784	3 004	3 872	63 192
1980	22 873	9 954	4 322	18 827	6 353	9 863	13 673	7 051	9 088	136 995
1984	28 448	14 416	6 621	29 239	9 574	13 158	19 241	9 985	13 578	194 673

Sources: C. H. Feinstein (1976) Statistical Tables of National Income, Expenditure and Output of the U.K. 1855–1965 (Macmillan); for years to 1965 – National Income and Expenditure (CSO); thereafter annual 'Blue Books'.

Table 3.7 Selected items of consumers' expenditure at constant 1984 prices, 1900–1984, United Kingdom (£ million)

Year	Food	Drink	Tobacco	Housing	Fuel + light	Clothing	Durables	Total
1900	15 495	11 824	2243	5 864	3116	3 415	1 639	58 543
1905	16 294	10 725	2367	6 413	3045	3 243	1 728	61 492
1910	16 326	9 301	2461	6 827	3257	3 520	1 831	64 507
1915	16 973	9 423	2992	7 221	3455	3 617	1 837	71 061
1920	16 844	8 055	3677	7 444	3307	3 819	1 382	65 334
1925	20 299	6 497	3553	7 729	3597	3 721	2 088	68 611
1930	21 836	5 769	4238	8 521	3907	3 989	2 305	74 699
1935	22 773	5 248	4674	9 289	4124	4 239	3 126	81 409
1940	19 056	5 344	5547	11 140	4564	3 738	6 593	71 567
1945	18 782	5 844	6981	11 768	4336	2 887	4 926	77 680
1950	27 154	5 438	7027	14 321	5312	4 797	2 537	93 393
1955	29 065	5 858	7859	14 928	5820	5 038	4 176	103 647
1960	31 459	6 764	8819	16 586	6785	6 062	6 060	119 179
1965	33 274	7 776	8414	19 061	8572	6 881	7 392	138 231
1970	33 049	10 335	8774	23 624	9266	7 700	7 488	151 128
1975	29 500	13 924	9097	29 492	9472	9 041	9 359	164 921
1980	29 147	14 740	8128	27 992	9712	10 304	15 509	182 765
1984	28 448	14 416	6621	29 239	9574	13 158	19 241	194 673

Sources: C. H. Feinstein (1976) Statistical Tables of National Income, Expenditure and Output of the U.K. 1855–1965 (Macmillan);
for years to 1965 – National Income and Expenditure (CSO);
thereafter annual 'Blue Books'.

Table 3.8   Selected items as percentages of total consumers' expenditure (current prices), 1900–1984, United Kingdom

Year	Food	Drink	Tobacco	Housing	Fuel+light	Clothing	Durables	Travel+ communication	Running cars	Total
1900	28.3	11.4	1.6	10.2	4.6	9.3	3.8	3.9	1.0	100.0
1905	28.9	9.9	1.8	11.2	3.6	9.0	3.9	4.1	0.9	100.0
1910	28.4	8.7	2.0	11.2	3.6	9.5	3.8	4.4	0.9	100.0
1915	30.4	7.5	2.1	9.5	3.5	8.1	3.7	3.9	0.8	100.0
1920	30.8	9.0	2.4	5.4	3.5	15.8	3.6	4.0	0.8	100.0
1925	32.0	8.7	3.0	8.4	4.1	11.1	4.2	5.1	1.1	100.0
1930	29.6	7.7	3.6	9.5	4.1	10.6	4.2	5.0	1.5	100.0
1935	26.8	6.9	3.9	10.6	4.2	9.9	5.2	4.7	1.9	100.0
1940	27.4	8.3	5.7	11.6	4.9	11.0	12.2	4.2	1.8	100.0
1945	21.9	11.0	8.8	9.6	4.1	8.4	9.4	5.1	0.6	100.0
1950	25.1	7.8	8.1	8.9	3.8	11.2	5.2	4.5	1.2	100.0
1955	27.6	6.3	6.7	8.6	4.0	9.9	7.1	4.2	1.9	100.0
1960	25.0	5.6	6.7	9.8	4.4	9.7	8.4	4.2	2.7	100.0
1965	22.2	6.2	6.2	11.1	4.7	9.0	8.2	4.1	4.0	100.0
1970	20.3	7.4	5.5	13.2	4.8	8.5	7.4	4.3	5.4	100.0
1975	19.1	7.7	4.3	14.6	4.6	8.4	7.6	4.8	6.1	100.0
1980	16.7	7.3	3.5	13.7	4.6	7.2	10.0	5.1	6.6	100.0
1984	14.6	7.4	3.4	15.0	4.9	6.8	9.9	5.1	7.0	100.0

Sources: C. H. Feinstein (1976) *Statistical Tables of National Income, Expenditure and Output of the U.K. 1855–1965* (Macmillan); for years to 1965 – *National Income and Expenditure* (CSO); thereafter annual 'Blue Books'.

Table 3.9 Distribution of income before tax, 1949–81/2, percentage received by various groups

Group	1949	1954	1957	1963	1968–9	1971–2	1974–5	1976–7	1978–9	1981–2
Top 1%	11.2	9.3	8.4	8.0	7.1	6.5	6.2	5.5	5.3	5.7
Top 2–5%	12.6	11.5	11.5	11.2	10.7	11.0	10.6	10.8	10.7	20.5
Top 6–10%	9.4	9.3	9.5	9.7	9.3	9.8	9.8	9.9	10.1	
Top 10%	33.2	30.1	29.4	28.9	27.1	27.3	26.6	26.2	26.1	26.2
Top 11–20%	14.1	15.1	15.1	15.4	15.4	15.9	15.8	16.2	16.5	50.0
Top 21–30%	11.2	12.4	12.6	12.6	12.9	13.2	13.1	13.3	13.5	
Top 31–40%	9.6	10.5	10.7	10.9	11.0	11.0	11.0	11.2	11.2	
Top 41–50%	8.2	8.9	9.1	9.1	9.4	9.2	9.3	9.1	9.2	
Top 51–60%	23.7	7.4	7.5	7.5	7.6	7.4	7.6	7.4	7.3	23.8
Top 61–70%		5.3	5.9	5.9	6.2	5.9	5.8	5.8	5.8	
Top 71–80%		10.3	4.4	4.4	4.7	4.5	4.6	4.6	4.5	
Top 81–90%			5.3	5.3	3.4	3.3	3.6	3.7	3.5	
Top 91–100%					2.3	2.3	2.6	2.5	2.4	

Sources: 1949–74/5: 'Trends in the Distribution of Income' in *Economic Trends* (HMSO, May 1978);
1976/7: *Social Trends 1980* (HMSO, 1980);
1978/9: *Social Trends 1982* (HMSO, 1982);
1981/2: *Social Trends 1985* (HMSO, 1985).

Table 3.10 Distribution of income after tax, 1949–81/2, percentage received by various groups

Group	1949	1968–9	1971–2	1974–5	1976–7	1978–9	1981–2
Top 1%	6.4	4.6	4.6	4.5	3.8	3.9	3.9
Top 2–5%	11.3	9.8	10.0	9.7	9.7	9.8	} 19.2
Top 6–10%	9.4	9.2	9.5	9.5	9.6	9.7	
Top 10%	27.1	23.6	24.1	23.2	23.1	23.4	23.1
Top 11–20%	14.5	15.5	15.9	15.8	16.0	16.3	
Top 21–30%	11.9	13.1	13.4	13.2	13.4	13.5	50.3
Top 31–40%	10.5	11.5	11.3	11.4	11.3	11.3	
Top 41–50%	9.5	9.7	9.4	9.4	9.3	9.3	
Top 51–60%		8.1	7.8	7.8	7.7	7.7	
Top 61–70%		6.6	6.4	6.4	6.6	6.4	
Top 71–80%	26.5	5.3	5.1	5.3	5.1	5.1	26.6
Top 81–90%		3.9	3.9	4.4	4.5	4.1	
Top 90–100%		2.7	2.7	3.1	3.0	2.9	

Sources: 1949–74/5: 'Trends in the Distribution of Income' in *Economic Trends* (HMSO, May 1978);
1976/7: *Social Trends 1980* (HMSO, 1980);
1978/9: *Social Trends 1982* (HMSO, 1982);
1981/2: *Social Trends 1985* (HMSO, 1985).

income. Table 3.10 shows that the share of the top 1 per cent in post-tax incomes has also fallen between 1949 and 1981–2, but again, the rest of the distribution is remarkably similar.

Tables 3.11 to 3.13

These tables are derived from the government's annual *Family Expenditure Survey* (FES). Table 3.11 shows that while in 1984 the poorest 10 per cent of households received 0.0 per cent of original income, they received 5.3 per cent of final income. The share of the poorest 10 per cent in final income has increased from 2.7 per cent in 1974 to 5.3 per cent in 1984 while that of the richest 10 per cent has fallen from 23.6 per cent to 21.7 per cent, indicating a slight increase in the redistributive impact of the combined tax and government expenditure system.

In comparing Table 3.11 with Table 1.6 (p. 00) note that Table 1.6 divides by fifths, not tenths, and uses 1976 as the base, not 1974. The 1974–9 Labour government introduced more stringent rates of tax on higher incomes. But the most important difference between Tables 1.6 and 3.11 is that the *Social Trends* table is re-ranked for each type of income. Thus Table 1.6 tells us that the poorest fifth ranked by original income in 1976 received 0.8 per cent of total original income and then re-ranked by final income received 7.4 per cent

Table 3.11 Distribution of original and final incomes, 1974–84, shares received by deciles, ranked by original income

Incomes	Year	Bottom 10%	2nd 10%	3rd 10%	4th 10%	5th 10%	6th 10%	7th 10%	8th 10%	9th 10%	Top 10%	
Original	1974	0.1	1.2	3.9	6.7	8.5	11.0	12.9	14.0	17.0	26.7	100.0
Final	1974	2.7	4.1	5.5	6.9	8.3	9.6	11.2	12.9	15.4	23.6	100.0
Original	1976	0.1	1.1	3.4	6.3	8.4	10.3	12.1	14.3	17.4	26.6	100.0
Final	1976	4.5	4.9	6.4	7.4	8.6	9.8	11.1	12.2	14.4	20.8	100.0
Original	1978	0.0	1.0	3.2	6.1	8.4	10.3	12.2	14.5	17.6	26.4	100.0
Final	1978	4.6	4.7	6.1	7.0	8.5	9.8	11.0	12.5	14.6	20.9	100.0
Original	1980	0.0	0.5	2.6	5.9	8.3	10.3	12.3	14.6	17.8	27.7	100.0
Final	1980	4.6	4.5	5.5	7.2	8.4	9.7	11.0	12.6	14.6	22.0	100.0
Original	1982	0.0	0.4	1.9	5.2	8.0	10.2	12.4	14.8	18.3	28.8	100.0
Final	1982	5.1	4.6	5.5	7.0	8.0	9.5	10.8	12.4	14.9	22.1	100.0
Original	1984	0.0	0.3	1.6	4.5	7.5	10.0	12.4	15.2	19.1	29.4	100.0
Final	1984	5.3	5.0	5.5	6.9	7.8	9.5	10.8	12.5	14.9	21.7	100.0

Notes: Comparison of this table with Table 1.6 should be made with reference to the text, p. 00.
Sources: Annual articles – 'The effect of Taxes and Benefits on Household Income' in *Economic Trends* (HMSO). Most recent issue in December 1985. Reproduced with the permission of the Controller of Her Majesty's Stationery Office.

Table 3.12　Summary of the effects of taxes and benefits, 1984

Average per household (£ per year)	Bottom 20%	Second 20%	Third 20%	Fourth 20%	Top 20%	Average
Original income	110	2480	7130	11 200	19 750	8130
plus cash benefits	3130	2400	1140	810	600	1620
Gross income	3240	4880	8260	12 010	20 350	9750
less income tax and employees NI	− 10	330	1380	2 430	4 740	1770
Disposable income	3250	4550	6880	9 580	15 610	7980
less indirect taxes	760	1300	1890	2 490	3 700	2030
Income after cash benefits and all taxes	2490	3250	4990	7 090	11 920	5950
plus benefits in kind	1330	1340	1370	1 520	1 560	1430
Final income	3820	4600	6370	8 610	13 480	7370

Source:　'The Effect of Taxes and benefits on Household Income' in *Economic Trends* (HMSO, December 1985) Table A. Reproduced with the permission of the Controller of Her Majesty's Stationery Office.

Table 3.13　Gini coefficients and final income, 1961–84

Year	Original income	Final income
1961	38.4	33.5
1963	39.7	33.9
1965	38.6	32.8
1967	38.2	32.2
1969	40.7	33.2
1971	41.7	33.4
1973	42.2	32.8
1976	44.3	30.2
1978	44.7	31.5
1980	45.9	32.3
1982	48.2	33.0
1984	49.9	32.4

Source:　Annual articles 'The Effect of Taxes and Benefits on Household Income' in *Economic Trends*. Most recent issue in December 1985. Reproduced with the permission of the Controller of Her Majesty's Stationery Office.

Table 3.14   Balance sheets of the personal sector, 1957–84, current prices, United Kingdom (£billion)

Assets	1957	1961	1966	1970	1975	1980	1984
Physical assets							
Stocks and work in progress	1.9	2.2	2.0	2.6	5.4	7.1	8.9
Vehicles, plant and machinery	1.3	1.8	1.5	2.0	5.4	14.6	17.9
Dwellings	12.4	16.6	35.0	49.9	137.5	322.8	485.6
Other developed land and buildings	} 2.1	} 3.6	1.9	2.7	12.2	21.0	25.6
Agricultural and other land			4.6	4.6	11.0	27.6	29.7
Consumer durables	2.8	4.0	11.4	16.1	38.2	74.7	98.2
Total physical assets	20.6	28.2	56.4	77.9	209.6	467.8	665.9
Financial assets							
Notes and coin			2.2	2.7	4.8	8.3	10.0
Bank deposits			7.3	9.8	19.4	37.4	59.0
National Savings	} 13.4	} 16.7	8.1	8.3	8.0	12.2	28.1
Building society deposits			5.8	10.1	22.5	49.6	90.5
UK ordinary shares	8.8	18.2	12.8	17.7	24.5	38.2	77.5
Life Assurance and pension funds	9.7	13.5	14.6	20.4	33.5	89.5	227.3
Total financial assets	40.9	59.2	70.2	88.0	140.5	296.2	569.6
Liabilities							
Bank loans	0.5	1.2	1.5	1.8	5.8	14.4	33.9
Loans for house purchase	3.5	4.9	7.3	11.2	25.0	52.3	107.9
Total liabilities	6.6	9.8	14.3	18.9	39.5	90.6	173.5
Net wealth	54.9	77.6	112.3	147.0	310.6	673.4	1062.0

Sources: 1957 and 1961: 'National Balance Sheets and National Accounting, a Progress Report' in *Economic Trends* (HMSO, May 1971);
1966 and 1970: 'Personal Sector Balance Sheets' in *Economic Trends* (HMSO, January 1978);
1975: Table S12 in *Financial Statistics* (HMSO, February 1982);
1980 and 1984: Table S2 in *Financial Statistics* (HMSO, February 1986).

of total final income. Table 3.11 on the other hand keeps households in the same cells throughout. In consequence it brings out the mildly *redistributive* impact of governmental taxes and benefits while Table 1.6 emphasises the *distribution* of households in an array of inequality which has lengthened over the past decade.

Table 3.12 provides more detailed results for 1984, for households grouped into blocks of 20 per cent by rank of original income. It is clear from this table that it is cash benefits which have the greatest impact on the income distribution in terms of reducing inequality. Table 3.13 presents Gini coeffi-

Table 3.15   Balance sheets of the personal sector, 1957–84, percentages of net wealth, United Kingdom

Assets	1957	1961	1966	1970	1975	1980	1984
Physical assets							
Stocks and work in progress	3.5	2.8	1.8	1.8	1.7	1.1	0.8
Vehicles, plant and machinery	2.4	2.3	1.3	1.4	1.7	2.2	1.7
Dwellings	22.6	21.4	31.2	33.9	44.3	47.9	45.7
Other developed land and buildings	} 3.8	} 4.6	1.7	1.8	3.9	3.1	2.4
Agricultural and other land			4.1	3.1	3.5	4.1	2.8
Consumer durables	5.1	5.2	10.2	11.0	12.3	11.1	9.2
Total physical assets	37.5	36.3	50.2	53.0	67.5	69.4	62.7
Financial assets							
Notes and coin			2.0	1.8	1.5	1.2	0.9
Bank deposits			6.5	6.7	6.2	5.5	5.6
National Savings	} 24.1	} 21.5	7.2	5.6	2.6	1.3	2.6
Building society deposits			5.2	6.9	7.2	7.4	8.5
UK ordinary shares	16.0	23.5	11.4	12.0	7.9	5.7	7.3
Life Assurance and pension funds	17.7	17.4	13.0	13.9	10.8	13.3	21.4
Total financial assets	74.5	76.3	62.5	59.9	45.2	44.0	53.6
Liabilities							
Bank loans	0.9	1.5	1.3	1.2	1.9	2.1	3.2
Loans for house purchase	6.4	6.3	6.5	7.6	8.0	7.8	10.2
Total liabilities	12.0	12.6	12.7	12.9	12.7	13.4	16.3
Net wealth	100.0	100.0	100.0	100.0	100.0	100.0	100.0

Sources: 1957 and 1961: 'National Balance Sheets and National Accounting, a Progress Report' in *Economic Trends* (HMSO, May 1971);
1966 and 1970: 'Personal Sector Balance Sheets' in *Economic Trends* (HMSO, January 1978);
1975: Table S12 in *Financial Statistics* (HMSO, February 1982);
1980 and 1984: Table S2 in *Financial Statistics* (HMSO, February 1986).

cients of original income, with the Gini coefficient rising from 38.4 in 1961 to 49.9 in 1984. Much of this is the result of a larger proportion of pensioners in the population, and increased unemployment. The Gini coefficient of final income has been much more stable, experiencing no very significant changes.

Tables 3.14 and 3.15

Table 3.15, which presents shares in net wealth, is the more easily interpreted of these two tables. The most striking change in the composition of physical assets has been the increase in the share of dwellings in net wealth from 22.6 per cent in 1957 to 45.7 per cent in 1984, which reflects the substantial increase in owner-occupation over this period. It is striking that the share of physical assets in net wealth has also increased substantially, from 37.5 per cent to 62.7 per cent. The share of UK ordinary shares has fallen from 16 per cent to 7.3 per cent, much of the difference being bought by life assurance and pension funds, equity in which has increased its share from 17.7 per cent to 21.4 per cent. The share of notes and coin fell from 2 per cent in 1966 to 0.9 per cent in 1984, that of National Savings from 7.2 per cent in 1966 to 2.6 per cent in 1984, while Building Society deposits increased their share from 5.2 per cent to 8.5 per cent. Loans for house purchase (a liability to be set off against assets) increased their share as owner-occupation grew.

Tables 3.16 and 3.17

Table 3.17 shows that the share of dwellings in national assets has increased, as it has in personal sector assets. The share of land, buildings and works has fallen correspondingly.

Tables 3.18 to 3.20

Table 3.18 demonstrates that there has been a substantial fall in the share of wealth held by the richest 1 per cent and the richest 5 per cent of the

Table 3.16 Physical assets in the United Kingdom for selected years, 1900–1957, at current prices (£billion)

Assets	1900	1910	1920	1927	1937	1948	1957	1966	1975
Dwellings	1.0	1.0	3.2	2.4	3.3	8.1	19.2	54.6	206.1
Land, buildings and works	3.4	3.3	9.5	6.0	5.8	10.5	17.0	41.1	144.2
Plant and equipment	0.6	0.8	2.9	1.6	2.1	4.0	15.0	28.8	97.5
Stocks and work in progress	0.7	0.8	3.5	1.8	1.7	5.2	7.7	12.7	35.0
Total	5.7	5.9	19.1	11.8	12.9	27.8	58.9	137.2	482.7

Sources: 1900–1948: J. Revell (1967) *The Wealth of the Nation* (Cambridge University Press) p. 64;
1975: 'National Balance Sheets and National Accounting, a Progress Report' in *Economic Trends* (HMSO, May 1971);
1966 and 1957: 'National and Sector Balance Sheets for the UK' in *Economic Trends* (HMSO, November 1978). Reproduced with the permission of the Controller of Her Majesty's Stationery Office.

Table 3.17 Physical assets in the United Kingdom for selected years, 1900–1975, percentages of total

Assets	1900	1910	1920	1927	1937	1948	1957	1966	1975
Dwellings	17.5	16.9	16.8	20.3	25.6	29.1	32.6	39.8	42.7
Land, buildings and works	59.6	55.9	49.7	50.8	45.0	37.8	28.9	30.0	29.9
Plant and equipment	10.5	13.6	15.2	13.6	16.3	14.4	25.5	21.0	20.2
Stocks and work in progress	12.3	13.6	18.3	15.3	13.2	18.7	13.1	9.3	7.3
Total	100.0	100.0	100.0	100.0	100.0	100.0	100.0	100.0	100.0

Sources: 1900–1948: J. Revell (1967) *The Wealth of the Nation* (Cambridge University Press) p. 64;
1957: 'National Balance Sheets and National Accounting, a Progress Report' in *Economic Trends* (HMSO, May 1971);
1966 and 1975: 'National and Sector Balance Sheets for the UK' in *Economic Trends* (HMSO, November 1978). Reproduced
with the permission of the Controller of Her Majesty's Stationery Office.

Table 3.18   Distribution of marketable wealth among the adult population, 1923–83, percentage received by various groups

Year	% of total wealth held by			
	Top 1%	Top 5%	Top 10%	Top 50%
1923	61	82	NA	NA
1925	61	82	NA	NA
1930	58	79	NA	NA
1938	55	77	NA	NA
1950	47	74	NA	NA
1954	45	72	NA	NA
1960	34	59	NA	NA
1966	33	56	69	97
1971	31	52	65	97
1976	24	45	60	95
1980	20	39	52	94
1983	20	40	54	96

Sources: 1923–60: A. B. Atkinson and A. Harrison (1978) *The Distribution of Wealth in Britain* (Cambridge University Press) Table 6.5; 1966–83: *Inland Revenue Statistics 1985* (HMSO, 1986). Reproduced with the permission of the Controller of Her Majesty's Stationery Office.

Table 3.19   Distribution of marketable wealth, including occupational pension rights among the adult population, 1971–83, percentage received by various groups

Year	% of wealth held by				
	Top 1%	Top 5%	Top 10%	Top 25%	Top 50%
1971	27	46	59	78–83	90–96
1976	21	40	53	75–81	89–93
1980	17	33	46	69–73	90–94
1983	18	34	46	69–73	89–93

Sources: 1966–83: *Inland Revenue Statistics 1985* (HMSO, 1986). Reproduced with the permission of the Controller of Her Majesty's Stationery Office.

Table 3.20　Distribution of marketable wealth, including occupational and state pension rights among the adult population, 1971–83, percentage received by various groups

| Year | % of wealth held by | | | | |
	Top 1%	Top 5%	Top 10%	Top 25%	Top 50%
1971	21	37	49	69–72	85–89
1976	14	27	37	58–61	80–85
1980	12	24	35	55–58	79–83
1983	12	25	35	57–60	80–84

Sources:　1966–83: *Inland Revenue Statistics 1985* (HMSO, 1986). Reproduced with the permission of the Controller of Her Majesty's Stationery Office.

population since the beginning of the century. This is true of the richest 10 per cent since 1966, but as yet the bottom 50 per cent show little sign of benefitting. Table 3.19 illustrates the point that including occupational pension rights in our measure of wealth further reduces the inequality, and shows the bottom 50 per cent starting to gain. Going still further and adding state pension rights strengthens this point (see Table 3.20). For 1983 the top 1 per cent hold only 12 per cent of wealth including state and occupation pension rights, compared with 20 per cent of marketable wealth; the bottom 50 per cent hold 16–20 per cent compared with 4 per cent.

Notes

1. Thanks are due to the Department of Economics, Research School of social Sciences, at the Australian National University. This chapter was written during a visit there in summer 1986.
2. Central Statistical Office (1985) *United Kingdom National Accounts* (HMSO); W. Beckerman (1968) *An Introduction to National Income Analysis* (Weidenfeld).
3. In one or two special cases, services produced without payment are included in output, and a payment is therefore imputed and included (see Central Statistical Office, 1985).
4. For a discussion of these problems see W. Beckerman (1968).
5. C. H. Feinstein (1976). *Statistical Tables of National Income, Expenditure and Output of the U.K. 1855–1965* (Macmillan).
6. See W. F. F. Kemsley, R. N. Redpath and M. Holmes (1980) *Family Expenditure Survey Handbook* (HMSO).
7. See A. B. Atkinson (1983) *The Economics of Inequality* (Oxford University Press) pp. 45–7.

8. *The Wealth of the Nation* (1967) (Cambridge, University Press) p. 64.
9. See 'National and Sector Balance Sheets for the UK' in *Economic Trends* (1978) (HMSO, November) pp. 82–100.
10. A. B. Atkinson and A. Harrison (1978) *The Distribution of Wealth in Britain* (Cambridge University Press) Table 6.5.

4 The Labour Force

Robert Price and George Sayers Bain

Labour force statistics cover a wide variety of topics.[1] This chapter is necessarily highly selective and focuses on a number of key topics which are of particular interest and relevance to sociologists: the structure and composition of the occupied population, unemployment, hours of work, wage rates and earnings, the cost-of-living and retail price indices, trade union membership, and industrial disputes. Statistics on other aspects of the labour force, such as labour mobility and turnover and vacancy rates, are not discussed here, partly because of lack of space but also because of the absence of adequate historical data.

THE OCCUPIED POPULATION

The Census of Population provides a generally satisfactory picture of the historical development of the labour force. The first Census was carried out in 1801,[2] but the occupational and industrial classification systems used prior to 1911 varied very widely and are difficult to make consistent with the post-1911 systems. Consequently, the following analysis is confined to the period 1911–81. From the vast amount of information provided by the Census on the labour force, three aspects have been identified here as being of particular interest to sociologists: occupational composition, sex composition, and participation rates.

Occupational composition

The most striking characteristic of the occupational structure of Britain as presented in Table 4.1 is the rapid growth, in both absolute and relative terms, of the non-manual labour force and the commensurate decline in the manual labour force. Between 1911 and 1981, the number of non-manual workers increased by 287 per cent while the number of manual workers declined by 11 per cent. While the number of non-manual workers increased steadily over the whole 70-year period, with a particularly rapid increase in the decade 1971–81,[3] the number of manual workers was on a slow downwards trend from 1931 onwards, again with an acceleration of the trend in the final decade.[4]. The non-manual share of the labour force increased from 18.7 per cent to 52.3 per cent of the total between 1911 and 1981, while the manual share declined from three-quarters of the labour force (74.6 per cent) in 1911 to under one-half (47.7 per cent) in 1981.

The third section of the labour force, the employers and proprietors, which was identified up to 1966, was always small and showed a tendency to decline as businesses became incorporated. After 1966 Census data make it extremely difficult to identify a figure for employers and proprietors that is consistent with the earlier series. From 1971, therefore, an alternative form of presentation has been adopted which is of comparable sociological interest. The self-employed within each occupational group have been identified separately, thus allowing the identification of new trends in the structure and organisation of economic activity which involve the adoption of self-employed status. As can be seen from Table 4.1, between 1971 and 1981 there was a small but

Table 4.1(a)   The occupied population of Great Britain by major occupational groups, 1911–81

Occupational groups	Number of persons in major occupational groups, 1911–81 (000s)							
	1911	*1921*	*1931*	*1951*	*1961*	*1966*	*1971*	*1981*
Employers and proprietors	1 232	1 318	1 407	1 117	1 139	832	—	—
							(1 003)	(1 193)
Non-manual workers	3 433	4 094	4 841	6 948	8 478	9 461	11 072	13 278
							(703)	(809)
(a) *Managers*	631	704	770	1 245	1 268	1 514	2 460	3 489
							(151)	(172)
(b) *Higher professionals*	184	196	240	435	718	829	945	1 218
							(74)	(135)
(c) *Lower professionals and technicians*	560	679	728	1 059	1 418	1 604	1 938	2 681
							(0.9)	(0.2)
(d) *Forepersons and inspectors*	237	279	323	590	682	736	754	1 042
							(31)	(38)
(e) *Clerical and related employees*	832	1 256	1 404	2 341	2 994	3 262	3 547	3 687
							(43)	(40)
(f) *Sales employees*	989	980	1 376	1 278	1 398	1 516	1 428	1 161
							(840)	(721)
Manual workers	13 685	13 920	14 776	14 450	14 022	14 393	13 949	12 128
Total occupied population	18 350	19 332	21 024	22 515	23 639	24 686	25 021	25 406

Note: Figures in brackets for 1971 and 1981 give numbers of each category that were recorded as self-employed at those Censuses.

Sources: This table is based on Bain (1970: Table 2.1) and Routh (1965: Table 1), updated from the Censuses of Population of 1966, 1971 and 1981. For a discussion of the way in which the original table was constructed, see Bain (1970: 189–90).

Table 4.1(b)   The occupied population of Great Britain by major occupational groups, 1911–81

Occupational groups	Major occupational groups as a % of total occupaltion populaltion 1911–81 *(percentages)*							
	1911	*1921*	*1931*	*1951*	*1961*	*1966*	*1971*	*1981*
Employers and								
proprietors	6.7	6.8	6.7	5.0	4.7	3.4	—	—
Non-manual								
workers	18.7	21.2	23.0	30.9	35.9	38.3	44.3	52.3
(a) *Managers*	3.4	3.6	3.7	5.5	5.4	6.1	9.8	13.7
(b) *Higher*								
professionals	1.0	1.0	1.1	1.9	3.0	3.4	3.8	4.8
(c) *Lower professionals*								
and technicians	3.1	3.5	3.5	4.7	6.0	6.5	7.7	10.6
(d) *Forepersons*								
and inspectors	1.3	1.4	1.5	2.6	2.9	3.0	3.0	4.1
(e) *Clerical and*								
related employees	4.5	6.5	6.7	10.4	12.7	13.2	14.2	14.5
(f) *Sales*								
employees	5.4	5.1	6.5	5.7	5.9	6.1	5.7	4.6
Manual								
workers	74.6	72.0	70.3	64.2	59.3	58.3	55.7	47.7
Total occupied								
population	100.0	100.0	100.0	100.0	100.0	100.0	100.0	100.0

Note: Figures in brackets for 1971 and 1981 give numbers of each category that were recorded as self-employed at those Censuses.

Sources: This table is based on Bain (1970: Table 2.1) and Routh (1965: Table 1), updated from the Censuses of Population of 1966, 1971 and 1981. For a discussion of the way in which the original table was constructed, see Bain (1970: 189–90).

significant increase in self-employment among non-manual workers, particularly in the managerial and professional groups, and a similar decline in manual self-employment.

There have also been marked differences in the growth of the various occupational groups which make up the non-manual labour force. The growth of the clerical and related work force has been the most obvious feature of the overall growth of non-manual work since the early part of the century. From 1911 to 1971, clerical work increased by 326 per cent, and rose by 6.5 percentage points to 14.2 per cent of the occupied population. However, the period from 1966 onwards, and most particularly the decade 1971–81, were characterised by a much more rapid growth of managerial and professional than of clerical occupations. From 1966 to 1981, managerial jobs increased by 130 per cent, professional jobs (higher and lower) by 60 per cent, and clerical

Table 4.1(c)   The occupied population of Great Britain by major occupational groups, 1911–81

Occupational groups	*Growth indices of major occupational groups 1911–81 (1911 = 100)*							
	1911	*1921*	*1931*	*1951*	*1961*	*1966*	*1971*	*1981*
Employers and proprietors	100	107	114	91	92	68	—	—
Non-manual workers	100	119	141	202	247	276	323	387
(a) Managers	100	112	122	192	201	240	390	553
(b) Higher professionals	100	107	130	236	390	451	514	662
(c) Lower professionals and technicians	100	121	130	189	253	286	346	479
(d) Forepersons and inspectors	100	118	136	249	288	311	318	440
(e) Clerical and related employees	100	151	169	281	360	392	426	443
(f) Sales employees	100	99	139	129	141	153	144	117
Manual workers	100	102	108	106	102	105	102	89
Total occupied population	100	105	115	123	129	135	136	138

Note: Figures in brackets for 1971 and 1981 give numbers of each category that were recorded as self-employed at those Censuses.

Sources: This table is based on Bain (1970: Table 2.1) and Routh (1965: Table 1), updated from the Censuses of Population of 1966, 1971 and 1981. For a discussion of the way in which the original table was constructed, see Bain (1970: 189–90).

jobs by only 13 per cent. With 13.7 per cent of the occupied population in 1981, managerial occupations were almost as numerous as clerical and related jobs; managerial and professional jobs taken together were twice as numerous as clerical jobs in 1981, whereas in 1966 there had been only 20 per cent more managerial and professional jobs than clerical. At the other end of the scale, the absolute number of salespersons has been falling rapidly since 1966 and their share of the labour force in 1981 was lower than at any Census since 1911.

Sex composition

The steady increase in female labour force participation since the Second

World War has been the subject of substantial comment and investigation.[5] Table 4.2 reflects the well-known pattern of inter-war stability in labour force participation by women, with just under 30 per cent of the labour force being female, and the steadily increasing share from 1951 to 1981. In the latter year women formed some 39 per cent of the total occupied population, their share having grown by a third since the inter-war period.

The proportion of women among manual workers has shown a remarkable stability over the 70-year period under consideration here and, with a few fluctuations between the beginning and end of the period, has been at much the same level in the period 1966–81 as it was in 1911. By contrast, the proportion of women in the non-manual labour force has increased steadily, from just under 30 per cent in 1911 to almost one-half in 1981. The growth of the proportion of women workers in the clerical and sales categories reflects the pattern of occupational segregation that has developed in this country, as elsewhere, since the early part of the century (Hakim, 1979). Among clerical and related workers, the most significant substitution of women for men occurred during the two world wars, although there would seem to have been a quickening of the pace of substitution in the most recent decade (1971–81). For sales staff, the Second World War is also a watershed for gender substitution, but in this case the decade 1971–81 was clearly the period when, along with a growth of supermarkets, a decline in the 'corner shop', and in the

Table 4.2   The percentage of female workers in major occupational groups in Great Britain, 1911–81

Occupational group	1911	1921	1931	1951	1961	1966	1971	1981
Employers and proprietors	18.8	20.5	19.8	20.0	20.4	23.7	21.7	24.2
Non-manual workers	29.8	37.6	35.8	42.3	44.5	46.5	46.2	42.8
(a) *Managers*	19.8	17.0	13.0	15.2	15.5	16.7	18.5	21.4
(b) *Higher professionals*	6.0	5.1	7.5	8.3	9.7	9.4	10.0	13.0
(c) *Lower professionals and technicians*	62.9	59.4	58.8	53.5	50.8	52.1	51.9	55.0
(d) *Forepersons and inspectors*	4.2	6.5	8.7	13.4	10.3	11.4	12.8	23.6
(e) *Clerical and related employees*	21.4	44.6	46.0	60.2	65.2	69.3	71.9	78.1
(f) *Sales employees*	35.2	43.6	37.2	51.6	54.9	58.7	59.4	77.8
All manual workers	30.5	27.9	28.8	26.1	26.0	29.0	28.6	28.7
Total occupied population	29.6	29.5	29.8	30.8	32.4	35.6	36.0	38.9

Sources: This table is based on Bain (1970: Table 2.3) and the 1966, 1971 and 1981 Censuses which were classified on a similar basis to the 1961 Census. For a discussion of the way in which the original table was constructed, see Bain (1970: 189–90).

total sales labour force, the most marked feminisation of the labour force took place.

The proportion of managerial, higher professional and supervisory jobs taken by women has been rising in recent years but still remains at levels that imply substantial under-representation of women in these occupations. In the case of managerial and supervisory jobs, women take approximately half the number that could be expected if they were represented in proportion to their overall share of the labour force; for higher professionals they take only one-third. Women have always been in a majority in the lower professional and technician category because of the preponderance of two majority-female occupations – teaching and nursing – in this category. The decline in the proportion of women in this group over the years can be largely accounted for by the influx of men into these occupations, although here, too, the 1971–81 period was one in which the traditional female dominance was reasserted.

Participation rates

Table 4.3 shows the number of persons in the labour force, and in the total population, who were above the compulsory school age at each of the Censuses, together with the participation rates or the percentage of the population of working age recorded as being in the labour force.[6] The underlying changes in participation rates have been the subject of detailed analysis elsewhere,[7] but a few key points can be made.

The overall male participation rate has declined steadily since 1911, primarily because of reductions in the proportion of the male population active in the labour force at either end of the age spectrum. In the period immediately after compulsory education, an increasing proportion of young males have been remaining in full-time education and training for longer periods; and at the other end of the spectrum, larger numbers of men are surviving to retiring age and leaving the labour force. This latter factor may have become more important in recent years due to the increase in early retirements and 'voluntary' permanent redundancies. For women, there has been a significant rise in the overall participation rate since 1951, with the rate in 1981 being 39 per cent higher than in the earlier year. In absolute terms, the number of economically active males in 1981 was virtually the same as in 1951, while the number of economically active females had increased by over three million (51 per cent).

Because of the rising proportion of women in the labour force, the increase in the female rate has offset the decline in the male rate, so that the total participation rate has remained at 60–61 per cent since 1921, with the exception of the apparently aberrant year 1966.[8] The structure of female labour force participation is investigated further in Tables 4.4, 4.5 and 4.6, which analyse the number of females in the labour force and in the population

Table 4.3 The labour force, total population, and participation rates by sex –
Great Britain, 1911–81

Year	(1) Labour force 14, 15 and 16 years and over (000s)	(2) Total population 14, 15 and 16 years and over (000s)	(3) Participation rate (1) as a % of (2)
Males			
1911	12 581	13 451	93.53
1921	13 612	14 826	91.81
1931	14 789	16 341	90.50
1951	15 649	17 862	87.61
1961	16 232	18 811	86.29
1966	15 994	19 030	84.05
1971	15 884	19 496	81.47
1981	15 526	19 961	77.78
Females			
1911	5 225	14 793	35.32
1921	5 573	16 827	33.12
1931	6 265	18 321	34.20
1951	6 561	20 045	32.73
1961	7 782	20 758	37.49
1966	8 863	21 011	42.18
1971	9 138	21 439	42.62
1981	9 879	21 700	45.53
Total			
1911	17 806	28 244	63.04
1921	19 185	31 653	60.61
1931	21 054	34 662	60.74
1951	22 210	37 907	58.59
1961	24 857	39 569	62.82
1966	25 857	40 041	64.58
1971	25 022	40 935	61.12
1981	25 405	41 661	60.98

Note: The labour force is here defined as the 'economically active population' and includes not only employees, but those classified as employers or proprietors, the self-employed, members of the armed forces, and persons reported as unemployed or otherwise out of work. Certain amendments have been made to the Census returns in order to increase the comparability of the figures over the period since 1911. In the Census for 1911 the population of working age as then defined covered persons aged 10 years and over; in 1921 those aged 12 years and over; in 1931, those aged 14 years and over; and in 1951, 1961 and 1966 those aged 15 years and over. Children aged from 10 to 14 years have therefore been excluded from the returns for 1911, and children aged 12 years and 13 years from the returns for 1921. In that year and in 1931, however, young persons of 14 and 15 years of age were grouped together in the tables and cannot be separated, so that the figures for those years unavoidably contain 14-year-olds and the table must be used bearing this in mind. For 1971 and 1981, following the raising of the school leaving age, the labour force and total population figures only include persons over 16 years of age. The labour force figures given here differ slightly from those in Table 4.1, partly because of the age adjustment and partly because the 'inadequately described occupations' were included here but had to be excluded from Table 4.1 because of its occupational classification.

Source: CSO – Census of Population of England and Wales and Scotland for the various years.

Table 4.4   The female labour force by age groups and marital status – Great Britain, 1911–81

Age	Year	Single (000s)	Married (000s)	Widowed and divorced (000s)	All (000s)
14 or 15–24	1911	2428	57	0.2	2487
	1921	2682	70	3.6	2755
	1931	2840	101	1.6	2943
	1951	2016	316	2.7	2335
	1961	1837	431	2.3	2270
	1966	1892	505	3.5	2401
	1971	1607	622	6.2	2235
	1981	1801	522	19.8	2343
25–35	1911	939	218	30	1187
	1921	927	206	52	1185
	1931	1018	320	25	1364
	1951	589	694	48	1331
	1961	392	819	25	1236
	1966	312	925	31	1268
	1971	303	1095	48	1446
	1981	444	1472	151	2067
35–44	1911	372	209	87	668
	1921	426	209	90	725
	1931	474	249	80	803
	1951	434	793	102	1328
	1961	304	1131	88	1523
	1966	254	1456	86	1796
	1971	199	1512	89	1801
	1981	154	1764	194	2112
45–54	1911	199	144	127	469
	1921	258	154	119	531
	1931	315	178	120	613
	1951	406	618	170	1195
	1961	355	1056	203	1613
	1966	273	1406	212	1890
	1971	234	1602	212	2048
	1981	153	1617	231	2001
55 and over	1911	120	84	210	414
	1921	178	94	205	477
	1931	239	105	199	542
	1951	288	237	247	772
	1961	331	472	337	1139
	1966	313	772	423	1508
	1971	250	930	428	1608
	1981	135	910	310	1355
All ages 14 or 15 and over	1911	4058	712	455	5224
	1921	4470	733	469	5672
	1931	4885	953	426	6265
	1951	3733	2658	570	6961

continued overleaf

170   *British Social Trends since 1900*

Table 4.4—*continued*

Age	Year	Single (000s)	Married (000s)	Widowed and divorced (000s)	All (000s)
	1961	3220	3908	655	7782
	1966	3044	5063	756	8863
	1971	2593	5761	783	9138
	1981	2686	6286	906	9879

Note: For the years 1911, 1921, 1931 and 1951, the totals given in Tables 4.4 and 4.5 respectively for the female labour force and the female population are slightly different from those given in Table 4.3. This is because it was necessary to exclude persons classified in the Scottish Census for those years under the heading 'Age Not Stated'. In 1911 the Scottish figures for four age groups had to be derived by sub-dividing the groups 24–44 years and 45–64 years according to the ratios observed respectively for the 25–34/35–44 and 45–54/ 55–64 age groups in the England and Wales Census for the same year. The age divisions shown in the table were chosen to permit the maximum comparability over the six Censuses with the minimum of statistical manipulations of this kind, since the age classifications used by the Census vary from year to year and also between those for England and Wales and for Scotland in the same year.

Source: CSO – Census of Population of England and Wales and Scotland for the various years.

Table 4.5   The female population by age groups and marital status – Great Britain, 1911–81

Age	Year	Single (000s)	Married (000s)	Widowed and divorced (000s)	All (000s)
14 or 15–24	1911	3324	475	3	3 802
	1921	3796	551	7	4 354
	1931	3750	546	3	4 299
	1951	2383	863	4	3 250
	1961	2366	1 031	4	3 401
	1966	2571	1 160	6	3 737
	1971	2449	1 372	12	3 833
	1981	2700	973	36	3 709
25–34	1911	1276	2 197	46	3 519
	1921	1216	2 199	112	3 527
	1931	1266	2 427	46	3 740
	1951	678	2 842	77	3 591
	1961	438	2 778	37	3 293
	1966	352	2 694	47	3 093
	1971	353	2 854	79	3 286
	1981	518	3 044	243	3 805
35–44	1911	567	2 104	143	2 814
	1921	630	2 358	199	3 187

Table 4.5—*continued*

Age	Year	Single (000s)	Married (000s)	Widowed and divorced (000s)	All (000s)
	1931	655	2 452	177	3 284
	1951	536	3 084	159	3 779
	1961	358	3 110	122	3 590
	1966	297	2 996	116	3 409
	1971	234	2 791	126	3 151
	1981	188	2 766	274	3 228
45–54	1911	340	1 451	276	2 067
	1921	432	1 833	296	2 561
	1931	493	2 091	339	2 923
	1951	543	2 613	315	3 471
	1961	435	2 989	304	3 728
	1966	332	2 821	293	3 446
	1971	284	2 820	286	3 390
	1981	188	2 514	331	3 033
55 and over	1911	348	1 166	1078	2 592
	1921	486	1 494	1219	3 199
	1931	657	1 975	1442	4 074
	1951	970	2 826	2159	5 955
	1961	1030	3 369	2389	6 788
	1966	1051	3 625	2650	7 326
	1971	1025	3 870	2883	7 778
	1981	824	4 027	3074	7 925
All ages 14 or 15 and over	1911	5854	7 393	1546	14 793
	1921	6560	8 434	1833	16 827
	1931	6821	9 492	2007	18 320
	1951	5109	12 228	2709	20 046
	1961	4626	13 276	2856	20 758
	1966	4602	13 296	3112	21 010
	1971	4345	13 707	3387	21 439
	1981	4419	13 322	3959	21 700

Note: See Note to Table 4.4.
Source: CSO – Census of Population of England and Wales and Scotland for the various years.

of working age, as well as female participation rates by age and marital status.

The increase in the female labour force has come mainly from a striking rise in the participation rates of married women of all ages coupled with their increase both absolutely and as a proportion of the female population. In 1911 less than 10 per cent of married women were working; in 1961 some 30 per cent were at work; by 1981 47 per cent were economically active. Tables 4.4 and 4.6 show clearly the major structural shift which occurred in the numbers and proportion of married women working between 1931 and 1951, and it appears that much of the shift occurred during and immediately following the Second

Table 4.6   Female participation rates by age and marital status – Great Britain, 1911–81 (percentages)

Marital status	Year	15–24	25–34	35–44	45–54	55 and over	All ages 14 or 15 and over
Single	1911	73.05	73.59	65.61	58.53	34.48	69.32
	1921	70.65	76.23	67.62	59.72	36.63	68.14
	1931	75.73	80.41	72.37	63.90	36.38	71.62
	1951	84.60	86.87	80.97	74.77	29.69	73.07
	1961	77.64	89.50	84.92	81.61	32.14	69.61
	1966	73.59	88.64	85.52	82.23	29.78	66.15
	1971	65.62	85.84	85.04	82.39	24.39	59.68
	1981	66.70	85.71	81.92	81.38	16.38	60.78
Married	1911	12.00	9.92	9.93	9.92	7.20	9.63
	1921	12.70	9.37	8.86	8.40	6.29	8.69
	1931	18.50	13.19	10.16	8.51	5.32	10.04
	1951	36.62	24.42	25.71	23.65	8.39	21.74
	1961	41.80	29.48	36.37	35.33	14.01	29.44
	1966	43.53	34.34	48.60	49.84	21.30	38.08
	1971	45.34	38.37	54.17	56.81	24.03	42.03
	1981	53.65	48.36	63.77	64.32	22.60	47.19
Widowed and divorced	1911	56.67	65.22	60.84	46.01	19.48	29.43
	1921	51.43	46.43	45.23	40.20	16.82	25.59
	1931	53.33	54.35	45.20	35.40	13.80	21.23
	1951	67.50	66.67	64.15	53.97	11.44	21.04
	1961	57.50	67.57	72.13	66.78	14.11	22.93
	1966	58.33	65.96	74.14	72.36	15.96	24.29
	1971	51.67	60.76	70.64	74.13	14.85	23.12
	1981	55.00	62.14	70.80	69.79	10.09	22.89
All females	1911	65.61	33.73	23.74	22.74	15.97	35.32
	1921	63.23	33.60	22.75	20.73	14.91	33.71
	1931	68.46	36.45	24.45	20.97	13.33	34.19
	1951	71.86	37.06	35.17	34.40	12.96	34.73
	1961	66.76	38.00	42.42	43.29	16.79	37.49
	1966	64.24	41.00	52.68	54.88	20.58	42.19
	1971	58.31	44.01	57.13	60.41	20.67	42.62
	1981	63.17	54.32	65.43	65.97	17.10	45.52

Source: Derived from Tables 4.4 and 4.5; the authors are indebted to Jackie Johns of the University of Manchester Institute of Science and Technology for the compilation of the series for 1911–66.

World War. In 1951 single women still accounted for 54 per cent of the female labour force; by 1961 they represented only 41 per cent of working women; and by 1981 they accounted for only 27 per cent of the total number of women at work. Put the other way round, while only 14 per cent of the female labour force was married in 1911, by 1981 66 per cent, almost two-thirds of working women, were married.

While part of the increase in female labour force participation can be accounted for by the increase in the proportion of married women in the female population (up from 50 per cent in 1911 to 62 per cent in 1981), by far the greater part of the explanation lies in a significant increase in the length of female labour force participation. Hakim has shown how the 'two-stage work profile' of women has become increasingly marked by shorter median periods of non-participation for child-bearing and rearing and greater proportions of women returning to work after the child-bearing/rearing break (Hakim, 1979:3–17).

UNEMPLOYMENT

The two primary sources of historical information on unemployment in Great Britain are the trade unions and the Department of Employment. Available material on unemployment gathered by trade unions dates from 1851, and although its accuracy and coverage are far from ideal, it remained the only source of information until 1913 when the Labour Department of the Board of Trade (the predecessor of the Ministry of Labour which was formed in 1917) began to collect unemployment statistics based on the National Insurance Act of 1911. Since the trade unions operated the 1911 Act, they were still the primary source of information until it was superseded by the Unemployment Insurance Act of 1920 which was operated by the Ministry of Labour (now the Department of Employment). This Act began to operate in 1921, but the Department regards 1923 as the first year for which reliable unemployment statistics can be provided.[9]

Table 4.7 is based upon these two sources and gives the percentage rate of unemployment in the United Kingdom from 1900 to 1984. It also gives an additional series for 1920–47 derived from the work of Feinstein on national income and expenditure (Feinstein, 1972: Table 57) who has adjusted the basic series to take account of the variations in coverage of the unemployment insurance series discussed below.

The major trends in unemployment during the twentieth century are well known and require little detailed commentary here. Unemployment was at its lowest during the two world wars and was consistently high during the inter-war period. From the end of the Second World War to the end of the 1960s, unemployment averaged less than 2 per cent, although certain regions of the country were still relatively seriously affected. From the early 1970s, unemployment was consistently higher than in the previous period, rising to record levels from 1979 onwards due to the combination of world recession and the monetarist economic policies of the Thatcher Government. By 1984–5, unemployment was not only at levels unprecedented in the post-war era but was also probably somewhat higher on a comparable basis than in the depths of the depression in1931–2.

The slightly tentative note struck in the last sentence reflects the difficulties

Table 4.7   The percentage rate of unemployment – United Kingdom, 1900–1984

Year	Official series	Feinstein	Year	Official series	Feinstein	Year	Official series
1900	2.5		1940	9.7	3.3	1980	7.4
1901	3.3		1941	6.6	1.2	1981	11.4
1902	4.0		1942	2.4	0.5		
1903	4.7		1943	0.8	0.4	1982	12.1
1904	6.0		1944	0.7	0.4	1983	12.9
1905	5.0		1945	1.2	0.5	1984	13.1
1906	3.6		1946	2.5	1.9		
1907	3.7		1947	3.1	1.4		
1908	7.8						
1909	7.7		1948	1.8	1.3		
1910	4.7		1949	1.6	1.2		
1911	3.0		1950	1.5	1.3		
1912	3.2		1951	1.2	1.1		
1913	2.1		1952	2.1	1.6		
1914	3.3		1953	1.8	1.5		
1915	1.1		1954	1.5	1.2		
1916	0.4		1955	1.2	1.0		
1917	0.6		1956	1.3	1.1		
1918	0.8		1957	1.6	1.3		
1919	2.1		1958	2.2	1.9		
1920	2.0		1959	2.3	1.8		
1921	12.9	11.3	1960	1.7	1.5		
			1961	1.6	1.4		
1922	14.3	9.8	1962	2.1	1.9		
1923	11.7	8.1	1963	2.6	2.2		
1924	10.3	7.2	1964	1.7	1.5		
1925	11.3	7.9	1965	1.5	1.3		
1926	12.5	8.8	1966	1.6	1.5		
1927	9.7	6.8	1967	2.5	2.2		
1928	10.8	7.5	1968	2.5	2.3		
1929	10.4	7.3	1969	2.5	2.3		
1930	16.0	11.2	1970	2.6	2.4		
1931	21.3	15.1	1971	3.5	3.2		
1932	22.1	15.6	1972	3.8	3.4		
1933	19.9	14.1	1973	2.7	2.3		
1934	16.7	11.9	1974	2.6	2.5		
1935	15.5	11.0	1975	4.2	3.9		
1936	13.1	9.4	1976	5.7	5.3		
1937	10.8	7.8	1977	6.2	5.7		
1938	13.5	9.3	1978	6.1	5.5		
1939	11.6	5.8	1979	5.7	5.3		

Sources and Notes: The figures for 1900–12 are the percentage unemployed in certain trade unions and are taken from Mitchell and Deane (1962); those for 1913–21 are the percentage unemployed in certain trade unions as adjusted by Hilton (1923) and cited by LCES; those for 1922–47 are the insured unemployed as a percentage of the insured labour force as given by the Ministry of Labour and associated with the reliability and internal consistency of the unemployment series and these difficulties require considerable comment. The reliability of the series is most in doubt prior to 1922 when the figures were derived from the returns of those unions which operated unemployment benefit schemes. Since relatively few unions operated such schemes, and those that did generally restricted their membership to crafstmen, the resulting unemployment percentages are clearly not the same as those prevailing among the labour force as a whole. Despite this limitation, these figures possess considerable utility. First, they are the only quantitative measure of unemployment available for the period. Secondly, although the figures are not a good guide to the *volume* of unemployment, expert opinion holds that they do give a reasonable indication of *fluctuations* in unemployment.[10]

The figure for the year 1921 is perhaps the most unreliable. The 1921 figure in Table 4.7 is based on the 'crude' trade union return of 14.8 per cent, which was adjusted by Hilton to give 12.9 per cent. But other sources give higher estimates. Hines's estimate is 15.56 per cent, Routh's is 16.6 per cent, and Beveridge's is 17 per cent. Feinstein, on the other hand, gives a *lower* figure of 11.3 per cent (Hines, 1964: 250–51; Routh, 1965: 110; Beveridge, 1944: 47; Feinstein, 1972: Table 57). There are at least three reasons for the confusion: first, the introduction of the Unemployment Insurance Act of 1920 which did not produce reliable figures until 1923. Secondly, the Irish Treaty of 1920 which required the separation of the unemployed in Southern Ireland from those in the rest of the United Kingdom. Thirdly, the largest recorded annual increase in unemployment – from about 400 000 to 2 500 000 – which the 1920 Act had great difficulty coping with. Hilton's estimate for 1921 is given in Table 4.7 partly because it is comparable with the figures given for the earlier years and partly because, unlike some of the other estimates, the manner in which it was derived is clearly shown.

The internal consistency of the series is an even greater problem than its reliability. For the unemployment percentages reflect not only the changing demand for labour but also the changing occupational coverage of the unemployment insurance legislation. The proportion of the labour force covered by the legislation increased from about 20 per cent in 1920 to over 90 per cent in the post-1948 period. The legislation was originally confined to those workers who were most susceptible to unemployment but was continuously extended to workers who were less and less likely to be unemployed. In other words, each extension of the coverage of the insurance scheme

adjusted by LCES to obtain greater comparability across a period which saw several changes in the coverage of the unemployment insurance legislation; those for 1948–84 are the number registered as unemployed as a percentage of the estimated total number of employees as published by the Department of Employment. The series compiled by Feinstein was published in Feinstein (1972: Table 57) and updated on a consistent basis to 1979.

generally added proportionately more to the number insured than to the number unemployed with a consequent depressing effect on the percentage unemployed. Thus when making historical comparisons, it must be remembered that the unemployment percentages for the period 1920–47 are overstated relative to those for the post-1948 period. Feinstein's series shown in Table 4.7 has been compiled on a labour force base that is as consistent as possible with the post-1948 series, and provides an approximation of the lower rates of unemployment that would have been recorded if the insurance scheme coverage had been on the same basis as after 1948 (Feinstein, 1972: Table 57).

From 1948 to 1981 the series is generally internally consistent but there is still a tendency for it to under-record the actual amount of unemployment. All those drawing unemployment benefit are included, but for groups not entitled to draw benefit (school-leavers, newly-arrived immigrants, and married women either paying the lower rate of National Insurance available up to 1977 or not insured at all), registration with the Department of Employment was voluntary. They were likely to register, and hence be counted in the series, only if they felt that the Employment Exchange/Jobcentre could help them. Thus the series does not, as Lewes has noted, 'measure all spare labour available'. However, 'this is necessarily a vague term, since higher pay or more congenial work may well attract some who would prefer to remain "unemployed" under existing conditions' (Lewes, 1967:29).

Since 1980 the government has made a series of adjustments to the method of compilation of unemployment statistics which have had the effect of significantly reducing the numbers recorded as unemployed. These downward adjustments have also to be set alongside the number of workers covered by 'special employment measures' and the Youth Training Scheme, who would otherwise be unemployed, if a roughly comparable series to the 1948–81 period is to be constructed.[11] The main changes in compilation affecting the annual series have been to change the basis of the count from those 'registered for work' to those claiming benefit and seeking work (October 1982), the exclusion of those seeking part-time work (October 1982) and those aged 59 and over not in receipt of benefit (April 1983), the removal of the requirement that unemployed men over age 60 should register for work (June 1983), and the introduction of a two-week 'delay' in making the monthly count (March 1986). On the labour force side, the figure on which the percentage unemployed is calculated was increased from March 1986 by the inclusion of an estimate for the self-employed in the total labour force. As a consequence of these changes, the series is not consistent from 1981 onwards. Estimates of the degree of variation introduced by these changes are inevitably difficult to validate, but a conservative estimate of their effects on the rate of unemployment for 1981–5 is a reduction of at least three percentage points.[12] One additional consequence of these changes is that the *rate of change* of unemployment after 1981 cannot be measured with accuracy.

Over the long period covered by these figures it is not altogether easy to accept the official conclusion that 'the series available since 1921 may be regarded as a continuous series of approximately comparable figures and the fluctuations in them as adequate indications of economic change' (CSO, HMSO, 1958: 14). But it seems safe to take the series as reasonably comparable within the three periods 1900–21, 1922–47 and 1948–81. After 1981, as indicated earlier, there is a degree of internal discontinuity which reduces the comparability of the three years concerned. The real problems in relation to the earlier periods arise when comparisons are made not within but between them; but since no more internally consistent series is available, such comparisons have to be made, albeit with caution and qualification.

HOURS OF WORK

The only sources of detailed regular figures of hours worked are the Department of Employment's series on 'normal' weekly hours and hours actually worked. Normal weekly hours are defined as:

> those laid down in voluntary collective agreements between organisations of employers and workpeople by Joint Industrial Councils or other similar bodies or in statutory orders under the Wages Councils Acts, the Agricultural Wages Acts and the Catering Wages Act. The hours are the normal weekly hours in respect of which all rates used in the calculations of the index rates of wages are payable and in the case of individual industries are combined in the same proportions as are those rates. Generally for day workers the normal hours are exclusive of mealtimes but for shift workers an allowance for mealtimes is included in the normal number of hours (CSO, 1958: 36).

Weekly hours worked are the hours actually worked, including overtime and short-time worked as a result of agreement with management, but excluding individual absences due to sickness or voluntary reasons.

Systematic aggregate[13] data on normal weekly hours begin in 1920 while those on weekly hours actually worked begin in 1943 although data are available for the odd year prior to that date. The two series are given in Table 4.8.

The figures are based on a voluntary return and apply only to manual workers. The normal weekly hours series currently covers most industries and services except domestic service, commerce and finance. But the weekly hours actually worked series excludes the following industries: agriculture; coal mining; railways and London Transport; distribution, commerce, and finance; domestic service; catering; and entertainment. The range of industries covered by the two series has varied over time, and this has slightly lessened their internal consistency, although not seriously.

British Social Trends since 1900

Table 4.8   Hours of work of manual workers – United Kingdom, 1900–1985

Year	Normal weekly hours	Actual weekly hours	Year	Normal weekly hours	Actual weekly hours
1900	—	54	1943	47.2	50.0
1901	—	—	1944	47.2	48.6
1902	—	—	1945	47.5	47.4
1903	—	—	1946	46.8	46.2
1904	—	—	1947	44.9	45.2
1905	—	—	1948	44.8	45.3
1906	—	—	1949	44.7	45.4
1907	—	—	1950	44.7	46.1
1908	—	—	1951	44.6	46.3
1909	—	—	1952	44.6	45.9
1910	—	54	1953	44.6	46.3
1911	—	—	1954	44.6	46.7
1912	—	—	1955	44.6	47.0
1913	—	—	1956	44.6	46.8
1914	—	—	1957	44.6	46.6
1915	—	—	1958	44.5	46.2
1916	—	—	1959	44.4	46.6
1917	—	—	1960	43.7	46.2
1918	—	—	1961	42.8	45.7
1919	—	—	1962	42.4	45.3
1920	46.9	—	1963	42.4	45.4
1921	46.9	—	1964	42.2	45.8
1922	47.0	—	1965	41.4	45.3
1923	47.0	—	1966	40.7	44.3
1924	47.1	45.8	1967	40.5	44.3
1925	47.0	—	1968	40.5	44.5
1926	47.6	—	1969	40.4	44.6
1927	47.6	—	1970	40.3	43.9
1928	47.6	—	1971	40.2	43.2
1929	47.6	—	1972	40.1	43.5
1930	47.3	—	1973	40.0	43.9
1931	47.4	—	1974	40.0	43.4
1932	47.6	—	1975	40.0	42.2
1933	47.6	—	1976	40.0	42.6
1934	47.5	—	1977	40.0	43.0
1935	47.4	47.8	1978	40.0	43.0
1936	47.4	—	1979	40.0	42.8
1937	47.2	—	1980	39.7	42.0
1938	47.2	46.5	1981	39.6	42.1
1939	47.2	—	1982	39.1	42.0
1940	47.2	—	1983	39.0	42.4
1941	47.2	—	1984	39.0	42.5
1942	47.2	—	1985	38.9	42.8

Sources: The figures for actual weekly hours for 1900 and 1910 are tentative and are supplied by the LCES (nd); those for 1924, 1935, 1938, and 1943–50 are from the half-yearly inquiry into earnings, the results of which were published in the *Ministry of Labour Gazette*; those for 1951–68 are from the

WAGE RATES AND EARNINGS

The Department of Employment currently collects and publishes a vast array of earnings data disaggregated by industry, region, sex, manual and non-manual groups, and adult and youth workers. Contemporary analysis of wage and earnings trends has been particularly facilitated by the *New Earnings Survey* which was launched in 1968 and which, unlike other Department of Employment surveys, covers all industries, all occupations and all sizes of establishment. The detail asked for in the *New Earnings Survey* on the make-up of earnings and the reasons for fluctuations in pay is also much greater than in other surveys, and for this reason has become the most common resource for academic labour-market analysis.

Over the long term, however, there are just two basic series that have been compiled on an approximately comparable basis since the latter part of the nineteenth century: those covering the weekly money wage rates and weekly money earnings of manual workers.[14] The index of weekly wage rates measures the average movement in full-time basic rates of pay agreed in national collective agreements or Wages Council Orders. It thus takes no account generally of fluctuations due to overtime or short-time, or the consequences of local bargaining where bonuses, piecework earnings, local agreements and productivity supplements may all affect earnings levels. The main qualification to this is that the compilation of the index after 1947 did take into account movements in piece-rates in those industries where there was an 'appreciable amount of piecework' (DEP, 1971: 8). A further reservation to be entered against the wage-rate series is that, as Devons points out:

> average earnings may increase because people move to the more highly paid occupations and industries or because of regrading and more rapid promotion. But since the wage-rate index uses a fixed set of weights in combining the changes in different industries into an average, it takes no account of such movements (Devons, 1961: 205).[15]

Prior to 1938, and especially before 1914, wage rates and earnings were very close in most industries. In consequence, the distinction between the two concepts was not always clearly drawn, and in these early years the indices may show a greater degree of similarity than was actually the case. Since 1938, and particularly since the Second World War, the growth in the importance of

---

same inquiry, the results of which were published in DEP (1969:68). The figures for normal weekly hours for 1920–50 are calculated from the Index of Normal Weekly Hours using the actual averages available for some years, details of which are given in the *Ministry of Labour Gazette* (September 1957:330–1); those for 1951–68 are from DEP (1969:68); those for 1969–83 are from DE (1978:109), the *Employment Gazette*, and *New Earnings Surveys*.

Table 4.9   Index of money wage rates and earnings of manual workers in the
United Kingdom, 1900–1984 (1930 = 100)

Year	Weekly wage rates	Weekly wage earnings	Year	Weekly wage rates	Weekly wage earnings
1900	49.0	49.0	1943	144.0	191.0
1901	48.0	49.0	1944	153.0	198.0
1902	48.0	48.0	1945	159.0	196.0
1903	48.0	48.0	1946	172.0	207.0
1904	47.0	46.0	1947	178.0	221.0
1905	47.0	46.0	1948	187.0	239.0
1906	48.0	48.0	1949	193.0	249.0
1907	48.0	50.0	1950	195.9	262.9
1908	48.0	49.0	1951	212.5	289.5
1909	48.0	49.0	1952	229.0	312.3
1910	48.0	49.0	1953	240.7	331.6
1911	49.0	50.0	1954	251.1	353.2
1912	50.0	51.0	1955	268.0	386.0
1913	52.0	52.0	1956	289.2	416.9
1914	52.0	52.0	1957	303.9	436.2
1915	56.0	56.0	1958	314.9	451.2
1916	61.0	62.0	1959	323.2	471.7
1917	72.0	74.0	1960	331.5	502.2
1918	93.0	99.0	1961	345.2	532.7
1919	121.0	120.0	1962	358.0	551.6
1920	162.0	148.0	1963	370.9	574.8
1921	130.0	142.0	1964	388.3	624.5
1922	101.0	110.0	1965	405.2	674.7
1923	100.0	98.0	1966	424.2	714.1
1924	102.0	102.0	1967	440.1	742.3
1925	102.0	103.0	1068	469.2	803.3
1926	103.0	102.0	1969	494.0	870.4
1927	103.0	103.0	1970	555.2	988.6
1928	101.0	101.0	1971	619.3	1097.6
1929	101.0	101.0	1972	732.1	1270.4
1930	100.0	100.0	1973	820.4	1462.8
1931	99.0	99.0	1974	988.9	1755.4
1932	97.0	97.0	1975	1250.6	2166.6
1933	96.0	96.0	1976	1458.4	2452.2
1934	96.0	97.0	1977	1554.8	2662.8
1935	98.0	100.0	1978	1773.7	3030.0
1936	100.0	103.0	1979	2039.1	3515.8
1937	104.0	—	1980	2406.4	4176.5
1938	106.0	109.0	1981	2652.0	4628.3
1939	106.0	—	1982	2834.0	5064.8
1940	119.0	141.0	1983	2994.7	5526.6
1941	128.0	154.0	1984	—	5971.7
1942	137.0	174.0			

Sources: The wage-rate figures for 1900–1938 are from Phelps Brown and Hopkins
(1950:226); those for 1939–1949 are from Ministry of Labour data as cited
by LCES (nd); those for 1950–68 are from DEP (1969:8); those for 1969–76
are from DE (1978); and those for 1977–83 are from *Employment Gazette*
(December 1983). The wage-earnings figures for 1900–49 are from Bowley
(1937 and 1952); those for 1950–68 are from DEP (1969:8); and those for
1969–84 are from the *Employment Gazette*.

piece-rate bargaining, and the development of establishment and company bargaining, have caused wage rates and earnings to be clearly distinguished. These developments have also, however, gradually reduced the relevance of the wage-rate series. As increasing numbers of firms in both manufacturing and services sectors have broken away from national agreements and adopted company or enterprise specific wage structures and systems, the value of the wage-rate index as an indicator of across-the-board agreed changes in wages had diminished. The series was discontinued as an economy measure in December 1983.[16]

The series on average weekly earnings takes into account the total monetary remuneration of employees, including overtime, premium payments, bonuses and commission, but generally excluding income in kind. It covers the production industries (manufacturing, public utilities and construction), transport and communication, and public administration, although there have been several changes in coverage in recent years, which mean that there is a degree of discontinuity after 1970. Using Board of Trade and Department of Employment survey data, reasonably reliable wage and earnings indices can be constructed for the period 1860 to the present. Table 4.9 provides a series for wages and earnings from 1900 to 1984.

The following minor reservations should be borne in mind. First, both series are constructed by weighting industries and occupations according to their contribution to the labour force. Since these weights are periodically adjusted to take into account changes in the relative importance of different industries and occupations, there is an inevitable reduction in the internal consistency of the series over the whole period. Secondly, there is a certain lack of comparability between the two series since the industrial coverage of the wage-rate series is substantially more comprehensive than the coverage of the earnings series. Thirdly, the reliability of the official wage-rate series in the immediate post-First World War period has been questioned by Routh (1965: 110–11). He gives the following figures for 1919–22: 110.0, 144.0, 150.0, 110.0.

THE COST-OF-LIVING AND RETAIL PRICES

A cost-of-living and retail price index for the United Kingdom for the period 1900–84 is given in Table 4.10. The principal methodological question affecting the compilation and the interpretation of the index is the nature of the weightings used to produce a composite figure for average price and cost movements.

For the pre-1914 period, for which no official data exist, the most frequently quoted source, and the one used in Table 4.10, is Bowley's work on wages and real incomes (Bowley, 1937: 118–26). His index is weighted according to a 1904 Board of Trade survey of working-class consumption patterns. In 1914 an official 'cost-of-living' index was started, with the weightings still largely based on the 1904 family budget survey, but modified to take into account the

Table 4.10   The cost of living in the United Kingdom,
1900–1984 (1930 = 100)

Year	Index	Year	Index	Year	Index
1900	58.1	1929	104.3	1956	247.8
1901	57.6	1930	100.0	1957	257.0
1902	57.6	1931	92.4	1958	264.6
1903	58.1	1932	90.3	1959	266.0
1904	58.7	1933	89.2	1960	268.8
1905	58.7	1934	89.2	1961	278.0
1906	59.2	1935	92.4	1962	289.8
1907	60.9	1936	94.6	1963	295.7
1908	59.2	1937	100.0	1964	305.4
1909	59.8	1938	98.9	1965	320.0
1910	60.9	1939	101.0	1966	332.5
1911	62.0	1940	114.5	1967	340.5
1912	63.6	1941	124.7	1968	356.6
1913	65.3	1942	132.3	1969	375.9
1914	63.6	1943	138.0	1970	400.0
1915	79.5	1944	140.6	1971	437.6
1916	91.3	1945	145.7	1972	468.6
1917	113.9	1946	150.8	1973	511.8
1918	130.1			1974	593.8
1919	140.8	1947	159.0	1975	737.5
1920	170.9	1948	169.8	1976	859.8
1921	126.8			1977	995.8
1922	115.0	1949	174.9	1978	1078.9
1923	112.8	1950	180.5	1979	1223.2
1924	115.0	1951	197.1	1980	1442.9
1925	111.8	1952	215.0	1981	1614.5
1926	110.7	1953	221.8	1982	1753.5
1927	105.3	1954	225.9	1983	1833.7
1928	105.3	1955	236.0	1984	1925.1

Sources: The cost-of-living index for 1900–39 is derived from
Phelps Brown and Hopkins (1950:276, 281), which in
turn is based on Bowley's index for 1900–14 and the
Ministry of Labour's for 1914–39. For 1940–68, the
index is derived from LCES (nd), which in turn is
based on R. G. D. Allen's estimates for 1940–7 and the
Ministry of Labour's for 1947–9. For 1950–68, the
index is derived from DEP (1969). For 1969–84 it is
derived from the *Employment Gazette*.

estimated distribution of expenditure in 1914. It covered only those goods and
services which were regarded as the 'necessities of life', and was intended to
measure the changes in the cost of maintaining the pre-1914 minimum or
subsistence standard of living for working-class households.[17] Almost from
the outset the index was criticised on the grounds that it was based on an
excessively narrow and normative definition of the 'necessities of life' and that

the weights based on the 1904 family expenditure survey did not reflect current working-class consumption patterns. By 1937–8 these criticisms had convinced the Ministry of Labour that the index should be completely revised, and a further expenditure survey of working-class families was undertaken. But the outbreak of the Second World War delayed the introduction of a new index until 1947.

Despite the chorus of criticism, the fact remains that this index is the only continuous and consistent source of cost-of-living changes for the years 1914–39. And the opinion of most statisticians, including Devons (1961: 184–5), is that, except for the period 1939–47, it is a reasonable guide to *movements* in the cost of living. Hence it provides the basis for the cost-of-living series in Table 4.10 for the period 1914–39. For the period 1939–47, the official index is completely inadequate (Ministry of Labour and National Service, 1947). Fortunately, two reliable private estimates have been made by Allen and Seers. Both their series are based on the 1937–8 weights used in the Interim Index of Retail Prices and, although their methods differ slightly, the resulting series are very similar. That constructed by Allen is used in Table 4.10.[18]

In 1947 the Ministry of Labour abandoned the Cost-of-Living Index in favour of an interim Index of Retail Prices. The weights used in the new index were based on the consumption patterns revealed by the 1937–8 expenditure survey adjusted to take account of changes in prices between 1937–8 and 1947. In 1952 the basis of the Interim Index was revised with weights based on estimates mainly from the national income 'Blue Book' of working-class patterns of expenditure in 1950 valued at 1952 prices (Ministry of Labour and National Service, 1952).

This index continued until 1956 when it was replaced by the current Index of Retail Prices with weights based on the results of the 1953–4 family expenditure survey adjusted to correspond with the level of prices ruling in 1956. The 1953–4 expenditure survey, unlike those of 1904 and 1937–8, was not restricted to working-class households but was based on a random sample of the vast majority of households. Since 1962 the weights have been revised each January on the basis of family expenditure surveys for the three years ended in the previous June, valued at the prices prevailing at the date of revision.[19]

The basic character of the index, as reflected in its compilation and weightings, has thus changed considerably over the years. Until the Second World War it was very much a 'cost-of-living' index. That is, it attempted to measure the cost of maintaining the 1914 subsistence living standard of manual workers. During the post-war period it has instead attempted to measure changes in the price of things on which people *actually* spend their money, rather than merely those things which are necessary to maintain a minimum living standard. Moreover, since 1956 the index has taken into account the expenditure patterns not only of manual workers but also of most white-collar workers. These changes in the way the index has been weighted lessen its comparability over long periods. Even its comparability since 1948 has been somewhat compromised by the frequent changing of weights. It is doubtful, as Lewes (1967: 78) has noted, whether any index of this sort can really meaningfully represent long-term price changes when the 'basket of goods' being priced is changing greatly.

In fact, it is doubtful whether any single index, however weighted, can adequately reflect changes in the cost of living. Given wide variations in expenditure patterns according to such factors as family size, income level, and social habits, and variations in the extent to which the prices of different goods and services change, then an index number which measures the average change in the cost of living may not be relevant for particular groups because their pattern of expenditure differs from that assumed in the index. A possible remedy for this difficulty would be to have separate indices for different social groups and geographical regions. To a limited extent this does exist. The general index of retail prices excludes households in the top 3–4 per cent of the income distribution and also, more significantly,those pensioner households where at least three-quarters of total income is derived from pensions or social security benefits. Separate indices have been published since 1968 for one- and two-person pensioner households, both excluding housing costs.[20]

Nevertheless, there has been a growing tide of dissatisfaction with the existing indices from pressure groups and other bodies representing the elderly, the low-paid, and other low-income groups, since it is felt that the indices do not adequately reflect the expenditure patterns of these sectors of the population. For example, the strong effect of changes in mortgage rates and petrol prices on the general index clearly reduces its relevance to tenant households and those who predominantly use public transport. Other criticisms of the general index have reflected technical assessments of, for example, improved quality of goods and the speed at which expenditure patterns change. A substantial reconstruction of the index is likely to occur in early 1987 following a report by the government's Retail Prices Index Advisory Committee.[21]

Finally, the Tax and Prices Index introduced by the government in 1980 should be mentioned. This index measures the cost of living taking account of changes in direct tax and National Insurance contributions. Although given great prominence in government publications in the early months of its existence, it has steadily fallen into disuse since it started to show a less favourable picture of inflation than the general index. It is still published monthly among the background economic indicators in Table 0.1 of the Labour Market Data section of the *Employment Gazette*.

TRADE UNION MEMBERSHIP

The only comprehensive source of trade union membership data for the United Kingdom is the Department of Employment. The Labour Department of the Board of Trade, as it was known at the time, began the collection and publication of union membership data in 1892, although some partial data are available for some years before that. Throughout the period from 1892, the Department has sought to include in its series all organisations which 'are known to include in their objects that of negotiating with employers with a view to regulating the wages and working conditions of their members'. No distinctions have been drawn between manual and non-manual organisations, TUC-affiliated or non-affiliated bodies, or internal 'staff associations' and external unions. In more recent years, organisations which have been judged to meet the 'negotiating' and 'regulating' criteria set out by the Department have been included, even when they have not seen fit to apply for certification by the Registrar of Trade Unions under the 1971 Industrial Relations Act or the Certification Officer under the 1974 Trade Union and Labour Relations Act.

Thus the series is very comprehensive, deficient in coverage only in so far as relevant organisations failed to come to the notice of the Department or failed to make accurate membership returns. Indeed, it can be argued that in some respects it is *too* comprehensive, including as it does a number of bodies representing professional employees in the public sector with very limited collective bargaining functions (for example, the Association of Public Service Finance Officers and the New Towns Chief Officers Association) and a number of other associations with only weak representative functions. The Headmasters Conference, for example, is included, and many explicitly employer-dominated staff associations have been included over the years. On the other hand, it is arguable that the series fails to meet its own 'negotiating' and 'regulating' criteria by the omission of powerful professional bodies such as the Law Society, and the British Medical Association, which have a major influence on the terms and conditions of their members. In fact, the BMA is formally recognised by the state in bargaining with the DHSS over the pay and conditions of doctors employed in the National Health Service.

Three small reservations should be entered about the accuracy of the series in Table 4.11. First, it represents the aggregate of the membership of individual unions, and people who are members of more than one union are, therefore, counted more than once in the totals. The precise extent of this distortion is unknown but is unlikely to be large. Secondly, the series includes the total membership of UK-based unions operating in the Irish Republic and elsewhere overseas. Total union membership outside the UK was only 26 016 in 1984. Thirdly, since it is a self-reported series, there can be no guarantee of accuracy in any individual year. Unions' own knowledge of their membership size is frequently imperfect, but they may also make a deliberately inflated return to the Department for reasons of prestige or a deliberately understated return in order to minimise affiliation fees to the TUC. Some unions return the same rounded membership figure for several years in succession; others make no return and are credited by the Department with the same total as in the previous year. By and large, the series presented in Table 4.11 can be

Table 4.11 Union membership by sex – United Kingdom, 1900–1984

Year	Males			Females			Total		
	Actual membership (000s)	Potential membership (000s)	Density of membership (%)	Actual membership (000s)	Potential membership (000s)	Density of membership (%)	Actual membership (000s)	Potential membership (000s)	Density of membership (%)
1900	1869	11 194	16.7	154	4 763	3.2	2 022	15 957	12.7
1901	1873	11 325	16.5	152	4 775	3.2	2 025	16 101	12.6
1902	1857	11 433	16.2	156	4 833	3.2	2 013	16 267	12.4
1903	1838	11 541	15.9	156	4 890	3.2	1 994	16 433	12.1
1904	1802	11 649	15.5	165	4 948	3.3	1 967	16 599	11.9
1905	1818	11 757	15.5	180	5 005	3.6	1 997	16 765	11.9
1906	1999	11 865	16.8	211	5 063	4.2	2 210	16 932	13.1
1907	2263	11 973	18.9	250	5 120	4.9	2 513	17 098	14.7
1908	2230	12 080	18.5	255	5 178	4.9	2 485	17 264	14.4
1909	2214	12 188	18.2	263	5 235	5.0	2 477	17 430	14.2
1910	2287	12 296	18.6	278	5 292	5.3	2 565	17 596	14.6
1911	2804	12 404	22.6	335	5 350	6.3	3 139	17 762	17.7
1912	3027	12 453	24.3	390	5 380	7.2	3 416	17 841	19.1
1913	3702	12 502	29.6	433	5 410	8.0	4 135	17 920	23.1
1914	3708	12 551	29.5	437	5 440	8.0	4 145	17 998	23.0
1915	3867	12 600	30.7	491	5 470	9.0	4 359	18 077	24.1
1916	4018	12 649	31.8	626	5 500	11.4	4 644	18 155	25.6
1917	4621	12 698	36.4	878	5 530	15.9	5 499	18 234	30.2
1918	5324	12 747	41.8	1209	5 560	21.7	6 533	18 312	35.7
1919	6601	12 796	51.6	1326	5 591	23.7	7 926	18 391	43.1
1920	7006	12 845	54.5	1342	5 621	23.9	8 348	18 469	45.2
1921	5627	12 894	43.6	1005	5 651	17.8	6 633	18 548	35.8
1922	4753	12 334	38.5	872	5 470	15.9	5 625	17 804	31.6
1923	4607	12 436	37.0	822	5 528	14.9	5 429	17 965	30.2
1924	4730	12 539	37.7	814	5 587	14.7	5 544	18 125	30.6
1925	4671	12 641	37.0	835	5 645	14.8	5 506	18 286	30.1

1926	4407	12 743	34.6	812	5 703	14.2	5 219	18 446	28.3
1927	4125	12 847	32.1	794	5 762	13.8	4 919	18 609	26.4
1928	4011	12 950	31.0	795	5 821	13.7	4 806	18 771	25.6
1929	4056	13 054	31.1	802	5 880	13.6	4 858	18 934	25.7
1930	4049	13 158	30.8	793	5 938	13.6	4 842	19 096	25.4
1931	3859	13 261	29.1	765	5 997	13.4	4 624	19 259	24.0
1932	3698	13 302	27.8	746	6 038	12.8	4 444	19 340	23.0
1933	3661	13 343	27.4	731	6 078	12.4	4 392	19 422	22.6
1934	3854	13 384	28.8	736	6 119	12.0	4 590	19 503	23.5
1935	4106	13 425	30.6	761	6 159	12.0	4 867	19 585	24.9
1936	4495	13 466	33.4	800	6 200	12.4	5 295	19 666	26.9
1937	4947	13 507	36.6	895	6 240	12.9	5 842	19 748	29.6
1938	5127	13 548	37.8	926	6 281	14.3	6 053	19 829	30.5
1939	5288	13 589	38.9	1010	6 321	14.7	6 298	19 911	31.6
1940	5493	13 630	40.3	1119	6 362	16.0	6 613	19 992	33.1
1941	5753	13 671	42.1	1412	6 402	17.6	7 165	20 074	35.7
1942	6151	13 712	44.9	1716	6 443	22.1	7 866	20 155	39.0
1943	6258	13 753	45.5	1916	6 484	26.6	8 174	20 237	40.4
1944	6238	13 794	45.2	1848	6 524	29.5	8 087	20 318	39.8
1945	6237	13 835	45.1	1638	6 565	28.3	7 875	20 400	38.6
1946	7186	13 876	51.8	1618	6 605	25.0	8 803	20 481	43.0
1947	7483	13 917	53.8	1662	6 646	24.5	9 145	20 563	44.5
1948	7691	13 778	55.8	1672	6 954	25.0	9 363	20 732	45.2
1949	7645	13 828	55.3	1674	6 954	24.0	9 318	20 782	44.8
1950	7605	13 937	54.6	1684	6 954	24.1	9 289	21 055	44.1
1951	7742	13 906	55.7	1789	7 118	23.7	9 530	21 177	45.0
1952	7797	13 966	55.8	1792	7 271	24.6	9 588	21 252	45.1
1953	7749	14 001	55.3	1778	7 286	24.6	9 527	21 352	44.6
1954	7756	14 123	54.9	1810	7 351	24.2	9 566	21 658	44.2
1955	7874	14 224	55.4	1867	7 535	24.0	9 741	21 913	44.5
1956	7871	14 389	54.7	1907	7 689	24.3	9 778	22 180	44.1
1957	7935	14 487	54.8	1894	7 791	24.5	9 829	22 334	44.0
1958	7789	14 512	53.7	1850	7 848	24.1	9 639	22 290	43.2
1959	7755	14 426	53.8	1868	7 778	23.8	9 623	21 866	44.0
1960	7884	14 556	54.2	1951	7 440	25.1	9 835	22 229	44.2
1961	7911	14 699	53.8	2005	7 672	25.4	9 916	22 527	44.0
					7 827	25.6			

continued overleaf

Table 4.11 —continued

Year	Males			Females			Total		
	Actual membership (000s)	Potential membership (000s)	Density of membership (%)	Actual membership (000s)	Potential membership (000s)	Density of membership (%)	Actual membership (000s)	Potential membership (000s)	Density of membership (%)
1962	7960	14 909	53.4	2054	7 971	25.8	10 014	22 879	43.8
1963	7963	14 999	53.1	2104	8 022	26.2	10 067	23 021	43.7
1964	8044	15 013	53.6	2174	8 153	26.7	10 218	23 166	44.1
1965	8084	15 089	53.6	2241	8 295	27.0	10 325	23 385	44.2
1966	8003	15 072	53.1	2256	8 472	26.6	10 259	23 545	43.6
1967	7908	14 935	52.9	2286	8 412	27.2	10 194	23 347	43.7
1968	7836	14 772	53.0	2364	8 431	28.0	10 200	23 203	44.0
1969	7972	14 640	54.5	2507	8 514	29.4	10 479	23 153	45.3
1970	8444	14 497	58.2	2743	8 553	32.1	11 187	23 050	48.5
1971	8382	14 366	58.3	2753	8 518	32.3	11 135	22 884	48.7
1972	8452	14 316	59.0	2907	8 645	33.6	11 359	22 961	49.5
1973	8450	14 260	59.3	3006	8 984	33.5	11 456	23 244	49.3
1974	8586	14 125	60.8	3178	9 214	34.5	11 764	23 339	50.4
1975	8600	14 243	60.4	3427	9 333	36.7	12 026	23 576	51.0
1976	8825	14 401	61.3	3561	9 474	37.6	12 386	23 875	51.9
1977	9071	14 415	62.9	3775	9 654	39.1	12 846	24 069	53.4
1978	9238	14 413	64.1	3874	9 810	39.5	13 112	24 223	54.1
1979	9432	14 377	65.6	3857	10 073	38.3	13 289	24 449	54.4
1980	9156	14 438	63.4	3790	10 193	37.2	12 947	24 632	52.6
1981	8354	14 465	57.8	3752	10 087	37.2	12 106	24 551	49.3
1982	—	14 246	—	—	9 924	—	11 593	24 170	48.0
1983	—	14 085	—	—	9 947	—	11 337	24 032	47.2
1984	—	13 961	—	—	10 233	—	11 086	24 194	45.8

Sources: For 1900–1974, data are drawn from Bain and Price (1980: Table 2.1). For 1975–84, the membership series is derived from the trade union membership statistics published annually by the Department of Employment; and the potential membership series is compiled from the annual Census of Employment with the addition of the unemployed as estimated by the Department of Employment.

confidently treated as an accurate representation of both the absolute levels and the direction and magnitude of year-to-year changes in union membership in the UK, although it seems probable that female members are understated and male members overstated as a result of estimating errors by unions.

Of perhaps even greater interest than actual union membership is the ratio of this to potential union membership, a ratio generally referred to as the 'density' of union membership. The main difficulty in obtaining historical density figures is that, prior to 1948, the Department of Employment (then the Ministry of Labour) collected statistics only on the number of 'insured employees', not on all employees. The only source of information on all employees prior to 1948 is the decennial Census of Population. Thus the potential membership series prior to 1948 in Table 4.11 was obtained by taking the total occupied population of the UK – excluding employers, the self-employed and the armed forces, but including the unemployed – for each Census year, using linear interpolation for intervening years. From 1948, annual labour force statistics are available and have been used.

The general trends in union membership and density in the twentieth century can be summarised relatively succinctly. There was a steady growth in membership and density from 1906 to 1913; after a pause in 1914, both series climbed rapidly to record levels of 8.3 million members and a density of 45.2 per cent in 1920. This peak was followed by two years of precipitate decline which then led to more than a decade of steady erosion of membership. The bottom of the trough was reached in 1933 with a density of 22.6 per cent – roughly half the level of 1920 – and a membership of 4.4 million. The upswing that began gently in the mid-1930s continued to gather pace during the Second World War, peaking in 1948 at the same density level coincidentally as in 1920, 45.2 per cent, but with 9.4 million members due to the growth in the labour force. From 1948 to 1968, membership rose slowly in absolute terms but failed to keep pace with the growth of the labour force, thus resulting in a slight decline in density to 43–44 per cent. The period 1969 to 1979 was a period of dramatic sustained growth: membership increased by 3 million to 13.3 million and density rose to a peak of 54.4 per cent in 1979. Density stood at over 50 per cent for each year from 1974 to 1980. Since then, union membership and density have declined. Membership stood at a little over 11 million in 1984, a fall of over 2 million from its 1979 peak but still higher than at any time prior to 1969. If the unemployed are excluded from the potential membership figure, density moved from 57 per cent at the 1979 peak to 52.3 per cent in 1984, indicating that unions are still substantially as representative of the employed labour force at the end of the period as at the beginning.

Trends in male and female membership have generally followed aggregate membership trends with female membership and density at a lower overall level. Nevertheless, the final period of membership growth noted above (1969–79) was characterised by a substantially greater increase in female union density than in male density. Indeed, the aggregate increase in membership came almost in equal measure from male and female employees despite the still significantly lower share of total employment taken by women. Since 1982, however, separate series for male and female membership have no longer been published because of the increasing number of unions unable to provide an accurate disaggregation of their membership by sex.

Finally, Table 4.12 gives the membership of unions affiliated to the TUC and the Labour Party and expresses it as a percentage of total union membership given in Table 4.11. It will be seen from these series that the TUC has increased in representativeness over much of the century with only very few and relatively short-lived periods when the proportion of total union membership in the TUC actually declined. The 1960s and 1970s have seen the affiliation of almost all the major non-affiliated public sector unions such as NALGO (National and Local Government Officers Association), the NUT (National Union of Teachers), the IPCS (Institution of Professional Civil Servants) and the SCPS (Society of Civil and Public Servants), resulting in an affiliated membership of around 90 per cent of total union membership. As far as union membership affiliated to the Labour Party is concerned, Table 4.12 reveals the substantial negative impact of replacing 'contracting out' by 'contracting in' in the 1927 Trade Disputes Act, and the positive impact of

Table 4.12   Union membership affiliated to the TUC and the Labour Party, 1900–1984

Year	Membership affiliated to TUC (000s)	TUC membership as a proportion of total union membership (%)	Union membership affiliated to Labour Party (000s)	Union membership affiliated to Labour Party as a proportion of total union membership (%)
1900	1 200	59.3	353	17.4
1901	1 400	69.1	455	22.5
1902	1 500	74.5	847	42.1
1903	1 423	71.4	956	47.9
1904	1 541	78.3	855	43.5
1905	1 555	77.9	904	45.3
1906	1 700	76.9	975	44.1
1907	1 777	70.7	1050	41.8
1908	1 705	68.6	1127	45.4
1909	1 648	66.5	1451	58.6
1910	1 662	64.8	1394	54.3
1911	2 002	63.8	1502	47.8
1912	2 232	65.3	1858	54.4
1913	—[1]	—	—[2]	—
1914	2 682	64.7	1572[3]	37.9
1915	2 851	65.4	2054	47.1

Table 4.12—*continued*

Year	Membership affiliated to TUC (000s)	TUC membership as a proportion of total union membership (%)	Union membership affiliated to Labour Party (000s)	Union membership affiliated to Labour Party as a proportion of total union membership (%)
1916	3 082	66.4	2171	46.7
1917	4 532	82.4	2415	43.9
1918	5 384	80.9	2960	45.3
1919	6 505	82.1	3464	43.7
1920	6 418	76.9	4318	51.7
1921	5 129	77.3	3974	59.9
1922	4 369	77.7	3279	58.3
1923	4 328	79.7	3120	57.5
1924	4 351	78.5	3158	57.0
1925	4 366	79.3	3338	60.6
1926	4 164	79.8	3352	64.2
1927	3 875	78.8	3239	65.8
1928	3 673	76.4	2025[4]	44.2
1929	3 744	77.1	2044	42.1
1930	3 719	76.8	2011	41.5
1931	3 613	78.1	2024	43.8
	3 368	75.8	1960	44.1
1933	3 295	75.0	1899	43.2
1934	3 389	73.8	1858	40.5
1935	3 615	74.3	1913	39.3
1936	4 009	75.7	1969	37.2
1937	4 461	76.4	2037	34.9
1938	4 669	77.1	2158	35.7
1939	4 867	77.3	2214	35.2
1940	5 079	76.8	2227	33.7
1941	5 433	75.8	2231	31.1
1942	6 042	76.6	2206	28.0
1943	6 642	81.3	2237	27.4
1944	6 576	81.3	2375	29.4
1945	6 671	84.7	2510	31.9
1946	7 540	85.7	2635	29.9
1947	7 791	85.2	4386[5]	48.0
1948	7 937	84.8	4751	50.7
1949	7 883	84.6	4946	53.1
1950	7 828	84.3	4972	53.5
1951	8 020	84.2	4937	51.8
1952	8 088	84.4	5072	52.9
1953	8 094	85.0	5057	53.1
1954	8 107	84.7	5530	57.8
1955	8 264	84.8	5606	57.6
1956	8 305	84.9	5658	57.9
1957	8 337	84.8	5644	57.4
1958	8 176	84.8	5628	58.4
1959	8 128	84.5	5564	57.8

continued overleaf

Year	Membership affiliated to TUC (000s)	TUC membership as a proportion of total union membership (%)	Union membership affiliated to Labour Party (000s)	Union membership affiliated to Labour Party as a proportion of total union membership (%)
1960	8 299	84.4	5513	56.1
1961	8 313	84.0	5550	56.1
1962	8 315	84.1	5503	56.5
1963	8 326	83.8	5507	55.4
1964	8 771	87.0	5502	54.6
1965	8 868	87.1	5602	55.0
1966	8 787	86.9	5539	54.8
1967	8 726	87.5	5540	55.6
1968	8 875	88.3	5364	53.3
1969	9 402	89.7	5462	52.1
1970	10 002	89.4	5519	49.3
1971	9 895	88.9	5559	49.9
1972	10 001	88.0	5425	47.8
1973	10 022	87.5	5365	46.8
1974	10 364	88.1	5787	49.2
1975	11 036	91.8	5750	47.8
1976	11 516	93.0	5800	46.8
1977	11 865	92.4	5913	46.0
1978	12 128	92.5	6260	47.7
1979	12 173	91.6	6450	48.5
1980	11 601	89.6	6427	49.6
1981	11 006	90.9	6282	51.9
1982	10 510	90.7	6189	53.4
1983	10 082	88.9	6116	53.9
1984	9 855	88.9	n.a.	n.a.

Notes:
1. No TUC Congress was held in 1914 and hence no affiliation figures for 1913 were published.
2. Figures for Labour Party affiliations for 1913 are not available for reasons connected with the Osborne Judgment of 1909 which restrained unions from using their funds for political purposes.
3. The 1913 Trade Union Act partially reversed the Osborne Judgment. From 1914 to 1927 unions were able to establish separate political funds, with a specific political levy on members, and objectors were given the right to 'contract out' of paying the levy.
4. The Trade Disputes Act of 1927 replaced 'contracting out' with 'contracting in' for the period up to 1946. That is, members wishing to pay the levy had to specifically indicate this wish to the union.
5. The 1927 Act was repealed in 1946 and 'contracting in' was replaced by 'contracting out', as had obtained in the 1914–27 period.

Sources: The TUC's affiliated membership is taken from its Annual Reports. Union membership affiliated to the Labour Party was obtained from Cole (1948:480) and from the Labour Party's Annual Conference Reports.

reversing this provision in 1946. There have been no new affiliations to the Labour Party since the Post Office Engineering Union in 1964 and, despite the reballoting required by the 1984 Trade Union Act, no disaffiliations. The changing proportion of members in Labour Party affiliated unions thus simply reflects the changing proportion of total membership accounted for by affiliated unions.[22]

INDUSTRIAL DISPUTES

Detailed information on strikes and lockouts is available from 1888 when the Board of Trade began publication of an annual *Report on Strikes and Lockouts*. This was published up to 1913 and included details of each industrial dispute resulting in a stoppage of work. A monthly article on strikes has appeared in the *Ministry of Labour Gazette* (now the *Employment Gazette*) since 1893, and since 1914 the *Gazette* has also provided a more detailed annual analysis. Comprehensive national data are thus available on the three main dimensions of dispute activity: the number of strikes, the number of workers involved, and the number of working days 'lost'. Further breakdowns by industry and by region, as well as by size and length, are available for much of the period after the Second World War and some years between 1919 and 1939 (CSO, 1978; Durcan, McCarthy and Redman, 1983). Analyses of the causes of disputes and the results and methods of settlement have also been published from time to time in the *Abstracts of Labour Statistics* and, as far as causes are concerned, are still published monthly in the *Employment Gazette*.[23] The accuracy and interpretation of these data have been the subject of considerable debate and academic commentary (Turner, 1969; McCarthy, 1970; Silver, 1973; Edwards, 1983), but a few key points can be restated here by way of qualification to the data provided in Table 4.13.

The first important problem is understatement. The Department excludes all strikes not connected with terms and conditions of employment. Stoppages for 'political' reasons such as the anti-conscription, anti-war and anti-'intervention' strikes at the end of the First World War, and the major strikes against the Industrial Relations Act 1971 are excluded. A more substantial exclusion are all strikes involving fewer than ten workers or lasting less than a day, unless the strike involves a total of at least 100 working days 'lost'. This means that a number of lightning strikes, one- and two-hour demonstration strikes, and rolling strikes are excluded. The only large-scale systematic survey of dispute activity in manufacturing industry suggested that there are one and a half times as many strikes lasting less than a day as there are strikes of a day or more, and hence that the *number* of strikes in the official series represents only about a quarter of the total number of strikes in this sector (Brown, 1981: 98–100). A further understatement occurs because it is not obligatory to report a dispute to the Department of Employment; many disputes that meet

Table 4.13 Industrial disputes in the United Kingdom, 1900–1984

Year	All industries				% Strikes lasting less than 3 days	Excluding coal-mining			
	No. of stoppages	Workers involved (000s)	Days lost (000s)	D/W		No. of stoppages	Workers involved (000s)	Days lost (000s)	D/W
1900	633	189	3 088	16.3		511	n.a.	2 648	n.a.
1901	631	180	4 130	22.9		455	n.a.	2 388	n.a.
1902	432	255	3 438	13.5		271	49	1 043	21.3
1903	380	114	2 320	20.4		267	56	1 105	19.7
1904	346	84	1 464	17.4		246	42	866	20.6
1905	349	94	2 368	25.2		266	53	1 239	23.4
1906	479	218	3 019	13.8		398	136	2 226	16.4
1907	585	148	2 148	14.5		498	98	1 618	16.5
1908	389	296	10 785	36.4		253	n.a.	9 510	n.a.
1909	422	301	2 687	8.9		227	31	518	16.7
1910	521	515	9 867	19.2		310	220	4 391	20.0
1911	872	962	10 155	10.6		702	823	6 090	7.4
1912	834	1463	40 890	27.9		687	358	9 329	26.1
1913	1459	689	9 804	14.2		1296	486	8 506	17.5
1914	972	449	9 878	22.0		814	177	6 160	34.8
1915	672	453	2 953	6.5		593	155	1 312	8.5
1916	532	284	2 446	8.6		465	223	2 135	9.6
1917	730	821	5 647	6.9		602	554	4 476	8.1
1918	1165	1132	5 875	5.2		1018	764	4 710	6.2
1919	1352	2586	34 969	13.5		1140	1680	27 528	16.4
1920	1607	2024	26 568	13.1		1397	610	9 144	15.0
1921	763	1829	85 872	47.0		616	578	13 179	22.8
1922	576	556	19 850	35.7		421	438	18 604	42.5
1923	628	407	10 672	26.2		442	219	9 489	43.3
1924	710	616	8 424	13.7		520	480	6 861	14.3
1925	603	445	7 952	17.9		439	315	4 499	14.3
1926	323	2751	162 233	59.0		260	1701	15 799	9.3
1927	308	114	1 174	10.3		198	41	486	11.9

Year								
1928	302	124	1 388	11.2		205	42	936	22.3
1929	431	534	8 287	15.5		278	455	7 711	16.9
1930	422	309	4 399	14.2		272	160	3 736	23.4
1931	420	492	6 983	14.2		273	211	4 135	19.6
1932	389	382	6 488	17.0		278	330	6 201	18.8
1933	357	138	1 072	7.8		245	66	626	9.5
1934	471	134	959	7.2		328	61	594	9.7
1935	553	279	1 955	7.0		336	79	587	7.4
1936	818	322	1 829	5.7		548	141	977	6.9
1937	1129	610	3 413	5.6		672	218	1 917	8.8
1938	875	275	1 334	4.9		512	102	637	6.2
1939	940	337	1 356	4.0		536	132	791	6.0
1940	922	299	940	3.1		541	110	435	4.0
1941	1251	362	1 079	3.0		781	207	744	3.6
1942	1303	457	1 527	3.3	77.3	777	205	687	3.4
1943	2785	559	1 808	3.2	80.6	942	265	918	3.5
1944	2194	826	3 714	4.5	80.9	941	258	1 234	4.8
1945	2293	532	2 835	5.3	77.2	987	289	2 194	7.6
1946	2205	530	2 158	4.1	77.8	876	313	1 736	5.5
1947	1721	623	2 433	3.9	76.2	668	315	1 521	4.8
1948	1759	426	1 944	4.6	78.6	643	237	1 480	6.2
1949	1426	434	1 807	4.2	76.8	552	186	1 053	5.7
1950	1339	303	1 389	4.6	76.5	479	161	958	6.0
1951	1719	379	1 694	4.5	74.7	661	244	1 344	5.5
1952	1714	416	1 792	4.3	79.2	493	143	1 132	7.9
1953	1746	1374	2 184	1.6	79.8	439	1206	1 791	1.5
1954	1989	450	2 457	5.5	80.6	525	246	1 989	8.1
1955	2419	671	3 781	5.6	81.1	636	317	2 669	8.4
1956	2648	508	2 083	4.1	81.6	572	267	1 581	5.9
1957	2859	1359	8 412	6.2	82.2	635	1094	7 898	7.2
1958	2629	524	3 462	6.6	83.1	666	276	3 012	10.9
1959	2093	646	5 270	8.2	78.1	786	454	4 907	10.8
1960	2832	819	3 024	3.7	76.7	1166	581	2 530	4.4
1961	2686	779	3 046	3.9	73.7	1228	530	2 309	4.4
1962	2449	4423	5 798	1.3	72.6	1244	4268	5 490	1.3
1963	2068	593	1 755	3.0	75.3	1081	440	1 429	3.2

continued overleaf

196

Table 4.13—continued

Year	All industries					Excluding coal-mining			
	No. of stoppages	Workers involved (000s)	Days lost (000s)	D/W	% Strikes lasting less than 3 days	No. of stoppages	Workers involved (000s)	Days lost (000s)	D/W
1964	2524	883	2277	2.6	75.3	1466	711	1975	2.8
1965	2354	876	2925	3.3	68.8	1614	759	2513	3.3
1966	1937	544	2398	4.4	68.0	1384	494	2280	4.6
1967	2116	734	2787	3.8	65.6	1722	693	2682	3.9
1968	2378	2258	4690	2.1	61.0	2157	2228	3636	2.1
1969	3116	1665	6846	4.1	62.3	2930	1520	5807	3.8
1970	2906	1801	10980	6.1	54.9	3746	1683	9890	5.9
1971	2228	1178	13551	11.5	50.7	2093	1155	13488	11.7
1972	2497	1734	23909	13.8	48.5	2273	1393	13111	9.4
1973	2873	1528	7197	4.7	49.1	2572	1481	7107	4.8
1974	2922	1626	14750	9.1	42.8	2736	1320	9125	6.9
1975	2282	809	6012	7.4	40.6	2070	781	5960	7.6
1976	2016	668	3284	4.9	46.7	1740	630	3214	5.1
1977	2703	1166	10142	8.7	41.0	2441	1113	10054	9.0
1978	2471	1042	9405	9.0	42.4	2133	938	9210	9.8
1979	2080	4608	29474	6.4	42.0	1782	4555	29361	6.4
1980	1330	834	11964	14.3	51.4	1028	748	11812	15.8
1981	1338	1513	4266	2.8	55.5	1036	1415	4031	2.8
1982	1528	2103	5313	2.5	60.1	1125	1878	4939	2.6
1983	1352	574	3754	6.5	55.6	997	441	3270	7.4
1984	1206	1464	27135	18.5	51.7	1128	1183	4652	3.9

Note: D/W series gives the average number of days lost per worker involved in the year.
Sources: All industries: 1900–1936 from Ministry of Labour (1937:127); 1937–84 from the annual article in the *Employment Gazette*.
Excluding coal-mining: Number of stoppages and number of days lost up to 1976 Smith *et al.* (1978); from 1976 Edwards (1983:211).
Number of workers involved from *Employment Gazette*.

the Department's criteria are not reported, and the same survey suggested that only 62 per cent of strikes eligible for inclusion were, in fact, reported (Brown, 1981: 98–100). Finally, all other forms of dispute such as 'go-slows', overtime bans, or working to rule, are excluded, because of the obvious difficulties of definition and measurement and the practicalities of reporting that would be involved.

The second important problem is the ambiguity of classification involved in the various measures used. It is, for example, sometimes difficult to distinguish between a single strike which spreads from one firm or area to another, and a series of separate sympathetic strikes. Thus year-to-year comparisons in the number of strikes or their 'average' size may be badly distorted. It is also difficult to know with precision how many workers are actually involved, or precisely when certain groups stopped work or started again. The actual numbers of days 'lost' may thus be distorted, as may the distribution of those days between workers 'directly' and 'indirectly' involved. This distinction has been retained for many years, but there is an inevitable arbitrariness in the recording employers' assessment of who is actually involved in the primary dispute and who has been laid off as a consequence.[24]

The implications of these difficulties for the interpretation of strike trends have been discussed at length by Edwards (1983: 210). As far as the underrecording of small strikes is concerned, he argues that:

> while the ... published figures do not measure the true number of strikes, these figures can be used to examine broad trends. Since recording practices have remained largely the same the figures should pick up the same sort of strikes from one year to the next, so that changes in the number recorded reflect real changes in the number of strikes coming within the Department's criteria. More detailed breakdowns must, however, be treated with caution.

The figures for workers involved and days 'lost' tend to be more accurate measures than the estimate of the number of strikes. This is because workers involved and days lost are concentrated in a few large stoppages. The data presented in Table 4.13 are based on the form of presentation used by Edwards. The main indices of strike activity (number, workers involved, days 'lost') for the years 1900–1984 are shown, both including and excluding coal mining. In certain periods, the trend of strikes in coal mining has been very different from other industries, and the aggregate figures thus obscure the picture elsewhere in the economy. Comprehensive accounts of British strike trends can be found in Hyman (1984), Smith *et al.* (1978), and Edwards (1983).

Notes

1. For a more complete discussion of historical labour force statistics and of their strengths and weaknesses, see Devons (1961: chapters 2 and 3) and Lewes (1967: chapter 2). For discussions of contemporary series, see Buxton and MacKay (1977) and CSO (1986a: chapter 5).
2. See CSO (1951) for a discussion of each Census prior to 1951.
3. The abolition of an 'employers and proprietors' category from 1971 and its replacement with data on self-employment may have slightly distorted the relative rates of growth of the manual and non-manual categories after that date.
4. The decline in the manual share of the labour force from 1971 to 1981 represents its most rapid rate of decline since the 1911 Census; since the Census was carried out in early 1981, the full effects of the recession on manufacturing employment are not reflected in these figures.
5. See, for example, Blaxall and Reagan (1976), Myrdal and Klein (1968), and Mackie and Patullo (1977).
6. Participation rates are sometimes computed on the basis of the whole population instead of the population of working age, which is in this context the population 'at risk'. The usefulness of computing on the basis of the whole population lies in calculating the ratio of active to dependent persons in the economy, and in international comparisons where the definition of the population of working age may vary. Since neither of these conditions applies here the population of working age is used. It should be noted that in British official publications the term 'activity rate' is normally used instead of the term 'participation rate'.
7. The best surveys of British trends in labour force participation are to be found in Hakim (1979) and Hunt (1968). See also Gales and Marks (1974).
8. The higher participation rate recorded for 1966 was accounted for in the first edition of this volume by the under-recording of part-time women workers in the 1961 Census. This was corrected at the 1966 Census. If this was an appropriate and accurate correction, it would seem that the continued subsequent growth of part-time work has been counterbalanced by the declining levels of participation due to longer periods in full-time education and earlier retirements.
9. For a comprehensive analysis of unemployment statistics, see Garside (1980). Only aggregate unemployment data are discussed here, but it should be noted that official series are currently available which classify unemployment data by region, occupation, industry, age, sex, and duration. See the *Employment Gazette* for details of these series.
10. See Committee on Industry and Trade (1926: 219–20, 244–5) and Beveridge (1944: 40–46).
11. Numbers benefiting from special employment measures at the end of March 1986 were 357 000; 265 219 YTS trainees were recorded at the same date. (Both figures exclude Northern Ireland.) A proportion of these people would probably have been employed in the absence of the special schemes, so any estimate made for the purposes of compiling a consistent series must inevitably be tentative (*Employment Gazette*, May 1986: 173–4).
12. See, for example, the report in *The Guardian*, 14 August 1986, where the Unemployment Unit is reported as calculating a figure of 3.8 million unemployed (15.4 per cent) as against the official figure of 3.2 million (11.7 per cent) published by the Department of Employment. For an official statement, see *Economic Trends* (CSO, June 1986).
13. The data are also available on a disaggregated basis by sex, age groups, industry, and region. For details, see the *Employment Gazette*.

14. For information on other series, see Devons (1961: 193–205), Lewes (1967: 31–6), DEP (1971), and the *Employment Gazette.*
15. No official analysis is published of the contribution made by each of these factors to the differential movement of rates and earnings, although up to 1948 the Ministry of Labour used to make estimates of the effect on average earnings of the changes in the distribution of the labour force by industry, sex, and age.
16. However, the details of wage rates, hours and other conditions of service included in national collective agreements for manual workers are still published in a loose-leaf form by the Department of Employment. See *Time Rates of Wages and Hours of Work* published annually by the Department of Employment Statistics Division.
17. For a detailed explanation of this index, see Ministry of Labour and National Service (1944).
18. See a series of articles by R. G. D. Allen in the LCES *Bulletin,* 25 (11 August 1947), 74–6; 26 (18 February 1948), 18–19; and 27 (February 1949), 15–17. See also Seers (1949a and 1949b).
19. For a detailed explanation of this index, see Ministry of Labour (1967).
20. See the *Employment Gazette* (HMSO, monthly) for these pensioner indices.
21. For a comprehensive review of the deficiencies of the retail price index, see Institute of Fiscal Studies (1986) and the *Observer,* 18 May 1986. For the Committee's report, see CSO (1986b); see also *Employment Gazette* (September 1986): 373–9.
22. For a comprehensive survey of union membership trends, see Bain and Price (1983).
23. See CSO (1958: 45) for detailed information on the early sources of statistics on strikes.
24. Workers laid off in *other* plants than the one where the dispute occurs are *not* included in the series.

References

ALLEN, R. G. D. (1947, 1948, 1949) *London and Cambridge Economic Service Bulletin,* 25, 26, 27. (London: Times Newspapers Ltd.)
BAIN, G. S. (1970) *The Growth of White-Collar Unionism* (Oxford: Clarendon Press).
BAIN, G. S. and PRICE, R. J. (1980) *Profiles of Union Growth: A Comparative Statistical Portrait of Eight Countries* (Oxford: Blackwell).
BAIN, G. S. and PRICE, R. J. (1983) 'Union Growth: Dimensions, Determinants, and Destiny', in Bain (ed.) *Industrial Relations in Britain* (Oxford: Blackwell) 3–33.
BEVERIDGE, W. H. (1944) *Full Employment in a Free Society* (London: Allen & Unwin).
BLAXALL, M. and REAGAN B. (eds) (1976) *Women and the Workplace: The Implications of Occupational Segregation* (Chicago: University of Chicago Press).
BOWLEY, A. L. (1937) *Wages and Income in the United Kingdom Since 1860* (Cambridge: Cambridge University Press).
BOWLEY, A. L. (1952) 'Index-Numbers of Wage-Rates and Cost of Living', *Royal Statistical Society Journal,* Series A, 115(4) (September): 500–506.
BROWN, W. (ed.) (1981) *The Changing Contours of British Industrial Relations: A Survey of Manufacturing Industry* (Oxford: Blackwell).
BUXTON, N. and MACKAY, D. (1977) *British Employment Statistics* (Oxford: Blackwell).

CENTRAL STATISTICAL OFFICE (CSO) (1951) *Census Reports of Great Britain, 1801–1931* (London: HMSO).

CENTRAL STATISTICAL OFFICE (CSO) (1958) *Labour Statistics* (London: HMSO).

CENTRAL STATISTICAL OFFICE (CSO) (1978) *Labour Statistics* (London: HMSO).

CENTRAL STATISTICAL OFFICE (CSO) (1986a) *Guide to Official Statistics*, 5th edn (London: HMSO).

CENTRAL STATISTICAL OFFICE (CSO) (1986b) *Methodological Issues Affecting the Retail Price Index*, Cmnd 9848 (London: HMSO).

COLE, G. D. H. (1948) *A History of the Labour Party Since 1914* (London: Routledge).

COMMITTEE ON INDUSTRY AND TRADE (1926) *Survey of Industrial Relations* (London: HMSO).

DEPARTMENT OF EMPLOYMENT (DE) (1978) *British Labour Statistics: Yearbook 1976* (London: HMSO).

DEPARTMENT OF EMPLOYMENT AND PRODUCTIVITY (DEP) (1969) *Statistics on Incomes, Prices, Employment and Production*, no. 29 (June) (London: HMSO).

DEPARTMENT OF EMPLOYMENT AND PRODUCTIVITY (DEP) (1971) *British Labour Statistics: Historical Abstract 1886–1968* (London: HMSO).

DEVONS, E. (1961) *An Introduction to British Economic Statistics* (Cambridge: Cambridge University Press).

DURCAN, J., McCARTHY, W. E. J. and REDMAN, G. (1983) *Strikes in Post-War Britain* (London: Allen & Unwin).

EDWARDS, P. K. (1983) 'The Pattern of Industrial Action', in Bain (ed.) *Industrial Relations in Britain* (Oxford: Blackwell) 209–34.

FEINSTEIN, C. (1972) *National Income, Expenditure and Output of the United Kingdom 1855–1965* (Cambridge: Cambridge University Press).

GALES, K. and MARKS, P. (1974) 'Twentieth Century Trends in the Work of Women in England and Wales', *Journal of the Royal Statistical Society*, Series A, 137 (I): 60–74.

GARSIDE, W (1980) *The Measurement of Unemployment* (Oxford: Blackwell).

HAKIM, C. (1979) *Occupational Segregation*, Department of Employment Research Paper no. 9 (London: HMSO).

HILTON, J. (1923) 'Statistics of Unemployment Derived from the Working of the Unemployment Insurance Acts', *Royal Statistical Society Journal*, 86 (March): 154–205.

HINES, A. G. (1964) 'Trade Unions and Wage Inflation in the United Kingdom, 1863–1961', *Review of Economic Studies*, 31 (October): 221–52.

HUNT, A. (1968) *A Survey of Women's Employment* (London: HMSO).

HYMAN, R. (1984) *Strikes*, 3rd edn (London: Fontana).

INSTITUTE OF FISCAL STUDIES (1986) *The RPI and the Cost of Living*, IFS Report Series no. 22 (London: Institute of Fiscal Studies).

LEWES, F. M. M. (1967) *Statistics of the British Economy* (London: Allen & Unwin).

LONDON AND CAMBRIDGE ECONOMIC SERVICE (LCES) (nd) *The British Economy: Key Statistics 1900–1966* (London: Times Newspapers).

McCARTHY, W. E. J. (1970) 'The Nature of Britain's Strike Problem'. *British Journal of Industrial Relations*, 8 (July): 224–36.

MACKIE, L. and PATULLO, P. (1977) *Women at Work* (London: Tavistock).

MINISTRY OF LABOUR (1937) *Twenty-Second Abstract of Labour Statistics of the United Kingdom*, Cmd 5556 (London: HMSO).

MINISTRY OF LABOUR (1967) *Method of Construction and Calculation of the Index of Retail Prices*, Studies in Official Statistics no. 6 (London: HMSO).

MINISTRY OF LABOUR AND NATIONAL SERVICE (1944) *The Cost of Living Number: Method of Compilation* (London: HMSO).

MINISTRY OF LABOUR AND NATIONAL SERVICE (1947) *Interim Report of the Cost of Living Advisory Committee*, Cmd 7077 (London: HMSO).

MINISTRY OF LABOUR AND NATIONAL SERVICE (1952) *Interim Index of Retail Prices: Method of Construction and Calculation* (London: HMSO).

MITCHELL, B. R. and DEANE, P. M. (1962) *Abstract of British Historical Statistics* (Cambridge: Cambridge University Press).

MYRDAL, A. and KLEIN, V. (1968) *Women's Two Roles: Home and Work*, 2nd edn (London: Routledge).

PHELPS BROWN, E. H. and HOPKINS, S. V. (1950) 'The Course of Wage-Rates in Five Countries, 1860–1939', *Oxford Economic Papers*, New Series, II(2) (June): 226–96.

ROUTH, G. (1965) *Occupation and Pay in Great Britain* (Cambridge: Cambridge University Press).

SEERS, D. (1949a) *Changes in the Cost of Living and the Distribution of Income Since 1938* (Oxford: Blackwell).

SEERS, D. (1949b) *The Levelling of Incomes Since 1938* (Oxford: Blackwell).

SILVER, M. (1973) 'Recent British Strike Trends: A Factual Analysis', *British Journal of Industrial Relations*, 11 (March): 66–104.

SMITH, C. T. B., CLIFTON, R., MAKEHAM, P., CREIGH, S. W. and BURN, R. V. (1978) *Strikes in Britain: A Recent Study of Industrial Stoppages in the United Kingdom*, Department of Employment Manpower Papers 15 (London: Department of Employment).

TURNER, H. A. (1969) *Is Britain Really Strike-Prone? A Review of the Incidence, Character and Costs of Industrial Conflict* (London: Cambridge University Press).

5 Social Mobility

Kenneth Macdonald and John Ridge

Since the first edition of this chapter in 1972, impressive development has occurred in the 'state of the art'. We then noted the lack of authoritative data, and tried to assemble some fragments from a variety of sources: their deficiency has been largely remedied by the major study of England and Wales carried out from Nuffield College, Oxford in 1972 (Goldthorpe *et al.* 1980), extended in some respects to 1983 (Goldthorpe and Payne, 1986). The British Election studies, reworked by Heath *et al.* (1985), now provide a complementary source: in particular it allows comparison of the social mobility of women with that of men. The paradigm of analysis that we sketched in 1972 has been superseded by developments of log-linear modelling, which at that date was little known and less used by sociologists. As a result, the literature on social mobility has become even more complex technically: fortunately there is now an excellent substantive introduction and review (Heath, 1981), while the basic elements of log-linear models are covered by Gilbert (1981). In this chapter we summarise some of the main findings on trends in England and Wales, then discuss a related, but as yet unresolved, question – whether it is appropriate to treat industrial societies as homogeneous units.

REPLICATING GLASS

To provide information on trends in mobility was, of course, a major aim of the 1972 Oxford survey of men living in England and Wales (the study hereafter abbreviated to OMS). The obvious and preferred method is to compare results from two or more studies at different points in time. This committed OMS to 'replicating Glass'; that is, collecting and coding data in such a way that direct comparisons could be made with the earlier national study carried out in 1949 by Glass and his associates (Glass, 1954). However, as we argued in the first edition of this chapter, the 1949 study proved ill-suited to such a use. In particular, it was impossible to reproduce adequately the coding scheme used for converting occupational data into class or status categories (Macdonald, 1974). Hope (1981) details the results of a careful comparison: discrepancies between the 1949 and 1972 reports by members of a cohort represented in both samples suggest that differences in method between the two studies will confound and obscure any real changes (see also Goldthorpe *et al.*, 1980: p. 86, fn 6).

BIRTH COHORT ANALYSIS

Anticipating the difficulty of replication the OMS group had designed their sample so as to allow birth cohort analysis. This chiefly involved a sample size large enough to give a statistically adequate representation of a number of narrow age-bands.[1] Following Blau and Duncan (1967) respondents' 'origin' was specified as father's occupation at son's age 14 (not simply father's last or main occupation). To help reduce the effect of differences in length of career between age-groups, 'destination' was specified both as current occupation and as the occupation held ten years after starting work.

There are well-known difficulties in cohort analysis based on recall by members of different age-groups: differential recall bias, differential mortality, emigration, immigration. 'Here, as elsewhere in mobility research, it is easier to appreciate the likelihood of sizeable errors, both random and systematic, than to estimate them or to devise suitable corrections', (Duncan, 1965: 492). The only practical course is that suggested by Goldthorpe *et al.* (1980): 'We can only hope that what we would think *prima facie* likely is in fact the case: namely that any such distortions will not be of a magnitude capable of affecting significantly the major results that we report' (p. 68).

Birth cohort analysis aims to distinguish the effects of differences in age from those due to differences in location in time. But time differences are inextricably confounded with the possible effect of changes in the 'meaning' of cohort-membership at different times. A cohort's life-chances can be seen as influenced by a competition with members of all other age-groups, at each stage in that cohort's life. But cohort analysis removes that context, or at least assumes it is the same for all cohorts. This seems unrealistic. It may well be that the conditions of competition between age-groups vary from time to time: one might, for example, suspect that the chances of young people *relative to* those of older people were better in the 1960s than in the 1980s. But if this were the case we could not distinguish it from a (possibly distinct) overall change in the structure of opportunity between the two periods (from a 1980 sample we would necessarily *not* get a full sample of the 1960 population, only at best a sample of those who were then within a specific age-group). This limitation means that results are potentially ambiguous, for 'cohort' cannot simply be equated with 'time'.

MEASURES OF CLASS POSITION

Regardless of the feasibility of 'replicating Glass', the OMS group sought to replace Glass's status categories (based on the Hall-Jones 'prestige' scale) with a scheme of class categories reflecting similarities in the work and market situations of different occupations (the details and further references are given in Goldthorpe *et al.*, 1980: 39–42). The seven categories of the Goldthorpe scheme are often collapsed into three; a 'service' class of the two professional, administrative and managerial categories (I and II), an 'intermediate' class combining the clerical and sales (III), self-employed (non-professional) (IV) with technician and supervisor (V) categories, and a 'working' class of skilled (VI) and other (VII) manual workers (including farm labourers). Both versions are used in our tables and figures.

We use present (1972) occupation as our measure of destination. This reintroduces a confounding of age with time effects. However, the alternative (occupation ten years after starting work) has its own problems: in particular, there is a high level of missing data for the age-groups for whom this career-point coincided with National Service in the Second World War. Goldthorpe *et al.* (1980) have used both measures and compared the results. They conclude (pp. 69–71) that age effects can be largely ignored for those over 35, and that 1972 occupation can be used to measure destination provided that care is taken in interpreting effects among the youngest age-group, for whom present occupation is less adequate as a pointer to the class category of future occupations.

THE GENERAL MODEL

Table 5.1 summarises the experience of the OMS sample (restricted to those who were living in England and Wales at age 14). It is at once obvious that the outflow into the service class is quite high, and that this is bound to happen, because there are considerably more service-class destinations than origins (of the whole sample, 25 per cent were in the service class in 1972, but only 12 per cent had originated there). In other words, there has been a shift in the occupational structure. We cannot assess it very well from this table, since the distribution of origins refers to no well-defined time in the past, and reflects differences in fertility between classes (Duncan, 1966). Fortunately the shift is also clearly visible in Census data (Goldthorpe *et al.* 1980, Table 2.3), although the occupational categories are not identical.[2] In Table 4.1 of this volume Price and Bain bring the story up to 1981: the changes have continued, and in some cases accelerated (the recent shrinkage of the manual category is particularly marked).

As well as considering the absolute levels of mobility (the actual events that generated Table 5.1), we should also look at the equality of opportunity to share in the expansion of the service class. In Table 5.1 there seems to be a marked advantage to those from the service class in their access to it: 60 per cent of those with service origin are in the service class in 1972, compared with 29 per cent from the intermediate, and only 16 per cent from the working class. The traditional method for assessing equality of opportunity has been some variant on the comparison of actual mobility with the frequencies expected from a baseline model of 'perfect mobility' (in Glass's phrase). The aim is to

Table 5.1   Intergenerational mobility for men born 1908–47: outflow
(row) percentages

Origin	Destination			
	Service	*Intermediate*	*Working*	*All*
Service	60	26	14	12
Intermediate	29	37	34	32
Working	16	27	57	56
All	25	30	44	100

Notes: OMS sample, restricted to men living in England and Wales at
age 14.
For details of class schema, see Goldthorpe, *et al.* (1980: 39–
42).
Origin = occupation reported for father at respondent's age 14.
Destination = occupation in 1972.

separate out the effect of shifts in the occupational structure; in terms of the table, to 'control for the marginals'. As has been evident for some time (Duncan, 1966), variants on the χ^2 approach do not succeed in doing this. Instead, it has proved more effective to approach inequality of opportunity directly by calculating odds-ratios (Goldthorpe *et al.*, 1980: 77–82). For example, we can compare the chance ('odds') of going from the service class to the service class, rather than to the working class, with the odds on the same pair of destinations for those who start in the working class. In Table 5.1 the odds on a service-class destination are much better than evens for those from the service class (60:14), but quite the other way round for those from the working class (16:57). This particular aspect of difference in relative mobility chances can be summarised as the ratio of these odds, about 15 in this case: if the chances of the two origin classes were equal, the ratio would of course be 1.[3] A major advantage of conceiving of relative chances of mobility as odds-ratios is that they can readily be represented in log-linear models of the mobility table (Hauser, 1978: but see also the cautionary discussion in Macdonald, 1983a).

The pattern of relative mobility chances ('fluidity') in the OMS data has been analysed in this way by Goldthorpe *et al.* (1980: Chapter 3). They find that the absolute mobility observed is very largely a product of the shift in occupational structure (as reflected in the change in marginals), and that there remain considerable inequalities between origin classes in their access to, in particular, service-class positions: those of service-class origin are markedly more likely to be found in the service class than are men originating elsewhere. Their analysis of the patterns of mobility among all seven classes also reveals a distinctively high tendency for positions in class IV (the petty bourgeois group) to be inherited.

TRENDS TO 1972

We can now turn to the examination of trends in both absolute and relative mobility. Goldthorpe *et al.* (1980, Table 3.1, p. 70) present an outflow table of origin by the three possible destination measures. Our own analyses (Tables 5.2–5.5) refer to a slightly different subset of the OMS sample, those whose origin and destination are both located in the occupational structure of England and Wales: note that we here amalgamate the seven classes into three (Service, Intermediate and Working).

Outflow tables such as these can be regarded as a presentation of the origin-destination relation standardising for size of origin but not of destination class. Each row of percentages carries two (not three) distinct values, so we can represent each row as one point in a two-dimensional space.

A convenient mapping is the so-called triangular graph (for example, Dickinson, 1973, pp. 35–7), seen in Figure 5.1, where the value on a variable is measured along a line from a vertex, perpendicular to the opposite side (the vertex representing the value of 100 per cent on its associated variable, the opposite side representing zero). Simple geometry requires that the three

Table 5.2   Intergenerational mobility for men born 1908–17: outflow (row) percentages

	Destination			
Origin	*Service*	*Intermediate*	*Working*	*All*
Service	55	29	16	10
Intermediate	23	40	37	32
Working	14	29	57	59
All	21	33	47	100

Notes: As for Table 5.1.

Table 5.3   Intergenerational mobility for men born 1918–27: outflow (row) percentages

	Destination			
Origin	*Service*	*Intermediate*	*Working*	*All*
Service	61	24	15	11
Intermediate	30	39	31	33
Working	16	28	56	56
All	26	31	43	100

Notes: As for Table 5.1.

Table 5.4 Intergenerational mobility for men born 1928–37: outflow (row) percentages

	Destination			
Origin	Service	Intermediate	Working	All
Service	69	21	10	11
Intermediate	33	38	29	31
Working	17	30	53	58
All	28	32	40	100

Notes: As for Table 5.1.

Table 5.5 Intergenerational mobility for men born 1938–47: outflow (row) percentages

	Destination			
Origin	Service	Intermediate	Working	All
Service	64	23	13	15
Intermediate	30	35	35	32
Working	18	23	59	53
All	29	27	44	100

Notes: As for Table 5.1.

values thus defined have a constant sum – which is precisely the arithmetic constraint imposed by the percentages. Were a caste system in operation the point corresponding to the 'service' row (for example) would lie at the 'service' vertex (100 per cent self-recruitment). 'Perfect mobility', in the χ^2 sense, would mean that each row would be plotted in the same place (that of the 'all' row).[4]

In Figure 5.1 there appears to be some slight movement in the location of the class configuration in this space, though it remains fairly stable. In the trajectory for the service class it is likely that the marked kink with the youngest cohort reflects the immaturity of their careers. Otherwise, the overall movement of each class simply echoes that of the 'perfect mobility' points.

These, being simply the destination marginals, can be more directly presented. In Figure 5.2 we display for present (1972) occupation the proportions in each of the three broad classes for each of the four 10-year age-groups. The expansion of the service class is clear, and it seems likely that the apparent increase in the working class reflects simply the lack of worklife mobility by the youngest group: their mature destinations would show instead a more marked increase in the service class. Figure 5.3 shows that 'forced' mobility (reflecting the differences between origin and destination distributions) has

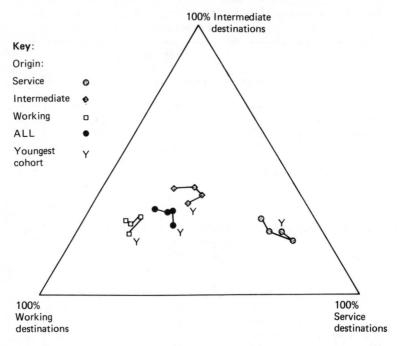

Figure 5.1   Triangular graph of OMS cohort outflow: by three origin classes and origin marginal, Tables 5.2–5.5

Notes:
See text for details of interpretations. For each origin class the lines join the four cohorts in a trajectory from oldest to youngest (Y). The triangle is equilateral.

increased more rapidly than has total mobility (the proportion of the sample who have moved out of their origin class by 1972), which in itself suggests that fluidity has if anything decreased over time. Again it is likely that the reversal of the trend with the youngest cohort simply reflects the lack of time they have had for mobility.

It looks then as if the continuing transformation of the occupational structure has led to modest increases in absolute mobility. But this tells us nothing about any changes in the relative chances of access by those from different origin classes. Of the many odds-ratios that could be calculated, an interesting one is that contrasting the odds that service-class men remain service class rather than enter the working class with the odds that working-class men enter the service class rather than remain working class. For the two oldest cohorts the (logged) value is 1.15 (a considerable inequality, bearing in mind that 'perfect mobility' corresponds to a logged value of 0): there is a sharp rise to 1.34 for those born in 1928–37, but the log odds-ratio then falls to 1.23 for the youngest cohort. If we allow for the immaturity of this last group,

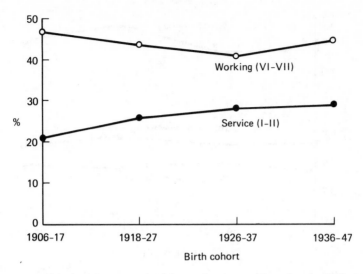

Figure 5.2 Percentage with occupations in service or working class in 1972, by birth cohort (from Tables 5.2–5.5)

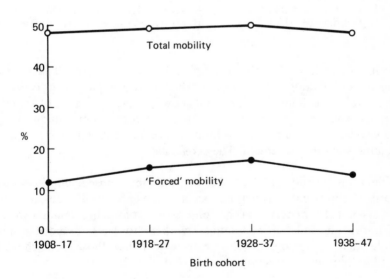

Figure 5.3 Overall mobility rates by birth cohort (in percentages)

Notes:
'Forced' mobility = index of dissimilarity between marginals of Tables 5.2–5.5.
Total mobility = per cent off diagonal, Tables 5.2–5.5.

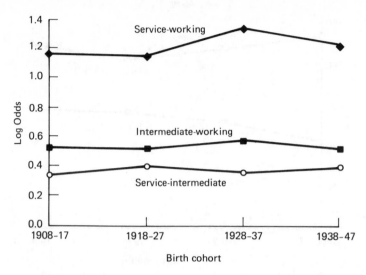

Figure 5.4   Symmetrical log odds-ratios, by birth cohort

Notes: Where S = *Service*, I = *intermediate*, W = *Working*, we calculate the odds-ratios
from the (Origin → Destination) cells, raw or percentaged, in Tables 5.2–5.5.
Read 'A:B' as 'the ratio of A to B' (*i.e.* 'A divided by B') – so the odds-ratio is a
ratio of ratios (or odds).

Service-Working	= [(S→S):(S→W)]	:	[(W→S):(W→W)]
Service-Intermediate	= [(S→S):(S→I)]	:	[(I→S) :(I→I)]
Intermediate-Working	= [(I→I) :(I→W)]	:	[(W→I):(W→W)]

we would expect the odds-ratio to go up, and continue this rise. The other two
'symmetrical' log odds-ratios (those in which only a single pair of classes are
involved) have much lower values, and show less clear evidence of trend: see
Figure 5.4. Thus the hypothesis of no change ('constant social fluidity') seems
broadly consistent with the data (Goldthorpe *et al.* 1980: pp. 80–1), although
some interesting trends remain. They conclude:

> If, then, one were pressed to pick out the most consequential change in
> relative mobility patterns that has occurrred over recent decades, one might
> well suggest the tendency, in the context of a contracting manual working
> class, for the sons of nonmanual workers to have 'avoided' manual
> employment to a progressively greater extent than those men who origi-
> nated within this contracting class. (p. 84).

THE PICTURE IN DETAIL

So we can conclude from log-linear modelling that there is no evidence overall for major and significant divergences from a common pattern of origin-destination interchange within the time period available. But so far we have only looked at the broad pattern of movement between the three amalgamated classes. If we move to the finer detail of the seven categories it is possible that there remain interesting (that is, interpretable) over-time shifts within the pattern of origin-destination movement. A possible tool would be to examine spatial representations based on multi-dimensional scaling of cohort-by-cohort dissimilarity measures between occupations.

There are two main traditions in the generation of such measures. The more prevalent (for example, Blau and Duncan, 1967: 67–75) involves the calculation of absolute percentage differences, typically on outflow data. These measure the percentage of sons from, say, categories A and B who would have to change their occupational destination for the outflow patterns from A and B to be identical. The other tradition would look at the interchange between two categories: Lauman (1966), for example, takes both the conditional probability given an A father of a B son, and the conditional probability given a B father of an A son, and feeds these to a program designed to merge asymmetric measures.

The two emphases could in principle yield divergent results: doctors and dentists, for example, might have similar patterns of extra-professional association but strong intra-profession self-recruitment. Thus they would appear closer on an outflow-pattern than on an interchange measure.

We have analysed the OMS cohort data using both approaches. The interchange measure we have upgraded to the (logarithm of) the pairwise (symmetrical) odds-ratio (see Macdonald, 1983a, p. 220), believing it to be better to contrast the exchange odds rather than average the entry probabilities. Since multi-dimensional scaling solutions are liable to varieties of local minima problem, we have undertaken both analyses using both Kruskal's stress formula 1 and Guttman's coefficient of alienation. With one exception all routes concur in returning, for each cohort, the straightforward configuration depicted in Fig 5.5.[5] For clarity, we have shown only the aggregate solution.

Given the matrix of dissimilarities between classes in terms of their outflow distributions, the program has calculated the implied distances that would be consistent with its input. There is a clear major dimension, ranking the classes in the expected way: VI and VII form a clear working class, but the affinity of I and II as a service class is not quite as clear. The second (vertical) dimension serves to underline the distinctive character of the petty bourgeois grouping, class IV. The picture is plausible and unsurprising: its notable feature in the context of trends in relative mobility patterns is that it applies almost equally well to all four cohorts.[6]

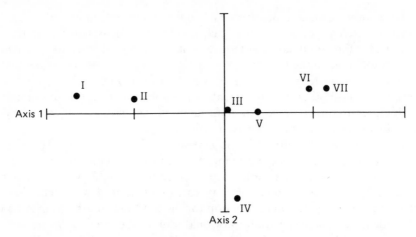

Figure 5.5   Outflow dissimilarity solution, aggregate OMS sample

Notes: for details see text page 211.
Class I, II – Professional, managerial
Class III – Routine white collar
Class IV – Petty bourgeois, including farmers
Class V – Foremen, etc.
Class VI, VII – Working.

AFTER THE RECESSION ...

The basic finding, then, is that there has been no increase in equality of opportunity or 'openness' of British society[7] in the period up to 1972, despite the opportunity that structural transformation and relatively low unemployment would seem to have offered. The implications for the recession beginning in 1973 are of great interest. It could be argued that this period would have seen a marked decline in openness: a reduction in the performance of the economy would halt structural transformation, stopping the engine of social mobility, and (as also by increasing the risk of unemployment) greatly increase the tenacity with which those in advantaged positions would work to transmit them to their children. The result might be a sudden increase in the perception of inequality (hitherto masked by high levels of absolute mobility, as well as overall increases in standard of living), with obvious political implications. But in fact the period seems not to have been marked by a shift to the left electorally, with few signs of a 'crisis of legitimacy'. It is obviously desirable to extend the OMS study forward in time to explain the failure of this expectation.

This difficult task has been carried out ingeniously, albeit laboriously, by Goldthorpe and Payne (1986). In collaboration with Social and Community Planning Research they were able to recode occupational data from the

British General Election study of 1983 (Heath *et al.*, 1985) into the OMS categories (and, for a sample, *vice versa*, as a check on the validity of recoding). From this it was possible to generate various versions of an origin-destination table (destination specified as 1983 occupation) for comparison with the experiences of the OMS sample as a whole. They find that there has been no change in the pattern of relative mobility chances between the two studies. On the assumptions of our previous paragraph, this seems highly unlikely. But in fact, as Goldthorpe and Payne go on to show, those assumptions are wrong. The rates of absolute mobility have remained high, indeed, 'forced' mobility has if anything risen. In particular, the service class has continued to grow in relative size, while the working class has contracted. But what has happened, of course, is that unemployment has gone up sharply, and has 'removed' from the occupational structure (and thus from competition) a large group of men in predominantly working-class occupations. For the remainder, the benign effects of structural transformation have continued: shifts in industrial structure away from manufacturing towards such 'services' as finance and tourism have been shifts from areas of predominantly working-class to areas of intermediate and service-class occupations. But in 1983, unlike 1972, it is not possible to ignore unemployment in the analysis of social mobility: Goldthorpe and Payne (1986: 18) conclude:

> In sum, then, one could say that the return of mass unemployment, in the British context at least, has had the general effect of 'raising the stakes' in the mobility 'game'. In particular, the chances of becoming mobile out of the working class or of avoiding mobility into it have taken on a still greater importance than before for the standard and style of life that an individual may anticipate. This is so because to occupy a working-class position so greatly increases the risk of experiencing the rather decisive form of downward social mobility that becoming – and perhaps for long remaining – unemployed must be taken to represent.

LOG-LINEAR MODELS

We now turn to a parallel analysis of data from some of the British Election studies. This has been made possible by the recoding by Heath *et al.* of the earlier datasets into the revised Goldthorpe class schema used in the 1983 survey (Heath *et al.*, 1985)[8]: the principles of the revision are described by Goldthorpe and Payne (1986: fn 2). In this and subsequent sections we make more detailed references to the results of log-linear modelling of multi-way tables: a brief review of the principles may be helpful.

The central narrative can be simply presented. Suppose as an illustration that we have a (realistically complex) table of origin by destination by region by cohort; let us use the shorthand of *ODRC* to refer to that table and, for example, OD to the aggregate origin by destination table within it (aggregated across region and cohort). Then the question is: how much information do we need to generate a set of expected values which are compatible with the full observed $ODRC$ table. If we could get by with knowing simply the aggregate two-way tables (such as OD), and from their cross-hatching produce a reasonable facsimile of the observed $ODRC$, this would be to say, amongst other things, that we do not need to assume that the connection between origin and destination varies by cohort (that is, we do not need to know ODC) and, *a fortiori*, we do not need to assume that mobility varies by cohort within region.

Models are specified by writing down the knowledge that they invoke (and note that, if we know ODC we, by implication, know OD, OC and DC). Attached to each model is a measure of how well it fits the data: conventionally this is provided by a statistic called G^2, with associated degrees of freedom. For our purposes we could, without much distortion, read G^2 as if it were χ^2, but the effective interpretation of the G^2 in relation to its degrees of freedom is provided by the associated 'p' value, which gives the probability that the presented model might have generated the observed data.

A fairly straightforward technology, though the statistics may often decline to adjudicate decisively between competing substantive models. Computationally, the modelling program starts with an 'estimated' $ODRC$ table of identical cells, and iteratively imposes upon it the information provided by the terms of the model. The more familiar χ^2 for a two-way table is simply an elementary instance of the technique: it involves fitting to (for example) an OD table, the model O,D; asking can we account for the observed value simply by knowing the distributions of the variables involved, or need we assume some OD interaction?

COMPARING MEN AND WOMEN

Goldthorpe and Payne (1986), as we have noted earlier, used the 1983 Election study in conjunction with the 1972 OMS to get two time-points for the study of trends, thus avoiding the problems of single-sample cohort analysis. In the same spirit we can treat the Election studies of 1964, 1974 and 1983 as points on a possible trend-line of changes in mobility patterns.

As a first step, we must find out whether the 1972 and 1974 mobility tables are actually as similar to each other as they should be, given their dates. We have 7640 men in our 1972 subset, and 877 men with classifiable occupations and aged 20–64 in the 1974 sample. They can be combined to give a table ODP (P referencing the two points in time): the model OD, OP fits very well, with a G^2 of 36.9 (42df, $p < 0.69$).[9] In other words there is overall a pattern of association between O and D (as expected), and also some significant difference between the two O distributions. But, crucially, we do not need to suppose that the OD pattern is different in the two studies (we do not need the term *ODP* in the model). The observed origin distributions are not in fact widely different:

Class	I	II	III	IV	V	VI	VII	
1972	6	5	7	13	12	29	27	100%
1974	4	9	7	12	8	34	26	100%

This is a satisfactory result: although there may be some query over the similarity of the origin distributions, there are no grounds for believing we have differing estimates of the origin-destination table in the temporally-adjacent OMS and 1974 samples.

As well as avoiding the problems of interpreting age-groups as cohorts, a further advantage of using the election studies is that we have data on women as well as men.

We can first ask whether the Election studies support our OMS conclusion that there are no changes over time in the patterns of relative mobility among men. Taking men (all ages, and with classifiable occupations) separately in a table *ODT* (origin by destination by timepoint = 1964, 1974 and 1983), we can fit the data very well with the model *OD*, *OT*, *DT* ($G^2 = 66.6$, with 72 *df*: $p < 0.66$). That is, all we need to postulate is that there is a constant pattern of relative mobility chances *OD*, and that both the origin and destination distributions change over time.

The same lack of change holds for women: the model *OD*, *OT*, *DT* fits satisfactorily, although less closely than for men ($G^2 = 91$, with 72 *df*: $p < 0.07$). However, it is worth noting that in both cases the percentage misclassified by the fitted model is low (5.3 per cent of men, and only 4.6 per cent of women), suggesting that there is little to be gained by supposing in either case that there really are trends over time. To make a more direct comparison of the experiences of men and women, we must amalgamate them into a single analysis.

We therefore include a variable *S* to capture any gender differences, and analyse the four-way table *ODST* (*S* = male/female, with *T* again being the three timepoints: 1964, 1974, 1983), with those with non-classifiable occupations again removed (reducing *N* from 6500 to 5014). A good fit is obtained with the very parsimonious model *OD*, *OT*, *DT*, *DS*, *TS* ($G^2 = 223.5$, with 210 *df*: $p < 0.25$), which misclassifies 6.3 per cent of the sample. This suggests that we need not suppose any changes in relative mobility patterns over time, nor any differences in the relative mobility patterns of men and women (at least for those with classifiable jobs). Both origin and destination distributions shift over time, and the destinations of women (but not their origins)[10] differ from those of men. This last result deserves emphasis. The women's destination distribution differs sharply from that of men in each study, but the difference is largely constant over time: the term *DS* representing this difference is by far the most important in terms of G^2 reduction. The aggregate distributions are:

Class	I	II	III	IV	V	VI	VII	
M	13	14	10	10	11	21	21	100%
F	3	18	47	3	2	5	23	100%

The most striking features are the concentration of women in the routine clerical occupations of Class III, and in the unskilled manual Class VII. Thus the absolute mobility of women over the period as a whole is largely a

Table 5.6　Intergenerational mobility of women – British General Election studies outflow (row) percentages

1964

	Destination				
Origin	*Service*	*Intermediate*	*Working*	*All*	*(N)*
Service	36	55	9	9	(33)
Intermediate	14	54	32	33	(115)
Working	9	46	45	58	(205)
All	13	49	38	100	(353)

1974

	Destination				
Origin	*Service*	*Intermediate*	*Working*	*All*	*(N)*
Service	54	38	8	13	(71)
Intermediate	15	58	26	27	(149)
Working	12	52	35	60	(325)
All	19	52	29	100	(545)

1983

	Destination				
Origin	*Service*	*Intermediate*	*Working*	*All*	*(N)*
Service	43	52	5	18	(246)
Intermediate	25	55	20	31	(409)
Working	14	53	33	51	(684)
All	23	53	24	100	(1339)

Notes:　From British Election Studies files, recosded to OMS class scheme. See text p. 213

movement from working-class origins to routine non-manual destinations: the outflow percentages for each time-point are given in Table 5.6 (collapsed into the three broad classes) and are compared with men's outflow patterns in the triangular graph of Figure 5.6. But despite this distinctive pattern of absolute mobility, the model suggests that women's relative chances of access to destinations, given origins, are not significantly different from men's.

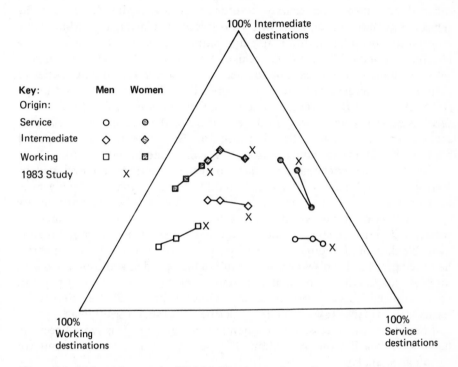

Figure 5.6   Triangular graph of British Election study outflows: three origin classes by sex; 1964, 1974 and 1983

Notes: See text S for details of interpretation. Lines join the samples in a trajectory from 1964 through 1974 to 1983 (x), for each origin class separately for men and woman.

As far as trends are concerned, there is a reasonable agreement with the OMS finding of changes in absolute mobility rates that are very much larger than changes in relative mobility; the hypothesis of 'constant social fluidity' is still consistent with the data, although there remain specific trends not significant in a global model. And it is also of interest that, at least with these data, and at this global level, we have located no strong evidence either of trends in women's (relative) social mobility or of differences from men's.

INTERNATIONAL COMPARISONS

A further striking development since 1972 has been the proliferation of national studies in broadly the same spirit as OMS, influenced to varying degrees by the major American study by Blau and Duncan (1967) and its successor (Featherman and Hauser 1978). In principle, these offer to one another a valuable interpretative context. In practice, however, differences in coding conventions and other design features make comparison difficult at other than a gross and usually uninformative level. This defect is being remedied by the continuing CASMIN-Project of the University of Mannheim. A group of sociologists, in a major international collaboration, have assembled into a standard form a data archive of national studies. This has already led to a number of publications focused on the search for communalities in patterns of intergenerational fluidity, including Erikson and Goldthorpe (1985, 1986), and the precursor studies by Erikson *et al.* (1979, 1982, 1983). Work is currently under way on the extension of these analyses to take into account the role of educational institutions in determining the rate and patterns of mobility in industrial societies (König and Müller, 1986).

The theory of 'convergence' among industrial societies as developed by Kerr *et al.* (1960) can, if interpreted literally, bring comparative analyses to bear on the measurement of trends. For if mobility rates and patterns are correlated with (if not generated by) levels of economic development, a society's mobility history could be reconstructed from the more readily available data on the course of its economy, at least once a 'calibration curve' had been produced. This is surely fanciful. In fact, the detailed comparisons so far made suggest that there are major common elements in the fluidity patterns of a number of societies (Erikson and Goldthorpe, 1985). Certainly there seems little evidence (over a range of societies) that such variation as is found can be related at all closely to economic development. This would seem to have some bearing on the notion of a society as a meaningful unit for sociological analysis.

The argument that industrial societies are essentially homogeneous is certainly crucial to many of the analyses presented by Blau and Duncan (1967). It is precisely this claim that has been strongly contested by critics, particularly Crowder (1974), arguing that functionalist models assume homogeneity, and prompt techniques of analysis that deny the reality of deviant and disadvantaged groups. If industrial societies are in fact mosaics of social groupings with different experiences, control over resources and so on, then it is surely improper to treat societies as units for the study of, *inter alia*, trends in patterns of relative social mobility. It could be argued that from one point of view the restriction of samples to men, characteristic of the '1970s' studies, is an admission of heterogeneity: women's experiences are assumed to be different. But if men are socially distinct from women, could not some men be similarly distinct from others? In fact Duncan himself rejected the assumption of homogeneity in his classic quantitative assessment of black disadvantage in the USA (Duncan, 1968). In England and Wales the OMS data give some support (limited by subgroup size) to the claim that members of immigrant groups are differently and significantly discriminated against in mobility chances (Heath and Ridge, 1983).

However, the image of a mosaic is seriously inconsistent with the claim of a common pattern among industrial societies. Suppose that a society is in fact composed of a set of subgroups with different mobility patterns: our particular concern in this chapter is with the set of subgroups formed by different cohorts. An aggregate similarity to another society could only come about if it were the case *both* that the mobility patterns of each subgroup were identical across societies *and* that both socieities had the same distribution of people across subgroups. Otherwise we would have to assume an amazing coincidence of differing compositional effects 'cancelling out'. It follows that we have to regard the fact of cross-national similarity as setting a rather low upper limit to the amount of variation within societies: in other words, there seems to be an *a priori* case for expecting little sign of trends in patterns of relative mobility, since trends are themselves a form of variation within society.[11] We might hypothesise that it is nevertheless within such limited variation that we should look for explanations of the idiosyncratic residuals in particular societies' mobility patterns that remain once the 'core pattern' has been extracted.[12] This, of course, does not help us to identify the relevant subgroups (they might well not be age-based), still less their differences in pattern of mobility. With this in mind, we turn to a comparison of mobility patterns between OMS sample members living in London and the South-East at age 14, and those living elsewhere at that age.

DISAGGREGATION

As we noted earlier, the relevance of regional to trend analysis is quite direct: the over-time varying economic fortunes of regions (in particular the differing nature of their employment base) might have produced over-time within-region variations in mobility pattern which would be obscured in the aggregate analysis.

There are many possible routes to the classification of region: the definitive British classification for the analysis of mobility has yet to be located, and it would not be within the scope of this chapter to present discussion in the detail needed to constitute an advance. Accordingly we have retreated to an 'incontestable' split of 'London and the South-East' against the 'rest'. Were there to exist different regional mobility trajectories, London and the South-East would surely show one such. We have taken OMS data, selecting 'region

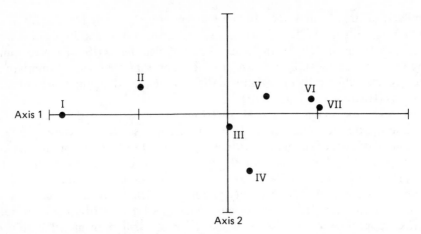

Figure 5.7   Outflow dissimilarity solution, OMS samples in London and the South-
East at age 14

Notes: As Figure 5.5. See text p. 000.

at age 14' as the appropriate regional allocation for our present purposes: did
subsequent careers depend on this point of origin, and were such dependencies
structured over time?

In log-linear formulation, this would imply that to fit the data *ODCR*
(where *R* indexes London and the South-East versus the rest and *C* stands for
cohort) we would need to include amongst others the terms *ODR* and *ODC*. In
fact the latter is not needed. We can achieve a satisfactory fit with the model
ODR, OC, DC, RC ($G^2 = 275.9$ with 252 *df*: $p < 0.14$). In other words, there is a
small but significant region effect on patterns of origin-destination movement,
represented by the need to include the term *ODR*. The drop in G^2 when we add
ODR to the model involving only two-way terms is clearly significant: G^2
decreases by 52.7 with 36 *df*: $p < 0.04$ (although the overall per cent misclassified – which a log-linear model does not formally minimise – drops only from
7.1 to 6.5). The two-way terms in the model imply that, as we would expect,
both origin and destination distributions shift across cohorts (there is little
difference between cohorts in regional distribution, and the term *RC* could be
omitted from the model without much loss). In addition, both origins and
destinations differ significantly between regions (in the model fitting all two-
way terms both are highly significant and are implied in *ODR*). But there is no
reason to suppose that relative mobility chances differ by cohort, even when
we disaggregate by region: the terms *ODC* and *ODCR* are not needed to
achieve a satisfactory fit.

As a first step to the interpretation of this difference between regions in
terms of relative social mobility we present in Figure 5.7 a map of the implied
distances among the seven classes, using the *MDSCAL* method deployed

earlier. It turns out that the configuration for those from England and Wales outside London and the South-East is indistinguishable from that for the whole sample as shown in Figure 5.5. But in Figure 5.7, for those in London and the South-East at age 14, at least one interesting difference can be seen. The structure overall is, of course, much the same, but it is noticeable that class IV has moved closer to, in particular, class III, while the similarity of classes III and V is less marked. One obvious interpretation would turn on the relative absence of farmers, with their distinctive outflow pattern, from London and the South-East. In London and the South-East 21 per cent of those with class IV origins are in class IV in 1972: elsewhere the figure is 31 per cent. But equally this attenuated distinctiveness of the petty bourgeois class in London and the South-East may reflect their greater access to the more plentiful class I positions in that region (19 per cent of destinations in London and the South-East, 12 per cent elsewhere: entered by 20 per cent of petty bourgeois men in London and the South-East, 11 per cent elsewhere).[13]

DETECTING TRENDS: A CAVEAT

Given that at best mobility tables integrate over a non-trivial time-period, there will remain the speculation that there may be recent changes – possibly even sizeable changes – which, since they are only represented in the experience of a small proportion of the sample (the youngest), though present, do not disturb the fit of the 'constant social fluidity' model. One response (a response reacting to the ease with which sociology can generate speculations – *entia non sunt multiplicanda praeter necessitatem*) would be to refrain from speculation. But there may be merit in attempting some location of the size of the problem.

Suppose we take the origin-destination table for the youngest cohort, modify each symmetrical odds-ratio by some factor x, rescale the resulting table to the original marginals, and replace the observed cohort by this modified cohort in the overall table. Where x is greater than unity this is equivalent to postulating a greater than observed closure in the recent cohort. We can observe the impact of this ploy upon the fit of the 'constant social fluidity' model as we change the value of x from 1.1 to 1.5 (from a 10 per cent to a 50 per cent increase in 'closure'). G^2 moves from its observed value of 116 ($p < 0.29$) to 115 ($p < 0.31$) for a 10 per cent increase in closure, and to 124 ($p < 0.14$) for a 50 per cent increase. There are more extreme transformations which also yield models compatible with the data. Consider applying the method to all four cohorts, generating two alternative versions of a marked change in closure across age-groups: when we fit the 'constant social fluidity' model to the resulting tables we find:

G^2 129.5 $p < 0.08$ ($x = 1.4, 1.2, 1, 0.8$ for cohorts 1, 2, 3, 4)
G^2 131.3 $p < 0.06$ ($x = 0.8, 1, 1.2, 1.4$, for cohorts 1, 2, 3, 4)

Each of these last two applications only misclassifies 5 per cent of cases (and the worst case accounts for around 93 per cent of the G^2 under independence – taking the model O, D, C as a baseline).

In amelioration, we should note that there are ways to detect such trends in odds-ratios. For example, we can look at selected residuals, or specify an explicit effect model: for a detailed discussion of such an attempt in the American context, see Macdonald (1983b). The multi-dimensional scaling strategies we used earlier may not be sensitive to temporal changes in the absolute, as opposed to the relative, distances between occupations (cf. 'Could you tell if the universe doubled in size last night?'). But we can take the 21 values of the pairwise (symmetrical) odds-ratios within each cohort and examine them for trends across cohort. The more extreme of the above modifications produce clear trend pictures, though distortions of the most recent cohort are more difficult to detect.

We can apply the same strategy to the observed data. The means of the logarithms of the symmetrical odds-ratios over the seven classes give the following monotonic trend:

Cohort   1908–17   1918–27   1928–37   1938–47
              1.54   1.68   1.72   1.75

If we amalgamate the cohorts, to produce a dataset of 84 symmetrical odds-ratios, and run regressions predicting their values as a function of cohort and occupational category, we find a cohort 'effect' of 0.07, being the increment in 'closure' at each cohort transition.

There are two points being made. First, at the level of data available, given quite large true shifts in closure over time, we would be unable to demonstrate that a 'constant social fluidity' model was incompatible with such data (and this is more acute if we postulate very recent change). Secondly, despite the fit of the constant social fluidity model, there are indications in the OMS data of increasing closure in recruitment as measured by the odds-ratios; the magnitude of the effect is not huge, but is consistent.

CONCLUSION

Overall, then, we may conclude that there is no compelling evidence of uniform and general changes over time in patterns of relative mobility in England and Wales. The specific changes that have taken place are in the direction of reduced openness: that is, of increased inequality of opportunity as between the different classes. In particular, in the period since 1972 it seems that unemployment has become a significant factor in differentiating the working class from other groups.

Notes

We are indebted to John Goldthorpe, Anthony Heath and Hiroshi Ishida for their helpful comments on an earlier draft of this chapter.

1. This was an important factor in the decision to restrict the sample to men. The experiences of men and women would have to be analysed separately (certainly in the period up to 1972), giving in effect two samples. It was feared that neither would be large enough for cohort or other subgroup analyses. The project's grant was sufficient only for one sample from a single population.

2. The Census data also suggest an explanation for what has been held to be a defect of Glass's 1949 study, that it produced origin and destination distributions almost identical to each other. In fact, the rapid growth of the service class was only just beginning in 1949, and would not be likely to be reflected in the experience of the 1949 sample.

3. In practice, odds-ratios are calculated from frequencies, not percentages, and are usually converted to logarithms. Details of the calculation of symmetrical or pairwise odds-ratios are spelt out in the notes to Figure 5.4.

4. This emphasises again that the 'old' mobility ratio – based on a comparison with perfect mobility in this sense – fails to 'control for the marginals'.

5. The exact co-ordinates are those of a virtually zero-stress Kruskal solution (with neatly linear Shepard diagram of distances against dissimilarities) from the absolute percentage differences for the aggregate origin-destination table. Odds-ratio analyses are very similar, except perhaps for a tendency to place skilled and unskilled manual closer together. Our overall result agrees with Mitchell and Critchley (1985) though from a different perspective. The (non-trend) interesting feature is that the petty bourgeois (class IV) are in fact further from their nominal 'neighbouring' classes than they would be were the display fully linear.

6. The only deviation arises from the multi-dimensional scaling analysis of the pairwise odds in the oldest cohort. It refuses to yield a well-fitting two-dimensional solution, but can be persuaded to converge (with a Kruskal stress of .0004) to a three-dimensional configuration in which the first two dimensions replicate the configuration of Figure 5.4, and the third dimension exists mainly to segregate 'manual foremen and technicians' from the rest.

7. For a broadly comparable study of Scotland in the same tradition, see Payne *et al.* (1981): the basic mobility table from these data is discussed by Goldthorpe *et al.* (1980: Table A.6 and p. 291). Whelan and Whelan (1984) give a thorough analysis of the available Irish data.

8. We are indebted to Anthony Heath for suggesting and permitting this use of the data, and for providing the necessary tabulations. Copies of the data were supplied by the ESRC Data Archive at the University of Essex. The earlier surveys were organised by David Butler (Nuffield College, Oxford) and Donald Stokes (University of Michigan), and from 1970 by a team at the University of Essex (including Ivor Crewe, Bo Sarlvik, James Alt and David Robertson).

9. Interestingly OP and DP are not providing interchangeable information: with OD, DP we get $G^2 = 58.9$, $p < 0.43$; OD, OP, DP gives $G^2 = 25.6$ and $p < 0.90$.

10. Unsurprisingly, since origin for both men and women is defined in terms of the occupation of the head of the household in which they grew up.

11. Alternatively, we might question the 'fact' of similarity itself. König and Müller (1986) suggest that, at least for France and West Germany, the OD similarity conceals different national patterns of transition between origin, education, entry to the labour market and current occupation. It remains to be seen whether this finding applies more generally.

12. Erikson and Goldthorpe (1986) are the first to have presented a fully-worked example of such analysis, with a 'core model' applied to the relative mobility patterns in nine industrial nations.
13. To carry this further we would need to specify this claim in an explicit effect model which is then fitted to the data. We do not undertake this here, since our concern is simply to gain some sense of the possible impact on trends of regional effects.

References

BLAU, P. M. and DUNCAN, O. D. (1967) *The American Occupational Structure* (New York: Wiley).

CROWDER, D. N. (1974) 'A critique of Duncan's Stratification Research; *Sociology*, 8.

DICKINSON, C. G. (1973) *Statistical Mapping and the Presentation of Statistics* (London: Edward Arnold).

DUNCAN, O. D. (1965) 'The trend of occupational mobility in the United States', *American Sociological Review*, 30: 491–8.

DUNCAN, O. D. (1966) 'Methodological Issues in the Analysis of Social Mobility', in Smelser, N. J. and Lipset, S. M. (eds) *Social Structure and Mobility in Economic Development* (Chicago: Aldine Press).

DUNCAN, O. D. (1968) 'Inheritance of Poverty or Inheritance of Race?', in Moynihan, D. P. (ed.) *On Understanding Poverty* (New York: Basic Books).

ERIKSON, R. and GOLDTHORPE, J. H. (1985) 'A Model of Core Fluidity in Industrial Nations', CASMIN Working Paper no. 5, University of Mannheim.

ERIKSON, R. and GOLDTHORPE, J. H. (1986) 'National Variation in Social Fluidity' CASMIN Working Paper no. 9, University of Mannheim.

ERIKSON, R., GOLDTHORPE, J. H. and PORTOCARERO, L. (1979) 'Intergenerational Class Mobility in Three Western European Societies', *British Journal of Sociology*, 30: 415–41.

ERIKSON, R., GOLDTHORPE, J. H. and PORTOCARERO, L. (1982) 'Social Fluidity in Industrial Nations', *British Journal of Sociology*, 33.

ERIKSON, R., GOLDTHORPE, J. H. and PORTOCARERO, L. (1983) 'Intergenerational Class Mobility and the Convergence Thesis', *British Journal of Sociology*, 34.

FEATHERMAN, D. L. and HAUSER, R. M. (1978) *Opportunity and Change* (New York: Academic Press).

GILBERT, G. N. (1981) *Modelling Society* (London: Allen & Unwin).

GLASS, D. V. (ed.) (1954) *Social Mobility in Britain* (London: Routledge).

GOLDTHORPE, J. H. and PAYNE, C. (1986) 'Trends in Intergenerational Class Mobility in England and Wales, 1972–1983' *Sociology*, 20 (1): 1–24.

GOLDTHORPE, J. H., with LLEWELLYN, C. and PAYNE, C. (1980) *Social Mobility and Class Structure in Modern Britain* (Oxford: Clarendon Press).

HAUSER, R. M. (1978) 'A structural model of the mobility table', *Social Forces*, 56 (March): 919–53.

HEATH, A. F. (1981) *Social Mobility* (London: Fontana).

HEATH, A. F., JOWELL, R. and CURTICE, J. (1985) *How Britain Votes* (Oxford: Pergamon).

HEATH, A. F. and RIDGE, J. M. (1983) 'Social Mobility of Ethnic Minorities', *Journal of Biosociological Science, Suppl.*, 8: 169–84.

HOPE, K. (1981) 'Trends in the Openness of British Society in the Present Century', in

Treiman, D. J. and Robinson, R. (eds) *Research in Social Stratification and Mobility*, 1.

KERR, C. *et al.* (1960) *Industrialism and Industrial Man* (Cambridge: Harvard University Press).

KÖNIG, W. and MÜLLER, W. (1986) 'Educational systems and Labour Markets as Determinants of Worklife Mobility in France and West Germany', *European Sociological Review*, 2 (2): 73–95.

LAUMANN, E. O. (1966) *Prestige and Association in an Urban Community* (New York: Bobbs–Merrill).

MACDONALD, K. I. (1974) 'The Hall-Jones Scale: a Note on the Interpretation of the Main British Prestige Coding', in Ridge, J. M. (ed.) *Mobility in Britain Reconsidered* (Oxford: Clarendon Press).

MACDONALD, K. I. (1983a) 'On the Interpretation of a Structural Model of the Mobility Table', *Quantity and Quality*, 17: 203–24.

MACDONALD, K. I. (1983b) 'Return to Indianapolis: a comment on the logic of model construction', *American Journal of Sociology*, 89: 683–7.

MITCHELL, J. C. and CRITCHLEY, F. (1985) 'Configurational Similarity in Three Class Contexts in British Society', *Sociology*, 19.

PAYNE, G. *et al.* (1981) 'Social Mobility and Occupational Change', in Gaskin, M. (ed.) *The Political Economy of Tolerable Survival* (London: Croom Helm).

WHELAN, C. T. and WHELAN, B. J. (1984) *Social Mobility in the Republic of Ireland: a Comparative Perspective* (Dublin: The Economic and Social Research Institute, Paper no. 116).

6 Schools

A. H. Halsey

In education, as in every other aspect of social structure, the problem arises of translating published official statistics into social indicators. Education has to be thought of sociologically as the organisation of the more formal aspects of socialisation. Throughout the twentieth century formal socialisation has grown in importance in the double sense that it has taken up more of the time of more people at each stage of its development. One result has been an increased production of official statistics which have changed their character in response to changes in the structure of education and to changes in the preoccupations of administrators and policy makers.

We have confined ourselves for the most part to statistics on English and Welsh schools. The Scottish system is distinctive both in its history and its structure. The English system is a complex of deceiving names. Schools may be defined as full-time educational institutions for children up to the statutory leaving age and for those who stay on voluntarily in the same institutions. Some definitions may help the reader to distinguish between the different kinds.

Administratively and financially there is a basic distinction between the public and the private sector, but there are also hybrid arrangements. Public sector schools are maintained by local education authorities who pay for them partly from local rates and partly from general grants provided by the central government. Independent schools in the private sector may be recognised as efficient after inspection by Her Majesty's Inspector of Schools. Then there are the hybrids or voluntary schools, established mainly by religious denominations, which are assisted by funds from central government. Among these 'aided schools' are those for which two-thirds of the managers or governors are appointed by the voluntary body and one-third by the local authority. The authority pays maintenance and running costs and teachers' salaries while the managers are responsible for the exterior of the building, improvements, enlargements and alterations. Religious instruction and the appointment of teachers are controlled by the managers or governors. 'Controlled' schools are those for which one-third of the governors or managers are appointed by the voluntary body and two-thirds by the local authority.

All costs are borne by the authority which appoints the teachers. Religious instruction follows the agreed syllabus with the addition of two periods of denominational instruction if the parents agree. By 'special agreement', authorities may consent to pay between half to three-quarters of the cost of building a new school or enlarging an existing (usually secondary) voluntary school. The status of the school then becomes similar to that of an aided school.

Before 1976 there were direct grant schools – about 170 in England and Wales – receiving direct grant from central government for scholarship of pupils. In 1975, however, these schools were required to elect either to enter the maintained sector or to become independent. About a quarter chose to enter the maintained sector and the direct grant scheme was phased out over the following five years.

Schools may also be divided according to the age range of their pupils. There are four stages: pre-primary up to age 5; primary from 5 to 11; secondary from 11 until the pupil leaves school; and further education which covers all education and training after full-time schooling ends.

Within the stages, the following types of school may be distinguished:

1. **Nursery schools, day care centres and playgroups** providing education for children below compulsory school age, that is, under five.
2. **Infants' schools**, for children aged 5 to 7.
3. **Junior schools** for those aged 7 to 11. In Scotland the distinction between infant and primary schools is generally not made.
4. In England and Wales **Middle schools** take children from first schools and lead on, in most cases, to comprehensive upper schools. They cover varying age ranges between 8 and 14. Depending on their individual age range they are deemed either primary or secondary.
5. **Secondary modern schools**, providing for children aged 11 to 15.
6. **Secondary technical schools**, providing for selected children aged 11 plus.
7. **Secondary grammar schools**, providing for children aged 11 plus who are selected as capable of a relatively exacting academic schooling. This tripartite division between secondary modern, secondary technical and grammar schools largely gave way during the 1970s to
8. **Comprehensive schools**, providing education for all secondary pupils in a given district.

   But provision of maintained secondary schools in the area of a local authority may include any combination of types of school. Comprehensive schools now account for over 90 per cent of pupils in a variety of patterns as to forms of organisation and the age range of the pupils attending. Scotland has a few schools which are part comprehensive and part selective, that is, comprehensive in intake but selective as regards level of courses offered. In Northern Ireland secondary education normally begins when pupils reach the age of 11. They transfer from primary schools on the basis of two tests compiled and marked by the Department of Education for Northern Ireland. Parents who do not wish their children to take the tests may transfer them to secondary (intermediate) schools. Most successful pupils in the tests go to secondary (grammar) schools and the remainder to secondary (intermediate) schools.

In the earlier part of the century there were:

9.   **All-age-schools** containing children of both primary and secondary age.
10. Finally there are **Special schools**, either day or boarding, providing education for children who are so seriously handicapped, physically or mentally, that they cannot profit fully from education in normal schools. Some special schools are run by voluntary bodies. They receive some grant from the DES but rely mainly on fees charged to the LEAs for pupils sent to them. Hospital special schools provide for children who are spending a period in hospital.

The term 'further education' is used generally to cover all education after the period of compulsory schooling. There is overlap between the work of secondary schools and colleges of further education preparing pupils for 'A' level examinations. The term higher education covers all advanced courses (including teacher-training courses) to universities and institutions of further education, that is, those leading to qualifications above 'A' level, Scottish Certificate of Education 'H' grade, and ordinary national diploma or their equivalents.

SOURCES OF USEFUL STATISTICS

Government statistics

A range of statistical volumes and bulletins on education are produced by the Department of Education and Science, the Scottish Education Department, the Welsh Office and the Department of Education for Northern Ireland. Regional analysis of some of this material is produced in *Regional Trends*. A selection of material, mostly on a United Kingdom base, appears annually from 1970 in *Social Trends*.

From 1900 to 1914 statistics were published separately as parliamentary papers. 1901 figures are taken from *Statistics of Public Education 1900–1* (1902) Cd 1139, 1911 figures are taken from *Statistics of Public Education 1910–1911* (1912–13) Cd 6551. From 1915 to 1960 statistics were published together with the annual report of the department.

1921, 1931 and 1938 figures are taken from *Education* – the Annual Reports of the Board of Education for the appropriate years, published as parliamentary papers. The 1951 figures are taken from *Education in 1951* (1951) the Annual Report and Statistics of Education of the Ministry of Education, Cmd 8554.

Since 1961 statistics have been published separately from the annual report, in several parts, and as departmental papers. From 1961 figures are taken from the appropriate volumes of *Statistics of Education*.

List 69 and *List 71* are selected local authority statistics on education published from 1956 as departmental publications.

15 to 18 (1959) Report of the Central Advisory Council for Education (England) (Chairman: Sir Geoffrey Crowther).

Half Our Future (1963) Report of the Central Advisory Council for Education (England) (Chairman: John Newsom).

For a convenient selection of earlier official documents see J. Stuart Maclure (1965) *Educational Documents: England and Wales 1816–1963* (Chapman & Hall).

Higher Education (1963) Appendix 1 (Cmnd 2154–1) and Appendix 2 (B) (Cmnd 2154 11–1) of the Report of the Committee on Higher Education (Chairman: Lord Robbins).

Children and their Primary Schools (1966) A Report of the Central Advisory Council for Education (England), 2 vols (Chairman: Lady Plowden).

Public Schools Commission First Report (1968) (Chairman: Sir John Newsom).

Public Schools Commission Second Report (1970) (Chairman: Professor D. V. Donnison).

Other sources

Banks, O. (1955) *Party and Prestige in English Secondary Education* (Routledge).

Halsey, A. H., Health, A. F. and Ridge, J. M. (1980) *Origins and Destinations* (Oxford University Press).

Institute of Municipal Treasurers and Accountants, *Education Statistics*, published annually since 1948.

Kalton, G. (1967) *The Public Schools* 2nd edn (Longmans).

Kelsall, R. K. (1957) *Report on an Enquiry into Applications for Admissions to Universities 1955–6*, Committee of Vice-Chancellors and Principals of the Universities of the United Kingdom).

National Childrens' Bureau – see particularly K. Fogelman, (ed.) (1983) *Growing Up in Britain: Papers from the National Child Development Study* (Macmillan). This study is based on a follow-up of all births in England, Scotland and Wales in the week 3–9 March 1958. A wide range of information has been collected on the 17 000 babies born in that week. There have been four sweeps – at birth, at age 7, 11 and 16 and at 21. The fourth sweep is still being analysed.

Maurice Scott (1980) Net Investment in Education in the United Kingdom 1951–71, *Oxford Review of Education*, 1(6): 21–30.

Vaizey J. and Sheehan J. (1968) *Resources for Education* (Allen & Unwin).

For basic data on numbers in school, their ages and the types of school we have used the primary sources – the annual statistics published by the government department responsible for education. However, these are somewhat unsatisfactory for the beginning of our period, because at the time the idea of financial accountability was dominant in the collection of government statistics, so that only government financed services were included. The idea that planners and others need to have information about all types of education has developed during the period along with the growth in the amount and variety of educational services so that the scope of the statistics has also increased.

As can be seen from the notes to Table 6.1, in 1901 only numbers in public elementary schools were counted. By 1911, children in grant-aided secondary schools and 'recognised efficient' independent schools were also counted along with all those in maintained schools. However, it was not until 1961 that children in 'other independent' schools were included, so that all children in school were covered by the government statistics. Trends in the use of private

Table 6.1   Children in all listed[1] schools as a proportion of the total population in certain age groups, 1901–1984, England and Wales (percentages)

Year	Age 2–4 (incl.)	Age 5–11 (incl.)	Age 12–14 (incl.)	Age 15–18 (incl.)	Age 2–18 (incl.)
1900–1901	2.8	89.3	41.5	0.3	49.6
1910–11	67.2		57.5	1.5	51.0
1920–1	67.3		65.8	3.2	52.4[2]
1930–1	8.8	91.7	73.0	6.0	54.1[2]
1937–8	10.0	92.4	74.5	6.6	53.7
1950–1	7.7	97.2	93.1	12.5	58.3
1960–1	10.8	99.9	99.9	19.6	66.0[3]
1970–1	11.5	100.0	100.0	20.8	58.8
1980–1	27.2	100.0	100.0	37.1	66.0
1983–4[4]	41.1	100.0	100.0	37.3	

Notes:
1. 'Listed schools': 1901 public elementary schools; 1911, 1921, 1931, 1938 public elementary schools, grant-aided secondary schools, and 'recognised efficient' independent schools; 1951 LEA maintained schools, direct grant and 'recognised schools'; 1961–84 the same schools as in 1951 with the addition of 'other independent schools'.
2. Not including estimated numbers in independent schools in 1921 and 1932.
3. A small number of 19-year-olds are shown in the *Statistics of Education* and not included here.
4. Figures for United Kingdom. Ages as at 31.8.83.
Sources: 1901 and 1911 figures from *Statistics of Public Education 1900–1*, and *1910–11*; 1921, 1931, 1938, and 1951 figures from *Education in* (given year), Annual Reports and Statistics of Education of the Board (Ministry) of Education; 1961 and 1971 *Educational Statistics for the UK 1983/4*.

education must be derived from estimates made in 1921 and 1933 and the later figures.

A minor though difficult problem is that, up to the reorganisation of education following the 1944 Education Act, figures for grant-aided second-ary schools were given in a less detailed breakdown than those for public elementary schools, and also in groups which did not correspond to the post-1944 end-on system with the change to secondary school at 11. No detailed age-group breakdowns were given for 'recognised efficient' independent schools before 1951.

There is a lack of data on regional variations in expenditure per pupil in the Ministry of Education's annual published statistics until the most recent volumes. However the Institute of Municipal Treasurers and Accountants has published since 1948 selected statistics including expenditure per pupil for all the county boroughs, and counties with average expenditure for county boroughs and English and Welsh counties.

Our tables on trends in total educational expenditure and its distribution between different stages and types of school rely heavily on the work of Maurice Scott.[1]

The statistics do not give pupil/teacher ratios for the pre-1944 period but we have calculated them from the number of teachers and number of pupils given. Similarly we have calculated the percentage of certificated and uncertificated teachers. Again there is a lack of published information on regional variation until the most recent years.

Information about the number of pupils staying on beyond the statutory school-leaving age and the proportion of leavers going on to further education is scanty for the pre-1944 period. The government gives leaving age figures only for those leaving grant-aided secondary schools. Olive Banks gives some figures for the proportion going on to further education from the same schools and also some indication of regional variation in 1925–6.[2] The post-1944 statistics, however, progressively cover more schools.

The government statistical publications do not include information on class differences in chances of receiving selective education and differential class achievement except for the supplement to the *Statistics of Education 1961*. Most of our information is based on surveys undertaken as private academic research, or for government committees. We rely mainly on the national survey conducted by the Oxford Mobility Research Group in 1972.[3]

Five basic questions may be asked of the statistics in this chapter:

How many children are there in what kind of schools?
What resources of money, teachers etc. have been spent on them?
What are children's educational attainments?
When did the children leave and for what destinations?
What is the relation between social origin and educational or occupational destination?

CHILDREN AND SCHOOLS

Compulsory schooling is from age 5. A typical school at the beginning of the century was a public elementary all-age school recruiting pupils at 5 or under and keeping them to the statutory leaving age. As may be seen from Table 6.1, which shows the percentage enrolment of various age-groups, full-time attendance often stopped at 12 when children were permitted to work half-time. But the statutory age was raised generally to 14 in 1921, to 15 in 1947 and to 16 in 1972–3. Table 6.1 is not based on a complete enumeration.[4] It clearly shows, however, a rising proportionate enrolment among children in the pre-school years and, more dramatically, among those aged 15 to 18.

The 1902 Education Act inaugurated a national system of secondary schools though, at that time, this was conceived as an education for the minority. Secondary schools were linked to the universities rather than to 'elementary' or primary schools. After 1902 the endowed grammar schools of earlier foundation received grants of public money and many new maintained secondary schools were built. Children entered these schools at age 7 or 8 and usually stayed till age 15 or over. Fees were charged. Thus in the early years of the century the elementary and secondary systems were parallel rather than integrated. An important link was established in 1907 when grants to secondary schools were made dependent on the establishment of 25 per cent of free places for pupils recruited from public elementary schools. This is the origin of the 'scholarship' or "11-plus' examination. Higher grade schools had been set up by some of the School Boards established under the 1870 Education Act, thus putting secondary education 'end-on' to primary education. The emphasis in these schools was on science and technology or crafts. Under the 1902 Act, counties and county boroughs became the responsible educational authorities instead of the School Boards with some lower-level authorities retaining responsibility for elementary schools (these are the 'Part III' authorities, the reference being to the part of the Act which made provision for them). After 1902 the higher grade schools, in the main, did not survive, but were assimilated into secondary education.

Tables 6.2 and 6.3 show the gradual increase of public, and the decline of private, provision in the twentieth century. Glennester and Wilson[5] estimated that there were 2.5 million pupils in private schools in the 1850s. A century later, in 1951, this had shrunk to 564 000 (480 000 at independent schools and a further 84 000 at the direct grant schools), representing 9.2 per cent of the school population, a share which continued to decline to 1978 when it was 5.8 per cent. But then in the following years some sign of reversal appeared, raising slightly both absolute numbers and proportions. In 1981 they were 499 000 and 6.2 per cent (Table 6.3). Overall, the historical fact is of small proportions in marketed schooling over the century following the first major interventions of the state through the 1870 Act, and of decline to 1978.

But the market covers an enormous heterogeneity of competitive enterprises of widely varying character and quality. At the apex of the hierarchy are the famous public schools. Their definition has shifted. Sociologically the important clue to the meaning of the adjective 'public' to describe these schools is that they were, prototypically in the case of Westminster, an alternative child-rearing device to the private tutor in the aristocratic household. The original seven studied by the Clarendon Commission of 1861 were the core of the system as it developed in the nineteenth century. They were Charterhouse, Eton, Harrow, Rugby, Shrewsbury, Westminster and Winchester, but already the definition had to be modified so as to include the two famous upper-class day schools, St Pauls and Merchant Taylors.

Subsequent redefinitions were always in the direction of enlargement. The Taunton Commission (1864) added some newcomers, and some endowed grammar schools. The compilers of the first *Public Schools Yearbook* in 1889 agreed on 25. By 1962 the nuclear seven were still at the heart of the system and T. W. Bamford was suggesting the figure of 106 boarding schools as a maximum, including 14 of the direct grant schools.[6] In 1968 the Public Schools Commission[7] adopted the less stringent, if administratively more convenient, definition of membership of the Headmasters' Conference, or the Governing Bodies Association, or the Association of Governing Bodies of Girls' Public Schools, and there were 288 such schools when the Newsom Commission was appointed, including 11 in Scotland. The Commission noted, however, that there were over 1000 other independent schools for children mainly of secondary school age, and over 1800 preparatory and pre-preparatory schools. Public schools, as Newsom defined them, accounted for only 1.4 per cent of all pupils, compared with 1.5 per cent in direct grant schools, 5.5 per cent in all independent schools, and 93 per cent in maintained schools (excluding special schools).

In the 1980s the definition shifted again. John Rae[8] notes that there were over 2000 independent schools in Britain in 1981, of which 1350 were recognised as efficient by the Department of Education and Science, and of these just over 1000 were members of the Independent Schools' Information Service. In 1983 there were more than 2500 independent schools in Britain with 1352 in membership of ISIS. That membership is Rae's criterion for defining the wider boundary of those public schools which had previously claimed the prestigious title 'public'. Rae also identifies 210 public schools defined as having membership of the Headmasters' Conference. He also uses the term 'Great Schools' when he wants to refer to the handful of famous schools, by which he appears to mean the Clarendon schools, 'that from the early nineteenth century have been uppermost in the minds of opponents and supporters alike when they have spoken of public schools'.

Led by the 'Great Schools', the private system reached the height of its expansion at the end of the nineteenth century. Since then it is its tail and not the head which has withered. The Great Schools and the public schools including the direct grant schools which went independent when the list was

Table 6.2 Numbers and proportions of children in different types[1] of schools in certain age groups, 1901–84, England and Wales (000s)

	Age 2–4 no.	Age 2–4 %	Age 5–11 no.	Age 5–11 %	Age 12–14 no.	Age 12–14 %	Age 15–18 no.	Age 15–18 %	Age 2–18 no.	Age 2–18 %
1901										
Public elementary and special	618	100	4316		836		8		5778	
1911										
Public elementary and special	351	100	4613	99.2	1096	92.5	7	17.4	6067	97.4
Grant-aided secondary	neg.	n.a.	38	0.8	89	7.5	33	82.6	161	2.6
Total	351	n.a.	4651	100.0	1185	100.0	40	100.0	6228	100.0
1921										
Public elementary	177	100	4421	99.2	1258	87.2	8	8.8	5865	94.2
Grant-aided secondary	neg.	—	94	0.8	186	12.9	82	91.2	362	5.8
Total	177	—	4515	100.0	1444	100.0	90	100.0	6227	100.0
1931[2]										
Public elementary	159	100	4382	98.3	1024	83.9	29	17.6	5594	93.2
Grant-aided secondary	neg.	—	75	1.7	200	16.1	136	82.4	411	6.8
Total	159	—	4457	100.0	1224	100.0	165	100.0	6005	100.0
1938[2]										
Public elementary and special	166	100	3734	98.0	1190	79.4	33	18.5	5123	91.6
Grant-aided secondary	neg.	—	76	2.0	248	20.6	145	81.5	470	8.4
Total	166	—	3810	100.0	1438	100.0	178	100.0	5593	100.0
1951										
LEA primary, all-age and special	177	97.4	3454	97.2	431	20.5	4	1.5	4067	66.5
LEA grammar and technical	neg.	—	2	—	396	18.8	176	63.7	574	9.4
LEA modern comprehensive and other secondary	—	—	3	—	1132	53.9	48	17.4	1159	19.0
Direct grant	2	0.8	19	0.5	51	2.4	24	8.6	96	1.5
Independent 'recognised'	3	1.8	77	2.2	92	4.4	24	8.8	220	3.6
Total	182	100.0	3555	100.0	2102	100.0	276	100.0	6115	100.0
1961										
LEA primary, all-age and special	203	89.4	3683	94.3	320	10.6	5	1.0	4211	55.0

School type	No.	%	No.	%	No.	%	No.	%	No.	%
LEA grammar and technical	—	—	—	—	536	17.7	274	54.4	811	10.6
LEA modern comprehensive and other secondary					1914	63.4	104	20.7	2018	26.4
Direct grant	1	0.6	20	0.5	63	2.1	38	7.4	122	1.6
Independent 'recognised'	5	2.4	100	2.6	128	4.3	67	13.2	300	3.9
Other independent	17	7.6	102	2.6	59	1.9	16	3.2	195	2.5
Total	226	100.0	3906	100.0	3019	100.0	504	100.0	7658	100.0
1971										
LEA primary, all-age, special and nursery	261	93.8	4591.2	95.5	256.6	9.1	9.7	1.0	5119	58.2
LEA grammar and technical	—	—	—	—	362	12.8	248.5	28.0	611	6.9
LEA other secondary	—	—	21.7	0.5	2005	70.9	506.9	57.0	2533	28.7
Direct grant and recognised independent	6.5	2.3	124	2.6	184.7	6.6	118	13.2	433.6	4.9
Other independent	10.7	3.8	66.8	1.4	19	0.7	6.3	0.7	103	1.2
Total	278.5	100.0	4805	100.0	2828	100.0	889.6	100.0	8799.6	100.0
1981										
Maintained primary nursery and special	451.5	94.6	3824.2	92.4	129	4.0	20.3	1.6	4425	48.9
Grammar	—	—	—	—	82	2.6	52.1	4.2	134.1	1.5
Other secondary	—	—	130.2	3.1	2778.1	87.0	1037	84.3	3945.3	43.6
Independent	25.5	5.3	183.6	4.4	204.9	6.4	120.4	9.8	534.4	5.9
Total	477	100.0	4138.0	100.0	3194	100.0	1229.8	100.0	9038.8	100.0
1984										
Maintained primary nursery and special	492.2	94.9	3312.1	92	117.1	3.9	22.2	1.8	3943.6	47.3
Grammar	—	—	0.1	—	70.5	2.3	48.1	4	118.7	1.4
Secondary	—	—	116.8	3.2	2620.6	87.0	1020.4	84.3	3757.4	45
Independent	26.3	5	170.2	4.7	202.6	6.7	119.1	9.8	518.2	6.2
Total	518.5	100.0	3599.2	100.0	3010.4	100.0	1209.8	100.0	8337.9	100.0

Notes: 1. Detailed age-group breakdowns are not given for 'Independent Recognised' schools before 1951. No figures are given in the *Statistics of Education* for other independent schools before 1961 except for the 1921 estimated figures.

2. In 1931 and 1938 the number of children in age groups 2–4 and 15–18 were estimated by dividing the age groups given in the statistics into equal years.

Sources: 1901 and 1911 figures from *Statistics of Public Education 1900–1*, and *1910–11*; 1921, 1931, 1938 and 1951 figures from *Education in* (given year), Annual Reports and Statistics of Education of the Board (Ministry) of Education; 1961 from *Statistics of Education* for subsequent years.

Table 6.3   Full-time pupils by age and type of school 1951–81, England and Wales (percentages)

	School	Age[3] 5–10	Age[3] 11–15	Age[3] 16+	All[3]
1951[1]	Maintained	93.1	88.9	62.1	90.8
	Direct grant	0.4	2.4	9.3	1.4
	Independent	6.5	8.7	28.7	7.8
	Total %	100.0	100.0	100.1	100.0
	No. (000s)	(3614)	(2404)	(131)	(6149)
1956[1]	Maintained	94.0	89.5	67.2	91.7
	Direct grant	0.4	2.5	10.0	1.4
	Independent	5.5	8.1	22.8	6.9
	Total %	99.9	100.1	100.0	100.0
	No. (000s)	(4312)	(2657)	(165)	(7134)
1961	Maintained	94.3	91.2	71.9	92.2
	Direct grant	0.5	2.2	9.1	1.5
	Independent	5.2	6.5	19.0	6.2
	Total %	100.0	99.9	100.0	99.9
	No. (000s)	(3907)	(3140)	(253)	(7300)
1966	Maintained	95.1	91.2	77.7	92.7
	Direct grant	0.5	2.6	7.6	1.6
	Independent	4.5	6.2	14.7	5.7
	Total %	100.1	100.0	100.0	100.0
	No. (000s)	(4204)	(3049)	(354)	(7607)
1971	Maintained	96.0	92.3	81.8	93.9
	Direct grant	0.4	2.4	6.9	1.5
	Independent	3.6	5.2	11.2	4.6
	Total %	100.0	99.9	99.9	100.0
	No. (000s)	(4804)	(3300)	(418)	(8522)
1976	Maintained	96.2	93.3	86.2	94.4
	Direct grant	0.4	2.1	5.4	1.4
	Independent	3.4	4.7	8.5	4.3
	Total %	100.0	100.1	100.1	100.1
	No. (000s)	(4738)	(3998)	(574)	(9310)
1981[2]	Maintained	95.3	93.4	82.2	93.8
	Independent	4.6	6.6	17.8	6.2
	Total %	99.9	100.0	100.0	100.0
	No. (000s)	(3903)	(3794)	(383)	(8080)

Notes:
1. For 1951 and 1956 the figures for independent schools not recognised as efficient were estimated.
2. The figures for 1981 relate to England only, not England and Wales as for earlier years.
3. Age is that at 1 January for the year in question except for 1981 when it is at 31 August 1980. The numbers are those attending school in January. For 1951–71 the 11–15 group thus includes some pupils over the school-leaving age; for 1976 and 1981 the 16+ group includes some pupils under the school-leaving age.

Source: *Statistics of Education.*

withdrawn in 1975, are full and flourishing, albeit partly at the expense of their weaker market competitors. But the private market as a whole shrank relative to the state sector as the twentieth century advanced, at least until 1979.

A crucial distinguishing feature of the private sector is its retention of pupils beyond the minimum school-leaving age into the sixth form. The private sector is more heavily weighted by sixth-formers and much less by children of primary school age, than is the state sector. Nevertheless, the increase in sixth form attendance at state schools is a still more dramatic development of the school system since 1950. Table 6.3 shows the trends over the post-war period. The private sector has gained in relative strength among older pupils but, in the same period the advance of the state sector has been most rapid. From having nearly 40 per cent of the older pupils in 1951 the private sector declined to less than 20 per cent in 1981. Private school pupils are now outnumbered 4 to 1 even at the sixth form level.

At the primary stage (5 to 10), there was a decline in absolute numbers attending private schools before the Second World War and this has continued since, despite the fact that until the mid-1970s the size of the age group was on the increase. The decline is both absolute and relative, and it is probably not rash to infer that there was over this period a continued decline in the popularity of private primary education. This continued decline, however, took place largely among the schools 'not recognised as efficient' in the formal language of the DES. At the secondary school stage (11 to 15), the absolute numbers in the private sector stayed relatively steady between 1951 and 1981, beginning at 268 000 and ending at 251 000. Meanwhile the state sector expanded hugely, first with the two 'baby booms' of 1946 and 1961, and then with the raising of the school-leaving age in 1972–3. From 2 136 000 in 1951 the numbers rose to 3 047 000 in 1971 and then to 3 731 000 in 1976, before declining again as the bulge passed through the secondary schools to 3 543 000 in 1981. Thus there were roughly stable numbers in the private sector coupled with an enormous expansion in the absolute numbers of the state sector and the consequent increase in the latter's relative share.

Finally, with respect to the trends at 16 plus, Table 6.3 shows that the most dramatic decline in the private sector's share has taken place in this age group despite the fact that the absolute numbers increased by over one-third between 1951 and 1981. This was in part due to the increased birth-rate and the raised school-leaving age, but mainly to a trend towards attendance beyond minimum school-leaving age. It was, above all, the trend towards longer school careers which swelled the state schools' sixth forms. In 1951 about 12 per cent of pupils in the state sector stayed on at school to the age of 16 compared with about 60 per cent in the private sector, and perhaps 6 per cent from the state sector were staying on into the sixth form (that is, to age 17) compared with 40 per cent in the private sector. By 1981 all pupils, in both sectors were obliged to stay to 16, but the proportion staying on to 17 had increased in the state sector from 6 to 20 per cent and in the private sector from 40 to 70 per cent.

Table 6.4 Type of school – county[1] and voluntary[2] 1900–1984 England and Wales (percentages)

	1900	1930	1938	1950	1960	1971	1981	1984
Primary and all-age[3] schools or departments[4]								
County	34.4	52.6	55.8	54.8	59.5	64.0	65.1	65.0
Church of England	52.7	39.7	36.4	37.0	32.3	26.4	24.6	24.7
Roman Catholic	5.7	6.1	6.5	7.1	7.4	8.8	9.5	9.6
Other	7.2	1.6	1.2	1.1	0.8	0.7	0.6	0.6
All primary schools or departments	100.0	100.0	100.0	100.0	100.0	100.0	100.0	100.0
	(31 313)	(30 429)	(29 224)	(23 133)	(23 488)	(23 054)	(20 993)	(20 001)
Secondary[5] schools or departments[4]								
County	—	51.8	55.3	83.8	85.3	81.5	80.2	80.2
Church of England	—	—	—	5.6	4.3	3.9	5.1	5.4
Roman Catholic	—	6.4	6.6	3.9	5.8	10.1	10.8	10.5
Others	—	41.9	38.1	6.6	4.5	4.4	3.9	3.9
All secondary	—	100.0	100.0	100.0	100.0	100.0	100.0	100.0
		(1 354)	(1 398)	(4 765)	(5 801)	(5 295)	(4 654)	(4 444)

Notes:
1. Buildings provided and schools wholly maintained by the local education authority. County schools were previously known as council or board schools.
2. Schools maintained by the local education authority but buildings provided by a voluntary organisation. For details see p. 226.
3. In 1900, 1930 and 1938 public elementary schools and, subsequently, maintained primary schools.
4. Departments with a separate head teacher.
5. In 1930 and 1938 secondary schools on the grant list, subsequently maintained secondary schools.
Source: Statistics of Education.

Table 6.5 Status of voluntary schools, 1960–84, England and Wales (maintained only)

	1960		1971		1981		1984	
	Primary and all-age schools and departments	Secondary schools and departments	Primary and all-age	Secondary	Primary and all-age	Secondary	Primary and all-age	Secondary
Church of England								
aided	3174	139	2502	117	2076	117	1994	118
controlled	4393	83	3598	65	3101	102	2955	103
special agreement and not determined	18	27	3	29	1	19	1	19
Roman Catholic								
aided	1725	254	2020	420	1201	426	1910	392
controlled	1	1	1	—	1	—	1	—
special agreement	1	90	1	117	1	79	1	76
Others								
aided	57	93	42	84	41	60	41	56
controlled	139	165	117	148	89	119	80	115
special agreement	—	1	—	1	—	1	—	1
All voluntary schools								
aided	4956	486	4564	621	4118	603	3946	566
controlled	4533	249	3806	213	3191	221	3036	218
special agreement and not determined	19	118	4	147	2	99	2	96
Total	9508	853	8374	981	7311	923	6984	880

Note:
1. See p. 226 for definition of voluntary schools.
2. Figures for 1981 and 1984 England only.
Source: Statistics of Education.

Both sectors, therefore, kept many more pupils for longer, but they were starting from different base lines and remained clearly differentiated even in 1981, despite the transformation of the state sector. In the private sector a sixth-form career has now become the norm, and while these sixth-formers are vastly outnumbered by those in state sixth forms, it is still only a small minority of state school pupils who stay on to this stage of education.

Within the state sector the school system is historically a fusion of religious and secular foundations.[9] Table 6.4 shows the rising importance of the secular schools over the course of the century and Table 6.5 shows the status of voluntary schools (aided, controlled or special agreement) from 1960 to 1984.

The main division of schools at the beginning of the century was between elementary and secondary. Reform has been in the direction of replacing this distinction by a division between primary and secondary schools. After 1907 there was a gradual increase in the secondary proportion of 12 to 14-year-olds (from 7.5 per cent in 1911 to 20.6 per cent in 1938). Then the 1944 Act abolished the elementary schools and made state secondary schools end-on to primary schools. Hence the figures for 1951 look very different. Only 20.5 per cent of the 11 to 14-year-old group remained in LEA primary all-age and special schools with 18.8 per cent in LEA grammar and technical and 53.9 per cent in secondary modern and comprehensive schools. The remainder were in direct grant (2.4 per cent) and independent schools recognised as efficient (4.4 per cent). By 1984 the process was nearly complete – only 3.9 per cent of 11 to 14-year-olds were in primary all-age and special schools with 87 per cent in moderns and comprehensives and only 2.3 per cent in grammar and technical schools.

Thus for those aged 11 the secondary replaced the primary school. But there are divisions within secondary education. Some secondary schools are selective. The proportion of 13-year-olds in such selective schools rose from 1911 (4.7 per cent) to 1951 (22.6 per cent). After 1961 the trend was in the opposite direction with the rise of the comprehensive school. By 1976 three-quarters of pupils in public secondary schools were in comprehensives. By 1984 the percentage was 82 (in Scotland and Wales 96).

EXPENDITURE AND RESOURCES

Allocation of resources is the responsibility of local education authorities, but throughout the century there has been a trend towards increasing centralisation of policy-making and administration. Under the Education Act of 1918 the responsibility for developing a national system of public education was placed on the local authorities, and it was not until the 1944 Act that this duty was formally transferred to the Minister of Education acting through local education authorities. From the passing of the 1918 Act, specific percentage grants were made by the Board of Education in respect of approved expenditure by education authorities, and in this way financial support was given automatically to local initiative which fell within the provisions of the Act and the grant regulations. This left the way open to a good deal of regional and local variations in educational development and expenditure.

Since 1920 there has been a marked growth of monetary and of real expenditure on education. Table 6.6 summarises this trend to 1983. At 1948 prices government expenditure rose from £106 million in 1919–20 to £943 million in 1983. As a percentage of Gross National Product (GNP) the rise was from 1.2 to 6.3 in 1975, falling back to 5.2 in 1983.

Table 6.6   General government expenditure on education, 1919/20–1983, UK

	Expenditure at current prices (£m)	Expenditure at 1948 prices (£m)	Index (1948 = 100)	Expenditure as percentage of GNP (%)
1919–20	69	106	41	1.2
1924–5	88	148	57	2.0
1929–30	103	169	65	2.2
1934–5	102	174	67	2.2
1939–40	127	182	70	2.0
1944–5	150	150	58	1.2
1947–8	259	259	100	2.4
1948	284	284	100	2.4
1950	347	307	108	2.6
1955	547	367	129	2.8
1960	917	458	161	3.6
1965	1 585	563	198	4.4
1970	2 532	705	248	4.9
1975	6 626	905	319	6.3
1980	12 121	935	329	5.3
1983	15 583	943	332	5.2

Sources: 1919–20 to 1947–8 – J. Vaizey, 1958, *The Costs of Education* Allen and Unwin; for GNP – C. H. Feinstein, 1967, *National Income, Expenditure and output of The United Kingdom 1855–1965* (Cambridge University Press); 1948 to 1983 – National Income & Expenditure 'Blue Books'.

The overall growth in expenditure was accompanied by large structural changes (Table 6.7(a)(b)). These were partly a direct result of legislation and of the changing financial and organisational framework of public education in the present century. For instance, the advent of 'free' secondary education stemming from the Acts of 1907 and 1944 undoubtedly was an important reason for the increasing weight of secondary schools in the total (as was the movement of elementary school pupils aged about 11 into secondary schools).

Table 6.7(a)   Composition of public education expenditure by sector, 1920–67, England and Wales (percentages)

	1920	1930	1940	1950	1955	1965	1967
Primary	57.4	56.4	54.8	37.3	38.9	28.1	27.5
Secondary	20.0	19.4	19.1	27.4	28.3	32.2	31.7
Teacher training	0.9	0.8	0.6	2.0	1.7	3.4	3.9
Further and adult	5.0	4.9	4.9	7.5	7.9	12.2	12.5
Universities	5.2	5.9	6.7	8.0	8.2	9.9	10.5
Special schools	2.3	2.5	2.7	1.5	1.9	2.0	2.0
Meals	0.4	0.5	1.1	7.2	6.2	5.9	6.0
Health service	1.8	2.8	3.4	3.5	2.1	1.8	1.7
Administration and inspection	7.1	7.0	6.8	5.7	4.9	4.5	4.4
Total	100.0	100.0	100.0	100.0	100.0	100.0	100.0

Sources: 1920–1965: Vaizey, J. and Sheehan, J, (1968) *Resources for Education* (Allen & Unwin) 1967: *Statistics of Education* (1967) vol. 5.

Table 6.7(b)   Public authorities education and related expenditure (current and capital) by type of service, England and Wales (percentages)

	1952–3	1959–60	1969–70	1979–80	1983–4[1]
Primary (incl. nursery)	34.0	27.2	24.6	23.8	22.6
Secondary	26.0	33.8	28.2	30.7	31.6
Special schools	1.6	2.2	2.3	3.7	4.1
Further and adult	8.8	10.5	13.7	16.2	18.1
Teacher training	3.5	2.4	4.9	0.8	0.9
Universities	8.8	9.1	13.4	12.4	11.5
School health	1.7	1.6	1.3	0.2	0.2
Meals and milk	9.6	7.1	5.2	5.1	3.4
Youth and PT	1.1	1.0	1.2	1.2	1.3
Transport	1.6	1.3	1.1	1.7	1.6
Administration and inspection	3.5	3.7	3.7	4.1	4.4
Other		0.1	0.3	0.2	0.2
Total	100.0	100.0	100.0	100.0	100.0

Note:
1. England
Source: *Statistics of Education.*

But the long-term and pervasive nature of the trends suggests that deeper social forces were at work. Educational change would appear to be self-sustaining: as more achieve certain levels of education they transmit awareness of the value of education to their contemporaries and to their children. Also, the development of the economy and the increasing demand for more specialised and more complex skills made the demand for education all the greater. Thus there has been a steady rise in the shares of secondary, higher, further and adult education in total spending. Of course, diminishing *shares* of total expenditure were generally accompanied by increases in the *absolute* magnitude of real expenditure, as the overall growth in the provision of educational resources was so large.

In economic terms the meaning of educational expansion is best translated into a measure of net investment in education. Such a measure has been attempted for the first time by Maurice Scott for the period 1951–71. His calculations also produce some related measures of total expenditure, the stock of 'useful education', cumulative costs, prices of inputs into education and average costs per pupil in different types of educational institution. We have numbered the tables [6.8 to 6.14] in this chapter and Scott writes as follows:[10]

The whole of expenditure on education cannot be regarded as investment in the sense of adding to the *'useful stock'* of past expenditures, since a large part of it is needed merely to *maintain* the existing stock. As people retire, or die, the education which they have received is lost, so far as its direct contribution to measured output is concerned. It has to be replaced by education given to new entrants into the work force. Net investment occurs, broadly speaking, when the new entrants outnumber those leaving or when they are, on average, more highly educated. In order to define the concept with sufficient precision to enable one to measure it, we must now consider more carefully what is meant by the 'useful stock' of past expenditure, and what the expenditure required to maintain it means.

By the *'useful stock'* I mean the total amount spent on the education of those currently at work multiplied by their rate of work. The total amount spent, since it is to be added up for all those at work, must be measured at a common price level. The way I have chosen to do this, for each year for which estimates of net investment were made (i.e. 1950/51 to 1970/71, these being years from 1st April to 31st March which were used throughout the study), is to estimate how much it would have cost, in the prices of that year, to provide the same resources as were used to educate each member of the work force. Thus, for example, I take (in principle) a man aged 51 in 1950/ 51 who received his education between, say, 1905/06 and 1917/18 (when we may suppose he left school for good). For each of these years I take the actual amount spent on his *formal* education at school, and I update it to the prices of 1950/51 by multiplying it by an index of the costs of inputs into education (teachers, books, buildings, etc.). I then add up the amounts spent on him, now all expressed at 1950/51 prices, and that gives me his 'embodied education' (with an important qualification made below). However, one further step is required to get the 'useful stock', which is to multiply this value of 'embodied education' by the man's rate of work, expressed as so-many hours per annum in 1950/51. This last step is necessary, since hours of work can differ very greatly, and since there would otherwise be an ambiguity in the notion of 'a member of the work force.' Am I a member if I work one hour per year? The only way to overcome this ambiguity is to measure the stock, not in terms of so-many pounds of embodied education, but in terms of so-many pound hours.

The above description of the 'useful stock' leaves some loose ends which must now be tied up. First, the reason for confining attention to education embodied in those actually at work has already been given: I want to relate the estimates to national output as officially measured. However useful education embodied in married women working at home, for example, may be, or however much it may contribute to the enjoyment of life of those who have retired, these persons' work or enjoyment does not feature in national output as officially measured.

Secondly, attention is confined to *formal* education, comprising primary and secondary schooling, but public and private, universities and full-time further education (notably teacher training). Part-time education and all training on-the-job is not included on grounds of expediency: the task of making the present estimates was quite enough, but it would, in principle, be desirable to extend them.

Thirdly, the description so far given refers to what I call 'explicit' expenditure on education. It can be argued, as many have, that there is another important component of the cost of education, namely the earnings foregone by those being educated. At each stage in the process, there is a choice between staying on at school, or university etc., or taking a job. To choose the former involves sacrificing the latter, and the output thereby lost is a real cost of staying on. I have attempted to allow for this by estimating the amount of earnings foregone. Thus, to return to the example of the man aged 51 in 1950/51, I have estimated the value of earnings foregone for each of the yers he spent at school, valuing them at the level of earnings in 1950/51, and have then added them to his embodied explicit education to get the total cost of his embodied education. While this seems to me a reasonable way to measure the cost, some may wish to exclude foregone earnings. To cater for them, and because the estimates of explicit expenditure are in any case of interest in themselves, I have shown the two elements of educational cost separately in what follows.

Table [6.8] sets out the main estimates of total expenditure on education, maintenance expenditure and net investment, with separate estimates for explicit expenditure and foregone earnings. The figures are given only for three selected years as this suffices to show the main points, which are as follows. First, at the start of the period maintenance expenditure was much larger in relation to total expenditure than it was at the end of the period. Secondly, the consequence of this was that net investment rose much faster than total expenditure. Thirdly, although foregone earnings were nearly as great as explicit expenditure, they formed a much lower proportion of net

Table 6.8   Total expenditure, maintenance and net investment in education in the
United Kingdom

	Year	Total expenditure	£m, current prices Maintenance	Net investment[1]
Total	1950–1	474	319	155
	1960–1	1268	716	552
	1970–1	3404	1685	1719
Explicit [expenditure][2]	1950–1	253	149	104
	1960–1	687	337	350
	1970–1	1833	789	1044
Foregone earnings[3]	1950–1	221	170	51
	1960–1	581	379	202
	1970–1	1571	896	675

Notes:
1. Net investment = total expenditure *less* maintenance.
2. Explicit expenditure is conventional current expenditure, both private and public, on full-time formal education, excluding costs of school meals and boarding, and excluding costs of research in universities. Allowance is made for interest and amortisation on buildings.
3. Foregone earnings are the estimated earnings for work foregone by those staying on at school or place of higher education.
Source: Maurice Scott (1980) (see p. 229).

investment. Another way of putting this is to say that much more of foregone earnings was maintenance. The reason for this is that, by definition, foregone earnings at a given year's prices, e.g. 1950/51, are the same for a given age (e.g. at 15 years of age) for all members of the work force. Whether I am 20 or 60 years old in 1950/51 my foregone earnings at age 15 are the same, being the earnings foregone by someone aged 15 in 1950/51 who is staying on at school. By contrast, with explicit expenditure, more is being currently spent on education for each child at each age than was spent on the education of present members of the work force. Hence the maintenance component of explicit expenditure is smaller.

In Table [6.9], net investment in education is expressed as a percentage of other relevant magnitudes. From 1950/51 to 1970/71 it increased from 9 to 17% of total other investment in the economy, and from 1.3 to 3.8% of total output.

In Table [6.10], the estimates of net investment are expressed in real terms. The correct way to do this, in the writer's opinion, is to measure the quantity of consumption foregone to undertake this investment, and this is shown in the first two columns of the table. Measured in this way, the volume of net investment increased roughly five times from 1950/51 to 1970/71. The conventional way to measure the volume is to deflate each

Table 6.9   Net investment in education in the United Kingdom in relation to total other investment and total output

		Net investment in education as a percentage of:	
	Year	Gross domestic capital formation at market prices (1)	Gross National Product at factor cost (2)
Total	1950–1	8.9	1.3
	1960–1	11.5	2.4
	1970–1	17.0	3.8
Explicit	1950–1	5.9	0.9
	1960–1	7.3	1.5
	1970–1	10.3	2.3
Foregone earnings	1950–1	2.9	0.4
	1960–1	4.2	0.9
	1970–1	6.7	1.5

Note: Net investment in education has been related to so-called *gross* domestic capital formation because, in the writer's opinion, the latter is the best readily available measure of *net* investment (other than in 'human capital') from the point of view of society as a whole. For a similar reason, Gross National Product was used in column (2). See Maurice Scott's 'Investment and growth', *Oxford Economic Papers*, November 1976.

Source: Maurice Scott, (1980) (see p. 229).

component of value by an appropriate price index. We have attempted to do this in the last two columns of the table, where explicit expenditures are deflated by a specially constructed price index of educational inputs (teachers, books, buildings etc.), and foregone earnings are deflated by an index of wages rates. Measured in this way, net investment increased rather more slowly: about three times from 1950/51 to 1970/71. The increase was slower because educational costs rose faster than consumer goods and services prices over this period (see Table [6.13]).

We turn now to some related estimates. The total useful stock of education, measured at constant *costs*, is compared in Table [6.11], with total man-hours worked, total population and national output at constant prices. For this purpose, we have taken the sum of all education 'embodied' in those at work multiplied by their hours of work, thus getting pound-hours of education cost, shown in the table at 1960/61 prices. The stock so measured can be regarded as one factor tending to increase the productivity of the work force. Column (3) shows that, for each man-hour worked on average, there was available a stock of 'embodied' education costing £845 at 1960/61 prices in 1950/51. This had risen by 43% to £1205 at 1960/61 prices in 1970/71. Over the same period, average output per man-hour rose by

Table 6.10   Net investment in education in the United Kingdom at constant 1960–1
prices

Year	Deflating by consumer price index (£m 1960/1 prices)		Deflating by index of educational costs	
	(1) Total	(2) Explicit	(3) Total	(4) Explicit
1950–1	216	144	284	188
1960–1	552	350	552	350
1970–1	1147	697	944	586
	As multiples of 1950/1 rates of net investment			
1950–1	1.000	1.000	1.000	1.000
1960–1	2.560	2.426	1.946	1.860
1970–1	5.318	4.827	3.327	3.112
	Rates of growth, per cent per annum			
1950–1 to 1960–1	9.9	9.3	6.9	6.4
1960–1 to 1970–1	7.6	7.1	5.5	5.3
1950–1 to 1970–1	8.7	8.2	6.2	5.8

Notes: Columns (1) and (2) show the growth in net investment in education measured
in terms of the quantity of consumption sacrificed to obtain it. Columns (3)
and (4) show the growth in net investment in education measured in terms of
the quantity of inputs (teachers, books, buildings etc. and man-hours of work
foregone) required to obtain it.

Source: Maurice Scott, (1980) (see p. 229).

83% (obtained by dividing column (6) by column (2)). It follows that the
stock:output ratio fell, and this is shown in column (7). One could interpret
that column as showing the number of hours it took a pound's worth of
'embodied education' to 'produce' a pound's worth of output, on average.
Of course, one cannot attribute all production to the educational stock in
this way. Finally, column (5) of Table [6.11] shows that there was an
increase in the stock per head of population of 21% from 1950/51 to 1970/
71.

Reference has already been made to the increasing amounts of education
received by succeeding generations. In Table [6.12] are given the amounts of
education received by members of the work force of different ages and sex in
April 1971, the amounts being measured at 1960/61 costs. A note to the
table explains the meaning of the figures.

Several interesting points emerge. First, the *explicit* education received by
a typical worker aged 20 more than tripled in real terms in the first 60 years
of this century. Thus, at age 20, a typical male worker in 1909 (whose age in
1971 would thus be 82) had received altogether education costing £235
explicitly (i.e. not counting foregone earnings). By 1969, a typical 20-year-
old worker had received education costing £769 explicitly. The contrast is

Table 6.11 Stock of 'useful education' in relation to other magnitudes

Year	Stock of 'useful education' (1960/1 cost) £ mn × mn hours p.a. (1)	Man-hours worked in year (000mn.) (2)	Stock per man-hour (£ at 1960/1 cost) (3)	Population end of year (Millions) (4)	Stock per head (Million £−hours 1960/1 cost) (5)	National output in year (£000 mn. 1960/1 prices p.a.) (6)	Stock output ratio (hours) (7)
Total stock							
1950–1	40.75	48.20	845	50.2	0.812	18.10	2251
1960–1	48.12	48.48	993	52.7	0.913	23.25	2070
1970–1	54.56	45.26	1205	55.5	0.983	31.05	1757
Explicit stock							
1950–1	19.31	48.20	401	50.3	0.384	18.10	1067
1960–1	23.35	48.48	482	52.7	0.443	23.25	1004
1970–1	27.39	45.26	605	55.6	0.493	31.05	882

Notes:
Col. (3) = (1) ÷ (2) × 1000
Col. (4) = (1) ÷ (5)
Col. (5) = (1) ÷ (4)
Col. (6) = Gross National Product at factor cost.
Col. (7) = (1) ÷ (6) × 1000
Source: Maurice Scott, (1980) (see p. 229).

less marked for the total cost of education received, including foregone earnings, but the increase was still large: about $2\frac{1}{2}$ times, from £550 to £1409 for the male worker. Secondly, as a higher proportion of young people stayed on longer at school, or went to university or other places of further education, the averages increased faster with age. Thus, the oldest male workers in Table [6.12] at age 20 had, on average, received only £30 more 'explicit' education than on average at age 15. The youngest male workers in Table [6.12] at age 20 had received £215 more 'explicit' education than at age 15. Thirdly, females throughout received on average the same or less education than males. So far as 'explicit' education is concerned, the sex-differences were not very marked, although they widened with age within any one cohort, being negligible when the cohort was 15 but appreciable at age 25. Foregone earnings were also lower for females.

Table 6.12 Cumulative cost of education received during their lives by workers of different ages at April 1971 at 1960–1 prices

Mean age of 5-year cohort at April 1971 (1)	Mean age of cohort in col. (1) at which cumulative cost is given in cols (3) to (6) (2)	Total Male (3)	Female (4)	Explicit Male (5)	Female (6)
82	15	433	430	205	204
	20	550	547	235	235
	25	615	576	260	245
67	15	539	535	293	289
	20	690	675	331	325
	25	756	715	349	336
52	15	601	593	327	322
	20	883	846	412	399
	25	960	887	439	414
37	15	679	675	419	417
	20	1111	1069	564	521
	25	1239	1163	613	587
22	15	863	858	554	548
	20	1409	1373	769	755

Cumulative cost per worker of education received at 1960/1 prices by those at work (£)

Note: The figures in cols (3) to (6) show, for example, that an average worker drawn from a cohort of male workers whose ages last birthday in April 1971 ranged from 80 to 85, and so with mean age 82, would have received, when the mean age of that cohort was 15 (i.e. in 1904) an amount of education costing altogether £433 at 1960/1 prices thus far in his life. Of that amount, £205 would have been 'explicit' expenditure and the rest foregone earnings. When the mean age of the cohort was 20 (i.e. in 1909) he would have received altogether £550, and so on.

Source: Maurice Scott, (1980) (see p. 229).

In order to estimate maintenance expenditure, we had to estimate the cost of replacing education in the 'useful stock'. It was assumed that this required the same quantity of inputs as had been required to provide the education in the first place, so that, for example, if X hours of a teacher's work of a given grade had been provided in, say, 1900, then X hours of a similar teacher's work was required to replace it in, say, 1960. Alternatively, if exactly the same bundle of inputs was not used, then a bundle *costing the same amount* in some given base year was deemed equivalent. No allowance, in fact, was made for changes in the productivity of educational inputs. Conversations with educationalists suggested to me that it was a matter of some controversy whether productivity had increased or not, it being next to impossible to measure changes in the quality of education provided by a given bundle of inputs. In view of this, the only practical solution seemed to be to measure everything at cost.

In order to do this, estimates of changes in the prices of inputs were required, which could be used to deflate expenditures at current prices so as to bring them to a common price basis. In order to keep the computations manageable, only one price index was constructed and this is shown in Table [6.13]. In principle, it would have been better to have had separate price index numbers for each type of educational establishment. Most care was devoted to measuring the changing 'price' of teachers, since these comprised about two-thirds of the weight of the index.

Table 6.13　　Prices of inputs into education and consumer goods and services prices 1901–71

Year	Index numbers of prices (1960/1 = 100)		Rate of increase between years per cent p.a.	
	Inputs into education	Consumer goods and services	Inputs into education	Consumer goods and services
1900–1	12.0	19.4	1.0	0.5
1913–14	13.7	20.7	8.8	6.6
1923–4	31.9	39.3	−0.2	−0.6
1938–9	31.1	36.0	4.2	7.6
1944–5	39.8	55.8	21.9	3.0
1945–6	48.5	57.5	2.6	4.6
1950–1	55.1	71.9	6.1	3.4
1960–1	100.0	100.0	5.9	4.1
1970–1	178.2	149.8		
1900–1 to 1970–1			3.9	3.0

Note:　　Inputs into education comprise teachers, administrators, unskilled labour, heating, lighting, miscellaneous purchases including books, and buildings. The weights used reflect the share of the item in total expenditure on education, with about two-thirds of the weight given to teachers. The index of consumer prices is that estimated by Feinstein, linked to the 'Blue Book' series at 1950/51.

Source:　　Maurice Scott, (1980) (see p. 229).

The table shows that the prices of inputs into education rose at about 4% per annum over the first 70 years of the century, or about 1% per annum faster than the prices of consumer goods and services. This faster rate of increase occurred in most periods, but there were erratic movements over shorter periods, in particular during and just after the Second World War.

The index of input prices has been used in Table [6.14] to show changing costs per pupil at the main educational establishments distinguished in the analysis. Estimates were also made for further educational establishments, and for private schools after the Second World War, but these are not shown. According to the estimates, inputs per pupil have fairly consistently increased for primary education, the only reductions taking place during the Second World War. Secondary education, however, apparently suffered during the First World War as well, as also did universities. The last, in particular, are much affected by composition changes and capacity utilisation. Thus the weight of Oxford and Cambridge was much greater before 1914, and capacity was much under-used in 1944/45, leading to high average

Table 6.14   Average costs per pupil in terms of inputs at 1960–1 prices
(£)

Year	Primary school	Grant list	Secondary school LEA younger	LEA older	University
1900–1	22	112	—	—	387
1913–14	30	139	—	—	387
1923–4	32	101	—	—	219
1938–9	44	119	—	—	312
1944–5	41	103	—	—	345
1945–6	38	—	61	109	282
1950–1	43	—	68	122	376
1960–1	52	—	77	135	466
1970–1	58	—	97	158	567

Notes: Costs at current prices were divided by the price index of inputs into education given in Table 6.13 to give the above costs at 1960/1 prices. Primary schools were state-maintained or assisted schools catering for pupils up to ages varying from about 11 to 14. Secondary schools on the grant list were assisted by the state, and in some cases wholly the responsibility of the Local Education Authorities (LEAs). Only LEA schools are shown for post-war years. 'Younger' means 'under 15 years of age' until 1960/1 inclusive. For 1970/71 'younger' means 'under 16 years of age'. Costs include teaching, administration (both Central and Local Government as well as school administration), books and materials, cleaning and maintenance, heating and lighting and imputed rent, but exclude meals, milk, transport, youth services, board and lodging and, for universities, exclude research costs.
Source: Maurice Scott, (1980) (see p. 229).

Table 6.15 Pupil to teacher ratios by type of school, 1901–84, England and Wales

	Public elementary	Grant-aided secondary
1901	48.5	n.a.
1911	37.4	16.0
1921	35.5	16.6
1931	33.1	19.0
1938	30.9	18.8

	All primary	Secondary modern	Grammar	Comprehensive	Other	Total secondary	Direct grant grammar	Independent recognised efficient	other independent
1951	30.0	22.4	18.1	19.7	—	20.6	19.0	13.7	—
1961	28.6	21.7	18.3	18.9	—	20.4	17.8	13.2	18.3[1]
1971	26.9	19.0	16.7	17.5	17.0	17.9	16.4	12.8	13.9
1981	22.7	17.3	16.2	16.4	16.3	16.4	12.5		
1984	22.2	17.0	15.9	16.0	15.5	16.0	11.6		

Notes: 'Teachers' includes all adult teachers qualified or unqualified but excludes student teachers, pupil teachers and probationer teachers. From 1951–68 part-time teachers are taken into account as two part-time equivalent to one full-time teacher.
1. Part-time teachers not taken into account.

Sources: Statistics of Public Education, 1901, 1911; Annual Report of Board of Education 1920–21 and 1930–31; Education in 1931 and Statistics of Public Education. Statistics of Education, 1961, 1984.

Table 6.16 Percentage distribution of classes by size, 1910–84, England and Wales (percentages)

	1910	1930	1938	1950	1961	1971	1981	1984
Primary[1]								
Up to 20 pupils	—	9.2	10.0	10.2	10.0	6.8	20.5	21.6
21–30 pupils	—	20.0	22.0	22.8	27.0	29.2	56.3	58.6
31–40 pupils	—	30.8	37.3	38.2	48.7	61.6	22.3	17.2 (Eng. 31–36 only)
41–50 pupils	—	33.3	29.2	27.5	14.2	3.2	} 0.8	} 2.4
51 and over	—	6.6	1.4	1.3	0.1	0.1		
41 and over	—	39.9	30.6	28.8	14.3	3.3		
Secondary[2]								
Up to 15 pupils	34.2	} 19.0	} 26.4	4.2	4.2	13.9	} 43.4	} 29.7
16–20 pupils	18.6	} 13.4		6.7	7.4	15.6		
21–25 pupils	19.4	19.9	17.4	13.2	12.8	14.6	19.2	21.9
26–30 pupils	21.9	26.7	32.6	23.6	23.3	27.0	26.9	33.0
31–35 pupils	5.8	20.6	23.3	28.1	32.5	23.4	8.9	10.3
36–40 pupils				17.1	16.7	3.7	0.5	0.4
41–50 pupils	} 0.1	} 0.4	} 0.3	6.9	2.9	0.5	} 1.0	} neg.
Over 50				0.1	0.1	1.3		
31 and over	5.9	21.0	23.6	52.2	52.2	28.9	10.4	10.7

Notes:
1. Public elementary schools in 1930 and 1938, maintained primary schools in 1950 and 1961.
2. Secondary schools on the grant list in 1910, 1930 and 1938, maintained secondary schools in 1950 and 1961.
Source: Statistics of Education.

costs in that year, which fell sharply in 1945/46 as demobilisation got under way. In interpreting the university figures one has to remember that the price index of inputs is probably not very accurate for them, since changes in university salaries have at times diverged markedly from those of school teachers. Consequently, some of the falls and rises in university costs per pupil are probably due to changes in relative rates of pay. The university figures before 1923/24 are also unreliable because of the paucity of readily available statistics of cost.

The 1950s and 1960s were a period of remarkable expansion in education in the United Kingdom. A much larger slice of the growing national output was devoted to expanding that 'useful stock' of education. Costs per pupil at all types of educational establishment increased both in terms of real inputs (teachers, buildings etc.) and, even more so, in terms of the consumption sacrificed to obtain these inputs. As a result, the average worker received much more education, measured in terms of costs, than this father or grandfather. Even if we were to stop all further net investment, merely maintaining the existing stock would now require an appreciably larger fraction of national output than just after the Second World War.

All this, however, is in terms of measurable quantities, namely costs. It

Table 6.17   Teachers qualifications in different types of school, 1901–67, England and Wales (percentage of total teachers)

| | Public elementary | | Grant-aided secondary | |
	Certificated	Uncertificated and supplementary	Graduate	Non-graduate
1901	55.7	44.3	—	—
1911	62.7	37.3	57.4	42.6
1921	70.3	29.7	63.5	36.5
1931	74.7	25.3	74.1	25.9
1938	79.2	20.8	78.4	21.6

Percentage of graduate teachers in different types of school

	Primary	Modern	Grammar	Direct grant grammar
1951	3.2	14.0	76.8	67.4
1961	3.8	17.3	78.2	70.0
1971	4.8	29.1	73.8	63.0
1979	12.9	47.0	79.1	65.6
1983	19.8	55.9	82.2	28.1[1]

Notes: Based on full-time teachers. 1951 onwards, no figures given for unqualified teachers.
   1.   All direct grant schools: nursery, special, unattached.
Source: *Statistics of Public Education 1900–1, 1910–11*; *Education* – Annual Report of Board of Education 1920–1; *Statistics of Education*, 1961–83.

says nothing about the quality of the education provided per unit cost, although that is undoubtedly of the first importance.

Teaching quality is obviously one aspect. Pupil/teacher ratios by type of school are given in Table 6.15 and class sizes in Table 6.16. Note the slow and steady amelioration in public elementary schools between 1901 and 1938. But this of course disguises variations between particular schools. Note also the better teacher/pupil ratios in secondary schools and especially those in the private sector.

Quality and turnover of teachers is also important. We seem to have no statistics on class of degree among graduate teachers. The trend of formal qualifications is shown in Table 6.17. There was a steady rise in certification among teachers in public elementary schools up to 1938 and a slowly rising proportion of graduate teachers in all types of school up to 1985.

SOCIAL CLASS, LENGTH OF SCHOOLING AND EDUCATIONAL ATTAINMENT[11]

Leaving age varies with the type of school attended (Table 6.18). Figures for the inter-war period show the growing tendency for both boys and girls to stay in the grant-aided secondary schools until they were at least 16. After the war, when secondary education of some kind became universally available, the variation in leaving age between different types of school becomes clear. Direct grant and independent schools had the highest proportion staying on until 18 or more, followed by the grammar schools, though the difference between the different types of institution lessened while the leaving age for all children rose. From 1971 the age-basis of calculation shifted to 31 August of the previous year (which disguises the continuing trend). From 1972–3 the school leaving age was 16, but a fairly steady growth in the number of pupils, particularly girls, who choose to stay on is evident. In England and Wales in 1983, 30 per cent of boys and 22 per cent of girls stayed on for an extra year compared with 23 and 21 per cent respectively in 1967. About a fifth of both boys and girls in 1983 stayed for two extra years.

The rising numbers of qualified secondary school pupils which we described above appear in Table 6.19. Over the period 1961–81 the state sector acquired a greater share of the certificates at both O-level and A-levels. But there was a significant exception. Despite its falling share of successful candidates the private sector managed to hold its own in the competition for three or more A-levels – the crucial competition for university entrance. The private schools produced 29 per cent of those obtaining three or more A-levels in 1981 despite the fact that in the previous 20 years their share of pupils aged 17 + fell from 29 per cent to 19 per cent. As Table 6.20 makes plain, the private schools managed to extract an increasing quality of examination performance from

Table 6.18 Proportion of children leaving school at different ages by type of school, 1920–67, England and Wales (percentages)

Year	Type of school	14 and under 16		16 and under 18		18 and over		Total	
		Boys	Girls	Boys	Girls	Boys	Girls	Boys	Girls
1920	Grant-aided secondary	55.1	45.9	44.9	54.1	—	—	100	100
1931	Grant-aided secondary	27.7	28.9	58.1	53.8	14.2	17.3	100 (35 299)	100 (32 377)
1938	Grant-aided secondary	25.0	26.9	62.5	59.8	12.6	13.4	100 (43 288)	100 (38 168)
1951	Grammar	20.1	23.8	60.2	60.2	19.7	16.0	100 (45 453)	100 (45 164)
	Technical	61.1	52.8	38.3	46.4	0.5	0.8	100 (16 215)	100 (8 567)
	Bilateral, multilateral and comprehensive	69.7	68.9	25.7	26.9	4.6	4.3	100 (3 599)	100 (3 439)
	All-age and modern	98.3	98.0	1.7	1.8	neg.	0.2	100 (178 188)	100 (175 802)
	Direct grant	10.4	14.1	60.3	63.4	29.4	22.4	100 (5 120)	100 (5 536)
1961	Grammar	8.2	12.6	56.4	60.7	35.2	26.7	100 (52 713)	100 (54 505)
	Technical	27.5	27.3	64.6	65.6	7.9	7.2	100 (11 917)	100 (6 857)
	Bilateral, multilateral and comprehensive	65.6	63.0	29.2	31.5	5.2	5.5	100 (17 062)	100 (16 286)
	Other maintained secondary[1]	73.7	71.9	24.6	26.6	1.8	1.5	100 (13 890)	100 (15 034)
	Direct grant	4.4	7.2	46.3	55.2	49.2	37.7	100 (7 040)	100 (6 751)
	Independent recognised efficient	5.7	12.8	49.2	68.6	45.1	18.5	100 (14 326)	100 (13 431)

Year									
1971	Grammar	19.2	23.8	54.7	58.4	26.0	17.8	100 (45 630)	100 (47 680)
	Comprehensive	65.0	66.1	28.0	28.6	6.9	5.2	100 (108 690)	100 (102 680)
	Modern and all-age	84.6	85.2	14.9	14.4	0.4	0.4	100 (117 710)	100 (110 100)
	Technical and other secondary	59.9	61.9	33.1	33.7	7.0	4.4	100 (20 770)	100 (118 780)
	Direct grant	11.2	14.3	58.5	63.8	30.3	21.9	100 (7 780)	100 (7 620)
	Independent and grant-aided	61.5	63.2	29.7	30.7	8.8	6.1	100 (315 330)	100 (298 090)
1979	Grammar	30.2	34.8	62.5	62.4	7.2	2.8	100 (13 350)	100 (14 100)
	Comprehensive	76.7	73.6	21.4	25.3	1.8	1.2	100 (301 340)	100 (290 810)
	Sixth-form college	4.1	2.0	81.8	89.1	14.1	8.9	100 (12 280)	100 (12 090)
	Other secondary	91.4	88.5	8.0	11.3	0.5	0.2	100 (37 900)	100 (36 360)
	Direct grant	14.1	15.6	73.2	78.9	12.7	5.3	100 (7 020)	100 (5 270)
	Independent	21.8	38.6	65.2	54.2	13.0	7.1	100 (17 420)	100 (13 820)
1983	Grammar	25.7	28.6	65.3	67.4	9.0	3.9	100 (10 090)	100 (11 210)
	Comprehensive	72.0	68.0	25.6	30.1	2.3	0.1	100 (330 240)	100 (321 840)
	Other secondary	87.9	83.7	11.3	15.8	0.8	0.6	100 (25 020)	100 (23 410)
	Independent	19.0	29.2	67.2	62.4	13.7	8.4	100 (24 580)	100 (19 130)

Note: 1. Excluding leavers from secondary modern and all-age schools for which information is not available.

Sources: Annual Report of Board of Education 1920; Annual Report and Statistics of Education, 1931, 1938, 1951; *Statistics of Education*, pt 2, 1961; *Statistics of Education*, vol. 2, 1971; *Statistics of Education* school-leavers, CSE and GCE, vol. 2, Table 2, 1979 (England only); *Statistics of Education*, school-leavers, CSE and GCE, Table C2, 1983 (England only).

Table 6.19   Achievements of school-leavers by type of school (percentages)

	School	1 or more O-levels	5 or more O-levels	1 or more A-levels	3 or more A-levels
1961	Maintained	78.1	72.9	69.0	68.7
	Direct grant	7.5	9.6	12.4	15.9
	Independent	14.4	17.5	18.6	15.4
	Total	100.0	100.0	100.0	100.0
	No. (000s)	167.5	93.5	50.5	26.0
1966	Maintained	81.4	76.2	73.8	72.6
	Direct grant	6.3	8.4	10.5	12.4
	Independent	12.3	15.4	15.7	15.0
	Total	100.0	100.0	100.0	100.0
	No. (000s)	219.4	129.9	85.2	43.2
1971	Maintained	83.6	78.0	76.3	72.5
	Direct grant	6.3	8.8	10.1	13.0
	Independent	10.2	13.1	13.7	14.5
	Total	100.1	99.9	100.1	100.0
	No. (000s)	231.8	132.4	102.6	51.4
1976	Maintained	86.1	78.1	76.6	72.3
	Direct grant ⎱ Independent ⎰	13.9	22.0	9.5 13.9	12.3 15.4
	Total	100.0	100.1	100.0	100.0
	No. (000s)	284.8	138.1	112.2	60.0
1981	Maintained	87.6	79.5	77.0	70.9
	Direct grant ⎱ Independent ⎰	12.4	20.5	23.0	29.1
	Total	100.0	100.0	100.0	100.0
	No. (000s)	333.0	161.0	120.8	68.6

Source: Statistics of Education.

the same number of pupils. In 1961 only two-fifths of the leavers from private schools had any A-levels, and less than one-fifth had three or more. By 1981 63 per cent left with at least one A-level, and as many as 45 per cent had three or more. A remarkable improvement in academic output had been achieved in these 20 years.

Improvement of this kind was not paralleled in the state schools. The output of A-levels increased tremendously in absolute terms and considerably in proportionate terms (from 6.1 per cent with one or more A-levels in 1961 to 13.5 per cent in 1981). But there was no matching of the private sector shift towards the achievement of three A-levels.

In consequence there was a clear sense in which inequality as between state and private secondary schooling increased over these two decades. The inequality in question is that the chances of emerging with three A-levels from a private school compared with a state school widened between 1961 and 1981. The chances were, of course, unequal at the earlier date. The point is

Table 6.20 School-leavers' achievements at A-level (percentages)

School	None attempted	Candidates' achievements 0	1,2	3+	Total Percentage	Number (000s)
1961						
Maintained	93.1	0.8	3.0	3.1	100.0	(571.2)
Direct grant	49.7	5.0	15.4	30.0	100.0	(13.8)
Independent	61.0	5.2	19.3	14.5	100.0	(27.8)
Direct grant and independent	57.3	5.1	18.0	19.6	100.0	(41.6)
1966						
Maintained	87.8	1.3	5.5	5.4	100.0	(578.0)
Direct grant	35.4	4.8	24.0	35.9	100.1	(14.9)
Independent	50.1	5.7	22.8	21.4	100.0	(30.3)
Direct grant and independent	45.2	5.4	23.2	26.2	100.0	(45.2)
1971						
Maintained	84.3	2.0	7.2	6.5	100.0	(572.0)
Direct grant	28.4	4.5	23.8	43.4	100.1	(15.4)
Independent	39.8	6.2	25.3	28.6	99.9	(26.0)
Direct grant and independent	35.6	5.6	24.7	34.1	100.0	(41.4)
1976						
Maintained	85.2	1.9	6.4	6.5	100.0	(664.5)
Direct grant	26.9	4.8	21.1	47.1	99.9	(15.7)
Independent	38.5	4.2	23.4	33.9	100.0	(27.2)
Direct grant and independent	34.3	4.4	22.6	38.7	100.0	(42.9)
1981						
Maintained	84.6	1.9	6.4	7.1	100.0	(689.9)
Independent	33.0	4.0	17.7	45.3	100.0	(44.1)

Source: *Statistics of Education.*

that, after two decades of clear progress in both sectors, they were more unequal. The inequality in 1961 in terms of odds ratios was 7.6.[12] The odds shortened slightly during the 1960s, but by 1981 were distinctly longer than originally (see Table 6.21).

Inequality, it appears, has been changing its form. The older form was essentially inequality of chances of entry to the sixth form; thereafter the attrition of working-class pupils was relatively minor. But by 1981 the door of the sixth form had become relatively less important – and, indeed, the success of the state comprehensives has largely been that of encouraging vastly greater numbers to pass through. The new inequality is that among sixth-formers the private schools have forged ahead much faster in their capacity to prepare A-level candidates for high performance in their examinations. The state sector

Table 6.21   Chances of obtaining three or more A-levels in state and private schools, 1961–81

School	Percentage of leavers with three or more A-levels				
	1961	*1966*	*1971*	*1976*	*1981*
State	3.1	5.4	6.5	6.5	7.1
Private (including direct grant)	19.6	27.2	34.1	38.7	45.3
Odds ratios	7.6	6.2	7.4	9.1	10.8

Source: Calculated from statistics in Table 6.20.

has expanded its sixth-form numbers; the private sector has kept its numbers stable and dramatically improved their performance. In the process the selection procedures of the private schools have, we suspect, changed, just as the sharp increase of state school numbers will have changed the kind of children admitted to comprehensive sixth forms.

The association between class and academic achievement has been well established by studies throughout the century. The most recent study of England and Wales was by Halsey, Heath and Ridge,[13] and Tables 6.22 to 6.29 are taken from this source. The class schema used is as follows. Class I includes higher-grade professionals, administrators, managers and proprietors. Class II includes lower-grade professionals, administrators and managers, supervisors and higher-grade technicians. Classes I and II are termed the *service* class. Class III includes clerical, sales and rank-and-file service workers. Class IV includes small proprietors and self-employed artisans (the 'petty bourgeoisie'). Class V includes lower-grade technicians and foremen (the 'aristocracy of labour'). Classes III, IV and V together are termed the *intermediate* class. Class VI includes skilled manual workers in industry. Class VII includes semi- and unskilled workers in industry. Class VIII includes agricultural workers and smallholders. Classes VI, VII and VIII together are termed the *working* class.

Table 6.22 shows the changing class chances of access to selective schools (defined to include the technical and grammar schools of the state sector, as well as all schools in the private sector).

Chances of admission to selective schools generally increased at all levels of the class structure in the case of boys born between 1923 and 1932, and between 1933 and 1942, but then actually fell back again in the case of the birth cohorts 1943 to 1952 to levels very like those, in most cases, of a generation earlier.

The expansion of selective schooling is described in Table 6.23. In terms of the percentage of boys in each birth cohort who were 'first generation' in grammar or technical schools compared with their parents (defined as both having attended non-selective schools) expansion should decrease the number of first-generation schoolboys. The table shows that there was a considerable

Table 6.22   Attendance at selective schools by birth cohort (percentages)

| Father's class[2] | Birth cohort | | | | |
	1913–22	*1923–32*	*1933–42*	*1943–52*	*All*
I, II (Service)	69.7	76.7	79.3	66.4	71.9
	124[1]	*108*	*107*	*112*	*111*
III, IV, V (Intermediate)	34.9	44.0	43.3	37.1	39.6
	55	*52*	*47*	*54*	*51*
VI, VII, VIII (Working)	20.2	26.1	27.1	21.6	23.7
	0	*0*	*0*	*0*	*0*
All	29.6	37.0	38.8	34.8	35.0
(No.)	(1873)	(1897)	(1890)	(2351)	(8011)

Notes:
1.   Figures in italics give log distances – a form of disparity ratio in which the ratio P_{ik}/P_{jk} is converted to $\log_e P_{ik} - \log_e P_{jk}$.
      See Halsey *et al.* (1980) 37 (as in *Source*).
Source: Halsey, A. H., Heath, A. F. and Ridge, J. M. (1980) *Origins and Destinations* (Oxford University Press) Table 4.9.

Table 6.23   'First generation' pupils at selective schools by birth cohort percentages

| Respondent's secondary schooling | Year of birth | | | |
	1913–22	*1923–32*	*1933–42*	*1943–52*
Technical	86.1	78.6	75.9	63.6
Grammar	80.2	67.1	69.9	54.5
Direct grant	66.7	55.2	39.3	31.7
Independent non-HMC[1]	54.8	53.1	51.2	27.8
Independent HMC[1]	36.0	27.6	22.9	15.8
All selective	78.1	69.2	65.1	49.9

Note:
1.   Head Masters' Conference.
Source: As Table 6.22.

decline. The fall was largest in the case of the private and direct grant schools where the proportions halved. It was smallest in the case of the technical schools; even in the most recent cohort (birth 1943 to 1952) over one-half were still 'first generation' pupils. Recruits to the post-war state selective schools were still, more often then not, new to their academic tradition.

Table 6.24 shows trends in school attendance and school examinations for the four birth cohorts. During the period covered by the study there was a great increase in the numbers staying on to 15, mainly because of the raising of the school-leaving age in 1947. There was also a high rate of growth in school attendance at 16, 17 and 18 years of age throughout the post-war period. The apparent stagnation of the pre-war years was followed by a continuing boom in school attendance after the war. True, the highest increases occurred among the 1933-42 cohort who were entering secondary education in 1944 and were thus having to make decisions about school-leaving from 1948 onwards. But substantial increases were also recorded by the 1943–52 cohort who were making their decisions in the late 1950s and early 1960s. Over the period as a whole the percentage of each cohort staying on until 16 or later increased by 185 per cent. Given that the size of the cohorts themselves also increased, this means that the actual numbers who stayed on increased by 242 per cent. This figure can be put in perspective by noting that Britain's gross national product over the comparable 30 years increased by only 52 per cent, that the intake into the private schools increased by only 75 per cent and that even the intake into the grammar schools increased by only 138 per cent. Thus there were general increases in provision but the increases were greater among the more selective and prestigious forms of secondary education. Grammar school places doubled, but the numbers entering the sixth form more than trebled and the numbers staying on to complete a sixth-form course rose fourfold.

There is a general characteristic of educational expansion in advanced industrial countries since the Second World War; the higher the educational level the faster the rate of growth. This phenomenon appears also in the pattern of examination successes. Table 6.24 shows that the percentage of the cohort obtaining O-levels (or School Certificate before the war) increased by

Table 6.24   Trends in school attendance and school examinations

		1913–22	*1923–32*	*1933–42*	*1943–52*
Percentage staying on at school until	15	22.8	27.5	94.8	100.0
	16	15.6	18.1	31.0	44.4
	17	8.3	7.8	14.5	23.7
	18	3.4	4.0	7.7	14.2
Percentage obtaining	O-level	11.9	14.0	23.2	34.0
	A-level	2.1	3.6	7.1	15.1
Success rates	O:16	0.76	0.77	0.75	0.77
	A:18	0.62	0.90	0.92	1.06

Note: The first four rows indicate the percentage of boys staying at their secondary schools until the age indicated or a higher one. To obtain the percentage *leaving* at a given age we have to subtract from the percentage given for that age the percentage for the next higher age. For example, in the 1943–52 cohort the percentage leaving at 15 was 100−44.4 = 55.6

We have computed the A-level success rate for the proportion of those staying on until 18 because relatively few people who left at 17 obtained A-levels before doing so. 4.8 per cent of those who obtained an A-level pass (or Higher School Certificate) left school at 16 or earlier; 15.8 per cent left at 17; 63.7 per cent at 18; and 15.7 per cent left at 19 or later.

Source: As Table 6.22.

186 per cent while that obtaining A-levels (or Higher School Certificate before the war) increased by 619 per cent.

The distribution of increased school attendance beyond the minimum leaving age between different social classes is shown in Table 6.25. There were very different rates of increase at social class levels and also a decline in class differentials. The proportion of boys from service class homes who stayed on to 16 or later increased by 50 per cent, the proportion from the intermediate class increased by 200 per cent and that from the working-class by 240 per cent. The distance between the classes shrank accordingly, the service class/working-class log distance[14] shrinking from 174 to 91, and the intermediate/working-class log distance shrinking from 56 to 43. Thus expansion was associated with decreasing inequality. The picture given by Table 6.25 is not, however, a simple one of linear trend towards equality of class chances. The distance between classes first rose and then fell. The maximum inequality, as measured by the log distance, occurred not in the earliest cohort but in the 1923–32 cohort. And it should be noted that the difference, measured in straightforward percentage terms, between the service and working class was actually greater at the end of the period than at the beginning. The difference started at 43 percentage points, widened to 51 and fell back marginally to 47 in the youngest cohort. Table 6.26 shows the trends in school attendance at age 18 plus.

Table 6.25 Trends in school attendance: percentage staying on until 16 or later

| Father's social class | Birth cohort | | | |
	1913–22	1923–32	1933–42	1943–52
I, II (Service)	52.4 *174*[1]	61.0 *185*	77.3 *136*	78.6 *91*
III, IV, V (Intermediate)	16.1 *56*	23.9 *91*	34.6 *56*	48.5 *43*
VI, VII, VIII (Working)	9.2 *0*	9.6 *0*	19.8 *0*	31.6 *0*

Note:
1. Figures in italic give log distances (see Table 6.22, Note 1).
Source: As Table 6.22.

Table 6.26 Trends in school attendance: percentage staying on until 18 or later

| Father's social class | Birth cohort | | | |
	1913–22	1923–32	1933–34	1943–52
I, II (Service)	15.7 *162*[1]	20.0 *216*	32.2 *214*	38.2 *179*
III, IV, V (Intermediate)	6.1 *68*	6.2 *99*	5.9 *44*	14.4 *81*
VI, VII, VIII (Working)	3.1 *0*	2.3 *0*	3.8 *0*	6.4 *0*

Note:
1. Figures in italic give log distances (see Table 6.22, Note 1).
Source: As Table 6.22.

Table 6.27 Attendance at university by birth cohort (percentages)

Father's social class	1913–22	1923–32	1933–42	1943–52
I, II (Service)	7.2	15.9	23.7	26.4
	208[1]	*258*	*233*	*214*
III, IV, V (Intermediate)	1.9	4.0	4.1	8.0
	75	*120*	*58*	*95*
VI, VII, VIII (Working)	0.9	1.2	2.3	3.1
	0	*0*	*0*	*0*
All	1.8	3.4	5.4	8.5
No.	(1846)	(1879)	(1856)	(2246)

Note:
1. Figures in italic give log distances (see Table 6.22, Note 1).
Source: As Table 6.22.

Trends in class access to the universities are shown in Table 6.27. Comparing the development of secondary schools (Table 6.22), it appears from Table 6.27 that university expansion kept pace with the growth of the service classes, and that 'Robbinsian expansion' was an effective response to the post-war baby boom. The familiar picture emerges, as with educational expansion generally, that though the fastest rates of growth almost always accrue to the working class, the greatest absolute increments of opportunity went to the service class. Trends in class access to part-time further education and to post-secondary education as a whole are shown in Table 6.28. It emerges that the

Table 6.28(a) Percentage attending part-time further education by social class and birth cohort

Father's social class	1913–22	1923–32	1933–42	1943–52
I, II (Service)	50.0	46.2	59.3	45.1
III, IV, V (Intermediate)	40.3	41.7	55.1	57.2
VI, VII, VIII (Working)	29.9	36.9	46.4	50.8

Table 6.28(b) Percentage attending any form of post-school education by social class and birth cohort

Father's social class	1913–22	1923–32	1933–42	1943–52
I, II (Service)	60.6 *65[1]*	64.4 *50*	77.1 *44*	73.9 *30*
III, IV, V (Intermediate)	43.5 *32*	48.0 *21*	60.4 *19*	67.4 *21*
VI, VII, VIII (Working)	31.5 *0*	38.9 *0*	49.9 *0*	54.6 *0*

Note:
1. Figures in italic give log distances (see Table 6.22, Note 1).
Source: As Table 6.22.

part-time further education class access has slowly changed with expansion from the familiar positive correlation of class and opportunity to an inverse relation for those born after the Second War. Thus, in the earlier decades it was not usefully seen as an alternative route for the working class so much as an extension of class-biased educational opportunity. For the last cohort, the alternative-route description is more accurate. Nevertheless, any description has to be placed in the context of the whole structure of educational opportunity beyond school, and then it appears that expansion has brought a slow and steady diminution of class inequality. The log distance of the service from the working class fell from 65 to 30. In the same process the gap in rate of journeying decreased. An extra 13 of every 100 service-class boys travelled educationally beyond school compared with an extra 23 working-class boys.

We can sum up the changing educational experience of boys born between 1913 and 1952 in Table 6.29. There were trends towards the amelioration of early childhood disadvantages in the double sense that the typical child of the later cohorts was more likely to come from a service-class home or, if from the working class, to have been born into rather better material circumstances, to have had rather better educated parents and fewer siblings. As a supplier of children, the service class increased from less than 1 in 10 in the first cohort (born in 1913–22) to approximately 1 in 5 in the fourth (born 1943–52). Material goods in any case became less certain discriminators between families both across and within classes. Children stayed longer in schools and went on in larger proportions and numbers to post-secondary education. The rates of change varied. The private sector of both primary and secondary education expanded in proportion to the number of children in the intermediate post-war years, but thereafter attendance at private primary schools fell away and private secondary schooling ceased to grow. Meanwhile various forms of selective secondary education expanded before and even after the Second War, but it should be noted that the expansion was greatest and sustained longest in the case of grammar schools, whereas the proportion of children in technical schools fell among those who reached the secondary stage after the war. Only among the youngest cohort was there the beginning of the development of comprehensive secondary schooling which, by the 1980s, dominated the scene.

Finally, we should note that post-secondary schooling in universities, colleges of higher and further education also expanded throughout the century. Accordingly, the costs of the education of the average boy rose through the period in terms of both the amount of money spent on him and the length of his educational career. But investment was proportionately higher at the higher levels of secondary and post-secondary education. Thus, what is essential for the understanding of theories concerning equality and social selection, the nature of educational expansion was such as to maintain, and indeed to increase, the cost of the longest, compared with the shortest, possible educational career.

Table 6.29 A review of changing experience from 1913 to 1972: percentage of each age-group having the specified attribute

	Born			
	1913–22	1923–32	1933–42	1943–52
At respondent's age 14				
Class origin: service	9.1	10.2	12.2	17.7
intermediate	28.5	27.4	29.7	30.3
Domestic amenities: telephone	7.4	9.7	16.3	25.4
refrigerator	2.2	3.8	16.2	46.4
inside lavatory	37.2	50.9	61.3	82.1
fixed bath or shower	37.5	56.8	67.7	86.4
House tenure: owned	19.6	24.7	27.5	36.0
council house	18.7	26.6	31.9	39.2
Number of siblings (average)	3.3	3.0	2.5	2.2
Father's education				
Private primary	3.1	3.0	2.8	3.3
Private secondary[1]	2.3	2.3	3.3	4.0
Selective secondary	6.6	9.8	14.3	23.1
Any exam or qualification	1.9	2.0	2.7	5.3
Respondent's own education				
Private primary	5.2	5.1	7.1	5.7
Private secondary[1]	5.0	5.4	7.5	7.3
Private, excluding direct grant	3.7	3.8	5.8	5.5
Grammar school	10.6	13.6	20.2	21.0
Any selective secondary[2]	29.0	36.2	38.2	34.4
School-leaving age (average)	14.5	14.6	15.4	15.8
Ordinary School Certificate/O-level	11.9	14.2	23.1	34.0
Higher School Certificate/A-level	2.1	3.6	6.9	14.4
Entered university	1.8	3.4	5.4	8.4
No. (=8529)	(2035)	(2053)	(1990)	(2451)

Notes:
1. Independent schools (whether Headmasters' Conference Schools or not) and direct grant schools.
2. Including technical schools.

Notes

1. Maurice Scott (1980) 'Net Investment in Education in the United Kingdom 1951–71', *Oxford Review of Education*, 1(6): 21–30.
2. Olive Banks (1968) *The Sociology of Education* (Batsford).
3. See A. H. Halsey, A. F. Heath, and J. M. Ridge (1980) *Origins and Destinations* (Oxford University Press).
4. See notes to Table 6.1. It is noteworthy that there have been considerable fluctuations in the child population. For the United Kingdom in 1901 there were 8 million children aged 5–14. Fertility fell during the slump years of the 1930s to bring the total down to 6.7 million in 1941. It increased to a high point of 9.2 in 1976 and then dropped again in subsequent years to roughly the same figure in 1986 as it had been at the beginning of the century.
5. H. Glennester and G. Wilson (1970) *Paying for Private Schools* (Allan Lane) 13–17.
6. T. W. Bamford (1967) *Rise of the Public Schools – A Study of Boys', Public Boarding Schools in England and Wales from 1837 to the Present Day* (Nelson) 268–9.
7. Public Schools Commission (1968) *First Report*, vol. 1 (HMSO).
8. J. Rae (1981) *The Public School Revolution: Britain's Independent Schools 1964–1979* (Faber).
9. See M. Cruickshank (1963) *Church and State in English Education* (Macmillan).
10. The following pages [384–394] are reproduced from Maurice Scott (1980) 'Net Investment in Education in the United Kingdom 1951–71', *Oxford Review of Education*, 1(6): 21–30.
11. The discussion in pp. 255–260 and Tables 6.20 and 6.21 are taken from A. H. Halsey, A. F. Heath, and J. M. Ridge (1985) 'The Political Arithmetic of Public Schools' in G. Walford (ed.) *British Public Schools* (Falmer Press). The Tables were extracted from *Statistics of Education*.
12. The odds ratio measures the relative chances that pupils entering different types of school will succeed or fail in the competition to achieve three or more A-levels.
13. A. H. Halsey, A. F. Heath and J. M. Ridge (1980) *Origins and Destinations* (Oxford University Press).
14. See Table 6.22, Note 1.

7 Higher Education

A. H. Halsey

Given that the 1944 Education Act legislated secondary education for all, the most general term for all education beyond school is post-secondary. The Robbins Report on Higher Education, which appeared in 1963, was a landmark in the definition of higher education. But the underlying framework for interpreting the trends is the shape and pace of movement towards universal post-secondary education. Various phrases are used in the literature to describe different kinds of post-school education including higher education, further education, and adult education. There are no absolute clear dividing lines between institutions, and this chapter refers mainly to statistics on the universities, and to statistics on advanced courses in further education. Statistics on universities for Great Britain and Northern Ireland are published in a convenient form from 1966 (*Volume VI, Statistics of Education*, and for recent years by the University Grants Committee (UGC) as *University Statistics*). This form of publication took the place of the University Grants Committee's *Returns from Universities and University Colleges* which were previously published in command paper form up to and including the statistics for 1965–6 (Cmnd 3586). There are also useful publications by the Universities' Central Council on Admissions (UCCA) and the University Statistical Service.

The general twentieth-century story is one of expansion, and is illustrated in Figure 7.1, showing the highest qualification level of the population by age in

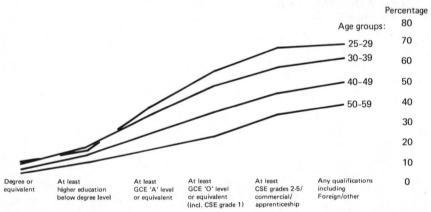

Figure 7.1   Highest qualification level of the population: by age, 1984, Great Britain

Sources: *Labour Force Survey*, 1984, Department of Employment; *Social Trends*, no. 16, chart 3.19. Reproduced with the permission of the Controller of Her Majesty's Stationery Office.

1984. Age grades appear as 'geological strata' with rising levels of qualifications attained. In 1984, 70 per cent of the population in the 25–29 age group held an educational qualification, whereas only 39 per cent of those aged 50–59 did so.

It is convenient to recognise the importance of the Robbins Report of 1963, and accordingly to divide the story into four main sections:

1. The growth of higher education up to 1963.
2. Developments since the Robbins Report.
3. Development of the universities from 1900.
4. Students in post-secondary education.

GROWTH OF HIGHER EDUCATION 1900 TO 1963

The Robbins Committee[1] defined higher education for their purposes as follows: 'In the main we have concentrated on the universities[2] in Great Britain and those colleges, within the purview of the Ministry of Education and the Scottish Education Department, that provide courses for the education and training of teachers or systematic courses of further education beyond the advanced level of the General Certificate of Education (in Scotland, beyond the higher grade of the Scottish Certificate of Education) or beyond the Ordinary National Certificate or its equivalent.'[3]

The definition is further elucidated by a consideration of further education which embraces 'in addition to the colleges of advanced technology, the advanced work undertaken at a great number of technical and commercial colleges and schools of art, but it excludes the initial stages of much professional and other education provided in such colleges'.[4]

An indication of the growth of higher education is provided in the Robbins Report (Table 53, p. 199). Using the definition referred to above, and including part-time as well as full-time study, the outlays of central and local government (in respect of teaching and other services, rent and maintenance of buildings, apparatus and materials, student grants and building development) on higher education in Great Britain rose from (at 1962–3 prices) £26m in 1937–8 to £90m in 1954–5 and to £219m in 1962–3. The percentage of 17-year-olds receiving full-time education in Great Britain had risen from 1 per cent in 1870 to 2 per cent in 1902 to 4 per cent in 1938 and to 15 per cent by 1962.

The pattern of higher education as described by Robbins in 1962, and using his definitions, may be summarised as follows. At the turn of the century nearly all full-time higher education had been provided by universities: the courses then given in teacher-training colleges and colleges of education involved only two years of study and the standard of instruction was correspondingly restricted. The training colleges had grown substantially in

British Social Trends since 1900

Table 7.1   Students in full-time higher education, 1900/1–1962/3,
Great Britain

Year	University	Teacher training	Further education	All full-time higher education
1900–01	20 000	5 000	—	25 000
1924–5	42 000	16 000	3 000	61 000
1938–9	50 000	13 000	6 000	69 000
1954–5	82 000	28 000	12 000	122 000
1962–3	118 000	55 000	43 000	216 000

Notes: Figures for further education in 1924–5 and 1938–9 are
approximate. The table does not include full-time advanced
students in the colleges of music and other colleges mentioned
in paragraph 8 of Chapter 1 of Higher Education.
Part of the large increase in teacher training between 1954–5
and 1962–3 was due to the lengthening of the training college
course in England and Wales.
Source: Higher Education, p. 15, Table 3.

Table 7.2   Percentage of age group[1] entering full-time higher
education, 1900–1962, Great Britain

Year	University	Teacher training	Further education	All full-time higher education
1900	0.8	0.4	—	1.2
1924	1.5	1.0	0.2	2.7
1938	1.7	0.7	0.3	2.7
1954	3.2	2.0	0.6	5.8
1955	3.4	2.0	0.7	6.1
1956	3.5	2.1	0.8	6.4
1957	3.9	2.2	0.9	7.0
1958	4.1	2.4	1.2	7.7
1959	4.2	2.8	1.3	8.3
1960	4.1	2.7	1.5	8.3
1961	4.1	2.5	1.7	8.3
1962	4.0	2.5	2.0	8.5

Note:
1.   See Note 5 on p. 295.
Source: Higher Education, p. 16, Table 4.

the years before the Robbins Committee, both because of rising standards of entry and, in England and Wales, because of the introduction of three-year courses in 1960. The stature of some colleges engaged in further education had also grown dramatically in the 1950s. While the number of university students had slightly more than doubled since before the war, the number in training colleges and colleges of education had increased just over fourfold. But even more striking had been the marked increase in the number of full-time students in advanced courses in further education. This group had been negligible at the beginning of the century but by 1962 constituted a fifth of all full-time students in higher education. Most part-time higher education was provided in institutions of further education. In 1962–3 there were 54 000 advanced students attending these institutions for at least one day a week (compared with 29 000 in 1954–5): most of them were released by their employers for the purpose. Another 54 000 advanced students attended only in the evening. In the universities the number of part-time students was 9000 (over two-thirds of them at post-graduate level) compared with 6000 before the war. Students in training colleges and colleges of education were almost always full-time. The trends are presented in Table 7.1. They may also be presented in terms of percentages of the age group.[5] For those entering full-time higher education courses they are given in Table 7.2.

HIGHER EDUCATION SINCE 1963

The Robbins Report heralded accelerated growth in higher education. In 1962 there were 31 British universities, 10 colleges of advanced technology, 150 teacher-training colleges and upwards of 600 technical colleges and other institutions of further education in which about 33 000 students were enrolled on courses of higher education standard. Robbins set targets for 1973 of 219 000 university students, 122 000 teacher-trainees in (renamed) colleges of education, and 51 000 in technical colleges on advanced courses. These targets were reached by 1970 and surpassed by over 40 000 in the case of the technical colleges. Between 1963 and 1970–71 the total student population in full-time higher education doubled to 457 000. In this period the colleges of advanced technology were given university charters, seven new universities were founded in England and one in Scotland, where in addition two others were formed from leading technical institutions. The colleges of education doubled their student places, but many have since been drawn into the polytechnic system with their students reading for Bachelor of Education degrees.

In 1964 the Secretary of State for Education and Science, C. A. R. Crosland, announced a 'binary policy' for higher education – a division between the autonomous 44 universities and a 'public sector' led by 30 polytechnics.

The number of advanced students in the polytechnics or 'public sector' institutions has grown considerably – to 215 000 in 1970–71 and further to

Table 7.3 Higher education – full-time students: by origin, sex, and age, United Kingdom

(000s)

Students	Males					Females				
	1970–1	1975–6	1980–1	1982–3	1983–4	1970–1	1975–6	1980–1	1982–3	1983–4
Full-time students by origin[1]										
From the United Kingdom Universities										
– undergraduate	128.3	130.1	145.1	142.4	138.0	57.0	73.6	96.2	100.0	98.6
– post-graduate	23.9	23.2	20.7	19.3	20.0	8.0	10.2	11.3	10.9	11.4
Public sector higher education	102.0	109.3	111.9	133.4	141.9	113.1	120.1	96.4	115.4	124.0
Total full-time UK students	254.2	262.6	277.7	295.1	299.9	178.2	203.9	203.9	226.3	234.0
From abroad	20.0	38.6	40.7	34.8	34.5	4.4	9.9	12.6	12.0	12.1
Total full-time students	274.2	301.2	318.4	329.9	334.4	182.6	213.8	216.5	238.3	246.1
Full-time students by age[2]										
18 or under	28.7	31.7	50.3	52.4	51.1	30.4	30.5	41.6	45.9	44.9
19–20	99.0	104.6	117.8	127.6	130.5	82.3	90.0	89.7	100.7	106.3
21–24	104.6	108.7	95.6	97.8	98.5	44.5	59.8	53.5	58.5	60.6
25 or over	42.0	56.1	54.5	52.2	54.3	25.3	33.4	31.5	33.1	34.4

Notes:
1. Origin is on fee-paying status except for European Community students domiciled outside the United Kingdom who from 1980–81 are charged home rates but are included with students from abroad.
2. In 1980 measurement by age changed from 31 December to 31 August.
Source: Social Trends, no. 16, Table 3.12. Reproduced with the permission of the Controller of Her Majesty's Stationery Office.

Table 7.4 Higher education – part-time students: by type of establishment, sex, and age, United Kingdom   (000s)

Students	Males					Females				
	1970-1	1975-6	1980-1	1982-3	1983-4	1970-1	1975-6	1980-1	1982-3	1983-4
Part-time students by establishment										
Universities	18.1	19.3	22.6	22.6	23.1	5.7	7.0	10.7	12.4	13.2
Open University[1]	14.3	33.6	37.6	40.7	41.6	5.3	22.0	30.1	33.8	34.6
Public sector higher education										
– part-time day courses	69.8	80.2	110.5	112.6	113.1	6.7	15.4	30.8	35.1	38.6
– evening only courses	39.8	35.0	35.1	31.3	32.2	5.0	5.8	15.2	16.2	16.8
Total part-time students	142.0	168.1	205.8	207.2	210.0	22.7	50.2	86.8	97.5	103.2
Part-time students by age										
18 or under	—	—	11.8	8.8	8.3	—	—	3.2	2.8	2.8
19–20	—	—	33.9	35.8	33.8	—	—	7.5	7.8	7.8
21–24	—	—	48.3	48.0	47.3	—	—	16.0	17.6	17.4
25 or over	—	—	111.7	114.6	120.5	—	—	60.1	69.3	75.3

Note:
1. Calendar year beginning in second year shown. Excludes short course students up to 1982–83 in 1983–84 short course students are included apart from 6000 not separately available by sex.
Source: *Social Trends*, no. 16, Table 3.13. Reproduced with the permission of the Controller of Her Majesty's Stationery Office.

266 000 in 1983–4 (Table 7.3). Putting together all full-time higher education students in universities and public sector institutions from the UK and abroad the numbers rose from 457 000 in 1970–71 to 581 500 in 1983–4 (Table 7.3). In addition, by 1983–4 there were 313 000 part-time higher education students in the universities and the public sector institutions (Table 7.4). As percentages of the relevant age group, new entrants to full-time higher education are shown in Table 7.5 for the period 1970–84.

Table 7.5   Higher education – home students entering full-time and sandwich courses for the first time: by age, Great Britain (000s and percentages)

Students	1970–1	1975–6	1980–1	1981–2	1982–3	1983–4
New students (000s)						
Aged under 21	102.6	107.4	113.5	120.4	125.0	123.7
Aged 21 or over	27.3	31.4	33.7	36.5	36.5	37.3
Total	129.9	138.8	147.2	156.9	161.5	161.0
New students aged 21 or over as a percentage of all new students	21.0	22.6	22.9	23.3	22.6	23.2
New students aged under 21 as a percentage of the average of 18- and 19-year old populations	13.7	13.6	12.7	13.5	13.5	13.3

Source: *Social Trends*, no. 16, Table 3.14. Reproduced with the permission of the Controller of Her Majesty's Stationery Office.

It is possible to compare the Robbins plan with the actual experience in the period 1962–80. The comparison of programme and performance is taken from the recent work by John Carswell.[6] Carswell compares a number of aspects of the proposals of the Robbins Committee in terms of full-time student numbers down to 1980 with the outcome in that year (Table 7.6 to 7.9). The first line of each table gives the 1962 position as stated in the Robbins Report.

All the figures refer to full-time students at degree level (or equivalent) and above, and include full-time students at advanced level in further education. Overseas students, who formed between 9 and 12 per cent of the whole student body at different times during the period, are included. Since part-time students are not included the tables do not show the contribution of the Open University. The figures are for Great Britain, and do not include Northern Ireland.

Table 7.6 gives the overall picture divided by 'sectors'. The colleges of

Table 7.6 Development of the 'sectors', 1962–80, Great Britain (000s full-time students)

Students	UGC institutions	'Public sector' institutions	Total
(1) Actual 1962	130	86	216
(2) Addition for 1967 proposed by Robbins Committee	67	45	112
(3) Total (1) + (2)	197	131	328
(4) Actual 1967	200	179	379
(5) Further addition proposed by Robbins Committee for 1980	149	81	230
(6) Robbins proposal for 1980 (3) + (5)	346	212	558
(7) Actual 1980	301	223	524
(8) Difference between programme and performance	− 45	+ 11	− 34

Notes:
1. All the entries in the first column include the colleges of advanced technology, though they did not in fact become universities until 1964.
2. The entries in the second column bring together further education to advanced level in England and Wales and the equivalent in Scotland, and teacher training in Great Britain as a whole. Lines 2, 6 and 7 should be read with the important reservations that (i) the Robbins Report much overstated the need for teacher training, and (ii) further education expanded far more quickly than the Robbins Committee had proposed. While these departures in opposite directions almost cancel each other out, the components of the figures 212 in line 6 and 223 in line 7 are very different.
3. Line 7 includes advanced courses.
Source: J. Carswell (1985) *Government and the Universities in Britain* (Cambridge University Press) Appendix 1.

advanced technology appear in the 'university sector' figures for 1962, though they did not join the UGC Grant List until afterwards. The 'public sector' institutions include polytechnics, other further education institutions offering advanced courses, colleges of education in England, Scotland and Wales, Central Institutions in Scotland, and the two specialised higher educational institutions still financed by the Department of Education and Science – the Royal College of Art and the Cranfield Institute.

The table shows that overall performance came within 6 per cent of programme, and at mid-term considerably exceeded it but, as between the 'sectors', the programme was not achieved in the way the Robbins Report proposed. The last line of the table does not indicate a failure on the part of the UGC institutions to achieve the Robbins objective, but reflects the subsequent decision to develop further education on a much larger scale than the Robbins Report had proposed, with a consequent redistribution of both numbers and resources.

Table 7.7 Science/technology contrasted with all other subjects, Great Britain (000s full-time students)

Students	UGC institutions		'Public sector' institutions		Totals all institutions		Grand total all institutions, all subjects
	Science/ technology	*Other subjects*	*Science/ technology*	*Other subjects*	*Science/ technology*	*Other subjects*	
(1) Actual 1962	59	71	26	60	85	131	216
(2) Addition to 1980 proposed by Robbins Committee	136	80	38	88	174	168	342
(3) Robbins proposal for 1980 ((1)+(2))	195	151	64	148	259	299	558
(4) Actual 1980	112	188	64	160	176	348	524
(5) Difference between programme and performance	−83	+37	nil	+12	−83	+49	−34

Notes:

1. Lines 2 and 3 have been estimated on the basis that the Robbins Committee intended that about two-thirds of the additional places which they proposed in universities and further education should go to science/technology; and that in teacher-training colleges the balance of subjects should remain unchanged.

2. Line 5 should be read bearing in mind that the Robbins 'target' for further education, which envisaged successive transfers of further education institution to the 'university sector', was almost at once superseded by the 'binarist' policy of developing the 'public sector' separately.

3. Line 4 includes advanced courses.

Source: J. Carswell (1985).

Table 7.7 contrasts the proposed and actual expansion of student numbers in science/technology and in 'other subjects' taken as a whole. The short-hand 'science/technology' is taken as including mathematics, physics, chemistry, biology and all forms of engineering and computer studies, but excludes medicine, dentistry and veterinary studies.

The table shows that the numbers fell short by about 25 per cent in science/technology over the 20-year period, and that, despite the cut-back in teacher training, 'other subjects' exceeded the objective by about 17 per cent in compensation. These 'other subjects' include business studies, economics and medicine as well as the humanities, and it should be noted that, because of the length of the medical course, medical students bulk larger *in any given year* in relation to 'opportunity' at one end or graduate output at the other, than most other groups.

Table 7.8   Male and female students at degree and advanced level, all subjects and all types of institution in Great Britain (000s full-time students)

	Students	*Women*	*Men*	*Total*
(1)	Actual 1962	68	148	216
(2)	Addition to 1980 proposed by Robbins Committee	185	157	342
(3)	Robbins proposal for 1980 ((1)+(2))	253	305	558
(4)	Actual 1980	214	310	524
(5)	Difference between programme and performance	−39	+5	−34

Notes:
1. The additional places in line 2 have been estimated on the basis that the additions assigned by Robbins to the universities and further education were to be equally divided between the sexes, but that two-thirds of the extra places assigned to teacher training would be filled by women. Although the rundown of teacher training was largely compensated by the development of further education institutions, the difference between lines 3 and 4 for women students should be read with this in mind.
2. Line 4 includes advanced courses.
Source: J. Carswell (1985).

Table 7.8 shows the intended and actual distribution of places between the sexes, so far as the former can be estimated from the Report. Broadly speaking, over the nineteen-year period, the number of women students trebled, and that of men doubled, so that women rose from just over 30 per cent of the student body to more than 40 per cent. This growth, however, was mainly in non-science subjects, as is shown in Table 7.9, which contrasts the growth in science/technology numbers as between the sexes. It shows that the expansion came very near the objective in respect of men (though here

Table 7.9   Science/technology at degree or advanced level, distribution between male and female students, all types of institution in Great Britain (000s full-time students)

Students	Women	Men	Total
(1) Actual 1962	12	73	85
(2) Addition to 1980 estimated by reference to			
Robbins Report	87	87	174
(3) Estimated target for 1980 on basis of			
Robbins Report ((1) + (2))	99	160	259
(4) Actual 1980	28	148	176
(5) Difference between programme and			
performance	−71	−12	−83

Source: J. Carswell (1985).

students from overseas played an important part), so that almost the whole of the short-fall in science/technology shown in Table 7.8 is attributable to the absence of the women students who had been hoped for. The number of women students in science/technology did indeed more than double over the period, but the base in 1962 was so low that this made little difference. The prognostications required it to expand by more than eight times.

Finally the inauguration of the Open University should be mentioned; it began in 1970, teaching partly by radio and television, partly by correspondence courses and partly by tutorial and summer school groups. There are no formal qualifications for entry. By 1983–4 the Open University had over 76 000 part-time students including those on short courses (Table 7.4).

Summing up the post-Robbins period it may be said that within the framework of expansion, the main feature has not been the growth of full-time, male undergraduates reading science or technology in universities. The really spectacular growth has been of women studying the arts and humanities or part-time students in public sector colleges and at the Open University. Up to 1981 the overseas student numbers also increased dramatically but then fell back. Numerically higher education, including part-time study, is now dominated by the public sector institutions.

THE UNIVERSITIES 1900–85[7]

The British universities developed slowly in the nineteenth century and entered the twentieth century as a restricted and élite group of institutions. In England, Oxford and Cambridge stood at the centre, the University of London had emerged as a federation of heterogeneous colleges in the capital, and university charters were being granted to colleges in the major provincial cities. Scotland, meanwhile, had four well-established universities. The system as a whole mustered only 20 000 students out of a population of 40 million.

In the twentieth century there has been more substantial growth from this tiny base. The number of students has risen from 25 000 before the First World War to twice as many between the wars and over ten times as many at the present time, so that in 1983–4 there were over 300 000 university students on full-time or part-time courses.

Although the growth of the universities has been continuous throughout the century, and although the two wars accelerated the trends, it is clear that social and economic developments after the Second World War surpassed all previous pressures towards expansion and continued to do so up to the end of the 1970s. In the 1980s, however, confidence in universities has faltered. From 1981 cuts were imposed in government funding, and government planning for the 1990s assumes contraction rather than expansion.

The older class conceptions of education eroded rapidly in the post-war years. Statistics of inequality of educational opportunity became popular knowledge and turned access to the universities into an almost commonplace criterion of distributive justice. This motif was strengthened by the economic aim of eliminating waste of potential talent in the work force, and particularly by the insistent attack on the assumption of a restricted 'pool of ability' which came to be seen increasingly as a rationalisation for preserving class privileges. In this process the ideological defence of an élite system of universities was seriously undermined, and policy for the development of higher education came to be seen more in terms of economic feasibility. Only after the end of the post-war period in the mid-1970s did the tide of expansion meet increasingly serious resistance from governments concerned to reduce public expenditure.

The course of expansion had three phases. The first began around the turn of the century with the foundation of the civic universities and continued after the First World War until the depression years of the 1930s. The second, which was more rapid, occurred after the Second World War. Unlike its predecessor, it did not fade out, but instead formed the basis for the third phase in the 1960s and 1970s. At the beginning of the first period Oxford and Cambridge were numerically, as well as academically and socially, preponderant. By the end of it, just before the Second World War, they had been surpassed in numbers of students and staff by the major redbrick universities, and overtaken by London. Within the first decade of the century Birmingham, Bristol, Leeds,[8] Manchester[9] and Sheffield[10] gained charters as independent universities: together with the nineteenth-century foundation at Durham and its Newcastle constituent, they began to lead the expansion of the British university system and have continued to do so ever since.

The second period of growth after the Second World War included the granting of independent charters to the former provincial university colleges at Nottingham, Southampton, Hull, Exeter and Leicester.[11] The last-named became independent in 1957, bringing the total number of British universities to 21. Meantime, the establishment of the University College of North Staffordshire at Keele,[12] without tutelage from London, was the precursor of a much publicised movement at the end of the 1950s to found new universities with independence *ab initio*. The first of these, Sussex,[13] admitted its first students in 1961. Subsequently East Anglia, York, Essex,[14] Kent, Warwick and Lancaster have received charters, and four new Scottish universities have been formed, one at Strathclyde (out of the Royal College of Science at Glasgow), one at Stirling, Heriot-Watt in Edinburgh and one at Dundee. The bulk of the expansion between 1947 and 1964 was borne by the established universities in the industrial provincial cities, by London, by Wales and by the ancient universities in England and Scotland.

THE FORMER CATS

Numerically another important addition was the translation of nine English colleges of advanced technology (CATs) to university status.[15] Their incorporation into the university system during the three or four years after the Robbins Report produced a group which is larger than either the new English universities, the ancient English colleges or the University of Wales.

The CATs were designated in 1957 (except for Bristol, which was elevated in 1960, and Brunel, in 1962) and were taken from the control of the local education authorities, who had nurtured them from their nineteenth-century origins, to be given independent status under the direct control of the Ministry of Education in 1962. Robbins's recommendation that they be upgraded to university status was accepted (though not the linked proposal for the creation of five Special Institutions for Scientific and Technological Education and Research) and all except Chelsea, which was absorbed into the University of London, received an independent charter. Only two of them retained the technological label in their titles – Loughborough University of Technology and Bath University of Technology. The Bradford Institute of Technology became the University of Bradford; Northampton College of Advanced Technology became the City University; Battersea College of Technology became the University of Surrey and moved to Guildford; Brunel College moved ten miles away from Acton to a larger site near Uxbridge as Brunel University.

UNIVERSITY FINANCE

The growth of reliance on the state for financial support expresses itself dramatically in Table 7.10 which shows the income of universities from 1920–84 distributed by its source. There are two essential features of the statistics. First, the rate of growth in the 1960s, associated with the Robbins enquiry and

Table 7.10 Sources of university income, 1920–1984, United Kingdom: sources as percentage of total income

Year	Total income of universities (£)	Parliamentary grants	Grants from LAs	Fees	Endowments	Donations and subscriptions	Other sources[1]
1920–1	3 020 499	33.6	9.3	33.0	11.2	2.7	10.2
1923–4	3 587 366	33.5	12.0	33.6	11.6	2.5	4.8
1928–9	5 174 510	35.9	10.1	27.8	13.9	2.4	9.9
1933–4	5 593 320	35.1	9.2	32.8	13.7	2.4	6.8
1938–9	6 712 067	35.8	9.0	29.8	15.4	2.6	7.4
1946–7	13 043 541	52.7	5.6	23.2	9.3	2.2	7.0
1949–50	22 009 735	63.9	4.6	17.7	5.7	1.7	6.4
1953–4	31 112 024	70.5	3.6	12.0	4.3	1.6	8.0
1955–6	38 894 000	72.7	3.1	10.8	3.8	0.9	8.7
1961–2	74 113 000	76.5	2.1	9.0	2.7	0.9	8.9
1964–5	124 161 715	79.9	1.4	8.1	1.9	0.6	8.1
1967–8	216 204 321	72.9[2]	0.9	7.4		1.7	17.1[2]
1967–8[3]	216 624 712	73.8	0.9	7.4	1.2	0.5	16.2
1969–70	258 919 000	73.2	0.7	7.3		1.7	16.0
1979–80	1 266 564 000	63.1	Not shown sep.	15.9		0.9	20.1
1983–4	1 982 782 000	61.8		13.1		1.2	23.9

Notes:
1. Includes payment for research contracts from 1955–6.
2. The amount of parliamentary grant shows an apparent drop in 1967–8 because, for that year only, grants from the Exchequer are distinguished in the statistics. Grants and payments for research from other government departments are included in 'other sources'. Previously all parliamentary grants had been grouped together.
3. From 1967–8 the figures are for Great Britain only. Parliamentary grants are Exchequer grants and grants from government departments. (Payments for research included in 'other'.) From 1969 the total is net income, that is, exclusive of repayment of Selective Employment Tax.

Sources: 1920–68: UGC Returns;
1967–68: Statistics of Education, 1968, vol. 6, p. xviii.
1969–70: Statistics of Education, 1970, vol. 6, p. xviii.
1979–80: University Statistics, 1980, vol. 3, Table 2;
1983–84: University Statistics, 1983–4, vol. 3, Table 2.

the redefinition of higher education, which increased the number of universities from 24 to 44 in the following ten years, dwarfed all previous experience. Secondly, an increasing proportion of university income is provided by the state. By 1983–4 the income from fees, endowments, donations and subscriptions had fallen to 14.3 per cent compared with 46.9 per cent in 1920–21.

Since the creation of the University Grants Committee (UGC) the total income of the universities on the grant list has risen from just over £3 million in 1920–1 to nearly £2000 million in 1983–4.

UNIVERSITY STAFF

The academic professions, like the institutions in which they serve, have evolved in response to the changing structure of society, having developed from the pre-industrial traditions of Oxford and Cambridge, where they constituted a tiny group oriented to the customs and demands of the clerical and aristocratic classes to which, at least by the seventeenth century, they largely owed their existence. The academic career began to change in the second half of the nineteenth century with the development of professionalism, specialisation and expansion. The nineteenth-century developments were of small numerical importance. At the end of the century there were about 800 Oxford and Cambridge dons, 500 teachers in the provincial redbrick universities, a similar number in Scotland and less than 250 in London. Tables 7.11 to 7.13 give a numerical outline of the distribution of university teachers between different types of university, different grades or academic ranks, and different faculties or subjects. They demonstrate the shift away from traditional conceptions, the elongation of the professions and their increasing specialisation.

The number of university teachers in Britain has grown from rather under 2000 at the beginning of the century to over 40 000 at the present day. The statistics, however, are unusually imperfect because of changes in administrative habits during the course of the century and especially because of the vagaries of Oxford and Cambridge records. The main source from 1919 is the UGC in its *Annual and Quinquennial Returns*. Only from 1965–6 (Cmnd 3586) is it possible, for the first time, to discover an exact count of the number of university teachers irrespective of the source of funds for their employment. The effect is to produce a jump in the numbers at this point through the inclusion for the first time of staff paid from other than general university funds. They numbered 3429 out of the total of 25 294 in 1975–6.

The growth has been continuous but it accelerated sharply in the 1960s following acceptance of the Robbins Report. There were now more university teachers than there were students before the First World War. We have divided the universities into 8 groups, each group differing according to its character, age and location (Table 7.11). By 1968 the largest group, employing

Table 7.11   Distribution of full-time staff among university groups, 1961–84, Great Britain (percentages)

University group	Full-time staff					
	1961–2	*1964–5*	December *1968*	*1971*[1]	*1981–2*	*1984*
Major redbrick	32.4	32.7	25.9	25.0	24.0	23.6
London	23.6	21.7	20.1	19.1	18.6	18.7
Scotland	15.5	16.2	15.5	15.8	14.8	14.5
Minor redbrick	10.2	10.6	9.7	9.3	10.6	10.3
Oxford and Cambridge	10.4	8.6	8.1	8.9	7.5	8.8
Ex-CATs	—	—	8.0	7.9	9.2	8.7
New English	1.0	3.2	6.8	7.6	9.0	9.1
Wales	6.9	6.9	5.9	6.4	6.4	6.2
Total Great Britain	100.0	100.0	100.0	100.0	100.0	100.0
Grand total	14 276	18 352	30 755	35 059	42 840	42 058

Note:
1.   31 December 1971.
Sources: Calculated from UGC Returns and information from the UGC. The two earlier years include staff at Oxford and Cambridge who were paid only partly from university funds since they also did college work. The 1968 figures include those not financed at all from university funds – 223 at Oxford and 49 at Cambridge.
1971 – *Statistics of Education*, vol. 6, Table 36.
1981–2 – *University Statistics 1981–2*, vol. 1, UGC, Table 27.
1983–4 – *University Statistics 1983–4*, Table 27.

more than a quarter of all university teachers,was made up of the major redbrick universities in the larger provincial industrial cities.[16] The second largest group, with a fifth of the university teachers, was formed by the constituent colleges of the University of London.[17] Third in order, and accounting for 15.5 per cent of all university teachers, were the 7 Scottish institutions.[18] Fourth came the minor redbrick universities[19] which between them employed 9.7 per cent of all university teachers. Oxford and Cambridge came next with 8.1 per cent and they were closely followed by the former English colleges of advanced technology.[20] The new English universities occupied the seventh place[21] with 6.8 per cent of all academic staff and last came the University of Wales[22] accounting for 5.9 per cent of university teachers. The relative size of the groups has remained stable to the mid-1980s, except that the new English universities have risen above Oxford and Cambridge (Table 7.11).

The pattern of growth from 1910 in each of the seven university groups is set out in Table 7.12. Though they have changed their relative numerical

Table 7.12 Full-time academic staff by university group and rank, 1910–84, Great Britain (percentages)

University group/rank	1910–11[1]	1919–20[2]	1929–30	1938–9	1949–50	1959–60	1963–4	1971	1981–2	1983–4
Major redbrick										
Professors	30	28	21	18	13	11	10	10.0	9.8	9.2
Readers and Senior Lecturers	—	—	6	6	14	16	17	19.3	23.3	22.8
Lecturers and Assistant Lecturers	70	72	63	66	60	61	56	63.2	58.2	58.5
Others	—	—	9	10	13	12	17	7.6	8.7	9.4
Total	(626)	(849)	(1081)	(1349)	(2743)	(4148)	(5456)	(8565)	(10 271)[3]	(9927)
London[4]										
Professors	31	31	21	19	14	13	14	13.3	12.8	12.0
Readers and Senior Lecturers	—	—	16	16	22	26	26	21.3	22.1	21.5
Lecturers and Assistant Lecturers	69	69	56	57	55	54	51	61.0	54.6	55.3
Others	—	—	7	8	9	7	9	4.4	10.5	11.2
Total	(202)	(601)	(856)	(1057)	(2146)	(3072)	(3750)	(6505)	(7961)	(7876)
Minor redbrick										
Professors	27	31	21	16	12	11	11	10.8	10.3	9.4
Readers and Senior Lecturers	—	—	10	8	7	8	14	18.4	20.7	20.2
Lecturers and Assistant Lecturers	73	69	61	59	65	64	59	64.6	57.7	59.8
Others	—	—	9	17	16	16	16	6.1	11.2	10.8
Total	(104)	(151)	(258)	(324)	(842)	(1236)	(1699)	(3181)	(4524)	(4342)
Wales										
Professors	42	37	24	23	17	14	12	9.6	10.2	9.5
Readers and Senior Lecturers	—	—	6	12	16	14	15	17.8	22.1	22.3

Lecturers and Assistant Lecturers	58	63	55	58	60	60	57	66.5	57.0	57.6
Others	–	–	15	16	7	12	15	6.9	10.7	10.6
Total	(143)	(178)	(301)	(371)	(512)	(799)	(1121)	(2184)	(2738)	(2620)
Scotland[5]										
Professors	32	35	23	22	13	11	10	9.4	10.2	9.8
Readers and Senior Lecturers	–	–	8	7	15	20	21	19.7	24.2	22.9
Lecturers and Assistant Lecturers	68	65	68	69	65	66	64	64.9	56.3	56.5
Others	–	–	1	2	7	4	5	5.9	9.3	10.8
Total	(403)	(498)	(553)	(718)	(1439)	(2120)	(2600)	(5412)	(6333)	(6089)
English new universities										
Professors						14	14	10.9	10.6	9.4
Readers and Senior Lecturers						4	13	15.8	20.6	20.2
Lecturers and Assistant Lecturers						80	60	69.6	63.3	63.3
Others						3	13	3.7	5.5	7.0
Total						(108)	(331)	(2602)	(3859)	(3836)
Oxford and Cambridge										
Professors								9.0	8.6	6.9
Readers and Senior Lecturers								7.9	6.8	6.0
Lecturers and Assistant Lecturers								82.0	80.1	82.5
Others								1.1	4.4	4.6
Total								(3052)	(3202)	(3706)
Ex-CATs										
Professors							4.3 (1965–6)	8.4	8.4	7.7
Readers and Senior Lecturers								20.2	23.2	22.2
Lecturers and Assistant Lecturers								68.8	62.3	60.7
Others								2.6	6.0	9.3
Total								(2738)	(3952)	(3662)

continued overleaf

Table 7.12—continued

University group/rank	1910–11[1]	1919–20[2]	1929–30	1938–9	1949–50	1959–60	1963–4	1971	1981–2	1983–4
All universities in Great Britain except Oxford and Cambridge										
Professors	31	31	22	20	13	12	12	10.6	10.5	9.8
Readers and Senior Lecturers	–	–	10	9	16	18	19	19.4	22.6	21.9
Lecturers and Assistant Lecturers	69	69	61	62	60	61	57	64.4	57.9	58.2
Others	–	–	8	9	11	10	13	5.6	9.0	10.1
Grand totals	(1478)	(2277)	(3049)	(3819)	(7682)	(11 483)	(14 927)	(31 186)	(39 638)	(38 352)

Notes:
1. Figures in Group A for these years include the staff of the Merchant Venturers' Technical College, formed as part of Bristol University, 'to afford preparation for an industrial or commercial career'.
2. For 1919–20 Heads of Departments are counted as Professors. The numbers may then include some non-professorial Heads of Departments.
3. Including Manchester Business School and University of Manchester Institute of Science and Technology.
4. From 1971 includes the London Business School.
5. The Board of Education Report for 1910–11 gives only staff numbers at Dundee University College. Staff numbers for Scotland have been calculated from the calendars of the Scottish Universities for 1910–11.

Sources: UGC Returns – information from the UGC and *Statistics of Education* up to 1964;
 1971 – *Statistics of Education*, vol. 6, 1971, Table 36;
 1981–2 – *University Statistics 1981–2*, vol. 1, UGC, Table 27.

positions, every group has increased its numbers. The exact number of dons at Oxford and Cambridge at the beginning of the century is not known, but there were probably about 800, including all university teachers and college fellows. There were 471 resident MAs at Oxford in 1900 and 3446 undergraduates. Oxford's total academic staff in 1922 was 357 rising to 1127 in 1964–5 with 9450 students. At Cambridge the number of dons primarily engaged in teaching and research, with or without college fellowships, rose from 458 in 1928 to 1001 in 1959 when there were 8997 students. The Scottish full-time academic staff numbered 498 in 1920 and 2600 in 1963–4.

Oxford and Cambridge, numerically the strongest group in the early 1900s, gradually lost their lead. Our estimate is that academic staff at Oxford and Cambridge increased from 800 at the beginning of the century to something like 1000 in the 1930s. In the major redbrick universities the increase was from 626 in 1910 to 1349 in 1938–9 and in London from 202 to 1057.

By 1981 the number of university teachers had reached a peak. Between 1981–2 and 1983–4 the number of dons at Oxford and Cambridge rose from 3202 to 3706, but in all the other groups there was a slight fall (Table 7.12).

The elongation of the university professions

The academic staff of the British universities, taken as a whole, form a hierarchy headed by a professoriate of only 10 per cent. The shape of the hierarchy, which is shown in Table 7.12, developed historically from the collegiate guilds of masters in the Oxford and Cambridge colleges, and the established professorial system of the Scottish universities.

The academic hierarchy has been elaborated and regularised during the twentieth century. The sharpest drop in the proportion of professors took place during the 1920s (from nearly a third to little more than a fifth), though the fall has been continuous throughout the period for all the groups included in the statistics.

Before 1920 the ranks below the professorship were neither equivalent from one university to another, nor distinguished in the Board of Education statistics. Many of them carried low status and low pay, but, as may be seen in the table, the proportion in the main career grade – the lectureship – has risen. Thus there have been two rather conflicting processes at work. On the one hand the hierarchy has been lengthened with the creation of a non-professorial staff and a corresponding decrease in the proportion of professorial chairs; and on the other, within the non-professorial ranks, there has been a tendency towards up-grading with a corresponding decrease in the proportion of assistant lecturers. From the 1960s there has been renewed pressure to increase the proportion of senior posts. In 1967 the UGC announced that, in any given university, senior posts (including professorships, senior lectureships and readerships), could be filled to a maximum of 35 per cent of the total academic staff.[23]

Moving down the ranks, the numerical proportions for all universities in 1983–4 were, professors 9.8 per cent, readers and senior lecturers 21.9 per cent, lecturers and assistant lecturers 58.2 per cent, leaving 10.1 per cent in posts of various kinds outside the main hierarchy.

These figures exclude Oxford and Cambridge whose staffs are classified in the same terms as those for other universities. This means that the great bulk are classified as lecturers, which is misleading in that many college teaching fellows have a salary and status superior to that of lecturers elsewhere. Moreover, the fact that Oxford and Cambridge have no senior lectureships is of no significance in the context of the collegiate staff structure. The proportion of professors and readers is relatively low, partly because some college dons have equivalent positions.

London has a higher proportion of professors and readers, partly because of the strength of the medical faculty. Apart from London, the differences in the proportion of senior staff among the several types of university institution are quite small. It is very close to 31 per cent or 32 per cent for all universities except Oxford and Cambridge. However, the figures for 1965–6 show that the ex-CATs were exceptional in their low proportion of professors; they had only 4.3 per cent in that year. This reflected the recent promotion of these institutions from the ranks of the technical colleges where professorships do not exist and where staffing is different in both nomenclature and structure. The distribution of ranks in the former colleges of advanced technology had moved much closer to those in the other types of university during the 1970s (Table 7.12).

Specialisation and the changing balance of studies

University studies in the twentieth century have widened in scope, and the balance between the faculties has also shifted. The first change, however, has been continuous, while the second has fluctuated. Widening the scope of studies has meant that university teachers have specialised increasingly in their academic interests, choosing between research and teaching, and between undergraduate and graduate supervision. One crude but dramatic illustration of the widening range of specialisms may be derived from the UGC's statistics in the branches of study pursued by advanced students. In 1928, 123 subjects were distinguished: a quarter of a century later there were 382. In the meantime, economics had been divided into economics, industrial economics, econometrics and economic history; the number of branches of engineering had risen from 7 to 22, and such subjects as Ethiopic studies, fruit nutrition, immunology, personnel management, medical jurisprudence and space science had appeared.

The changing balance of studies since the First World War is shown in Table 7.13. After the war the arts faculties expanded, especially at the expense

Table 7.13 Academic staff or students, by faculty, 1919–84, Great Britain (percentages)

Faculty	1919–20[1]	1928–9	1938–9	1949–50	1961–2	1970–1	1980–1[3]	1983–4
Arts[2] } Social Studies	38.7	53.3	44.8	43.6	{ 25.5 8.4	21.3 15.5	19.6 17.1	18.4 16.3
Pure Science	18.3	16.7	15.5	19.8	26.3	28.3	26.6	27.0
Applied Science Technology }	16.4	11.1	12.6	16.0	19.5	} 14.6	15.1[4]	15.7
Agriculture Forestry }						} 3.3[5]	2.5	2.4
Medicine Dentistry Veterinary science }	26.6	18.9	27.1	20.6	20.2	} 17.0	19.0	20.2
Total numbers	(43 018)	(44 309)	(50 246)	85 421	(13 104)	(34 103)	(43 017)	(42 058)

Notes: Student numbers are given for the years 1919–20, 1928–9, 1938–9, and 1949–50 and *include* Oxford and Cambridge. Staff numbers are given for the year 1961–2 and *exclude* Oxford and Cambridge lecturers and below.

1. Oxford and Cambridge student numbers were not included in the UGC Returns for 1919–20. These numbers were taken from the Returns for 1922–3, the first year they were included, and added to the numbers for other universities given in the 1919–20 Returns.
2. Including Education.
3. Full-time only.
4. Including architecture and other vocational/professional subjects.
5. Includes veterinary science.

Sources: UGC Returns and *University Statistics.*

of medicine and the applied sciences. In the 1930s the trend was reversed and the arts faculties have been in relative decline ever since. By the end of the 1920s they constituted half of the academic staff, they now account for less than one-fifth.[24] The social studies expanded much more rapidly than the other faculties in the 1960s. Between 1961–2 and 1966–7 social studies teachers increased by 155 per cent, compared with 46.5 per cent for university staff as a whole. The pure science faculties declined during the inter-war period, but rose steadily after the Second World War to become the largest faculty group. Medicine has declined relatively throughout the period, sharply in the 1920s with a recovery at the end of the 1930s, and with oscillations since the Second World War. The applied sciences and technology were proportionately more significant after the First World War than at any subsequent point until 1950, and even with the incorporation of the former CATs these subjects still accounted for less than a fifth of all academic staff in 1966–7.[25] They are now of comparable scale to the social sciences.

None the less, it is clear that the traditional stereotype of the academic as an arts don is seriously inaccurate: and this was already so at the time of the Robbins Report. By 1968 the arts faculties made up only one-sixth of the total. The largest single faculty was pure science (29 per cent), the remainder in descending order of size, were arts, medicine and dentistry, applied science, social studies, education and last agriculture, forestry and veterinary science. Thus, even assuming that half the social scientists were 'pure', nearly 50 per cent of academics worked in some kind of natural or social-science-based technology. The technologist, thus broadly defined, has the most plausible claim to be thought of as the typical university teacher.

STUDENTS IN HIGHER EDUCATION

We have already referred to the increase in the number and proportion of students in full-time higher education since 1900. Here we look more closely at sex and social class, at the type of institution attended, and the type of course pursued.

In 1920, women constituted well under one-third of all full-time university students; in 1939 they made up less than a quarter, but they had risen to nearer 40 per cent by 1983–4. Thus the trend over the past decade has been towards equalisation. Oxford and Cambridge traditionally had an especially small proportion of women but by 1980–81 they held 30 per cent of the places.

It can be calculated from Table 7.3 that between 1970–71 and 1983–4 the number of women in full-time higher education rose by 34.8 per cent compared with 22.0 per cent for men. But the expansion of opportunities for women in higher education has been markedly in part-time rather than full-time studies where the percentage growth over the same period was 354.6 for women and 47.9 for men.

Trends in the relation between class origin and university entrance are set out in Table 7.14.[26] The figures in the table reflect the fact that the universities expanded throughout the century but especially in the 1960s, that is, for those born between 1943 and 1952. It appears that the university expansion kept pace with the growth of the service or professional and managerial classes and that 'Robbinsian expansion' was an effective response to the post-war baby boom. The familiar picture also emerges, as with educational expansion generally, that though the fastest *rates* of growth almost always accrue to the working class, the greatest absolute increments of opportunity go to the upper middle class.

Table 7.14   Attendance at university by birth cohort (percentages)

Father's social class[1]	1913–22	1923–32	1933–42	1943–53
I, II (Service)	7.2	15.9	23.7	26.4
	208[2]	258	233	214
III, IV, V (Intermediate)	1.9	4.0	4.1	8.0
	75	120	58	95
VI, VII, VIII (Working)	0.9	1.2	2.3	3.1
	0	0	0	0
All	1.8	3.4	5.4	8.5
No.	(1846)	(1879)	(1856)	(2246)

Notes:
1. For details of this class schema see above p. 409.
2. Figures in italics give log distances – a form of disparity ratio in which the ratio P_{ik}/P_{jk} is converted into the distance measure $\log_e P_{ik} - \log_e P_{jk}$ (See *Origins and Destinations*, p. 37).
Source: A. H. Halsey, A. F. Heath and J. Ridge (1980) *Origins and Destinations* (Oxford: Clarendon Press), Table 10.8.

The general pattern which has emerged from sociological research on education is that the origins of the modern education system can be described as a minimal education for the majority, with further opportunity for the minority. For a minority within that minority the golden road to high opportunity was provided by selective secondary education and by the universities. Educational expansion has developed the system in two main ways – by raising the output of children qualified to go beyond secondary education, and by differentiating the opportunities available to those, whether qualified or not, who stayed past the minimum school-leaving age. All forms of post-secondary education have been selective in the sense of not being universal. And there has been a correlation between class origin and selective educational destination.

Trends in class access to part-time further education and to post-secondary education as a whole are shown in Table 7.15. For part-time further education

Table 7.15(a) Percentage attending part-time further education by social class and birth cohort

Father's social class	1913–22	1923–32	1933–42	1943–52
I, II (Service)	50.0	46.2	59.3	45.1
III, IV, V (Intermediate)	40.3	41.7	55.1	57.2
VI, VII, VIII (Working)	29.9	36.9	46.4	50.8

Table 7.15(b) Percentage attending any form of post-school education by social class and birth cohort

Father's social class	1913–22	1923–32	1933–42	1943–52
I, II (Service)	60.6 *65*[1]	64.6 *50*	77.1 *44*	73.9 *30*
III, IV, V (Intermediate)	43.5 *32*	48.0 *21*	60.4 *19*	67.4 *21*
VI, VII, VIII (Working)	31.5 *0*	38.9 *0*	49.9 *0*	54.6 *0*

Note:
1. Figures in italic give log distances (see Table 7.14).
Source: See Table 7.14.

Table 7.17 Full-time students by type of faculty, 1919–82, Great Britain (percentages)

Faculty	1919–29[1] Men	1919–29[1] Women	1929–30 Men	1929–30 Women	1938–9 Men	1938–9 Women
Arts (including theology, fine art, music, economics and education)	23.8	54.6	44.8	74.7	38.7	64.7
Social Studies (including social, administrative and business studies)	—	—	—	—	—	—
Pure Science	19.4	15.2	17.1	15.0	15.2	15.9
Medicine (including health and dentistry)	33.4	28.6	23.3	8.8	30.3	17.3
Technology (including engineering, applied chemistry, architecture, etcetera)	21.3	0.5	12.5	0.5	13.6	0.8
Agriculture (including forestry, horticulture and veterinary science)	2.0	1.1	2.2	0.9	2.3	1.3
Total	100.0 (24 768)	100.0 (9 183)	100.0 (32 682)	100.0 (12 921)	100.0 (38 368)	100.0 (11 634)

Notes:
1. Excluding Oxford and Cambridge.
2. Birmingham figures include two-year teacher-training figures.
3. Figures for United Kingdom.

Table 7.16   Universities – home candidates and acceptances: by social class, 1981 and 1984, United Kingdom (Percentages and 000s)

	Candidates			Acceptances		
	1981	*1984*	*1986*	*1981*	*1984*	*1986*
Percentage in each social class:						
Professional	23.1	19.5	18.2	24.5	22.1	20.4
Intermediate	47.8	47.3	47.6	48.9	48.2	48.2
Skilled non-manual	9.7	10.6	11.5	9.1	10.1	10.7
Skilled manual	13.5	14.1	13.8	12.3	12.4	12.5
Partly skilled	4.8	7.2	7.6	4.2	6.2	6.9
Unskilled	1.1	1.3	1.4	1.0	1.1	1.2
Total (= 100%) (000s)	133.2	141.2	135.7	67.2	65.8	69.8
Not classified (000s)	16.1	15.3	16.9	7.3	5.9	7.1

Sources: *Universities Central Council on Admissions Statistical Supplements.*

1950–1		*1960–1*		*1971–2*[3]		*1981–2*	
Men	*Women*	*Men*	*Women*	*Men*	*Women*	*Men*	*Women*
37.2[2]	63.0[2]	25.4	52.7	15.3	40.8	14.6	37.3
—	—	11.5	9.4	21.0	22.6	22.5	25.1
21.1	17.0	25.5	21.7	28.5	22.1	26.0	19.4
21.1	16.6	14.5	13.6	9.7	10.8	10.5	12.0
15.8	1.1	19.5	1.3	23.9	2.6	24.2	4.3
4.9	2.4	3.6	1.3	1.5	1.1	2.1	1.9
100.0	100.0	100.0	100.0	100.0	100.0	100.0	100.0
(65 831)	(19 483)	(81 330)	(26 369)	(45 438)	(21 903)	(152 497)	(100 874)

Sources: *Returns from Universities and University Colleges.*
Statistics of Education, vol. 6, Table 10.
1981–2 – *University Statistics*, vol. 1, Table 1.

Table 7.18   Term-time residence of full-time students, 1920–80, Great Britain
(percentages)

| Year | In colleges or halls of residence | | | In lodgings | | | At home | | |
	Men	Women	Total	Men	Women	Total	Men	Women	Total
1920–1	4.2	27.9	10.2	43.0	22.4	37.5	52.8	49.7	52.0
1929–30	20.6	35.9	24.9	39.4	16.5	32.9	40.0	47.6	42.1
1938–9	21.4	37.3	25.1	37.5	19.2	33.2	41.1	43.5	41.7
1950–1	20.0	38.9	24.3	42.3	28.4	39.1	37.7	32.7	36.6
1960–1	23.5	39.3	27.4	54.3	39.7	50.7	22.2	21.0	21.9
1971–2	37.9	41.4	39.7	43.1	40.2	41.7	16.7	15.9	16.3
1979–80	46.4	46.4	46.4	35.8	34.1	35.0	14.1	15.0	14.6

Note:
1. Excluding Oxford and Cambridge students.
Sources: UGC; *Returns from Universities and University Colleges*; 1971–2 and 1979–80 *Statistics of Education*, vol. 6.

class access has slowly changed with expansion from the familiar positive correlation of class and opportunity to an *inverse* relation for those born after the Second War. Thus in the earlier decades it was not usefully seen as an alternative route for the working class so much as an extension of class-biased educational opportunity. For the last cohort, born during and after the war, the alternative route description is more accurate. For the whole structure of educational opportunity beyond school it appears that expansion has brought a slow and steady diminution of class inequality. This trend is shown by the log distances in the table: that between the service class and the working class fell from 65 to 30 as between those born in 1913–22 and those born in 1943–52.

Inequality of class access remains. As may be seen from Table 7.16, comparatively high proportions of candidates from the professional and intermediate social classes as defined by the Registrar General were accepted into the university in 1984. The proportion of accepted candidates from the homes of manual workers was 19.7 compared with 22.1 per cent from the professional classes. The relevant population proportions may be estimated at 30 per cent and 6 per cent respectively.

The relative numerical importance of different faculties has also changed substantially since 1920 (Table 7.17). Pure science has been the most popular faculty for men since 1960, followed by technology and social studies while in 1920 medicine was the largest faculty followed by the arts and then technology. For women the pattern is slightly different; the arts faculties have by far the largest number of students, followed by social studies and then pure

Men	Other Women	Total	Men	Women	Total
—	—	—	100.0	100.0	100.0
			(23 939)	(8 687)	(32 626)
—	—	—	100.0	100.0	100.0
			(32 682)	(12 921)	45 603)
—	—	—	100.0	100.0	100.0
			(38 368)	(11 634)	(50 002)
—	—	—	100.0	100.0	100.0
			(65 831)	(19 483)	(85 314)
—	—	—	100.0	100.0	100.0
			(81 330)	(26 369)	(107 699)
2.3	2.6	2.4	100.0	100.0	100.0
			(165 278)	(69 707)	(234 985)
3.7	4.4	4.1	100.0	100.0	100.0
			(185 481)	(107 257)	(292 738)

science; and it was arts subjects that were also most popular among women in 1920, with medicine coming next but attracting only half as many.

University students may live at home or in halls of residence or in lodgings; Table 7.18 shows the extent of the move away from living at home. The number and proportion in halls of residence or colleges has increased very substantially since 1920 and has in effect replaced the home-based student.

Notes

1. This Report, together with its five appendices, constitutes a comprehensive description of higher education in Great Britain in 1963. See *Higher Education*, Report and Appendices, Cmnd 2154. The Committee was appointed by the Prime Minister under the Chairmanship of Lord Robbins 1961–3.
2. That is, those institutions whose charters empower them to grant degrees. There are now (1986) 46 such institutions including the Open University, the University College of Buckingham, the Cranfield Institute and the Royal College of Art.
3. *Higher Education*, Report, chap. 1, para. 6.
4. Ibid., para. 7.
5. Entrants in any given year are of various ages. The method used in the Robbins report was to express the number of each age as a percentage of the total number of that age and then to sum the percentages. This gives a weighted percentage of a composite age group.
6. John Carswell (1985) *Government and the Universities in Britain* (Cambridge University Press) Appendix 1.
7. For an account of the evolution of the universities and the academic professions in Britain, see A. H. Halsey and M. Trow (1970) *The British Academics* (Faber).
8. A. H. Shimmin (1945) *The University of Leeds* (Cambridge University Press).

9. H. B. Charlton (1951) *Portrait of a University 1851–1951* (Manchester University Press).
10. A. D. Chapman (1955) *The Story of a Modern University: A History of the University of Sheffield* (Oxford University Press).
11. J. Simmonds (1958) *New University* (Leicester University Press).
12. W. B. Gillie (1960) *A New University: A. D. Lindsay and the Keele Experiment* (Chatto and Windus).
13. Sir John Fulton (1964) *Experiment in Higher Education* (Tavistock Pamphlet no. 8) and David Daiches (ed.) (1964) *The Idea of a New University: An Experiment in Sussex* (Andre Deutsch).
14. A. E. Sloman (1964) *A University in the Making* (British Broadcasting Corporation).
15. These are Aston, Bath, Bradford, Brunel, Chelsea, City, Loughborough, Salford and Surrey.
16. These were Birmingham, Bristol, Durham, Leeds, Liverpol, Manchester (including the School of Business Studies and the Institute of Technology), Newcastle and Sheffield, most of which received their charters within a few years of the turn of the nineteenth century and twentieth century.
17. London received its charter in 1836, mainly on the basis of the recently formed University and King's colleges; in 1968 it was composed of 31 self-governing schools and 14 institutes directly controlled by the university. We also include the Graduate School of Business Studies.
18. Aberdeen, Edinburgh, Glasgow, Heriot-Watt, St Andrews, Strathclyde and Stirling. St Andrews, founded in 1410, was the oldest of these, with an additional college at Dundee founded in 1881. Aberdeen Edinburgh, and Glasgow were fifteenth and sixteenth-century foundations. The Royal College of Science and Technology at Glasgow goes back to 1796 but received a charter as the University of Strathclyde in 1964. Stirling was new, admitting its first (107) students in 1967.
19. Exeter, Hull, Leicester, Nottingham, Reading and Southampton. With the exception of Reading all were at one time provincial colleges preparing students for the examinations of the University of London. They received their charters between 1948 and 1957. Reading was founded in 1926.
20. Aston, Bath, Bradford, Brunel, Chelsea, City, Loughborough, Salford and Surrey.
21. East Anglia, Keele, Sussex, York, Lancaster, Kent, Essex and Warwick.
22. It received its charter in 1893, though several of its constituent colleges dated from earlier in the nineteenth century. Aberystwyth was founded in 1859, Bangor in 1885, Cardiff in 1885 and Swansea in the 1920s. St David's College, Lampeter, also received grants from the University Grants Committee under a scheme agreed in 1961 through the University College of South Wales, Cardiff.
23. 'The ratio is to be applied to the total numbers of full-time academic staff wholly paid from general university funds ... The ratio is calculated for each university "across the board" ... The actual distribution of the number of senior posts within each university between the different faculties and departments is entirely a matter for the university itself to decide.' UGC, *University Development 1962–67*, para. 77.
24. It should be noticed, however, that the decline was not as marked after 1950 as may appear from Table 7.13 since before 1959 the social studies were included with arts subjects.
25. The figures in Table 7.13 up to 1950 are based on the distribution of students and therefore in comparing the relative importance of subjects over time we have implicitly assumed that staff/student ratios were equal between faculties.
26. From A. H. Halsey, A. F. Heath and J. Ridge (1980) *Origins and Destinations* (Oxford: Clarendon Press).

8 Electors and Elected

David Butler

This chapter covers some of the most readily defined or quantifiable aspects of the political process in Britain – the legal and social composition of the electorate, the votes recorded at parliamentary elections and the social and party composition of the House of Commons and the Cabinet. It is important to stress that quantifiable statements about political institutions are far from representing the whole truth about them.

All sorts of considerations that are relevant to balanced discussion of the evolution or the efficacy of the central instruments of British government are left untouched in this chapter, simply because they cannot be reduced to tables or other irrefutable statements of fact. The bibliographical references do, however, include some general evaluative and analytical writing.

ELECTORAL FRANCHISE

Parliamentary

In 1900 there were 6 731 000 names on the parliamentary electoral roll (approximately 58 per cent of the male population over 21). In 1986 the number was 43 392 000 (almost equal to the total population over 18). In 1900 only men were entitled to vote and the franchise qualifications – under the Representation of the People Acts of 1867 and 1885, and the Registration Act of 1885 – limited the number, mainly by requiring 12 months' residence and occupancy of premises worth £10 a year; on the other hand some people could vote in more than one constituency, through having business premises or university qualifications or a second residence. By the Representation of the People Act of 1918, the qualifications were simplified and the vote was extended to almost all women over 30; by the Representation of the People Act of 1928, women were placed on a virtually equal footing with men. By 1931 the electorate was equal to 94 per cent of the adult population – although, since there were 137 000 university electors (0.5 per cent of the total) and 365 000 business electors (1.4 per cent), and since there were some inaccuracies in the register, the proportion of the adult population able to vote cannot have exceeded 90 per cent. The Representation of the People Act of 1945 – and special wartime factors – greatly curtailed the business qualification and there were only 49 000 business electors entitled to vote in 1945; on the other hand, graduates on the lists for the 12 university constituencies now numbered 217 000.

By the Representation of the People Acts of 1948 and 1949, all plural voting was abolished. The 1950 register was equivalent to 99 per cent of the adult population (although a 1950 study by the Government Social Survey suggested that about 4 per cent of the names were there in error; a 1967 study found a similar rate of inaccuracy; a 1982 study found that errors had risen to 7 per cent).[1]

By the Representation of the People Act of 1969, the voting age was lowered to 18 – although it was estimated that less than 70 per cent of the population between 18 and 21 were inscribed in the first register which came into force on 15 February 1970. The 1982 OPCS (Office of Population and Census Statistics) study showed that omissions varied by area; young blacks in city centres had only a 50 per cent chance of getting on the register.

Local government

From 1889 to 1945 the local government franchise was confined to householders or occupiers of business premises, and from 1918 onwards, their wives (until 1928, only if over 30). By the Representation of the People Act of 1945, the parliamentary and local government franchises were assimilated. The business vote, although eliminated for parliamentary purposes in 1948, continued for local government purposes until the Representation of the People Act of 1969 when, except for the City of London, it was abolished.[2]

ELECTORAL ADMINISTRATION

General

From 1900 to 1918 electoral arrangements were governed primarily by the Representation of the People Act, 1867, as modified by the Ballot Act, 1872, the Corrupt Practices Act, 1883, the Franchise Act, 1884, the Registration Act, 1885, and the Redistribution of Seats Act, 1885. The Representation of the People Act, 1918, the Equal Franchise Act, 1928, the Representation of the People Act, 1948 (consolidated in 1949), the Representation of the People Act, 1969, and the Representation of the People Act, 1985, constitute the only major legislation in the century.[3]

Redistribution

The Redistribution of Seats Act, 1885, left the House of Commons with 670 members. The 1885 Act, while removing the worst anomalies, specifically rejected the principle that constituencies should be approximately equal in size. This princple was, however, substantially accepted in the Representation of the People Act, 1918, on the recommendation of the Speaker's Conference of 1917, although Wales, Scotland and Ireland were allowed to retain disproportionate numbers of seats. The 1918 Act increased the size of the House of Commons to 707, but this fell to 615 to 1922 on the creation of the Irish Free State. Population movements produced substantial anomalies in representation and the Redistribution of Seats Act, 1944, authorised the immediate subdivision of constituencies with more than 100 000 electors, which led to 25 new seats being created at the 1945 election and raised the number of MPs to 640. It also provided for the establishment of Permanent Boundary Commissioners to report every three to seven years. The Boundary Commissioners' first recommendations were enacted in the Representation of the People Act, 1948 (with the controversial addition by the Government of 17 extra seats as well as the abolition of the 12 university seats), and the 1950 Parliament had 625 members. The next reports of the Boundary Commissioners, given effect by resolutions of the House in December 1954 and January 1955, increased the number of constituencies to 630. The controversy caused by these changes led to the Redistribution of Seats Act, 1958, which modified the rules governing the Boundary Commissioners' decisions and asked them to report only every 10 to 15 years. The Boundary Commissioners started their revision in 1965; when their recommendations came before Parliament in 1969, the Labour Government insisted upon their rejection. The Conservative Government gave effect to them in October 1970.[4] As a result the House of Commons had 635 members from 1974 to 1983. The next redistribution, started in 1976, was only completed, after some litigation, just in time for the 1983 election. It increased the House from 635 to 650 members.

REFERENDUMS[5]

The only referendum at the national level took place on 5 June 1975 when, on a 64.5 per cent turnout, the United Kingdom voted 64.5 per cent 'Yes' and 35.5 per cent 'No' to stay within the European Community.

On 1 March 1979 referendums were held in Scotland and Wales on measures for devolution. In Scotland 32.9 per cent of the electorate voted in favour and 30.8 per cent against; 36.3 per cent did not vote. Since the Scotland Act required the support of '40 per cent of the electorate' the 'Yes' was insufficient. In Wales the vote was 11.9 per cent 'Yes' and 46.9 per cent 'No' with 41.1 per cent not voting.

EUROPEAN ELECTIONS[6]

Direct elections to the European Parliament took place in 1979 and 1984. The results for the United Kingdom are listed in Table 8.1(b).

ELECTION RESULTS: SOURCES

The only official record of election results is to be found in Parliamentary Papers on election expenses published 6 to 12 months after each election. Since these make no acknowledgement of parties, they are of limited analytic use. However, results are in a number of other sources.

The official returns, listing candidates' votes and expenses, issued as Parliamentary Papers after every General Election, except 1918, are: 1901 (352) lix, 145; 1906 (302) xcvi, 19; 1910 (259) lxxiii, 705; 1911 (272) lxii, 701; 1924 (2) xviii, 681; 1924–5 (151) xviii, 775; 1926 (I) xxii, 523; 1929–30 (114) xxiv, 755; 1931–2 (109) xx, I; 1935–6 (150) xx, 217 1945–6 (128) xix, 539; 1950 (146) xviii, 311; 1951–2 (210) xxi, 841; 1955 (141) xxxii, 913; 1959–60 (173) xxiv, 1031; 1964–5 (220) xxv, 587; 1966–7 (162) iv, I; 1970–1 (305) xxii, 41; 1974–5 (60); 1974–5 (478; 1979–80 (374); 1983–4 (130).

The Times House of Commons (published after every election since 1880 except for 1906, 1922, 1923 and 1924).

The Constitutional Year Book (published annually 1885–1939. Until 1919 it gave every result since 1885; after 1919 it only gave post-1918 results and after 1931 only results since 1923 or 1924.)

British Electoral Facts 1832–1985 by F. W. S. Craig (Political Reference Publications, second edition 1985). (This gives national totals, together with much else.)

British Parliamentary Election Results by F. W. S. Craig (Political Reference Publications, separate volumes for 1885–1918, 1918–49, 1950–70, 1974–). (These volumes record all constituency results with percentages. They constitute easily the most authoritative and convenient source of electoral data.)

British Political Facts 1900–1985 by D. and G. Butler (Macmillan, 1986). (This gives national totals and other electoral data.)

The British Voter 1885–1966 by M. Kinnear (Batsford, 1968).

British Parliamentary Constituencies: a Statistical Compendium by I. Crewe and A. Fox (Faber, 1984).

The Almanac of British Politics by R. Waller (Croom Helm, second edition, 1984).

From 1945, the results of each election have been analysed in statistical appendices to the Nuffield College series of studies, *The British General Election of 1945* by R. B. McCallum and Alison Readman (OUP, 1947), *The British General Election of 1950* by H. G. Nicholas, (Macmillan, 1951), *The*

British General Election of 1951 by D. E. Butler (Macmillan,1952), and subsequent volumes for each election by D. Butler and various co-authors (all published by Macmillan).

A valuable source on pre-1914 election statistics is *Social Geography of British Elections 1885–1910* by H. Pelling (Macmillan, 1967).

A general bibliography on British electoral statistics and psephological studies is to be found in the chapter by D. Butler and James Cornford in S. Rokkan and J. Meyriat (eds), *International Guide to Election Statistics* (Mouton, 1969).

ELECTION RESULTS: STATISTICS

Tables 8.1 to 8.3 are taken from *British Political Facts 1900–1985* because they provide a simple series compiled on the same basis for the whole century.

It is, however, impossible to present election statistics in any finally authoritative way. British law makes no acknowledgement of the existence of political parties, and in most general elections the precise allegiance of at least a few of the candidates is in doubt. This, far more than arithmetic error, explains the discrepancies between the figures provided in various works of reference.

Such discrepancies, however, are seldom on a serious scale (except, perhaps, for 1918). Election figures suffer much more from being inherently confusing than from being inaccurately reported. The complications that arise from unopposed returns, from plural voting, from two-member seats, and, above all, from variations in the number of candidates put up by each party, are the really serious hazards in psephological interpretation.

In Table 8.1(a) an attempt is made to allow for these factors by a column which shows the average vote won by each opposed candidate (with the vote in two-member seats halved, and with university seats excluded). This still gives a distorted picture, especially when, as in 1900 or 1931, there were many unopposed candidates or when, as in 1929, 1931, or 1950, there was a sharp change in the number of Liberals standing; in 1918 the situation was so complicated that any such statistics are omitted, as they are likely to confuse more than to clarify; for other elections they should be regarded as corrective supplements to the cruder percentages in the previous column rather than as substitutes for them.

The turn-out percentages are modified to allow for the distorting effect of the two-member seats which existed up to 1950.

To simplify classification, some arbitrary decisions have been made. Before 1918 candidates have been classified as Conservative, Liberal, or Irish Nationalist, even if their designation had a prefix such as Tariff Reform, or Independent, but only officially sponsored candidates are classed as Labour. From 1918 onwards, candidates not officially recognised by their party have

Table 8.1(a) General election results, 1900–1987, United Kingdom

	Total votes	MPs elected	Candidates	Unopposed returns	% Share of total vote	Average % vote per opposed candidate
1900 (28 Sept.–24 Oct.)						
Conservative	1 797 444	402	579	163	51.1	52.5
Liberal	1 568 141	184	406	22	44.6	48.2
Labour	63 304	2	15	—	1.8	26.6
Irish Nationalist	90 076	82	100	58	2.5	80.0
Others	544	—	2	—	0.0	2.2
Elec. 6 730 935	3 519 509	670	1102	243	100.0	—
Turnout 74.6%						
1906 (12 Jan.–7 Feb.)						
Conservative	2 451 454	157	574	13	43.6	44.1
Liberal	2 757 883	400	539	27	49.0	52.6
Labour	329 748	30	51	—	5.9	39.9
Irish Nationalist	35 031	83	87	74	0.6	63.1
Others	52 387	—	22	—	0.9	18.8
Elec. 7 264 608	5 626 503	670	1273	114	100.0	—
Turnout 82.6%						
1910 (14 Jan.–9 Feb.)						
Conservative	3 127 887	273	600	19	46.9	47.5
Liberal	2 880 581	275	516	1	43.2	49.2
Labour	505 657	40	78	—	7.6	38.4
Irish Nationalist	124 586	82	104	55	1.9	77.7
Others	28 693	—	17	—	0.4	15.4
Elec. 7 694 741	6 667 404	670	1315	75	100.0	—
Turnout 86.6%						
1910 (2–19 Dec.)						
Conservative	2 420 566	272	550	72	46.3	47.9
Liberal	2 295 888	272	467	35	43.9	49.5
Labour	371 772	42	56	3	7.1	42.8

Irish Nationalist	131 375	84	106	53	2.5	81.9
Others	8 768	—	11	—	0.2	9.1
Elec. 7 709 981	5 228 369	670	1191	163	100.0	—
Turnout 81.1%						

1918 (Sat., 14 Dec.) Result announced 28 Dec. 1918)

Coalition Unionist	3 504 198	335	374	42	32.6	
Coalition Liberal	1 455 640	133	158	27	13.5	
Coalition Labour	161 521	10	18	—	1.5	
(Coalition)	(5 121 359)	(478)	(550)	(69)	(47.6)	
Conservative	370 375	23	37	—	3.4	
Irish Unionist	292 722	25	38	—	2.7	
Liberal	1 298 808	28	253	12	12.1	
Labour	2 385 472	63	388	1	22.2	
Irish Nationalist	238 477	7	60	25	2.2	
Sinn Fein	486 867	73	102	—	4.5	
Others	572 503	10	197	—	5.3	
Elec. 21 392 322	10 766 583	707	1625	107	100.0	
Turnout 58.9%						

1922 (Wed., 15 Nov.)

Conservative	5 500 382	345	483	42	38.2	48.6
National Liberal	1 673 240	62	162	5	11.6	39.3
Liberal	2 516 287	54	328	5	17.5	30.9
Labour	4 241 383	142	411	4	29.5	40.0
Others	462 340	12	59	1	3.2	28.3
Elec. 21 127 663	14 393 632	615	1443	57	100.0	—
Turnout 71.3%						

1923 (Thu., 6 Dec.)

Conservative	5 538 824	258	540	35	38.1	42.6
Liberal	4 311 147	159	453	11	29.6	37.8
Labour	4 438 508	191	422	3	30.5	41.0
Others	260 042	7	31	1	1.8	27.6
Elec. 21 281 232	14 548 521	615	1446	50	100.0	—
Turnout 70.8%						

continued overleaf

304

Table 8.1(a)—*continued*

	Total votes	MPs elected	Candidates	Unopposed returns	% Share of total vote	Average % vote per opposed candidate
1924 (Wed., 29 Oct.)						
Conservative	8 039 598	419	552	16	48.3	51.9
Liberal	2 928 747	40	340	6	17.6	30.9
Labour	5 489 077	151	512	9	33.0	38.2
Communist	55 346	1	8	—	0.3	25.0
Others	126 511	4	16	1	0.8	29.1
	16 639 279	615	1428	32	100.0	—
Elec. 21 731 320						
Turnout 76.6%						
1929 (Thu., 30 May)						
Conservative	8 656 473	260	590	4	38.2	39.4
Liberal	5 308 510	59	513	—	23.4	27.7
Labour	8 389 512	288	571	—	37.1	39.3
Communist	50 614	—	25	—	0.3	5.3
Others	243 266	8	31	3	1.0	21.2
	22 648 375	615	1730	7	100.0	—
Elec. 28 850 870						
Turnout 76.1%						
1931 (Tue., 27 Oct.)						
Conservative	11 978 745	473	523	56	55.2	62.9
National Labour	341 370	13	20	—	1.6	
Liberal National	809 302	35	41	—	3.7	
Liberal	1 403 102	33	112	5	6.5	28.8
(National Government)	(14 532 519)	(554)	(696)	(61)	(67.0)	—
Independent Liberal	106 106	4	7	—	0.5	35.8
Labour	6 649 630	52	515	6	30.6	33.0
Communist	74 824	—	26	—	0.3	7.5
New Party	36 377	—	24	—	0.2	3.9
Others	256 917	5	24	—	1.2	21.9
	21 656 373	615	1292	67	100.0	—
Elec. 29 960 071						
Turnout 76.3%						

1935 (Thu., 14 Nov.)

	Total Votes	MPs Elected	Candidates	Unopposed	% Share	% Votes
Conservative	11 810 158	431	585	26	53.7	54.8
Liberal	1 422 116	21	161	—	6.4	23.9
Labour	8 325 491	154	552	13	37.9	40.3
Independent Labour Party	139 577	4	17	—	0.7	22.2
Communist	27 117	1	2	—	0.1	38.0
Others	272 595	4	31	1	1.2	21.3
Elec. 31 379 050	21 997 054	615	1348	40	100.0	—

Turnout 71.2%

1945 (Thur., 5 July) (Result announced 26 July 1945)

	Total Votes	MPs Elected	Candidates	Unopposed	% Share	% Votes
Conservative	9 988 306	213	624	1	39.8	40.1
Liberal	2 248 226	12	306	—	9.0	18.6
Labour	11 995 152	393	604	2	47.8	50.4
Communist	102 780	2	21	—	0.4	12.7
Common Wealth	110 634	1	23	—	0.4	12.6
Others	640 880	19	104	—	2.0	15.4
Elec. 33 240 391	25 085 978	640	1682	3	100.0	—

Turnout 72.7%

(1950) (Thu., 23 Feb.)

	Total Votes	MPs Elected	Candidates	Unopposed	% Share	% Votes
Conservative	12 502 567	298	620	2	43.5	43.7
Liberal	2 621 548	9	475	—	9.1	11.8
Labour	13 266 592	315	617	—	46.1	46.7
Communist	91 746	—	100	—	0.3	2.0
Others	290 218	3	56	—	1.0	12.6
Elec. 33 269 770	28 772 671	625	1868	2	100.0	—

Turnout 84.0%

1951 (Thu., 25 Oct.)

	Total Votes	MPs Elected	Candidates	Unopposed	% Share	% Votes
Conservative	13 717 538	321	617	4	48.0	48.6
Liberal	730 556	6	109	—	2.5	14.7
Labour	13 948 605	295	617	—	48.8	49.2
Communist	21 640	—	10	—	0.1	4.4
Others	177 329	3	23	—	0.6	16.8
Elec. 34 645 573	28 595 668	625	1376	4	100.0	—

Turnout 82.5%

continued overleaf

Table 8.1(a)—continued

	Total votes	MPs elected	Candidates	Unopposed returns	% Share of total vote	Average % vote per opposed candidate
1955 (Thu., 26 May)						
Conservative	13 286 569	344	623	—	49.7	50.2
Liberal	722 405	6	110	—	2.7	15.1
Labour	12 404 970	277	620	—	46.4	47.3
Communist	33 144	—	17	—	0.1	4.2
Others	313 410	3	39	—	1.1	20.8
Elec. 34 858 263	26 760 498	630	1409	—	100.0	—
Turnout 76.7%						
1959 (Thur., 8 Oct.)						
Conservative	13 749 830	365	625	—	49.4	49.6
Liberal	1 638 571	6	216	—	5.9	16.9
Labour	12 215 538	258	621	—	43.8	44.5
Communist	30 897	—	18	—	0.1	4.1
Others	224 405	1	56	—	0.8	10.0
Elec. 35 397 080	27 859 241	630	1536	—	100.0	—
Turnout 78.8%						
1964 (Thu., 15 Oct.)						
Conservative	12 001 396	304	630	—	43.4	43.4
Liberal	3 098 878	9	365	—	11.2	18.5
Labour	12 205 814	317	628	—	44.1	44.1
Communist	45 932	—	36	—	0.2	3.4
Others	302 982	—	98	—	1.1	7.9
Elec. 35 892 572	27 655 002	630	1757	—	100.0	—
Turnout 77.1%						
1966 (Thu., 31 Mar.)						
Conservative	11 418 433	253	629	—	41.9	41.8
Liberal	2 327 533	12	311	—	8.5	16.1
Labour	13 064 951	363	621	—	47.9	48.7
Communist	62 112	—	57	—	0.2	3.0

	Votes	Seats	Candidates		%	%
Others	390 577	2	89	—	1.5	8.6
Elec. 35 964 684	27 263 606	630	1707	—	100.0	—
Turnout 75.8%						
1970 (Thu., 18 June)						
Conservative	13 145 123	330	628	—	46.4	46.5
Liberal	2 117 035	6	332	—	7.5	13.5
Labour	12 179 341	287	624	—	43.0	43.5
Communist	37 970	—	58	—	0.1	1.1
Others	865 329	7	195	—	3.0	7.9
Elec. 39 342 013	28 344 798	630	1837	—	100.0	—
Turnout 72.0%						
1974 (Thu., 28 Feb.)						
Conservative	11 868 906	297	623	—	37.9	38.8
Liberal	6 063 470	14	517	—	19.3	23.6
Labour	11 639 243	301	623	—	37.1	38.0
Communist	32 741	—	44	—	0.1	1.7
Plaid Cymru	171 364	2	36	—	0.6	10.7
Scottish Nat. P.	632 032	7	70	—	2.0	21.9
National Front	76 865	—	54	—	0.3	3.2
Others (G.B.)	131 059	2	120	—	0.4	2.2
Others (N.I.)[1]	717 986	12	48	—	2.3	25.0
Elec. 39 798 899	31 333 226	635	2135	—	100.0	—
Turnout 78.7%						
1974 (Thu., 10 Oct.)						
Conservative	10 464 817	277	623	—	35.8	36.7
Liberal	5 346 754	13	619	—	18.3	18.9
Labour	11 457 079	319	623	—	39.2	40.2
Communist	17 426	—	29	—	0.1	1.5
Plaid Cymru	166 321	3	36	—	0.6	10.8
Scottish Nat. P.	839 617	11	71	—	2.9	30.4
National Front	113 843	—	90	—	0.4	2.9
Others (G.B.)	81 227	—	118	—	0.3	1.5
Others (N.I.)[1]	702 094	12	43	—	2.4	27.9
Elec. 40 072 971	29 189 178	635	2252	—	100.0	—
Turnout 72.8%						

continued overleaf

	Total votes	MPs elected	Candidates	Unopposed returns	% Share of total vote	Average % vote per opposed candidate
1979 (Thu., 3 May)						
Conservative	13 697 690	339	622	—	43.9	44.9
Liberal	4 313 811	11	577	—	13.8	14.9
Labour	11 532 148	269	623	—	36.9	37.8
Communist	15 938	—	38	—	0.1	0.9
Plaid Cymru	132 544	2	36	—	0.4	8.1
Scottish Nat. P.	504 259	2	71	—	1.6	17.3
National Front	190 747	—	303	—	0.6	1.6
Ecology	38 116	—	53	—	0.1	2.0
Workers Rev. P.	13 535	—	60	—	0.1	0.5
Others (G.B.)	85 338	—	129	—	0.3	1.3
Others (N.I.)[1]	695 889	12	64	—	2.2	18.8
Elec. 41 093 264	31 220 010	635	2576	—	100.0	—
Turnout 76.0%						
1983 (Thu., 9 Jun.)						
Conservative	13 012 315	397	633	—	42.4	43.5
Liberal	4 210 115	17	322	—	13.7	27.7
Social Democrat	3 570 834	6	311	—	11.6	24.3
Alliance	(7 780 949)	(23)	(633)	—	(25.4)	(26.0)
Labour	8 456 934	209	633	—	27.6	28.3
Communist	11 606	—	35	—	0.04	0.8
Plaid Cymru	125 309	2	36	—	0.4	7.8
Scottish Nat. P.	331 975	2	72	—	1.1	11.8
National Front	27 065	—	60	—	0.1	1.0
Others (G.B.)	193 383	—	282	—	0.6	1.4
Others (N.I.)[1]	764 925	17	95	—	3.1	17.9
Elec. 42 197 344	42 197 344	650	2579	—	100.0	—
Turnout 72.7%						

1987 (Thu., 11 Jun.)

	Votes	MPs	Candidates		%	%
Conservative	13 750 525	376	633	—	42.2	43.2
Liberal	4 173 354	17	327	—	12.9	13.2
Social Democrat	3 167 798	5	306	—	9.7	9.9
(Alliance)	(7 341 152)	(22)	633	—	(22.6)	(23.1)
Labour	10 029 944	229	633	—	30.8	31.5
Plaid Cymru	123 589	3	36	—	0.4	7.3
Scottish Nat. P.	416 873	3	71	—	1.1	14.0
Green	89 753	—	133	—	0.3	1.4
Others (G.B.)	37 576	—	106	—	0.1	0.6
Others (N.I.)	730 152	17	77	—	2.2	22.1
	32 529 564	650	2324	—	100.0	—

Elec. 43 181 321
Turnout 75.3%

Note:

1. From 1974 onwards, no candidates in Northern Ireland are included in the major party totals although it might be argued that some independent Unionists should be classed with the Conservatives and that Northern Ireland Labour candidates should be classed with Labour.

Sources: D. and G. Butler, *British Political Facts 1900–1985; The Times House of Commons* (1987).

Table 8.1(b) Direct elections to European Parliament, 1979, 1984 (United Kingdom)

1979 (Thur., 7 June)

	% Turnout	% votes Con.	Lab.	Lib.	Nat.	Other	Seats Con.	Lab.	Lib.	Nat.	Other
England	31.3	53.4	32.6	13.2	—	0.8	54	12	—	—	—
Wales	34.4	36.6	41.5	9.6	11.7	0.6	1	3	—	—	—
Scotland	33.7	33.7	33.0	13.9	19.4	—	5	2	—	1	—
Great Britain	32.1	50.6	33.1	13.1	2.5	0.7	60	17	—	1	—
Northern Ireland[1]	55.7	—	—	0.2	—	99.8	—	—	—	1	3
United Kingdom	32.7	48.4	31.6	12.6	2.5	4.9	60	17	—	1	3

Electorate 41 152 763   Votes cast 13 446 083

1984 (Thu., 14 June)

	% Turnout	% votes Con.	Lab.	Alln.	Nat.	Other	Seats Con.	Lab.	Alln.	Other
England	31.6	43.1	35.0	20.4	—	1.5	42	24	—	—
Wales	39.7	25.4	44.5	17.4	12.2	0.5	1	3	—	—
Scotland	33.0	25.7	40.7	15.6	17.8	0.2	2	5	—	1
Great Britain	31.8	40.8	36.5	19.5	2.5	0.8	45	32	—	1
Northern Ireland[1]	63.5	—	—	—	—	100.0%	—	—	—	3
United Kingdom	32.6	39.9	36.0	19.1	2.4	5.6	45	32	—	4

Electorate 42 493 274   Votes cast 13 998 274

Note:
1. In Northern Ireland the election was conducted by Single Transferable vote.
Sources: F. W. S. Craig, *Europe Votes 2* (1985); D. Butler and D. Marquand, *European Elections and British Politics* (1981); D. Butler and P. Jowett, *Party Strategies in Britain* (1985).

been classified with 'Others' (except that in 1935 Ind. Lib. are placed with Lib.). Liberal Unionists have been listed as Conservatives throughout. Liberal National, National Labour, and National candidates are listed with Conservatives except in 1931.

SOCIAL BASES OF PARTY STRENGTH

Since the advent of opinion polls a large amount of data about the background of voters have become available. Table 8.4, based on National Opinion Polls (NOP) 1964 findings, illustrates the broad picture, which had only changed a little during the first 20 years that such data were available. The MORI (Market and Opinion Research International) findings of 1983 show a new picture.

Data of this sort are discussed in the local studies of voting conducted in the 1950s, notably:

M. Benney, R. H. Pear and A. P. Gray (1956) *How People Vote* (Routledge & Kegan Paul).

R. S. Milne and H. C. Mackenzie (1955) *Straight Fight* (Hansard Society).

R. S. Milne and H. C. Mackenzie (1958) *Marginal Seat* (Hansard Society).

On a national scale the Gallup Poll have published their findings in a monthly Bulletin since 1960. NOP have done the same since 1963. Summaries of opinion poll findings are to be found in:

R. R. Alford (1964) *Party and Society* (John Murray).

J. Blondel (1963) *Voters, Parties and Leaders* (Penguin).

J. Bonham (1954) *The Middle Class Vote* (Faber).

R. L. Leonard (1968) *Elections in Britain* (van Nostrand).

P. G. J. Pulzer (1967) *Political Representation and Elections* (Allen & Unwin).

R. Rose (1965) *Politics in England* (Faber).

There is the special treatment of working-class voting using specially collected survey material in:

R. T. McKenzie and A. Silver (1968) *Angels in Marble* (Heinemann).

E. A. Nordlinger (1962) *The Working Class Tories* (McGibbon & Kee).

J. H. Goldthorpe, D. Lockwood, F. Bechhofer and J. Platt (1968) *The Affluent Worker* (vol. II, *Political Attitudes*) (CUP).

A comprehensive academic study of voting behaviour, involving nationwide sample surveys, is provided in:

Table 8.2 General election results by regions, 1900–87

	1900	1906	Jan. 1910	Dec. 1910	1918	1922	1923	1924	1929	1931
County of London										
Conservative	51	19	33	30	Coal.	43	29	39	24	53
Liberal	8	38	25	26	53	9	11	3	2	4
Labour	—	2	1	3	Op.	9	22	19	36	5
Others	—	—	—	—	9	1	—	1	—	1
Rest of S. England										
Conservative	123	45	107	103	Coal.	130	89	150	111	156
Liberal	32	107	46	49	149	23	48	5	18	4
Labour	—	3	2	2	Op.	9	27	10	35	5
Others	—	—	—	1	16	3	1	—	1	—
Midlands										
Conservative	60	27	49	50	Coal.	53	45	64	35	80
Liberal	27	59	31	30	67	17	17	2	5	3
Labour	1	2	8	8	Op.	17	25	21	47	4
Others	—	—	—	—	20	—	—	—	—	—
Northern England										
Conservative	98	31	45	50	Coal.	82	57	101	51	146
Liberal	55	102	86	82	121	27	48	9	10	9
Labour	—	20	22	21	Op.	60	64	59	108	15
Others	1	1	1	1	50	2	2	2	2	1
Wales										
Conservative	6	—	2	3	Coal.	6	4	9	1	11
Liberal	27	33	27	26	20	10	12	10	9	8
Labour	1	1	5	5	Op.	18	19	16	25	16
Others	—	—	—	—	15	1	—	—	—	—
Scotland										
Conservative	36	10	9	9	Coal.	13	14	36	20	57
Liberal	34	58	59	58	54	27	22	8	13	7
Labour	—	2	2	3	Op.	29	34	26	37	7
Others	—	—	—	—	17	2	1	1	1	—
Ireland										
Conservative	19	16	19	17	Coal.	10	10	12	10	10
Liberal	1	3	1	1	1	—	—	—	—	—
Labour	—	—	—	—	Op.	—	—	—	—	—
Others	81	82	81	83	100	2	2	—	2	2
Universities										
Conservative	9	9	9	9	Coal.	8	9	8	8	8
Liberal	—	—	—	—	13	3	2	3	2	2
Labour	—	—	—	—	Op.	—	—	—	—	—
Others	—	—	—	—	2	1	1	1	2	2
Totals										
Conservative	402	157	273	272	Coal.	345	258	419	260	521
Liberal	184	400	275	272	478	116	159	40	59	37
Labour	2	30	40	42	Op.	142	191	151	288	52
Others	82	83	82	84	229	12	7	5	8	5
Total seats	670	670	670	670	707	615	615	615	615	615

Notes: In 1918 all Coalition and all non-Coalition candidates are listed together. In fact a substantial number of the 48 Conservatives who were elected without the Coupon worked with the Government. Virtually no Coupons were issued to Irish candidates but 23 of the 101 non-University seats in Ireland went to Unionists.
The vertical lines indicate redistribution of seats.
Northern England includes Cheshire, Lancashire, Yorkshire, and all counties to their north.

	1935	1945	1950	1951	1955	1959	1964	1966	1970	Feb. 1974	Oct. 1974	1979	1983	1987
(GLC)														
	39	12	12	14	15	18	10	6	9	42	41	50	56	57
	1	—	—	—	—	—	—	—	—	—	—	—	2	3
	22	48	31	29	27	24	32	36	33	50	51	42	26	23
	—	2	—	—	—	—	—	—	—	—	—	—	—	—
	147	88	144	153	171	157	134	169	136	128	146	168	171	
	3	3	1	—	—	1	3	4	2	5	5	3	5	3
	15	91	54	46	42	34	46	67	34	21	29	13	3	3
	—	3	—	—	1	—	—	1	1	—	—	—	—	—
	67	24	35	35	39	49	42	35	51	43	40	57	70	67
	1	—	—	—	—	—	—	—	—	—	—	—	—	—
	19	64	59	59	57	47	54	61	45	54	58	41	30	33
	—	2	—	—	—	—	—	—	—	1	—	—	—	—
	106	43	61	69	75	77	53	44	63	47	44	53	68	63
	5	2	1	2	2	2	—	2	—	4	3	4	6	4
	60	128	107	99	90	88	114	121	104	112	117	107	89	96
	—	—	—	—	—	—	—	—	—	1	—	—	—	
	11	4	4	6	6	7	6	3	7	8	8	11	14	8
	6	6	5	3	3	2	2	1	1	2	2	1	2	3
	18	25	27	27	27	27	28	32	27	24	23	22	20	24
	—	—	—	—	—	—	—	—	1	2	3	2	2	3
	43	29	32	35	36	31	24	20	23	21	16	22	21	10
	3	—	2	1	1	1	4	5	3	3	3	3	8	9
	20	37	37	35	34	38	43	46	44	40	41	44	41	50
	5	5	—	—	—	1	—	—	1	7	11	2	2	3
	10	9	10	9	10	12	12	11	8	—	—	—	—	—
	—	—	—	—	—	—	—	—	—	—	—	—	—	—
	—	—	—	—	—	—	—	—	—	—	—	—	—	—
	2	3	2	3	2	—	—	1	4	12	12	12	17	17
	9	4	—	—	—	—	—	—	—	—	—	—	—	—
	1	1	—	—	—	—	—	—	—	—	—	—	—	—
	—	—	—	—	—	—	—	—	—	—	—	—	—	—
	2	7	—	—	—	—	—	—	—	—	—	—	—	—
	432	213	298	321	344	365	304	253	330	297	277	339	397	376
	20	12	9	6	6	6	9	12	6	14	13	11	23	22
	154	393	315	295	277	258	317	363	287	301	319	269	209	229
	9	22	3	3	3	1	—	2	7	23	26	16	21	23
	615	640	625	625	630	630	630	630	630	635	635	635	650	650

Midlands includes Hereford, Worcs., Warwickshire, Northants., Lincs., Notts., Leics., Staffs., Salop, Derbyshire.

Southern England includes the rest of England, except for the County of London (the old L.C.C. area), but from 1974 the seats in the outer areas of the Greater London Council are classed with the County of London and not with the rest of S. England.

Source: As for Table 8.1

Table 8.3   By-elections, 1900–1987, United Kingdom

	Total[1] By-elections	Changes	Con. +	Con. −	Lib. +	Lib. −	Lab. +	Lab. −	Others +	Others −
1900–1905	113	30	2	26	20	4	5˙	—	5	—
1906–9	101	20	12	—	—	18	5	—	3	2
1910	20	—	—	—	—	—	—	—	—	—
1911–18	245	31	16	4	4	16	2	4	10	8
1918–22	108	27	4	13	5[2]	11[2]	14	1	4	2
1922–3	16	6	1	4	3	1	2	—	—	1
1923–4	10	3	2	1	—	1	1	1	—	—
1924–9	63	20	1	16	6	3	13	1	—	—
1929–31	36	7	4	1	—	1	2	4	1	1
1931–5	62	10	—	9	—	1	10	—	—	—
1935–45	219	30	—	29	—	—	13	1	17	—
1945–50	52	3	3	—	—	—	—	—	—	3
1950–1	16	—	—	—	—	—	—	—	—	—
1951–5	48	1	1	—	—	—	—	1	—	—
1955–9	52	6	1	4	1	1	4	—	—	1
1959–64	62	9	2	7	1	—	6	2	—	—
1964–6	13	2	1	1	1	—	—	1	—	—
1966–70	38	16	12	1	1	—	—	15	3	—
1970–4	30	9	—	5	5	—	2	3	2	1
1974	1	—	—	—	—	—	—	—	—	—
1974–9	30	7	6	—	1	—	—	—	—	—
1979–83	20	7	1	4	4	—	1	2	1	2
1983–7	31	6	—	4	4[3]	—[3]	1	1	1	1

Notes:
1. Up to 1918, and to a lesser extent to 1926, the number of by-elections is inflated by the necessity for ministers to stand for re-election on appointment. In 53 such cases the returns were unopposed.
2. In 1918–22 Opposition Liberals won 5 seats and lost 2. Coalition Liberals lost 9.
3. Alliance
Sources: As for Table 8.1.

D. Butler and D. Stokes (1974) *Political Change in Britain* (Macmillan, 2nd edn).
B. Sarlvik and I. Crewe (1983) *Partisan Dealignment in Britain* (CUP).
A. Heath, R. Jowell, and J. Curtice (1985) *How Britain Votes* (Pergamon).
See also R. Rose and I. McAllister (1986). *Voters begin to Choose* (Sage).
and M. Franklin (1984), *The Decline of Class Voting in Britain* (Oxford).

MEMBERS OF PARLIAMENT

There are considerable difficulties in drawing up tables about the backgrounds of MPs. Some are very reticent about themselves and a few are actively

Table 8.4(a) Party support by sex, age and social class, 1964, (percentages)

	All	Sex		Age				Class			Trade union	
		Men	Women	21–4	25–34	35–54	55+	ABC1	C2	DE	Member	Non-member
All	100	48	52					39	39	31		
Cons.	43	38	46	40	40	41	48	65	34	31	28	48
Lab.	45	52	42	49	48	46	41	20	54	59	62	38
Lib.	11	8	12	11	11	12	11	13	11	9	9	12
Other	1	2	1	1	1	1	1	1	1	1	1	1

Source: National Opinion Poll (1964) (12 000 in combined sample).

Table 8.4(b) Party support by sex, age and social class, 1987

	All	Sex		Age				Class			Trade union	
		Men	Women	18–24	25–34	35–54	55+	ABC1	C2	DE	Member	Non-member
All	100	48	52	14	19	33	34	43	27	30	23	77
Cons.	43	43	43	37	39	45	46	54	30	30	30	47
Lab.	32	32	32	40	33	29	31	18	36	48	42	29
Alln.	23	23	23	21	25	24	21	26	22	22	26	22
Other	2	2	2	2	3	2	2	2	2	2	2	2

Source: MORI (1987) (23 396 in combined sample).

Table 8.5   Interests represented by Conservative and Liberal MPs, 1900–1910. Percentages of all interests represented (some members representing several interests) (percentages)

	Landowners	Commerce and industry	Legal and professional	Others	Total
	Con.	*Con.*	*Con.*	*Con.*	
1900	20	52	18	10	100
1906	17	64	11	8	100
1910 Jan.	26	53	12	9	100
	Lib.	*Lib.*	*Lib.*	*Lib.*	
1900	9	58	29	4	100
1906	8	65	23	4	100
1910 Jan.	7	66	23	4	100

Source: J. A. Thomas, *The House of Commons 1900–11* (1958).

Table 8.6   Main occupation of MPs, 1918–51 (percentages)

	Conservative				Labour			
	1918–35 *(average)*	1945	1950	1951	1918–35 *(average)*	1945	1950	1951
Employers and managers	32	32½	30½	32½	4	9½	9½	9
Rank and file workers	4	3	3	4½	72	41	43	45
Professional workers	52	61	62	57½	24	48½	46½	45½
Unpaid domestic workers	—	½	—	—	—	1	1	½
Unoccupied	12	3	4½	5½	—	—	—	—
	100	100	100	100	100	100	100	100

Source: J. F. S. Ross, *Electors and Elected*, p. 440.

misleading. The classification of education and occupation leaves many borderline dilemmas. These problems are discussed at various points in the main sources on the subject.

W. L. Guttsman (1963) *The British Political Élite* (McGibbon & Kee).
J. F. S. Ross (1944) *Parliamentary Represenation* (Eyre & Spottiswoode, 2nd edn; *Elections and Electors* (1955) (Eyre & Spottiswoode).
The Nuffield Studies of each election since 1945.
J. A. Thomas (1939) *The House of Commons 1837–1901* (University of Wales). *The House of Commons 1900–1911* (1958) (University of Wales).

Age

The average age of members has been very constant. At the beginning of every Parliament from 1918 to 1983 it has lain between 48½ and 52. The average age of Labour members has always been slightly higher than the rest.

Occupation

Details of the interests represented by members of the pre-1914 parliaments are provided by J. A. Thomas. Table 8.5 is based on W. L. Guttsman's adaptation of Thomas's figures.[7]

For the interwar and immediate post-1945 period J. F. S. Ross offers a summary of occupations (Table 8.6), while since 1951 the Nuffield studies reach results using a slightly different definition of occupation (Table 8.7).

Table 8.7   Main occupations of MPs, 1951–87 (percentages)

| | | | | | *Conservative* | | | | | | |
| | | | | | | Feb. | Oct. | | | |
	1951	1955	1959	1964	1966	1970	1974	1974	1979	1983	1987
Professional	41	46	46	48	46	45	44	46	45	45	42
Business	37	30	30	26	29	30	32	33	34	36	37
Misc.	22	24	23	25	23	24	23	20	20	19	20
Workers	—	—	1	1	1	1	1	1	1	1	1
	100	100	100	100	100	100	100	100	100	100	100

| | | | | | *Labour* | | | | | | |
| | | | | | | Feb. | Oct. | | | |
	1951	1955	1959	1964	1966	1970	1974	1974	1979	1983	1987
Professional	35	36	38	41	43	48	46	49	43	42	40
Business	9	12	10	11	9	10	9	8	7	9	8
Misc.	19	17	17	16	18	16	15	15	14	16	22
Workers	37	35	35	32	30	26	30	28	36	33	29
	100	100	100	100	100	100	100	100	100	100	100

Sources: D. and G. Butler, *British Political Facts 1900–1985*, p. 178; D. Butler and D. Kavanagh, *The British General Election of 1987* (Macmillan 1988).

Education

The educational background of Conservative and Labour members of Parliament is shown in Table 8.8.

Table 8.8   Education of Conservative and Labour MPs 1906–87 (percentages)

	Conservatives		Labour	
	Public School	*University educated*	*Public School*	*University educated*
1906	67	57	0	0
1910 Jan.	74	58	0	0
1910 Dec.	76	59	0	0
1918	81	49	3	5
1922	78	48	9	15
1923	79	50	8	14
1924	78	53	7	14
1929	79	54	12	19
1931	77	55	8	17
1935	81	57	10	19
1945	85	58	23	32
1950	85	62	22	41
1951	75	65	23	41
1955	76	64	22	40
1959	72	60	18	39
1964	75	63	18	46
1966	80	67	18	51
1970	74	64	17	53
1974 Feb.	74	68	17	56
1974 Oct.	75	69	18	57
1979	77	73	17	57
1983	70	71	14	53
1987	68	70	14	56

Sources: Data for 1906 and 1910 are based on J. A. Thomas, *The House of Commons 1906–1911* (1958). From 1918 to 1950 J. F. S. Ross provides the data on university education in *Elections and Electors* (1955) and on public school education for Conservatives. The figures for Labour public schoolboys up to 1935 have been calculated afresh for this table. All figures from 1951 onwards are taken from the Nuffield studies. See also C. Mellors, *The British M.P. 1945–1975* (1978).

Sex

Women's candidature for, and membership of, the House of Commons since 1918 are shown in Table 8.9.

THE CABINET

Table 8.10 shows the social and educational background of the Cabinet formed by each new Prime Minister on coming to office (except that Asquith's is not given for 1908 but for 1 August 1914; new wartime governments are omitted in 1915, 1916 and 1940; so is Baldwin's in 1923; MacDonald's

Table 8.9   Women candidates and MPs, 1918–87

	Conservative		Labour		Liberal (Alln.)		Other		Total	
	Cands	MPs	Cands	MPs	Cands	MPs	Cands	MPs	Cands	MPs
1918	1	—	4	—	4	—	8	1	17	1
1922	5	1	10	—	16	1	2	—	33	2
1923	7	3	14	3	12	2	1	—	34	8
1924	12	3	22	1	6	—	1	—	41	4
1929	10	3	30	9	25	1	4	1	69	14
1931	16	13	36	—	6	1	4	1	62	15
1935	19	6	35	1	11	1	2	1	67	9
1945	14	1	45	21	20	1	8	1	87	24
1950	28	6	42	14	45	1	11	—	126	21
1951	29	6	39	11	11	—	—	—	74	17
1955	32	10	43	14	12	—	2	—	89	24
1959	28	12	36	13	16	—	1	—	81	25
1964	24	11	33	18	25	—	8	—	90	29
1966	21	7	30	19	20	—	9	—	80	26
1970	26	15	29	10	23	—	21	1	99	26
1974 Feb.	33	9	40	13	40	—	30	1	143	23
1974 Oct.	30	7	50	18	49	—	32	2	161	27
1979	31	8	52	11	51	—	76	—	210	19
1983	40	13	78	10	(115)	—	87	—	280	23
1987	46	17	92	21	(105)	2	84	1	327	41

Sources: F. W. S. Craig, *British Electoral Facts* (2nd edn, 1985); *The Times House of Commons* (1987).

National Government is given for its termination in 1935, not its inception in 1931; and Thatcher's Government is reassessed as it existed on 30 September 1986.

The class composition of governments is largely drawn from the table on p. 78 of W. L. Guttsman, *The British Political Élite*. Aristocrats are those who had among their grandparents the holder of a hereditary title. Working class are those whose fathers appear to have had a manual occupation while they were growing up.

Schools are classified as Public Schools if they are members of the Headmaster's Conference.

The Oxbridge column includes three Oxford men to every Cambridge one: there is not much difference between parties in this although Mr Wilson's 1964 Cabinet was the only one in this century to contain no Cambridge men.[8]

Table 8.10 Social and educational composition of British Cabinets, 1895–1986[1]

Date	Party	PM	Cabinet size	Aristo crats	Middle class	Working class	Public school		University educated	
							All	Eton	All	Oxbridge
Aug. 1895	Con.	Salisbury	19	8	11	—	16	7	15	14
Jul. 1902	Con.	Balfour	19	9	10	—	16	9	14	13
Dec. 1905	Lib.	Campbell-Bannerman	19	7	11	1	11	3	14	12
Jul. 1914	Lib.	Asquith	19	6	12	1	11	3	15	13
Jan. 1919	Coal.	Lloyd George	21	3	17	1	12	2	13	8
Nov. 1922	Con.	Bonar Law	16	3	12	1	14	8	13	13
Jan. 1924	Lab.	MacDonald	19	3	5	11	8	—	6	6
Nov. 1924	Con.	Baldwin	21	9	12	—	21	7	16	16
Jun. 1929	Lab.	MacDonald	18	2	4	12	5	—	6	3
Aug. 1931	Nat.	MacDonald	20	8	10	2	13	6	11	10
Jun. 1935	Con.	Baldwin	22	9	11	2	14	9	11	10
May 1937	Con.	Chamberlain	21	8	13	—	17	7	16	13
May 1945	Con.	Churchill	16	6	9	1	14	7	11	9
Aug. 1945	Lab.	Attlee	20	—	8	12	5	2	10	5
Oct. 1951	Con.	Churchill	16	5	11	—	14	7	11	9
Apr. 1955	Con.	Eden	18	5	13	—	18	10	16	14
Jan. 1957	Con.	Macmillan	18	4	14	—	17	8	16	15
Oct. 1963	Con.	Home	24	5	19	—	21	11	17	17
Oct. 1964	Lab.	Wilson	23	1	14	8	8	1	13	11
Jun. 1970	Con.	Heath	18	4	14	—	15	4	15	15
Mar. 1974	Lab.	Wilson	21	1	16	4	7	—	16	11
Apr. 1976	Lab.	Callaghan	23	1	15	7	8	—	15	12
May 1979	Con.	Thatcher	22	3	19	—	20	6	18	17
Sept. 1986	Con.	Thatcher	22	5	17	—	15	4	20	13
Average 23 Cabinets										
13 Con. Cabinets			19	7	12½	3	17	7½	14	13
6 Lab. Cabinets			20½	1½	9½	9	7	½	11½	7½
2 Lib. Cabinets			19	6	11½	1	11	3	14½	12½

Note: 1. This table is largely based on W. L. Guttsman, *The British Political Elite* (1963). Aristocrats are those who had among their grandparents the holder of a hereditary title. Working class are those whose fathers appear to have had a manual occupation when they were growing up. Schools are classified as Public Schools if members of the Headmasters' Conference. See also *British Political Facts, 1900–1985*.

Notes

1. See P. Gray and T. Corlett (1950) *The Electoral Register as a Sampling Frame* (Central Office of Information); P. Gray and F. A. Gee (1967) *Electoral Registration for Parliamentary Elections* (HMSO); T. Todd and P. Butcher (1982). *Electoral Registration 1981* (OPCS).
2. For details on changes in franchise qualifications see the successive editions of Parker's *Election Agent and Returning Officer* (Knight). See also B. Keith-Lucas (1953) *The English Local Government Franchise* (Blackwell), D. Butler (1962) *The British Electoral System since 1918* (Oxford), and the Representation of the People Acts of 1883, 1918, 1928, 1945, 1948, 1949, 1969 and 1985. A convenient summary of franchise qualifications at any given time is to be found in *Whitaker's Almanack* or (up to 1939) in *The Constitutional Year Book*.
3. There have been five major inquiries into electoral questions:
   1908–10 Royal Commission on Electoral Systems.
   1917 Speaker's Conference on Electoral Reform.
   1930 Ullswater Conference on Electoral Reform.
   1943–4 Speaker's Conference on Electoral Reform.
   1965–8 Speaker's Conference on Electoral Law.
4. The problems of electoral administration are dealt with in the reports of the Speaker's Conferences on Electoral Reform of 1917, 1943–4 and 1965–8, and the Ullswater Conference of 1930 (see Cd 8463/1917; Cmd 3636/1930; Cmd 6534/1944; and Cmd 6543/1944, Cmnd 2917 and 2932/1966; Cmnd 3202 and 3275/1967 and Cmnd 3550/1968. See also the Report of the Home Affairs Committee, HC 32/1982/3.
   See also the reports of the Boundary Commissioners (Cmd 7260, 7274, 7270, 7231 of 1947, Cmd 9311–14 of 1954. Cmnd 4084, 4085, 4086, and 4087 of 1969, and Cmnd 8753 of 1982 and Cmnd 8797, 9172, and 9176 of 1983. See also the judgement of Lord Justice Oliver in *R. v. Boundary Commission ex parte* Foot and others for a lucid exposition of the status of Boundary Commissions (1 All England Law Reports 1099 (1983)).
   See also H. L. Morris (1921) *Parliamentary Franchise Reform in England from 1885 to 1918* (New York), D. Butler (1955) 'The Redistribution of Seats', *Public Administration*, Summer, 125–47, and R. Waller (1983) 'The 1983 Boundary Commission', *Electoral Studies*, December. See also R. L. Leonard (1968) *Elections in Britain* (Van Nostrand).
5. See D. Butler and U. Kitzinger (1976) *The 1975 Referendum* (Macmillan).
6. See D. Butler and D. Marquand (1981) *British Politics and European Elections* (Hutchinson).
   D. Butler and P. Jowett (1985) *Party Strategies in Britain* (Macmillan).
   The Times Guide to the European Parliament 1979.
   The Times Guide to the European Parliament 1984.
7. *The British Political Élite*, p. 104.
8. Other sources of value in this area are:
   Richard Rose (1969) *Class and Party Divisions*, University of Strathclyde Occasional Paper No. 1.
   F. M. G. Willson (1959) 'The Routes of Entry of New Members of the British Cabinet 1868–1958', *Political Studies*, VII (Oct.) 222–32.
   Leon Epstein (1962) 'British Class Consciousness and the Labour Party', *J. British Studies*, III.

9 Urbanisation and Local Government

Bruce Wood

The link between urbanisation and local government was central to the Victorian local government structure. The twin Local Government Acts of 1888 and 1894 recognised the town unit as deserving of its own local authority, whether designated as county borough, municipal borough or urban district. These Acts consolidated earlier legislation including the Borough reforms of 1835, and the creation of urban and rural sanitary districts in the 1840s–1870s. Indeed, the recognition of towns can be traced back much further with the granting of charters and of parliamentary representation.

There was, then, an immediate link between urbanisation and local government at the turn of the century, a link which was to last without serious challenge until 1974. The local government structure, in principle, saw towns in terms of their built-up area. In practice it is true that there were some boroughs and urban districts which did include open countryside within their boundaries, but these were anomalies. The definition of urban which predominated was one of 'bricks and mortar', and we shall see later that the outward growth of towns into adjacent areas classified as 'rural' led to pressure from those towns for boundary extensions or for the award of county borough status.

A first definition of urbanisation can thus be constructed as one based on the built-up area of a town, and measurable by analysing the areas and status of the different kinds of local authority. Such measurement had to end in 1974, because the Local Government Act, 1972 was based on this approach only in the case of the conurbations. However, the built-up area definition of urbanisation does remain measurable, and a special 1981 Census report was based on it.

This first definition alone is no longer satisfactory. In 1888 and 1894 personal mobility, certainly at the daily level, was extremely restricted. Workers tended to live close to the factories, mills and other places of employment. Shopping was a local activity, and journeys of any length to seek entertainment were a rarity. Only a few of the more affluent sections of society had the resources, of time as well as money, which enabled them to be regularly mobile. The built-up area concept of urbanisation thus broadly matched the general pattern of life.

Nowadays this traditional concept needs to be supplemented by a second one based more on personal habits than on physical factors. Our second

322

definition of urbanisation involves recognition of the growing interdependence of town and country during the twentieth century. This sociogeographic approach measures change in such habits as the journey to work, to shops, and to entertainment and leisure facilities. In these and other respects most towns no longer cater only for the inhabitants of the immediate built-up area.

If mass mobility, rural commuting, and suburban sprawl have rendered the Victorian concept of a town to some extent redundant, they have also played a part in introducing the need to recognise a third concept of urbanisation. Since the mid-1960s public policy has become increasingly concerned with the 'inner city', the Victorian core of many cities. This core has typically been experiencing losses of population and of jobs. It has sometimes been the scene of riots, and it contains a population seen by governments to be suffering from urban deprivation. A battery of social, economic and physical policies have been designed to alleviate this so-called 'urban problem', and the inner city concept of urbanisation thus constitutes a third definition which requires our attention.

The aim of this chapter is to examine these three definitions of urbanisation in turn, and to indicate developments in the twentieth century in relation to each of them. The data available do not always allow a full and detailed exposition of trends, particularly in the case of the second and third definitions, because they have not been continually recognised. The first general data problem is thus one which cannot be overcome. It is the absence of particular statistics which are ideally needed to illustrate the pace of change.

A second general problem in compiling statistical evidence concerns the areas for which data are normally available. The existence of this problem helps to link the main sections of the chapter. Most census data, and most other government statistics, are collected on the basis of whole local government areas. This results in two important drawbacks.

First, statistics normally lack geographical continuity. Local government boundaries have not remained unchanged since the turn of the century. Though 1974 represents a total break of continuity, the problem can be seen throughout the century. Cities like Birmingham and Manchester, and many smaller towns, all had boundary changes from time to time, as was to be expected given that the principle behind the local government structure was one of built-up areas being within the town unit. The final section of the chapter is devoted to a detailed exploration of the many boundary changes. For the time being the important point is that these boundary changes are both a help to us (in that they give a broad measure of the physical growth of towns) and a hindrance (because time-series can only be constructed and trends analysed with extreme caution).

The second drawback follows on immediately from this first one. The boundary changes are not as helpful as they might be because, in practice, they only rarely matched exactly the pattern of urban development. For one thing, such changes tend inevitably to occur after the physical development has taken place. In addition, for long periods there was what amounted to a moratorium on such changes taking place. This moratorium, partly a reflection of opposition to boundary extensions to towns by 'rural' local authorities and their inhabitants (who had no wish to be classified as 'urban' and often to pay higher rates as a result), meant that many rapidly growing suburbs did not become recognised as parts of towns. Municipal boundaries frequently did not reflect the true urban limits of a town, and the bricks-and-mortar definition cannot be measured with total confidence or precision. Nor can the sociogeographic definition, particularly when the movement of people across boundaries is being examined. For example, the Halewood factory of Ford Motor Company – developed to provide large-scale employment for Liverpudlians – lay within, and on the edge of, a 'rural district' outside the city. Census journey-to-work statistics as a result gave the misleading impression that the whole rural district was a major employment centre, whereas this was true of just one small corner of it, a corner which ought realistically to have been included in the neighbouring town unit of local government. More common was the reverse of this example – the building of very large residential housing estates just outside the boundaries of a town, boundaries which could not easily be altered due to the moratorium.

These two major general difficulties must be kept in mind throughout the chapter. In later sections they will be re-emphasised when they are particularly pertinent, and other more specific statistical problems will also be raised.

URBANISATION (1) – BRICKS-AND-MORTAR

Urban area

Visually it is clear that virtually all towns have grown in area this century. Thus, on the first definition of urbanisation, towns are today more significant and important than they were at the turn of the century. Indeed, in several places – notably the seven conurbations or 'metropolitan areas' – a number of originally separate towns have completely coalesced to form one continuous large urban area.

Such developments are best illustrated statistically in figures found in the decennial census reports. As mentioned earlier, these refer to whole local authority areas – whole boroughs and urban districts in the data presented here. Bearing in mind the problem that local government boundaries tended not to keep pace with physical developments, Table 9.1 (which thus underestimates the true rate of urbanisation) indicates that the urban area has increased by around 45 per cent since 1901, until in 1981 it accounted for more than one-seventh of England and Wales. (Though local government was reformed in 1974, the 1981 Census reports included some data based on 1971 boundaries. Whether this happens again in 1991 remains to be seen.)

Table 9.1   Urban area,
1901–81, England and Wales

Year	Urban area (acres)
1901	3 748 987
1911	4 015 701
1931	4 504 928
1951	5 273 917
1961	5 323 656
1981	5 492 344

Note: England and Wales
total area = 37 363 262
acres (1981)
Sources: Census Preliminary
Reports.

Urban population

Towns may only cover one-seventh of the surface of England and Wales, but in terms of population they are, of course, far more dominant. Table 9.2 shows that more than three-quarters of the population were living in 'towns' (whole urban local authority areas) in each census year.

In absolute numbers the urban population rose by almost exactly 50 per cent in the period 1901–81, from 25.1 million to 37.7 million. Yet Table 9.2 also shows that the proportion of urban dwellers has remained fairly static, rising to a peak of almost 81 per cent in 1951 but falling back to under 77 per cent in 1981. This partly reflects the almost complete absence of local government boundary changes in provincial England and Wales after the war (see the last section of the chapter for details), and partly the development of retirement and long-distance communting homes in rural areas such as East Anglia. A further significant factor has been population decline. From 1971 to 1981 the aggregate population of towns actually fell for the first time ever, by 742 000 or 1.9 per cent.[1] But over a longer period there has been a much more significant drop in the population of the inner areas of many major cities. Urban population of the inner areas of many major cities. Urban population decline has resulted from planned suburban, new town and overspill schemes which were deliberately designed to reduce population density through slum clearance and rehousing at lower densities as well as from the unplanned voluntary migration of some city dwellers. In several cases the rate of population decline has been dramatic. The County of London, for example, contained 4 536 541 people in 1901 but by 1981 under 2.5 million. In the provinces the City of Salford declined, even more sharply, from 221 000 to under 100 000. In both these cases the boundaries involved remained stable,

Table 9.2   Urban population 1901–81, England and Wales

Year	Total population (000s)	Urban population (000s)	Urban %
1901	32 528	25 058	77.0
1911	36 070	28 163	78.1
1931	39 952	31 952	80.0
1951	43 758	35 336	80.8
1961	46 105	36 872	80.0
1981	49 011	37 691	76.9
1981 (new)	49 155	44 111	89.7

Note: The difference in Total population for the two 1981 definitions is because the Census Preliminary Report for 1981
covers 'population present' but the Key Statistics Report is
for 'usually resident'.

Sources:
1.   1901 to 1981 – Census Preliminary Reports.
2.   1981 (new definition) – *Census 1981: Key Statistics for Urban Areas.*

but in most towns truly comparable figures are less easy to obtain due to boundary changes. We will see when considering the third definition of urbanisation that population decline is viewed as one important indicator of urban deprivation.

So far, then, we have observed an increase of over 12 million town dwellers this century. They live in an urban area which has grown by 45 per cent but still represents only one-seventh of the total land area. We have also come across the suggestion that a moratorium on local government boundary changes has caused the urban area to be underestimated when using whole local authority areas. The last line in Table 9.2 appears to confirm that this suggestion is indeed a fact. A special 1981 Census Report introduced a new definition of urban area, based on the extent of urbanisation indicated on Ordnance Survey maps.

This new definition begins by defining 'urban land' (this includes roads, car parks, airports and areas such as golf courses when they are entirely surrounded by built-up sites) and includes in any 'urban area' a continuous area of urban land of 50 acres or more, plus separate areas if they are less than 50 metres apart. There must be a minimum population of 1000 in the 'urban area'.[2]

Clearly this can be seen to be a much more rigorous bricks-and-mortar definition than is the use of whole local authority areas. As can be seen from Table 9.2, it results in just under 90 per cent of the population being classified as 'urban', instead of 77 per cent. That this measure seems to be in some way scientific is not in doubt; that the apparent science accurately represents what most people would think of as 'urban' is far less certain. A minimum population of only 1000, for example, results in some quite small, remote villages being categorised as 'urban'. Not everyone would agree that places like Amergate (Derbyshire), Aspatria (Cumbria), Crawley Down (Sussex) or Bruton (Somerset) are 'towns': the census is right to describe the inclusion of at least the 289 urban areas with a population of under 2000 as 'a somewhat arbitrary matter'.

The 1981 report was the second special study of urbanisation undertaken in conjunction with a census. The 1951 Census General Report, also a 'one-off' exercise, used rather different criteria and produced very different results.[3] The 1951 definition of 'urban' covered whole wards or parishes with a population density of more than ten persons per acre.

Table 9.2 shows 35.3 million inhabitants of urban local authorities in 1951, but the special survey classified only 31.5 million as urban. Using the density definition, the urban proportion of the population was only 72 per cent as against 80 per cent using the traditional administrative areas definition. This contrasts sharply with the special 1981 definition, which found a larger urban population than did the traditional analysis. Clearly there is no agreement amongst statisticians and demographers as to exactly what constitutes urbanisation!

The size of towns

Boundary changes make it exceedingly difficult to obtain fully comparable data on the numbers of towns in different population categories at intervals since 1900. Table 9.3 highlights the problem, and has to be interpreted with great care if it is not to give a misleading picture. Two very obvious false impressions which the raw data can give are that 150 towns 'disappeared' between 1931–61, and that 900 towns suddenly appeared between 1961–81!

The 1931–61 changes merely reflected the success of a series of County

Table 9.3   Towns by population size, 1901–81, England and Wales

Year	Total number of 'towns'	Under 10 000	10 to 50 000	50 to 200 000	200 000 to 1 million	Over 1 million
		Number with a population of				
1901	1122	686	361	61	13	1
1931	1120	591	416	94	17	2
1961	965	333	450	162	18	2
1981 (new)	1852	1372	357	93	26	4

Sources: As Table 9.2.

Reviews held in the 1930s under the 1929 Local Government Act. We will see in the final section that these reviews of district councils led to the merger of many small urban districts into larger neighbouring towns, and the 'demotion' of only 42 towns which became parishes within a rural district. The dramatic rise in the number of towns in 1981 arises from the Special Census report with its more liberal definition of 'urban areas'.

Despite these problems of comparability, particularly in the case of 1981, Table 9.3 and Table 9.4 (which gives the proportions living in different sizes of town) do reveal some interesting points about trends in urbanisation. In particular they show that the great growth has been in middle-sized towns, with populations between 50 000 and 200 000. By 1961 such towns accounted for not far off 40 per cent of the urban population, a proportion which had almost doubled since the turn of the century. In contrast, the larger cities were of declining importance: towns of over 200 000 inhabitants accounted for 36.3 per cent of the urban population in 1901, but only 28.6 per cent by 1961, even though their numbers had risen from 14 to 20. This is now the second time that there had been an indication of population decline in big cities, and a particular look at the conurbations will clarify the extent of this depopulation.

Table 9.4　Proportion of urban population living in towns of various sizes, 1901–61, England and Wales

Year	Percentage of urban population living in towns of				
	Under 10 000	*10 to 50 000*	*50 to 200 000*	*200 000 to 1 million*	*Over 1 million*
1901	12.4	29.7	21.6	18.2	18.1
1931	8.5	28.1	27.3	19.2	16.9
1961	4.7	28.9	37.9	16.9	11.7

Sources:　Census Reports, 1901, 1931, 1961.

The conurbations

Government statisticians did not officially recognise the existence of 'conurbations' until a special Census Report in 1951.[4] Earlier academic studies had provided some data, but not with enough precision to allow trends to be analysed with any great confidence.

The 1951 Report recognised six conurbations and drew their boundaries extremely tightly, to include only whole local authorities and only built-up areas. In the context of our first definition of urbanisation this happens to be extremely convenient, but many were critical that nearby commuter towns and 'rural suburbs' had been excluded. The inclusion in the study of only six conurbations was also a conservative approach for academic researchers included up to 95 areas as 'conurbations'.[5] On the other hand, the six could be said to stand on their own in terms of population size.

The 1974 reform of local government also recognised conurbations, which were given a different structure of local government and entitled 'metropolitan areas'. A seventh area, South Yorkshire, was added, and the boundaries of many of the others were more than marginally different from those used in the 1951 Census. Tyne and Wear, for example, included the Sunderland area. West Midlands covered Coventry, and Greater Manchester embraced Wigan.

Because of these 1974 reforms, which incidentally were also criticised because the boundaries of the metropolitan areas were alleged to be drawn too tightly, trend data for the whole period 1901–81 is not available. Instead it is necessary to break the period into two, and the conurbations into those recognised in 1951 and those which emerged from the reforms of local government in Greater London (1965) and in the rest of England and Wales (1974). This is done in Tables 9.5 and 9.6.

It is ironic that the conurbations were not officially recognised by statisticians until they were beginning to decline in importance – in terms of population, at any rate. In Table 9.5 the trend is traced from 1871 in order to show that the period of relative growth of the conurbations was already over by 1901, when 54 per cent of the urban population lived in them, and they accounted for 41 per cent of the total population of England and Wales. Both these proportions declined in the period 1901–61. It should be noted that there were some boundary changes in this period, but the 1951 Census was content to describe their impact as being 'comparatively small'.

Table 9.5 The conurbations' population, 1871–1961, England and Wales

Area	Population (000s)				
	1871	*1901*	*1931*	*1951*	*1961*
Greater London	3889.5	6 586.3	8 215.7	8 348.0	8 182.6
SELNEC[1]	1385.9	2 116.8	2 426.9	2 422.7	2 427.9
West Midlands	968.9	1 482.8	1 933.0	2 237.1	2 346.6
West Yorkshire	1064.3	1 523.8	1 655.4	1 692.7	1 703.7
Merseyside	690.2	1 030.2	1 346.7	1 382.4	1 384.2
Tyneside	346.1	677.9	827.1	835.5	855.3
Conurbation totals	8344.9	13 417.8	16 404.8	16 918.4	16 900.2
Conurbation % of urban totals	–	54	51	48	46
Conurbation % of England & Wales totals	37	41	41	39	37

Note:
1. SELNEC = South-East Lancashire and North-East Cheshire.
Sources: Census 1951 and 1961.

Table 9.6   The conurbations' population 1961–81, England and Wales

Area	Population (000s)		
	1961	*1971*	*1981*
Greater London	7 992.4	7 452.3	6 696.0
Greater Manchester	2 719.9	2 729.0	2 594.8
West Midlands	2 731.9	2 793.3	2 644.6
West Yorkshire	2 005.4	2 067.7	2 037.5
Merseyside	1 718.2	1 656.5	1 513.1
Tyne and Wear	1 243.8	1 211.7	1 143.2
South Yorkshire	1 303.3	1 322.5	1 301.8
Conurbation totals	19 714.9	19 233.0	17 931.0
Conurbation % of England and Wales totals	42.8	39.5	36.6

Source: Census Preliminary Reports.

A further trend became increasingly marked towards the end of the period. In some conurbations population decline had become absolute as well as relative. In Greater Manchester (officially entitled SELNEC – South-East Lancashire and North-East Cheshire) this had already happened before 1951. By 1961 Greater London was experiencing depopulation, and most of the others were static. Table 9.6 picks up the story for the 'new' post-1974 conurbations, or metropolitan areas. All except West Yorkshire suffered population loss in the 1961–81 period. Greater London's loss of a massive 1.3 million represented an absolute population decline of some 16 per cent; Merseyside lost 12 per cent and Tyne and Wear 8 per cent. Not surprisingly the conurbations accounted for only 36.6 per cent of the total population in 1981 as against 42.8 per cent in 1961. We will see when analysing the third definition of urbanisation – the deprived inner city – that this absolute population decline is particularly marked in that part of the conurbations.

Planned urbanisation – 'new towns'

The genesis of the 'new town' idea of planned new settlements can be traced back to at least 1816, when Robert Owen built New Lanark. Sir Titus Salt's Saltaire (1853) and Sir George Cadbury's Bourneville (1879) were other nineteenth-century pioneer developments, whilst Ebenezer Howard's 'Garden City Association' paved the way for the new towns of Letchworth, Hampstead Garden Suburb and Welwyn. The first signs of local authority activity in this field were probably in the interwar period at Becontree (LCC) and Wythenshawe (Manchester CB).

Following the recommendations of the Reith Committee,[6] the New Towns

Act, 1946, placed the responsibility for the planning and construction of new towns upon separate development corporations, appointed by the Minister. These were given extensive powers to acquire and develop land and to provide certain public utility services, although the county council remained the planning authority for the area, and the provider of schools, health and other personal social services.

Table 9.7   Area and population of the New Towns, England and Wales

New Town	Area (acres)	Population			
		Original	1961	1971	1981
1. *London Ring designated 1946–9*					
Basildon	7 818	25 000	53 780	77 287	94 791
Bracknell	3 304	5 140	20 533	34 067	49 024
Crawley	6 047	9 000	54 047	67 843	72 684
Harlow	6 395	4 500	53 701	78 092	79 523
Hatfield	2 350	8 500	20 516	25 359	25 150
Hemel Hempstead	5 977	21 200	54 954	70 085	76 954
Stevenage	6 252	6 700	42 984	67 078	74 507
Welwyn	4 317	18 500	35 179	40 448	40 727
2. *Others designated 1947–50*					
Aycliffe	3 111	60	12 395	20 203	24 518
Corby	4 401	15 700	36 097	47 991	47 623
Cwmbran	3 155	12 000	30 788	41 065	44 316
Peterlee	2 785	200	13 331	21 846	22 919
Totals for Original New Towns	55 912	126 500	428 305	591 364	652 736
3. *Second wave, designated 1961–4*					
Redditch	7 181	—	31 409	37 709	63 693
Runcorn	7 247	—	28 436	35 921	64 412
Skelmersdale	4 124	—	10 344	26 739	39 400
Telford	19 281	—	61 150	79 451	103 646
Washington	5 572	—	20 127	25 240	49 986
4. *Third wave, designated 1968–70*					
Central Lancashire	35 054	—	228 198	235 638	247 870
Milton Keynes	21 891	—	32 269	46 499	96 546
Newtown	1 490	—	5 021	5 616	8 651
Northampton	19 926	—	124 100	133 673	157 217
Peterborough	15 921	—	75 891	87 568	115 544
Warrington	18 402	—	116 730	126 801	135 946
Totals for Second and Third Wave New Towns	156 089	—	733 675	840 855	1 082 911

Source: *Census 1981*: New Towns, Part I, Table 3.

New towns were seen by the post-war government as a means of dispersing both population and jobs from the conurbations which were under severe pressure at that time – notably Greater London and Tyneside. The progress of new towns is summarised in Table 9.7 and it can be seen that the new town movement has been in three waves. During the years 1946–50 twelve new towns were designated by the Minister, no less than eight of them specifically to relieve London. No further designations took place until 1961, since when, in two separate phases, a further eleven new towns have been approved.

As the table shows, the original new towns experienced their major population explosion in the 1950s, when they more than trebled in size, but continued to grow rapidly up to 1971. Experience varied in the period 1971–81, with Hatfield and Corby actually having very marginal declines in population, and three or four others stabilising. About half a million people had moved to this first wave of new towns, and this was close to the targets for which they had been told to plan.

The second and third wave of new towns were, in general, growing rapidly in the 1970s though Central Lancashire and Warrington showed only modest population increases. The totals show an increase of about 30 per cent in that period, and that something in excess of a quarter of a million people had been attracted to the later designations by 1981, and they had not completed their growth at that time. However, the plans of several were slowed down by government in the 1980s as a result of priority being increasingly given to policies designed to combat urban deprivation following the recognition of our third definition of urbanisation, to be discussed below.

However, the 1946 Act did not relieve local authorities of all their powers to deal with overspill. The Town Development Act 1952 was designed to supplement the work of the New Towns Act by allowing for help to be given to small towns chosen for planned population expansion. Under the 1952 Act, 'exporting' authorities assist the 'importing' area in the planning of developments and provision of the necessary services, without an *ad hoc* development corporation being established.

Some 66 formally agreed schemes were signed in the 1950s and 1960s. They involved the provision of 160 000 homes for some half a million people. Half were negotiated by the Greater London Council and its predecessors, and these London agreements were widely spread geographically, from Bodmin to Burnley, although the vast majority were within 75 miles of the capital. The other main exporting authorities were Birmingham (with 15 schemes), Liverpool (4), Manchester-Salford (4), Wolverhampton (4), Bristol (4), and Newcastle (2 schemes).[7]

Before the Second World War the progress of urbanisation was largely dependent on market forces, and can therefore be described as spontaneous in character. The last 40 years has witnessed a new approach, with the development of planned urbanisation taking place alongside the former pattern. Something like 1.25 million people have moved to new towns or other planned developments designed to take 'overspill' population. It should, of course, be realised that this actually has little effect on the data relating to the first definition of urbanisation because most of those people have merely transferred from one urban unit to another. The main effect has been on the urban area. Table 9.1 showed large increases in the period up to 1951, but an increase of only 220 000 acres in the period 1951–81. Much of this was the result of planned developments – the new towns alone encompass more than 200 000 acres and several of them did not obtain 'urban' local government status until after 1951. Hatfield and Bracknell, exceptionally, remained classified as 'rural' until 1974, despite their obvious urban character.

URBANISATION (2) – THE SOCIOGEOGRAPHIC APPROACH

The Victorian local government structure was based on a clear distinction between town and country, and this was widely seen as an accurate reflection of the prevailing social conditions. G. C. Broderick, a leading observer, concluded in 1885 that 'no readjustment of [local government] boundaries can be satisfactory which ignores the manifold and increasing differences between urban and rural districts'.[8] The first definition of urbanisation, relying on these boundaries, was thus seemingly valid.

The twentieth century has witnessed a much less clearly defined frontier between town and country. Table 9.2 indicates that the proportion of the population living in urban areas had changed very little in the period 1901–81. Yet there is considerable disagreement between official statisticians as to the accuracy of its data: special surveys in 1951 and 1981 concluded that the 'true' urban population might be as high as 90 per cent or as low as 70 per cent. What constitutes urban had become a matter of dispute.

Agriculture

One indisputable fact is that the proportion of the economically active population engaged in agriculture – the most traditional and obvious rural occupation – has fallen dramatically. But Table 9.8 possibly slightly exaggerates the extent of the fall because any time-series of occupational classifications faces problems of redefinition. On the one hand, the 1901 figure was probably a little low because the system of classifying 'labourers' was not very rigorous until the 1911 and 1921 censuses, which appeared to record an absolute rise in the numbers of farm workers. On the other hand, technological change has caused a growth in agricultural engineers, and in self-employed contractors for tasks like harvesting, and it is possible that some of these do not get correctly categorised under 'agriculture'. But these are essentially minor points – the very considerable decline in agricultural employment is

Table 9.8   Agricultural employment,
1901–81, England and Wales

Year	% of employed population engaged in agriculture, fishing and forestry
1901	9
1931	6
1961	4
1981	2

Source: Census Reports.

undeniable. The proportion has dropped at least fourfold, and in absolute numbers the 1.2 million in 1901 has fallen to only about 400 000.

Even in rural areas agriculture is the occupation of a minority. The 'new' 1981 definition of urban areas left only 10 per cent of the population outside them. In these remaining rural areas one person in seven (14.1 per cent) of those economically active was classified under agriculture. In the 'rural' parts of Powys the proportion just topped 30 per cent; in five other counties the figure was between 20 and 25 per cent. But these are the figures for only the deeply rural parts of these counties. In Powys as a whole the agricultural industry employed only 18.9 per cent of these economically active, a figure a long way above the next two counties (Dyfed 11.1 per cent, Lincolnshire 10.0 per cent).[9]

This very sharp decline in agricultural employment to extremely low figures even in the most apparently rural of areas offers a clear indication of the unsuitability of the 'bricks-and-mortar' definition of urbanisation as a measure of social change, for in Table 9.2 the proportion of the population living in urban areas was found to be fairly constant at between 77 and 81 per cent. In 1900 it may have been substantially correct to equate 'rural' and 'agricultural'. Today 'rural' may signify habitation at low densities, but it no longer indicates a peculiar or particular way of life centred on farming.

Transport

If any one factor has caused this change, it can only be growth in personal mobility caused by the invention and spread of mechanised transport facilities. Even in the nineteenth century this was having its effect through the provision of railways, and early in the present century trams and buses increased rapidly in numbers. More recently the motor car has become a means of mass mobility, and the combined effect of all these developments has been to break down the barriers between town and country. Some indication of these changes appears in Table 9.9 which gives the number of motor vehicles at various dates from 1904 (the first year that licences were compulsory).

Like almost all time-series, Table 9.9 has to be read with some caution though its overall message of increased means of personal mobility, particularly after the Second World War, is quite clear. This mobility is truly personal in that it is flexible. The decline of public transport is not fully revealed in the table because tram-cars and trains are excluded from the public transport figures. Had they been included, the table would show a much steeper fall for there were many thousands of tram-cars and miles of now disused railways in the interwar period. Secondly, the data for 1978 onwards is not strictly comparable with that for earlier years due to a change in registration procedures with the opening of a national centre at Swansea. The new data is in one respect more accurate because it is a complete count whereas earlier figures were based on samples, but in another respect marginally less accurate because the count is taken on one particular day whereas the samples were over a whole month of registrations. Finally, definitions of certain types of vehicle have changed, particularly in the case of 'light goods', which used to be styled 'vans'. The Highway Statistics for 1981, for example, give a figure of 11 643 000 private cars and light goods for the year 1968, whereas the identical publication in 1969 showed 10 816 000 – a difference of more than 800 000 through retrospective reclassification.

Table 9.9   Motor Vehicles Licensed, 1904–81, Great Britain

Year	*Private cars and light goods*	*Motor cycles, mopeds, etc.*	*Public transport*	*All vehicles*
1904	8 465	—	5 345	17 810
1934	1 308 425	548 461	85 129	2 403 856
1948	1 960 510	559 313	127 625	3 728 432
1958	4 548 530	1 519 935	95 680	7 959 725
1968	11 643 000	1 228 000	99 000	14 447 000
1978	15 166 000	1 194 000	110 000	17 772 000
1981	16 421 000	1 371 000	110 000	19 355 000

Note: Scotland is included in this table, but it accounts for only some 7 per cent of vehicles.
Source: Department of Transport, *Highway Statistics*.

Journey to work

Of more relevance to an examination of the sociogeographic definition of urbanisation would be a series of tables indicating the precise effects on the town–country dichotomy of this increase in the means of mobility. Ideally, one would like data indicating changes in shopping, entertainment, leisure and working habits so that the growing links between town and country could be measured with precision. However, because mass transportation is largely a post-war phenomenon, this type of material is almost completely unavailable for the early part of the century, with the single exception of journey-to-work statistics, which were first collected on a national basis as part of the 1921 Census. For the rest, all that can be done is to give some indication of the present extent to which the traditional boundaries of town and country mask individual shopping and leisure habits. The marked lack of interest in, for example, shopping and entertainment habits shown by social geographers in the early part of the century is probably in itself sufficient indication of their relative unimportance at the time.

Though the very wealthy had 'commuted' for many decades, the mass movement of people to work has a far shorter history. From the viewpoint of this study, the 1974 reform of local government also effectively ended the era for which trends could be analysed because the new administrative boundaries no longer recognised town and country as separate units, and Rural District Councils were abolished.

The figures in Table 9.10, however, give a good indication of the change in journeying to work over a 45-year period. They were specially calculated for the (Redcliffe-Maud) Royal Commission on Local Government in England as part of its review of the interdependence of town and country, and they analyse workplace movements for every Rural District Council.

Before the results of Table 9.10 are considered, some words of warning about the data are essential, even though they do not significantly undermine the outcome of the analysis. First, the 1921 Census was delayed for administrative reasons until mid-June (instead of the 'normal' April date). By then, of course, the holiday season was under way. As the census recorded journey to work on the basis of 'enumerated population' rather than 'usual residence' (much more satisfactory, and used in later census reports), the 1921 figures somewhat exaggerate the level of movement in certain areas. For example, a Bolton mill-worker enumerated on holiday in Blackpool would appear in the report as a commuter from Blackpool to Bolton. This could not happen in the case of the 1966 Census, because the use of 'usual residence' as a basis for the workplace tables means that our mill-worker would be excluded from the Blackpool figures and placed back in his 'home' town. Thus the 1921 figures are, at the outset, a little on the high side, and the Census Report estimated that in over 50 rural districts the 'enumerated' population was over 3 per cent more than the 'normal' population due primarily to the presence of holiday-makers at the time of enumeration.

Secondly, figures for both years are slightly low because of the form in which the data are analysed in the Workplace volumes. For each of the two years the numbers travelling into towns have been abstracted for each individual rural district. In 1921, only movements of 25 or more persons to a

Table 9.10 Rural to urban workplace movements, 1921 and 1966, England and Wales

Year	Economically active: all RD's	Of these work in urban areas (No.)	(%)	No. of RD's	No. with proportions travelling into urban areas of						
					0– 10%	10– 20%	20– 30%	30– 40%	40– 50%	50– 60%	Over 60%
1921	3 045 900	425 200	14.0	663	363	158	81	38	14	6	3
1966	4 315 700	1 600 300	37.1	472	42	75	105	89	75	56	30

Source: Table based on Table 6, Appendix 2, vol. 3 of Report of Royal Commission on Local Government in England 1966–9 (1969) Cmnd 4040. Figures for Welsh rural districts added from 1921 and 1966 Census Workplace Tables.

town were included in the tables, and in 1966 the figure was 50 or more (or, rather 5 or more as in the latter year a 10 per cent sample was used). The correct figures for both years should, therefore, be somewhat higher – slightly more so in the case of 1966 than 1921.

A third reservation (by now familiar) concerns the nature of urban and rural boundaries in the two years. It will later be seen that in 1921 urban district boundaries were a far better reflection of the limits of built-up areas than was the case in 1966, as up to 1921 boundary changes took place frequently, whereas from 1945 there has been a comparative 'freeze' on such changes. Consequently the 1966 boundaries do not fully reflect the outward growth of towns since the war, and some journeys to work from 'rural' to urban areas in this year will be short ones from housing estates just outside the towns' limits.

Finally, mention must be made of the particularly large non-response to this question in 1921, when in some areas more than 15 per cent did not record their place of work. As the response rate in 1966 was far higher, this problem has been overcome by including in both years only those respondents who gave a classifiable answer. The total numbers of economically active in rural districts in 1921 given in the table is thus somewhat reduced, but at least the data for the two years are more truly comparable as a result.

Bearing these points in mind (and, if anything, they roughly cancel each other out when making a comparison between the two years), Table 9.10 gives a clear indication of the growing extent to which the inhabitants of rural districts rely on towns for their employment. In view of the decline in numbers employed in the traditional rural occupation of agriculture, seen earlier in Table 9.8, this trend is to be expected. However, the extent of the 1966 dependence on towns for work was, perhaps, surprising. About two in five working rural dwellers travelled daily into urban areas to their job, or, proportionately, more than two and a half times as many as in 1921. In 1921, one rural district in eleven recorded a daily flow into towns of over 30 per cent of its economically active population for employment purposes. By 1966 this was happening in 250 of the 472 districts, and in 30 of these over 60 per cent of workers were travelling into towns. At the other end of the scale only a handful of areas (42 out of the 472) recorded a flow of less than 10 per cent, whereas more than half of the districts fell into this category at the earlier date.

Shopping and leisure

Information on shopping, leisure and entertainment habits is not available for the early part of the century, and even the recent data is somewhat piecemeal and difficult to obtain. Statistical evidence of historical trends cannot, therefore, be presented. All that can be done is to give some indication of people's habits today, in order to try to give an insight into the links between town and country.

There is no data available comparable to that for journeying to work. Census of Distribution statistics relate to shopping turnover in urban centres but do not draw catchment areas around towns. Researchers therefore have to make estimates from them about the extent to which shoppers come from outside the town. When surveying the extent of town–country interdependence in the late 1960s, the Redcliffe-Maud Royal Commission sponsored two related pieces of research which built on Census of Distribution data: detailed studies of shopping habits in the Kent and Guildford areas,[10] and a national Community Attitudes Survey.[11]

Some 59 per cent of respondents in the Community Attitudes Survey stated that for food and household goods they or their families had at least one large shopping 'expedition' each week, the proportion varying only from 58 to 62 per cent according to the type of area in which they lived. Forty-four per cent of all respondents undertook this 'expedition' without leaving their local authority, but in the case of rural district inhabitants this was true of only 22 per cent (as against 54 per cent for county boroughs and 50 per cent for urban districts and municipal boroughs). This again indicates the considerable mobility of those residing in rural areas, though no details were given of exactly where they went to shop.

The Kent and Guildford data was analysed by the Greater London Group (London School of Economics). They applied the findings to the rest of the South-East in order to arrive at a shopping 'map' for the region. Two of the conclusions which emerged are particularly noteworthy: first, catchment areas for shopping appeared to be rather smaller than those for journeying to work, and, secondly, the shopping centres had changed little in relative importance between 1950 and 1961 (apart from the development of the new towns). If anything, the shopping centres in 1961 were receiving a little more of their trade from out-of-town shoppers than in 1950.

The Community Attitudes Survey also posed 'a battery of questions' on the frequency of visiting certain types of public entertainments, and their location. Of the results, the most significant for this study is that 52 per cent of rural inhabitants did not pursue any of the 12 types of entertainment listed (cinema, theatre, football, dance halls, etc.) within their local authority area. This reply was given by only 17 per cent and 27 per cent of respondents in the case of county boroughs and of urban districts/municipal boroughs respectively.

Most of the data presented so far emphasises the dependence of rural areas on urban centres – for work, leisure, shopping and so on. In one instance, however, it is the urban dweller who is reliant for the pursuit of his interests on rural areas. Of the 12 types of entertainment used in the questionnaire, only 2 could be considered from the replies to be 'frequently-indulged pastimes'. As many as 58 per cent of respondents claimed to go 'into the countryside' for pleasure or recreation at least once a month; 36 per cent used public parks or gardens this often but, of the other 10 items listed, only 3 (cinema, bingo, and soccer, rugby or cricket matches) attracted a response rate of more than 10 per cent for frequent participation (soccer, etc., recording 17 per cent, bingo 12 per cent, cinema 10 per cent). Thus the major source of entertainment of the English population appears to be the drive or walk into the countryside, and it is primarily this (plus the provision of foodstuffs by the agricultural industry, and the fact that trade from rural areas increases the prosperity of the towns) which justifies the phrase 'interdepenence of town and country'.

To sum up, trend data to give a full analysis of the sociogeographic definition of urbanisation are simply not available in the case of many of the social habits which one would like to investigate. However, most, if not all, of these habits rely to a large extent on the growth of mobility, and licensing statistics for motor vehicles illustrate the post-1945 growth of mass mobility by road. Trend statistics for the employment structure and, in a slightly more limited fashion, for journeying to work, amply illustrate this second concept of urbanisation, based on patterns of living rather than patterns of development. More recent evidence on such factors as shopping and leisure provides additional, but not unexpected, support for the theory that urban and rural areas have, during this century, had steadily growing links. Although a figure cannot be given, it is safe to say that large numbers of those living in areas officially designated for local governmental purposes as 'rural', and therefore classified as such under the first definition of urbanisation, in effect live under the direct and constant influence of the town and may therefore be said to be 'urbanised'.

URBANISATION (3) – URBAN DEPRIVATION AND THE INNER CITY

Our exploration of the first two definitions of urbanisation has revealed a fairly clear pattern of change. Urban growth since 1900 has largely been on the edges of cities, in adjacent rural areas, and in planned overspill schemes. There new houses have been constructed, the invention of the mass-produced motor car has enabled residents to travel freely to work and shop in the cities, and the picture is the opposite of decline.

This 'suburbanisation' of urban Britain, partly created by social engineering designed deliberately to reduce the congestion of the inner cities, and partly the result of market forces as wages rose and the middle classes sought modern housing near green fields, is particularly clear in Table 9.6. The seven conurbations had a population loss of 1.8 million in the period 1961–81. Earlier, individual examples of Victorian cities – inner London and Salford – which had halved in size, were quoted. Places like Salford, Islington, Hackney, inner Liverpool and Birmingham, and many more have become publicly recognised by politicians of all opinions as constituting a third category of urbanisation: urban deprivation.

Urban deprivation is not new. The Victorians had had to cope with poverty, squalor and disease in the then rapidly expanding industrial cities. The social engineers of the post-war decades, with their visions of new and expanded towns, were also seeking deliberately to depopulate the inner cities in order to allow redevelopment at lower densities. Their concern was essentially physical, for they were able to work within a welfare state which would take care of poverty, illness and family problems.

Something went wrong, as became dramatically apparent when Brixton and other areas experienced riots in the 1980s. This is not the place to elaborate on the different theories as to the cause of what became increasingly recognised from the late 1960s as 'the inner city problem', theories which can be social, economic, physical, political, or even administrative. Our concern is to identify the extent of urban deprivation by investigating the criteria which have been developed by public policy-makers seeking to design new policies to alleviate the problem.

As the 1985 Archbishop of Canterbury's Commission on Urban Priority Areas put it, 'they are places which suffer from economic decline, physical decay, and social disintegration. These factors interlock and together they describe multiple and relative deprivation'. Three kinds of blight – economic, physical and social – characterise areas of urban deprivation.[12]

Social statisticians have not found it easy to transform such descriptions into clear policy advice through the use of hard data. Deprivation is 'relative', and there is no clear cut-off point where it can be confidently stated that areas below the line are 'deprived' and those above it are not. Social geography does not reveal the extremes implied – even the apparently most deprived urban areas still contain considerable numbers of residents in the top social classes, in good jobs, and with affluent standards of living, for example. One early policy experiment, the designation of Educational Priority Areas, identified schools which were to receive additional resources due to the nature of the catchment area. Later, research revealed that most of the pupils in these schools were not those who the designers of the policy had thought of as deprived, and most of the pupils at whom the policy was aimed were not in EPA schools![13]

The eight statistical criteria used by government for identifying urban deprivation, listed in Table 9.11, are certainly not value-free. The fifth, on housing amenities, is an excellent example because it actually represents the values and priorities of a much earlier period. Redeveloped inner cities, with their unpopular modern tower and medium-rise blocks, are full of houses or flats with baths and indoor toilets (the so-called 'basic amenities'). Yet residents remain extremely dissatisfied and still have major housing problems – dampness, lack of insulation against noise or the cold, structural faults, poor landscaping, lack of supervised play space, and many others. The official

Table 9.11   Government indicators of urban deprivation, 1984

Indicator	How measured	Source
1. *Unemployment*	% economically active residents who are unemployed	1981 Census
2. *Overcrowding*	% households living at more than 1 per room	1981 Census
3. *Single-parent households*	% households with one or more single-parent families with child(ren) aged 0–15	1981 Census
4. *Pensioners living alone*	% households with only one pensioner, living alone	1981 Census
5. *Lacking basic amenities*	% households without exclusive use of bath and inside W.C.	1981 Census
6. *Ethnic origin*	% residents where head of household born in New Commonwealth or Pakistan	1981 Census
7. *Population change*	% change (i.e. decline) 1971–81	1981 Census
8. *Standardised mortality rate 1980*	Ratio of locally-adjusted death rate to the national rate	OPCS *Vital Statistics*

Source: Department of the Environment, Inner Cities Directorate (1984) *Census 1981 Information Note 2 – Urban Deprivation.*

definition of housing deprivation used by government does not provide for this and so can be criticised as not adequately reflecting the values of the public at large.

Other criteria are equally controversial. Some imply the existence of a problem because there are immigrants, pensioners or one-parent families in an area, and this can be interpreted as insulting. Population decline does not have to be a bad thing – after all, it was a target of planners until quite recently in many areas. But to examine every indicator separately is rather to miss the point of the exercise, which is to attempt to locate areas suffering from multiple deprivation. The indicators are constantly being improved by academic and government researchers. Indeed, the Economic and Social Research Council has sponsored research using as many as 70 indicators, which should produce a more refined map of deprivation when it is completed.[14] But the dependence on a decennial census for almost all the data means that most indicators become increasingly outdated as only some can be updated between census years.

The indicators listed in Table 9.11 were weighted and processed by the Department of Environment to produce an overall 'score' for each borough or district. Again, the weighting, and hence the score, will reflect the values of those undertaking the exercise (how important is unemployment relative to ethnic origin or single-parenthood?). In 1985 the government accepted the findings of the Department of Environment's researchers, updating only the unemployment indicator, and used the resulting 'league table of deprivation' to disqualify some authorities from continuing to receive funds under the 'traditional urban programme', a system of grants begun in 1968. Less than 80 of the 400 English councils qualified even to apply for funds, whereas previously applications were unrestricted.[15]

The indicators in Table 9.11 were processed statistically and every local authority was ranked on each of the eight. In Table 9.12 those authorities which emerge as the most deprived are listed, using the number of times they appear among the worst ten authorities in England.

London boroughs dominate the list, which contains only Knowsley and Manchester in the provinces. This domination reflects the physical scale of London, which results in many boroughs having no suburban areas whatsoever. Most of the provincial big cities like Liverpool, Birmingham and Newcastle, have, within their administrative boundaries, at least a few of their suburbs, and this affects their 'score' on any index of deprivation.

The inclusion of Knowsley (a large area of post-war municipal overspill housing on the edge of Liverpool) as one of the most deprived parts of Britain raises the important point that urban stress areas are not just inner cities. Outer estates, often huge and impersonal, are also suffering acutely from multiple deprivation.

Table 9.12   Comparison of key indicators of deprivation

Local authority	No. of times in worst ten	Indicators concerned
1. *Hackney*	5	Population loss; non-whites; lacking amenities; single parents; overcrowding
2. *Lambeth*	4	Population loss; non-whites; single parents; overcrowding
3. *Brent*	3	Non-whites; overcrowding; single-parents
4. *Hammersmith*	3	Population loss; lacking amenities; overcrowding
5. *Haringey*	3	Non-whites; lacking amenities; single parents
6. *Islington*	3	Population loss; lacking amenities; single parents
7. *Kensington and Chelsea*	3	Population loss; lacking amenities; overcrowding
8. *Knowsley*	3	Unemployment; single parents; overcrowding
9. *Manchester*	3	Unemployment; population loss; single parents
10. *Newham*	3	Non-whites; lacking amenities; overcrowding
11. *Tower Hamlets*	3	Non-whites; single parents; overcrowding
12. *Wandsworth*	3	Non-whites; lacking amenities; single parents

Source: See Table 9.11.

Table 9.12 has deliberately been constructed to exclude the very detailed statistical data which is harder to absorb than are the rankings. In Table 9.13 the percentage values for six of the eight indicators are given for Hackney (the five cited in Table 9.12 plus a sixth, unemployment, where Hackney also fared badly). In order to give some indication of the full extent of relative deprivation, Hackney figures are placed alongside those of the authority ranked in 100th position. It should be noted that there are in fact over 360 districts and boroughs in England, and the median scores would have been for the 180th authority, giving even greater variances from Hackney. However, there is clearly no significant deprivation in many districts, so an arbitrary decision to select the 100th ranked was taken on the basis that the government officially recognises 78 areas (listed in Table 9.14) as suffering from a scale and intensity of urban deprivation sufficient to be eligible for urban aid funding.

Table 9.13   Deprivation in Hackney

Indicator	Hackney's ranking	Hackney's amount	Amount of 100th authority
1. Single-parents	1	10.6% households	5.2% (Barking)
2. Overcrowding	2	4.0% households	3.2% (Doncaster)
3. Non-whites	3	28.0% households	2.5% (Brighton)
4. Housing amenities	5	11.9% Lack bath/wc	4.9% (Tameside)
5. Population change	7	18.1% decline (1971–81)	0.9% decline (Bradford)
6. Unemployment	15	15.3% in 1981	10.0% (Wandsworth)

Source: See Table 9.11.

That Hackney and the other 11 areas listed in Table 9.12 are truly deprived is very apparent. The difference between Hackney and the 100th ranked area is never less than 50% (unemployment), and on two indicators (non-whites and population loss) is tenfold and twentyfold. On the other three Hackney scores are between double and treble the 100th area. Flesh is put on the bare bones of these statistics in a recent study of Hackney sub-titled 'Life Under the Cutting Edge'.[16]

This third definition of urbanisation has been the focus of a great deal of government attention for almost twenty years. Many policy initiatives and experiments have been taken in a bid to tackle urban deprivation.[17] But despite this activity there are clear signs that this is not a definition of urbanisation which will shortly become redundant: there is widespread agreement that urban deprivation has not been significantly reduced by this battery of public policies, indeed, that its scale and intensity has continued to increase.

Table 9.14   Authorities eligible to apply for urban programme funds, 1986–7, England

Partnership areas	Programme authorities	Other designated districts	Undesignated eligible districts
1. Birmingham	1. Blackburn	1. Barnsley	1. Bristol
2. Hackney	2. Bolton	2. Burnley	2. Calderdale
3. Islington	3. Bradford	3. Doncaster	3. Camden
4. Lambeth	4. Brent	4. Ealing	4. Corby
5. Manchester	5. Coventry	5. Greenwich	5. Derby
6. Salford	6. Hammersmith and Fulham	6. Haringey	6. Derwentside
7. Newcastle	7. Hull	7. Hartlepool	7. Dudley
8. Gateshead	8. Knowsley	8. Langbaurgh	8. Ellesmere Port
	9. Leeds	9. Lewisham	9. Grimsby
	10. Leicester	10. Newham	10. Halton
	11. Middlesborough	11. Rotherham	11. Hyndburn
	12. North Tyneside	12. St Helens	12. Kensington and Chelsea
	13. Nottingham	13. Sefton	13. Kirklees
	14. Oldham	14. Southwark	14. Lincoln
	15. Rochdale	15. Walsall	15. Luton
	16. Sandwell	16. Wigan	16. Pendle
	17. Sheffield		17. Plymouth
	18. South Tyneside		18. Preston
	19. Sunderland		19. Rossendale
	20. Tower Hamlets		20. Scunthorpe
	21. Wandsworth		21. Sedgefield
	22. Wirral		22. Stockton
	23. Wolverhampton		23. Stoke
			24. Tameside
			25. Trafford
			26. Waltham Forest
			27. Wear Valley
			28. West Lancashire
			29. Westminster
			30. The Wrekin

Note: In addition, the government is funding 2 Urban Development Corporations (Docklands, Liverpool) and 17 Enterprise Zones in England.

Sources:
1. *Faith in the City* – Report of the Archbishop of Canterbury's Commission (1985) 11.
2. Letter from Department of Environment dated 28 July 1985 to Associations of Local Authorities.

LOCAL GOVERNMENT REFORM

The 1888 and 1894 reforms of local government were based on the twin principles of the democratisation of all local authorities and of the recognition of a town-country dichotomy in local administration. It is this latter feature which will be explored here. Thus the 1888 Act created counties and county boroughs as separate authorities, and the 1894 Act organised the county areas on a similar basis by retaining municipal (or non-county) boroughs and the separate urban and rural districts which had first been fully recognised two decades earlier in the 1872 Public Health Act. These authorities survived until the reforms of the mid-1960s (in Greater London) and of 1974 (in the remainder of England and Wales). In the intervening period there were a host of changes in the detailed blueprint of boundaries, as will be seen later, but these did not dent, indeed they were basically in accord with, the original principle of the division between town and country.

It would be wrong to pretend that the 'original' (that is, 1888 and 1894) boundaries were an absolutely accurate reflection of the urban geography of England and Wales at that time. Some boroughs and urban districts contained considerable rural tracts, while others were already overspilling their limits, as was evidenced by a number of requests for boundary extensions in the early years after 1888. Borough and urban district limits were only a rough approximation of the extent of the built-up area of a town; but, as a measure of this, data for these areas are the best available (apart from the special studies in 1951 and 1981 referred to earlier). Furthermore, subsequent changes are a more satisfactory guide to urban development in that no borough was likely to obtain a boundary extension bringing in to its area sizeable tracts of rural land. If anything, changes since 1888 failed to keep pace with urban development, and the use of municipal aggregates as a measure of the growth of urbanisation tends to underestimate rather than exaggerate the growth of towns. The reason is largely to be found in the varying and, at times, extremely complex procedures for obtaining boundary changes, and these will be referred to when appropriate.

County boroughs

Because of the contemporary political and parliamentary situation, the final 1888 Act bore rather less resemblance than usual to the original Bill. A major part, relating to the establishment of district and parish councils, had to be dropped completely due to the shortage of time. In 22 night sittings at the Committee Stage, clauses relating to the proposed decentralisation of parliamentary and Local Government Board functions were whittled away, as also were controversial sections on licensing.[18] In all some 1900 amendments to the original Bill were proposed.[19]

Other effective amendments related to the creation of county boroughs as entirely autonomous units of government. The Bill listed only ten, all with a population in excess of 150 000; but even at the first reading debate, the government speaker (Ritchie, President of the Local Government Board) forecast that 'many attempts will be made by Hon. Members who represent boroughs other than those I have named to have their boroughs also included in the Schedule'. He was right, and during the passage of the Bill, the government gave way to pressure by reducing the qualifying limit to 100 000, then to 50 000 (and almost to as low as 25 000!). The Parliamentary Secretary to the Board at that time said later that 'we came to the 50 000 line for a reason which very often obtains in the House of Commons – because we could not help ourselves'.[20]

The result of this political infighting was the creation of 61, instead of 10, county boroughs. The Act also recognised that subsequent demographic changes would necessitate the revision of boundaries from time to time. Table 9.15 summarises the consequences of such revisions. Initially a flexible system was established whereby a county borough could obtain a boundary extension either by promoting a Local Act, or through the making of a Provisional Order – following a public inquiry held by a Departmental Inspector – by the Minister responsible (a provisional order had later to be approved in a compendious Act of Parliament). New county boroughs could be created in similar fashion, provided that the population qualification of 50 000 had been obtained.

Table 9.15   County boroughs, 1888–1974, England and Wales

Year	Number of CBs	Area		Population	
		Total (acres)	% of England and Wales	Total (000s)	% of England and Wales
1888	61	308 000	0.8	—	—
1891	64	347 889	0.9	7 588.5	26.2
1901	67	420 006	1.1	9 141.3	28.1
1931	83	760 007	2.0	13 308.5	33.3
1961	83	907 267	2.4	13 651.0	29.6
1974	83	1 058 700	2.8	14 027.2	26.0

Sources: Census Reports, 1891–1971.

The 61 original county boroughs covered an area of 308 000 acres in 1888, but within a year of the passing of the Act, both the numbers and extent of county boroughs began to be increased. In 1889, one new county borough (Oxford) was established, and the addition of 839 acres to Swansea marked the opening of a period of regular and frequent changes,[21] a period which ended in the mid-1920s with new legislation following recommendations of the Onslow Commission. By then 20 other towns had joined with Oxford as new creations, and these had taken out of county council control some 100 000 acres and 1.3 million population.[22]

Even more important was the rate of county borough extensions. From

1889 to 1922 there were no less than 109, covering around 250 000 acres and 1.7 million population.[23] The total effect on counties by these changes was thus the loss of more than one-third of a million acres and three million population. Particularly hard-hit were Lancashire (minus 667 000 population) and Staffordshire and the West Riding (both losing around 400 000). In all, however, 27 of the 61 provincial counties were affected.[24]

During this period the extension of the county borough system of government was effected without too much difficulty, and demographic changes were matched fairly closely by administrative reforms. Exactly two-thirds of the requests for county borough status or boundary extensions were granted by Parliament,[25] but county council opposition to such changes grew as time went by. Counties felt they were being robbed of their most important areas, and pressure from them helped cause the government to establish the Onslow Commission to look into these and other municipal problems in 1923. The review had two crucial outcomes as far as this study is concerned: the establishment of County Reviews of district boundaries (to be considered in the next section), and the passage of the Local Government (County Boroughs and Adjustments) Act 1926. This raised the qualifying limit for new creations to 75 000, and abolished the more popular Provisional Order method of obtaining boundary extensions except where all parties were in agreement. The aim was to curtail the rate of change.

As far as new creations were concerned, the 1926 Act was completely successful. Only Doncaster (1927) was made a county borough between 1926 and the establishment of the 1958 Local Government Commission (and this town was fortunate in that its Private Bill was passed just before the 1926 Act came into force). Doncaster increased the total number of County Boroughs to 83 from the original 61 and 1888. The rate of boundary extensions was also severely curtailed after 1926, in terms of their effect on the counties, though not in terms of the number of alterations. Between 1927 and 1958 some 229 000 acres of territory were included in county boroughs, an estimated 325 000 population being involved.[26] The actual number of extensions remained high, largely due to the initiation of County Reviews by the 1929 Act. Thus from 1929 to 1937 there were no fewer than 154 extensions (and 26 small diminutions) of the areas of 47 of the 83 county boroughs, or rather more than in the whole of the period 1888–1922.[27]

From 1958 onwards came a third and brief phase in the history of county boroughs. In both of the periods from 1888 to 1958, changes in status and area came only on the initiative of the authorities involved. From 1958 to 1966 the initiative passed to two committees created by government: the Local Government Commissions for England and for Wales.

One reason for the reduction in the spate of county borough creations and extensions after 1926, apart from the more difficult legislative process involved, was the attitude of the government. This was particularly the case after the Second World War, when for more than a dozen years the future of the local governmental system was under review by successive governments. From 1945 to 1958 only those local bills which were relatively non-controversial were supported by the government – others, such as the attempts of Ealing, and other large boroughs in Middlesex and Essex, to obtain county borough status, failed due to government opposition to piecemeal changes at a time when the whole structure of local government was under review.

The results of this lengthy review were seen in the establishment in 1957 and 1958 of the two Local Government Commissions and of a Royal Commission on London's local government. None of the three could themselves alter the pattern of local authorities: all were limited to recommending changes to the government. In the case of the first two, restrictive terms of reference severely limited the scope of potential recommendations to the minimum. The existing structure was, in provincial England and Wales, taken for granted – only details could be changed (apart from within the five conurbations). In London, the Herbert Commission had a freer hand.

Governmental reception of the proposals of these three bodies varied considerably. The London blueprint was in many ways accepted – though the 1963 London Government Act was a considerably amended version of the 1960 Herbert Report.[28] In Wales, little happened as a result of the Commission's report. In provincial England a number of piecemeal alterations took place, notably in the West Midlands conurbation.

Despite the problems of restricted terms of reference, the effects of changes since 1958 on county boroughs were not inconsiderable. Three disappeared into the area covered by the Greater London Council – Croydon, West Ham and East Ham. Three new ones – Luton, Solihull and Torbay – were created. Thirty English and Welsh county boroughs obtained boundary extensions, and the 1.3 million population involved was more than four times the number transferred in the whole of the 1926–58 period.[29] Had the Commissions completed their work, the changes would have been even greater. They were wound up prematurely on the appointment of the Redcliffe-Maud Royal Commission on Local Government in England, with its far wider terms of reference. Its 1969 Report was much amended before Parliament passed the 1972 Local Government Act which led to the new structure of 1974.[30]

The history of county boroughs from 1888 to 1974 was, therefore, one of a steady stream of new creations and of boundary extensions. Indeed, only three county boroughs remained unchanged in area since their creation (excluding the new ones of the 1960s). In all, about 4.5 million people were transferred and, as Table 9.15 shows, the area of county boroughs more than trebled. Yet the proportion of the population living in these big towns changed little in the 85 years, and fell quite sharply from a peak in the 1920s as inner city populations began to decline and Britain became more suburbanised with voluntary movement out to the immediate suburbs and the surrounding rural catchment areas.

County councils and London

The detailed pattern of county government, in contrast to that of the county boroughs, remained much more stable. Amalgamations, new creations, and even minor boundary changes, were comparatively few and far between. As a result, the main changes to county boundaries since the 1888 Act stemmed from the expansion of the county borough form of government, already explored in detail. The creation of a new county borough, or extension of an existing one, normally adversely affected a neighbouring county council, and it has already been seen that by this process more than 4.5 million people and around 700 000 acres were at one time or another transferred from the counties to the county boroughs.

Sixty-one administrative counties were named in the 1888 Act, under which a number of geographical counties were divided into two or three separate administrative ones. Such divisions (for example, of Yorkshire and Lincolnshire into three, of Sussex, Northamptonshire and others into two) normally reflected the previous holding of separate quarter sessions – for county councils were the successors to quarter session government by the county's justices – though one of the more bizarre amendments proposed to the Bill in the House of Lords sought the creation of a county (in several detached parts) of the Kent Cinque Ports. This was only narrowly defeated, by 35 votes to 32!

The Act also established the county of London, based on the boundaries of its immediate predecessor, the Metropolitan Board of Works. This county was unique in that it was the only one carved out from a number of ancient counties, consisting as it did of parts of Kent, Surrey and Middlesex.

As with county boroughs, the 1888 Act made additional provision for the subsequent division or amalgamation of counties, as well as for more minor boundary changes. In the event, little attempt was made to use these, the only new county created after 1888 being the result of the separation of the Isle of Wight from the county of Southampton (only officially called Hampshire in 1959) in 1890. One or two other tentative suggestions were mooted (for example, for a new county in South Wales), but no other definite applications were made.[31]

As Table 16 shows, from 1890 until the 1960s the number of county councils remained stable, at 62. The mid-1960s saw the creation of the Greater London Council, and as a result the London and Middlesex counties disappeared. In the East Midlands the review of the Local Government Commission led to the amalgamations of Cambridgeshire and the Isle of Ely (created as two separate counties in 1888), and of the Huntingdonshire and the Soke of Peterborough (the latter had been separated from Northamtonshire in 1888). Proposals for further amalgamation, covering Rutland, Lincolnshire and Wales, were abandoned with the establishment of the Redcliffe-Maud Commission.

Although it was well known that county boundaries in many areas were in need of revision, the 1888 Act did not contain any provision for a general

Table 9.16   County councils, 1891–1986, England and Wales

| | | Population | | | Number with a population of | | |
| | | Total | % of England | Under | 50 000– | 200 000– | Over |
Year	Number	(m)	and Wales	50 000	200 000	1 million	1 million
1891	62	21.4	73.8	4	27	28	3
1901	62	23.4	71.9	4	25	30	3
1931	62	26.6	66.7	5	19	32	6
1961	62	32.5	70.4	4	18	33	7
1971	59	34.5	70.7	4	15	33	7
1981	54	48.5	100.0	—	2	40	12
1986	47	31.8	63.8	—	2	38	7

Note: LCC and GLC are included as counties in the table.
Sources:
1.   Census Reports, 1891–1981.
2.   Municipal Year Book, 1986.

review. It was not until the 1929 Local Government Act (following the Onslow Reports) that substantial progress was made through the creation of statutory County Reviews. The 1931 Census reported that several hundred changes resulted, affecting 14 800 acres and 20 300 people in 22 counties.[32] The early 1960's Local Government Commission reviews offered the next chance of an overhaul of provincial county boundaries, but only a handful of proposals were implemented. The most important changes were in the London area, where the new Greater London Council absorbed between 28 and 46 per cent of the populations of Kent, Essex and Surrey, and some 4 per cent of Hertfordshire (as well as the whole of London and Middlesex counties).[33]

The counties of England and Wales, despite losing significant areas and populations to the county boroughs, continued to grow steadily in the 1888–1974 period, and their proportion of the total population can be seen in Table 9.16 to have changed little. Most counties increased in size, though a few declined. The London County Council was depopulated by a massive one and a half million; other losses, mainly in Wales, were on a similar scale.

The 1974 reforms, also included in Table 9.16, were entirely based on a county–county district system of government. Some 39 non-metropolitan and 6 metropolitan counties were established in provincial England (the latter lasting only until their abolition, along with the Greater London Council, in 1986), and a further eight non-metropolitan counties covered Wales. The 1986 abolitions apart, changes to county boundaries since 1974 have been rare and extremely minor, despite the 1972 Act creating a review system led by an independent Local Government Boundary Commission. As we have seen throughout most of the century, there is almost always opposition to any proposals for boundary changes.

County districts and parishes

With between 350 and 1650 districts, and 10 000 to 15 000 parishes involved, a detailed analysis of change this century is clearly impracticable. But a brief summary of events will be sufficient to reveal the main points relating to urbanisation.

The period 1888 to 1986 can, broadly speaking, be divided into five sections. First, from 1888 to 1929 there was a period best described as a 'free-for-all' where structural change was piecemeal and dependent on local initiative. Secondly, under the 1929 Act each county council had to undertake a review of urban and rural district, and parish boundaries, and there followed a decade of fairly comprehensive reform. Thirdly, the period of the post-war embargo on almost all alterations, discussed earlier, was ended by the establishment of the Local Government Commissions in 1958. Their work on the boundaries of the major authorities, the fourth period (1958–66), was due to be supplemented by a further round of County Reviews, but these had scarcely started when the Redcliffe-Maud Commission was appointed. Fifthly, from 1974 the new districts and parishes have had few alterations, though the Local Government Boundary Commission is proceeding to review them. Table 9.17 gives the numbers of authorities at dates which as far as possible reflect this division of the history of district and parish reform into five episodes.

The table makes it clear that it was in the 1930s and through the 1974 reforms that the most dramatic changes took place. However the relatively static numbers of county districts in the period up to 1929 masks a high level of activity – it is just that amalgamations, creations, absorptions and so on tended to cancel each other out at that time. This was revealed in evidence to the Onslow Commission by the Ministry of Health, whose main witness produced figures to show that 55 new municipal boroughs had been given charters between 1889 and 1927, while 27 had disappeared (three into neighbouring county boroughs, and 24 had themselves become county boroughs). During this same period, 270 new urban districts were formed, but this number was largely cancelled out by 193 reductions in numbers (caused by 58 urban districts obtaining borough charters, 66 being swallowed by county boroughs and 27 by municipal boroughs, extensions; 38 being amalgamated with neighbouring urban districts; three being transferred to rural districts, and one to a metropolitan borough). Finally, all but three of the 118 new rural districts were a direct result of the provisions of the 1894 Act, whereby any rural sanitary authority crossing a county boundary was divided into two rural districts. Thirty-eight rural districts had been absorbed into boroughs, urban districts or neighbouring rural areas.[34]

Despite this considerable volume of change, to which should be added more than 400 other orders (up to 1922) relating to alterations to district boundaries,[35] the Onslow Commission still saw an urgent need for a general review of

Table 9.17   County districts and parishes, 1891–1986, England and Wales

Year	Total districts	Municipal boroughs	Urban districts	Rural districts	Total parishes
1891	1522	238	709	575	—
1929	1713	256	781	647	14 259
1940	1387	278	602	478	12 350
1961	1384	317	564	474	10 890
1971	1283	259	522	469	n.a.
1986	402	—	—	—	11 012

Notes:
1. The Total of Districts after 1891 includes 29 metropolitan boroughs (abolished 1965) and 33 London boroughs (from 1965) which do not appear in the breakdown of types of district.
2. In 1986 there were 333 non-metropolitan and 36 metropolitan districts, outside London.
3. 1891 was the nearest date to 1894 for which figures were available. As the number of Urban Sanitary Districts was rising steadily at the time, the total of 709 for that year underestimates the number existing when the 1894 Act was passed. The number of Rural Sanitary Districts in 1891 includes over 100 which crossed county boundaries and were made into two or more separate Rural Districts under the provision of the 1894 Act (see text).

Sources:
1. *Census Reports – 1891*: Area, Houses and Population Tables, vol. I, Tables 3, 6 and vol. II, Tables 2, 3; *1931*: General Report, 69–71, and Table 34; *1961*: Age, Marital Condition and General Tables, Table 6.
2. Municipal Year Book, 1971 and 1986.

district and parish boundaries. With no fewer than 66 boroughs, 302 urban districts, and 126 rural districts having a population of less than 5000, such a recommendation was not particularly radical or surprising.[36] The 1929 Act ordered all counties to undertake such a review, though municipal boroughs managed somehow to obtain their exclusion from these provisions.

Table 9.17 clearly shows the results of the reviews, amounting to a reduction in numbers of 326 county districts and almost 2000 civil parishes. Many of the smallest districts were merged, though a later study indicates that the reviews were far more successful in some areas than in others, depending on the attitude taken by the county council concerned.[37] Overall, the proportion of boroughs and urban districts containing fewer than 5000 population fell from 35 per cent to 25 per cent. As far as parishes were concerned, the results were equally patchy, for as many as 118 detached parts remained even after these county reviews (instead of 868 before then). Twenty-nine counties continued to contain at least one parish which was in two pieces, though 66 of the 118 divided parishes were in Essex and Northumberland alone.[38]

Following the Second World War, a period of relative stability took place, with the few alterations that took place being, for the most part, the result of voluntary agreement. Two or three small urban districts voluntarily merged with neighbouring rural authorities, and a roughly similar number of new ones were created due to the rise of the new towns. In comparison with the hectic decade before 1939, however, peace reigned supreme in the field of local government boundaries.

Despite numerous official reports, scarcely more happened in the fourth period, 1958–66. Although, as the table indicates, a further hundred reductions in the number of districts took place, the vast bulk of this was accounted for by three sets of reforms – those in Greater London, the West Midlands conurbation and Shropshire. The net reduction in authorities in these three areas was about 50, 30 and 20 respectively.

The 1958 Act also instigated a second round of county reviews, but, in the event, only Shropshire's was completed, and only five other counties got even as far as producing reports, before the 1966 clampdown on changes following the establishment of the Redcliffe-Maud Commission. The only real effect of the few reviews that got off the ground was the creation of a new type of authority. The rural borough was the name given to a municipal borough which was merged into a rural district, and the rural borough, although to all intents and purposes a mere parish council, retained its mayor and town clerk. With so few county reviews being completed, there were only seven rural boroughs – five in Shropshire and one each in Cornwall and Devon – though after 1974 many other former municipal boroughs obtained the comparable status of Town Council when they became part of the much larger districts created under the provisions of the Local Government Act 1972.

Notes

1. *Census 1981: Preliminary Report on Towns.*
2. *Census 1981: Key Statistics for Urban Areas*, 9.
3. *Census 1951: General Report*, 83.
4. *Census 1951: Greater London and Five Other Conurbations.*
5. 95 were analysed in T. W. Freeman (1959) *The Conurbations of Great Britain* (Manchester University Press).
6. Ministry of Town and Country Planning, New Towns Committee (1946) *Interim Report*, Cmd 6759, para. 8.
7. Ministry of Housing and Local Government (1969) *Report for 1967 and 1968*, Cmnd 4009, 72.
8. Quoted in *Lipman* (1949) 133.
9. *Census 1981: Key Statistics for Urban Areas*, Summary Table 3.
10. *Research Study 1.*
11. *Research Study 9.*
12. *Archbishop of Canterbury's Commission*, para. 1.17.
13. See especially *Educational Priority*, 3(7) (HMSO, 1975).
14. The researchers are D. Eversley and I. Begg.
15. Letter from Department of Environment to Local Authority Associations, 28 July 1985.

16. P. Harrison (1985) *Inside the Inner City* (Penguin).
17. The main initiatives are reviewed in J. Higgins, N. Deakin, J. Edwards and M. Wicks (1983) *Government and Urban Poverty* (Blackwell).
18. Redlich and Hirst (1970) 1: 201.
19. Local Government Board (1888–9) *Eighteenth Report*, 17.
20. Royal Commission on Local Government 1923–9 (1925) *Minutes of Evidence*, Long, Q.8786 (hereafter referred to as the Onslow Commission).
21. By 1891 nearly 40 000 acres had been added through three new creations and several extensions (see Table 15).
22. Onslow Commission, *1st Report*, Cmd 2506, para. 373.
23. *Ibid.*, para. 374.
24. *Ibid.*, para. 377.
25. *Ibid.*, table on p. 164.
26. Royal Commission on Local Government in England 1966–9 (1969) *Report*, Cmnd 4040, vol. 3, appendix 1, para. 15. Figures adjusted to take into account extensions to Cardiff and Newport in Wales.
27. *Census 1931, General Report*, 67–9.
28. See *Rhodes* (1970) for a full account.
29. Note 26, paras 17–19.
30. See Wood (1976) for a full account.
31. *Minutes of Evidence* (1923–9), Gibbon (Ministry of Health) 82–3.
32. *Census 1931, General Report*, 66–7.
33. Note 26, para. 30.
34. *Minutes of Evidence* (1923–9), Robinson, paras 12, 19, 27, 278–80.
35. Ibid., Gibbon, 81.
36. Onslow Commission (1928) *2nd Report*, Cmd 3213, para. 19.
37. Richards (1965).
38. *Census 1931, General Report*, 73–4 and Table 36.

Sources of data

1. *Official Documents* (published by HMSO)
   Census Reports 1891–1981
   Department of Trade, *Census of Distribution and Other Services*
   Department of Transport, *Highway Statistics*
   General Register Office, *Registrar-General's Annual Estimates of the Population of England and Wales and of Local Authority Areas*
   Local Government Board, *Annual Report* (especially for 1888–9; 1893–4; 1894–5)
   Local Government Boundary Commission, *Reports* (various, from 1973)
   Local Government Commission for England, *Reports 1–9* (1961–5)
   Local Government Commission for Wales, *Report and Proposals* (1962)
   New Towns Act 1965, *Reports of the Commission for the New Towns and of the Development Corporations* (Annual – published as House of Commons Papers)
   Royal Commission (Onslow) on Local Government 1923–9 (1925) *First Report*, Cmd 2506; *Second Report* (1928) Cmd 3213; *Minutes of Evidence* (1923–9).
   Royal Commission (Redcliffe-Maud) on Local Government in England 1966–9 (1969) *Report Studies 1*, 'Local Government in South East England' (1968); *Research Studies 9*, 'Community Attitudes Survey: England' (1969)
   Royal Commission on Local Government in Greater London 1957–1960 (1960) *Report*, Cmnd 1164

2. *Acts of Parliament*
   Local Government Act 1888
   Local Government Act 1894
   Local Government (County Boroughs and Adjustments) Act 1926
   Local Government Act 1929
   New Towns Act 1946
   Town Development Act 1952
   Local Government Act 1958
   Local Government Act 1963
   Local Government (Termination of Reviews) Act 1967
   Local Government Act 1972
   Local Government Act 1985

3. *Other Sources*
   Archbishop of Canterbury's Commission on Urban Priority Areas (1985) *Faith in the City* (Church House Publishing).
   V. D. Lipman (1949) *Local Government Areas 1834–1945* (Blackwell).
   Municipal Year Book (annual).
   J. Redlich and F. W. Hirst (1970) *The History of Local Government in England* (Macmillan).
   G. Rhodes (1970) *The Government of London: The Struggle for Reform* (Weidenfeld).
   P. G. Richards (1965) 'Local Government Reform: The Smaller Towns and the Countryside', *Urban Studies*, 2(2).
   B. Wood (1976) *The Process of Local Government Reform 1966–74* (Allen & Unwin).

10 Housing

Julia Parker and Catriona Mirrlees

Trends in housing are divided into four main sections.

1. The size of the housing stock at successive points in time, and its relation to the population – for example, its density of occupation in terms of persons per room.
2. The age, structural condition, tenure and available amenities of dwellings at successive points in time.
3. The rate of building.
4. Aspects of housing finance.

There are three main types of statistics: census data, survey data, and housing returns and other records made by local authorities and government departments. The technical volume of the 1977 government publication *Housing Policy* is a useful source of information relating to the existing stock and also containing some historical data. Census reports from 1901 to 1981 record the number of houses available (occupied and vacant), the size of the population and the size of the household in relation to the size of the dwelling. Information about various aspects of housing and its relationship to households has become more varied and elaborate with each successive census. From 1931 separate housing reports have been issued.

There is a lack of survey data covering the whole of England and Wales for the period up to 1947. Since then, however, the Government Social Survey, established during the war, has conducted a number of surveys – in 1947 of Great Britain, in 1960 and 1964 of England and Wales, in 1965 of Scotland with the Scottish Development Department, and in 1967 the house condition survey of England and Wales with the Ministry of Housing and Local Government. Similar studies have continued through the 1970s and the results are now published by the Department of the Environment.

The Joseph Rowntree Memorial Trust has supported three national housing surveys, the first in 1958, and four local studies, and also enquiries into the ownership and management of rented houses. We have not made use of their information because the general data are similar to that obtained from the census reports and government surveys and often the analyses are too detailed for our purposes.

Local authority returns and other records give details of the number of houses built and are fairly complete since 1919.

How satisfactory are the figures available?

357

SIZE OF HOUSEHOLD STOCK AND DENSITY OF OCCUPATION

Size

Although figures do cover the whole of our period beginning with the census of 1901, and show the broad trends, there are discontinuities between the figures for 1901 and those for subsequent census dates. The 1901 Census did not distinguish between private families (subsequently called households since all members do not need to be related), and institutional or non-private households, so that it is not possible to say what proportion of the total population was living in private households. Also each separate building was counted as a house, so that the excess of households over dwellings (in the sense of self-contained dwellings, either house or flat), and the number of households sharing dwellings, is not known. The number of structurally separate dwellings was first distinguished in 1921, but an estimate of the number of such dwellings in 1911 was given in the housing report of the 1931 Census, so that figures for the number of dwellings and number of private households are on the same basis from 1911 until 1971. In that year the definition of dwelling changed from accommodation having independent access to the street to living areas having no rooms, corridors or other circulation areas shared. We cannot tell precisely how this affected the statistics, but we assume the total of separate dwellings would appear to increase in 1971 as accommodation without independent access would then be counted. In 1981 there was no count of dwellings, only of 'household spaces'.

In 1981 the definition of household also changed. It was extended to include people sharing a living room, rather than referring only to a group sharing catering arrangements. Again, it is not clear how this would affect the statistics. We assume it would mean a drop in the number of units counted as separate households. Some measure of the consequences of the altered definition is provided by Table 10.7 which shows a sharp reduction both in shared dwellings and sharing households between 1971 and 1981. The 1981 figures exclude an unknown number of dwellings and households that would have been counted as shared or sharing in 1971.

Density of occupation

Again, the figures are not very satisfactory before the 1921 Census. The number of persons per room was taken as a rough guide to overcrowding, and households living at densities of more than two to a room were regarded as overcrowded. In 1901 figures showing the percentage of households living at more than two people to a room refer only to those living in one to four rooms. This understates the true figure as there were probably some over-crowded households living in more than four rooms. A similar difficulty occurs in 1911 when the percentage of families with more than two people to a room is based on those living in one to nine rooms. Neither report gives the proportion of the population living at densities of more than two per room. From 1921 onwards figures show the average density of occupation of families of different sizes and the proportion of households living at varying densities. In order to get comparable figures from 1911 we have taken in Table 10.4 'over one and a half persons per room' as the highest measure of density as the 1961 and later census reports do not give the proportions of families more crowded than this. In 1966 there was, however, a change in the definitions of rooms to be counted which would have exaggerated the reduction in the numbers living at high densities;[1] the kitchen was always counted as a room, whereas in previous census reports it was only counted as a room if it was used for eating meals. In 1971 and 1981, however, kitchens less than '6 feet' wide were excluded which presumably makes the figures more comparable with the figures for 1961 and before.

Another measure of overcrowding was proposed in 1931 relating the number of bedrooms available to the type of family, in terms of age, marital status and sex, occupying them. This was not applied to data covering the whole of England and Wales, however, until the social survey report *The Housing Situation in England and Wales in 1960* so that we have not used it in this chapter. A measure of psychological, if not necessarily physical, over-crowding is the number of households sharing dwellings. Figures go back to 1921 and an estimate was made in 1931 of the approximate number of households sharing in 1911. We do not know the position in 1981 as there was no count of dwellings.

Moreover, the census definition of a household, as a single person catering for himself or a group sharing housekeeping or a living room, is in some ways inadequate. It means, for instance, that a young married couple living with parents, and whether eating with them or not, would not be counted as a separate sharing household in spite of the fact that they would probably regard themselves as such.

Census figures also analyse some data by region. Unfortunately the major regions listed have been differently defined at different dates throughout the period with which we are dealing. Nevertheless, we have regrouped the regions to cover approximately the same areas as in 1931 to permit some geographical comparisons through time.

AGE, STRUCTURAL CONDITION AND AMENITIES OF DWELLINGS

Age

None of the census reports have included this information, and no compre-

hensive figures on the age of the total stock of dwellings at any one time seem
to exist, though a rough division into pre-1919 and post-1919 houses could be
made by adding the number of new houses built and subtracting those pulled
down, as figures exist for new houses built and old ones pulled down from that
date. The first of the Government Social Survey housing studies, *The British
Household*, estimated the proportion of houses built before and after 1919 for
a sample covering Great Britain. Unfortunately the published tabulations do
not give a regional analysis, so we could not obtain an age distribution for
England and Wales to compare with later available figures. However, the
Social Survey study of Scottish housing, and the house condition surveys of
England and Wales of 1967 and later years, by the Ministry of Housing and
Local Government, do allow us to illustrate the national trend.

Structural condition

The Ministry of Housing and Local Government reports in its quarterly
publication *Housing Statistics Great Britain*, No. 9, April 1968, that the house
condition survey of England and Wales of 1967 was the first comprehensive
survey designed to assess the structural fitness of houses. Previous estimates of
'unfit' houses were made by totalling local authority returns on numbers of
'unfit' houses. These were unreliable because not uniformly based, and often
referred only to houses on current slum clearance programmes.

Amenities

The Census of 1951 was the first to seek information about the amenities
available to households. The 1947 survey also covered certain amenities, but
as the tabulations refer to Great Britain as a whole, and as the amenities dealt
with do not correspond exactly with those of the census reports, we have not
included them in our tables. Although the area covered (England and Wales)
is the same for the censuses of 1961 and later years, the amenities referred to in
their schedules differ, so that we have selected items to be as comparable as
possible. Nor are currently listed amenities entirely relevant to the 1980s. In
1981 hot water tap and outside WC were dropped, but they were not replaced
by any others – for example, central heating – which might reflect rising living
standards and expectations.[2] To give a regional comparison we have again
amalgamated the standard regions of the 1951 and later censuses to be
approximately similar to those of 1931.

Tenure

This is an important aspect of the housing situation as different types of tenure

represent differences in security and potential capital assets. In the 1920s and
1930s, the growth of the building society movement resulted in a considerable
increase in the number of owner-occupiers, and the building of local authority
houses resulted in substantial numbers of local authority tenancies. The
Government Social Survey report of 1947 analysed tenure by regions, so that
we can extract figures for England and Wales to correspond approximately
with those in the census reports for 1961 (the first census for which tenure
figures were obtained). A regional comparison has been made by grouping
census regions to correspond approximately with those used in the 1947
survey. Comparisons made in 1961 and later years between tenures for
numbers of shared dwellings, density of occupation and amenities available,
are also used.

BUILDING

On the whole figures are reasonably complete since 1919. Local authorities
have been obliged to make returns to the central department and records of
the number of new houses built by private builders are also good from 1919, as
the post-war government was aware of the importance of the whole house-
building programme. We have tried to present all the figures in totals for the
same five-year periods, but this has not always been possible where a new type
of policy (for example, 'improvement grants') began in the middle of one of
our periods, or where the records we have been able to discover do not make
this breakdown.

COSTS

The overall amount of government and local authority expenditure on
housing is documented, but it is more difficult to get a clear picture of amounts
spent on individual items. A complete record of government contributions for
the improvement and conversion of older houses exists, but the statistics
published by the government do not give local authority contributions in
respect of this item before 1961, probably because they were small. Furthermore, official housing statistics do not include the substantial tax relief on
mortgage interest payments accorded to owner-occupiers, a concession now
commonly considered as an additional element in public expenditure on
housing.[3]

The amount of money loaned, and the number of mortgages granted by
building societies, are available over our period, though only since 1960 are
the number of new mortgages distinguished from total mortgages in the year
which normally included a few remortgages on existing ones. Figures for local
authority loans for house purchase are available from 1959, and for insurance
companies only from 1966.

Costs of housing to occupiers have not been documented in a form which makes it possible to construct tables to show the trend over the whole of our period. Reports on surveys of family expenditure conducted by the Board of Trade and the Ministry of Labour appeared in 1904, 1912, 1918, 1937–8, 1953–4 and 1967, but it is not possible to construct a table showing the proportion of income spent on housing over that time. The 1904 and 1912 surveys cover towns in England and Wales, the 1937–8 survey the United Kingdom, and the other surveys Great Britain. More importantly, the 1904 and 1912 surveys give a range of rents, according to size of property and not average rents, and a range of incomes according to type of enployment without relating the two. The 1918, 1937–8 and the 1953–4 surveys give average rents but not average incomes of the sample concerned. It is possible to relate rents to the figures for average weekly wages, but these may not have been the average weekly wage of the people in the sample, and the figures obtained seem to be too much subject to error to be put in tabular form. The pre-war surveys dealt only with working-class expenditure, and therefore ignored the cost of mortgage payments. All these surveys gave rents including rates. The figures derived from the 1967 survey are more satisfactory, as they give rents and mortgage payments as a proportion of the total household income, and of the income of the head of the household of the groups concerned. But rates are not included so the figures are not strictly comparable with the earlier ones. We have, however, been able to construct a table showing trends between 1967 and 1983 using data from later Family Expenditure Surveys. Some regional comparisons are also available from 1969.

NOTES ON TABLES

Housing stock and density of occupation

Tables 10.1 and 10.2 show the increases in dwellings, households, total population and population in private households. The count of dwellings for 1971 and 1981 is probably inflated, compared with earlier years, as a result of the change in definition, and the 1981 figure for households is based on a new definition which would result in a lower estimate than for earlier years. The percentage of the population in private households (Table 10.2) has not changed much over the period varying between 95 and 97 per cent with a slight upward trend since the 1930s.

Table 10.3 summarises changes in the size of dwellings and of families, in the density of occupation and in the proportion of families and population living at high densities. The size of dwellings changed little over the period 1921 to 1981 in spite of a considerable drop in the average family size. Density of occupation has declined steadily and so has the proportion of families living at high densities, the latter dropping to under 1 per cent by 1981. Since 1921

Table 10.1 Stock of dwellings, number of households and population, 1901–81, England and Wales (000s)

Census year	Buildings used as habitations (occupied and vacant)[1]	Dwellings for private families (or households) occupied and vacant	Occupied habitations dwellings	Families or separate occupiers[2]	Private families (or households)[3]	Population Total	Population In private families (or households)
1901	6710	–	6 449	7037	–	32 528	–
1911	7550	c. 7 691	–	8005	7 943	36 070	34 776
1921	7798	7 979	9 123	–	8 739	37 887	36 180
1931	–	9 400	12 080	–	10 233	39 952	38 042
1951	–	12 389	14 332	–	13 118	43 758	41 840
1961	–	14 646	16 348	–	14 890	46 166	44 543
1971[4]	–	17 024	18 121	–	16 779	48 750	47 296
1981[5]	–	19 192	–	–	18 326	49 155	47 948

Notes:

1. In the Census of 1901 and 1911 all separate buildings were counted as 'houses', so that a block of flats was counted as one house. In 1921 the term 'structurally separate dwelling' was introduced and subsequently used as the unit counted. It means a dwelling occupied by a private household with independent access to the street or to a public hall. The figure given for 1911 is an estimate given in the 1931 Census housing report.

2. The 1901 report counted those filling in the schedule as 'occupiers' and did not distinguish between private and non-private establishments. From 1911 onward a 'private family or household' is a group of persons, whether related or not, who live together and benefit from common housekeeping, or any person living alone who is responsible for his own needs.

3. For 1961 onwards this figure is corrected for households absent on census night.

4. The definition of dwelling changed in 1971. Previously 'structurally separate living accommodation with independent access to the street', it became 'living space with no rooms, corridors or other circulation areas shared'.

5. The census did not make a direct count of dwellings in 1981. Estimates have been made using the method suggested by the DoE (*Housing and Construction Statistics, 1974–1984*). The number of shared dwellings is calculated by assuming that on average 100 'not self-contained' household spaces are equivalent to 30 separate dwellings (20 in some areas of London).

   Prior to 1981, people living at the same address were counted as belonging to the same household only if they were catered for by the same person for at least one meal a day. In 1981 the definition was extended to include everyone who shared a living room, whether or not they had common catering arrangements. The 1981 figures, therefore, include an unknown number of households that would have been counted separately under the 1971 definition.

Sources: Census of England and Wales 1931, 1961, 1971 and 1981, *Housing Reports;*
Housing and Construction Statistics, 1974–1984;
Housing Policy Technical Volume, part 1.

Table 10.2   Proportion of the population[1] in private households, 1911–81, England and Wales

	Population in private households	Population in non-private households[2]	Total population	Percent of total population
1911	34 776 402	1 294 090	36 070 492	96.4
1921	36 179 946	1 706 753	37 886 699	95.5
1931	38 042 464	1 909 913	39 952 377	95.2
1951	41 840 000	1 918 000	43 758 000	95.6
1961	44 542 828	1 623 172	46 166 000	96.5
1971	47 296 180	1 453 395	48 749 575	97.0
1981	47 947 757	1 206 930	49 154 687	97.5

Notes:
1. As present on census night, that is, not corrected for absent residents and visitors. In 1981 figures for 'usual residents' were estimated and given for comparison. This showed 'usual residents in private households' as 47 806 003 and 'resident [present and absent] total population' as 48 521 596.
2. Includes population enumerated in communal establishments; and campers, vagrants etc.
Sources: Census of England and Wales 1931, 1951, 1961, 1971 and 1981, *Housing Reports*.

overcrowding has dropped sharply. In 1981 only 0.6 per cent of households were living at a density of more than one and a half persons per room compared with 16.3 per cent in 1921 and the number living at less than half a person per room has multiplied by five (Table 10.4). The proportion of households living at a density of from half to one person per room, the biggest group, rose gently until 1961 and has since been falling.

Table 10.5 simply documents the well-known fact that larger families tend to be more crowded than smaller families. There is, however, considerable geographical variation in households living at high densities (Table 10.6); Greater London and the Eastern region retain their respective positions with the largest and smallest number of overcrowded households and the differences have become more marked as the absolute numbers have declined. Greater London had nearly five times as many crowded households as the Eastern region in 1981, compared with under three times as many in 1931. Other areas have made slight shifts in relative positions, the North becoming slightly less crowded compared, for example, with the South-East.

Although the number of persons in relation to habitable rooms is not an entirely satisfactory way of measuring overcrowding, the clear reduction in density of occupation suggests a considerable improvement in the standard of housing as far as simple overcrowding is concerned. Even Greater London has only 1.4 per cent of overcrowded households by this standard. However,

Table 10.3 Average size of dwellings and density of occupation, 1901–81,
England and Wales

Census year	Average size of dwelling (occupied rooms)[1]	Private families per dwelling[2]	Average size of families	Average density (persons per room)	Percentage of families at more than 2 per room[3]	Percentage of population at more than 2 per room
1901	—	1.1	4.6	—	5.6[4]	—
1911	—	1.0 (approx.)	4.4	—	5.6[5]	—
1921	5.1	1.1	4.1	0.9	5.7	9.6
1931	5.1	1.1	3.7	0.8	3.9	6.9
1951	4.7	1.1	3.2	0.7	1.2	2.2
					more than 1.5 per room	more than 1.5 per room
1961	4.8	1.0	3.0	0.7	2.8	5.3
1971	5.0	1.0	2.9	0.6	1.4	2.9
1981	5.0[6]	1.0	2.7	0.5	0.6	1.3

Notes:
1. Rooms were defined in 1931, 1951 and 1961 as usual living rooms including bedrooms, and kitchens if used for eating, but excluded sculleries, landings, lobbies, closets, bathrooms, store rooms, offices and shops. In 1971 and 1981 kitchens less than 6 feet wide were excluded.
2. In 1901 the unit counted was 'separate occupiers', not private families.
3. From 1961 figures for numbers living at a density of more than two per room were no longer given.
4. Understated because based on occupancies of 1–4 rooms only.
5. Based on 1–9 room occupancies, so slightly understated.
6. Average number of rooms per 'household space'.
Sources: Census of England and Wales 1931, 1951, 1961, 1971 and 1981, *Housing Reports*.

Table 10.4 Density of occupation: proportion of households living at different
densities of persons to a room,[1] 1911–81, England and Wales

	1911[2]	1921	1931	1951	1961	1971	1981
Over 1.5	16.9	16.3	11.4	5.1	2.8	1.4	0.6
1 up to and including 1.5	18.5	17.6	14.6	10.9	7.5	4.5	2.7
0.5 up to and including 1	53.4	53.5	58.7 ⎫	84.0	64.1	59.8	40.5
Less than 0.5	11.2	12.6	15.3 ⎭		25.6	34.3	56.1
	100.0	100.0	100.0	100.0	100.0	100.0	100.0

Notes:
1. See notes to Table 10.3 for definition of 'room'.
2. Based on occupancies of 1–9 rooms only.
Sources: Census of England and Wales 1931, 1951, 1961, 1971 and 1981, *Housing Reports*.

Table 10.5   Average density of occupation of families of different sizes, 1921–81, England and Wales

Persons in family	Persons per room					
	1921	*1931*	*1951*	*1961*	*1971*	*1981*
1	0.34	0.33	0.30	0.28	0.25	0.25
2	0.50	0.48	0.49	0.49	0.42	0.41
3	0.68	0.67	0.69	0.70	0.59	0.57
4	0.85	0.85	0.87	0.88	0.74	0.70
5	1.02	1.03	1.03	1.05	0.89	0.84
6	1.20	1.20	1.20	1.22	1.04	0.99
7	1.37	1.38	1.36	1.40	1.20	1.14
8	1.53	1.53	1.52	1.56	1.35	1.28
9	1.67	1.67	1.66	1.75	1.50	1.41
10	1.77	1.76	1.81			
11	1.81	1.79	1.94	1.98		
12	1.77	1.72	2.03			
13	1.68	1.54			1.73	1.62
14	1.50	1.24	2.05			
15+	1.01	0.78				
All families	0.91	0.83	0.74	0.66	0.58	0.54

Sources: Census of England and Wales, 1931, 1951, 1961, 1971 and 1981, *Housing Reports*.

Table 10.6   Density of occupation by region,[1] 1931–81: proportion of households living at more than 1.5 persons per room, England and Wales

	1931	*1951*	*1961*	*1971*	*1981*
England and Wales	11.5	5.1	2.8	1.4	0.6
Greater London	15.0	5.8	4.4	2.9	1.4
London and South-East	11.5	4.6	3.1	1.8	0.8
North	14.3	6.5	3.0	1.3	0.6
Midlands	9.7	4.9	2.6	1.3	0.6
East	5.7	3.2	1.9	0.5	0.3
South-West	6.5	3.6	2.0	0.7	0.4
Wales	10.1	5.0	2.3	0.8	0.4

Note:
1. The composition of the standard regions was changed at each successive census. For this table regions have been combined to give approximately the same areas covered as the six regions used in 1931. The Greater London conurbation is not one of the standard regions and remains more nearly the same area throughout. It is included in the South-East region.
Sources: Census of England and Wales, 1931, 1951, 1961, 1971 and 1981, *Housing Reports*.

Table 10.7   Number and percentage of shared dwellings: number and percentage of sharing households, 1911–81, England and Wales

Year	Shared dwellings	Percentage of all dwellings	Number of sharing households	Percentage of all households	Average density (persons per room) of sharing households
1911[1]	—	—	1 250 000	15.7	—
1921[2]	753 000	—	1 732 000	19.8	—
1931	838 695	9.2	1 948 555	19.0	2.7
1951	798 694	6.6	1 871 923	14.3	0.9
1961	349 521	2.4	885 778	6.1	0.9
1971	270 815	1.7	637 050	3.9	0.7
1981	81 143[3]	0.4	234 849[4]	1.3	0.6

Notes:
1. The figure for 1911 is an estimate given in the 1931 *Housing Report*.
2. The 1931 *Housing Report* considers that the 1921 figure was somewhat under-stated.
3. Calculated using method described in Table 10.1. The sharp drop in shared dwellings between 1971 and 1981 reflects the similar drop in sharing households which, in turn, reflects the changed definition of households.

    The 1981 figures exclude an unknown number of shared dwellings or sharing households that would have been included in 1971. See Table 10.1, note 4.
4. The number of households living in 'not self-contained' household spaces.
Sources: Census of England and Wales, 1931, 1951, 1961, 1971 and 1981, *Housing Report*.

Table 10.8   Percentage of households sharing a dwelling by region,[1] 1951–77, England and Wales

Region	1951	1961	1971	1977[2]
England and Wales	14.3	6.1	3.9	—
Greater London	34.2	19.7	13.4	7.3
London and South-East	25.5	15.7	7.4	4.8
North	7.1	2.3	1.5	1.9
Midlands	8.9	2.5	1.6	1.8
East	7.4	2.1	1.5	2.9
South-West	14.0	4.6	3.8	3.2
Wales	15.9	5.4	2.5	—
England	14.2	6.1	3.9	3.1

Notes:
1. Regions are not strictly comparable due to boundary changes, particularly those of 1979. See also Table 10.6, note 1.
2. No count of shared dwellings was made in the 1981 Census.
Sources: Census of England and Wales, 1951, 1961 and 1971 *Housing Reports*; *National Dwelling and Housing Survey, 1978*.

measured by our other standard of overcrowding, the sharing of dwellings, improvements have been less marked (Tables 10.7 and 10.8). The position worsened between 1911 and 1921 and did not recover noticeably until after 1931. Even in 1971, 4 per cent of all households were sharing a dwelling, and 13 per cent in Greater London. As we have already noted, the two-thirds drop in both shared dwellings and sharing households between 1971 and 1981 may be largely attributable to changed definitions.

The condition of dwellings

We have little information about the structural condition of dwellings but Table 10.9 suggests three things:

1. The conservative nature of the estimates of unfit houses derived from slum-clearance programmes, which seem to have been based to a large extent on what the local authorities felt that they could achieve with the resources at their disposal.
2. Changing criteria of fitness reflecting higher public expectations about what consitutes a satisfactory dwelling as living standards rise.

Table 10.9   Number of unfit dwellings, 1934–81,[1] England and Wales

Year	Number	
1934	266 851	
1937	377 930	Based on slum-clearance programmes
1939	472 000	
1960	622 000	Based on local authority returns, often linked to
1965	820 000	current slum-clearance programmes
1967	1 836 000	
1971	1 244 000	Estimates of English and Welsh house condition
1976	1 262 000	surveys
1981	1 206 900	

Note:
1. Before 1967 national estimates of the numbers of unfit dwellings were based on returns made by local authorities, but local definitions varied so the results were unsatisfactory. In 1965, for instance, local authority returns suggested 820 000 unfit dwellings, whereas the national survey of 1967 counted more than twice as many.

Sources: M. Bowley (1945) *Housing and the State* (Allen & Unwin);
Housing Statistics Great Britain 9;
The Housing Situation in 1960, Government Social Survey, ss. 319;
House Condition Survey 1971 (England and Wales);
English House Condition Survey 1981;
Welsh Housing Statistics 1;
Welsh Housing Statistics 2.

3. The deterioration of old property which may have been structurally sound at the beginning of the period, but which has been allowed to decay in spite of slum clearance and improvement schemes. It is not possible, unfortunately, to deduce from these figures how much property was omitted from slum-clearance programmes which would have been classified as unfit by the standards of the public health inspectors in 1967, and how much was originally fit and has subsequently deteriorated.

No figures were obtained giving an estimate, for England and Wales, of the proportion of older houses – say more than 30 years old – in the total stock in the 1930s. As this was a time of considerable building activity, it is likely that the proportion of older houses would be declining. However, Table 10.10 shows that in 1947, according to a sample survey, 68.3 per cent of houses in Great Britain were built before 1919, and this proportion was probably similar to 1939 owing to the virtual building standstill during the war. By 1984 the proportion of pre-1919 houses had dropped to 28.7 per cent in England and Wales. The proportion of interwar dwellings had also fallen as the post-war building programme has got under way. Half of the housing stock in 1984 had been built since 1945.

Table 10.10   Age of dwellings, 1947–84 (estimated), England and Wales (percentages)

Year	Pre-1919	1919–44	1945–70	Post-1970
1947 (Great Britain)	68.3	3.17	—	—
1967	38.4	27.1	34.5	—
1971	35.8	24.1	40.1	
1981	29.7	21.6	34.2	14.5
1984	28.7	21.0	33.5	16.8

Sources: 1947 based on sample data from P. G. Gray, *The British Household*, Government Social Survey, 1947;
1967 sample data are from the *House Condition Survey (England and Wales)* 1971, *Housing Statistics Great Britain* 10;
1971, 1981, 1984 estimates are based on census data from 1851 to 1981, estimated rates of new construction before 1919, and assumed ages for losses from the dwelling stock; *Housing and Construction Statistics*, 1974–84.

The distribution of old and new dwellings among the main tenure groups appears in Table 10.11. Owner-occupiers increased their holding of old property from one-quarter to nearly 60 per cent between 1938 and 1975, while the share of 'other tenures', mainly private renters, fell from three-quarters to just over one-third. This reflects the practice of building societies in the 1930s of lending mainly for new houses, older houses were usually privately rented and not sold, because rent control imposed in 1919 made it difficult to evict

370

Table 10.11 Stock of housing by tenure and age (estimated), 1938–75, England and Wales

		Age of dwelling							
		Pre-1919		1919–44		Post-1914		All dwellings	
Year	Tenure	(millions)	(%)	(millions)	(%)	(millions)	(%)	(millions)	(%)
1938	Owner-occupied	1.90	24.9	1.80	47.4	—	—	3.70	32.4
	Rented from local authority/new town	0.02	0.3	1.10	28.9	—	—	1.12	9.8
	Other tenures	5.70	74.8	0.90	23.7	—	—	6.60	57.8
		7.62	100.0	3.80	100.0	—	—	11.42	100.0
1960	Owner-occupied	2.9	41.4	2.4	57.1	1.1	32.4	6.4	43.8
	Rented from local authority/new town	0.2	2.9	1.2	28.6	2.2	64.7	3.6	24.7
	Other tenures	3.9	55.7	0.6	14.3	0.1	2.9	4.6	31.5
		7.0	100.0	4.2	100.0	3.4	100.0	14.6	100.0
1971	Owner-occupied	3.3	54.1	2.6	61.9	3.1	45.6	9.0	52.6
	Rented from local authority/new town	0.3	4.9	1.2	28.6	3.4	50.0	4.9	28.7
	Other tenures	2.5	41.0	0.4	9.5	0.3	4.4	3.2	18.7
		6.1	100.0	4.2	100.0	6.8	100.0	17.1	100.0
1975	Owner-occupied	3.4	57.6	2.7	64.3	3.8	48.1	9.9	55.0
	Rented from local authority/new town	0.3	5.1	1.2	28.6	3.7	46.8	5.2	28.9
	Other tenures	2.2	37.3	0.3	7.1	0.4	5.1	2.9	16.1
		5.9	100.0	4.2	100.0	7.9	100.0	18.0	100.0

Source: Housing Policy Technical Volume, part 1.

Table 10.12   Stock of dwellings by tenure and condition (estimated), 1967, 1971,
1976 and 1981, England and Wales

Year	Tenure	Number of unfit dwellings (000s)	% of all unfit dwellings	% of all dwellings (fit and unfit)	% unfit of tenure type
1967[1]	Owner-occupied	556	30.3	50.8	7.0
	Rented from local authority/new town	72	3.9	27.1	1.7
	Other tenures	1118	60.9	21.4	33.2
	Closed[2]	90	4.9	0.7	79.6
		1836	100.0	100.0	—
1971	Owner-occupied	355	28.5	53.0	3.7
	Rented from local authority/new town	58	4.7	28.0	1.2
	Other tenures	645	51.8	16.5	22.9
	Closed[2]	24	1.9	0.1	100.0
	Vacant	162	13.0	2.4	39.5
		1244	100.0	100.0	—
1976	Owner-occupied	313	35.3	55.2	3.1
	Rented from local authority/new town	53	5.9	29.0	1.0
	Private rented	521	58.7	15.8	18.2
		887	100.0	100.0	—
1981	Owner-occupied	539	44.7	57.0	5.0
	Rented from local authority/new town	71	5.9	28.1	1.3
	Private rented	401	33.2	11.6	18.1
	Vacant	196	16.2	3.3	31.3
		1207	100.0	100.0	—

Notes:
1. The 1967 figures are taken from *Housing Statistics Great Britain*, 9. Estimates in these tables are based on the House Condition Survey carried out in February and March 1967 by the Ministry of Housing and Local Government. This was the first large-scale survey of its kind. Details are given in *Economic Trends* for May 1968. See Table 10.9, note 1 for unsatisfactory nature of earlier estimates.
2. Closed under Housing or Planning Acts.
Sources: *Housing Statistics Great Britain*, 9;
House Condition Survey 1971 England and Wales;
English House Condition Survey 1976;
Welsh Social Trends 1978;
English House Condition Survey 1981;
Welsh Housing Statistics 1983.

Table 10.13 Stock of unfit dwellings by region (estimated), 1967–81, England and Wales

Region	Year	Unfit dwellings (000s)			Percentage of unfit dwellings[1]	Unfit dwellings as a percentage of total stock of permanent dwellings in the area[1]
		In or adjoining clearance areas	Not in potential clearance areas	All[1]		
Northern, Yorks. *and Humberside,* *and North-West*	1967	578	184	762	41.5	15.1
	1971	400	140	540	43.4	10.1
	1976	192	190	382	42.7	7.1
				(506)	(40.1)	(9.4)
	1981[2]	131	304	435	36.0	7.8
South-East	1967	139	199	338	18.4	6.4
	1971	92	139	231	18.6	4.0
	1976	69	126	195	21.8	3.1
				(326)	(25.8)	(5.2)
	1981[2]	108	251	359	29.7	5.4

Rest of England and Wales	1967	382	354	736	40.1	13.7
	1971	231	242	473	38.0	8.0
	1976	107	210	317	35.5	4.9
				(429)	(34.0)	(6.6)
	1981²	100	232	413	34.2	6.0
England and Wales	1967	1099	737	1836	100.0	11.7
	1971	723	521	1244	100.0	7.3
	1976	368	526	894	100.0	4.9
				(1262)		(7.0)
	1981²	339	787	1207	100.0	6.3

Notes:

1. Figures in brackets are re-estimates of 1976 figures published in 1981 survey report; percentages in brackets are recalculations based on these estimates.

2. 1981 estimates are calculated on the basis that approximately 30 per cent of dwellings were judged to be in or adjoing clearance areas in England and Wales by the survey inspectors.

Sources: *Housing Statistics Great Britain, 9;*
House Condition Survey 1971 (England and Wales);
English House Condition Survey 1976;
Welsh Social Trends 1978;
English House Condition Survey 1981;
Welsh Housing Statistics (1983).

sitting tenants. Since the Second World War building societies have been encouraged to lend more money on older houses, and more old property has become available for sale as the privately-rented sector has declined. In 1975 owner-occupiers held two-thirds of the interwar dwellings, most of the remainder belonging to the local authorities, and only 7.9 per cent remaining in the privately-renting sector. At the same time 95 per cent of the newer post-war houses were shared almost equally between owner-occupiers and local authorities.

The next couple of tables give details of the condition of dwellings in relation to tenure and geography. The owner-occupied sector contained 45 per cent of all unfit houses in 1981, a higher proportion than in 1967. By contrast, most unfit dwellings, 60 per cent, were to be found in the privately-rented sector in 1967 but only 33 per cent in 1981 (Table 10.12). This reflects the dwindling number of houses available to rent privately (Table 10.18). A far higher proportion of privately-rented dwellings than of other occupied property were classified as unfit in 1981, as in earlier years. The local authorities have barely any unfit houses, not surprisingly, as nearly three-quarters of their dwellings have been built since the Second World War.

The South-East remains a comparatively favoured area with 30 per cent of all unfit dwellings, and 5 per cent of its total stock unfit, whereas the North has 36 per cent of all unfit dwellings and 8 per cent of its stock unfit. But a sharp drop in the proportion of unfit dwellings in the north has reduced regional

Table 10.14   Proportion of all households who share or lack certain amenities, 1951–81, England and Wales (percentages)

Type of amenity	1951 Share the amenity	Lack	1961 Share	Lack	1971 Share	Lack	1981[1] Share	Lack
Hot-water tap	—	—	1.8	21.9	2.0	6.4	—	—
Fixed bath	8	37	4.6	22.0	3.4	8.7	1.3	1.9
WC[2]	13	8	5.8	6.9	4.0	1.1	1.2	2.8

Notes:
1. In 1981 a reduction in the number of households classified as sharing their amenities occurred when the definition of a household was changed and groups of people who were previously considered as being in separate households were considered as one household.
2. For 1951 and 1971 this refers to either internal or external WC. In 1961, to internal WCs and external WCs that are attached to the dwelling. In 1981 only inside WCs are considered. For comparison, the National Dwelling and Housing Survey that refers to England only estimates that in 1977 2.7 per cent of households shared an inside/outside WC and 0.3 per cent lacked the use of any at all.
Sources: Census of England and Wales 1951, 1961, 1971 and 1981, *Housing Reports*; *National Dwelling and Housing Survey 1978*.

Table 10.15   Proportion of sharing households who share or lack certain amenities, 1951–81, England and Wales (percentages)

Type of amenity	1951 Share	Lack	1961 Share	Lack	1971 Share	Lack	1981[1] Share	Lack
Hot-water tap	—	—	25.4	37.9	32.4	16.1	—	—
Fixed bath	57	28	55.0	30.1	49.8	16.7	60.9	6.3
WC[2]	77	2	69.9	1.4	53.9	0.4	59.3	4.4

Notes:
1. As no count of households sharing dwellings was made in 1981, these figures are for the percentage of households living in 'not self-contained' accommodation sharing or lacking the amenity.
2. See Table 10.14, note 2.

Sources: Census of England and Wales 1951, 1961, 1971 and 1981, *Housing Reports*.

differences considerably since 1967 (Table 10.13). For England and Wales as a whole, the number of unfit houses has dropped from nearly 12 to just over 6 per cent of the total stock. Tables 10.14 to 10.17 show the availability of certain amenities during the period 1951 to 1981 to all households and to all households who share dwellings. There were substantial improvements over the period, the proportion of all households sharing or lacking a bath or WC falling to 1 or 2 per cent. The figures for 1981 may, however, suggest a greater improvement than actually occurred as a result of the altered definition of

Table 10.16   All households and sharing households who have the exclusive use of listed[1] amenities, 1951–81, England and Wales (percentages)

Household type	1951	1961	1971	1981[2]
All households	52	69.3	82.1	95.3
Sharing households	11	10.7	26.8	29.2

Notes:
1. The census report lists vary. The 1951 list is: piped water, cooking stove, water closet and fixed bath; the 1961 list: cold-water tap, hot-water tap, fixed bath and WC; the 1971 list: hot-water supply, fixed bath/shower, and WC; the 1981 list: fixed bath/shower and inside flush toilet.
2. 'Sharing households' is restricted to those living in 'not self-contained accommodation'. Thus the households classified in 1971 as sharing dwellings but having self-contained accommodation are not included. Had the 1971 definition been retained the number of sharing households would have been greater.

Sources: Census of England and Wales, 1951, 1961, 1971 and 1981, *Housing Reports*.

household which meant that groups of people previously considered as separate were regarded as one unit. Sharing households remain at a great disadvantage, two-thirds sharing or lacking bath or WC in 1981, a deterioration in the position ten years earlier (Table 10.15). The comparison with all households for possession of a selected group of amenities appears in Table 10.16.

Regional differences in standards of amenity are not very marked (Table 10.17). Wales and Greater London have tended to be rather below average for the period 1951–81, and the North marginally above. The South-West has moved from a below average position to become the region with the highest standards.

Table 10.17   Proportion of households with certain[1] amenities by region,[2] 1951–81 (percentages)

Region	1951	1961	1971	1981
England and Wales	52.0	69.3	82.1	95.3
Northern	54.1	71.4	81.2	95.7
Midlands	51.2	70.1	82.3	95.5
London and South-East	53.2	67.4	82.7	95.1
South-West	49.0	68.3	85.8	96.1
East	50.0	71.3	82.2	95.5
Wales	40.0	64.2	77.5	93.3
Greater London	51.0	62.2	75.7	93.0

Notes:
1.   Listed amenities as in note to Table 10.16.
2.   Regions as in Table 10.6.
Sources: Census of England and Wales, 1951, 1961, 1971 and 1981, *Housing Reports*.

Tenure

Tenure is useful as a basis for analysing housing statistics, rather than income or social class. Of the three main tenure groups, owner-occupiers tend to have the higher incomes but they also have other advantages compared with the average council or private tenant. They have complete security and a safe investment free of capital gains tax which has proved particularly valuable over recent years when house prices have risen more rapidly than general living costs.[4] Home owners also have substantial public help towards their housing costs in tax relief granted on mortgage interest payments. During 1983–4 this amounted to £2341 million, compared with a total of £1521 million paid in subsidies by central and local government for publicly rented dwellings (Table 10.27, note 1).

The attractiveness of home ownership, rising real incomes, and the increasing availability of loans from building societies have resulted in a sixfold increase in the proportion of the population who are owner-occupiers since the beginning of the century, and an even steeper decline in the privately-rented sector. High building and repair costs and rent controls have helped to make renting dwellings to private tenants a poor economic proposition for landlords and successive Acts from 1957, decontrolling rents and attempting to extend more security to tenants, have further discouraged private landlords and brought more property into the market for sale for owner-occupation. Furthermore, the sale of council houses has also been increasing, particularly since 1980 when tenants received a statutory right to buy their council dwellings, encouraged by generous discounts. This, and the sharp drop in new building since the end of the 1970s, led to a fall in the proportion of people renting from local authorities in 1983 for the first time during the century.

The tables on tenure (Tables 10.18 to 10.21) show the growth of owner occupancy, the lesser growth of local authority tenancy, the dramatic decline in private tenancies, and some regional differences within these general trends. London stands out with less owner-occupation, and more private renting, than elsewhere, and the South-East has the highest proportion of owner-occupiers, and fewer local authority tenants. Average density of occupation also varies by tenure. In 1961 local authority property was the most densely occupied, except for shared dwellings rented furnished, which had an average density of just over one person a room. By 1981 densities for all categories had dropped, but local authority dwellings were then more crowded than privately-rented furnished property. Local authority houses remain the best equipped with amenities, though standards in the owner-occupied sector are now very similar, having improved far more rapidly since 1966. Privately-rented dwellings are also now better served with amenities, though they lag well behind the other tenure groups.

Table 10.18   Housing stock by tenure (estimated), 1914–83, England and Wales (percentages)

Tenure	1914	1938	1951	1960	1971	1981	1983
Owner-occupied	10	32	31	44	50	58	62
Rented from local authority or new town corporation	—	10	17	25	28	29	26
Rented from private landlord and miscellaneous	90	58	52	31	22	13	12

Sources: *Housing Policy Technical Volume*, part 1;
Census of England and Wales 1971 and 1981 *Housing Reports*;
Housing and Construction Statistics, 1983.

Table 10.19   Regional[1] comparisons of households by tenure, 1947–81, England and Wales (percentages)

Region	Year	All tenures	Owner-occupiers	Renting from local authority or new town corporation	Renting from private person[2]	Other tenures[3]
England and	1947[4]	100	27	12	58	3
Wales	1961	100.0	42.3	23.7	27.8	6.2
	1971	100.0	50.2	28.0	21.6	0.2
	1981	100.0	58.1	28.8	11.0	2.1
North	1947[4]	100	26	13	55	6
	1961	100.0	40.9	25.8	27.6	5.7
	1971	100.0	49.0	31.6	19.3	0.1
	1981	100.0	55.9	32.8	9.7	1.6
Midlands and	1947[4]	100	32	11	55	2
Wales	1961	100.0	42.9	26.8	23.4	6.9
	1971	100.0	51.4	31.0	17.6	0.1
	1981	100.0	59.1	30.3	8.6	2.0
South and East	1947[4]	100	29	11	56	4
(excl. Greater	1961	100.0	43.6	28.3	20.5	7.6
London)	1971	100.0	55.7	24.0	20.1	0.2
	1981	100.0	63.4	23.4	10.3	3.0
Greater London	1947[4]	100	23	13	63	1
	1961	100.0	36.6	18.3	42.0	3.1
	1971	100.0	40.4	24.9	34.1	0.6
	1981	100.0	48.6	30.7	19.2	1.5

Notes:
1. Later figures have been combined so that they refer to areas approximately equivalent to those used in the *British Household* study of 1947.
2. Includes companies (1966) and housing associations (1971, 1981).
3. For 1971 this category includes only 'not stated'. For 1981 the other tenures were 'rented with business' and 'rented by virtue of employment'.
4. Figures for 1947 are not sufficiently exact to allow rounding to decimal points.
Sources: 1947 figures are from P. G. Gray, *The British Household*, Government Social Survey, 1947;
Census of England and Wales 1961, 1971 and 1981, *Housing Reports*.

Building rates

Tables 10.22 to 10.26 document housing performance in both the public and private sector from 1919. Figure 10.1, based on data from Table 10.22, shows how the overall rate of building fluctuated between the five-year periods due to economic and political factors, the local authority and private building rates moving independently of each other at times, chiefly for political reasons. The immediate pre-war years were a major building period, only exceeded by the

Table 10.20 Density of occupation, persons per room, by type of tenure in all dwellings and shared dwellings, 1961, 1971 and 1981, England and Wales

Tenure	1961		1971		1981	
	All dwellings	*Shared dwellings*	*All dwellings*	*Shared dwellings*	*All dwellings*	*Shared[1] dwellings*
Owner-occupied	0.59	0.69	0.54	0.57	0.51	—
Rented from local authority	0.83	0.93	0.70	0.73	0.62	—
Rented unfurnished	0.64	0.83	0.54	0.67	0.48	—
Rented furnished	0.82	1.11	0.73	0.86	0.58	—

Note:
1. No count of shared dwellings was made in the 1981 Census of England and Wales.
Sources: Census of England and Wales 1961, 1971 and 1981, *Housing Reports.*

Table 10.21 Proportion of households with certain amenities by tenure, 1966, 1971 and 1981, England and Wales (percentages)

Amenities	Year	All tenures	Owner-occupied	Rented from local authority or new town corporation	Rented[1] from a private person	Other[2] and not stated
With shared hot tap	1966	2.1	1.0	0.6	6.3	0.9
	1971	2.0	0.8	0.4	7.1	8.4
	1981	—	—	—	—	—
With no hot tap	1966	12.5	6.9	4.6	34.2	8.1
	1971	6.4	3.7	2.1	18.0	13.0
	1981	—	—	—	—	—
With shared fixed bath	1966	4.3	1.9	1.0	12.7	1.4
	1971	3.4	1.0	0.7	12.4	14.6
	1981	1.3	0.3	0.6	8.8	1.0
With no fixed bath	1966	14.9	9.6	3.2	40.3	11.1
	1971	8.7	5.8	2.1	24.3	13.8
	1981	1.9	1.4	0.4	8.5	1.2

With shared inside WC	1966	4.1	1.4	0.9	14.1	1.4
	1971	3.3	0.8	0.5	12.4	15.3
	1981	1.2	0.2	0.3	8.7	1.0
With no inside WC	1966	19.7	14.8	9.0	42.7	16.9
	1971	12.1	9.0	6.3	26.8	12.4
	1981	2.8	2.2	1.5	9.7	2.1
With shared outside WC	1966	1.9	1.0	0.6	5.7	0.5
	1971	0.7	0.3	0.1	2.4	1.7
	1981	–	–	–	–	–
With no WC (inside or outside)	1966	1.8	1.5	0.5	3.1	4.3
	1971	1.1	1.1	0.2	2.4	2.6
	1981	–	–	–	–	–
With exclusive use of hot water, fixed bath and[3] inside WC[3]	1966	72.4	81.1	87.8	35.3	79.3
	1971	82.1	88.5	91.7	54.7	65.4
	1981	95.3	97.2	97.6	79.2	96.5

Notes:
1. See Table 10.19, note 2.
2. See Table 10.19, note 3.
3. 1981 figures refer only to 'exclusive use of fixed bath and inside WC', not exclusive use of hot water.
Sources: Sample Census of England and Wales 1966 *Housing Report*;
Census of England and Wales 1971 and 1981 *Housing Reports*.

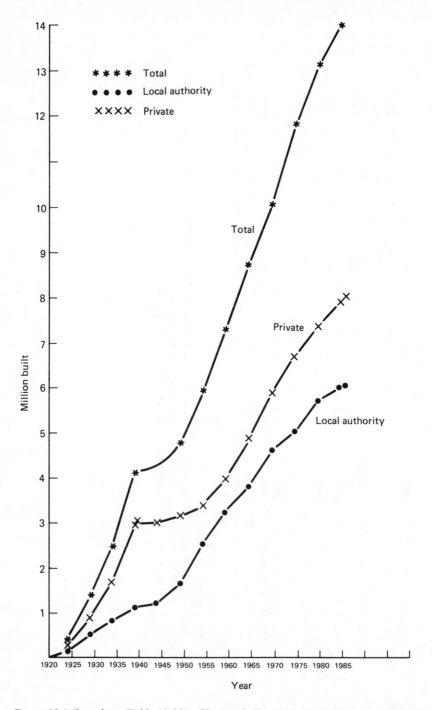

Figure 10.1 (based on *Table* 10.22)   Houses built, 1919–85, England and Wales

Labour administration of the second half of the 1960s. Private builders have been the major suppliers of dwellings since 1919, apart from the decade after the end of the war when private building was strictly controlled. By the end of the 1950s the private sector had almost regained its predominance and has had the larger programme ever since. All house building slowed down in the 1970s and has slumped in the first half of the 1980s, with the local authority sector cut by over 50 per cent. The private sector has been less severely restrained, building for owner-occupation being encouraged by the generous tax relief for occupiers.

Table 10.23 shows action under the local authority slum-clearance programmes. Between 1934 and 1939, demolitions were running at about 50 000 a year, with about 200 000 people moved each year. No subsequent five-year period has reached this rate of rehousing. During the war slum clearance ceased entirely, and was restarted afterwards much later than the house building programme. It was not until the late 1950s that it approached the 1934–9 rate. Since 1970 the number of houses demolished has been falling. Tables 10.23 and 10.24 may be read with Table 10.9 (number of unfit dwellings) to show how action has failed to keep pace with slum-clearance plans and estimates of unfit dwellings.

Table 10.24 shows the considerable amount of repair work on older houses, first, emergency work on war-damaged houses, secondly repairs carried out at the instigation of local authorities. The latter involved over a million houses during the four-year period from 1951 to 1954, though the rate has fallen

Figure 10.1   Houses built, 1919–85, England and Wales
(values used in graph are from Table 10.22)

	Local authority	Private	Total
1924	176 914	221 543	398 457
1929	503 267	894 887	1 398 154
1934	789 617	1 699 138	2 488 755
1939	1 136 457	2 969 050	4 105 507
1944	1 211 957	3 044 550	4 256 507
1949	1 644 055	3 170 867	4 814 922
1954	2 556 860	3 399 483	5 956 343
1959	3 245 445	4 022 507	7 267 952
1964	3 791 174	4 901 263	8 692 437
1969	4 552 348	5 884 601	10 436 949
1974	5 088 908	6 714 648	11 803 556
1979	5 729 566	7 382 078	13 111 644
1984	6 023 568	7 955 708	13 979 276
1985	6 047 242	8 101 543	14 148 785

* * *   Total
● ● ● ●   Local authority
x x x x   Private

Table 10.22   Permanent houses built in five-year periods,
1919–84 and in 1985, England and Wales

Years	Local authority	Private builders[1]	Total
1919–24	176 914	221 543	398 457
1925–9	326 353	673 344	999 697
1930–4	286 350	804 251	1 090 601
1935–9	346 840	1 269 912	1 616 752
1940–4	75 500	75 500	151 000[2]
1945–9	432 098[3]	126 317	558 415
1950–4	912 805	228 616	1 141 421
1955–9	688 585	623 024	1 311 609
1960–4	545 729	878 756	1 424 485
1965–9	761 174	983 338	1 744 512
1970–4	536 560	830 047	1 366 607
1975–9	640 658	667 430	1 308 088
1980–4	294 002	573 630	867 632
1985	23 674	145 835	169 509

Notes:
1. Including 431 669 built between 1919 and 1939 with the aid of subsidy.
2. This figure is for the period September 1939 to March 1944. The Ministry of Health *Annual Reports* give no figure for completed permanent houses for the rest of 1944. There was an embargo on the building of new houses during the period.
3. From 1945 onwards figures in this column include houses built by New Town Development Corporations and by Housing Associations and Government Departments, but exclude temporary houses built by local authorities.
Sources: J. B. Cullingworth, *Housing and Local Government in England and Wales* (Allen & Unwin 1966);
Housing Statistics Great Britain 12;
Ministry of Health *Annual Report*, Cmnd 6562, for year ended 31.3.44;
Ministry of Health *Annual Report*, Cmnd 6744, for year ended 31.3.45;
Housing and Construction Statistics 1973, 1976, 1974–84;
Local Housing Statistics England and Wales 1986.

sharply since the mid-1960s. Nearly four and a half million dwellings have been improved with the help of public money since the end of the 1940s. The number of improvement grants rose rapidly in the 1960s and, after falling back in the later 1970s, the level remains relatively high, reflecting a shift in government policy away from demolition and in favour of renovation. It is noticeable that a much higher proportion of grants goes to the private sector and to owner-occupiers (Table 10.25).

There has been a marked change in the size of houses built since the war,

Table 10.23   Slum clearance, houses/dwellings[1] demolished or closed, 1930–84, England and Wales

	Total houses demolished or closed	Parts of buildings closed	Persons/families[2] moved
Up to March 1934[3]	27 564	—	91 109
April 1934 to March 1939	245 272	—	1 001 417
1940–4[4]	nil	—	—
1945–9[5]	29 350	3850	98 950
1950–4	60 532	5913	211 090
1955–9	213 402	8571	682 228
1960–4	303 621	5514	833 746
1965–9	339 419	4253	896 352
1970–4	309 214	3997	256 028
1975–9	208 817	—	143 680
April 1979–April 1984	112 243	—	—

Notes:
1. Houses for this purpose mean whole buildings, not structurally separate dwellings within a building. Where only some of the dwellings within a building were closed this is listed under 'parts of building closed'. From 1975 only a count of dwellings demolished or closed was made. The figures thus include separate dwellings deemed unfit and closed in a building in which other dwellings remain occupied.
2. Persons moved up to and including 1974; 'families moved' for the period 1975–9.
3. Including approximately 11 000 houses demolished and 17 000 people moved up to 1930 (Ministry of Health *Annual Report*, 1931–2).
4. Authorities were asked to postpone all slum-clearance plans during the war (Ministry of Health *Summary Report*, 1939–41).
5. Based on estimates given in *Housing Statistics Great Britain*, 6 (see notes and definitions no. 7).
Sources: M. Bowley (1945) *Housing and the State* (Allen & Unwin);
Housing Statistics Great Britain, 6, 12;
Housing and Construction Statistics nos 1, 17, 32, 1974–84.

with a fourfold increase in the proportion of single bedroom dwellings. The proportion of large houses has also increased to 15 per cent of all those built in 1984, though local authorities continue to build very few with more than four bedrooms (Table 10.26). Private builders have consistently provided the larger dwellings, local authorities increasingly those with one or two bedrooms.

Housing trends during this century, then, reveal the number of dwellings rising from roughly 6.5 million to 19 million, a period when population rose by 50 per cent. The outcome of these trends is the virtual disappearance of overcrowding and of households sharing a dwelling. But while the building programme has necessarily added substantial numbers of relatively new houses, more than one-quarter of the total stock in 1984 had been built before 1919. Slum clearance and, more recently, the improvement of older dwellings, have dealt with some of the worst conditions, so that very few households now

Table 10.24   Houses[1] or dwellings[2] made fit,[3]
1945–84, England and Wales

Period	No. of houses or dwellings
1945–9	883 591
1945 to March 1951	510 301
March 1951 to end 1954	1 197 930
1955–9	1 247 895
1960–4	1 096 618
1965–9	470 681
1970–4	215 464
April 1974–pril 1979	94 614
April 1979–April 1984	56 077

Notes:
1. Houses for this purpose means whole buildings, not the separate dwellings within them.
2. Number of dwellings from 1970. A house may contain more than one dwelling.
3. 'Made fit' – for figures 1945–9 of war-damaged houses this means simply making weathertight and habitable. Other figures refer to houses/dwellings made fit having been deemed to be so far defective in one or more of the matters of the Housing Acts 1936 and 1957 as to be not reasonably suitable for occupation.

Sources: Ministry of Health *Report* for year ended 31 March 1949;
Ministry of Housing and Local Government *Reports*;
Housing Statistics Great Britain, 12, 19;
Housing and Construction Statistics, 1971–81 and 1974–84.

lack basic amenities, though sharing households fare badly in this respect and the privately-rented sector is poorly served compared with the other main tenure groups. Moreover, in 1981 there remained over one million unfit dwellings, 6 per cent of the total stock.

The tables in this chapter demonstrate the great improvement in housing standards for the mass of the population. For a minority, however, conditions remain very poor. The limited regional comparisons that we have been able to make suggest persistent geographical differences in type of tenure, the possession of amenities, the proportion of sharing households, and of unfit dwellings. But the regional analyses conceal the particularly bad conditions in

Table 10.25 Improvement grants approved paid,[1] 1949–84,
England and Wales

	Local[2] authority dwellings	Private[3] owners	Housing associations
		No. of dwellings	
1949–58	9 846	150 023	
1959	16 213	62 783	
1960–4	180 054	430 724	
1965–9	157 197	409 812	
1970–4	402 356	836 389	27 334
1975–9	250 496	266 974	67 989
1980–4	360 001	779 105	76 478

Notes:
1. Before 1975 figures refer to grants *approved*. After 1975 to grants *paid* to private owners and work *completed* on housing association and local authority dwellings.
2. Figures for Welsh housing revenue account dwelling renovations are not available for 1976 onwards.
3. From 1981 includes grants to tenants in both public and private sectors.
Sources: *Housing Statistics Great Britain*, 12, 19;
Housing and Construction Statistics 1971–81 and 1974–84.

the poorest districts of large towns. We have no statistics which would allow construction of trend tables, but the social and economic problems of the inner cities have received more attention over the last decade and some comparisons are possible for recent years which give a measure of the extreme deprivation of the poorest urban areas.[5] For instance, Inner Birmingham had 12 per cent and several of the Inner London boroughs over 8 per cent of their households overcrowded, with more than one person per room, compared with a national average of just over 3 per cent in 1981.[6] Our regional analysis, however, shows Greater London generally as the area with most overcrowding, on a more stringent definition, but even so with only just over twice the national average (Table 10.6). Again, our regional analysis shows 7 per cent of Greater London households lacking certain amenities compared with a national average of 5 per cent (Table 10.17). But DoE figures for 1981 show inner areas of London, Birmingham, Manchester and Liverpool with a proportion of households lacking the exclusive use of basic amenities two or three times the average for England and Wales.[7] In a similar way our figures for the regional distribution of sharing households show Greater London as worst off with rather over twice the average proportion for England and Wales. But, using a different method of comparison, Inner London in 1971

Table 10.26 Public and private houses and flats completed by number of bedrooms, selected years, 1945–84, England and Wales (percentages)

Year	Local authorities and new towns				Private owners				Local authorities, new towns and private owners			
	1	2	3	4 or more	1	2	3	4 or more	1	2	3	4 or more
1945–60	10.0	29.6	58.0	2.4	—	—	—	—	—	—	—	—
1961	26.1	32.0	39.9	2.0	1.8	35.1	59.6	3.5	4.2	29.7	62.6	3.5
1966	26.5	34.7	36.6	2.2	2.0	25.0	67.3	5.7	3.1	21.9	69.6	5.5
1971	31.2	29.9	34.7	4.1	2.0	18.6	69.8	9.7	13.6	23.1	56.0	7.5
1976	31.9	25.7	38.4	4.0	3.6	23.1	58.2	15.1	17.0	24.3	48.9	9.8
1981	39.7	28.3	27.3	4.7	6.8	22.4	50.4	20.5	18.8	24.5	42.0	14.7
1984	44.0	32.5	21.0	2.4	13.0	29.8	39.5	17.7	18.6	30.3	36.1	15.0

Sources: *Housing Statistics Great Britain*, 12;
Housing and Construction Statistics 1972 and *1974–84*.

had a heavy concentration of enumeration districts with the highest incidence of sharing, 56 per cent, though containing only 9 per cent of all urban enumeration districts in Great Britain. Other English conurbations also had disproportionately large numbers of the worst enumeration districts on many indicators of deprivation.[8]

Apart from inner city dwellers there is another group who have obviously not shared in the general improvement in housing standards – those who have no house at all. Homeless people have been regarded at different times as the responsibility of welfare or housing authorities, but in 1977 local housing departments were given the duty to provide accommodation for homeless households in certain priority groups. Since that time the number of house-holds accepted as homeless by the local authorities has risen by nearly 150 per cent to reach almost 90 000 and many more apply unsuccessfully for help (Table 12.7). This is the group with the most acute housing problem of all and the growing numbers reflect increasing unemployment and decreasing public spending.

Housing costs

Tables 10.27, 10.28 and 10.29 show the growth of government and local authority contributions to permanent housing since 1919 through direct subsidies. The direct subsidies do not, however, represent the total cost to public funds. The government foregoes tax revenue by allowing income tax relief on mortgage payments made by owner-occupiers for instance, which, as will be seen in the footnote to Table 10.27, amounted to far more in 1983–84 than central and local government subsidies to public housing.

Table 10.30 documents the rapid growth of building societies, who were lending money on about a quarter of a million new houses in 1938 and on over one and a half million in 1984. Their growth allowed the growth in home ownership already discussed. Figures for loans for house purchase from insurance societies are only available from 1966, and from local authorities from 1959 (Tables 10.31 and 10.32), but the number of loans and amounts lent from both sources are considerably less than the building society figures and have probably only been significant since 1960.

Perhaps the most difficult area to document in housing cost is that of the variation in rents during the century, and between different areas. Owing to the inflation of currency, the most satisfactory way of seeing trends in rent would be to show them as a proportion of household income. This has not been possible for the earlier years as we have explained in the discussion on sources. Only tentative information is available. From the 1905 survey it seems likely that approximately 13 per cent to 15 per cent of the head of household's income was spent on rent (including rates), and in the 1937–8 survey it was still approximately 15 per cent (using the 1938 average manual

Table 10.27   Cost[1] of housing subsidies, 1919–47, England and Wales, 1949–84, United Kingdom (£ millions)

| | Central government subsidies to: | | | |
Year	Local authorities	Public corporations and housing associations	Local authority subsidies to housing	Total public subsidies
England and Wales				
1919–20	0.2	—	0.5	0.7
1930–1	11.9	—	3.0	14.9
1936–7	14.0	—	3.8	17.8
1941–2	15.3	—	5.2	17.5
1946–7	17.5	—	7.0	25.5
United Kingdom				
1949–0	33.9	2.0	14.4	50.3
1952–3	43.6	2.7	18.8	44.4
1955–6	64.2	3.8	27.0	95.0
1958–9	71.5	4.3	29.0	104.8
1961–2	78.2	6.7	45.5	120.4
1964–5	88.6	8.6	52.7	149.9
1967–8[2]	121	13	69	203
1970–1	200	23	95	318
1973–4	299	44	89	432
1976–7	987	171	185	1343
1979–80	1533	311	413	2257
1982–3	567	346	582	1495
1983–4	474	395	651	1520

Notes:
1. Figures in this table do not include central government contributions to housing benefits and mortgage tax relief. In 1983–4 housing benefit payments amounted to £1665 million while mortgage interest relief at source (MIRAS), introduced in 1983, cost £2341 million.
2. Figures for 1967–84 not sufficiently exact to allow rounding to decimal points.
Sources: Ministry of Health *Annual Report* 1938–9;
    Annual Abstract of Statistics 1937, 1942, 1947, 1964, 1965, 1971, 1985;
    Local Government Financial Statistics 1919–47.

worker's weekly earnings given in the Ministry of Labour *Gazette*). However, Wendt[9] quotes the Political and Economic Planning Committee's unpublished housing report as estimating that, before the war, a working-class family spent approximately 12 per cent of its total income (that is including income of other family members) on rent, and this declined to 8 per cent or 9 per cent by 1950. It is not stated whether rates are included.

Table 10.33 shows the more detailed figures derived from the later surveys – mean and median rents (minus rates) as a proportion of head of household

Table 10.28   Improvements grants[1] for private
owners and housing associations,[2] 1959–84, England
and Wales

Year or period	No. of dwellings	Amount approved or paid (£000s)
1959	43 277	8 654
1960–4	385 753	64 514
1965–9	374 434	71 796
1970–4	713 200	389 715
1975–9	366 974	406 522
1980–4	779 105	2 283 394

Notes:
1. Up to 1970 includes discretionary grants approved and standard grants paid in respect of the dwellings by local authorities. After 1970 amounts are grants paid.
2. From 1981 figures include grants to tenants in both public and private sectors.

Sources: Housing Statistics Great Britain, 12;
Housing and Construction Statistics 17, 1974–1984.

Table 10.29   Improvement grants in selected years, 1951–79, England and Wales
(£thousand)

Year	Government contributions		Year	Local authority grants for private owners[1]	
	Local authority dwellings	Private owners		Discretionary[2]	Standard[3]
1951–2	1	1		—	—
1955–6	33	182		—	—
1960–1	345	2 478	1961	8 824	4107
1965–6	1 428	7 232	1966	7 353	5760
1970–1	4 200	13 100	1971	24 694	7830
1975–6	31 000	82 700	1976	67 460	4295
1978–9	31 200	101 000	1979	94 446	4987

Notes:
1. Includes some grants to housing associations.
2. Approved up to 1970 and paid from 1971.
3. Grants paid. Includes repairs and special grants for 1971, 1976 and 1979.

Sources: Housing Statistics Great Britain, 12;
Housing and Construction Statistics 31.

Table 10.30　Building societies:[1] number of mortgages and amount advanced annually, 1910–84, Great Britain

Year	Total advanced during year (£000s)	Total number of advances on mortgages during year	Total advanced on new mortgages (£000s)	Number of new mortgages
1910	9 292	—	—	—
1920	29 095	—	—	—
1930	88 767	159 348	- -	—
1938	137 020	232 294	—	—
1941	9 950	22 406	—	—
1950	269 717	302 145	—	—
1960	559 398	387 406	544 686	326 125
1966	1 244 750	535 512	1 204 200	444 170
1969	1 546 894	538 114	1 499 630	456 764
1972	3 618 588	887 740	3 445 937	672 928
1975	4 893 399	794 000	4 711 199	643 000
1978	8 795 122	1 181 000	8 251 348	820 000
1981	12 000 207	1 096 000	11 099 916	754 000
1984	23 769 900	1 657 700	21 958 800	1 119 900

Note:
1.　Societies with assets exceeding £1 million in 1969 and 1972, exceeding £2 million in 1975, 1978 and 1981, and exceeding £6 million in 1984.
Sources:　1910–66: *Annual Reports* of Chief Registrar of Friendly Societies, Part 5: *Building Societies*; Chief Registrar of Friendly Societies, *Statistical Summary of Building Societies*.
　　　　　1969–84: *Annual Reports* of Chief Registrar of Friendly Societies, Part 2: *Building Societies*.

Table 10.31　Loans for house purchase[1] by insurance societies, 1966–84, United Kingdom

Year	No. of dwellings	£(millions)
1966	—	147.0
1969	39 750	179.6
1972	24 750	149.0
1975	21 670	240.4
1978	16 960	202.2
1981	15 270	283.9
1984	16 470	387.1

Note:
1.　Up to 1976 amounts paid include some 'topping up' loans.
Sources:　British Insurance Association Sample Survey reported in:
　　　　　Housing Statistics Great Britain, 12.
　　　　　Housing and Construction Statistics 5, 1974–84.

Table 10.32   Housing loans by local authorities, 1959–84, England and Wales

Year	For house purchase[1]		Other housing loans[2]	
	Number of dwellings	£(millions)	Number of loans	£(millions)
1959	44 699	55.0	4 946	1.9
1960	47 864	67.0	10 928	3.3
1963	57 617	104.0	12 115	4.5
1966	46 229	109.0	18 791	9.9
1969	19 096	42.2	15 633	20.6
1972	45 202	132.9	35 031	57.7
1975[3]	101 952	636.1	42 948	157.0
1978	27 315	154.5	33 570	215.1
1981	4 050	34.6	15 845	159.7
1984	1 425	15.9	13 295	168.2

Notes:
1. To private persons.
2. To private owners for conversion, alterations, repairs or improvements; and to housing associations. Welsh authorities' power to approve new loans to housing associations was withdrawn in 1975 and loans (with prior approval) ceased during 1981.
3. Up to and including 1975 figures are for loans reported by local authorities during the period. Later figures are rounded estimates of loans made including adjustments for returns not received.
Sources: *Housing Statistics Great Britain*, 12;
         Housing and Construction Statistics 5, 20, 1974–84, 24.

and total household incomes. Divergence between the mean and the median reflects a skewed distribution formed by a small proportion of households with relatively very high housing expenditure. The proportion of mean rent to total household income seems to have remained fairly steady until 1982 when it increased by over 3 per cent, with private rents taking a slightly smaller proportion of incomes than local authority ones. Mortgage repayments represent a rather higher proportion of a generally higher income. Regional variations in the cost of houses over the past 15 years appear in Table 10.34. For England and Wales average prices have multiplied by six since 1969. The South-East has consistently had the highest prices and has also experienced the sharpest increase over the years, with the South-West in second place. Houses have been, and remain, considerably cheaper in the North and Midlands.

Table 10.33   Rents[1] or mortgage[2] payments as a proportion of head of household income[3] and of total household income (estimated),[4] 1967–82, Great Britain (percentages)

Rents/mortgage	Year	As percentage of head of household income		As percentage of total household income	
		Mean[5]	Median	Mean[5]	Median
Local authority rents	1967	11.9	10.3	8.2	7.2
	1970	13.6	11.0	9.5	7.7
	1972	13.5	10.0	9.4	7.0
	1974	12.4	10.0	9.0	7.0
	1976	10.9	8.6	8.1	5.9
	1978	11.2	9.0	8.3	6.0
	1980	12.3	9.0	9.0	7.0
	1982	16.7	14.0	12.6	10.0
Private rents	1967	11.4	9.1	8.6	6.8
	1970	11.8	9.1	9.4	6.9
	1972	11.4	9.0	8.9	7.0
	1974	10.4	7.0	8.1	6.0
	1976	10.4	7.5	8.0	5.5
	1978	10.6	8.0	8.6	5.0
	1980	11.0	9.0	8.9	6.0
	1982	14.4	11.0	11.5	8.0
Mortgage payments	1967	13.1	11.8	10.8	9.7
	1970	14.0	12.3	10.9	9.9
	1972	12.6	11.0	10.0	9.0
	1974	14.8	12.0	11.5	9.0
	1976	13.5	10.6	10.2	8.0
	1978	13.2	10.0	9.7	8.0
	1980	14.8	12.0	10.8	9.0
	1982	17.1	13.0	11.8	9.0

Notes:
1. Rents are exclusive of rates and service charges but water charges are included up to 1974. Sums received from subletting have been deducted.
2. Excluding endowment mortgage payments.
3. Incomes are gross. Since 1974 the income of an owner-occupier no longer includes a notional estimate (based on the rateable value of the dwelling) of income derived from ownership.
4. The estimates relate to a relatively small sample of households and some are subject to substantial sampling error. In the later years only selected tenures were surveyed, and thus the tables are not a complete coverage of all households.
5. The mean of the individual ratios: the average mortgage payment as a percentage of the average income would generally be lower.

Sources: Family Expenditure Surveys 1967–1982 reported in:
   Housing Statistics Great Britain 12;
   Housing and Construction Statistics, 2 (1972), 8 (1973), 15 (1975), 23 (1977), 31 (1979), 8 Part 2 (1981), 1973–83.

Table 10.34   Average dwelling prices[1] 1969–83, regions of England and Wales

Area	1969 (£)	1972 (£)	1975 (£)	1978 (£)	1981 (£)	1983[2] (£)
England	4674	7 529	11 935	15 618	24 589	28 500
North	3714	5 413	9 611	13 044	18 602	22 400
Yorks and Humberside	3436	4 880	9 013	12 099	19 202	22 000
North-West	3922	5 724	9 771	13 410	20 554	23 900
East Midlands	3791	5 621	9 989	12 810	19 465	23 200
West Midlands	4348	6 223	10 634	14 342	21 755	24 800
East Anglia	4298	7 031	11 909	13 968	23 060	27 100
South-West	4496	7 771	11 932	15 503	25 385	29 300
South-East (incl. Greater London)	5897	10 204	14 722	18 981	30 205	35 500[3]
Wales	4168	5 935	10 083	13 373	20 155	24 300

Notes:
1. Building Society mortgages on dwellings for owner-occupation. Variations in price do not necessarily indicate variations in price of comparable dwellings.
2. Excluding Local Authority sitting tenants.
3. Greater London 35 900, Rest of South-East 35 400.

Sources: *Regional Statistics*, 11 (1975);
              Regional Trends, 1980, 1983, 1985.

Notes

1. The extent of the reduction was also exaggerated by errors in enumeration, see *Social Trends*, Central Statistical Office, 1970, App. B, p. 167.
2. See Chapter 9, p. 341 *et seq.*, for shortcomings of indices of deprivation.
3. See Bernard Kilroy (1982) 'Public Expenditure on Housing', in Alan Walker (ed) *Public Expenditure and Social Policy* (Heinemann) for a comprehensive analysis of public spending on housing during the 1970s.
4. See Chapter 4, pp. 181–4 for changes in the cost of living index over the period, and Chapter 3, Tables 3.6, 3.7 and 3.8 for the disproportionate rise in housing expenditure.
5. See Chapter 9, pp. 340–5 for a discussion of urban deprivation and the inner city.
6. Figures from DoE, reproduced in *Faith in the City*, the report of the Archbishop of Canterbury's Commission on Urban Priority Areas (Church House, 1985), p. 19.
7. Figures from the DoE, reproduced in *Faith in the City*, p. 19.
8. Sally Holtermann, 'Areas of Urban Deprivation in Great Britain: an analysis of 1971 census data', *Social Trends*, no. 6 (CSO 1975).
9. P. F. Wendt (1962) *Housing Policy – the Search for Solutions* (University of California Press) p. 20.

Bibliography

BOARD OF TRADE (1908) *Enquiry by the Board of Trade into working class rents*, Cd 3864.

BOWLEY, M. (1945) *Housing and the State* (Allen & Unwin).

CENTRAL STATISTICAL OFFICE *Social Trends* (1970) no. 1.

Annual Abstract of Statistics, no. 84 (1935–1946) to date (HMSO).

Regional Statistics (formerly *Abstract of Regional Statistics*), annual publication to 1980, no. *11* (1975), *15* (1980).

Regional Trends (formerly *Regional Statistics*), annual publication from 1981 to date.

Welsh Social Trends, 1978 no. 2.

CHURCH HOUSE (1985) *Faith in the City*, The Report of the Archbishop of Canterbury's Commission on Urban Priority Areas.

CULLINGWORTH, J. B. (1965) *English Housing Trends*, Occasional Papers on Social Administration, no. 13 (Bell).

CULLINGWORTH, J. B. (1966) *Housing and Local Government in England and Wales* (Allen & Unwin).

DEPARTMENT OF THE ENVIRONMENT (DoE)

English House Conditions Survey 1976 (1978) part 1: *Report of the Physical Condition Survey*, Housing Survey Report no. 10 (HMSO).

English House Condition Survey 1981 (1982) part 1: *Report of the Physical Condition Survey*, Housing Report no. 12 (HMSO).

House Condition Survey 1971 (England and Wales) (1973) Housing Survey Report no. 9 (DoE).

Housing Policy Technical Volume (1977) part 1 (HMSO).

National Dwelling and Housing Survey 1978 (1979) (HMSO).

(Jointly with Scottish Development Department and Welsh Office)

Housing Statistics: Great Britain, quarterly from no. 20 (1971) to no. 24 (1972).

Housing and Construction Statistics, quarterly from no. 1 (1972) to no. 32 (1979), and no. 1 (part 1 and part 2 (1980) to date, annual publications 1971–81, 1972–1982, 1973–83, 1974–84.

(Jointly with Welsh Office)

Local Housing Statistics: England and Wales, published quarterly, no. 75 (1985), 76 (1986), 77 (1986).

GENERAL REGISTER OFFICE

Census reports of England and Wales.

General Report, England and Wales, 1901.

Housing Report, England and Wales, 1931.

Housing Report, England and Wales, 1951.

Housing Report, England and Wales, 1961.

Sample Census *Housing Report*, England and Wales, 1966.

GOVERNMENT SOCIAL SURVEY (earlier published by Central Office of Information)

The British Household by P. G. Gray (1947) unnumbered.

The Housing Situation in England and Wales in 1960, ss. 319.

The Housing Situation in England and Wales in 1964, ss. 372.

Scottish Housing 1965, by J. B. Cullingworth (1967) ss. 375 (undertaken for the Scottish Development Department).

HOLTERMANN, SALLY (1975) 'Areas of Urban Deprivation in Great Britain: an analysis of 1971 census data', *Social Trends*, no. 6 (CSO).

KILROY, BERNARD (1982) 'Public Expenditure on Housing,' in Alan Walker (ed.) *Public Expenditure and Social Policy* (Heinemann).
MINISTRY OF HEALTH   *Annual Reports*, part I, 1919 to 1952 inclusive. *Summary Report*, 1939–41.
MINISTRY OF HOUSING AND LOCAL GOVERNMENT (1964)
   Report for 1950–4; Annual Reports 1955 to 1964.
   Report for 1965–6.
   Handbook for Housing Statistics, 1965, 1966.
   Housing Returns for England and Wales, from 1946 monthly until 1948, then quarterly until 1966.
   Local Government Financial Statistics 1919–47.
(Jointly with Scottish Development Department and the Welsh Office)
   Housing Statistics Great Britain, quarterly from no. 2 (1966) – no. 19 (1970).
MINISTRY OF LABOUR (1940) *Labour Gazette*, December.
MINISTRY OF RECONSTRUCTION (1945) *Housing,* Cmnd 6609.
OFFICE OF POPULATION CENSUSES AND SURVEYS, LONDON
   Census reports of England and Wales.
   Housing Report, England and Wales, 1971.
   Housing and Household Report, England and Wales, 1981.
REGISTRY OF FRIENDLY SOCIETIES
   Annual Reports of the Chief Registrar (Great Britain).
   Part 5: *Building Societies* 1952–65.
   Statistical Summary: Building Societies.
   Part 2: *Building Societies* 1969–84.
WELSH OFFICE   *Welsh Housing Statistics*, annual publication no. 1 (1981) – no. 5 (1985) (HMSO).
WENDT, P. F. (1962) *Housing Policy – the Search for Solutions* (University of California Press).

11 Health

Klim McPherson and David Coleman

This chapter describes and analyses trends in physical health and the medical care of the physically ill. It depends upon three kinds of statistics: mortality rates and measures of prevalence of certain diseases as well as consultation rates; the supply of medical services in terms of institutions, doctors and nurses; and costs.

MORTALITY

Time series of deaths, and rates for different age and sex groups, are readily obtainable. It is more difficult to analyse death-rates by cause of death, over time, because definitions of diseases have changed and at different times different diseases have been classified in different ways. The Registrar-General uses the International List of Causes (revised in 1909 and subsequently), but for some time also gave tables using a short list of causes adopted in 1911 by his office and the Local Government Board. More recently the International Classification of Diseases (ICD) is used in its periodic revisions. We have therefore been selective, and show death-rates for particular diseases where definitions have not changed and which are, or were, important causes of death. Several annual publications of the Registrar-General (Office of Population Censuses and Surveys (OPCS) series DH), summary volumes in the same series, and more frequent *Monitors* give a complete statistical coverage. These and other medical data are summarised in the annual government publications, *Health Trends* (HMSO) and in the quarterly official journal and abstract *Population Trends* (HMSO).

We have not been able to show the changing distribution of death-rates by region or town, because boundary changes since 1900 make it very difficult to get consistent geographical areas for different dates. The reorganisation of the National Health Service in 1974 is a further, more recent, hindrance. Geographical variations at any one time can, however, be demonstrated; a decennial review has been published by the Registrar-General after every census since 1851.

General trends in mortality

The twentieth century has confirmed some long-term trends in mortality and begun some new ones. As with fertility, there is nothing particularly significant about the date 1900. None the less, the century as a whole has brought the

UK, and most other Western populations, close to the end of a mortality transition from high to low death-rates which began in the eighteenth century. There has been a correspondingly radical switch in the major causes of death and the ages at which most deaths occur. It should be mentioned straightaway that there is no evidence for any increase in natural life span – the peak age of mortality is still within a few years of what it was in 1841 (Benjamin and Overton, 1979).[3] What is apparent is the reduction of premature deaths and the development of a 'rectangular curve' of mortality where more and more deaths are concentrated at old age. In Britain, as in all developed societies, the twentieth century has seen the eclipse of classical infectious disease. Such diseases now account for a relatively trivial proportion of all deaths (less than 1 per cent). They have been replaced with diseases such as cancer and circulatory diseases which are much less tractable to modern preventive and curative medicine (see Table 11.1) and the burden of whose mortality is concentrated at older ages.

Mortality rates

Crude rates (Table 11.1) in mortality analysis are essential for the computation of rates of natural increase: that is, the excess of births over deaths. But they give no intuitive clue as to the magnitude of risk to the average individual, and are sensitive to changes in the age structure because of the very strong age-relation of mortality characteristic of all human populations, whatever their level of mortality (Table 11.2).

The expectation of life at birth, computed from age specific mortality rates, gives a better summary measure of the level and trend of mortality risks experienced by the population (Table 11.3). These have consistently shown higher death rates in the North and North-West for well over a century, for example. It is worth pointing out that Northern Ireland and Scotland have worse mortality levels than England and Wales (Table 11.4). Indeed, earlier this century female survival in Northern Ireland was scarcely superior to that of males – a pattern only found elsewhere in high mortality populations in the Third World. But Scottish rates have improved relative to those of England and Wales since the 1970s.

Another widely-used single index of mortality is the Standardised Mortality Ratio (SMR). Standardisation removes the effects of age structure by a comparison of actual deaths with those 'expected' on the hypothesis of constant age specific mortality rates (see Pollard, Yusuf and Pollard, 1981). The number of deaths 'expected' in each period are calculated by multiplying the population age-structure in each period by the reference, or standard, age specific mortality rates being used in comparison. The difference between the 'expected' deaths for each year and the actual number are expressed in proportion to those of the reference population set at 100, to allow an easy percentage comparison to be made (Table 11.1 shows this with reference population being that for 1950–52). All this 'indirect standardisation' tech-

Table 11.1 Deaths, death-rates and mortality comparisons, 1901–85 England and Wales

Period	Deaths			Crude rates per 1,000 living			Standardised[1] mortality ratios (1950–52 = 100)		
	Persons	Males	Females	Persons	Males	Females	Persons	Males	Females
1901–05	2 671 566	1 379 931	1 291 635	16.0	17.1	15.0	249	234	264
1906–10	2 577 208	1 326 425	1 250 783	14.7	15.6	13.8	221	208	234
1911–15[2]	2 598 719	1 344 171	1 254 548	14.3	15.4	13.3	205	195	215
1916–20[2]	2 589 333	1 340 340	1 248 993	14.4	16.5	12.8	190	180	199
1921–25	2 336 270	1 189 865	1 146 405	12.1	12.9	11.4	157	147	166
1926–30	2 386 721	1 217 610	1 169 111	12.1	12.9	11.4	145	137	153
1931–35	2 426 435	1 232 370	1 194 065	12.0	12.7	11.4	134	127	141
1936–40[2]	2 565 773	1 319 242	1 246 531	12.5	13.5	11.6	128	123	132
1941–45[2]	2 497 013	1 301 357	1 195 656	12.8	15.1	11.1	112	110	113
1946–50[2]	2 500 640	1 284 831	1 215 809	11.8	12.8	10.9	101	99	102

1951–55	2 571 153	1 325 747	1 245 406	11.7	12.5	10.9	97	98	95
1956–60	2 616 963	1 344 000	1 272 963	11.6	12.3	10.9	91	94	89
1961–65	2 766 372	1 415 447	1 350 925	11.8	12.4	11.2	90	95	87
1966–70	2 837 466	1 448 627	1 388 839	11.7	12.4	11.2	87	92	83
1971–75	2 914 762	1 474 783	1 439 979	11.9	12.4	11.4	85	89	81
1976–80	2 934 749	1 475 067	1 459 682	11.9	12.3	11.6	81	85	78
1985	590 734	292 327	298 407	11.8	12.0	11.7	–	–	–

Notes:

1. The standardised mortality ratio shows the number of deaths registered in the year of experience as a percentage of those which would have been expected in that year had the sex/age mortality of a standard period (1950–52) operated on the sex/age population of the year of experience.

2. For the years 1915–20 and from 3 September 1939 to 31 December 1949 for males, and from 1 June 1941 to 31 December 1949 for females, the mortality rates are based upon civilians only but, as in other years, the number of deaths include those of non-civilians registered in England and Wales.

Source: The Registrar-General's *Statistical Review for England and Wales for 1973, part I: Medical Tables. OPCS Mortality Statistics Serial Tables 1841–1980 Series DH1 No 15* (London: HMSO). OPCS Mortality Statistics 1985 Series DH1 No 17 (London: HMSO).

Table 11.2   Death rates per 1,000 population within sex and age groups, and infant mortality per 1,000 live births, 1901 to 1980, England and Wales

Period	All ages	Deaths under 1 year per 1,000 live births	1-4	5-9	10-14	15-19	20-24	24-34	35-44	45-54	55-64	65-74	75-84	85 and over
Males														
1901-05	17.1	151		3.68	2.14	3.20	4.39	5.89	9.74	17.0	32.4	65.3	137.6	274.6
1906-10	15.6	129		3.33	1.97	2.97	3.9	5.25	8.62	15.5	31.2	64.4	137.	283.0
1911-15¹	15.4	121		3.42	2.05	3.01	3.98	5.15	8.20	14.9	30.2	64.4	139.2	281.6
1916-20	16.5	101		3.81	2.41	3.91	6.60	8.58	9.07	14.0	27.9	62.0	139.4	267.8
1921-25	12.9	86		2.55	1.69	2.66	3.53	4.05	6.51	11.6	24.9	58.2	135.5	272.7
1926-30	12.9	77		2.48	1.61	2.58	3.30	3.68	6.18	11.6	24.4	58.3	135.4	298.4
1931-35	12.7	70	6.88	2.28	1.44	2.45	3.15	3.31	5.40	11.2	23.6	56.	135.2	278.8
1936-40¹	13.5	62	5.00	1.96	1.27	2.15	2.99	3.09	4.95	11.0	25.0	56.8	139.5	286.3
1941-45	15.1	56	3.72	1.69	1.20	2.22	5.00	4.16	4.81	9.85	23.1	51.7	121.6	226.4
1946-50	12.8	41	1.90	0.88	0.69	1.33	1.75	1.92	3.23	8.55	22.4	51.6	119.0	241.8
1951-55	12.5	30	1.23	0.55	0.48	0.86	1.23	1.39	2.71	7.93	22.5	54.6	126.7	265.8
1956-60	12.3	25	0.99	0.49	0.40	0.88	1.12	1.17	2.45	7.35	21.9	53.3	122.8	239.2
1961-65	12.4	23	0.94	0.47	0.41	0.95	1.11	1.11	2.46	7.38	21.7	54.0	121.3	253.2

1966–70	12.4	21	0.87	0.43	0.39	0.96	0.97	1.02	2.38	7.18	21.0	55.3	115.9	254.1
1971–75	12.4	19	0.75	0.39	0.35	0.88	0.99	0.97	2.22	7.22	20.2	51.4	116.3	242.4
1976–80	12.3	15	0.59	0.32	0.29	0.87	0.93	0.94	2.01	6.73	18.9	48.8	112.4	237.0
Females														
1910–05	15.0	124		3.79	2.24	3.02	3.66	5.04	8.05	13.1	25.4	54.8	119.9	249.4
1906–10	13.8	105		3.44	2.09	2.76	3.34	4.46	7.05	12.0	24.3	53.1	119.6	250.9
1911–15	13.3	97		3.37	2.11	2.75	3.25	4.08	6.46	11.4	22.7	51.7	117.5	254.4
1916–20	12.8	79		3.81	2.56	3.66	4.47	5.48	6.39	10.4	20.4	47.7	115.1	241.9
1921–25	11.4	66		2.41	1.72	2.56	3.11	3.59	5.03	8.79	18.7	45.5	112.9	241.2
1926–30	11.4	59		2.25	1.53	2.41	2.94	3.33	4.99	8.44	18.0	44.4	110.4	254.4
1931–35	11.4	54	6.23	2.07	1.37	2.22	2.77	3.09	4.33	7.96	17.0	42.8	108.9	245.0
1936–40	11.6	48	4.40	1.71	1.13	1.87	2.49	2.68	3.83	7.47	16.5	41.8	107.1	252.7
1941–45[1]	11.1	44	3.26	1.31	0.90	1.74	2.41	2.46	3.27	6.43	14.0	36.0	93.5	206.8
1946–50	10.9	32	1.62	0.64	0.54	1.05	1.54	1.76	2.56	5.51	12.8	34.4	93.2	208.9
1951–55	10.9	23	1.04	0.39	0.34	0.50	0.70	1.09	2.11	4.89	11.8	33.1	92.4	222.0
1956–60	10.9	20	0.82	0.33	0.27	0.38	0.52	0.81	1.83	4.46	10.9	36.7	86.4	212.5
1961–65	11.2	18	0.78	0.32	0.25	0.38	0.47	0.73	1.78	4.43	10.6	29.8	83.6	206.7
1966–70	11.2	16	0.70	0.28	0.25	0.39	0.44	0.65	1.68	4.34	10.3	28.0	77.5	203.0
1971–75	11.4	15	0.61	0.27	0.21	0.39	0.43	0.57	1.56	4.37	10.2	26.5	75.4	193.5
1976–80	11.6	12	0.48	0.22	0.20	0.34	0.40	0.56	1.39	4.11	9.11	25.3	70.8	192.8

Note: As Table 11.1, note 2
Source: OPCS Mortality Statistics Serial Tables 1841–1980 series DH1 No. 15 (London: HMSO).

Table 11.3 Expectation of life at birth and at ages of 1 year, 15 years, 45 years and 65 years, 1901 to 1982, England and Wales

Source	Year	Expectation of life at									
		Birth		Age 1		Age 15		Age 45		Age 65	
		Males	Females	Males	Females	Males	Females	Males	Females	Males	Females
(From English life tables)	1901–10	48.5	52.4	55.7	58.3	47.3	50.1	23.3	25.5	10.8	12.0
	1910–12	51.5	55.4	57.5	60.3	48.6	51.4	23.9	26.3	11.0	12.4
	1920–22	55.6	59.6	60.1	63.0	50.1	53.1	25.2	27.7	11.4	12.9
	1930–32	58.7	62.9	62.3	65.5	51.2	54.3	25.5	28.3	11.3	13.1
	1950–52	66.4	71.5	67.7	72.4	54.4	59.0	26.5	30.8	11.7	14.3
	1960–62	68.1	74.0	68.8	74.4	55.3	60.9	27.1	32.1	12.0	15.3
	1970–72	69.0	75.3	69.4	75.4	55.8	61.8	27.4	32.9	12.2	16.1
(From full life tables)	1972–74	69.2	75.6	69.6	75.7	56.0	62.0	27.6	33.1	12.3	16.3
	1973–75	69.5	75.7	69.8	75.8	56.2	62.1	27.7	33.2	12.4	16.4
	1974–76	69.6	75.8	69.8	75.8	56.2	62.1	27.8	33.2	12.4	16.4
	1975–77	69.9	76.0	70.0	76.0	56.4	62.3	27.9	33.3	12.5	16.5
	1976–78	70.0	76.2	70.1	76.1	56.5	62.4	28.0	33.4	12.5	16.6

1977–79	70.2	76.4	70.3	76.3	56.6	62.6	28.1	33.6	12.6	16.8
1978–80	70.4	76.6	70.4	76.4	56.8	62.7	28.3	33.7	12.8	16.8
1979–81*	70.8	76.9	70.7	76.7	57.0	63.0	28.5	33.9	12.9	17.0
1980–82	71.7	77.1	71.0	76.9	57.3	63.1	28.7	34.1	13.1	17.1
1981–83	71.3	77.4	71.2	77.1	57.5	63.3	28.9	34.2	13.2	17.3
1982–84	71.6	77.6	71.4	77.3	57.7	63.5	29.1	34.4	13.3	17.4
1983–85	71.8	77.7	71.6	77.4	57.9	63.6	29.2	34.5	13.4	17.5

Notes:

1. These life tables are provisional; mortality rates prior to 1961 are not precisely comparable to those of later years because the definition of the home population used for 1981 and 1982 differs from that used for previous years, and this affects the average for the periods 1979–81 and 1980–82.

2. A number of methodological changes were introduced into the construction of the life table from 1972–4. The most significant change is that the life table is compiled from mortality data by single years of age rather than the average for five-year age-groups (as in 'abridged' life tables compiled in previous years). Small differences between life tables based on the two methods should not be given too much prominence because differences can result from the methodological changes rather than fundamental changes in mortality.

Source: OPCS (1980) *Mortality Statistics* (London: HMSO).
OPCS (1987) Mortality Statistics 1985 Series DH1 no. 17 t. 22. (London: HMSO).

Table 11.4   UK expectation of life separately for England and Wales, Scotland, and Northern Ireland

English life table no.	Year	England and Wales		Scotland		N. Ireland	
		Expectation of life at birth					
		M	F	M	F	M	F
1	1841	40.2	42.2	—	—	—	—
2	1838–44	40.4	42.0	—	—	—	—
3	1838–54	39.9	41.9	—	—	—	—
	1861–70	—	—	40.3	43.9	—	—
4	1871–80	41.4	44.6	41.0	43.8	—	—
5	1881–90	43.7	47.2	43.9	46.3	—	—
6	1891–1900[1]	44.1	47.8	44.7	47.4	46.3	45.7
7	1901–10[2]	48.5	52.4	—	—	47.1	46.7
8	1910–12	51.5	55.4	50.1	53.2	50.7	51.0
9	1920–22[3]	55.6	59.6	53.1	56.4	55.4	56.1
10	1930–32[4]	58.7	62.9	56.0	59.5	57.8	59.2
	1945[5]	62.6	68.8	59.8	64.6	—	—
11	1950–52	66.4	71.5	64.4	68.7	65.5	68.8
	1955	67.5	73.0	—	71.8	—	—
12	1960–62[6]	68.1	74.0	66.1	72.6	—	—
	1965	68.5	74.7	66.5	73.0	67.9	73.5
	1969[7]	68.5	74.8	66.9	73.8	67.6	73.7
13	1970–72	69.0	75.3	67.5	73.8	67.2	73.6
	1972–74	69.2	75.6	67.2	73.7	67.2	73.5
	1973–75	69.5	75.7	67.4			

1974–76	69.6	75.8	67.8	74.3	66.8	73.7
1975–77	69.9	76.0	67.8	74.2	67.5	73.8
1976–78	70.0	76.2	68.3	74.6	67.8	74.1
1977–79	70.2	76.4	68.2	74.3	68.0	74.5
1978⁸–80	70.4	76.6	68.2	74.4	68.3	74.8
1979–81	70.8	76.9	68.7	75.1	68.8	75.1
1980–82	71.1	77.1	69.1	75.5	69.3	75.7
1981–83	71.3	77.4	69.2	75.3	69.8	76.0
1982–84	71.6	77.6	69.6	75.7	69.9	76.1
1983–85	71.8	77.7	69.9	75.9	70.1	76.4
1985	—	—	70.0	75.8	—	—

Abridged life tables

Notes:
1. 1890–92 ⎫
2. 1900–02 ⎬ Northern Ireland
3. 1925–27 ⎭
4. 1936–38
5. 1940–44 Scotland
6. 1961 Scotland
7. 1968–70 Northern Ireland
8. Scotland 1973 onwards: data for single years (central year of each group of three)

Sources: English data 1972–74 etc. from full life tables;
OPCS Mortality Statistics 1985 Series DH1 no. 17 t. 22 (London: HMSO);
Registrar General Scotland Annual Report 1985 table J1.1 (Edinburgh: HMSO);
Registrar General Northern Ireland Annual Report 1984 table V (Belfast: HMSO).

nique requires is total deaths at each period and the age structure at each period for the populations being compared, and a reference set of age specific rates.

Analysis of the rates for different age-groups shows that people under 45 have made the greatest proportionate gain, as would be expected (Table 11.2), but it is notable that the rates for older men – that is, over 55 – have decreased far less than those for older women. The fall in the infant mortality rate has been the most dramatic of all (Tables 11.5 and 11.6).

The changing importance of different diseases as causes of death may be seen from Table 11.7. Infectious illnesses are now very insignificant compared with 1900, while pneumonia, diseases of the heart, and cancer are all as important, or more important, than in the earlier years of the century. Infant mortality from infectious diseases and TB has now been almost eliminated, while congenital anomalies have become relatively more important and now account for one-third of all infant deaths (Table 11.8).

This can be seen to have been an important cause of the changing expectation of life at various ages. The expectation of the young has increased by over 20 years since 1900, but among the elderly the improvement is not so dramatic. This is a reflection of the increasing relative importance of life-threatening chronic diseases, which only become important during middle age. The principal causes of death are shown in Table 11.9 for the UK, and death-rates at selected ages in 1980 are shown in Figure 11.1.

Social, historical and demographic trends affecting mortality

The decline in mortality is generally regarded as a consequence of major social and economic trends: increase in real incomes, nutrition and housing; higher levels of education, a more interventionist state in welfare and income support; improvements in medicine and their wider availability to the population.

Neither the First or Second World War, nor the Depression, altered this decline in mortality in the UK. The advent of the National Health Service (NHS) after the Second World War appears to have accelerated it. In fact, the improvement in mortality from most conditions in infancy and at most other ages of life among the civilian population during the two World Wars is one of the more remarkable achievements of the century (Winter, 1985). The sharpened attention which food shortages gave to the balance and adequacy of the national diet appears to have more than compensated for shortages, deteriorating housing and for the absence of 40 per cent of the medical profession in the Royal Army Medical Corps (RAMC) in the First World War.

The continued improvement in mortality, especially infant mortality, during the depression years is more interesting, as wartime conditions no longer applied. Claims that infant mortality worsened during the depression (Brenner, 1975) appear to be misguided (Winter, 1983). The effects of unemploy-

Table 11.5   Infant mortality,[1] 1900–85, England and Wales

Year	Total live births	Deaths under 1 year	Rate per 1000 live births	Deaths under 4 weeks	Deaths under 1 week	No. of still-births[2]	Perinatal death-rate
1900	257 480	142 912	154	—	—	—	—
1910	267 721	94 579	105	—	—	—	—
1920	379 982	76 552	80	33 694	20 979	—	—
1930	648 811	38 908	60	20 060	14 267	27 577	62
1940	607 029	33 892	56	17 503	12 611	22 731	58
1950	697 097	20 817	30	12 917	10 606	16 084	38
1960	785 005	17 118	22	12 191	10 475	15 819	31
1970	784 486	14 207	18	9 661	8 326	10 345	23
1975	603 445	9 518	16	6 472	4 763	6 295	19
1980	656 234	7 899	12	5 323	4 042	4 773	13
1985	656 417	6 141	9	3 531	2 853	3 645	10

Notes:
1. Infant mortality rates are the number of deaths under one year per 1000 live births occurring in the year, except in the years 1931–56 when they were based on the related live births, that is, combined live births of the associated and preceding year to which they relate. Perinatal mortality rates are the number of deaths under one week plus stillbirths, per 1000 live and stillbirths.
2. Stillbirths not published until 1927.

Source: The Registrar-General's *Statistical Review for England and Wales*, part I, *Medical Tables*, for the relevant years up to 1970;
OPCS Mortality Statistics: Childhood and maternity 1976 Series DH3 no. 3;
OPCS Mortality Statistics: Childhood 1980 and 1985 Series DH3 nos. 8, 19;
OPCS Mortality Statistics Perinatal and Infant: Social and Biological factors. Series DH3 nos. 9, 19.

Table 11.6   Infant and perinatal mortality and live and stillbirth rates, 1901–85, England and Wales

Years	Deaths of infants under 1 year per 1000 live births			Perinatal mortality rates per 1000 total births	Live births per 1000 population	Stillbirth rates per 1000 total (live and stillbirths) births
	Total	Legitimate	Illegitimate			
1901–05	138	—	224	—	28.2	—
1906–10	117	113	210	—	26.3	—
1911–15	110	105	179	—	23.9	—
1916–20	90	85	140	—	21.5	—
1921–25	76	73	119	—	19.9	—
1926–30	68	65	103	—	16.7	—
1931–35	62	60	86	62.5	15.0	41
1936–40	55	54	71	59.2	14.9	38
1941–45	50	48	51	48.6	17.6	30
1946–50	36	36	34	39.8	18.4	24
1951–55	27	27	28	37.6	15.2	23
1956–60	23	22	26	34.9	16.4	21
1961–65	21	20	25	29.4	18.1	17
1966–70	18	18	23	24.6	16.9	14
1971–75	17	16	18	21.0	14.0	12
1976–80	13	13		15.6	12.4	9
1985	9	9	—	9.8	13.1	6

Notes: As for Table 11.5.
Source: OPCS Mortality Statistics Serial Tables 1841–1980 Series DH1 no. 15 t.1;
OPCS Mortality Statistics Perinatal and Infant: Social and Biological factors. Series DH3 no. 18.

Table 11.7 (a)   Standardised mortality ratios (base years 1950–52 taken as 100) 1901–78, England and Wales

Period	Tuberculosis (all forms)	Syphilis	Typhoid and paratyphoid fevers	Meningococcal infections	Cancer	Diabetes Mellitus	Diseases of the heart	Influenza	Pneumonia (all forms)	Peptic ulcer
1901–10	649	—	23 581	—	—	156	—	254	—	—
1911–20	541	—	8 926	246	—	162	—	605	—	90
1921–30	362	—	2 729	157	—	154	—	345	—	99
1931–39	245	—	1 180	343	97	176	—	222	—	110
1940–49	196	150	387	355	98	129	91	90	125	102
1950–59	60	80	59	82	101	88	94	69	105	93
1960–64	21	53	23	40	103	92	90	38	130	72
1965	16	51	44	34	104	98	87	9	128	63
1970	11	—	—	44	107	102	83	78	104	57
1975	9	—	14	55	110	105	82	15	180	62
1980	6	—	9	27	112	97	77	5	193	57

Source: The Registrar-General's *Statistical Review for England and Wales*, part 1, *Medical Tables*.

Table 11.7 (b) Death rates per million population at ages under 15 years

Period	Scarlet fever	Diphtheria	Whooping cough	Poliomyelitis	Measles
1901–10	271	571	815	—	915
1911–20	123	437	554	13	838
1921–30	64	298	405	11	389
1931–39	46	290	197	11	217
1940–49	7	112	111	11	62
1950–59	neg	1	17	9	13
1960–64	neg	neg	3	1	7
1965	neg	—	2	2	11
1970	—	—	1	—	3
1975	—	0	1	—	1
1978	—	—	1	—	2

Source: The Registrar-General's Statistical Review for England and Wales, part 1, Medical Tables.

Table 11.8   Death rate under 1 year per 1000 live births from various causes, 1891–1980, England and Wales

Cause of death	1891–1900	1910	1920	1930	1940	1950	1960	1970	1980
All causes	153.33	105.44	79.93	59.97	55.83	29.99	21.80	18.19	12.04
Common infectious diseases[1]	10.0	7.22	4.20	3.13	2.76	0.48	0.04	—	—
Tuberculous diseases[2]	7.92	3.91	1.47	0.90	0.59	0.17	0.01	—	—
Diarrhoea and enteritis[3]	27.05	12.64	7.98	5.43	4.37	1.65	0.44	—	—
Congenital, developmental and wasting diseases[4]	44.44	40.46	32.45	28.31	24.99	16.04	14.72	3.60[6]	3.22[6]
All other categories[5]	63.89	41.21	33.83	22.21	23.11	11.75	6.55	14.59[7]	8.82[7]

Notes:
1. Smallpox, chicken-pox, measles, scarlet fever, diphtheria, croup, whooping cough.
2. Tuberculosis – all forms.
3. All forms of diarrhoea, enteritis and gastritis.
4. Prematurity, congenital defects, starvation, debility, birth injury.
5. Remainder – including erysipelas, syphilis, meningitis, bronchitis, pneumonia, accidents and lack of care. See p. cxi of supplement to the 65th Annual Report of the Registrar-General, Part I, 1891–1900 for lists of causes in each category. For 1950 onwards we have grouped causes according to the above categories.
6. Congenital anomalies alone.
7. All causes except congenital.
Source: The Registrar-General's Annual Reports, and the Registrar-General's Statistical Review for England and Wales, part I, Medical Tables, for the relevant years; Mortality Statistics: Childhood (HMSO, 1980).

Table 11.9 Deaths by cause – England and Wales 1982, Scotland 1981 and Northern Ireland, 1980 (general causes and selected specific causes)

Cause	ICD	England and Wales				Scotland (%)		N Ireland (%)	
		M No.	(%)	F No.	(%)	M	F	M	F
All Causes	001–999	290 166	100.0	291 695	100.0	100.0	100.0	100.0	100.0
Circulatory system	390–459	139 717	48.2	144 529	49.5	50.6	53.5	51.5	53.6
Ischaemic heart disease	410–414	88 716	30.6	65 889	22.6	32.4	25.5	32.8	24.5
Acute myocardial infarction	410	62 157	21.4	42 256	14.8	26.4	19.6	24.0	19.1
Pulmonary circulation etc.	415–429	12 449	4.3	19 810	6.8	3.6	5.3	5.6	7.8
Cerebrovascular disease	430–438	26 235	9.0	42 793	14.7	11.1	17.6	9.8	16.8
Cerebral infarction	433,434	5 835	2.0	9 924	3.4				
Cancers	140–236	70 026	24.1	62 422	21.4	23.3	20.9	17.9	18.4
Trachea, Bronchus, Lung	162	25 962	8.9	8 870	3.0	9.5	3.5	5.9	1.9
Female breast	174		–	12 405	4.3	–	3.7	–	3.6
Genito-urinary organs	179–189	9 759	3.4	9 612	3.3	3.0	3.1	2.4	2.4
Cervix uteri	180		–	1 932	0.7	–	0.6	–	0.4
Other uterus	179,182		–	1 577	0.5	–	0.3	–	0.4
Ovary	183		–	3 577	1.2	–	1.1	–	0.9
Prostate	185	5 291	1.8		–	1.5	–	1.3	–
Bladder	188	2 968	1.0	1 275	0.4	0.9	0.5	0.6	0.3
Lymphatic (leukaemias)	200–208	4 215	1.5	3 749	1.3	1.2	1.2	1.4	1.3
Stomach	151	5 978	2.1	4 233	1.5	1.9	1.5	1.9	1.6

Cause	ICD								
Respiratory system	460–519	43 652	15.0	44 459	15.2	10.9	9.6	13.7	13.0
Pneumonia	480–488	22 611	7.8	33 918	11.6	4.9	6.6	6.7	9.1
Influenza	487	256	0.1	460	0.2	0.1	0.1	0.1	0.2
Chronic obstructive pulmonary disease	490–496	18 582	6.4	8 018	2.7	5.1	2.4	5.3	2.5
Bronchitis, emphysema, asthma	490–493	13 124	4.5	5 750	2.0	3.2	1.5	3.7	1.8
Injury and Poisoning	800–999	11 572	4.0	8 038	2.8	5.6	4.1	7.3	4.7
Motor-vehicle traffic accidents	E810–E819	3 684	1.3	1 557	0.5	1.6	0.6	2.4	0.9
Suicide	E950–E959	2 781	1.0	1 498	0.5	1.0	0.6	0.6	0.3
Homicide	E960–E969	178	0.1	167	0.1	0.2	0.1	0.7	0.1
	E980–E989	949	0.3	724	0.2	0.4	0.2	0.2	0.2
War	E990–E999	—	—	—	—			0.6	—
Infectious Diseases	001–139	1 138	0.4	978	0.3	0.5	0.4	0.4	0.4
Tuberculosis, respiratory	010–012	311	0.1	143	<0.1	0.1	0.1	0.2	0.1
Tuberculosis late effects	137	110	0.1	76	0.1				
Septicaemia	038	224	<0.1	248	<0.1	0.1	0.1	0.0	0.1

Source: OPCS (1983) *Monitor* DH2 83/84;
Registrar-General, Scotland (1982) Annual Report 1981, table C1.1 Edinburgh, HMSO
Registrar-General, Northern Ireland (1982) Annual Report 1980, Abstract 20, Belfast, HMSO

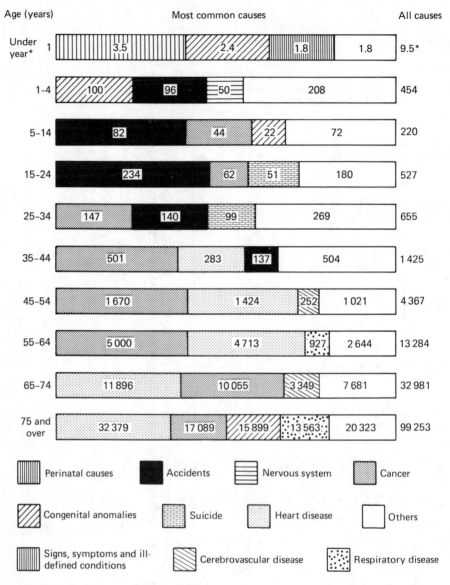

Figure 11.1   Main causes of death in each age-group, with death-rates per million
             population, 1985.

Source: OPCS Monitor DH2 86/2 Deaths by Cause, 1985. Fig. 4, (London, OPCS)

ment on mortality are, in fact, notoriously difficult to estimate (Stern, 1983) because of the two-way nature of the relationship, although it is not surprising that there is some evidence for worsened health in some of the large number of unemployed at present, most of whom have not, of course, become unemployed through ill health (Moser, Fox and Jones, 1985). The underlying trend in incomes, the decline in family size, improvement in hygienic knowledge and clinical practice seems none the less to have sustained continuous improvement in mortality in the population as a whole, both in the depression years and in the present high level of unemployment.

Infant mortality

Infant mortality has fallen throughout the century, starting about 1910 after little change in the nineteenth century. Smaller family size, improvements in midwifery, better knowledge of child care among mothers, and improved hygienic conditions in towns, are thought to be particular factors which helped start the decline at the beginning of this century. Most infant deaths were post-neonatal, associated with gastrointestinal infection. The influence of socialised medicine after the Second World War, together with the chance to use the new specifically curative drugs against bacterial disease (penicillins and the sulpha drugs) – the availability of which had been improved by the war – accelerated the pace of infant mortality decline for several years even though the increase in lung cancer and coronary thrombosis depressed improvements in adult mortality. Infant mortality continues to improve up to the present: the pace of change is much influenced by more effective intensive care and surgical and clinical practice for vulnerable babies. The social composition of the population and of birth cohorts is also becoming more favourable to lower mortality. Nowadays relatively fewer babies are born into larger families – the reversal of the position at the beginning of the century, which may have helped to explain the persistence then of high infant mortality rates. The trend in breast feeding is becoming more favourable (Martin and Monk, 1982). Relatively more babies are born into lower-risk middle-class families, partly as a result of a general shift in the occupational distribution away from manual work and also more effective and acceptable contraception. But higher risk births to women from the New Commonwealth now comprise 8 per cent of all births. Even so, Britain's place in the international infant mortality league table has deteriorated, a development of controversial significance (Short Report, 1980; Chalmers, 1983). Most infant mortality is now perinatal; associated with prematurity and congenital malformations. Forty per cent of post-neonatal deaths now fall under the 'cot death' or 'sudden infant death' syndrome which was not even specifically identified in the first edition of this book.

Mortality of children and young adults

Death rates in childhood, always the lowest in any human population, are now so low that further improvements are difficult to make and would in any case have little demographic consequence. Most deaths of older children and young adults now arise from accidents (particularly road accidents) and from premature forms of cancer such as leukaemia. The increase in this cause at all ages has been attributed to the liberal use of medical X-rays in the past; claims that low-level nuclear radiation from artificial sources is to blame are highly controversial. Although it cannot be ruled out, it has certainly not been demonstrated (NRPB, 1986). Only at adolescence and young adulthood are death rates low enough for suicide and violence to make any statistical impact (Figure 11.1). Road deaths have prevented much recent improvement in young adult mortality, which is much higher in males than in females.

Mortality in middle life and old age

Beyond these ages the improvements in age specific mortality rates are progressively less striking. Cervical cancer, associated with the sexual behaviour of women and/or their partners, and early deaths from lung cancer from smoking, are increasing causes of death among women in their 30s. Both are avoidable; and the former is curable, if diagnosed in its pre-cancerous state by cervical smear. In the 1980s 75 per cent of all deaths occur at over age 65 (compared to 34 per cent in the 1920s). In middle and old age most deaths are accounted for by circulatory disease, cancer, and chronic respiratory failure (bronchitis, emphysema and asthma). These are diseases characteristically associated with old age or with long-term exposure to damaging influences from behaviour or environment. These causes are by far the most important overall (51 per cent, 21 per cent and 14 per cent of all deaths, respectively). Some of the cancers (probably liver and cervical) and many of the pneumonias are caused by infectious organisms. But most of the latter are a consequence of an aged immune system in an individual terminally weakened by other conditions, rather than a primary cause of death.

Trends in mortality by social class

Social class differences in mortality are shown in Table 11.10. It is notable that males in the highest class have the lowest mortality rate up to 1932, but the third highest in the years 1949–53. During this later period class II had the most favourable rate and class V the worst – a position it has held consistently. The divergence from the norm for class V was, however, less than half what it had been in 1910–12, though rather more than the difference in 1930–32. Problems of interpretation arise from the changing definitions and from social restructuring itself. The Black Report, however, leaves little room for com-

Table 11.10 Mortality by social class: standardised mortality ratios[1] for men aged 20–64 from all causes 1910–12 to 1982–83 (percentages)

	1910–12[2,3]	1921–23	1930–32	1949–53	1949–53[4]	1959–63 unadjusted	1959–63 adjusted[5]	1970–72 unadjusted	1970–72 adjusted[5]	1979–80, 1982–83[6]	1976–81
Class I	88	82	90	98	86	76	75	77	75	66	66
Class II	94	94	94	86	92	81	—	81	—	76	77
Class III	96	95	97	101	101	100	—	99 (IIIN) 106 (IIIM))	—	94 (IIIN) 106 (IIIM)	105 (IIIN) 96 (IIIM))
Class IV	93	101	102	94	104	103	—	114	—	116	109
Class V	142	125	111	118	118	143	127	137	121	165	124

Notes: The table excludes non-civilians.

1. Standardised mortality ratio can be defined as the number of deaths registered in a standard period within a given social class grouping ages 20–64, as a percentage of the number that would have occurred if the death rates in each separate age-group in the social class groupings had been the same as in a standard population consisting of all males in England and Wales.

2. In 1910–12 for ages 25–65 inclusive, other years for ages 20–64 inclusive.

3. In 1910–12 miners, textile and agricultural workers were not included in the social class groupings. In 1930–32 minor changes were made in the classification of occupations into social class groupings. For the period 1949–53 there were some further changes in assignments of occupations to the social class groupings. The following table shows the 1949–53 figures grouped according to the classification of 1951 and the 1931 classifications.

4. Corrected figures as published in 'Registrar-General's *Decennial Supplement, England and Wales, 1961: Occupational Mortality Tables*' (London: HMSO) 1971: 22.

5. Occupations in 1959–63 and 1970–72 have been reclassified according to the 1950 classification.

6. Data from 1979–80, 1982–83 Decennial Supplement, based on 1980 Classification of Occupations. The Decennial Supplement warns that the social class data should not be regarded as reliable, especially for Class V which are exaggerated by bias (see Ch. 4).

7. Data from OPCS Longitudinal Study, ages 15–64 (see Fox, A. J. and Goldblatt, P. O. (1982) *Longitudinal Study: socio-demographic mortality differentials 1971–75* (London: HMSO).

Source: *The Black Report: Inequalities in Health* (1982) ed. Townsend, P. and N. Davidson. OPCS 1986 Occupational Mortality Decennial Supplement 1979–80, 1982–83 Series DS no. 6 Appendix IV (London HMSO); Fox, A. J., Jones, D. R., Moser, K. and Goldblatt P. O. 1985 'Socio economic diferential in mortality'. *Population Trends 40.*

Table 11.11 Standardised mortality ratio for women from all causes, 1930–32 to 1979–83, England and Wales

Class	1930–32[1] Married	1930–32[1] Single	1949–53[1] Married	1949–53[1] Single	1971–75[2] Married	1971–75[2] Single	1979–80, 82–83[1] Married	1979–80, 82–83[1] Single
All occupied and re-tired	100	100	100	100	100	100[2]	100	100
Class I	81	100	96	82	72	83	76	72
Class II	89	64	88	73	88	72	84	69
Class III N					94		93	80
M	99	95	101	89	98	111	110	110
Class IV	103	102	104	89	119		125	105
Class V	113	112	110	92	117	90	157	121
Unoccupied	134	122	95	142	144	161	49	208

Notes:

1. For ages 20–64 inclusive, married women classified by husband's social class.

Source: *Decennial Supplement* to the Registrar-General's *Statistical Review for England and Wales*, part II, *Occupational Mortality*;
OPCS 1986 Occupational Mortality 1979–80, 1982–83 Decennial Supplement, Series DS no. 6.

2. For ages 15–74 inclusive, married women classified by husband's social class.

Source: Fox, A. J. and Goldblatt, P. O. (1982) *Longitudinal Study. Socio-Demographic Mortality Differentials* (1971–75) (London: HMSO).

placency. The figures for women (Table 11.11) are more limited, but suggest a worsening in the relative position of married women and an improvement in that of single women in class I. Women in class V have the highest mortality rates apart from those described as unoccupied. Single unoccupied women were particularly vulnerable from 1949–53. Table 11.12 shows an analysis from the Black Report which indicates a progressive worsening of the relative position of the lower social classes among both sexes and at all ages since then.

Analysis of cause of death shows class V to suffer particularly from bronchitis and tuberculosis (TB) and relatively less from cancer, though the rate of deaths from this cause is still the highest in all social classes (Logan; Figure 11.2). Detailed analysis of recent trends, in particular death-rates, indicates a continuing change in the patterns of mortality by sex and dominant causes. Lung cancer, for instance, is increasing only among women but the social class differences among men continue to diverge (Table 11.13). Breast cancer is an increasingly important cause of death among women, indeed it is the most important cause among middle-aged women. However, Figure 11.4 shows that higher social classes suffer more than others, although this effect appears to be converging.

The drop in infant mortality for all the classes is apparent from Table 11.14, but in spite of a decrease of 50 per cent or more, the rate for class V in 1949–53 was still higher than it was for class I in 1921–3. The position of class V, in relation to the average, worsened between 1921 and 1953. More recent trends show no improvement in their relative position.

Table 11.15 reproduces a recent analysis from the 1981 Census and *Decennial Supplement* (1979–83), indicating a further deterioration in the relative position of manual workers in terms of their risk of death from all causes and for three of the most dominant causes. This will undoubtedly be a major concern of epidemiological and social research for the remainder of the twentieth century, particularly as the health and relative mortality of the unemployed attracts more research. Figure 11.5 shows that regional variations in mortality are not entirely explained by social composition.

In particular, as is normal in controversies of this kind, the debate becomes polarised around the issue of innate vulnerability versus environmental influence. It is also coherently argued that apparent social class differences in mortality experience, at least in part, can be attributed to (a) artefacts of coding both of occupation at death and occupational assignment to a particular social class; (b) differential social mobility, downwards of the less robust and upwards of the more robust; (c) changing meaning of a particular classification with time, thus class V defines a different social group in 1980 than it did in 1950. These latter problems have been extensively discussed by Fox *et al.* (1985). The hereditary argument has been forcefully made by Himsworth (in relation to childhood mortality) and discussed by Chalmers (1985). More recently Hart (1986) gives support to the argument of the Black report, which cites environmental influences as the strongest determinant of

Table 11.12 Mortality rates per 100 000, and as percentage of rates for occupational classes I and II (men and married women) 1951–71, England and Wales

Occupational class	Age	Men (rates per 100 000)			Married women (rates per 100 000)		
		1949–53	1959–63	1970–72	1949–53	1959–63	1970–72
I and II	25–34	124	81	72	85	51	42
III		148	100	90	114	64	51
IV and V		180	143	141	141	77	68
I and II	35–44	226	175	169	170	123	118
III		276	234	256	201	160	154
IV and V		331	300	305	226	186	193
I and II	45–54	712	544	554	427	323	337
III		812	708	733	480	402	431
IV and V		895	842	894	513	455	510
I and II	55–64	2 097	1 804	1 710	1 098	818	837
III		2 396	2 218	2 213	1 202	1 001	1 059
IV and V		2 339	2 433	2 409	1 226	1 229	1 131
		(as per cent I and II)			*(as per cent I and II)*		
I and II	25–34	100	100	100	100	100	100
III		119	123	125	134	125	121
IV and V		145	177	196	166	151	162
I and II	35–44	100	100	100	100	100	100
III		122	134	151	118	130	131
IV and V		146	171	180	133	151	164
I and II	45–54	100	100	100	100	100	100
III		114	130	132	112	124	128
IV and V		126	155	161	120	141	151
I and II	55–64	100	100	100	100	100	100
III		114	123	129	109	122	127
IV and V		112	135	141	112	138	135

Source: (1982) *The Black Report*.

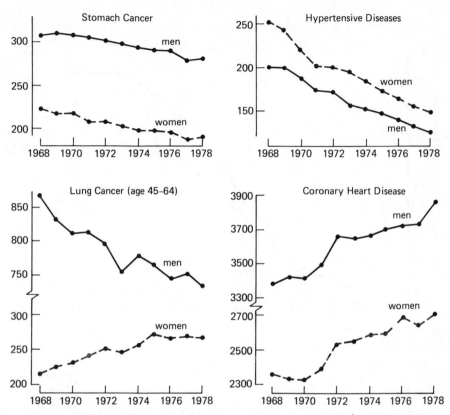

Figure 11.2   Changes in mortality for selected causes, England and Wales, 1968–78
(death-rates per million population)

Source: OPCS Mortality statistics, London HMSO, annually – Series D111.

life chances and argues that the social class gradient (notwithstanding these other considerations) is widening.

The major causes of death: circulatory disease, cancers and chronic lung disease

The emergence of cancer and circulatory disease deaths as the prime causes of mortality in the twentieth century also provokes much argument. To some extent their predominance as causes of death in older age follows the lifting of the burden of mortality at younger ages caused by the decline of tuberculosis, diphtheria and other infectious diseases. But circulatory disease and cancer mortality also has a dynamics of its own (Marmot, Booth and Beral, 1981), as the trend in social class differentials clearly shows (Logan 1976). To what extent should they be regarded as inevitable consequences of an affluent way of life, or of the fundamental process of ageing, or are they in part avoidable

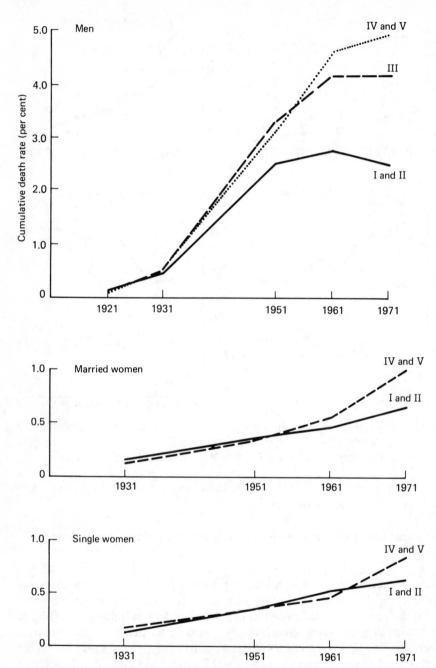

Figure 11.3   Lung cancer: cumulative death-rate per cent, ages 25–64, by social class groups.

Source: W. P. D. Logan (1976). *Cancer mortality by occupation and social class 1851–*

Table 11.13 Standardised mortality ratios for certain diseases for males aged 20–64 inclusive, 1910–72 (1910–12 aged 25–64 inclusive), England and Wales

Cause of death	Period	Social class				
		I	II	III	IV	V
All causes	1910–12	88	94	96	93	142
	1921–23	82	94	95	101	125
	1930–32	90	94	97	102	111
	1949–53	98	86	101	94	118
	1970–72	77	81	104	114	137
Respiratory TB	1910–12	86	87	109	92	152
	1921–23	49	84	98	100	140
	1930–32	61	67	100	104	125
	1949–53	58	63	102	95	143
	1970–72	26	47	173	124	254
Cancer	1910–12	99	91	101	96	131
	1921–23	80	92	99	96	123
	1930–32	83	92	99	102	115
	1949–53	94	86	104	95	113
	1970–72	75	80	204	116	131
Bronchitis	1910–12	41	68	95	98	184
	1921–23	27	55	94	120.	176
	1930–32	31	56[2]	92[2]	135[2]	156
	1949–53	34	53	98	101	171
	1970–72[1]	36	51	195	128	188

Notes:
1. In years 1970–72 'bronchitis' category includes asthma and emphysema.
2. These figures were read from a diagram and are therefore approximate.
Source: *Decennial Supplement* to the Registrar-General's *Statistical Review for England and Wales*, 1921, part II, *Occupational mortality, fertility and infant mortality*; 1931, part II, *Occupational mortality*; 1951, *Occupational mortality*, part II, vol. 1, commentary and vol. 2, tables.

consequences of an unsatisfactory personal environment or lifestyle? Until the 1960s death rates from these causes appeared to be increasing or at least not improving. More recently, as death rates have declined in the USA and to a lesser extent in the UK and other European countries, the view has gained ground that many of these premature deaths are preventable (Doll and Peto, 1975; Preston, 1982).

In the USA, whose death-rates from coronary artery disease once led the world, mortality has fallen by over a quarter since the 1950s. Many other

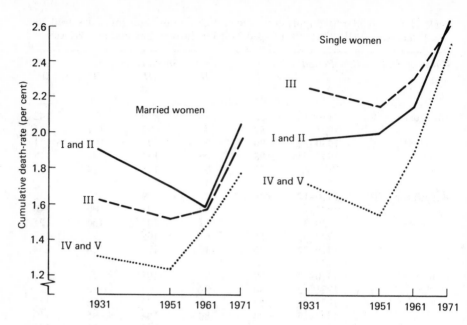

Figure 11.4   Breast cancer: cumulative death-rate per cent at ages 25–64, by social class group

Source: As Figure 11.3.

Western countries are following this example. But in Britain the trend in heart disease is only improving slowly, especially in social classes I and II (Ball and Purcell 1984). In those countries where smoking has not declined, where unsatisfactory diet persists and where drinking continues to increase, for example in Eastern Europe, and particularly in the Soviet Union, mortality trends from lung cancer and heart disease have been reversed: in these countries death-rates have been going up since the 1970s (Feshbach, 1982; Compton, 1985).

In the UK there is little to be pleased about as death-rates, especially from circulatory disease, are among the highest in the Western world (Table 11.16), with Scotland and Northern Ireland out in front (see also Table 11.9). In recent years the role of smoking in lung cancer and circulatory disease has been conclusively established. But the role of diet and exercise in the explanation of levels of heart disease (Committee on Medical Aspects of Food Policy 1984) and cancer and of their striking differences by social class and geographical origin still lacks the same quality of prescriptive evidence (Cummins, 1981).

A number of other major sources of mortality are also declining in mortality rate and in incidence – notably stomach cancer and stroke (see Figure 11.2). The former may be due to the much maligned preservatives in food, eliminat-

Table 11.14 Infant mortality rate (legitimate) by social class of father, 1921–81, England and Wales

Social class	1921–23	1930–32	1949–53	1964–65	1970–72	1976	1979	1981
				Rate per 1000 legitimate live births				
I	38	33	19	12.7	11.6	9.4	9.8	7.7
II	55	45	22		13.6	10.5	9.7	7.9
IIIN }	77	58	29	17.2	14.5	11.2	9.8	8.5
IIIM }					17.0	12.9	11.4	10.3
IV	89	67	34	20.8	19.6	13.3	14.3	12.6
V	97	77	41		30.7	22.3	18.7	18.8
All classes[1], including unemployed	79	62	30	17.5	17.7	13.3	11.8	10.2

Notes: Changes in classification of occupations as in previous tables.
1. After 1970 'all' includes illegitimate children.

Sources: *Decennial Supplement* to the **Registrar-General**'s *Statistical Review for England and Wales*, 1921, 1931, 1951;
  Studies on medical and population subjects, no. 19;
  Social Trends (1985) Table 7.2.

Table 11.15 SMRs for selected causes in Great Britain among men aged 20–64, for 1970–72 and 1979–83, categorised by manual or non-manual

Category	1970–72				1979–83			
	All causes	Lung cancer	Coronary heart disease	Strokes	All causes	Lung cancer	Coronary heart disease	Strokes
Manual	129	150	113	148	116	129	114	120
Non-manual	99	87	102	118	80	65	87	76
Manual/non-manual	1.30	1.72	1.11	1.25	1.45	1.98	1.31	1.58

Notes:
1. For each cause the Standardised Mortality Ratio (SMR) for 1979–83 is 100. The 1970–72 figures are standardised to the 1979–83 rates.
2. Categorisation by manual and non-manual is to overcome biases due to occupation description inconsistencies at death and at the 1981 Census.

Source: Marmot, M. G. and McDowall, M. E. (1986) 'Mortality Decline in Widening Social Inequalities', *Lancet*, ii: 274.

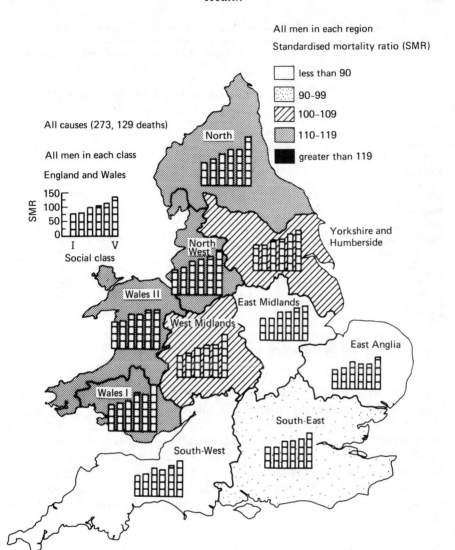

Figure 11.5 Mortality by social class and region: men aged 15–64, England and Wales.

Source: OPCS (1978) DS no. 1, fig. 8.7, p. 180.

Table 11.16   Cardiovascular disease – international comparisons

| | Persons aged 35–74 (death-rates per 100 000 1976–77) | |
| | M | F |
	Age-adjusted, US pop. 1940, ratio to E + W rate = 100)	
USA		
White	94	86
Non-white	118	166
Canada	87	79
Denmark	81	73
Norway	77	68
Sweden	75	67
Netherlands	73	67
England and Wales	100	100
Northern Ireland	124	132
Scotland	120	133
Belgium	84	86
France	57	55
FRG	82	82
Switzerland	63	61

Source: Computed from Wunsch and Lambert, 1981, Table 3.

ing many natural carcinogens generated by the decay of food. Although surgery and chemotherapy can provide complete remission of some cancers, many are still beyond cure once contracted. Cancer survival rates (as opposed to incidence) have only improved dramatically in a few conditions such as childhood leukaemias (OPCS (1981) *Cancer Statistics*). In these respects we know more about cancers than circulatory disease, because a national cancer registration system was set up in 1969, which enables records to be linked to subsequent mortality, or other life events, through the Longitudinal Study (LS).

The role of medicine

The role of medicine in the decline of mortality in the nineteenth and twentieth centuries is controversial (McKeown, 1976; Szreter, 1986; Keynes, Coleman and Dimsdale (in press)). The demographic impact of curative medicine has primarily been in mopping up the remaining infectious bacterial diseases after the Second World War. Although some diseases could be prevented by immunisation at the beginning of the century (for example, diphtheria, and smallpox since the eighteenth century) specific cures for bacterial diseases were not developed before the 1930s (sulpha drugs, antibiotics). Viral diseases remain incurable once contracted. Only a few hundred of these preventable deaths now occur each year. Prodigies of surgery and intensive care now save thousands of lives from accidents, prematurity or weakness caused by other conditions which in previous years would have been lethal. Primary preventive medicine has been more important than cure; eliminating or greatly reducing most serious viral conditions including the emergent twentieth century epidemic of poliomyelitis. Prevention can apply to accidental death as well. The worse carnage on the road was in the 1930s before the introduction of the driving test. Compulsory crash helmets for motorcyclists, seat belts, do seem to have reduced road traffic deaths among motorists and the gloomy critics' claim, that deaths among cyclists and pedestrians would increase to compensate as seat belts encourage more risky driving, has not been fulfilled.

Smoking and other habits

The late twentieth century resembles the late nineteenth and early twentieth century in the sense that mortality, now as then, is dominated by conditions incurable directly, but possibly avoidable by life-style. The single most important adverse mortality factor since 1900 has been the rise in cigarette smoking – effectively an invention of the twentieth century. Undoubtedly, this is a habit of affluence but not an inevitable part of it. It began at the beginning of the century among upper-class men. Cheap cigarettes and two World Wars made it standard among working-class men; women took up the habit later. The pattern of excess mortality from lung cancer, heart disease and bronchitis follows the same path a decade or two later (Royal College of Physicians, *Smoking or Health?* 1977). But in the last two decades a more mature affluence in most western industrial countries has started to abandon the habit, starting among better educated men. A majority of men in all social classes in the UK are now non-smokers (see Table 11.17) and the British trend in mortality from lung cancer is downwards (see Figure 11.2), as in all other developed societies where smoking has declined. But the persistence of high levels of smoking among women has retarded the pace of improvement of women's overall mortality levels, and enabled men to close the gap somewhat in expectation of life, according to new data in 1986 (Britton and Edison, 1986).

Much effort has gone into attempts to bring down death from circulatory disease and cancer rates in target groups in the UK and other western countries by altering smoking, drinking, eating and exercise habits, and blood pressure and cholesterol levels through drug treatment, though so far with only moderate success (Tunstall-Pedo and Hell, 1983). Attitudes are difficult to change fast; at the beginning of the century, the problem for many was an adequate diet, not an excessive one or obesity (Royal College of Physicians, 1983). The impact of prevention may be hampered by individual physiological and behavioural (type 'A' and 'B') variation in susceptibility to hazards. Two-thirds of smokers will not contract lung cancer, many people with fatty, sugary, salty diets do not get circulatory disease. This may be a chance

432

Table 11.17 Cigarette smoking by class, Great Britain

| Socioeconomic group | Percentage smoking cigarettes | | | | Ex-regular smokers | | Cigarettes/week/smoker | | | |
| | 1972 | | 1982 | | 1982 | | 1972 | | 1982 | |
Group description	M	F	M	F	M	F	M	F	M	F
Professional	33	33	20	21	34	21	102	75	108	73
Employers/Managers	44	38	29	29	39	19	126	86	139	97
Intermediate and junior non-manual	45	38	30	30	29	15	114	81	109	92
Skilled manual, own account	57	47	42	39	30	17	124	93	126	106
Semi-skilled manual, personal service	57	42	47	36	28	15	119	85	118	98
Unskilled manual	64	42	49	41	26	14	111	87	120	93
All	52	42	38	33	30	16	120	87	121	98

Source: OPCS *Monitor*, General Household Survey (GHS) 82/3: Cigarette Smoking 1972-1982.

phenomenon or a matter of unidentified biological susceptibility. If at least some of the more vulnerable individuals can be identified, as genetic research suggests is likely, more impressive improvements can be expected from a better target for preventive medicine. And if improvements in monoclonal antibody technique (an aspect of genetical engineering) allow cancer cells to be identified and destroyed by a new 'magic bullet' then there may be dramatic improvements in cancer death-rates. Surprisingly, though, the elimination of cancer mortality by itself will not affect average life expectancy by more than a couple of years.

New hazards

Some conditions have become more frequent this century, even allowing for earlier uncertainties about diagnosis. Leukaemia's rise may be a consequence of increased exposure to medical X-rays. The increase in skin cancers are likely to be a consequence of the fashion for sun-bathing, and cervical cancer from more adventurous sexual habits. The non-lethal diseases of gonorrhoea and herpes have certainly become more common for this reason. Most new lethal viruses (for example, lassa fever) are exotic imports which have not spread. AIDS is a spectacular exception to this rule. It is completely lethal, so far lacking both cure and easy prevention, and is spreading rapidly. So far its control depends very much on behaviour. It is demographically negligible at present in the UK (697 deaths and 1227 cases by December 1987) but it is rapidly spreading; cases are doubling every ten months. In the USA over a million people MAY BE infected with the virus. In the UK this figure may already be 50 000. It is potentially by far the most serious new twentieth century hazard to life. Only dramatic new preventative strategies hold any hope of reliably containing it.

Morbidity rates

Data on morbidity are fragmentary compared with the mortality statistics, and particularly so for the years before 1940. There are notification figures for some diseases, and some areas, from 1900, but notification of particular specified diseases only became compulsory for the whole of England and Wales in 1911. Notification figures are often an unreliable measure of the prevalence of disease. In the 1940s it may be that only two-thirds of measles cases, a quarter to a third of pneumonia cases and a fifth of a quarter of whooping-cough cases, for instance, were in fact notified (Stocks, 1949).

Alternative measures of sickness are hard to find. Tables 11.18 and 11.19 give some idea of the drop in the prevalence and seriousness of certain diseases since 1900. The trends are probably stronger than the figures suggest, since notification has become more comprehensive and more efficient in recent years. The analysis of reasons for which patients consult their doctors shows

434

Table 11.18 Notification rate for certain diseases per 1 000 000 living during stated years, 1900–83, England and Wales

Disease	1900[1]	1909[1]	1920	1930	1940	1950	1960	1967	1971	1980	1983
Smallpox	37	—	7	297	0.03	0.2	0.03	0.04	—	—	—
Scarlet fever	4 428	4 597	3 178	2 790	1 637	1 613	703	399	224	197	—
Diphtheria	2 313	1 538	1 848	1 858	1 160	22	2	0.1	0.31	0.09	—
Typhoid and para-typhoid fever	1 292	400	827	742	710	114	72	48	2.9	5.2	4.8
Puerperal fever and pyrexia	—	—	771	207	191	94	194	86	—	—	—
Erysipelas	—	—	427	460	329	174	65	29	—	—	—
Cerebro-spinal fever (meningococcal)	—	—	16	17	320	26	14	6	11	9	26
Poliomyelitis (paralytic and non-paralytic)	—	—	9	15	27	177	8	0.4	0.14	0.05	—
TB – respiratory	—	—	1 640	1 271	906	968	457	228	119	139	109
– non-respiratory	—	—	422	422	261	158	64	45	52	48	31
Whooping cough	—	—	—	—	1 344	3 599	1 278	693	339	405	46
Measles	—	—	—	—	10 266	8 385	3 482	9 514	2 704	2 629	2 041
Dysentery	—	—	360	135	716	394	946	456	192	60	—
Food poisoning	—	—	—	—	—	171	169	104	—	—	—
Ophthalmic neonatorum	—	—	274	—	110	44	23	13	—	—	—
Encephalitis	—	—	24	18	5	6	6	5	—	—	—
Pneumonia	—	—	1 034	1 279	1 200	699	318	123	—	—	—

Notes:
1. The population covered in 1900 was 13 244 000 and in 1909 was 19 422 000; subsequently it was the total population.
Source: Social Trends for relevant years. From 1971 figures refer to UK data.

Table 11.19 Notification rate and death-rate for selected diseases 1920–80, England and Wales (*N* = notification rate per million; *D* = death-rate per million)

Disease	1920 N	1920 D	1930 N	1930 D	1940 N	1940 D	1950 N	1950 D	1960 N	1960 D	1967 N	1967 D	1970 N	1970 D	1980 N	1980 D
Diphtheria	1 848	150	1 858	88	1 160	62	22	1	2	0.1	0.1	0	0.45	0.02	—	—
Measles	—	191	—	105	10 266	21	8 385	5	3 482	0.7	9 514	2	5 929	0.82	2 091	0.52
Pneumonia	1 034	991	1 279	696	1 200	734	699	421	318	548	123	675	—	—	—	—
TB – all forms	2 062	1 131	1 568	898	1 167	699	1 149	470	516	75	273	42	—	—	—	—

Notes: Notifications do not necessarily represent all the cases of a particular disease. This is particularly obvious in the case of pneumonia where the notification rate has continued to drop, but the death-rate has risen again since 1950, so that in 1967 it was considerably higher than the notification rate.

Source: *Annual Reports* of the Ministry of Health, part II;
The Registrar-General's *Statistical Review for England and Wales for 1967*, part I: *Medical Tables*;
On the State of Public health, a report of the Chief Medical Officer of the DHSS 1972–83.

Table 11.20 Analysis of a representative sample of insured patients consulting their doctor, 1916–33, by type of illness, Great Britain

Type of illness	Urban male and female 1916	Urban and rural male		Urban and rural female	
		1924	1933	1924	1933
Bronchitis, tonsilitis, colds, etc.	181.3	201.1	235.1	181.9	238.4
Influenza	76.1	137.3	126.0	115.9	106.9
Pneumonia	67.2	19.5	15.9	12.0	9.9
Debility, neuralgia, headache	56.0	36.1	35.1	77.5	70.3
Digestive	143.1	115.9	116.4	124.5	101.8
Septic condition	49.1	79.3	76.1	69.3	60.3
Lumbago, rheumatism, etc.	66.3	103.0	98.0	74.0	77.6
Organic heart	22.1	14.0	13.3	12.5	11.6
Anaemia	39.8	1.9	2.2	59.8	29.0
Genito-urinary system	28.4	15.7	17.3	45.1	51.9
Skin	47.1	33.3	44.4	43.6	55.4
Nerves and senses	67.0	42.9	55.8	50.3	59.8
TB	12.0	10.9	7.0	12.0	7.5
Cancer	–	2.1	2.0	1.6	1.4
Injuries and accidents	60.7	134.8	106.6	43.9	53.2
Others	81.6	52.2	50.8	76.1	65.0
Total	1 000.0	1 000.0	1 000.0	1 000.0	1 000.0

Notes: Analysis covers only insured people, who would have been relatively free from chronic illness. It is probable that services became increasingly fully used so that more minor complaints were treated.
Source: Political and Economic Planning (1937) *Report on the British Health Services*.

the most usual cases to have been bronchitis, tonsillitis and colds, or digestive disorders, for the period 1916–33 and there are no very marked changes in the consultation pattern – though pneumonia seems to have become less important at the end of the period (Table 11.20). In 1955–6 respiratory diseases remained the most important single cause for consulting the doctor (Table 11.21), but circulatory disease had increased by 1970–71. Analysis by social class shows class 1 with marginally the lowest standardised consultation rate in 1956, with little change by 1970–71 (Table 11.22). Class V had the highest consultation rates for bronchitis and cancer, but considerably lower rates relative to the other social classes for coronary diseases and TB (Table 11.23). The death-rate for class V for the listed diseases was relatively very high indeed, except for coronary diseases where the rate was higher for class I. This has now reversed and consultation ratios in 1970–71 begin to reflect this

Table 11.21   Patients consulting a GP: resulting diagnosis, 1955–56 and 1970–71, England and Wales (per 1000 consultations)

| | Patients | |
Diagnosis	*1955–56*	*1970–71*
Respiratory disease	231	189
Circulatory	53	85
Locomotor	67	68
'Symptoms'	75	67
Accidents	82	53
Skin troubles	84	65
Digestive troubles	86	54
Nervous troubles	95	69
Other	227	350
All	1 000	1 000

Notes: These were surveys of National Health practices widely distributed throughout England and Wales and to a fair degree representative.

Source: General Register Office, Studies on medical and population subjects, no. 14, vol.I: *Morbidity Statistics in General Practice* and *Morbidity Statistics in General Practice, 2nd National Study 1971–72*.

Table 11.22   Standardised[1] patient consulting rates by social class for males aged 15–64, 1955–56, 1970–71, England and Wales

| Social class | Consulting rates | |
	1955–56	*1970–71*
I	93	94
II	96	96
III	103	101
IV	99	101
V	99	104

Notes:

1.   The standardised patient consulting rate represents the number of men aged 15–64 who consulted their doctor per cent of the number 'expected' to have consulted on the basis of the patient consulting rates at corresponding ages of men of all social classes.

Source: General Register Office, Studies on medical and population subjects, no. 14, vol. II occupational;
No. 4b, *Socioeconomic Analysis*.

Table 11.23 Standardised[1] patient consulting rates for males aged 15–60, from May 1955 to April 1956, and standardised mortality ratios for males aged 20–64, from 1949 to 1953 (by illness and social class), England and Wales

Disease Class	Standardised patient consulting rates					Standardised mortality ratios				
	I	*II*	*III*	*IV*	*V*	*I*	*II*	*III*	*IV*	*V*
Respiratory TB	102	85	105	102	91	58	63	102	95	143
Malignant neoplasms	75	91	94	91	111	94	86	104	95	113
Coronary disease and angina	89	108	102	89	93	147	110	105	79	89
Bronchitis	49	70	99	118	146	34	53	98	101	171

Note:
1. See note 1 to Table 11.22.
Source: General Register Office, Studies on medical and population subjects, no. 14, vol. II occupational; General Practitioner survey.

Table 11.24 Standardised patient consulting ratios age 15–64, 1970–71, England and Wales

Listed diseases	Men Social class						Women (by husband's social class)					
	I	II	IIIN	IIIM	IV	V	I	II	IIIN	IIIM	IV	V
Neoplasms	94	80	107	105	105	110	107	104	111	93	92	119
Circulatory	96	101	111	93	102	99	82	95	92	101	110	120
Chronic bronchitis	29	53	67	110	133	205	59	66	50	104	135	172
Depressive neurosis	77	86	96	102	118	134	84	85	96	105	106	103
Anxiety neurosis	124	103	120	93	96	103	97	93	98	102	99	96

Source: Morbidity Statistics in General Practice 1970–71; No. 46, Socioeconomic Analysis.

Table 11.25 Rates of long-standing and acute illness and consultations per 1000 of occupational classes IV and V, as a percentage of class I (1971–76), England and Wales

Sex/class/health indicator	1971	1972	1973	1974	1975	1976
Males						
Class IV						
Long-standing illness	—	158	163	157	160	157
Acute sickness	126	133	110	134	102	80
GP consultations	133	132	125	146	129	91
Males						
Class V						
Long-standing illness	—	196	213	218	197	196
Acute sickness	155	181	129	150	85	102
GP consultations	143	175	164	147	121	125
Females						
Class IV						
Long-standing illness	—	274	214	182	197	176
Acute sickness	105	128	115	115	134	95
GP consultations	—	180	150	110	123	114
Females						
Class V						
Long-standing illness	—	320	276	204	253	246
Acute sickness	107	141	113	122	128	94
GP consultations	—	117	150	120	107	102

Source: Reports of the General Household Survey for relevant years (from The Black Report).

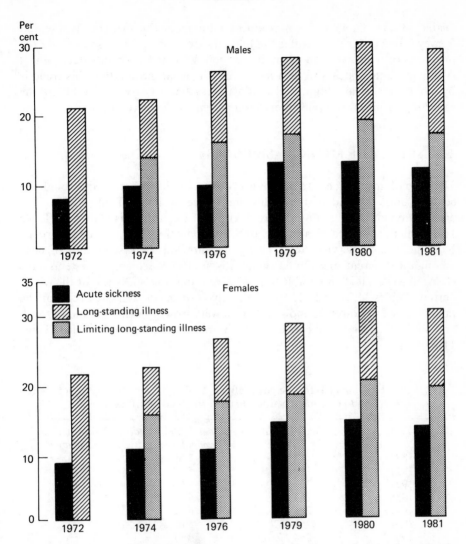

Figure 11.6   Trends in morbidity: proportioon of interviewees reporting long-stand-
              ing illness, limiting long-standing illness and acute sickness, Britain,
              1972–81

Note:
Data for acute sickness refers to the proportion of the sample who reported that their
usual lervel of activity had been restricted by illness or injury in the 14 days before
interview.

Source: General Household Survey (from OHE Compendium of Health Statistics 1986).

(Table 11.24). Table 11.25 reproduces data from the General Household Survey (GHS) which illustrates the limited extent of this data source and the problems of interpretation when disease codes are not uniformly determined. Although there appears to be a narrowing of social inequalities, this trend is by no means clear. Figure 11.6 illustrates that the overall trend in the reporting of illness to GHS interviewers seems to be increasing.

THE SUPPLY OF MEDICAL SERVICES

The ratio of hospital beds to population appears to have increased through the century until the end of the 1930s, and since declined (Table 11.26). The distribution of beds among different kinds of institution is shown in Table 11.27 which, of course, relates only to the period before the war and before the National Health Service Act. The figures showing the distribution of beds among the different specialities are unsatisfactory; classification systems have changed so that it is impossible to produce comparable statistics for the whole period (Tables 11.28 and 11.29). The analysis of out-patient statistics for the post-war years, however, shows a substantial growth in the volume of work and suggests a relative increase in this branch of the hospital service (Table 11.30).

Table 11.26 Hospital beds for the physically ill, 1891–1966: beds per 1000 population and percentage bed occupancy, England and Wales

Year	No. of beds[1]	No. per 1000 of total population	Percentage bed occupancy
1891	112 750	3.89	73
1911	197 494	5.48	77
1921	228 556	6.03	80
1938	263 103	6.41	77
1949	276 705	6.32	74
1961	266 882	5.06	79
1966	264 979	5.51	79

Note: 1. 1949–66 figures cover all staffed beds including those temporarily unavailable (because of redecorating, quarantine or illness of staff).
Sources: Robert Pinker (1966) *English Hospital Statistics 1861–1938* (Heinemann); Ministry of Health *Annual Reports*.

Some measure of the quantity of hospital care is the ratio of beds to the population, and here there is no strong evidence of improvement since the war (Table 11.31). Table 11.32 shows largely where these changes are happening; a reduction in mental illness beds as well as in general medicine somewhat compensated by small increases elsewhere. The number of hospital nurses has

Table 11.27 Number of beds for the physically ill and percentage distribution in voluntary, poor law and municipal hospitals, 1891–1938, England and Wales

Hospital type	1891		1911		1921		1938	
	No.	*Per cent*	*No.*	*Per cent*	*No.*	*Per cent*	*No.*	*Per cent*
Voluntary	29 520	26.2	43 221	21.9	56 550	24.7	87 235	33.2
Poor law								
infirmaries[1]	12 133	10.6	40 901	20.7	36 547	16.1	7 909	3.0
sick wards[2]	60 778	53.9	80 260	40.6	83 731	36.6	44 556	16.9
Municipal	10 319	9.2	33 112	16.8	51 728	22.6	123 403	46.9
Total	112 750	100.0	197 494	100.0	228 556	100.0	263 103	100.0

Notes:
1. Separate institutions.
2. In workhouse.
Source: Robert Pinker (see Table 11.26).

Table 11.28   Number of beds by specialty in voluntary and municipal hospitals, 1891–1938, England and Wales

Type of hospital	1891	1911	1921	1938
Teaching	7 228	8 284	9 584	12 610
General	15 189	21 677	28 736	90 462[1]
Infectious diseases	10 757	31 946	41 593	39 451
TB	1 075	5 500	13 546	23 457
Maternity	210	311	2 925	10 029
Other special	4 701	6 495	9 547[2]	20 686
Chronic and unclassified	679	2 120	2 347	13 943
Total	39 839	76 333	108 278	210 638

Notes:
1. Municipal general hospitals also include an unknown number of chronic sick.
2. The number of beds in other special municipal hospitals in 1921 is probably understated.
Source: Robert Pinker (see Table 11.26). No breakdown by specialty is given for Poor Law beds for the physically ill.

Table 11.29   In-patient beds by specialty, 1949–71, England and Wales

Department	1949		1961		1971	
	Beds allo-cated[1]	Waiting list	Beds allo-cated[2]	Waiting list	Available beds[1]	Waiting list
			(000s)			
All departments (excluding psychiatric beds)	276.7	491.5	266.9	465.4	—	—
Medical departments	96.8	29.3	72.2	12.4	58.0	10.1
Geriatrics and chronic sick	54.6	7.7	58.7	8.2	57.4	8.3
Surgical departments	57.5	375.2	72.3	367.4	71.8	386.0
Gynaecology, obstetrics & special baby care	24.7	59.1	28.4	63.8	31.7	77.6
Other specialist units	6.8	4.6	4.3	2.3	2.3	2.6
Pre-convalescent and convalescent	6.7	0.3	8.0	0.0	6.1	—
General practitioner units	7.9	7.8	11.0	9.7	10.9	3.6
Staff ward and unclassified	15.2	6.1	6.3	—	3.4	—
Private pay beds	6.6	1.5	5.6	1.6	—	—
Psychiatric[2]	198.7	6.1	211.5	9.0	178.0	5.4
Total (including psychiatric)	475.4	497.7	478.4	474.4	419.6	493.7

Notes:
1. See note 1, Table 11.26.
2. Includes abnormal, mentally ill and chronic sick under psychiatric care.

Table 11.30 Outpatients, 1949–71, England and Wales

Department	1949		1961		1971	
	New outpatients	Total attendances	New outpatients	Total attendances	New outpatients	Total attendances
All departments	6 148	36 112	13 346	42 398	15 792	46 268
Medical departments (a)	1 612	7 595	2 033	8 865	2 009	9 207
Geriatrics and chronic sick (b)	–	–	14	64	26	149
Surgical departments	3 334	11 989	3 853	14 581	4 108	16 186
Gynaecology, obstetrics and general baby care	629	2 668	1 077	4 198	1 312	5 170
Psychiatry – subnormality, mental illness, chronic sick under psychiatric supervision	97	466	172	1 274	214	1 573
Other specialties and unclassified	476	3 286	67	335	76	317
GP out-patients	–	–	135	403	172	526
Accident and emergency	–	10 108	5 995	12 678	7 873	13 139

Notes:
1. Figures for neurology and neurosurgery are given together and included in medical departments.
2. Geriatrics and chronic sick are included in appropriate specialties in 1949. In 1961 chronic sick are included in appropriate specialties.

Source: Ministry of Health *Annual Reports* for relevant years.

Table 11.31   Total available NHS hospital beds per 1000 population (selected years) United Kingdom

Year	Eng. & Wales	Scotland	N. Ireland	UK
1951	10.7	11.9	10.6	10.8
1961	10.3	12.3	11.7	10.6
1971	9.2	12.1	11.3	9.5
1981	7.7	11.2	11.3	8.1

Source: *Annual Abstract of Statistics* of Office of Health Statistics (1984) *Compendium of Health Statistics*, 5th edn.

nearly doubled, though in 1971 there were proportionately rather fewer who were fully qualified (Table 11.33).

The geographical distribution of hospital provision inherited by the NHS in 1948 has been much discussed. It was then largely determined by relative wealth leading to the coining of the 'Inverse Care Law' (Hart, J. T., 1971) which stressed the inverse relationship between expenditure and need, at least as measured by mortality. Before 1974 expenditure was not determined by staff norms, but largely by financing existing facilities. Hence the wealthier parts to the south (but also for different reasons, Scotland) received proportionally more resources. In 1974 the Resource Allocation Working Party (RAWP) mandated that expenditure should be in proportion to need (DHSS (1976) *Sharing Resources*). Thus a gradual equalisation is underway which in per capita terms will mean higher allocations to the poorer regions. Inequalities in need-related financial allocations are improving (Table 11.34), although probably not as rapidly as was originally hoped. Figure 11.7 shows the per capita allocation compared to the Target allocations calculated by RAWP. Generally, northern Regional Health Authorities 'should' receive more than they do and the London regions less. The Target allocations reflect differences in need measured by age structure of the population and mortality experience.

Table 11.35 shows the distribution of consultants among different specialties. Taking all doctors, including GPs, there has been a fairly steady increase during the century both absolutely and in relation to the rest of the population (Table 11.36), and the same is true of nurses (Table 11.37). There has been a similar increase in the number of doctors in general practice (Table 11.38) and a consequent decrease in the average size of GP lists (Table 11.39). In 1982 it was 2147 as opposed to 2436 in 1952.

COSTS

The increase in expenditure on the National Health Service and local authority welfare services, and the sources of finance, may be seen from Tables 11.40 and 11.41. The most dramatic rise, of course, in the 1970s is mostly

Table 11.32 NHS hospital beds – average available daily by specialty, 1965–81, England (000s)

Department	1965	1970	1975	1980	1981
Medical: Total	63.3	59.1	54.1	48.2	47.8
General medicine	32.0	30.8	29.5	27.9	28.2
Paediatrics	5.8	6.8	7.3	6.7	6.6
Infectious diseases	5.1	3.7	2.6	1.6	1.5
Diseases of the chest	13.9	10.8	7.4	4.2	3.8
Dermatology	2.1	2.0	1.8	1.7	1.6
Neurology	1.3	1.6	1.8	1.9	1.9
Cardiology	0.6	0.8	1.1	1.2	1.2
Physical medicine[1]	1.5	1.5	1.3	1.0	1.0
Genito-urinary medicine[2]	0.2	0.1	0.0	0.0	0.0
Rheumatology	0.8	1.0	1.3	2.0	2.0
Surgical: Total	67.7	70.4	69.9	66.8	66.2
General surgery	31.4	30.8	29.4	26.9	26.7
Ear, nose and throat[3]	6.3	5.9	5.5	4.9	4.8
T & O surgery	17.0	19.7	20.4	20.6	20.7
Ophthalmology	4.2	4.3	4.1	3.9	3.8
Radiotherapy	1.9	2.0	2.2	2.2	2.2
Urology	1.5	2.2	2.5	3.0	3.0
Plastic surgery	1.6	1.7	1.7	1.5	1.5
Thoracic surgery	2.2	2.1	2.0	1.6	1.6
Dental surgery	0.5	0.7	0.8	1.0	0.6
Neurosurgery	1.1	1.04	1.3	1.2	1.3
Gynaecology	9.4	10.5	10.3	9.8	9.7
Obstetrics	16.1	17.2	17.0	15.5	15.5
GP maternity	3.8	4.8	4.3	2.9	2.7
GP other medical	6.1	6.1	6.3	6.4	6.4
Mental illness	134.5	122.4	98.3	82.4	79.7
Mental handicap[4]	58.9	59.0	54.2	48.9	47.3
Geriatrics	54.7	57.2	55.6	54.9	55.5
Other	22.9	16.5	17.6	20.1	20.7
All specialties[5]	437.4	423.6	387.6	356.0	351.5

Notes: T&O = Traumatic and orthopaedic.
1. Including rehabilitation.
2. Prior to 1970, figures relate to sexually transmitted diseases.
3. Including tonsils, adenoids and others.
4. Prior to 1970, figures relate to subnormality and severe subnormality.
5. Excluding amenity beds.
Source: *Health and Personal Social Services Statistics*, CSO.

448

Table 11.33 Qualifications of nursing and midwifery hospital staff and percentage of total staff, 1949–77, England and Wales

Staff	1949[1] No.	Per cent	1961[1] No.	Per cent	1966 No.	Per cent	1971 No.	Per cent
Total	137 282	100.0	187 780	100.0	231 542	100.0	234 323	100.0
Registered nurses	44 460	32.4	62 291	33,.2	72 104	31.1	72 452	31.0
Student nurses	46 182	33.6	53 696	28.6	56 064	24.2	47 030	20.0
Enrolled nurses	14 369	10.5	13 428	7.2	29 147	12.6	32 717	14.0
Pupil nurses	1 658	1.2	6 085	3.2	14 373	6.2	20 347	8.7
Other nursing staff	21 792	15.9	40 689	21.8	46 036	19.9	47 922	20.5
State certified midwives	5 219	3.8	6 751	3.6	8 810	3.8	9 652	4.1
Pupil midwives	3 602	2.6	4 640	2.5	5 008	2.2	3 912	1.7

Note:
1. Two part-time counted as one full-time.
Source: DHSS, *Annual Reports* for relevant years.

Table 11.34 Total National Health Service expenditure[1] (net revenue and capital) per head of population by Regional Health Authorities and Health Boards,[2] 1974–75 to 1982–83, United Kingdom

Year ending 31 March

Area	1974–75	1976–77	1977–78	1978–79	1979–80	1980–81	1981–82	1982–83	% change 1974–82 at constant prices
United Kingdom	73	107	119	137	163	209	234	255	17
England[3]	72	105	116	133	158	203	226	245	16
Northern	68	99	110	130	153	196	217	249	18
Yorkshire	66	98	109	125	149	193	215	232	19
Trent	61	80	105	120	142	181	201	217	21
E Anglia	66	94	106	123	147	187	208	223	16
NW Thames	85	121	135	152	176	224	250	255	9
NE Thames	82	117	127	144	172	227	247	284	11
SE Thames	79	119	130	148	176	223	244	265	14
SW Thames	81	118	128	143	163	219	236	260	07
Wessex	65	96	107	121	143	185	204	225	15
Oxford	69	95	104	117	137	173	193	207	03
S Western	68	98	108	124	156	188	222	227	20
W Midlands	63	92	102	118	144	185	204	221	19
Mersey	74	108	120	136	161	206	228	249	14
N Western	68	102	116	135	162	209	238	259	28
Wales	76	109	123	141	167	213	237	251	15
Scotland	81	123	138	161	191	254	292	337	33
N Ireland[4]	92	128	143	164	200	253	292	335	17

Notes:
1. Excluding direct credits but includes income.
2. Includes Family Planning Clinic outlays.
3. Figures include Boards of Governors (London PGTHs).
4. Prior to 1976–77, figures include expenditures on Personal Social Services.

Sources: Health and Social Services Statistics, England, Wales, Scotland and Northern Ireland, from: Office of Health Economics 1986.

Table 11.35   Distribution of consultants by speciality, 1938–71, England and Wales

Specialty	1938–9		1949		1959		1967		1971	
	No.	Per cent	No.	Per cent	No.	Per cent	No.	Per cent	No.	Per cent
Total	1 620	100.0	5 316	100.0	7 031	100.0	9 341	100.0	9 856	100.0
General surgery and related specialities	375	23.1	1 126	21.2	1 308	18.6	1 522	16.3	858	8.7
Gynaecology and obstetrics	137	8.5	370	7.0	439	6.2	537	5.7	571	5.8
Ear, nose and throat	156	9.6	276	5.2	304	4.3	306	3.3	316	3.2
Ophthalmology	244	15.1	295	5.5	299	4.3	335	3.6	333	3.4
Orthopaedics	67	4.1	227	4.3	329	4.7	467	5.0	513	5.2
Anaesthesiology	76	4.7	459	8.6	791	11.3	1 117	12.0	—	—
General medicine and related specialities	291	18.0	1 217	22.9	1 577	22.4	2 102	22.5	905	9.2
Dermatology	51	3.1	114	2.1	140	2.0	160	1.7	162	1.6
Psychiatry	38	2.3	405	7.6	637	9.1	1 019	10.9	914	9.3
Pathology	64	4.0	454	8.5	629	8.9	1 030	11.0	545	5.5
Radiology and radiotherapy	121	7.5	373	7.0	578	8.2	746	8.0	759	7.7

Note: The 1938–9 data are drawn from a retrospective study of incomes made by Bradford Hill for the *Spens Report* on consultants and specialists. They do not include all specialities practising in 1938–9, merely those who were alive and who replied to a questionnaire in 1947. The data relate to Great Britain. The 1949–67 figures refer to the number of consultants under the National Health Service. 'General surgery and related specialities' include urology, neurosurgery, plastic and thoracic surgery, hospital dentistry and orthodontics. 'General medicine and related specialities' include chest diseases, neurology, cardiology, paediatrics, geriatrics, venerealogy, and social medicine. Comparable percentages for these subgroups are not available for 1938–9.

Source: Report of Interdepartmental Committee on Remuneration of Consultants and Specialists (*Spens Report*), pp. 22 and 25; and *Annual Reports* of the Ministry of Health for the relevant years.

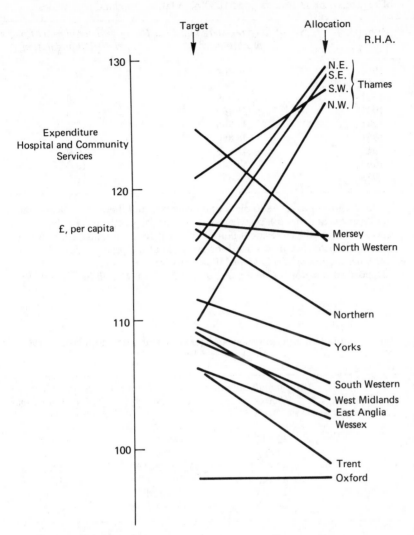

Figure 11.7 Difference between target allocation of funding for hospital and community services based on need and the actual allocation in year 1980–81 which remains somewhat determined by history

Table 11.36   Number of fully-registered medical practitioners 1901–78, and number of registered practitioners per 10 000 population, England and Wales

Year	No. of fully-registered medical practitioners	No. of registered practitioners per 10 000 population
1901	20 804	6.4
1911	22 241	6.2
1921	22 469	5.9
1931	26 469	6.6
1941	31 340	7.5
1951	38 850	8.9
1961	45 952	9.9
1968	52 346	10.8
1978	58 053	11.7

Note: England and Wales refers to place of registration and therefore reflects place of qualification and not place where the doctor is practising. Twelve months' service is required as a resident House Officer before full registration. Removal from the register occurs on death or evidence of malpractices, etc.

Source: *Medical Register (England and Wales)* for relevant years;
Report on the *Royal Commission on the National Health Service* (1979).

Table 11.37   Number of nurses (male and female) and total population, 1901–77, England and Wales

Year	Total population (000s)	Nurses (full-time equivalent)	No. of nurses per 1000 of total population
1901	32 538	69 200[1]	2.13
1921	37 887	122 804	3.24
1931	39 952	153 843	3.85
1951	43 745	207 771[2]	4.75
1961	46 205	267 320[2]	5.79
1977	49 440	340 980	6.90

Notes:
1.   1901 figures are Burdett's estimate. Other figures are from census data. Categories taken from 1921 and 1931 Censuses are 'midwives', 'sick nurses' and 'mental attendants'; from 1951 Census 'trained nurses and midwives', 'assistant nurses' and 'student nurses and probationer assistant nurses'. Health visitors and TB visitors are included in these 1951 categories and 'mental attendants' is dropped as an obsolete description. The 1961 Census has only one category – 'nurses'. Nurses here are those described as such in the census returns – not necessarily state registered nurses.
2.   Two part-time counted as one full-time. No adjustment was made for earlier years but probably there were few part-timers.

Source: Brian Abel-Smith (1966) *A History of the Nursing Profession* (Heinemann);
Census 1951, 1961, England and Wales, *Occupational Report*;
CSO (1983) *Annual Abstracts*.

Table 11.38   Number of general medical practitioners (GPs) by type, 1952–82, England and Wales

| | Index of number of GPs (1952 = 100) | | | | |
	Unrestricted	Restricted	Assistants	Trainees	All GPs
1952	100	100	100	100	100
1957	112	88	87	113	109
1962	118	76	59	77	110
1967	115	65	45	39	106
1972	122	44	35	102	111
1977	128	33	23	302	118
1982	140	23	16	557	131

Notes:
1. An unrestricted principal is a practitioner who provides a full range of general medical services and whose list is not limited to any group of persons.
2. A restricted principal is a practitioner who either (a), provides the full range of general medical services but whose list is limited to the staff of one or more hospitals or similar institutions in which he is employed or (b), provides maternity medical services and/or contraceptive services only.
3. An assistant is a practitioner who acts as an assistant to a principal.
4. A trainee is a practitioner employed for a maximum period of one year for the purposes of training in general practice and in respect of whom a training grant is paid.
Source: *Health and Personal Social Services Statistics*, CSO.

attributable to inflation. Local authority expenditure has risen proportionately more than central government expenditure, though within the latter, hospital costs have risen most steeply. Taxes and rates are still the overwhelmingly important source of finance.

The comparative figures showing the costs per patient for different types of hospital and distinguishing the teaching hospitals, speak for themselves (Table 11.42). One should, however, be cautious of costings in a system which is not costed by item of service, because some of the attributions of costs are arbitrary. It does remain true that, perhaps in part because item for service is not the dominant mode of finance, the health provision in the UK is very cheap relative to our wealth (Table 11.43). This is a very important feature of the macro-evaluation of health care because increasing use of the private sector (McPherson, Coulter and Stratton, 1985) may be, in part, a reflection of NHS provision which is keeping up with inflation, but not with the needs of an increasing proportion of elderly people, nor with the financial requirements of increasingly sophisticated medical technology. Rationing of effective curative services will inevitably become an important public question if we are to avoid spending a disproportionate amount of our GNP on health care.

Table 11.39 Number of unrestricted general medical practitioners and per 100 000 population,[1] 1951–81, United Kingdom

	Unrestricted principals – number				Rate per 100 000 population			
	England & Wales	Scotland	N. Ireland	UK	England & Wales	Scotland	N. Ireland	UK
1951	17 135	2 331	713	20 179	39.1	45.7	51.9	40.1
1956	19 180	2 555	734	22 469	42.9	49.9	52.5	43.9
1961	20 188	2 652	753	23 593	43.7	51.2	52.8	44.7
1966	19 844	2 570	750	23 164	41.5	49.4	50.8	42.5
1971	20 633	2 619	754	24 006	42.2	50.2	49.0	43.2
1976	21 837	2 820	727	25 384	44.4	54.2	47.3	45.4
1981	23 701	3 001	782	27 484	47.8	58.3	50.5	48.8

Notes:
1. Based on mid-year estimates.
2. At 31 March until 1973 and 1 July thereafter.
Sources: Health and Personal Social Services in England, Wales, Scotland and Northern Ireland, CSO.

454

Table 11.40   National health and personal social services: cost net from all sources of finance, 1958–59 to 1976–77, England and Wales

Source	England and Wales			England
	1958–59	*1968–69*	*1970–71*	*1976–77*
All services – £million	718	1 600	2 111	6 186
%	100.0	100.0	100.0	100. 0
Central Government Services	87.6	85.2	82.7	83.6
Central administrative	0.4	0.6	0.5	0.6
Health authority current[1]	51.4	50.5	50.0	56.8
capital	2.9	6.7	5.9	5.8
Administration of executive				
councils	0.6	0.6	0.6	—
General medical	9.2	7.5	7.5	5.1
Pharmaceutical	9.6	9.7	9.0	7.8
General dental	6.4	4.8	4.6	3.6
General ophthalmic	1.9	1.4	1.3	1.0
Welfare goods	3.5	2.2	1.9	0.3
Other	1.7	1.2	1.4	2.6
Local Authority Services	12.4	14.8	17.3	16.4
Personal social services[2]	4.0	5.5	11.8	16.4
Health	8.4	9.3	5.5	—

Notes:
1. Includes from 1974 administration of family planning clinics and local authority health services.
2. Prior to 1970–71 the costs quoted related to local authority welfare services.
Source: *Health and Personal Social Services Statistics for England* (1978) CSO.

Table 11.41   National health and personal services: source of finance, 1958–59 to 1976–77, England and Wales

Source	England and Wales			England
	1958–59	*1968–69*	*1970–71*	*1976–77*
All services – £ million	718	1 600	2 111	6 186
%	100.0	100.0	100.0	100.0
Central Government Services	87.6	85.2	82.7	83.6
Consolidated Fund	70.3	72.0	70.6	73.2
NHS contributions	12.9	10.2	9.2	8.4
Charges to recipients	4.3	2.7	2.7	1.8
Miscellaneous	0.1	0.3	0.2	0.2
Personal social services	12.4	14.8	17.3	16.4
Rates and grants	10.7	12.9	15.4	14.6
Charges to recipients	1.7	1.9	1.9	1.8

Notes: See notes for Table 11.40.

Table 11.42　Regional Health Authorities and Boards of Governors[1]: unit costs for years ended 31 March 1958–59 to 1976–77, England and Wales

Source	England and Wales			England
	1958–59	*1969–70*	*1970–71*	*1976–77*
Cost per in-patient week				
Teaching hospitals (acute)				
London	34.47	80.93	97.74	—
Outside London	28.69	73.33	88.58	—
Non-teaching hospitals				
Acute	23.85	54.44	65.03	240.45
Mainly acute	20.55	47.75	57.36	203.70
Chronic sick[2]	10.20	22.96	26.80	—
Maternity	24.63	57.07	65.62	248.43
Mental illness	6.96	17.67	21.46	81.27
Mental handicap	6.40	14.99	18.97	71.33
Cost per in-patient case[3]				
Teaching hospitals (acute)				
London	80.16	142.56	168.81	—
Outside London	54.99	105.54	123.39	—
Non-teaching hospitals				
Acute	48.50	81.92	94.54	317.61
Mainly acute	58.60	98.49	111.42	352.11
Maternity	37.22	60.16	66.72	234.32
Cost per out-patient attend-ance				
Teaching hospitals (acute)				
London	1.14	3.59	4.32	—
Outside London	0.97	3.03	3.46	—

Non-teaching hospitals				
Acute[4]	0.91	2.46	2.88	9.99
Mainly acute	1.04	2.67	3.12	9.96
Cost per out-patient case				
Teaching hospitals (acute)				
London	4.40	12.40	14.82	—
Outside London	3.04	8.66	9.98	—
Non-teaching hospitals				
Acute[4]	2.75	6.60	7.66	41.61
Mainly acute	3.41	7.90	9.22	42.10

Notes:

The types of hospitals are defined in the explanatory notes to the *Hospital Costing Returns* (HMSO) now called *Health Service Costing Returns*. For 1958–59 the costs are average for a limited number of hospitals, mainly the larger ones. A single system of costing was introduced from 1 April 1966, since when national average costs are shown. Figures for 1969–70 onwards are therefore not strictly comparable with those for 1958–59. The reorganisation of the National Health Service on 1 April 1974 brought teaching hospitals (except for certain postgraduate hospitals in London) under the overall administration of Regional Health Authorities. National averages from 1974–75 reflect both teaching and non-teaching costs. For this reason, and additionally due to redevised accounting procedures introduced also from 1 April 1974, costs are not comparable with those for earlier years.

1. Previous to 1974–75 Regional Hospital Boards and Boards of Governors. All years exclude hospitals administered directly by the Department of Health and Social Security.
2. The separate classification of hospitals for the chronic sick was discontinued from 1 January 1972.
3. Computed only for types of hospitals which have a relatively short average length of stay per in-patient case.
4. Acute hospitals with more than 100 beds.

Table 11.43 Total health care expenditure expressed as percentage of gross domestic product (GDP), 1960–83, selected OECD countries

	1960	1965	1970	1975	1977	1978	1979	1980	1981	1982	1983
Austria	4.4	4.7	5.3	6.4	6.6	6.9	6.9	7.0	7.2	7.3	6.9
Belgium	3.4	3.9	4.1	5.5	6.1	6.3	6.3	6.3	6.2	6.2	6.5
Denmark	3.6	4.8	6.1	6.5	6.7	6.6	6.6	6.8	6.8	6.8	6.6
Finland	4.2	4.9	5.6	5.8	6.6	6.6	6.3	6.3	6.4	6.6	6.6
France	4.3	5.3	6.1	7.6	7.8	8.2	8.3	8.5	8.9	9.3	9.3
Germany (W)	4.8	5.1	5.6	8.1	7.8	7.8	7.8	8.1	8.3	8.2	n.a.
Ireland	4.0	4.4	5.6	7.7	7.6	7.4	7.8	8.7	8.4	8.2	8.2
Italy	3.9	4.6	5.5	6.7	6.3	6.6	6.8	6.8	7.0	7.2	7.4
Japan	3.0	4.4	4.4	5.5	5.7	5.9	6.1	6.3	6.4	6.6	6.7
Netherlands	3.9	4.4	6.0	7.7	7.8	7.9	8.1	8.3	8.5	8.7	8.8
Norway	3.3	3.9	5.0	6.7	7.1	7.2	6.9	6.8	6.7	6.8	6.9
Sweden	4.7	5.6	7.2	8.0	9.2	9.3	9.1	9.5	9.6	9.7	9.6
Switzerland	3.3	3.8	5.2	7.1	7.2	–	7.0	7.2	–	7.8	–
UK	3.9	4.1	4.5	5.5	5.3	5.3	5.3	5.8	6.1	5.9	6.2
USA	5.3	6.1	8.0	8.6	8.9	8.9	9.0	9.5	9.7	10.6	10.8
Average (exc. UK)	4.0	4.7	5.7	7.0	7.2	7.4[1]	7.4	7.6	7.7[1]	7.9[1]	7.9[1]
UK as % below average	2	12	20	21	27	28	28	24	21	25	21

Notes:

n.a. = Figure(s) not available.

1. Average excluding country(ies) with no returns.

Sources: 'Measuring Health Care 1960–1983', Paris: Organization for Economic Co-operation and Development (1985).
From Health Expenditure in the UK, Office of Health Economics (1986).

References

Ball, K. P. and Purcell, H. (1984). 'Recent Trends in Coronary Mortality and their Implications for the UK: Are We Winning or Losing?' *Postgraduate Medical Journal*, 60: 1–46.

Benjamin, B. and Overton, E. (1979). Prospects for Increasing the Life Span', *Population Trends*, 23: 22–8.

Black, D., Morris, J. N., Smith, C., Townsend, P. (1980) Report of the Working Group on *Inequalities in Health* (The Black Report) (London, DHSS).

Brenner, M. H. (1979) 'Mortality and the National Economy: a Review and the Experience of England and Wales 1936–1976', *Lancet*, ii: 568.

Britton, M. and Edison, N. (1986). 'The Changing Balance of the Sexes in England and Wales, 1851–2001', *Population Trends, 46*: 22–5.

Chalmers, I. (1981) 'The Limitation of Audit by Death', in Chester, R., Diggory, P. and Sutherland, M. B. (eds) *Changing Patterns of Child Bearing and Child Rearing* (London: Academic Press) 39–56.

Chalmers, I. (1985) 'Short, Black, Baird, Himsworth and Social Class Differences in Fetal and Neonatal Mortality Rates', *Br. Med. J.*, 291: 231–2.

Committee on Medical Aspects of Food Policy (1984) *Diet and Cardiovascular Disease*, DHSS Report on Health and Social Subjects, no. 28 (London: HMSO).

Compendium of Health Statistics (1984) Annual Abstract of Statistics. Office of Health Economics, London.

Compton, P. A. 'Rising Morality in Hungary', *Population Studies, 39*, 71–86.

Cummins, R. O., Shaper, A. G. *et al.* (1981) 'Smoking and Drinking by Middle-aged British Men – Effects of Social Class and Town of Residence', *B.M.J.*, 283: 1497–1502.

DHSS (1976) *Sharing Resources for health in England.* Report of the Resource Allocation Working Party (RAWP) (London: HMSO).

Doll, R. and Peto, R. (1975) *The Causes of Cancer* (Oxford: Oxford University Press).

Feshbach, M. (1982) 'The Soviet Union: Population Trends and Dilemmas'. *Population Bulletin*, 37: 3 (Washington: Population Reference Bureau Inc.).

Fox, A. J. and Goldblatt, P. O. (1982) *Longitudinal Study: Sociodemographic Mortality Differentials 1971–75*, (London: HMSO).

Fox, A. J., Jones, D. R., Moser, K. and Goldblatt, P. O. (1985) 'Socioeconomic Differentials in Mortality', *Population Trends 40*.

Fox, A. J., Goldblatt, P. O. and Jones, D. R. (1985) 'Social Class Mortality Differentials: Artefact, Selection or Life Circumstances', *Journal of Epidemiology and Community Health*, 39: 1–8.

Hart, J. T. (1971) 'The Inverse Care Law', *Lancet* i: 405.

Hart, N. (1986) 'Inequalities in Health: The Individual Versus the Environment', *J. Roy. Stat. Soc.*, 149: 228–46.

Health Expenditure in the UK (1986) Office of Health Economics, London.

Himsworth, H. (1985) 'Epidemiology, Genetics and Sociology', *Journal Biosoc. Sci.*, 16: 159–76.

Keynes M., Coleman, D. A. and Dimsdale, N. H. (eds) (in press) *The Political Economy of Health and Welfare* (London: Macmillan).

Logan, W. P. D. (1976). *Cancer Mortality by Occupation and Social Class 1851–1971.* OPCS Studies on Medical and Population Subjects, no. 44 (London: HMSO).

McKeown, T., (1976) *The Role of Medicine: Dream, Mirage or Nemesis?* (Oxford: Basil Blackwell).

McKeown, T. (1976). *The Modern Rise of Population* (London: Edward Arnold).

McPherson, K., Coulter, A. and Stratton, I. (1985) *Increased use of Private Practice by Patients in Oxford Requiring Common Elective Surgical Operations, Br. Med. J.* 291: 797–9.

Marmot, M. G. and McDowall, M. E. (1986) 'Mortality Decline in Widening Social Inequalities', *Lancet*, ii: 274.

Marmot, M. G., Booth, M. and Beral, V. (1981) 'Changes in Heart Disease Mortality in England and Wales and Other Countries', *Health Trends*, 13: 33–8.

Martin, J. and Monk, J. (1982) *Infant Feeding 1980* (London: OPCS).

Medical Research Council Environmental Epidemiology Unit/OPCS (1983) *Trends in Cancer Mortality 1951–1980*, Series DH1, no. 11 (London: HMSO).

Measuring Health Care 1960–1983 (1985) Organisation for Economic Co-operation & Development, Paris

Moser, K. A., Fox, A. J. and Jones, D. R. (1984) 'Unemployment and Mortality in the OPCS Longitudinal Study', *Lancet*, ii: 1324.

National Radiological Protection Board (1986) *The Exposure to Radiation of the UK Population* (London: HMSO).

National Radiological Protection Board (1986) *The Risks of Leukaemia and Other Cancers in Seascale from Radiation Exposure* Addendum to NRPB.R171 (London: HMSO).

OPCS (1976) *Cancer Mortality 1911–1970*, Studies in Medical and Population Subjects, no. 29 (London: HMSO).

OPCS (1977) *Mortality Statistics: Childhood and Maternity 1976*, Series DH3, no. 3 (London: HMSO).

OPCS (1978) *Decennial Supplement on Occupational Mortality 1970–72*, Series DS, no. 1 (London: HMSO).

OPCS (1978) *Trends in Mortality 1951–1975*, series DH1 no. 3 (London: HMSO).

OPCS (1979) *Registrar-General's Decennial Supplement for England and Wales 1969–1973: Area Mortality Tables*, Series DS no. 3 (London: HMSO).

OPCS (1981) *Mortality Statistics: Perinatal and Infant: Social and Biological Factors*, Series DH3 no. 9 (London: HMSO).

OPCS (1981) *Mortality Statistics: Childhood 1985*, Series DH3 no. 19 (London: HMSO).

OPCS (1981) *Trends in Respiratory Mortality 1951–1975*, series DH1 no. 7 (London: HMSO).

OPCS (1981) *Cancer Statistics: Incidence, Survival and Mortality in England and Wales*, Studies in Medical and Population Subjects, no. 43 (London: HMSO).

OPCS (1982) *Monitor GHS 82/3: Cigarette Smoking 1972–1982* (London: HMSO).

OPCS (1985) *Mortality Statistics Serial Tables. Review of the Registrar-General on deaths in England and Wales 1841–1980*, Series DH1, no. 15 (London: HMSO).

OPCS (1986) *Mortality Statistics: Perinatal and Infant: Social and Biological Factors*, series DH3, no. 19 (London: HMSO).

OPCS (1986) *Monitor DH2, 86/2, Deaths by Cause 1985* (London: HMSO).

OPCS (1986) *Mortality Statistics: Childhood 1980*, Series DH3, no. 8 (London: HMSO).

OPCS (1986) *Occupational Mortality Decennial Supplement 1979–80, 1982–82*, Series DS, no. 6 (London: HMSO).

OPCS (1987) *Mortality Statistics 1985: Area*, Series DH5, no. 12 (London: HMSO).

OPCS (1987) *Mortality Statistics 1985*, Series DH1, no. 17 (London: HMSO).

Pollard A. H., Yusuf, F. and Pollard, G. N. (1981) *Demographic Techniques* (Oxford: Pergamon Press).

Preston, S. H. (ed.) (1982) *Biological and Social Aspects of Mortality and the Length of Life* (Liège: Editions Ordina for the International Union for the Scientific Study of Population).

Registrar General (1921) *Decennial Supplement on Occupational Mortality, Fertility, and Infant Mortality 1921* (London: HMSO).

Registrar General (1931) *Decennial Supplement on Occupational Mortality 1931* (London: HMSO).

Registrar General (1951) *Decennial Supplement on Occupational Mortality 1951* (London: HMSO).

Registrar General (1975) *Statistical Review for England and Wales 1973, Part I: Medical Tables* (London: HMSO).

Registrar General Northern Ireland (1986) *Annual Report 1984* (Belfast: HMSO).

Registrar General Scotland (1987) *Annual Report 1985* (Edinburgh: HMSO).

Royal College of Physicians (1977) *Smoking or Health?* (Pitmans Medical Publishing).

Royal College of Physicians (1983) 'Obesity: A Report of the Royal College of Physicians', *Journal of the Royal College of Physicians*, 17(1): 53–58.

Social Services Committee (1980) *Report on Perinatal and Neonatal Mortality* (The Short Report) (London: HMSO).

Stern, J. (1983) 'The Relationship between Unemployment, Morbidity and Mortality in Britain', *Population Studies*, *37*: 61–74.

Stocks, P. (1949) *Sickness in the Population of England & Wales 1944–47*, Studies in medical and population subjects no 2 (London: HMSO).

Szreter, S. (1986) *The Importance of Social Intervention in Britain's Mortality Decline 1850–1914: A Re-interpretation*, Centre for Economic Policy Research, Discussion Paper no. 121 (London: CEPR).

Townsend, P. and Davidson, N. (eds) (1982) *Inequalities in Health: The Black Report* (Harmondsworth: Penguin).

Tunstall-Pedo, H. D. and Hell, R. F. (1983) 'UK Heart Disease Prevention Project: Incidence and Mortality Results', *Lancet*, i: 1062–5.

Winter, J. M. (1983) 'Unemployment, Nutrition and Infant Mortality in Britain 1920–1950', in J. M. Winter (ed.) *The Working Class in Modern British History* (Cambridge: Cambridge University Press).

Winter, J. M. (1985) *The Great War and the British People* (London: Macmillan).

Wunsch, G. and Lambert, A. (1981) *Lifestyles and Death Styles. Differentials and Consequences of Mortality Trends.* Paper presented to British Society for Population Studies Conference, Exeter, 1981.

12 Welfare

Julia Parker and Catriona Mirrlees

We have examined the character and extent of the public welfare services in the following ways. First, we have tried to collect statistics for institutions, excluding hospitals. Secondly, we have tried to trace the development of domiciliary welfare services. Thirdly, we have gathered together figures relating to different kinds of cash grants, and fourthly, we have attempted some overall assessment of the costs of the welfare services as we have defined them. Finally, we have presented figures to indicate the changing value of some of the major cash benefits and to show the proportion of the population living on the poverty line.

It proved extremely difficult to assemble the required statistics, and in many cases the tables are very incomplete. For the most part we deal with statutory services, since there are no comprehensive statistics for voluntary services. Even for the statutory services, however, no single department of central government has been responsible for welfare, and attempts to trace developments, even in the same service, often entail searching through the records of several government departments.

The national statistics are unsatisfactory in several ways. Much social legislation has been permissive in its early stages, and the records are often either inadequate or non-existent for these periods because local authorities have not been required to make regular returns. Also there have been changes in the kind of information collected and in the methods of recording it. At certain times and for certain purposes, for instance, the old and the chronic sick, or the old and the handicapped, form a single category, but at other times and for other purposes they are distinguished. Further, the geographical areas for which figures are collected have changed frequently, so that it may be difficult to present statistics which accurately reflect developments. Minor problems also arise through changes in the form of publication. There are no uniform series which contain all the figures for the whole period; parliamentary papers change to departmental papers, or the same report may appear partly as a departmental and partly as a parliamentary publication.

INSTITUTIONS

In 1900 public social care and welfare services hardly existed. The Poor Law was designed only for the destitute and to be a deterrent, though the situation of paupers varied in the different Poor Law unions.[1] The Poor Law provided institutional care or outdoor relief in the form of cash grants. Institutions housed a wide range of persons with a wide variety of needs – children, the old, the sick, the mentally defective, single women with dependent children, the unemployed and so on. By 1900, however, some degree of specialisation was appearing. In some unions, notably in London, separate hospitals had developed which sometimes maintained very high standards of medical care; children might be placed in 'barrack schools', in cottage homes or even boarded out with foster parents; and in some cases old people had separate accommodation where they had more privacy, freedom and amenities.

Figures for the population in public institutions come from the annual returns on persons receiving poor relief, the annual reports of the Local Government Board, the Ministry of Health, the Home Office, and the Ministry of Education and for later years from the Department of Health and Social Security. It is not possible to give precise figures for the population of institutions for the years before the Second World War. Inmates were differently classified in different years and sometimes categories overlap – the old with non-able-bodied and able-bodied adults, for instance. In the early years sick children are not distinguished from healthy ones, and sick old people are not always distinguished from other sick adults. Therefore it is not possible to construct tables showing the numbers in particular age groups in institutions at different times. Nor is it always possible to distinguish the type of accommodation provided; there are no consistent figures showing the proportion of the sick in infirmaries or special sick wards, nor the number of old people in special institutions separated from the general mixed work-houses. In 1948 the Poor Law was formally abolished, and the inmates of Poor Law institutions were dispersed into various kinds of accommodation run by different departments of local government and by the hospital authorities. It is not possible to get an exact picture of trends in the proportion of people having residential care by comparing the number of children and old and handicapped people in local authority homes after the war with those in Poor Law institutions before the war, since the pre-war figures sometimes include an unstated proportion of hospital patients who would later appear in the hospital statistics. Thus an apparent drop in the numbers in residential homes represents to some extent a transfer of responsibility away from local government to the health authorities. The figures since the Second World War are much less complicated, and it is generally possible to show the fluctuations in the number of old people and children in different kinds of public accommodation since 1948.

DOMICILIARY WELFARE SERVICES

In some cases government departments have published statistics which indicate the development in domiciliary services since the 1900s or 1930s for different groups, such as the blind or the mentally ill; but generally the figures are incomplete. In other cases it is possible to get some idea of the growth of particular services (health visiting, home nursing and domestic help, for example), even though it may not be possible to say how far the service has benefited special groups of people; in the health visiting statistics visits to old people are not distinguished for earlier years, while figures for the domestic help service relate to different categories at different dates, so that groups distinguished in one year may be included in a single classification in another. Some services, such as welfare clinics and occupation centres for the mentally handicapped, were started by voluntary organisations, then supplemented by local authorities under permissive legislation and later in some cases taken over entirely by the local authorities as legislation became obligatory. Consequently figures sometimes distinguish voluntary organisation workers or clinics at first and later drop the distinction. Furthermore, statistics may relate to visits in one year and cases served in another, as with the home nursing service. At best, and even if they are consistent, the statistics give only a rough guide. They do not reveal the amount of attention given to each case in relation to need, so there is nothing to show how adequately individuals have been served.

DOMICILIARY CASH GRANTS

The number of persons having assistance and insurance payments under the Poor Law legislation, the Old Age Pensions Act of 1908, and the 1911 and later insurance Acts, can be discovered, for the most part, for the years before the Second World War as well as for the later period. The total figures are for Great Britain, but for the earlier years it has been necessary, in some cases, to refer to England and Wales for particular groups, as the Scottish statistics were not presented in the same way. Further, the early figures distinguish only persons entitled to sickness benefit, not those actually receiving it.

THE COST OF SERVICES AND BENEFITS

The cost of selected cash benefits has been analysed for Great Britain, as this was the easiest geographical unit to use for the whole period (with the exception of the figures for workmen's compensation which from 1900 to 1938 are for the United Kingdom). The tables for welfare services relate to England and Wales, but we return to the UK for comparisons between welfare services, education and health.

THE VALUE OF BENEFITS AND THE NUMBER OF PEOPLE IN POVERTY

We have used recent analyses of the Family Expenditure surveys to show the trends in the real value of selected benefits, their relation to one another and to average earnings. We have also used the same source to show the changes in the number and proportions of people living below, at and marginally above the supplementary benefit line, though even for the last decade the figures are not strictly comparable. A new method of estimating the number of people in poverty was introduced in 1979. This involved setting the supplementary benefit level at the average for the year, rather than adjusting it to represent the higher December figures after the annual uprating in November. The use of the lower yearly average would mean an apparent drop in the proportion of low income families in 1979 and later years.

NOTES ON TABLES

Institutions

The population in public institutions or supported in institutions by public authorities may be seen from Table 12.1. The numbers dropped through the first half of the century, rose again after 1950 and then dropped back in 1984. The proportion of the population in institutions was relatively high in 1910 but has since fluctuated around 3 per 1000. The difficulty of distinguishing between the healthy and the sick may be seen by comparing Tables 12.2 and 12.3. The former table shows the total number of persons in special institutions or wards for the sick or infirm, and the latter distinguishes sick and infirm according to the state of their health but not by institution. The number of sick and infirm tends to be greater when the distinction is by health rather than by institution, particularly for 1910, the earliest year when comparison is possible. Further, Table 12.3 refers only to adults, while Table 12.2 includes children, so that the real difference between those described as sick or bodily or mentally infirm, and those in special accommodation, must be greater than the figures suggest.

The number of old people in public residential accommodation has multiplied by more than five since 1900 (Table 12.4), and since 1930 they have represented an increasing proportion of the age group, officially extended in that year from people over 70 to include people over 65. There seems to have been a substantial increase in the number of old people in residential homes after the war, though the increase is obscured as the 1950 figures included young handicapped people.

It is less easy to trace the changing nature of the institutions inhabited by elderly people. In 1910 there were 1070, or just under 4 per cent of those in

Table 12.1 Persons supported by local authorities in institutions,[1] 1900–1984, England and Wales

Year	Men	Women	All adults	Children[2] In residential accommodation	In temporary accommodation	Total in institutions	Total excluding persons in infirmaries and Poor Law sick wards	Total excluding persons in infirmaries and Poor Law sick wards, per 1000 of total population
1900[3]	97 217	61 781	158 998	50 095		209 093	—[4]	—
1910	134 627	75 668	210 295	61 975	8 434	280 704	171 347	4.8
1920	69 671	62 202	131 873	53 631	4 812	190 316	110 819	2.9
1930	103 959	72 340	176 299	41 406	14 585	232 290	123 070	3.1
1938	84 425	56 493	140 918	28 693	4 887	174 498	101 491	2.5
1950	27 341	25 646	52 987	36 499	2 852	92 338	—	2.1
1960	35 007	51 886	86 893	30 346	4 125	121 364	—	2.7
1970	41 734	83 880	125 614	31 667	14 672	171 953	—	3.5
1980	38 101	98 236	136 337	41 100	—	177 437[5]	—	3.6
1984	34 058	94 935	128 993	24 972	—	153 965	—	3.1

Notes:

1. Institutions include Poor Law infirmaries, mixed workhouses, homes for the handicapped and children's homes and schools up to 1948. Small numbers were also supported in non-Poor Law institutions. Reformatory and industrial schools and asylums for the insane are not included. From 1950 institutions mean local authority welfare accommodation for the old and handicapped, children's homes, and temporary accommodation. Persons supported by local authorities in voluntary homes are also included. Those in hospitals managed by hospital boards and Home Office approved schools do not appear in the figures for institutions.

2. Children are defined as under 16 up to and including 1938; 1950 onwards they are under 18. Figures do not include children boarded out, in lodgings, residential employment or local authority hostels.

3. Vagrants are included with males as the male/female breakdown was not given in 1900.

4. Persons in sick wards and infirmaries were not distinguished in 1900.

5. Totals exclude children in temporary accommodation from 1980.

Sources: Local Government Board, *Poor Relief (Annual Returns)*, 1900–20;

Ministry of Health, *Poor Relief (Annual Returns)*, 1921–39;

Ministry of Health, *Annual Reports*, 1930–60;

Department of Health and Social Security, *Annual Report*, 1970;

Health and Personal Social Services Statistics for England, 1973 and 1986;

Health and Personal Social Services Statistics for Wales, 1985;

Children in Care in England and Wales, 1970 and 1980;

Home Office, *Seventh Report on the Work of the Children's Department*, 1955;

Home Office, *Annual Returns on Children in the care of Local Authorities in England and Wales*, 1960.

Table 12.2   Persons supported by the Poor Law in special institutions and wards in general institutions for the sick and mentally or physically handicapped (excluding asylums for the insane), 1910–38, England and Wales

Year	Separate Poor Law infirmaries	Separate Poor-Law institutions for the mentally infirm	Sick wards in general Poor Law institutions	Non-Poor Law institutions for mentally and physically handicapped	Total
1910	58 732	9 896	37 241	3 487	109 356
1920	23 288	7 711	43 053	5 445	79 497
1930	32 437	9 187	61 591	6 005	109 220
1938	9 034	6 097	50 773	7 103	73 007

Source: Local Government Board, *Poor Relief (Annual Returns)*, 1900–20;
Ministry of Health, *Poor Relief (Annual Returns)*, 1921–39.

Poor Law institutions, in separate homes for the aged rather than in the notorious general mixed workhouses. Figures for the separate homes are not given for the later years of the Poor Law administration, and it is only possible to distinguish different types of institution again after 1948. Since that date there has been some movement towards smaller homes for less than 35 people, though this seems to have quickly slackened off. There has been a much more marked trend towards homes taking from 35 to 70 people, and nearly two-thirds of all local authority residents lived in institutions of this size in 1970, while more than a sixth remained in larger institutions or premises shared with hospital authorities.

Table 12.3   Adults in Poor Law institutions and supported by the Poor Law in other institutions, 1900–38, England and Wales

Year	'Healthy'	'Sick and bodily infirm'	'Mentally infirm'[1]	Total[2]
1900	16 307	132 968		149 275
1910	24 916	175 423		200 339
1930	58 718	79 217	27 009	164 944
1938	54 792	51 193	24 712	130 697

Notes:
1. Not certified patients in mental institutions.
2. This total is less than the total figures for men and women given in Table 12.1 because it does not include vagrants who were not classified in this way. Vagrants totalled 9723 in 1900; 10 249 in 1910; 11 418 in 1930; 10 235 in 1938, and included a small number of children.
Sources: Local Government Board, *Poor Relief (Annual Returns)*, 1900–20;
Ministry of Health, *Poor Relief (Annual Returns)*, 1921–39.

Table 12.4 Old people[1] resident in institutions,[2] 1900–1980, England and Wales

Year	Poor Law institutions		Local authority homes			Joint user premises shared with hospital boards	Voluntary[5] homes and private homes	Total persons in public care	Total in age-group (000s)	Total in public care per 1000 of the age group
	General mixed workhouses	Homes for the aged poor	Less[3] than 35 beds	35–70[3] beds	Over 70[4] beds					
1900	25 024	—	—	—	—	—	168	25 192	888.08	28.0
1910	28 535	1 070	—	—	—	—	116	29 721	1 071.7	28.0
1920	20 643	—	—	—	—	—	91	20 734	1 313.04	16.0
1930	29 081	—	—	—	—	—	187	29 268	2 963.1	10.0
1938	24 998	—	—	—	—	—	1 427	26 425	3 720.0	7.0
1950[1]	11 818	—	—	19 222	—	13 057	5 980	50 077	—	—[6]
1960	—	—	15 189	20 846	21 592	6 887	9 367	73 881	5 458	14.0
1970 (England)	—	—	10 566	60 378	12 297	3 616	12 802 }	105 508	6 409	16.5
1970 (Wales)	—	—		5 600			249			
1980 (England)	—	—	1 001	102 890	223	50	15 923 }	126 327	7 422.3	17.0
1980 (Wales)	—	—		5 748			492			

Notes:
1. Old people are people over 70, up to and including 1920. After 1920 they are people over 65, except for 1950 when it is not possible to separate younger handicapped from old and handicapped. A very approximate estimate of numbers of younger handicapped might be 7000. In all years figures include those who were both old and handicapped.
2. Institutions include Poor Law mixed workhouses, voluntary homes for the handicapped and local authority welfare residential accommodation, but exclude Poor Law infirmaries and sick wards and institutions managed by hospital boards.
3. From 1970 'Less than 31 beds' and '31–70 beds'.
4. From 1960 these large homes include former mixed workhouses.
5. Figures are for people paid for by the Poor Law or local authorities. Totals in voluntary and private homes are not known until after the 1948 Registration Act.
6. The proportion of old people in public care was not given in 1950 because of the inclusion of younger handicapped people.

Sources: Local Government Board, Poor Relief (Annual Returns) 1900–20;
Ministry of Health, Poor Relief (Annual Returns) 1921–39;
Ministry of Health and Department of Health and Social Security Annual Reports; Health and Personal Social Services Statistics for England, 1982; Health and Personal Social Services Statistics for Wales, 1974 and 1982.

Table 12.5 Younger[1] handicapped people in welfare accommodation, 1950–80, England and Wales

Year	Local authority homes					Voluntary[4] homes and hospitals	Total in public care
	Less than 35 beds[2]	35–70 beds[2]	Over 70 beds[3]	Former mixed workhouses	Premises shared with hospital boards		
1950[5]		9 219		5 973	6 331	3 571	25 094
1960	785	1 428	3 671	—	1 623	3 168	10 675
1970 (England)	725	3 332	1 428	—	538	4 509	10 532 }
(Wales)			533			264	797 } 11 329
1980[6] (England)		305	4 962		36	4 359	9 321 }
(Wales)	86		25			237	689 } 10 010

Notes:

1. Under 65 years of age except 1950, see note 5. Figures may include a few children under 18. The Ministry only analyses figures into an under 30 years age-group, from 1960 onwards.
2. From 1970: 'Less than 31 beds' and '31–70 beds'.
3. From 1960 these large homes include former mixed workhouse premises.
4. People paid for by local authorities in voluntary accommodation.
5. 1950 figures include disabled over 65, as analysis of figures for people in welfare accommodation does not allow us to distinguish in this year. Also included are 49 children accommodated with people over 16.
6. From 1980 figures include short stay residents.

Sources: Ministry of Health Annual Reports for 1950 and 1960; Department of Health and Social Security Annual Report, 1970; Health and Personal Social Services Statistics for Wales, 1974 and 1981; Health and Personal Social Services Statistics for England, 1986.

Table 12.5 shows the number of younger handicapped[2] people in local authority care, since the war. It is not possible to distinguish this group in the earlier Poor Law statistics. The table is not very informative. The total number of people in care has remained steady during the 1960s and the 1970s but comparison with 1950 is impossible since the statistics for that year include unknown proportions of elderly people who were excluded in the later years. As for old people, there has been a marked move to homes with between 35 and 70 beds. A far higher proportion of handicapped than of old people are found in voluntary homes and hospitals – nearly a half, compared with 13 per cent of the elderly.

The number of adults and children in local authority accommodation as a result of homelessness has risen dramatically since 1949 (Table 12.6). The total had multiplied sixfold by 1973. After that date families were recorded rather than persons, but the upward trend has continued, albeit very unevenly, resulting in over 7000 families in temporary accommodation in 1985. The number of households accepted by the local authorities as homeless, however, is only a fraction of those who apply for help; less than a third in 1968, less than a quarter in 1972, though nearly two-thirds in 1976, the last year that applications were recorded for England (Table 12.7).

In 1900 there were over 75 000 children in public care, 57 000 were supported by the Poor Law – between a third and a half of them in general mixed workhouses, rather more in special institutions of different kinds and 13 per cent boarded out (Table 12.8). The number and proportion of children in public care dropped markedly after 1920, though the proportion boarded out rose. In 1938 there were still over 2000 children in the general mixed workhouses. After the Children Act of 1948 the terminology changed and public care of children became rather more humane. Perhaps because of the higher quality service and the greater readiness to take children into care temporarily, and because of the substitution of social for financial need as a criterion of eligibility, the number of children in public care rose both in absolute terms and as a proportion of the age group. A far higher percentage – nearly half of those in local authority care – were boarded out, and those in residential homes were all in special institutions for children. The general mixed workhouse had gone, though a number of the buildings were still being used, housing presumably some of the children in 'other local authority accommodation'. Over a quarter of all those in institutions were in homes taking not more than 12 children. After 1970, however, the picture changed in some important respects. There was a sharp increase of nearly one-third in the number of children coming into care. The proportion who were boarded out or placed in small homes fell, the numbers kept in reception centres doubled and those entrusted to friends or relatives multiplied by three.

Table 12.6 Number of persons and families resident in temporary accommodation[1] at a particular date, 1949–85, England and Wales

Month end	Greater London		Rest of England		England		Wales	
	Persons	*Families*	*Persons*	*Families*	*Persons*	*Families*	*Persons*	*Families*
December 1949	—	—	—	—	4 616	—	130	—
1959	—	—	—	—	5 790	—	90	—
1962	—	—	—	—	10 098	—	114	—
1965	7 613	—	4 567	—	12 180	—	231	—
1968[2]	9 791	2 016	8 466	1 507	18 257	3 523	592	101
1971	14 346	3 256	11 623	2 203	25 969	5 459	910	171
1973	—	—	—	—	27 416	6 401	1 190	227
June 1975	—	5 200	—	3 920	—	9 120	—	—
1977	—	3 420	—	2 920	—	6 340	—	—
1979	—	2 640	—	3 150	—	5 790	—	—
1981	—	2 245	—	2 777	—	5 022	—	—
1983	—	2 494	—	2 965	—	5 459	—	79
1985	—	2 105	—	4 834	—	6 939	—	285

Notes:

Figures from 1949 up to and including 1975 are for accommodation provided under Sections 21(I)(b) and 26(I)(b) of the National Assistance Act 1948 or the Children and Young Persons Act 1963. In 1977 the Housing (Homeless Persons) Act was implemented. The 1977 figures cover households resident in local authority temporary accommodation only, while figures for 1979 to 1985 refer to those families resident in hostels or bed and breakfast accommodation. The figures for 1985 are the total number of households in temporary accommodation and include those resident in local authority short-life dwellings.

2. 1968 figures for families exclude those with no children.

Sources: DHSS, *Health and Personal Social Services Statistics for England and Wales*, 1972; *Health and Personal Social Services Statistics for England*, 1974;
Welsh Office, *Health and Personal Social Services Statistics for Wales*, 1975;
DoE and Welsh Office, *Housing and Construction Statistics*, 18 (1976), 25 (1978), 32 (1979); *Local Housing Statistics, England and Wales*, 62 (1982), 68 (1984), 75 (1985).

Table 12.7 Number of households applying and/or accepted (A) for temporary accommodation, (B) as homeless[1] 1968–84 England and Wales

	Greater London		Rest of England		England		Wales	
	Applications	Acceptances	Applications	Acceptances	Applications	Acceptances	Applications	Acceptances
(A)								
1968	—	—	—	—	18,389	5 182	—	—
1970	—	—	—	—	24 592	5 926	1 066	294
1972	—	—	—	—	27 515	6 410	712	250
(B)								
1974	15 730	11 360	35 970	21 280	—	—	768	279
1976	16 580	12 400	—	38 680	52 550	33 680	768	279
1978	—	14 430	—	44 237	—	53 110	5 042²	3 204²
1980	—	16 676	—	51 172	—	60 913	8 277	5 446
1982	—	17 236	—	58 370	—	68 408	9 061	5 661
1984	—	25 180	—		—	83 550	8 845	4 999

Notes:

1. Homeless household figures are not strictly comparable due to (a) missing returns from variable districts and (b), introduction of 'new statistical systems' in 1977, 1980 and 1982.
2. Figure covers from April to December only as collection of statistics was not implemented until the second quarter of 1978 in Wales.

Sources: DHSS, *Health and Personal Social Services Statistics for England*, 1974;
  Welsh Office, *Health and Personal Social Services Statistics for Wales*, 1975;
  DoE, *Housing and Construction Statistics*, 18 and 20 (1976), 25 (1978), 32 (1979);
  Welsh Office, *Welsh Housing Statistics*, 5 (1985);
  DoE, *Local Housing Statistics*, 59 (1981), 62 (1982), 65 and 66 (1983);
  Regional Trends, 21 (1986).

Table 12.8 Children[1] in public care, 1900–1980, England and Wales

Children supported by the Poor Law

Year	Poor Law establishments				Non-Poor Law establishments			Total in institutions	Boarded out	Total supported by Poor Law	Children boarded out as a percentage of all children supported by the Poor Law	Children in reformatory and industrial schools[4]	Total number of children in public care	Children in public care per 1000 of the age group under 16[5]
	Workhouses	Grouped cottage homes	Scattered homes	Other schools and children's homes	Homes and hospitals for the mentally or physically handicapped	Voluntary[2] homes for the sick and handicapped	Training and industrial schools and other homes							
1900[6]	23 478	19 395				237	6 985	50 095	7 358	57 453	12.8	17 995	75 448	6.7
1910	15 834	11 640	7 366	13 607	3 067	1 322	9 139	61 975	8 813	70 788	12.4	16 307	87 095	7.4
1920	6 016	11 742	7 619	11 198	7 429	2 162	7 465	53 631	9 354	62 985	14.9	14 467	77 452	6.9
1930	4 703	9 484	7 398	10 270	1 286	1 486	6 779	41 406	8 186	49 592	16.5	5 946	55 538	5.5
1938	2 284	8 573	6 257	5 251	17	1 081	5 230	28 693	6 031	34 724	17.4	8 764	43 488	4.6

(For 1900 the figure 19 395 spans Grouped cottage homes, Scattered homes and Other schools and children's homes.)

Children in the care of local authorities

Year	Residential nurseries	Reception centres	Grouped cottage homes	Family group homes	Other local authority accommodation	Schools and homes for handicapped	In voluntary homes[2]	Total in institutions	In local authority hostels	In lodgings or residential employment	In care of friend or relative	Boarded out[3]	Total in local authority care	Percentage in local authority care boarded out	Children in approved schools[4]	Total in public care	Children in public care per 1000 of the age group under 18[5]

1952[7]	5 035	11 167	7 213	4 218	11 176	1 998	6 549	37 356	1 049	—	—	26 277	64 682	40.6	9 079	73 761	6.5
			Homes for not more than 12 children														
1960	3 543	1 586	5 064	14 053	2 243	3 857	30 346	953	1 746	—	28 684	61 729	46.4	7 770	69 499	5.8
1970	2 521	2 366	8 557	10 647	2 165	5 411	31 667	1 206	1 657	6 396	30 284	71 210	48.0	7 115[9]	78 325	5.8
1980[8]	700	5 200	8 600	20 400	3 000	3 200	41 100	1 600	1 900	18 500	36 900	100 000	37.0	—	100 200	8.1

Notes:

1. Children defined as under 16 up to and including 1938; after 1938 as under 18.
2. Totals of children in private and voluntary homes are not known before the Children's Act 1948. Figures given are only for children in voluntary homes supported by the Poor Law and local authorities. In 1949, 28 760 children were wholly in the care of voluntary bodies and in 1967, 10 839.
3. Not including a small number of 'care and protection' cases who were boarded out after the 1933 Children's Act.
4. After the 1933 Children's Act these were all known as Approved Schools.
5. Estimates of the population age groups are approximate as the Registrar-General's published figures are for five-yearly groups for some of the years shown.
6. Including children in Poor Law infirmaries and sick wards who have been excluded in subsequent years. Numbers of those in voluntary homes for sick and handicapped have been retained because the sick and handicapped are not separated in the published Poor Law figures and it was considered that the majority in these establishments would have been handicapped rather than acutely sick. The latter we have excluded where possible.
7. Detailed figures are not available for 1950 because of changes following the Children's Act of 1948.
8. Figures not strictly comparable with earlier ones due to a change in the method of collecting statistics in 1977.
9. After the implementation of the Children and Young Persons Act (1969) children who had previously been committed to an approved school were committed to the care of the local authority.

Sources: Local Government Board, *Poor Relief (Annual Returns)*, 1900–1920;
Ministry of Health, *Poor Relief (Annual Returns)*, 1921–39.
Home Office: *Annual Reports of the Inspector of Reformatory and Industrial Schools* 1900, 1910; *Fifth Report on the Work of the Children's Branch*, 1938; *Reports on the Work of the Children's Department*, 1955, 1961, 1961–3 and 1964–6; *Annual Returns on Children in the Care of Local Authorities in England and Wales* 1952, 1960;
Department of Health and Social Security: *Children in Care in England and Wales 1970 and 1980*; *Annual Report*, 1971; *Annual Abstract of Statistics* for relevant years.

Table 12.9 The expansion of the home nursing service, 1930–84, England and Wales

	Number of nurses employed			Type of case						Total cases during the year	Total population (000s)	Total cases as percentage of total population
Year	*Local authority*	*Voluntary organisa-tion*	*Total*	*Medical*	*Surgical*	*Maternal complica-tions*	*Infectious diseases*	*TB*	*Other*			
1930	37	1 990	2 027	—	—	—	—	—	—	72 487	39 801	0.18
1938	55	2 599	2 654	—	—	—	—	—	—	66 560	41 215	0.16
1950	5 811	2 587	8 398	—	—	*mostly chronic sick*	—	—	—	1 001 670	45 020	2.3
1960	8 634	1 688	10 322	643 261	173 838	10 561	3 235	13 811	52 913	897 619	45 775	2.0
1970	11 293 (9 292)[1]	—	—	—	—	573 000	—	—	—	1 031 500	48 680	2.1
1980[2]	15 338	—	—	—	—	1 505 300	—	—	—	3 604 100	49 244	7.3
1984	17 822	—	—	—	—	1 682 355	—	—	—	3 746 668	49 765	7.5

Notes:
1. Figures in brackets are the full-time equivalent of the number of employees.
2. Due to a change in definition in 1972 figures are not strictly comparable with earlier years.

Sources: Ministry of Health *Annual Reports* for 1930–60;
DoE, *Health and Personal Social Services Statistics for England*, 1977, 1982 and 1986;
Welsh Office, *Health and Personal Social Services Statistics for Wales*, 1982 and 1985;
Registrar-General's population mid-year estimates from *Annual Abstract of Statistics*, relevant years.

Domiciliary services

Statistics for the domiciliary welfare services are sketchy. For old and handicapped people, the major developments in the statutory services have come since the Second World War. Table 12.9 shows the expansion in the home nursing service since the 1930s with a very great rise in the number of nurses and cases dealt with in 1950. In 1970 over half the cases were people over 65, but it is not possible to distinguish old people in the earlier years. Figures for the domestic help service are available only since the war, the expansion is marked and the majority of recipients are old people, but it is not possible to see precisely how the service has been distributed among different groups (Table 12.10). Health visitors, too, have doubled the number of old people they visit since 1963 (Table 12.23), though the greater part of their work remains with young children. Again, single bedroom dwellings have been built largely, though not exclusively, for old people and the increasing proportion can be seen from Table 12.11. The same table also contains estimates of the number of old people receiving a range of different services; unfortunately the 1963 figures, based on a national survey, are not available for earlier years. However, the table does demonstrate how very small a proportion of old people benefit from domiciliary care.

The growth of community care for mentally ill and mentally subnormal people, now termed the mentally handicapped, may be seen from Tables 12.12 to 12.14. Since 1930 the number of mentally handicapped persons under local authority supervision has more than doubled. Nearly 50 000 people of all ages attended training courses in 1970 compared with 4000 before the war. By 1983 there were altogether over 14 000 places in local authority homes and hostels for adults, and a further 5000 places in voluntary homes and private households for the mentally handicapped of all ages. By 1970 there were ten times the number of people attending occupation centres as before the war and provision had doubled again by 1983, though later figures are calculated differently. The most dramatic increase in services, however, has been for the mentally ill after the 1959 Mental Health Act (Table 12.13).

Compared with services for the mentally ill, those for the blind were fairly well established in the 1930s (Table 12.15). Since 1930, the number of blind persons registered with local authorities has doubled, but the great majority of blind people are old and the increase in numbers largely reflects the growing proportion of old people in the population. Slightly more children under 5 were registered as blind in 1960 than in 1920, though the earlier figure probably reflects incomplete registration rather than a smaller prevalence of blindness among young children at that time. Local authorities keep registers of blind persons and of those with other types of physical handicap which give some indication of the level of services needed, though they are very incomplete. Persons able to work may also register as disabled at the local

Table 12.10   The expansion of the home help service, 1970–80, England and Wales

Year	Number of home helps employed (Total)	Type of case						Total cases¹ during the year	Total population (000s)	Total cases as percentage of total population
		Maternity	TB	Chronic sick	Old	Mentally disordered	Other			
1950	23 375	41 660	6 935	114 810				162 405	44 020	0.36
1960	49 314 (24 000)²,³	36 027	3 410	233 365		39 211		312 013	45 775	0.68
1970	70 000³ (approx) (32 994)	13 800	32 800		396 000	2 000	25 000	469 500	48 680	0.96
1980	97 110 (49 596)	5 570	48 221		698 562	4 862	30 703	787 918	49 244	1.6

Notes:
1. Figures may not add to totals due to rounding.
2. Full-time equivalents are given in brackets.
3. Approximate figures only.
Sources: As for Table 12.9.

Table 12.11 Domiciliary services for old people, 1963–83, England and Wales

Year	No. of 1-bed houses and flats completed by LAs in year	No. of old people's dwellings: tenders approved/completed by LAs in year[1]	Old people resident in sheltered housing[2]	Old people receiving				Total population 65 and over
				Homehelp[3]	Nursing[3]	Meals[4]	Chiropody[5]	
1963	27 079	—	35 894	258 000	46 000[6]	—[7]	423 000	5 617 600
1970	38 503	18 950	—	396 000	573 000	22 664 000	887 000	7 044 000
1980	28 565	7 451	—	698 562	1 505 354	43 624 000	1 434 785	7 255 200
1983								
(England)	14 251	7 591	—	—[8]	1 559 900	40 960 000	1 470 000}	7 500 400
(Wales)	714	—	—	45 850	90 392	1 892 000	113 913}	

Notes:
1. 1970 and 1980: number of dwellings for which tenders approved for local authorities; 1983: number of dwellings completed by local authorities.
2. Numbers receiving this service on a particular day in the year.
3. In 1963 figures refer to numbers receiving service on a particular day in the year, and from 1970 to number of cases over 65 in a year.
4. Number of meals served in recipient's own home, clubs and centres, by local authorities, during year.
5. In 1963 figures refer to numbers receiving this service on a particular day in the year and from 1970 to the number of over 65s treated in the year.
6. Bedfast only.
7. No local authority returns made as service was mainly the responsibility of the Women's Voluntary Service with some local authority support. In 1963 the WVS delivered 4.8 million meals to the elderly (Ministry of Health, *Annual Report*, 1964).
8. Local authority return 'Home Help Form SSDA 303' was discontinued in 1981.

Sources: Peter Townsend and Dorothy Wedderburn (1965) *The Aged in the Welfare State* (Bell);
Ministry of Health, *Health and Welfare: The Development of Community Care*, Cmnd 3022 (1966);
DHSS, *Health and Personal Social Services Statistics for England* 1977 and 1986;
Welsh Office, *Health and Personal Social Services Statistics for Wales* 1985;
Ministry of Housing and Local Government, *Housing Statistics*, no. 2 (1966);
DoE, *Housing and Construction Statistics*, 1970–80 and 1974–84.

Table 12.12 Domiciliary services for the adult mentally handicapped, 1930–83, England and Wales

	1930	1939	1950	1961	1970	1980	1983
Cases under LA supervision:							
Statutory	24 710	43 531	51 716 }	81 885	104 140	—	—
Voluntary	21 999	26 006	18 646 }			—	—
Occupation centres & clubs:							
Local authority	10	69 }	166	626	311	484	521
Voluntary	161	122 }		—	—	—	—
No. attending occupation centres:							
Aged under 16	— }	4 244 }	5 340	12 534	22 128	—	—
16 and over	— }	}		9 507	26 078	—	—
No. of places in occupation centres for adults				—	22 857[1]	44 963	49 583
No. resident in LA homes and hostels:							
Aged under 16	—	—	—	145	1 726	—	—
16 and over	—	—	—	453	4 959	—	—
No. of places in LA homes and hostels for adults	—	—	—	—	5 013	12 493	14 478
No. resident in voluntary homes and private households:							
Aged under 16	—	—	—	78	60	—	—
16 and over	—	—	—	289	544	—	—
No. of places in voluntary homes and private households[2]	—	—	—	—	—	3 746	5 046

Notes:
1. Excluding places in centres for adults and children.
2. England only.

Sources: *Annual Reports* of the Board of Control and Ministry of Health;
DHSS, *Digest of Health Statistics*, 1970; *Health and Personal Social Services Statistics for England*, 1974, 1977, 1982 and 1985;
Welsh Office, *Health and Personal Social Services Statistics for Wales*, 1974, 1983 and 1985.

Table 12.13   Domiciliary services for the adult mentally ill,[1] 1961–83,
England and Wales

	1961	1970	1980	1983
No. under LA supervision	40 036	100 517	—	—
Training/day centres				
No. attending	354	3 644	—	—
Places	—	—	5 339	5 825
LA residential homes and hostels				
Residents	734	3 828	—	—
Places	—	—	4 083	4 646
Voluntary homes and private households				
Residents	21	543	—	—
Places[2]	—	—	2 142	2 367

Notes:
1.   Services introduced following the 1959 Mental Health Act.
2.   England only.
Sources: DHSS, *Digest of Health Statistics*, 1970; *Health and Personal Social Services Statistics for England*, 1974, 1977, 1982 and 1985;
Welsh Office, *Health and Personal Social Services Statistics for Wales*, 1974, 1983 and 1985.

Table 12.14   Mental health staff,[1] 1961–83, England and Wales

	1961	1970	1980	1983
Mental health training centre and residential home staff (full-time equivalent)	2 081	7 482	19 632	24 139

Notes:
1.   Figures are not strictly comparable: In 1965 there was a change in the definition of mental health staff. 1980 and 1983 figures include some staff working in day centres for the physically handicapped and elderly.
Sources: DHSS, *Digest of Health Statistics*, 1970; *Health and Personal Social Services Statistics for England*, 1974, 1977, 1982 and 1985;
Welsh Office, *Health and Personal Social Services Statistics for Wales*, 1974, 1983 and 1985.

Table 12.15 Persons registered as blind and domiciliary services, 1920–80, England and Wales

Year	Number registered as blind					Blind persons employed[1]			
	0–4	5–15	16–64	65 and over and age un-known	Total	In workshops	In home-workers' schemes	Elsewhere	Home teachers[2]
1920	244	2 366	28 094		30 708	—	7 589	—	40
1930	—	—	—	—	56 853	2 956	1 573	5 025	441
1936	206	1 855	27 090	30 983	60 134	3 812	1 828	3 146	400
1950	356	1 364	32 877	46 723	81 320	3 185	1 465	4 985	591
1960	322	1 950	30 456	64 741	97 469	2 958	1 112	6 237	777
1970	2 100		27 700	73 200	103 000	1 875	685	6 123	855
1980	2 098		26 255	86 665	115 018	—	—	—	—

Notes:
1. 1970 figures are for England only. Figures unavailable for 1980.
2. Equivalent full time. 1970 figure for England only.

Sources:
Ministry of Health Annual Reports; Advisory Committee on the Welfare of the Blind, Annual Reports;
Ministry of Labour, Report of the Working Party on Workshops for the Blind, 1962;
Ministry of Labour, Annual Reports; Register of the Blind (unpublished, issued by Ministry of Health);
Department of Health and Social Security, Annual Report, 1970; Health and Personal Social Services Statistics for England, 1977 and 1986;
Welsh Office, Health and Personal Social Services Statistics for Wales, 1985.

employment exchanges, the object being to get extra help in finding a job. In all cases, registration is voluntary.

Community services seem to have maintained a fairly even level. The number of blind persons employed in workshops, or in their own homes, or in outside employment, has fallen slightly, though figures are not available for 1980. The trend perhaps reflects the increasing proportion of blind people who are elderly. The number of home teachers has risen as the number of blind people on the register has risen, though in 1970 the ratios of home teachers to blind persons was slightly higher than for earlier years. The increase in the register of the partially sighted may be seen from Table 12.16, but we have no statistics to indicate the extent of the services they receive.

Table 12.16   Persons registered as partially sighted, 1952–82, England and Wales

| Year | Persons on register by age | | | | Total |
	0–4	*5–15*	*16–65*	*65 and over and age unknown*	
1952[1]	80	1 665	3 632	5 849	11 226
1960	113	2 176	7 613	14 337	24 239
1970	2 700		10 900	23 800	37 400
1980	2 492		14 050	38 786	55 328
1982					
(England)	2 200		14 300	41 500	58 000
(Wales)[2]	—		—	—	4 546

Notes:
1.   1952 was the first year that figures were given.
2.   No age breakdown available.
Sources: Ministry of Health *Annual Reports*; *Health and Personal Social Services Statistics for England*, 1977 and 1986;
Welsh Office, *Health and Personal Social Services Statistics for Wales*, 1985.

Statistics for other types of physical handicap are scarce. Table 12.17 shows the numbers on the registers of handicapped persons maintained by local authorities – though these registers are notoriously incomplete. Some indication of the recent growth in the social work staff of the local authority welfare departments concerned with old people and the physically and mentally handicapped may be gained from Table 12.18. But the figures are not very informative. After 1971 social workers in the health and welfare departments joined childcare officers in the new social services departments and most took on a wider range of duties.

The development of domiciliary care for children may be seen both in the increasing number of children lacking normal family care who are boarded

Table 12.17 Persons registered as handicapped (deaf, deaf without speech and hard of hearing, and general classes[1]) 1955–80, England and Wales

Year	Under 16		16–64 inclusive		65 and over		Total
	Deaf and deaf without speech and hard of hearing	General classes	Deaf and deaf without speech and hard of hearing	General classes	Deaf and deaf without speech and hard of hearing	General classes	
1955[2]	2 849	4 509	16 597	35 121	5 262	5 931	74 052[3]
1960	3 462	5 405	22 592	66 319	9 427	21 641	128 846
1970	4 800	6 400	22 600	118 100	15 500	126 500	293 900
1980	4 483	20 903	27 511	324 726	35 702	614 493	1 027 818

Notes: Figures may not run to totals due to rounding.
1. Physical handicaps excluding blind or deaf.
2. The first year the register appeared in Ministry of Health Annual Reports.
3. Including some for whom age is not given.
Sources: As for Table 12.16.

Table 12.18 Social workers in local authority health, welfare and children's departments, 1956–69, and social services departments, 1971–83, England and Wales

Social workers	1956	1962	1967	1969	1971	1973	1975	1977	1979	1981	1983
Senior social workers (includes team leaders)	—	—	—	—	—	—	4 178 (4 069)[1]	4 775 (4 674)	5 283 (5 146)	5 276 (5 114)	5 041 (4 878)
Child welfare officers			—	3 450							
Social workers	2 438[2]	2 943[2]			10 928[4]	11 596 (11 137)	13 601 (12 644)	14 191 (13 160)	14 793 (13 715)	15 941 (14 733)	17 178 (15 815)
Trainee social workers			(6 063)[3]	(6 123)[3]		1 537 (1 535)	1 635 (1 629)	1 117 (1 117)	1 075 (1 067)	676 (672)	451 (446)
Welfare assistants	—	—				1 860 (1 779)	3 030 (2 880)	3 350 (3 145)	3 726 (3 450)	3 985 (3 671)	4 300 (3 935)
Community workers	—	—	—	—	—	—	293 (282)	434 (434)	575 (558)		
Management and supervisory	387	—	—	—	—	3 511[5] (3 495)	3 012 (3 010)	3 210 (3 209)	3 505 (3 499)	4 113 (4 094)	4 563 (4 531)

Notes:
1. Figures in brackets are the full-time equivalents.
2. These figures were dependent on local authority interpretation of the definition of a social worker and thus may include some child welfare officers, health workers and administrative staff.
3. Social workers employed by local authority health and welfare departments.
4. From 1971 figures for social workers include those previously employed in children's departments.
5. England only.

Sources: Younghusband Report (1959), Report of the Working Party on Social Workers in Local Authority Health and Welfare Services.
Ministry of Health, Health and Welfare: The Development of Community Care (1963);
DoE, Health and Personal Social Services Statistics for England relevant years;
Welsh Office, Health and Personal Social Services Statistics for England relevant years;
Home Office, Report on the Work of the Children's Department, 1967–9.

Table 12.19 Provision[1] of school meals[2] and milk,[3] 1910–80, England and Wales

Year	Number of main meals in a year[4]	Number of children served	Population aged 5–14 inclusive[5]	Percentage of population 5–14 served	Number of milk meals in a year	Percentage of population 5–14 receiving milk
1910	327 246	114 925	7 196 484	1.6	—	—
1920	11 867 934	148 082	7 178 752	2.1	—	—
1930	16 327 120	295 121	6 529 901	3.7	22 737 459	—
1938	26 819 108	687 855	—	—	114 961 182	
		Number served on a particular day		Percentage of pupils present taking meals	Number served on a particular day	Percentage of pupils present receiving milk
1950	—	2 408 000		51.3	4 377 600	84.5
1960	—	3 408 000		56.1	5 832 270	82.5
1970	—	5 148 000		67.9	8 967 000	91.5
1980 (England)	—	3 535 000		48.2	—	—[6]
1980 (Wales)	—	234 669		49.7	28 600	11.2

Notes:
1. In maintained/local authority schools only.
2. Total meals served: those paid for and those provided free.
3. Milk provided free only.
4. From 1910 to 1938 main meals included breakfasts, dinners and teas; from 1950 onwards, dinners only.
5. Population figures at census dates 1911, 1921 and 1931.
6. Figures unavailable. Free milk still served to some 'primary' and 'special' school children.

Sources: Board of Education and Ministry of Education Annual Reports and Statistics of Education vol. 5 up to 1972;
Dept. of Education and Science, Statistics of Education (Finance and Awards), 1982–3;
Board of Education, Report on the Working of the Education (Provision of Meals Act) 1906; Statistics of Education in Wales, no. 7 (1982);
CSO, Statistical Abstract for the United Kingdom, no. 81 (1936).

out with foster parents by the public authorities, rather than maintained in institutions (Table 12.8), and also in the growth of a variety of welfare services, often linked to health and education, available for all children. The growth in boarding out, which has been particularly marked since the war, means that there are now more than five times as many children in public care in foster homes as there were in 1900. And half as many again remain in the community in the care of friends or relatives. How far this latter development represents more enlightened policies or a breakdown in public services is uncertain.

Meanwhile, welfare services for all children were developing outside the Poor Law through the 1920s and 1930s – particularly in connection with education. The dramatic increase in the number of children having school meals and milk may be seen from Table 12.19. It continued until 1970, but since then government policies have led to the virtual disappearance of school milk and an abrupt drop in the number of children having school dinners.[3] School meals and milk began as a measure to improve the physical health of the children as did the school medical service.[4] Medical inspections were arranged for children first starting school and at intervals subsequently, and the number of routine inspections rose steadily with the school population until the 1950s when local authorities began to be more selective (Table 12.20). The growing provision for treatment may also be seen from the table. In the post-war period it is noticeable that, although the number of minor defects treated in the school clinics dropped very sharply, presumably as a result of the National Health Service, eye treatment increased and so did dental inspections. Speech therapy and child guidance also increased after 1950, but statistics are sparse.

The educational needs of handicapped children, too, have been gradually distinguished and provided for. In 1900 special schooling was limited to the blind and the deaf, and to the mentally defective and epileptic, but by 1966 the kinds of handicap separately provided for had multiplied to nearly a dozen types (Tables 12.21). There were just over 9000 children having special education in 1900; less than half the school boards made special arrangements at that time for handicapped children. By 1983 over 112 000 children were having special schooling – 1.6 per cent of all children under 16 compared with 0.1 per cent at the beginning of the century. Fewer blind children received special education in 1960 than in 1910, but there were slightly more children in schools for the deaf. The really dramatic increase, however, occurred for the mentally defective; less than 4000 children were having special education in 1900, and nearly 83 000 in 1983. By the latter date, among other types of children being distinguished for special attention, the most important numerically were the physically handicapped and the delicate, whose numbers have, however, dropped by a third since the late 1930s, and the maladjusted whose numbers have increased more rapidly than any other group, multiplying by 10 since 1950. Overall, by far the greater part of special provision in education is

Table 12.20(a) The school medical service, 1910–83, England and Wales

Year	No. of routine medical inspections	No. of children[1] aged 5–14	Percentage of children aged 5–14 inspected	No. of school nurses employed — No.	No. of school nurses employed — Full-time equivalent	No. of local authorities providing different facilities — Clinics	No. of local authorities providing different facilities — Dental services	No. of local authorities providing different facilities — Eye services
1910	1 377 000	7 196 484	19.1	632	—	30	—	70
1920	1 829 658	7 178 752	25.5	2 671	—	288	203	282
1930	1 770 779	6 529 901	17.1	5 485	—	316	310	313
1938	1 677 008	—	—	5 589	—	—	—	—
		No. of school pupils[2]	Percentage of pupils inspected					
1950	1 888 594	6 314 784	29.9	5 208	2 312	—	—	—
1956	2 139 000	7 619 814	28.1	6 999	2 667	—	—	—
1970	1 786 329	8 658 158	20.6	9 498	3 313	—	—	—
1980								
(England)	1 124 800	8 933 033	12.6	—	2 690	—	—	—
(Wales)	—	557 749	—	—	242	—	—	—
1983								
(England)	961 900	8 276 102	11.6	—	3 073	—	—	—
(Wales)	—	518 872	—	—	198	—	—	—

Table 12.20(b)   Different cases treated by local authorities

Year	Dental inspections	Percentage of pupils² inspected	Minor defects	Eye cases	ENT cases	Orthopaedic cases	Speech therapy cases	Child guidance cases
1938	3 225 376	—	1 072 204	275 999	—	—	—	—
1950	2 487 000	39.4	1 285 740	369 862	—	—	24 000	22 000
1960	3 595 000	47.2	605 000	560 000	150 000	129 000	56 000	36 000
1970	4 578 000	52.9	286 913	581 249	—	—	88 164	69 321
1980								
(England)	5 299 000	59.3	—	—	—	—	—	—
(Wales)	323 700	58.0	—	—	—	—	—	—
1983								
(England)	5 317 000	64.2	—	—	—	—	—	—
(Wales)	325 371	62.7	—	—	—	—	—	—

Notes:
1. Population figures are for census dates 1911, 1921 and 1931.
2. Includes those in maintained and non-maintained nursery, primary, secondary, and special schools.

Sources: *Annual Report* of the Board of Education.
Ministry of Education *Statistics of Education*;
DoE, *The Health of the School Child* 1969–70;
DHSS, *Health and Personal Social Services Statistics for England* 1977, 1982 and 1986;
Welsh Office, *Health and Personal Social Services for Wales* 1981 and 1985;
Statistics of Education Vol. 1, Schools 1972 and 1978;
DoE, *Statistics of Education: Schools*, 1983.

Table 12.21 Educational provision for handicapped children by type of handicap: children in special schools, 1900–1983,[1] England and Wales

Year	Blind or deaf Boarding	Day[3]	Blind Board-ing	Day[3]	Deaf Board-ing	Day[3]	Mentally defective[2] Board-ing	Day[3]	Epileptic Board-ing	Day[3]	Physically defective Board-ing	Day[3]	'Delicate' Board-ing	Day[3]	Autistic Board-ing	Day[3]
1900	3 330	2 069					3 751									
1910	2 295	4 183					509	11 094	464		331	4 087				
1920	3 161	4 984					15 361		496		11 809					
1930			1 872	2 775	2 784	1 912	1 984	14 552	609	—	5 338	6 010	2 572	7 702	—	—
1939			1 891	2 753	2 669	1 848	2 770	14 115	609	—	7 213	6 412	4 129	12 881	—	—
1950[4]			1 761	981	2 271	943	4 888	13 134	772	—	1 798	13 807	3 173	5 241	—	—
1960			2 996	838	3 334	2 563	9 363	23 284	696	—	2 473	7 961	3 130	4 363	—	—
1970[5]			1 770	1 007	2 629	2 453	8 719	45 017	604	—	2 319	8 856	2 244	2 880	—	—
1980			418	1 311	707	2 17:	5 844	78 593	102	414	974	9 907	1 231	2 838	99	357
1983			329	1 165	493	1 818	4 907	77 871	61	323	650	9 247	989	2 562	61	349

Year	With heart disease Board-ing	Day³	With pulmonary TB Board-ing	Day³	With ophthalmic defect Board-ing	Day³	With speech defect Board-ing	Day³	Maladjusted Board-ing	Day³	Total no. in special schools	Total in age group 5–15 inclusive (000s)	Percentage of age-group in special schools
1900	—	—	—	—	—	—	—	—	—	—	9 150	7 478	0.1
1910	—	—	—	—	—	—	—	—	—	—	22 963	7 864	0.3
1920	—	—	—	—	—	—	—	—	—	—	35 811	7 578	0.5
1930	196	20	1 711	585	254	—	—	—	—	—	50 856	7 190	0.7
1939	486	—	2 475	—	—	—	—	—	—	—	60 271	6 735	0.9
1950⁴	—	—	—	—	—	—	50	—	688	172	49 679	6 486	0.8
1960	—	—	—	—	—	—	83	—	1 347	256	62 687	7 560	0.8
1970⁵	—	—	—	—	—	—	92	6	2 509	1 541	82 646⁶	7 672	1.1
1980	—	—	—	—	—	—	96	952	3 899	5 559	115 474	7 054	1.6
1983	—	—	—	—	—	—	65	794	4 232	6 379	112 295	—	—

Notes:

1. 1900–1939 figures are number of places; 1950 onwards – number on roll.
2. Mentally defective children catered for by the local education authorities are now termed educationally subnormal.
3. Day pupils at boarding schools are counted with day pupils.
4. From 1950, following the Ministry's classification, children at hospital schools are counted as day children.
5. Figures for 1970 onwards refer to children in maintained special schools and do not include those in hospital schools.
6. The total for 1970 includes 77 children classed as having 'multiple' handicaps, 445 as being 'delicate and maladjusted' and 174 as being 'deaf and blind'.

Sources: Board of Education and Ministry of Education: *Annual Reports*, parts I and II; *Report on Schools for the Blind and Deaf*, 1898–1900; *Statistics of Public Education*;
DoE, *Statistics of Education: Schools*, for relevant years;
Population figures at census dates 1901 et seq. (1939 estimated figure);
CSO, *Annual Abstract of Statistics*, 1986.

Table 12.22   The health visiting service and child welfare clinics, 1920–83, England and Wales

Year	Number of health visitors employed				Total population (000s)	Ratio of health visitors to population	Total no. of visits	No. of children 0–1 visited	Percentage of children 0–1 visited	No. of clinics		No. of children 0–1 attending clinics
	Paid by local authority organisations	Paid by voluntary organisations	Total	Full-time equivalent						Local authority	Voluntary organisation	
1920	1 879	1 480	3 359	1 607	37 596	1:2300	—	—	—	1 061	993	—
1930	3 078	2 279	5 357	3 508	39 801	1:1135	—	—	—	2 113	822	—
1938	3 672	2 306	5 978	3 079	41 215	1:1340	8 694 489	—	66.2 (Eng.) 71.7 (Wales)	2 752	1 833	—
1950	5 897	233	6 130	4 011	44 020	1:1100	11 000 000	583 000	88.5	4 565	235	—
		No. of health visitors employed by LAs (full-time equivalent)					*Number of cases attended*					
1960	—	4 826[1]	7 203	4 826	45 775	1:950	12 207 000	613 000	71.1	5 651	280	516 000[2]
1970	—	5 914	—	—	48 680	1:823	4 431 800	822 600	104.9	—	—	618 000
1980	—	9 296	—	—	49 244	1:530	4 063 129	717 210	109.3	—	—	583 496
1983	—	10 076	—	—	49 654	1:493	4 090 308	676 373	107.5	—	—	530 673

Notes:
1. 1960 figures include those employed solely as TB visitors.
2. Figure for 1959.

Sources: Ministry of Health, *Annual Reports;*
DHSS, *Health and Personal Social Services Statistics for England*, 1977 and 1986;
Welsh Office, *Health and Personal Social Services Statistics for Wales* 1983 and 1985;
CSO, *Annual Abstract of Statistics*, for relevant years.

Table 12.23 Number of health visitors' cases by age and distinguishing certain disabilities, 1963–84, England and Wales (000s)

Year	Children born that year	Children born in previous five years	Persons aged 5 and under 65	Persons aged 65 and over	Total cases attended	Mentally discharged persons	Persons discharged from hospital	Tuberculosis households
1963	875.9	2 767.2	—	266.7	—	25.5	44.6	65.5
1971	834.7	2 485.3	746.1	454.2	4 520.3	29.4	54.3	26.5
1981	684.3	1 746.3	1 069.3	500.4	4 000.3	37.2	—	34.2
1984	682.6	1 774.6	1 279.9	483.7	4 220.7	34.3	—	22.3

Sources: DHSS, Health and Personal Social Services Statistics for England, 1973, 1977 and 1986; Welsh Office, Health and Personal Social Services Statistics for Wales, 1983 and 1985.

Table 12.24   Number of persons receiving assistance, 1900–1983, Great Britain

Year	Total	Outdoor relief[1] (included in total in column 1)		Old[2]		Sick	Unemployed	Non-contributory old age pensions
		Adults	Children	also with pension	Total			
1900	584 311	(350 327)	(158 190)	—	(152 843)	(292 660)	—	—
1910	622 837	(355 032)	(184 171)	—	(138 223)	(282 939)	—	607 000
1920	368 792	(167 469)	(138 380)	(6 284)	(8 621)	(104 958)	—	785 833
1930	1 356 293	(866 475)	(338 942)	99 231)	(143 376)	(271 351)	163 313[3]	1 373 331
1938	1 327 665	(835 442)	(270 552)	(226 756)	(225 130)	(439 746)	512 356[3]	1 789 207

Year	Total persons benefiting from assistance	Total no. of weekly allowances	Dependants		Supplementary benefits (National Assistance)								Non-contrib. pensions in payment without supplement
					Old		Sick		Unemployed		Others		
			Adults	Children	With contributory benefit	Without contributory benefit	With contributory benefit	Without contributory benefit	With contributory benefit	Without contributory benefit	With contributory benefit	Without contributory benefit	
1950	2 289 030	1 350 000	271 850	351 180	677 000	106 000	114 000	102 000	38 000	39 000	96 000	178 000	316 000
1960	2 724 000	1 857 000	385 000	436 000	1 075 000	111 000	139 000	128 000	43 000	85 000	65 000	211 000	46 000
1970	4 238 000	2 739 000	674 000	825 000	1 745 000	156 000	164 000	159 000	71 000	157 000	274 000		—[5]
1980	4 972 000	3 115 000	692 000[6]	1 165 000[6]	1 590 000	101 000	57 000	148 000	176 000	678 000	365 000		—
1983	—	4 353 000	—	—	1 570 000	85 000	79 000	162 000	205 000	1 621 000	631 000		—

Notes:

1. Figures in brackets are for England and Wales only as Scottish figures do not make this breakdown. The numbers in the categories do not add up to the numbers in the total column as they are not mutually exclusive. Nor do we give figures for other categories such as the mentally infirm where the method of classification changed during the period. Dependants are included, that is, where relief is given to the head of the family, the wife (if any) and children under 16 living with the head and dependent on him for support are counted. If outdoor relief is given exclusively to a wife or child, the head of the family is also counted as relieved, but other dependants are not.
2. The old are over 70 up to and including 1920; in 1930 and 1938 they are over 65.
3. Unemployed in England and Wales are added to the Scottish category 'Destitute and able bodied'.
4. Men over 65, Women over 60.
5. No longer separately counted.
6. Includes Northern Ireland figures.

Sources: Local Government Board, *Poor Relief (Annual Returns)* 1900–9; *Poor Relief (Annual Returns)* for relevant years;
Local Government Board for Scotland, *Annual Reports*;
Ministry of Health, *Annual Reports*;
National Assistance Board, *Annual Reports*;
CSO, *Statistical Abstract for the United Kingdom*, for relevant years;
DHSS, *Social Security Statistics*, 1976 and 1985.

Table 12.25 Number of persons[1] receiving insurance grants, 1900–1983, Great Britain

Year	Insurance benefits					War pensions	Workmen's[4] compensation cases of disablement in the year
	Contributory old age pensions	Widows,[2] orphans etc.	Entitled to[3] national health insurance benefits	Unemployment benefit including transitional benefit	Unemployment assistance		
1900	—	—	—	—	—	—	21 174
1910	—	—	—	—	—	—	378 340
1920	—	—	15 278 600	226 477	—	3 083 500[5]	381 966
1930	632 234	873 292	18 144 200	1 282 274	—	1 187 000	461 794
1938	815 642	1 100 080	20 034 200	1 031 933	560 863	882 000[6]	425 676

Year	Insurance benefits			Maternity benefit		Unemployment benefit[9]	Children attracting family allowances[10]	War pensions
	Retirement[7] pensions	Widows,[2] orphans, guardians, etc.	Average number[8] incapacitated by sickness and injury at one time during year	Industrial/ disablement pension	Maternity grants awarded during year	Maternity allowances awarded during year		

1950	4 152 000	474 000	917 000	59 000	757 000	124 000	226 000	4 756 000	1 047 423
1960	5 563 000	549 000	957 000	173 000	867 000	198 000	192 000	5 764 000	724 024
1970	7 363 000	551 268	978 000	207 000	829 000	233 000	305 500	6 955 000	519 000
1980	8 918 000	457 124[11]	1 096 000	196 000	664 000	351 000	708 750	13 304 000	354 000
1983	9 285 000	410 470	1 223 000	189 000[12]	658 000	330 000	953 250	12 750 000	314 000

Notes:
1. Figures refer to persons receiving payments on one day in the year unless otherwise stated in the heading or notes. Dependants are not included.
2. Widow's benefit (excluding widow's allowances), guardian's allowance, orphan's pensions and child's special allowances.
3. Numbers receiving benefit at any one time are not available. Benefits included sickness, disablement, maternity and medical benefit.
4. Workmen's compensation figures are for the United Kingdom. They do not include death benefit. The figure in the 1938 line is for 1935.
5. 1921 figures.
6. 1936 figures.
7. Men over 65, women over 60.
8. Not including death benefit.
9. Average number of claims current during the year.
10. Before April 1977 family allowance was payable to a family with two or more children. Child benefit, introduced April 1977, applies to all children.
11. 1979 figures.
12. 1982 figure.
Sources: CSO, *Statistical Abstract for the United Kingdom* relevant years.
Ministry of Labour, *Abstracts of Labour Statistics; Ministry of Labour Gazette;*
Treasury, *Return of Expenditure on Public Social Services;*
DHSS, *Social Security Statistics,* 1976 and 1985.

498

Table 12.26 Expenditure on income maintenance: assistance, non-contributory and insurance payments in £000s and as a percentage of all yearly spending on those benefits, 1900–1983, Great Britain

	Assistance			Insurance benefits						
Year	Poor Law outdoor relief	Non-contributory old age pensions	Unemployment allowances	Sickness, disablement, maternity	Unemployment	Old age contributory	Widows, orphans and guardians	Workmen's accidents	Compensation industrial diseases[1]	War pension
1900	3 166 (97.6%)							78 (2.4%)		
1910	4 684 (30.0%)	7 360 (54.1%)						2 108 (15.5%)	54 (0.4%)	
1920	5 416 (3.6%)	20 676 (13.7%)		10 089 (6.7%)	8 752 (5.8%)			4 857 (3.2%)	366 (0.2%)	100 949 (66.8%)
1930	15 616 (6.0%)	36 676 (14.0%)		19 303 (7.4%)	101 594 (38.9%)	16 363 (6.3%)	16 890 (6.5%)	5 127 (2.0%)	583 (0.2%)	49 205 (18.7%)
1938	19 380 (7.3%)	44 154 (16.7%)	41 309 (15.6%)	18 599 (7.1%)	51 662 (19.5%)	21 130 (8.0%)	24 305 (9.2%)	4 940[2] (1.9%)	546 (0.2%)	38 428 (14.5%)

	Supplementary benefits (National Assistance)				Insurance benefits						
Year	Weekly allowances	Non-contributory old age pensions	Single payments	Family allowances	Sickness[3] and maternity	Unemployment	Old age contributory pension and death grant	Widows, orphans and guardians	Industrial injury[1]	Industrial disablement pension and supplementation	War pensions

	Total expenditure on non-contributory benefits[4]									
1950	56 430 (9.4%)	25 230 (4.2%)	—	63 590 (10.6%)	74 032 (12.3%)	19 209 (3.2%)	250 534 (41.7%)	22 000 (3.6%)	9 162 (1.5%)	2 760 (0.5%)	78 084 (13.0%)
1960	166 200 (12.1%)	10 900 (0.8%)	4 250 (0.3%)	130 000 (9.5%)	150 649 (11.0%)	41 911 (3.1%)	662 172 (48.4%)	61 930 (4.5%)	18 032 (1.3%)	27 567 (2.0%)	95 501 (7.0%)
1970	593 000 (16.9%)	—	339 000 (9.7%)	420 680 (12.0%)	127 117 (3.6%)	1 638 791 (46.8%)	162 660 (4.6%)	33 381 (1.0%)	63 499 (1.8%)	124 000 (3.5%)
1980	3 007 000 (16.4%)	—	2 830 000 (15.5%)	1 730 488 (9.5%)	652 481 (3.6%)	8 830 500 (48.3%)	564 900 (3.1%)	46 548 (0.3%)	248 985 (1.4%)	375 000 (2.1%)
1983	8 055 000 (26.3%)	—	3 659 000 (11.9%)	2 240 637 (7.3%)	1 499 648 (4.9%)	13 565 791 (44.3%)	727 100 (2.4%)	46 469 (0.2%)	348 935 (1.3%)	504 000 (1.6%)

Notes:
1. Workmen's compensation figures 1900–38 are for the United Kingdom. The workmen's compensation and industrial injury figures do not include death benefits.
2. Figure for the year 1935–6.
3. Includes invalidity benefit from 1972. Invalidity benefit replaces sickness benefit if incapacity continues after 168 days in any period of interruption of employment.
4. Excluding family allowances and war pensions but including administration.

Sources: CSO, *Statistical Abstract for the United Kingdom*, for relevant years;
Ministry of Labour, *Annual Abstract of Labour Statistics*, for relevant years;
Annual Reports of the Local Government Board for England and Wales, the Scottish Local Government Board, the Ministry of Labour, the Ministry of Health, the Scottish Board of Health, the Ministry of Pensions, the Ministry of Pensions and National Insurance and the National Assistance Board;
DHSS, *Social Security Statistics*, 1976 and 1985.

now for mentally, rather than physically, handicapped children, a reversal of the position in the early years of the century.

The development of health visiting may be noted here as a service involving advice and information for families with young children. By 1930, 50 per cent of all infants under one year were visited, and this proportion had increased to 100 per cent by 1970 (Table 12.22). The number of clinics grew steadily up to the 1960s, but figures for later years are not available though the number of young children attending has levelled off. As the service has expanded the ratio of health visitors to the population has improved, but the figures for 1960 include women who were employed solely as TB visitors. However, and in spite of an increase in work with old people over the last 20 years, health visitors remain overwhelmingly concerned with child welfare (Table 12.23).

Cash grants

The number of persons receiving assistance or insurance grants is shown in Tables 12.24 and 12.25. Perhaps the most remarkable thing is that, in spite of the development of insurance benefits of all kinds, the number of people receiving public assistance payments increased from just over half a million in 1900 to nearly 5 million in 1980 – a rate of increase which far exceeded the rate of population growth. Most assistance and insurance payments are made to the old, and this tendency has become more marked as the proportion of old people in the population has grown. The other notable feature of the distribution of cash payments is the substantial drop in benefits to the unemployed after the depression years of the 1930s, and then the sharp upward trend again with the rising unemployment of the later 1970s and 1980s.[5]

The cost of services and benefits

The increasing expenditure on cash benefits is shown in Table 12.26. Poor Law relief, pretty well the only form of statutory benefit in 1900, fell dramatically to represent only 3.6 per cent of all cash payments in 1920, but since that date assistance grants have accounted for an increasing proportion of the total, reaching 26 per cent in 1983. Otherwise, insurance benefits and assistance have fluctuated with unemployment, war and population structure. Old age or retirement pensions are the most costly of all benefits, and expenditure has risen as the number of old people in the population has increased, and as contributory pension schemes have matured and have been extended to the whole population.

The total expenditure on cash payments has represented an increasing proportion of Gross National Product (GNP) from the beginning of the century, though with a slight falling back during the 1930s and the earlier position was not regained until the 1950s. The rapid rise in spending since then is illustrated in Table 12.27.

Table 12.28 shows the changing costs of selected welfare services, with the expenditure on particular items expressed as a proportion of the cost of all of them for different years. There has, of course, been a general shift from institutional provision to domiciliary services, institutional Poor Law relief representing 100 per cent of the cost of welfare services in 1900, while the most significant forms of institutional welfare provision remaining in 1982 accounted only for a third or so of the total. Proportionate spending on residential accommodation for old and handicapped people has more than doubled since 1950 to reach 26 per cent of all the items we list in 1982. Over the same period the proportion of the total going to school meals, milk and medical services dropped from 44 to 20 per cent. The share of children in care has remained fairly constant at 15 or 16 per cent.

Table 12.27   Total expenditure on social security benefits as a percentage of gross national product, 1900–1983, United Kingdom

	Total[1] expenditure on social security (£000s)	Gross National Product of United Kingdom (£000s)	Total expenditure as a percentage of Gross National Product (%)
1900	3 244	1 970 000	0.2
1910	13 606	2 231 000	0.6
1920	151 105	5 128 000[2]	2.9
1930	261 357	4 576 000	5.7
1938	264 453	5 175 000	5.1
1950	657 100	11 666 000	5.6
1960	1 498 900	22 875 000	6.6
1970	3 927 000	44 592 000	8.8
1980	23 508 000	199 027 000	11.8
1983	33 991 000	260 327 000	13.1

Notes:
1.   Figures up to and including 1938 exclude Northern Ireland.
2.   Figure for 1921.
Sources: 1900–1938: total expenditure on social security from Table 12.26;
   CSO, *Annual Abstract of Statistics*, for 1950–85; *National Income and Expenditure* 1964–74; *United Kingdom National Accounts* (1985);
   London and Cambridge Economic Services, *British Economy Key Statistics 1900–1964*.

We have also tried to express welfare spending, as distinct from cash grants, as a proportion of all local authority expenditure since the beginning of the century (Table 12.29). The figures should be treated very cautiously. Those for the period up to 1936 refer mainly to indoor relief under the Poor Law, with

502

Table 12.28 Local authority expenditure on certain welfare services in £000s and as a percentage of all yearly spending on those services, 1900–1982, England and Wales

Year	Poor Law indoor relief[1]	Maternity child welfare,[2] health visitors	Welfare of the blind	School meals, milk and medical services	Educational provision for handicapped children
1900–1901	5 903 (100%)	—	—	—	—
1905–06	7 317 (100%)	—	—	—	—
1910–11	7 871 (95.9%)	—	—	340 (4.1%)	—
1920–21	18 224 (79.1%)	1 904 (8.3%)	—	1 612 (7.0%)	1 294 (5.6%)
1925–26	16 411 (76.4%)	1 819 (8.5%)	—	2 011 (9.4%)	1 232 (5.7%)
1930–31	16 510[3] (68.6%)	2 782 (11.6%)	808 (3.4%)	2 295 (9.5%)	1 688 (7.0%)
1935–36	13 215[3] (56.8%)	3 411 (14.7%)	1 343 (5.8%)	3 076 (13.2%)	2 228 (9.6%)

Year	Residential accommodation for old, handicapped and temporary accommodation	Children in care (including boarded out)	Maternity and child welfare, health visitors[2]	Welfare of the blind	Welfare services for physically handicapped and old	Domestic help	Home nursing	School meals, milk and medical services	Educational provision for handicapped[4] children
1950–51	9 030 (11.3%)	12 120[5] (15.2%)	10 172 (12.7%)	2 320 (2.9%)	—	2 960 (3.7%)	4 173 (5.2%)	35 504 (44.4%)	3 635 (4.5%)
1960–61	21 070 (13.7%)	18 595 (12.1%)	13 784 (8.9%)	1 482 (1.0%)	1 209 (0.8%)	9 494 (6.2%)	7 883 (5.1%)	68 036 (44.1%)	12 725 (8.2%)
1970–71	63 613 (16.5%)	55 403 (14.4%)	35 006 (9.1%)	4 040 (1.0%)	17 401 (4.5%)	27 288 (7.1%)	20 130 (5.2%)	129 138 (33.5%)	33 831 (8.8%)

	Residential accommodation for the elderly, the younger physically handicapped, blind and deaf[6]		Day care support services for children	Adaptations to homes, provision of aids and telephones	Day centres and clubs for the elderly and occupational centres and clubs for others				
1980–81[7]	508 455 (25.9%)	329 195 (16.8%)	75 353 (3.8%)	15 355 (0.8%)	58 195 (3.0%)	213 325 (10.9%)	—	441 268 (22.5%)	323 470 (16.5%)
1982–83	605 776 (26.3%)	377 915 (16.4%)	99 753 (4.3%)	19 949 (0.9%)	74 764 (3.2%)	260 385 (11.3%)	—	464 754[8] (20.2%)	401 455 (17.4%)

Notes:

1. Total expenditure (including salaries and building costs) on the maintenance of paupers in Poor Law authority and non-Poor Law authority institutions. It excludes the maintenance of 'lunatics' in institutions and the cost of children boarded out. The latter is included in the cost of outdoor relief.
2. Maternity and child welfare figures 1920–38 include costs of midwifery as they are not separately distinguished. For figures 1950–70 midwifery costs are excluded.
3. Figures for cost of Poor Law general institutions and children's homes and schools, but now exclude costs of Poor Law hospitals and special institutions.
4. School milk was phased out during the 1970s. In 1970–71 total current spending on school milk was £13 347 000, in 1980–81 £6 340 000 and no longer separately recorded in 1982–3.
5. Figure for 1951–2, first available year.
6. Responsibility for providing temporary accommodation for homeless people was passed to Housing Departments during the 1970s. Administration costs are not included.
7. Following the coming into force of the Local Authorities Social Services Act (1970) from 1971 the personal social services are comprised of the former local welfare services and certain former local health services. Thus comparison of the 1980–1 and 1982–3 figures with previous years is not possible.
8. Welsh expenditure on school medical services unavailable.

Sources: Annual Reports of the Local Government Board of England and Wales;
CSO, *Statistical Abstract for the United Kingdom* and *Annual Abstract of Statistics* for relevant years;
Annual Reports of Ministry of Health;
Annual Reports of the Ministry of Education;
Home Office *Returns on Children in the Care of Local Authorities, England and Wales*;
DoES, *Statistics of Education*, vol. 5, 1968 and 1972;
Statistics of Education in Wales no. 10 (1985);
DoES, *Statistics of Education: Finance and Awards*, 1982–3;
DHSS, *Health and Personal Social Services Statistics for England* 1974 and 1986;
Welsh Office, *Health and Personal Social Services Statistics for Wales*, no. 12 (1985).

Table 12.29   Local authority expenditure on certain welfare services as a percentage of total local authority expenditure, 1900–1982, England and Wales

Year	Local authority current expenditure on welfare (£000s)	Total local authority current expenditure (£000s)	Welfare expenditure as a percentage of total expenditure (%)
	Indoor poor relief[1]		
1900–1	5 903	86 237	6.8
1905–6	7 317	111 340	6.6
1910–11	8 211	129 417	6.3
1920–21	20 128	343 155	5.9
1925–26	18 230	373 110	4.9
1930–31	20 100	432 704	4.6
1935–36	17 969	470 885	3.8
	Residential and welfare services[2]		
1950–51	27 424	887 361	3.1
1952–53	35 467	1 062 263	3.3
1954–55	39 927	1 225 337	3.3
1956–57	46 561	1 497 088	3.1
1958–59	53 872	1 731 287	3.1
1960–61	62 083	2 018 451	3.1
1962–63	75 926	2 446 859	3.1
1964–65	91 772	2 902 829	3.2
1966–67	119 032	3 621 425	3.3
1968–69	147 431	4 322 290	3.4
1970–71	199 397	6 185 508	3.2
1972–73	397 576	8 004 223	5.0
1974–75	763 973	11 734 287	6.5
1976–77	1 149 395	17 132 576	6.7
1978–79	1 464 710	21 409 787	6.8
1980–81	2 183 058	30 337 528	7.2
1982–83	2 643 923	36 124 321	7.3

Notes:
1. Expenditure (excluding that defrayed out of loans) on the maintenance of indoor paupers in Poor Law authority and non-Poor Law authority institutions, but excluding the maintenance of lunatics in institutions. From 1920–21 maternity and child welfare expenditure is included, and from 1930–31 blind welfare expenditure.
2. Provided under the National Assistance and Children's Acts of 1948 and after 1971 covering all services provided by local social services departments, including sheltered employment.

Sources: CSO, *Statistical Abstract for the United Kingdom*, for relevant years up to 1937; *Annual Abstract of Statistics*, for relevant years from 1938 to 1985; Local Government Board, *Annual Reports* from 1900 to 1912; *Annual Local Taxation Returns*, up to 1930–31;
Ministry of Health, *Local Government Financial Statistics* up to 1935–36;
Treasury, *Returns of Expenditure on Public Social Services*, 1922–38.

maternity and child welfare and blind welfare included in the later years. They do not include spending on welfare services connected with education, school meals, milk, medical services and arrangements for handicapped children. This group of educationally linked welfare services is also excluded from the figures for the post-war period which refer to arrangements made under the National Assistance and Children's Acts of 1948 to provide homes, supervision and care in the community for old and handicapped people and for children 'deprived of a normal home life'. After the reorganisation of local services in 1970 the figures also include expenditure that had formerly been a charge on the National Health Service – residential and domiciliary care for the mentally handicapped and the mentally ill, and for social work with hospital patients.[6] Thus there is a jump in local authority spending after 1971 that to some extent represents simply a transfer of spending from the health service accounts.

In Table 12.30 we show the trends in public spending on a range of social services since the last war. Insurance payments are the most costly programme, followed by education and the NHS. Insurance grants represented a similar proportion of social service spending in 1983 and in 1949 and so did education, but the NHS has lost ground, dropping by nearly a quarter. Housing's share of social services money has also fallen by one quarter since 1960. War pensions and non-contributory old age pensions have virtually ceased as those qualifying for them have died, and school meals and milk – always minor items in financial terms – have almost disappeared as a result of changing policies.

The highest rate of increase has been for personal social services, though they started with a relatively tiny share of all spending and remain with only 4 per cent. Otherwise, supplementary benefits took twice as large a proportion of resources in 1983 and family benefits had also risen markedly.

The value of benefits and people in poverty

The last three tables attempt some assessment of the changing value of benefits and of the number of people living around the official poverty line. Retirement pensions, invalidity benefit and long-term supplementary benefit have all become more generous in relation to unemployment benefit over the last 10 or 15 years and so, more recently, have family benefits. The relative value of death grants has dropped very sharply during the years since the war, and so to a much lesser extent has the maternity allowance (Table 12.31).

The changing value of four of the most important benefits, both in real terms and as a proportion of average earnings, may be seen in Table 12.32. The real value of insurance and supplementary benefits has roughly doubled since 1948, though retirement pensions have risen faster and unemployment benefit more slowly. Child support, including tax allowances until 1977, has

Table 12.30 Consolidated current and capital expenditure on social services and housing by the public sector, 1949–50 to 1983–84, United Kingdom

	1949–50		1960–61		1970–71		1980–81		1983–84	
	(£ million)	(Per cent)	(£ million)	(Per cent)	(£ million)	(Per cent)	(£ million)	(Per cent)	(£ million)	(Per cent)
Education	288.0	19.1	926.8	23.3	2 638	25.3	12 376	21.4	15 308	20.3
National Health Service	415.9	27.6	902.2	22.7	2 071	19.9	11 944	20.7	15 376	20.4
Local welfare services	—	—	32.9	0.8 }	274	2.6	2 468	4.3	3 164	4.2
Child care	13.7	0.9	26.6	0.7 }						
School meals and milk	63.9	4.2	67.5	1.7	132	1.3	479	0.8	519	0.7
Welfare foods			27.6	0.7	44	0.4	35	0.1	86	0.1
National insurance and industrial injuries	415.1	27.6	1 009.3	25.4	2 708	26.0	15 300	26.5	20 562	27.3
War pensions	81.8	5.4	96.9	2.4	127	1.2	424	0.7	533	0.7
Non-contributory old age pensions	28.9	1.9	11.4	0.3	3	0.1	41	0.1	42	0.1

Supplementary benefits[2]	65.9	4.4	174.7	4.4	544	5.2	2 983	5.2	5 934	7.9
Other non-contributory[3] benefits	—	—	—	—	—	—	501	0.9	1 030	1.4
Family benefits[4]	65.4	4.3	137.1	3.5	354	3.4	3 163	5.5	4 424	5.9
Administration of social security benefits[5]	—	—	65.3	1.6	186	1.8	1 096	1.9	1 466	1.9
Housing	67.7	4.5	494.6	12.4	1 339	12.8	7 025	12.1	6 977	9.3
Total	1 506.3	100.0	3 972.9	100.0	10 425	100.0	57 835	100.0	75 421	100.0

Notes:
1. Not separately distinguished.
2. Formerly 'National Assistance'.
3. This category includes the following benefits: attendance allowance, invalid care allowance, mobility allowance, invalidity pensions and lump sum payments to pensioners.
4. Child benefit replaced family allowance in 1977. The 1980–81 figure includes, in addition to child benefit, one parent benefit and family income supplement. In 1983–84 maternity grants are included in addition to the above.
5. For 1949–50 administration costs are included in the expenditure for individual benefits.

Sources: CSO, *Annual Abstract of Statistics,* for relevant years.

Table 12.31 The relative value of selected benefits, 1948–85, Great Britain

Date	Unemployment benefit	Sickness benefit	Retirement pension/ widow's pension	Invalidity benefit plus allowance[1]	Maternity allowance	Death Grant	Disablement pension[2]	Supplementary benefit Ordinary	Supplementary benefit Long-term	War pension[3]	Family income supplement[4]	Attendance allowance	Family allowances/ child benefit[5] 1 child	Family allowances/ child benefit[5] children
July 1948	100.0	100.0	100.0	—	138.5	—	173.1	92.3	—	236.9	—	—	—	19.2
August 1951	100.0	100.0	115.4	—	138.5	1 538.5	173.1	100.0	—	236.9	—	—	—	19.2
July 1952	100.0	100.0	92.3	—	110.8	1 230.8	169.2	107.7	—	220.3	—	—	—	15.4
May 1955	100.0	100.0	100.0	—	100.0	1 000.0	168.7	93.7	—	210.5	—	—	—	20.0
February 1958	100.0	100.0	100.0	—	100.0	1 000.0	170.0	90.0	—	203.2	—	—	—	16.0
April 1961	100.0	100.0	100.0	—	100.0	869.6	169.6	93.0	—	198.6	—	—	—	13.9
March 1963	100.0	100.0	85.2	—	100.0	740.7	144.4	85.2	—	169.2	—	—	—	11.9
January 1965	100.0	100.0	84.4	—	100.0	625.0	143.7	79.4	—	164.5	—	—	—	10.0
October 1967	100.0	100.0	100.0	—	100.0	666.7	150.0	95.6	105.6	187.3	—	—	—	8.9
November 1969	100.0	100.0	100.0	—	100.0	600.0	168.0	96.0	106.0	184.6	—	—	—	18.0

September 1971	100.0	100.0	116.7	100.0	500.0	166.7	96.7	105.0	180.7	66.7	—	—	15.0
October 1973	100.0	105.4	127.2	100.0	408.2	174.1	97.3	110.9	185.6	81.6	84.4	—	12.2
November 1975	100.0	119.8	145.0	100.0	270.3	196.4	98.2	123.4	204.0	72.1	95.5	—	13.5
November 1977	100.0	119.0	144.2	100.0	204.1	194.6	98.6	121.8	200.3	78.2	95.2	6.8	17.0
November 1979	100.0	125.9	152.4	100.0	162.2	205.4	98.9	128.1	209.9	83.8	100.5	21.6	43.2
November 1981	100.0	131.6	153.6	100.0	133.3	214.7	103.3	131.6	218.4	95.6	105.1	23.3	46.7
November 1983	100.0	125.9	147.0	95.9	110.9	205.5	99.1	126.1	205.5	96.1	100.6	24.0	48.1
November 1985	100.0	125.8	152.2	95.7	98.5	205.3	96.9	123.2	205.3	95.2	100.5	23.0	46.0

Notes:
1. Invalidity benefit has been taken at basic rate plus higher rate invalidity allowance.
2. Disablement benefit = 100 per cent rate.
3. War pensions: other ranks at 100 per cent rate.
4. Family Income Supplement is in respect of a married couple with children at maximum rate. From November 1985 children assumed to be aged 11 or under.
5. Family allowances/child benefit is in respect of 1- and 2-child families and does not include child tax allowances.

Sources: DHSS, *Social Security Statistics*, 1985.

Table 12.32 Equivalent value of selected benefits at 1985 prices and as a percentage of average earnings, 1946-84, Great Britain

Year[1]	Unemployment benefit[2]		Retirement pension[3]		Supplementary benefit (ordinary rate)[4]		Child support[5]			
	Equivalent at April 1985 prices (£)	As a % of average earnings of male manual workers (%)	Equivalent at April 1985 prices (£)	As a % of average earnings of male manual workers (%)	Equivalent at April 1985 prices (£)	As a % of average earnings of male manual workers (%)	Equivalent at November 1985 prices		As a % of average earnings of male manual workers	
							1 child family (£)	3 child family (£)	1 child family (%)	3 child family (%)
1946	—	—	15.56	19.1	—	—	3.37	11.27	4.4	14.6
1948	15.56	19.1	15.16	18.2	13.46	17.6	3.64	10.91	4.5	13.4
1951	13.23	15.9	15.39	18.3	14.07	18.2	4.00	11.88	4.6	13.7
1952	15.28	18.5	17.61	18.4	15.20	20.1	3.19	9.37	3.8	11.2
1955	17.65	18.6	19.49	19.8	15.41	17.8	4.10	13.64	4.2	14.1
1958	19.58	19.7	21.38	19.1	16.40	17.8	4.28	15.95	4.3	16.2
1961	21.38	19.1	23.30	20.4	18.83	17.8	4.52	16.94	4.0	14.9
1963	23.34	20.9			20.79	19.2	4.75	17.52	4.2	15.5

Year										
1965	26.20	21.6	26.10	21.4	23.60	20.3	5.90	19.12	4.8	15.6
1967	26.96	21.1	26.96	21.1	24.75	20.1	5.53	18.83	4.4	15.1
1969	26.86	20.0	26.86	20.0	24.71	19.2	5.01	18.51	3.8	14.1
1971	27.67	19.5	27.67	19.5	25.65	18.9	5.53	19.89	3.9	14.2
1973	28.43	18.2	29.98	19.2	26.72	17.7	4.72	16.84	3.0	10.8
1975	28.78	18.0	34.49	21.5	26.98	17.6	4.75	17.85	2.9	10.9
1977	29.33	19.4	34.92	23.1	27.40	19.2	4.79	15.74	3.2	10.5
1979	29.10	17.9	36.65	22.5	27.51	17.7	7.07	21.20	4.3	12.9
1981	27.41	17.4	36.06	22.9	27.87	18.0	6.47	19.42	4.1	12.2
1983	29.58	18.1	37.24	22.7	28.80	17.9	7.19	21.58	4.3	13.0
1984[6]	29.65	17.7	37.31	22.3	29.02	17.5	7.22	21.66	4.3	12.9

Notes:

1. Taken at various months of the year but November from 1975 onwards.
2. Man or single woman.
3. Man or woman on own insurance. From 1971 figures refer to benefit payable to the under 80s only.
4. Single householder.
5. The benefits relate to families on average earnings. Child support from April 1979 became child benefit only. Tax allowances were discontinued from that date.
6. 1984 figures are provisional. Due to the introduction of a new earning index, 1984 figures for percentage of average earnings may, in some cases, be higher than they would have been under the old measure.

Sources: **DHSS** *Social Security Statistics,* 1985;
CSO, *Abstract of Statistics,* 1985 (revised January 1986).

Table 12.33 Estimated numbers[1] of families and persons[2] with incomes[3] at or below 140 per cent of the supplementary benefit level,[4] 1972-83, Great Britain

Year	Situation	Income below supplementary benefit level		Receiving supplementary benefit		Income at or above supplementary benefit level but within 40% of it		Total		Total persons as a percentage of population
		Families (000s)	Persons (000s)	Families (000s)	Persons (000s)	Families (000s)	Persons (000s)	Families (000s)	Persons (000s)	(%)
1972	over pension age	—	980	—	—	—	—	—	—	—
	all ages	—	1 780	—	—	—	—	—	—	—
1973	over pension age	—	850	—	—	—	—	—	—	—
	all ages	—	1 600	—	—	—	—	—	—	—
1975	below pension age and single without children	260	260	340	340	290	290	890	890	
	and single with children	50	150	260	760	80	250	390	1 160	15.6
	and married without children	60	120	70	130	190	380	320	630	
	and married with children	130	570	120	550	710	3 200	960	4 320	
	over pension age	590	740	1 640	1 930	2 000	2 870	4 230	5 540	58.2
	all ages	1 090	1 840	2 430	3 710	3 270	6 990	6 790	12 540	23.1
1977	below pension age and single without children	390	390	390	390	390	390	1 170	1 170	
	and single with children	40[5]	110	320	900	90	290	450	1 300	18.5
	and married without children	50[5]	90	80	160	230	450	360	700	
	and married with children	160	670	150	700	880	2 600	1 1..	6 6..	

over pension age	620	760	1 700	2 000	2 150	3 010	4 470	5 770	59.9
all ages	1 260	2 020	2 650	4 160	3 730	7 840	7 640	14 020	25.8
1979									
below pension age and single without children	350	350	390	390	260	260	1 000	1 000	
and single with children	40[5]	110	320	900	70	200	430	1 210	12.7[4]
and married without children	40[5]	90	70	150	140	280	250	520	
and married with children	110	450	130	560	450	1 970	690	2 980	
over pension age	860	1 130	1 680	1 990	1 990	2 770	4 530	5 890	60.9[4]
all ages	1 420	2 130	2 590	3 980	2 910	5 470	6 920	11 580	21.3[4]
1981									
below pension age and single without children	560	560	640	640	530	530	1 730	1 730	
and single with children	60	170	370	990	90	280	520	1 440	20.3
and married without children	60	120	100	200	210	410	370	730	
and married with children	200	850	250	1 040	780	3 310	1 230	5 200	
over pension age	880	1 120	1 670	1 960	1 980	2 810	4 530	5 890	59.8
all ages	1 760	2 810	3 010	4 840	3 580	7 350	8 350	15 000	27.4

continued overleaf

514

Table 12.33—continued   Estimated numbers[1] of families and persons[2] with incomes[3] at or below 140 per cent of the supplementary benefit level,[4] 1972–83, Great Britain

Year	Situation	Income below supplementary benefit level		Receiving supplementary benefit		Income at or above supplementary benefit level but within 40% of it		Total		Total persons as a percentage of population
		Families (000s)	Persons (000s)	Families (000s)	Persons (000s)	Families (000s)	Persons (000s)	Families (000s)	Persons (000s)	(%)
1983	below pension age and single without children	700	700	1 000	1 000	1 560	1 560	3 260	3 260	
	and single with children	30	80	460	1 230	110	320	600	1 630	27.7
	and married without children	120	230	190	390	310	620	620	1 240	
	and married with children	170	690	390	1 640	940	3 920	1 500	6 250	
	over pension age	870	1 080	1 600	1 880	2 820	3 830	5 290	6 790	75.7
	all ages	1 880	2 780	3 640	6 140	5 740	10 250	11 260	19 170	35.7

Notes:
1. All figures rounded to the nearest 10 000.
2. The estimates relate only to people living in private households; families and persons in institutions are not sampled.
3. Income refers to net income less net housing costs, less travel to work expenses where appropriate.
4. 'A change in the method of estimating was introduced for 1979. In previous years, data recorded at interview, in what is a continuous survey, have been adjusted to represent the position at the end of the year by making assumptions about changes of income between the time of interview and December. As supplementary benefit scale rates have been uprated in November of each year and are normally at their highest relative to most other forms of income just after upratings, end of year estimates of low income families are close to the seasonal peak. It was therefore decided to take income as at the time of interview. This produces an annual average, and therefore provides a truer indication of the extent of low income. The 1979 estimates represent the average over the year and are therefore not directly comparable with estimates for earlier years' (Social Security Statistics, 1983).
   This change to a lower base line will reduce the number of people counted as having low incomes in 1979, relative to earlier years.
5. These figures are subject to very considerable proportionate statistical error.

Sources: A. B. Atkinson, The Economics of Inequality (1983);
   Analysis of Family Expenditure Survey in: Social Security Statistics, 1976, 1981, 1983 and 1985;
   DHSS, Low Income Families – 1983, (1986).

moved in, similar way, doubling its real value, though occasionally slipping below the 1946 level in the earlier years. If benefits are expressed as a percentage of average earnings, trends actually turn downwards or rise only marginally. The relative position of unemployment benefit has worsened, retirement pensions have improved and supplementary benefit has remained much the same. The value of child benefits for small families has barely changed in relation to earnings but for larger families there has been a downward trend.

The final table (12.33) shows the number of people and proportion of the population living at various income levels around the official poverty line. The figures reveal an upward trend since the early 1970s, only apparently interrupted in 1979 when the changed method of estimating income produced a smaller number of poor people. And the steepest increase, of nearly two-thirds, has been among the poorest – those living on or below the supplementary benefit standard. Among all poor people, those below pensionable age and single and without children have increased most quickly, multiplying three and a half times to reach over 3 million by 1983. There has also been a noticeable rise of nearly 50 per cent in the numbers of younger people with children and a smaller one of only 20 per cent among those over pensionable age. The final picture in 1983 shows 19 million people, 36 per cent of the population, living at or around the supplementary benefit level. Among them were nearly 7 million old people and nearly 8 million younger families with children. The rate of increase in the number and proportion of low income families has accelerated sharply since 1979.

Notes

1   The areas of local administration for the Poor Law, formed increasingly after 1834 by 'unions' of parishes.
2   Local authorities usually take into their institutions only persons so handicapped as to be unable to look after themselves and who have no relatives or friends who can support them.
3   After 1971 local authorities were no longer required to provide school milk for children over 7. In 1980 nutritional standards for meals were withdrawn and local authorities were free to act according to their discretion. Free school meals still had to be provided for children from families on supplementary benefit or receiving Family Income Supplement.
4   Bentley B. Gilbert (1966) *The Evolution of National Insurance in Great Britain: The Origins of the Welfare State* (Michael Joseph), Chapter 3.
5   For changing rates of unemployment see Chapter 4, especially Table 4.7.
6   A more detailed discussion and analysis of public spending on the personal social services through the 1970s is to be found in Adrian Webb and Gerald Wistow (1982) 'The Personal Social Services: Incrementalism, Expediency or Systematic Social Planning?', in Alan Walker (ed.) *Public Expenditure and Social Policy* (Heinemann).

References

ATKINSON, A. B. (1983) *The Economics of Inequality* (Oxford: Oxford University Press).
BOARD OF CONTROL, *Annual Reports*, 1900–49.
BOARD OF EDUCATION   *Annual Reports*, part I, 1900–38;
　Annual Reports, part II, the Report of the Chief Medical Officer of the Board of Education from 1921 onwards, published under the title *Health of the School Child*;
　Statistics of Public Education, annually, 1900–18;
　Report on Schools for the Blind and Deaf (1981) for the two years ending 31 August 1900, Cd 600.
　Report on the Working of the Education (Provision of Meals) Act 1906), Cd 5724.
CENTRAL STATISTICAL OFFICE
　Annual Abstract of Statistics (formerly the *Statistical Abstract for the United Kingdom*), 1946 to date;
　National Income and Expenditure, 1964–74;
　Regional Trends no. 21 (1986);
　Social Trends, no. 1 (1970);
　Statistical Abstract for the United Kingdom, annually, no. 50 (1902) to no. 82 (1937);
　United Kingdom National Accounts: The CSO Blue Book (1985).
DEPARTMENT OF EDUCATION AND SCIENCE (DoES) (before 1964 MINISTRY OF EDUCATION)
　Report of the Chief Medical Officer, *The Health of the School Child*, 1969–70;
　Statistics of Education: vol. 1, 1972 and 1978; vol. 5, 1968 and 1972;
　Statistics of Education in Wales, no. 7 (1982) and no. 10 (1985);
　Finance and Awards, 1982–3;
　Schools, 1983.
DEPARTMENT OF THE ENVIRONMENT (DoE) AND THE WELSH OFFICE
　Local Housing Statistics: England and Wales, quarterly 1966 to date;
　(With Scottish Development Department), *Housing and Construction Statistics*, quarterly, 1972 to date, 1979–80 and 1974–84.
DEPARTMENT OF HEALTH AND SOCIAL SECURITY (DHSS)
　Abstracts of Statistics (revised) 1986;
　Annual Reports, annually 1968 to 1977;
　Children in Care in England and Wales, annually, 1971 to date;
　Digest of Health Statistics, 1970;
　Health and Personal Social Services Statistics, 1972;
　Health and Personal Social Services Statistics for England, 1973 to date;
　Social Security Statistics, annually, 1972 to date.
　Low Income Families – 1983 (1986).
DEPARTMENT OF HEALTH FOR SCOTLAND (before 1929 SCOTTISH BOARD OF HEALTH), *Annual Reports*, 1929–61.
GILBERT, B. B. (1966) *The Evolution of National Insurance in Great Britain: The Origins of the Welfare State* (Michael Joseph).
HOME OFFICE
　Annual Reports of the Inspector of Reformatory and Industrial Schools, 1900–15;
　Fifth Report on the Work of the Children's Branch, 1938;
　Reports on the Work of the Children's Department, 1951, 1955 and 1961, 1961–3, 1964–6 and 1967–9;
　Annual Returns on Children in the Care of Local Authorities in England and Wales, 1952 to 1970;

LOCAL GOVERNMENT BOARD
    Annual Reports, 1900–19.
    Local Taxation Returns, annually, from 1900 to 1918.
    Poor Relief (Annual Returns), 1900–20.
LOCAL GOVERNMENT BOARD FOR SCOTLAND, *Annual Reports*, 1900–19.
LONDON AND CAMBRIDGE ECONOMIC SERVICES, *British Economy Key Statistics, 1900–1964.*
MINISTRY OF EDUCATION (formerly BOARD OF EDUCATION), *Annual Reports and Statistics of Education*, 1947–60.
MINISTRY OF HEALTH (took over the duties of the LOCAL GOVERNMENT BOARD in 1919)
    Annual Reports, part I, 1919–67;
    Annual Reports of the Advisory Committee on the Welfare of the Blind, 1919–36;
    Health and Welfare: The Development of Community Care, Cmnd 1973, (1963); revised to 1975–6, Cmnd 3022, (1966).
    Local Government Financial Statistics, up to 1935–6;
    Local Taxation Returns 1920–21 to 1930–31;
    Poor Relief (Annual Returns), 1921–39, 1946–7, 1947–8 and 1948.
    Register of the Blind, unpublished material;
    (Jointly with the DEPARTMENT OF HEALTH FOR SCOTLAND) *Younghusband Report* (1959) Report of the Working Party on Social Workers in Local Authority Health and Welfare Services.
MINISTRY OF HOUSING AND LOCAL GOVERNMENT (1966) Scottish Development Department and the Welsh Office, *Housing Statistics*, no. 2.
MINISTRY OF LABOUR
    Annual Abstract of Labour Statistics of the United Kingdom, 1900–1936;
    Annual Reports, 1923–60;
    Labour Gazette, monthly, 1900–1966;
    Report of a Working Party on Workshops for the Blind, 1962.
MINISTRY OF NATIONAL INSURANCE, *Annual Reports*, 1944–53.
MINISTRY OF PENSIONS, *Annual Reports*, 1918–52.
MINISTRY OF PENSIONS AND NATIONAL INSURANCE, *Annual Reports*, 1953–65.
NATIONAL ASSISTANCE BOARD, *Annual Reports*, 1948–65.
SCOTTISH BOARD OF HEALTH, *Annual Reports*, 1919–28.
SCOTTISH HOME AND HEALTH DEPARTMENT (formerly DEPARTMENT OF HEALTH FOR SCOTLAND), *Annual Report*, 1962.
TOWNSEND, P. and WEDDERBURN, D. (1965) *The Aged in the Welfare State*, Occasional Papers in Social Administration, no. 14 (Bell).
TREASURY, *Returns of Expenditure on Public Social Services*, annually, 1922–38.
UNEMPLOYMENT ASSISTANCE BOARD, *Annual Reports*, 1935–9.
WEBB, A. and WISTOW, G. (1982) 'The Personal Social Services: Incrementalism, Expediency or Systematic Social Planning?' in Alan Walker (ed.) *Public Expenditure and Social Policy* (Heinemann).
WELSH OFFICE
    Health and Personal Social Services Statistics for Wales, annually, 1974 to date;
    Welsh Housing Statistics, no. 5 (1985).

13 Religion

Peter Brierley

Religious statistics are intrinsically fascinating. They are more than a codifying of an interesting sociological phenomenon. They reflect in numerical terms a complex pattern of human behaviour, belief and understanding.

The New Oxford Illustrated Dictionary defines 'religion' as the 'human recognition of a super-human controlling power and especially from a personal God or gods entitled to obedience and worship'. The predominant religion in the United Kingdom is Christianity and all three broad historical streams of the the Christian faith are seen in this country – Protestantism, Catholicism, and the Orthodox Church. There are two established churches, the Church of England and the Church of Scotland, which are two of the many autonomous denominations in the Protestant group. Even the Catholic group has several components, from the dominant Roman Catholic Church to the smaller groups like the Old Catholics, or the Ukrainian Catholic Church. Likewise there are a number of distinct national groups within the Orthodox Church.

The Christian faith is not the only religious faith in this country. Hinduism, Islam, Buddhism, Sikhism are all present, as are more modern developments of these ancient creeds, like the Ahmadiyya Movement of the Muslims, and the Rastafarians. Also present in the United Kingdom, though growing less quickly in the 1980s than they did in the 1970s, are those religions which have some relationship to Christianity but which have departed from the fundamental tenets of traditional Christianity. The most common of these is to say that Jesus is not the Son of God. This so called 'non-Trinitarian' group includes the Jehovah's Witnesses, Mormons, Christadelphians, Christian Scientists, Theosophists, Church of Scientology, Unification Church (Moonies), the Worldwide Church of God and so on. But as this chapter indicates, there are very few non-Christian or extra-Christian groups outside the Jews publishing statistics relating to their activities.

Other elements of religiousness, the so-called 'common' or 'implicit' religion, general religiosity or superstition have not been included. This is for the pragmatic reason of definition (for there are few widely accepted in this broad area) and because, in practice, there is very little data available.

SOURCES OF INFORMATION

The bulk of available religious statistical data relates to the Christian faith.

Two key books have been used extensively – Robert Currie's massive *Churches and Churchgoers*, and the various editions of the *U.K. Christian Handbook* (UKCH). Robert Currie and Alan Gilbert provided this chapter and its data for the first edition of this book. Broadly their data sources account for the historical data up to 1970, and the UKCH for later figures. In most instances the information reproduced in these two volumes comes from the individual church or denominational headquarters directly.

Currie's data has been used selectively to give as much uniformity as possible with respect for the dates, and the quinquennial years since 1900 have therefore mostly been used. Many religious statistics change relatively slowly and this period is normally sufficient to monitor movements adequately.

The tables start with summaries of the membership, ministers and buildings of the larger denominations, followed by details of individual denominations. One table (Table 13.11) highlights recent figures for the many other smaller groups which exist.

Since 1980 three sets of publications – *Prospects for the Eighties* (covering English churches), *Prospects for Wales* and *Prospects for Scotland* – have given details of church attendance as opposed to church membership. The essence of these publications is reproduced in Table 13.12, and use is made of these figures to look at the nominalism present in Great Britain (Table 13.16) by defining this as the difference between membership and actual attendance. The age and sex of churchgoers (Table 13.22) also comes from these volumes.

For some tables, newly added in this edition, none of these volumes suffice. The specific source for each of these tables is given in appropriate notes. These tables cover the denominational allegiance of prison inmates, specific detail relating to Wales and Northern Ireland (published by the Welsh Office and Registrar General respectively), religious marriages, cremations, and some details from David Barrett's colossal *World Christian Encyclopaedia* (OUP, 1982) which gives some data for all denominations in every country in the world. A brief look at the publishing scene, and numbers of para-church agencies completes the list.

THE STRUCTURE OF THE CHURCHES' DATA COLLECTION SYSTEM

Each church body is totally autonomous, and what data it collects, and when, is entirely within its own purview and own authority structure. Needless to say, this varies from one body to another. An indication of the historical background and organisational structure of many of the major denominations, as well as several smaller groups, is given in the book *International Church Index* (Index Publications 1981) and not, therefore, repeated here.

The mechanism for all published data on individual church membership is a form completed annually by the minister or priest and sent to the appropriate headquarters. These forms vary considerably in the information requested, and in time of completion. The Anglicans and Roman Catholics gross up for non-response, but others, such as the Baptist Union of Great Britain and Ireland publish just the information actually received, repeating data of earlier years when no new information has been received. Only the Methodist church ensures that one year's return balances exactly with the previous years, not publishing their figures until the gains and losses experienced over a particular year matches the difference between the total of one year and the year before. Only the Anglican, Roman Catholic, Church of Scotland and Methodist data systems were computerised at the time of writing.

This is but the structural element of the problem of understanding what the data really indicates. The difficulty of defining religion at all leads to a second problem very familiar with social researchers. This is the conflict between beliefs, attitudes and behaviour. The New Testament, for example, defines pure religion in a behavioural dimension, that is, the visiting of 'orphans and widows in their affliction' and 'keeping oneself unstained from the world'. But can such behaviour actually be measured? The merits and demerits of qualitative research in measuring perceived actual behaviour will not be discussed here, but one observation may be pertinent. It is that quantitative assessments of church-going in this country must not be confused with attitudes towards the deity. There are essentially two elements, one of which is concerned with, simplistically, the number of people who say 'I believe in God', and the other which is concerned with the behavioural manifestation of that belief. Thus, one cannot infer the true religious following in Britain from market research studies that ask people simply the frequency with which they attend church. Expressed belief, church membership, church-going and other behavioural dimensions may all differ widely.

PROBLEMS OF DATA MEASUREMENT

A major problem is that of **diversity in terminology**, apparent from the descriptions given in individual sections. One of the most important words has unfortunately one of the greatest varieties of meaning – that is church membership. There is little agreement amongst the main Christian churches or non-Christian religions as to what this is. For example, some in the Church of England equate it with a person being on their 'Electoral Roll' (not to be confused with the local authority electoral roll). Any baptised adult (aged 16 or over) who has been to a particular church over the previous six months may ask to be put on it; if one should go to more than one Anglican church it is possible for that person to be on more than one Electoral Roll. The Church of Ireland and others publish communicant figures rather than membership figures. The Roman Catholics define membership as the Catholic population, that is those who were baptised in the Catholic church as infants. The Baptist church members on the other hand are those who have been baptised as adults, and certain West Indian churches require the speaking of tongues before admitting a baptised person into membership. The theological overtones implicit in many such definitions makes it extremely unlikely for any quick resolution of this problem.

Another example of terminology problems is seen in the use of the word 'church'. The majority of churches are specially-built structures in use regularly for the worship of God, but there are many hundreds of groups, who used to meet every Sunday in an ordinary house to worship God, which gave rise to the misleading title 'House Church Movement'. Many of these now meet in schools, or other hired halls; they are autonomous, self-governing churches, but have no obvious external sign of their existence. Hence even counting the number of churches in a particular locality is not straightforward, and the same is true of the buildings used by Buddhists, Hindus and others.

Diversity in timing is a further problem. The larger denominations all collect statistics from their churches on a regular basis, but the time when these figures are counted varies from one church to another. Roman Catholics count their mass attendance in the month of May, the Methodists their membership in October, and the Baptists quote their membership figures for the year ending in December. The Church of England counts its electoral roll numbers every November, though occasionally (as in 1975) it omits a year.

There are also **different periodicities.** The Methodists count their church membership every year, but church attendance figures only every third year. The Church of England has a major electoral roll revision every six years (this practice began in 1972, and was repeated in 1978 and 1984). At these revisions, all on the electoral roll *have* to sign on afresh. Inevitably the first count after the revision shows a drop from the previous count since those who have died or moved out of the parish are excluded.

These problems are compounded by a fourth – **lack of continuity.** The tables which follow frequently have gaps at certain periods. Thus trend analysis is hindered and, of course, the different definitions used make it impossible to compare truly across denominations, though within-denominational comparisons are more valid. In some instances to facilitate use, certain omitted figures have been estimated; such figures are all indicated.

The evaluation of forms requesting church statistics by church headquarter administrators varies from one church to another, but it is frequently undertaken **without professional assistance.** Thus published data is not always as accurate, comprehensive, or robust, as researchers and others might wish. Associated with this problem is also the fact that figures given by the same denomination at different times for ostensibly the same item (as 'numbers of members in 1970') may in fact be quite different! The differences often stem from the perception of the person answering the question. Does 'the number of ministers' include or exclude retired, but still active, ministers? chaplains? those assigned to administrative tasks? Often the researcher is at fault by not anticipating his/her request with sufficient clarity.

A further problem is the **absence of crucial data.** Certain types of information of major interest to researchers are rarely if ever collected in the macro, and thus geographical analyses, for example, are virtually inhibited. The socio-economic category of church-goers, often thought to be mainly middle class, has only been explored in sample surveys. Likewise, the ethnic origin of church members, and their political viewpoint. What kinds of job do church members have? What is their marital status? How many families go to church? Do church families have more children on average than non-church families? When church members move, do they continue their church membership? How far do they change denominations? All these are questions of concern, with varying answers in the massive sociological literature, which we are fortunate to possess in this country. Some answers naturally tend to be only for one or two groups or in one particular locality. This is not to castigate in any way the excellence of the steady stream of topical research that is undertaken, but emphasises the need for the background building studies against which smaller elements may be suitably interpreted and verified.

Underlying all these mechanical or sociopolitical features is one which is absolutely fundamental, which if corrected, might contain the seeds which would allow the plant of better statistics to grow. This is simply the fact that many clergy do not feel that numerate data is of use to them in their ministry, or believing they would feel threatened by such, tend to ignore it. Thus there is **little use of statistical information** by those who might naturally expect to apply it.

DOES IT MATTER?

Over the last 15 years British church membership has declined from 8.5 million to just under 7 million. In the same period the number of full-time ministers has decreased by 4 000, and 3 000 church buildings have closed. Yet against these depressing figures one needs to remember the 11 per cent of the adult population who go to church at least once a month, and a further 7 per cent who belong to a church but do not regularly attend. In addition some 46 per cent of the population would claim some notional allegiance to the church (mostly the Church of England). This leaves about 7 per cent who belong to the 'non-Trinitarian' churches and non-Christian religions, and 29 per cent who have no religious allegiance at all, which whilst still substantial proportions, are nevertheless minorities. (Estimated 1985 percentages.)

Two thousand six hundred religious books were published in 1986 leading the commentator in *The Listener* to say that 'these figures represent a significant subculture of belief in this country'. Such items of information, diffuse, diverse and discontinuous as they may be, nevertheless give us some information, some firm data, on which to appraise the religious scene in this country.

Exactly 100 years ago, A. T. Pierson wrote: 'Facts are the fingers of God. To know the facts . . . is the necessary condition of intelligent interest. Knowledge does not always kindle zeal, but zeal is "according to knowledge" and will not exist without it'. Perhaps these tables will in some small way help feed that knowledge, and yield that excitement and interest which such figures can surely generate.

Table 13.1 Church membership of larger denominations, 1900–1985

| Year | ANGLICAN | | | | PRESBYTERIAN AND CONGREGATIONAL | | | BAP-TISTS | METHODISTS | | | Total GB | Ireland | ROMAN CATHOLIC |
	C. of Eng.[1]	C. in Wales	Scot. Epis.	C. of Irel.[3]	C. of Scot.	Pres./Cong.	Total	BUGBI	England	Wales[6]	Scotland	MC		Great Britain
1900	2 796 000	141 008	116 296	296 000	661 629	1 283 499	1 945 128	365 275	728 289	33 926	8 191	770 406	27 745	—
1905	2 889 000	125 234	131 232	301 000	692 914	1 396 940	2 089 854	426 077	782 478	40 600	9 248	832 326	28 511	—
1910	3 391 000	152 654	141 732	306 000	714 039	1 394 934	2 108 973	418 194	791 961	39 562	9 770	841 294	29 357	2 339 038 (1913)
1915	3 375 000	157 089	144 159	311 000	721 137	1 402 741	2 123 878	411 490	775 837	38 721	9 561	824 119	27 795	2 433 655 (1916)
1920	3 323 000	159 957	144 489	315 000	739 251	1 416 687	2 155 938	404 544	752 302	39 751	9 668	801 721	27 247	2 501 937
1925	3 601 782	176 271	144 670	319 000	762 774	1 431 823	2 194 597	413 697	780 396	42 588	10 655	833 639	29 062	—
1930	3 656 630	184 604	134 066	323 000	1 271 095	899 616	2 170 711	405 808	788 183	42 118	11 161	841 462	30 087	2 813 244 (1931)
1935	3 598 522	195 744	130 028	326 000	1 288 648	888 912	2 177 560	400 638	759 835	52 065	13 698	825 598	30 757	2 933 294
1940	3 388 859	187 000E	124 498	329 000	1 278 297	865 032	2 143 329	381 841	728 470	49 879	13 843	792 192	31 053	2 989 665 (1939)
1945	2 989 704 (1947)	155 911	110 673	333 000	1 259 927	819 693	2 079 620	354 395 (1946)	690 088	48 735	13 836	752 659	31 193	3 036 826
1950	2 958 840	182 000E	108 502	336 000	1 271 247	781 812	2 053 059	337 203	683 823	47 033	13 959	744 815	31 933	3 557 059
1955	2 894 710 (1956)	176 000E	108 127	334 000	1 307 573	767 701	2 075 274	326 269	684 992	45 009	14 320	744 321	32 724	3 926 830
1960	2 861 887	182 864	97 038	331 000	1 301 280	732 640	2 033 920	317 360	672 916	41 721	13 952	728 589	31 909	4 495 157
1965	2 682 181 (1966)	165 273	97 175	326 000	1 247 972	691 483	1 939 455	294 360	639 028	38 543	12 776	690 347	30 996	4 875 825
1970	2 558 966	153 925	85 816	322 000	1 154 211	617 399	1 771 610	268 707	555 933	33 714	11 421	601 068		4 932 471
1975	1 912 000[2]E (1976)	133 107	44 741	300 000	1 041 772	674 771[4]	1 716 543[4]	181 798	503 400	28 935	9 183	541 518		4 996 310
1980	1 815 000[2]E	131 518	40 961	276 000	953 933	555 035[4]	1 508 968[4]	170 338	453 872	25 993	8 167	487 972		5 085 889
1985	1 672 000[2]E	116 911	37 000E	252 000	870 527	518 071[4]	1 388 598[4]	154 290 (1984)	406 534	22 525[5]	6 990	436 049	20 565[5]	5 023 736 (1974)

Notes: MC = Methodist Church, BUGBI = Baptist church of Great Britain & Ireland.

1. Electoral Roll.
2. Electoral Roll figures as supplied by the Church of England.

   1970 2 559 000
   1973 2 021 000
   1976 2 033 000
   1978 1 761 000
   1982 1 814 000
   1984 1 495 000

3. Estimated.
4. Change of basis, now includes Congregational Churches and United Reformed Church
5. Communicant members. Similar figures not available for 1970, 1975 or 1980.
6. From 1935 includes Primitive and United Methodists

Source: For sources see Tables 13.4, 13.5, 13.6, 13.7, 13.8, 13.9, 13.10.

525

Table 13.2 Number of ministers by larger denominations, 1900–1985

Year	ANGLICAN				BAPTISTS	METHODISTS	PRESBYTERIAN/CONGREGATIONAL					ROMAN CATHOLIC
	C. of Eng.	C. in Wales	Scot. Epis.	C. of Irel.			C. of Scot.	United Free Church of Scotland	Presbyterian Church of Wales	Cong.	URC	
1900	20 953	1 002	321 (1901)	—	1 963	4 087	1 828 (1901)	1 772	1 231	3 086	—	2 308
1905	20 571	967	—	—	2 074	4 419	—	—	1 248	3 095	—	2 580
1910	19 200E	972	349 (1911)	—	2 098	4 794	1 765 (1911)	1 604	1 310	3 104	—	2 758
1915	18 180 (1914)	985	—	—	2 080	4 878	—	—	1 230	3 091	—	2 949
1920	17 800E	975	326 (1921)	—	2 046	4 668	1 560 (1921)	1 563	1 156	—	—	2 998
1925	17 560	999	—	392 (1926)	2 020	4 773	—	1 492	1 156	—	—	3 114
1930	16 942	981	316 (1931)	—	2 017	4 765	2 751 (1931)	1 442 (1928)	1 147 (1929)	2 857	—	3 325
1935	17 193	981	—	—	2 020	5 201	—	—	1 120	2 846	—	3 909
1940	17 113 (1939)	—	316 (1941)	—	2 035	5 180	—	—	1 075 (1939)	2 804	—	4 468
1945	15 200E	—	—	—	1 886 (1946)	5 054	—	—	970	—	—	4 891
1950	13 500 (1951)	981	334 (1951)	378 (1951)	1 907	5 215	2 485 (1951)	—	913	—	—	5 078
1955	13 090 (1956)	950	—	—	1 945	5 053	—	—	839	—	—	5 317
1960	13 151	861	367 (1961)	—	2 049	5 075	—	—	759	—	—	5 637
1965	13 508	791	—	—	2 088	4 876	—	—	664	—	—	6 117 (1966)
1970	12 905 (1971)	737	325 (1968)	445	2 039	4 007E	1 754	77	346[2]	—	1 844 (1972)	6 245 (1971)
1975	11 176 (1977)	679	—	355	1 511	3 768E	1 588	76	276[2]	—	1 795	6 245
1980	10 563	674	—	330	1 393	3 506	1 536	73	220[2]	—	1 694	5 864
1985	10 074 (1984)	630	240E	364E	1 392 (1984)	3 425E	1 299	69	168[2]	—	1 303 (1984)	4 545

Notes: 1. URC = United Reformed Church.
2. Excluding retired ministers.

Source: For sources see Tables 13.4, 13.5, 13.6, 13.7, 13.8, 13.9, 13.10.

Table 13.3 Number of Churches by larger Denominations in Great Britain 1900–1985

| Year | ANGLICAN | | | BAPTIST | PRESBYTERIAN AND CONGREGATIONAL | | | | | | CATHO-LIC |
	C. of E.	C. in Wales	PCoE[2]		C. of Scot.	UFCoS[1]	URC	Cong.	EFCC[3]	Presbyterian Church of Wales[4]	
1901	17 468	—	326	2 710	1 828	1 630	—	4 876	—	2 953	1 886
1906	17 817	1 540	345	2 944	1 679	1 623	—	4 890	—	3 069	2 021
1911	18 026	—	354	3 047	1 643	1 545	—	4 910	—	3 128	2 179
1916	18 236	—	355	3 110	1 701	1 516	—	4 861	—	3 231	2 323
1921	18 270	—	352	3 019	1 704	1 482	—		—	3 264	2 377
1926	18 318	—	350	3 073	1 714	1 449	—	4 585	—	3 265	2 443
1931	18 417	1 751	353	3 122	2 920	—	—	4 671	—	3 201	2 685
1936	18 550	1 750	345	3 139	2 588	—	—	4 576	—	3 219	2 859
1941	18 666	1 693 (1939)	333	3 203	2 483	—	—	4 615	—	3 195	3 061
1946	—	—	334	3 215	2 410	—	—	4 516	—	3 133	3 242
1951	—	—	333	3 277	2 340	—	—	4 280	—	3 039	3 419
1956	17 980	—	326	3 200	2 280	—	—	4 188	—	3 036	—
1961	17 973	1 764 (1959)	318	3 215	2 093	—	—		—	3 010	—
1966	17 761	1 789 (1963)	312	3 211	2 166	—	—		—		—
1970	17 670	1 780	312	3 147	2 119	100	2 080 (1972)		—	1 300	4 047
1975	17 212	1 720	312	3 044	1 975	87	2 063		103	1 228	3 106
1980	16 984	1 675	311	2 762	1 852	84E	1 960		141	1 169	3 077
1985	16 582E	1 450	315	2 688	1 765	83	1 880		149	1 106	3 161

Notes:

1. United Free Church of Scotland.
2. Presbyterian Church of England, now the Scottish Episcopal Church.
3. Evangelical Fellowship of Congregational Churches.
4. Includes Churches, chapels and preaching places 1900–1961 churches only from 1970

Source: For sources see Tables 13.4, 13.5, 13.6, 13.7, 13.8, 13.9, 13.10.

Table 13.4 Detail of Church of England 1900–1985

Year	Electoral roll[1] (000s)	Easter Day communicants (000s)	Sunday School (000s)	Total parochial clergy[5]	Churches[3]
1900	2 796E	1 902	2 302	20 953 (1901)	17 468 (1901)
1905	2 889E	1 939	2 398	20 571	17 817 (1906)
1910	3 391E	2 212	2 437	—	18 026 (1911)
1915	3 075E	2 203	2 255	18 180 (1914)	18 236 (1916)
1920	3 323E	2 172	2 010	—	18 270 (1921)
1925	3 602	2 388	1 915	17 560	18 318 (1926)
1930	3 656	2 262	1 802	16 942	18 417 (1931)
1935	3 599	2 300	1 645	17 193	18 550 (1936)
1940	3 389	1 998	1 434 (1939)	17 113 (1939)	18 666 (1941)
1945	2 990 (1947)	1 729 (1947)	—	—	–
1950	2 959	1 848	—	13 500 (1951)	–
1955	2 895 (1956)	2 168 (1956)	1 308 (1956)	13 090 (1956)	17 980 (1956)
1960	2 862	2 159	1 039[4]	13 151	17 973 (1961)
1965	2 682 (1966)	1 899 (1966)		13 508	17 761 (1966)
1970	2 559	1 632		12 905 (1971)	17 670
1975[6]	1 912E	1 500E[2]		11 176	17 212
1980	1 815	1 526E		10 563	16 984
1985	1 672E[7]	1 468E (1982)		10 074 (1984)	16 582

Sources:

1. 1900–1924, data estimated using 1924–40 Communicant: Electoral Roll proportion trend.
2. 1975–82, Easter Day Communicants estimated from total Easter Week communicants using 1960–70 Easter week: Easter Day proportion trend.
3. 1901–66, Currie et al. (1977) Churches and Churchgoers; 1970–85 from Brierley (ed) UK Christian Handbook, 1987–8 edition.
4. This information is no longer collected because of the expense of doing so (per Church House).
5. Figures exclude non-stipendiary clergy and those working full-time in the prison, hospital or educational sectors. They cover beneficed clergy in the diocesan framework.
6. Six-year compulsory revisions began in 1972 and continued in 1978 and 1984.
7. This is an estimate rather than the official Electoral Roll figure because of the increasing tendency to use such figures for aiding the Church's financial structures.

Table 13.5   Detail of Church in Wales, 1900–1985

Year	Communicants[1]	Churches[3]	Sunday School[2]	Incumbencies[3]
1900	141 008	—	159 078	1 002
1905	125 234	1 540	164 584	967
1910	152 654	—	197 129	972
1915	157 089	—	196 435	985
1920	159 957	—	181 017	975
1925	176 271	—	179 942	999
1930	184 604	1 751	163 034	981
1935	195 744	1 750	147 475	981
1940	187 000 (1939)	1 693	—	—
1945	155 911	—	—	—
1950	182 000	—	—	981
1955	176 000	—	—	950
1960	182 864 (1959)	1 764	—	861
1965	165 273 (1963)	1 720	—	791
1970	154 700E[4]	1 780	—	737
1975	135 228 (1976)	1 720	—	679
1980	131 518	1 675	—	674[5]
1985	115 896	1 450	—	630

Sources:
1.   1900–1970 Currie *et al.* (1977). *Churches and Churchgoers*.
      1975–1985 Church in Wales.
2.   1900–1935 *Churches and Churchgoers*. No data after 1935.
3.   *Digest of Welsh Historical Statistics, Vol. 2* (1985). John Williams.

Notes:
4.   No figure given. The 1968 figure was 154 667, and the 1974 figure 137 326.
5.   The sources do not agree totally. Here they are reproduced:

Williams:	1965	791	Church	1974	750
	1968	770	in	1976	738
	1970	737	Wales:	1978	699
	1975	679		1979	688
				1980	674
				1981	665
				1982	658
				1983	643
				1984	636
				1985	630

Table 13.6 Detail of Church of Scotland 1900–1985

Year	Number on Roll	Communicants	Baptisms	Sunday School scholars	Ministers	Churches[1]
1900	661 629	474 929	39 256	222 944	1 828 (1901)	1 828 (1901)
1905	692 914	504 123	37 648	233 814	–	1 679 (1906)
1910	714 039	513 758	34 411	234 980	1 765 (1911)	1 643 (1911)
1915	721 137	495 932	31 335	211 129		1 701 (1916)
1920	739 251	509 541	35 812	193 616	1 560 (1921)	1 704 (1921)
1925	762 774	549 012	28 167	195 952		1 714 (1926)
1930[2]	1 271 095	892 300 (1932)	38 357	355 018	2 751 (1931)	2 920 (1931)
1935	1 288 648	919 313	38 083	341 223		2 588 (1936)
1940	1 278 297	835 432	35 005	244 494		2 483 (1941)
1945	1 259 927	734 405	37 843	247 244		2 410 (1946)
1950	1 271 247	863 174	43 266	281 108	2 485 (1951)	2 340 (1951)
1955	1 307 573	917 848	50 126	316 769		2 280 (1956)
1960	1 301 280	932 456 (1959)	50 631	297 192 (1959)		2 093 (1961)
1965	1 247 972	–	44 974	264 328 (1964)		2 166 (1966)
1970	1 154 211	769 247	35 371	220 873	1 754	2 119
1975	1 041 772	672 633	26 519	152 288	1 588	1 975
1980	953 933	582 379	22 848	120 360	1 536	1 852
1985	870 527	528 790	20 069	98 012	1 299	1 765

Notes:
1. Series refers to numbers of congregations 1932 onwards.
2. From 1930 on the figures include that part of the United Free Church of Scotland which amalgamated with the Church of Scotland.

Sources: Currie et al. (1977) Churches and Churchgoers, 1900–1970. 1975–1985 Church of Scotland.

Table 13.7   Details of the Baptist Union, 1900–1985

Year	Members[1]	Churches[4]	Sunday School Scholars	Pastors	Lay preachers
1900	365 275	2 710	525 136	1 963	5 436
1905	426 077	2 944	577 936	2 074	5 436
1910	418 194	3 047	572 686	2 098	5 564
1915	411 490	3 110	544 919	2 080	5 136
1920	404 544	3 019	508 759	2 046	5 026
1925	413 697	3 073	521 219	2 020	5 366
1930	405 808	3 122	477 929	2 017	5 333
1935	400 638	3 139	431 592	2 020	5 272
1940	381 841	3 203	372 174	2 035 (1939)	5 065 (1939)
1945	354 395 (1946)	3 215	297 293 (1946)	1 886 (1944)	4 453 (1944)
1950	337 203	3 277	317 688	1 907	4 424
1955	326 269	3 200	319 701	1 945	4 490
1960	317 360	3 215	259 742	2 049	4 382
1965	294 360	3 211	189 683	2 088	4 220
1970	268 707	3 147	190 315	2 039	4 219
1975	181 798	3 044	139 011[3]	1 511	3 432[2] (1974)
1980	170 338	2 762	122 548	1 393	—
1985	154 290 (1984)	2 688	109 684 (1984)	1 392 (1984)	—

Notes:
1. The series refers to the total membership of the Baptist Union of Great Britain and Ireland.
2. Lay preachers are not reported from 1975 onwards.
3. From 1975 onwards the figures refer to children under 14.
4. Figures for Baptist Union of Great Britain and Northern Ireland throughout England, Scotland, Wales and Northern Ireland.
Sources: 1900–1970 – Currie *et al.* (1977) *Churches and Churchgoers.*
        1975–85 – *Baptist Handbook.*

Table 13.8 Detail of The Methodist Church, 1900–1985

Year	Wesleyan Methodist[1]				Methodist New Connexion[1]			Bible Christians[2]			Primitive Methodist[3]			
	Members	SS	LPs	Mins	Members	SS	Mins	Members	SS	Mins	Members	SS	LPs	Mins
1900	410 384	967 046	19 956	2 202	31 782	84 465	195	27 572	42 485	168	186 466	460 632	16 459	955
1905	435 031	1 006 515	19 304	2 303	35 852	88 042	196	32 062	47 242	177	201 122	471 855	16 262	1 059
1910	439 230	980 165	19 578	2 455							206 016	470 839	16 241	1 093
1915	430 488	922 773	19 418	2 576							203 119	447 056	15 537	1 085
1920	413 206	849 861	18 457	2 520							200 175	424 452	14 383	1 044
1925	436 875	840 205	18 651	2 537							201 902	407 571	13 634	1 107
1930	445 735	763 075	18 870	2 562							201 491	368 782	12 909	1 092
1935														
1940														
1945														
1950														
1955														
1960														
1965														
1970														
1975														
1980														
1985														

Table 13.8 (contd.)

Year	United Meth. Free[1]			United Methodist[1]			Methodist Church[1]		Members by Country				Total Methodist Churches[3]			
	Members	SS	Mins	Members	SS	Mins	SS	LPs	England	Wales	Scotland	Ireland	Members	Ministers	Sunday School Attendance	LPs
1900	72 085	186 238	355						728 289	33 926	8 191	27 745	770 406	3 680	1 780 474	36 415
1905	78 411	193 362	366	148 988					782 478	40 600	9 248	28 511	832 326	3 905	1 843 966	35 566
1910				146 715	309 649	849			791 961	39 562	9 770	29 357	841 293	4 397	1 863 895	35 819
1915				142 230	285 681	817			775 837	38 721	9 561	27 795	824 119	4 478	1 752 500	34 955
1920				138 921	264 113	709			752 302	39 751	9 668	27 247	801 721	4 273	1 633 256	32 840
1925				141 619	253 242	713			780 396	42 588	10 655	29 062	833 639	4 357	1 596 885	32 285
1930				140 957	224 767	695			788 183	42 118	11 161	30 087	841 462	4 349	1 442 522	31 779
1935							1 187 056	34 412	759 835	52 065	13 698	30 757	825 598	4 674	1 281 611	34 412
1940							929 942	31 307	728 470	49 879	13 843	31 053	792 192	4 645	1 004 744	31 307
1945							717 021	28 144	690 088	48 735	13 836	31 193	752 659	4 514	776 629	28 144
1950							799 873	25 159	683 823	47 033	13 959	31 933	744 815	4 658	865 374	25 159
1955							769 733	23 605	684 992	45 009	14 320	32 724	744 321	4 518	831 088	23 605
1960							587 276	22 304	672 916	41 721	13 952	31 909	728 589	4 551	632 151	22 304
1965							482 420	20 991	639 028	38 543	12 776	30 996	690 347	4 377	518 282	20 991
1970									555 933	33 714	11 421	—	601 068	4 007E	—	—
1975									503 400	28 935	9 183	—	541 518	3 768E	237 989[4]	16 962[4]
1980									453 872	25 933	8 167	—	487 972	3 506	—	—
1985									406 534	22 525E	6 990	20 565	436 049E	3 425E	150 537[5]	13 984[5]

Notes: Abbreviations used: SS = Sunday School attendance; LP = Lay Preachers; Mins = Ministers.

1. Figures relate to England only.
2. Figures relate to England & Wales.
3. Figures relate to Great Britain.
4. 1974 figures.
5. 1983 figures.

Sources: 1900–1970: Currie et al. (1977) *Churches and Churchgoers.*
1975–85: Kindly supplied by Richard Smith, and from Brierley (ed.) *UK Christian Handbook*, 1987–8.

Table 13.9   Detail of United Reformed Church/Presbyterian/Congregational Churches, 1900–1985

Year	Free Church of Scotland (Commcts)	United Free Church of Scotland (Commcts)	Ref. Pres. Church of Scotland (Commcts)	Original Secession C. of S. (Commcts)	Presbyterian Church of Wales (Commcts)	Presbyterian Church in Ireland (Commcts)	(Active C's)	Reformed Pres. Church C. of I. (Commcts)	Presbyterian Church of England (Commcts)
1900	4 008	492 964	1 040 (1902)	3 611	158 114	106 630	–	3 709	76 071
1905	6 429	504 853	1 020 (1907)	3 000	189 164	106 366	70 177	3 894	85 215
1910	8 000 (1911)	506 693	1 000 (1911)	3 424	183 862	106 481	68 422	3 973	86 828
1915	8 096E	516 075	965E	3 492E	185 278	104 077	66 378	3 649	87 424
1920	8 192 (1919)	529 680	930 (1919)	3 561	187 220	104 778	65 854	3 619	83 710
1925	8 500 (1923)	536 407[1]	850 (1927)	3 022	189 323	109 224	68 853	3 440	85 109
1930	6 775E	16 577	800 (1931)	2 905	185 827	108 986	67 835	3 461	84 146
1935	5 542	21 286	790	2 753	182 221	113 811	80 013	3 535	81 715
1940	5 690E	23 574	795E	2 412E	178 245	118 203	83 090	3 469	76 815
1945	5 754E	23 863	800 (1947)	1 953	172 954	118 606	80 918	3 496	67 563
1950	5 619E	24 556	700E	1 908E	159 627	125 775	86 066	3 322	69 676
1955	5 909 (1957)	24 856	600 (1953)	1 813	150 077	133 422	93 842	3 389	69 651
1960	5 848E	23 157	589	–	136 716	136 554	99 084	3 327	71 329
1965	5 787E	20 710	568E	–	122 646	143 559	102 734	3 314	67 619
1970	5 726	17 248	548	–	108 064	141 072	98 504	3 250	59 473
1975	–	13 567	340	–	94 116	135 250E	97 040E	3 000E	–
1980	6 392	11 751	330	–	82 653	131 460E	94 850E	3 000E	–
1985	5 600E	9 764	280	–	77 000E	127 610E	92 590E	3 500E	–

Table 13.9 (contd.)

Year	United Reformed Church[2]	Congregational Federation of England (Members)	Evangelic Fellowship of Congregational Churches[22]	Congregational Union of Wales (Members)	Union of Welsh Dependents	Congregational Union of Scotland (Members)	Congregational Union of Ireland (Members)
1900	—	257 435	—	147 513	—	30 170	2 234
1905	—	278 649E	—	180 482	—	35 558	2 310
1910	—	287 952	—	168 693	—	35 660	2 368
1915	—	291 128	—	165 137	—	35 336 (1914)	2 084
1920	—	291 047E	—	165 294E	—	36 498	2 158E
1925	—	290 934 (1927)	—	165 513	—	37 270	2 231E
1930	—	286 716	—	162 781	—	38 337	2 305
1935	—	275 247	—	159 693	—	39 530	2 249
1940	—	259 876 (1939)	—	156 566	—	39 309	2 078 (1939)
1945	—	230 163	—	155 382	—	37 283	1 876
1950	—	209 590	—	144 078	—	35 030	1 731
1955	—	200 583	—	140 049	—	35 467	1 885
1960	—	193 341	—	127 242	—	34 537	—
1965	—	181 710	—	115 437	—	30 133	—
1970	192 136 (1972)	151 212	—	105 522	88 932[3]	25 284	2 030
1975	174 611	10 469	5 000		76 995[3]	20 255	2 003
1980	147 566	10 139	6 176		67 501[3]	20 988	2 130
1985	133 512 (1984)	10 335	6 254 (1983)		60 119[3]	19 920E (1983)	2 183 (1983)

Notes: Abbreviations used: Commcts = Communicants; Active C's = Active Communicants; Ref = Reformed; E = estimates

1. The majority of the United Free Church of Scotland amalgamated with the Church of Scotland.
2. The Presbyterian Church of England amalgamated with the majority of the English Congregationalists to form the United Reformed Church in 1972. A remnant however remained as the Congregational Federation, and a new group – the Evangelical Fellowship of Congregational Churches – was formed.
3. These figures relate solely to the Union of Welsh Independents, the earlier figures come from the Congregational Year Book which includes them.

Sources: Currie et al. (1977). *Churches and Churchgoers.*
UK Christian Handbook, ed. Brierley, 1978, 1982, 1984.

Table 13.10 Detail of Roman Catholic Church[3] 1900–1985

Year	Estimated Catholic population	Mass attendance	Baptisms	Adult conversions	Priests[1] Secular	Priests[1] Regular	Churches,[2] Chapels
1900	—	—	—	—	2 308	990	1 886
1905	—	—	—	—	2 580	1 359	2 021 (1906)
1910	2 339 038 (1913)	—	60 209 (1911)	3 609	2 758	1 544	2 179 (1911)
1915	2 433 655 (1916)	—	83 361	9 367	2 949	1 616	2 323 (1916)
1920	2 501 937	—	100 814	12 621	2 998	1 533	2 377 (1921)
1925	—	—	84 851	11 948	3 114	1 522	2 443 (1926)
1930	2 813 244 (1931)	—	83 494	11 980	3 325	1 686	2 685 (1931)
1935	2 933 294	—	82 871	11 648	3 909	1 806	2 859 (1936)
1940	2 989 665 (1939)	—	86 871 (1939)	10 646 (1939)	4 468	2 157	3 061 (1941)
1945	3 036 828	—	90 033	9 767	4 891	2 218	3 242 (1946)
1950	3 357 059	—	111 763	11 010	5 078	2 589	3 419 (1951)
1955	3 928 830	—	119 968	13 291	5 317	2 747	—
1960	4 495 157	—	147 977	14 803	5 637	2 959	—
1965	4 875 825	2 544 219 (1966)	158 366	10 308	6 117 (1966)	3 075 (1966)	—
1970	4 932 471	1 934 853	128 820	7 341 (1968)	5 942	2 980	4 047
1975	4 996 310	1 790 980	90 282	5 225	6 245	2 530	3 106
1980	5 085 889	1 964 602 (1981)	90 686	5 783	5 864	2 304	3 077
1985	5 023 736 (1984)	1 858 506 (1984)	84 740 (1984)	5 213	4 545[4]	2 173	3 161

Sources: Currie et al. (1977) Churches and Churchgoers.
Catholic Education Commission.
UK Christian Handbook, ed. Brierley, 1978, 1982, 1984.

Notes:
1. England and Wales only.
2. Excluding other buildings, such as convents, open for mass.
3. Great Britain only.
4. Secular priests for Scotland:

1970	1264
1975	1172
1980	1174
1985	1110

Table 13.11   Active Members of other churches

	1970	1975	1980	1985
African/West Indian				
Cherubim & Seraphim	150	200	200	300
Apostolic Faith	0	20	70	120
Other African	5 000	10 000	10 000	10 000
Church of God of Prophecy	2 074	2 800	5 290	5 125
New Testament Church of God	3 423	4 466	6 369	6 543
Ransom Church of God	20	36	60	100
Wesleyan Holiness	1 200	1 588	2 337	1 686
United Pentecostal Church	0	400	750	1 450
Other West Indian	20 000	40 000	40 000	40 000
Total	31 867	59 510	65 076	65 324
Independent churches not listed elsewhere				
Christian Brethren	80 000	73 000	68 000	70 000
Plymouth Brethren No. 4	12 500	11 500	10 500	10 500
Fellowship of Independent Evangelical Churches	20 760	19 820	21 923	30 150
Union of Evangelical Churches	2 000	2 000	1 500	1 400
Other Independent Churches	8 000	8 300	8 400	9 000
'House Church' movement	100	10 000	20 000	75 000
Other non-denominational churches	0	2 000	5 000	14 000
New Apostolic	1 000	1 200	1 400	1 532
Liberal Catholic	2 000	2 000	1 830	1 550
Independent Old Catholic Orthodox	150	150	150	150
Total	126 510	129 970	138 703	213 282
Lutheran				
Evangelical Lutheran	968	1 167	1 077	1 045
Lutheran Church in Ireland	100	85	30	0
Polish Evangelical Church of the Augsburg Confession Abroad	3 500	3 400	3 080	2 000
Latvian Evangelical	2 700	2 650	2 680	2 200
Estonian Evangelical	1 600	1 600	1 200	30
Other Lutherans	7 100	7 350	6 600	6 500
Total	15 968	16 252	14 667	11 775

Orthodox				
Oriental (Armenian)	350	450	450	500
Assyrian Church of the				
East	350	450	800	1 200
Bulgarian	300	300	300	300
Coptic	1 500	1 500	1 500	1 500
Estonian	500	500	500	500
Ethiopian	0	300	400	450
Greek, Archdiocese of				
Thyateria and GB	90 000	91 500	93 100	101 515
Indian Orthodox Syrian	0	0	100	186
Latvian	500	500	500	500
Polish	700	600	500	450
Rumanian	200	200	200	200
Russian Patriarchal	822	1 000	1 500	1 800
Russian outside Russia	2 000	1 800	1 300	1 000
Byelorussian Autocephalous	550	500	450	400
Serbian	1 000	1 550	2 000	2 300
Orthodox Syrian	300	210	100	100
Ukrainian Autcephalous	4 500	4 300	4 000	3 800
Total	103 572	105 660	107 700	116 701

Pentecostal/Holiness				
Apostolic	5 149	4 826	4 904	5 128
Assemblies of God	60 000	50 000	55 000	40 000
Elim Pentecostal	22 500	25 000	25 000	28 519
Emmanuel	229	251	370	300
Nazarene	3 561	3 665	3 792	4 300
Total	91 439	83 742	89 066	78 247

Other Protestants				
Moravian Church	4 725	4 550	4 052	2 647
Countess of Huntingdon	1 100	930	860	750
Religious Society of				
Friends	20 752	19 689	17 891	17 848
Salvation Army	91 799	92 661	74 505	59 108
Seventh Day Adventists	12 145	12 719	14 569	16 065
Churches for overseas				
nationals	4 385	4 598	6 757	8 522
Total	134 906	135 147	118 634	104 940

Note: Active Orthodox membership is taken as about 40 per cent of their community figure. In many African/West Indian Churches attendance is considerably greater than membership—perhaps by five times.

Source: *UK Christian Handbook*, MARC Europe 1987/88 edition.
Many of the figures are estimates, invariably indicated by ending in a zero.

Table 13.12   Adult[1] Church Attendance,[2] 1975–85

England (000s)	1975	1979	1984E[3]	% Annual change 1975/79	1979/84
Roman Catholic	1 418	1 310	1 166	−2.0	−2.3
Church of England	1 302	1 256	1 213	−0.9	−0.7
Methodist	454	447	438	−0.4	−0.4
Baptist	193	203	217	1.3	1.3
URC/Congregational	150	139	127	−1.9	−1.8
Independent	167	206	249	5.4	3.9
African/West Indian	55	66	83	4.7	4.7
Pentecostal/Holiness	78	88	103	3.0	3.1
Other	122	128	137	1.2	1.3
Orthodox	6	7	7	0.7	0.8
All churches	3 945	3 850	3 738	−0.6	−0.6

Wales (000s)	1978	1982	1985E[3]	% Annual change 1978/82	1982/85
Church in Wales	76	81	85	1.7	1.7
Roman Catholic	56	57	57	0.3	0.4
Presbyterian Church of Wales	40	37	35	−1.6	−1.5
Baptist	32	31	30	−1.1	−1.0
Union of Welsh Independents	26	25	24	−0.7	−0.6
Methodist	18	18	17	−1.0	−1.0
Others	29	32	34	2.0	2.1
All churches	277	280	282	0.3	0.3

Table 13.12 *(contd.)*

Scotland (000s)	1980	1984	% Annual change 1980/84
Roman Catholic	296	287	− 0.8
Church of Scotland	273	266	− 0.6
Independent	28	27	− 1.0
Baptist	22	21	− 0.9
Conservative Presbyterian[4]	19	17	− 2.5
Scottish Episcopal	15	16	2.2
Others	25	26	0.2
All churches	678	660	− 0.7

Notes:
1. Adult – that is those over 15 years of age.
2. Attendance is counted as being present at least once a month.
3. The 1984 and 1985 figures are estimated by extrapolating the 1975–9 and 1978–82 trends respectively in each country and then adding.
4. Includes 210 Free Church of Scotland churches, 77 Free Presbyterian Church of Scotland and 5 Reformed Presbyterian churches.

Sources: *Prospects for the Eighties*, Bible Society, 1980.
          Prospects for Wales, Bible Society and MARC Europe, 1983.
          Prospects for Scotland, National Bible Society of Scotland and MARC Europe, 1985.

Table 13.13 Density of church membership 1900–1985

Year	GB Population aged 15 and over (000s)	C. of E.	(%)	C. in W.	(%)	Scot. Epis.	(%)	C. of Scot.	(%)	Presb. & Conr.	(%)	Baptist	(%)	Methodist	(%)	Roman Catholic	(%)
1900	2 796 000		11.36	141 008	.57	116 296	.47	661 629	2.69	1 283 499	5.21	365 275	1.48	770 406	3.13	—	—
1905	2 889 000		10.99	125 234	.48	131 232	.50	692 914	2.64	1 396 940	5.32	426 077	1.73	832 326	3.17	—	—
1910	3 391 000		12.12	152 654	.55	141 732	.51	714 039	2.55	1 394 934	4.99	418 194	1.70	841 294	3.01	2 339 038 (1913)	8.36
1915	3 375 000		11.51	157 089	.54	144 159	.49	721 137	2.46	1 402 741	4.78	411 490	1.67	824 119	2.81	2 433 655 (1916)	8.30
1920	3 323 000		10.84	159 957	.52	144 489	.47	739 251	2.41	1 416 687	4.62	404 544	1.64	801 721	2.62	2 501 937	8.16
1925	3 601 782		11.20	176 271	.55	144 670	.45	762 774	2.37	1 431 823	4.45	413 697	1.68	833 639	2.59	—	—
1930	3 656 630		10.82	184 604	.55	134 066	.40	1 271 095	3.76	899 616	2.66	405 808	1.65	841 462	2.49	2 813 244 (1931)	8.33
1935	3 598 522		10.32	195 744	.56	130 028	.37	1 288 648	3.70	888 912	2.55	400 638	1.63	825 598	2.37	2 933 294	8.41
1940	3 388 859		9.46	187 000	.52	124 498	.35	1 278 297	3.57	865 032	2.41	381 841	1.55	792 192	2.21	2 989 665 (1939)	8.34
1945	2 989 704 (1947)		8.12	155 911	.42	110 673	.30	1 259 927	3.42	819 693	2.23	354 395	1.44	752 659	2.04	3 036 826	8.25
1950	2 958 840		7.82	182 000	.48	108 502	.29	1 271 247	3.36	781 812	2.07	337 203	1.37	744 815	1.97	3 557 059	9.40
1955	2 894 710 (1956)		7.50	176 000	.46	108 127	.28	1 307 573	3.39	767 701	1.99	326 269	1.33	744 321	1.93	3 926 830	10.17
1960	2 861 887		7.27	182 864	.36	97 038	.25	1 301 280	3.31	732 640	1.86	317 360	1.29	728 589	1.85	4 495 157	11.42
1965	2 682 181 (1966)		6.68	165 273	.41	97 175	.24	1 247 972	3.11	691 483	1.72	294 360	1.20	690 347	1.72	4 875 825	12.14
1970	2 558 966		6.24	153 925	.38	85 816	.21	1 154 211	2.82	617 399	1.51	268 707	1.09	601 068	1.47	4 932 471	12.03
1975	1 912 000 E		4.56	133 107	.32	44 741	.11	1 041 772	2.48	674 771	1.61	181 798	.74	541 518	1.29	4 996 310	11.91
1980	1 815 000 E		4.22	131 518	.31	40 961	.10	953 933	2.22	555 035	1.29	170 338	.69	487 972	1.14	5 085 889	11.84
1985	1 672 000 E		3.80	115 896	.26	37 000	.08	870 527	1.98	518 071	1.18	167 999	.68	436 049	.99	5 023 736	11.41

Note: The figures in each column under a percentage sign are the percentage of church members in a particular denomination of the adult population and are calculated by taking the proportion of the members over the population figures given in column one.

Thus, for the Church of England in 1900, $\frac{2\,796\,000}{24\,623\,000} = 11.36\%$

Source: Column 1, Office of Population Censuses and Surveys, *Historical Tables 1801–1981, England and Wales.* The population is for one year more than that started, thus the population of 24,623,000 for 1900 is actually for 1901.

Table 13.14 Churches 1900–85 and Churches per 100 000 population

Year	GB Population aged 15 & over (000s)	C. of E.	N	C. in Wales	N	BAPTIST	N	C. of Scot.	N	U.F.C.o.S.	N	Presbyterian Church of England	N	Congregational	N	Presbyterian Church of Wales	N	ROMAN CATHOLIC	N
1900	24 623	17 468	71	—		2 710	11	1 828	7	1 630	7	326	1	4 876	20	2 953	12	1 886	8
1905	26 282	17 817	68	1 540	6	2 944	11	1 679	6	1 623	6	345	1	4 890	19	3 069	12	2 021	8
1910	27 971	18 026	64	—		3 047	11	1 643	6	1 545	6	354	1	4 910	18	3 128	11	2 179	8
1915	29 332	18 236	62	—		3 110	11	1 701	6	1 516	5	355	1	4 861	17	3 231	11	2 323	8
1920	30 646	18 270	60	—		3 019	10	1 704	6	1 482	5	352	1	—		3 264	11	2 377	8
1925	32 160	18 318	57	1 751	5	3 073	10	1 714	5	1 449	5	350	1	4 585	14	3 265	10	2 443	8
1930	33 786	18 417	55	1 750	5	3 122	9	2 920	9	—		353	1	4 671	14	3 201	9	2 685	8
1935	34 870	18 550	53	1 693 (1939)	5	3 139	9	2 588	7	—		345	1	4 576	13	3 219	9	2 859	8
1940	36 829	18 666	52	—		3 203	9	2 483	7	—		333	1	4 615	13	3 195	9	3 061	9
1945	36 815	—		—		3 215	9	2 410	7	—		334	1	4 516	12	3 133	9	3 242	9
1950	37 828	—		—		3 277	9	2 340	6	—		333	1	4 280	11	3 039	8	3 419	9
1955	38 618	17 980	47	1 764 (1959)	5	3 200	8	2 280	6	—		326	1	4 188	11	3 036	8	—	
1960	39 360	17 973	46	1 789 (1963)	5	3 215	8	2 093	5	—		318	1	—		3 010	8	—	
1965	40 163	17 761	44	1 780	4	3 211	8	2 166	5	—		312	1	—		—		—	
1970	40 993	17 670	43	1 720	4	3 147	8	2 119	5	100	0	312	1	2 080[1]	5	1 300	3	4 047	10
1975	41 957	17 212	41	1 678	4	3 044	7	1 975	5	87	0	312	1	2 063[1]	5	1 228	3	3 106	7
1980	42 973	16 984	40	1 450	3	2 762	6	1 852	4	84	0	311	1	1 960[1]	5	1 169	3	3 077	7
1985	44 014	16 582	38	—		2 688	6	1 765	4	83	0	315	1	1 882[1]	4	1 106	3	3 161	7

Note:
1. United Reformed Church.

N = The number of churches per 10,000 population. Thus for the church of England in 1900, $\dfrac{17\,468 \times 100\,000}{24\,623\,000} = 71$

Table 13.15   Conversions 1900–1965[1]

Years[5]	Percentage of definite[2] conversions in a church context	Percentage of definite[2] conversions through spasmodic efforts[4]
1899–1908	31	15
1909–18	31	18
1919–28	41	21
1929–38	36	21
1939–48	31	22
1949–58	30	21
1959–68	27	24

Years	Percentage of definite[2] conversions through personal witness	Percentage of definite[2] conversions through a professional evangelist
1899–1908[5]	11	10
1909–18	5	5
1919–28	13	5
1929–38	16	7
1939–48	16	5
1949–58	13	15
1959–68	15	14

Years	Percentage of indefinite[3] conversions by the witness of a home or relatives	Percentage of indefinite[3] conversions influenced through personal witness outside home
1899–1908[5]	40	10
1909–18	43	12
1919–28	46	15
1929–38	33	21
1939–48	34	22
1949–58	25	26
1959–68	14	31

Years	Percentage of definite[2] conversions influenced by internal sensations[6]
1899–1908[5]	11
1909–18	15
1919–28	6
1929–38	8
1939–48	8
1949–58	14
1959–68	18

Years[5]	Percentage of definite[2] conversions influenced by the witness of home or relatives	Percentage of definite[2] conversions influenced by personal witness outside the home
1899–1908	50	11
1909–18	45	13
1919–28	35	17
1929–38	39	16
1939–48	27	25
1949–58	28	24
1959–68	20	31

Notes:

1. These tables reflect the results of a survey undertaken under the auspices of the Evangelical Alliance, published in *The Background Task* (Scripture Union 1968). This was based on 4083 personal interviews.
2. A 'definite' conversion is one in which the individual concerned knows the precise day on which day it occurred.
3. An 'indefinite' conversion is one where the exact timing is not known.
4. Spasmodic efforts are occasional evangelistic missions, crusades, etc., with no predefined pattern of recurrence.
5. People born in these years still alive in 1968.
6. Fear, conviction of sin, etc.

Table 13.16   Church nominalism 1975–85[1]

England (000s)	1975		1979		1984E	
	All members	Nominal members	All members	Nominal members	All members	Nominal members
Roman Catholic	3 513	2 095	3 530	2 220	3 563	2 397
Church of England	1 999	697	1 908	652	1 821	608
Methodist	515	61	473	26	426	− 12
Baptist	168	− 25	162	− 41	156	− 61
URC/Congrega-tional	190	40	166	27	140	13
Independent	137	− 30	169	− 37	220	− 29
African/West Indian	38	− 17	47	− 19	61	− 22
Pentecostal/Holiness	43	− 35	47	− 41	54	− 49
Orthodox	94	88	95	88	97	90
Other	141	19	142	14	143	6
All churches	6 938	2 893	6 739	2 889	6 681	2 943

Wales (000s)	1978		1982		1985E	
	All members	Nominal members	All members	Nominal members	All members	Nominal members
Church in Wales	141	65	138	57	135	50
Roman Catholic	125	69	130	73	133	76
Presbyterian Church of Wales	86	46	80	43	76	41
Union of Welsh Independents	70	44	65	40	62	38
Baptist	54	22	50	19	47	17
Methodist	28	10	25	7	23	6
Others	33	4	35	3	37	3
All churches	538	261	523	243	513	231

Scotland (000s)	1980		1984	
	All members	Nominal members	All members	Nominal members
Church of Scotland	954	681	908	642
Roman Catholic	816	520	815	528
Scottish Episcopal	41	26	40	24
Independent	37	9	35	8
Conservative Presby-terian	28	9	25	8
Baptist	19	− 3	20	− 1
Others	35	10	34	8
All churches	1 930	1 252	1 877	1 217

Notes:
1. This data is for adults only (i.e. over 15s).
2. Nominal church members are here defined as church members who do not attend at least once a month and are ascertained by subtracting church attenders from church members. This, however, will understate the numbers as some attenders are not church members. A negative number means that regular churchgoers are in excess of the number of members.

Sources: *Prospects Series*, MARC Europe, as given in Table 13.12.

Table 13.17 Religions of the population, 1901–1981, Northern Ireland

Year of enumeration	Total Population	Roman Catholic	Presbyterian	Church of Ireland	Methodist	Other denominations	Not stated
1901	1 236 952	430 390	399 562	316 825	44 134	47 971	1 070
1911	1 250 531	430 161	395 039	327 076	45 942	49 827	2 486
1926	1 256 561	420 428	393 374	338 724	49 554	52 177	2 304
1937	1 279 745	428 290	390 931	345 474	55 135	57 541	2 374
1951	1 370 921	471 460	410 215	353 245	66 639	63 497	5 865
1961	1 425 042	497 547	413 113	344 800	71 865	71 299	26 418
1971	1 519 640	477 921	405 717	334 318	71 235	87 938	142 511
1981	1 481 959	414 532	339 818	281 472	58 731	112 822	274 584

Source: Northern Ireland Census, 1981, Religion Report.

Table 13.18 Age structure of Church of England[1] clergy

Age-group	Year											
	1963		1968		1971		1978		1983		1984	
	No.	%	No.	%	No.	%	No.	%	No.	%	No.	%
<25	110	0.82	0	—	90	0.70	13	0.12	17	0.17	13	0.13
25–29	1 119	8.93	1 062	7.84	933	7.23	484	4.50	520	5.14	497	4.94
30–34	1 297	9.66	1 436	10.60	1 173	9.09	1 076	10.01	903	8.93	890	8.85
35–39	1 151	8.57	1 447	10.68	1 467	11.37	1 108	10.30	1 331	13.17	1 320	13.12
40–44	1 221	9.10	1 267	9.35	1 467	11.37	1 507	14.01	1 246	12.33	1 238	12.31
45–49	1 577	11.75	1 330	9.81	1 223	9.48	1 462	13.60	1 599	15.82	1 596	15.86
50–54	2 055	15.31	1 694	12.50	1 378	10.68	1 270	11.81	1 514	14.98	1 553	15.44
55–59	1 876	13.98	2 139	15.78	1 925	14.92	1 239	11.52	1 264	12.51	1 309	13.01
60–64	1 393	10.38	1 825	13.47	2 017	15.63	1 489	13.85	1 137	11.25	1 113	11.06
65–69	791	5.89	944	6.97	915	7.09	842	7.83	400	3.96	376	3.74
70–74	484	3.61	248	1.83	218	1.69	196	1.82	131	1.30	116	1.15
75–79	201	1.50	160	1.18	63	0.49	47	0.44	31	0.31	31	0.31
80–84	57	0.42	0	—	28	0.22	12	0.11	14	0.14	8	0.08
85–89	10	0.07	0	—	6	0.05	5	0.05	0	—	0	—
>90	1	0.01	0	—	2	0.02	3	0.03	0	—	0	—
Total	13 343		13 552		12 905		10 753		10 107		10 060	

Note:
1. These figures refer to full-time stipendary parochial Ministers only, i.e. those of incumbent status and assistant clergy.
Source: *Church of England Year Book and Church Statistics;* reproduced by permission of the Church Information office

Table 13.19 Welsh churches, 1900–1985

Year	Church in Wales			Baptists			Presbyterian Church of Wales[6]		
	Communicants[1]	Incumbents[2]	Churches	Members	Pastors	Churches[3]	Communicants	Ministers	Churches[4]
1900	141 008	1 002	—	106 566	543	1 757	158 114	1231	2 953 (1901)
1905	125 234	967	1 540	140 443	575	1 824	189 164	1248	3 069 (1906)
1910	152 654	972	—	128 038	593	1 938	183 862	1310	3 128 (1911)
1915	157 069	985	—	124 713	596	1 992	185 278	1230	3 231 (1916)
1920	159 957	975	—	125 068	567	1 983	187 220	1156	3 264 (1921)
1925	176 271	999	—	129 734	553	2 004	189 323	1156	3 265 (1926)
1930	184 604	981	1 751	125 704	531	2 013	185 827	1147 (1929)	3 201 (1931)
1935	195 744	981	1 750	122 735	535	2 002	182 221	1120	3 219 (1936)
1940	187 000E	981E	1 693 (1939)	115 833	538	2 014	178 245	1075 (1939)	3 195 (1931)
1945	155 911	981E	—	110 600E	473E	1 947	172 954	970	3 133 (1941)
1950	182 000E	981	—	105 922	467	1 987	159 627	913	3 039 (1946)
1955	176 000E	950	—	99 750	457	1 947	150 027	839	3 036 (1951)
1960	182 864	861	1 764 (1959)	93 114	450	1 948	136 716	759	1 412 (1956)
1965	165 273	791	1 789 (1963)	83 886	402	1 941	122 646	664	1 381
1970	153 925	737	1 780	72 097	366	—	108 064	346[8]	1 300
1975	133 107	679	1 720	59 021E	341E	—	94 116	276[8]	1 228
1980	131 518	674	1 675	52 067	306	825	82 653	220[8]	1 169
1985	116 911	630	1 450	47 500E	241	779	77 000E	168[8]	1 106

continued overleaf

Table 13.19 (contd.)

Year	Methodists Members[5]	Congregationalists and Welsh Ind. Members	Congregationalists and Welsh Ind. Ministers	Congregationalists and Welsh Ind. Churches	Roman Catholics Members	Roman Catholics Clergy	Roman Catholics Churches
1900	33 926	147 513	—	1 281	—	75	95
1905	40 600	180 482	—	1 306	—	95	112
1910	39 562	168 693	638	1 113 (1911)	54 055	103	123
1915	38 721	165 137	641	1 121	76 191	121	127
1920	39 751	165 294E	660	—	69 521	113	133
1925	42 588	165 513	—	—	92 430	122	143
1930	42 118	162 781	—	1 300	102 360	128	165
1935	52 065	159 693	—	1 320	103 345	133	182
1940	49 879	156 566	—	—	105 580	118	197
1945	48 735	155 382	—	1 353	105 775	157	211
1950	47 033	144 078	—	1 286	113 600	182	241
1955	45 009	140 049	—	1 308	115 100	192	208
1960	41 721	127 242	—	—	127 000	185	233
1965	38 543	115 437	—	—	138 300	187	249
1970	33 714	105 522 / 88 932[7]	362[7]	761[7]	142 881 (1971)	176	259
1975	28 935	76 995[7]	208[7]	751[7]	144 149 (1974)	158	270
1980	25 933	67 501[7]	200[7]	718[7]	125 700 (1978)	262[9]	268E
1985	22 525	60 119[7]	157[7]	683[7]	129 600 (1982)	200[9]	262

Notes:
1. 1975–85 supplied by Church in Wales.
2. 1980, 1985 from C. in W. figures.
3. Includes churches and chapels.
4. Includes churches, chapels and preaching places. Churches only after 1955.
5. From 1935 includes Primitive and United Methodists.
6. Also called Calvinistic Methodists.
7. These figures relate solely to the Union of Welsh Independants, whereas the earlier figures came from the Congregational Year Book which includes them but adds others.
8. Excluding retired ministers.
9. Including secular and regular clergy

Sources: Digest of Welsh Historical Statistics, Vol. 2 (1985) by John Williams. Churches and Churchgoers, Currie et al 1983 UK Christian Handbook, MARC Europe, 1987/88 and 1983 Editions for some 1980 and 1985 figures.

Table 13.20 Marginal Protestants 1970–85

Protestant group	Members				Ministers				Buildings			
	1970	1975	1980	1985	1970	1975	1980	1985	1970	1975	1980	1985
Aladura International Church	80E	300E	300	500	1	10	10	10	1	1	1	2
Christadelphians	21 000	25 000	22 000	20 000	–	–	–	–	379[2]	400[2]	360[2]	330[2]
Church of Christ Scientist	22 000E	17 000	15 000	13 500	–	–	–	–	311	294	261	238
Jehovah's Witnesses	61 913	79 586	83 521	101 200	7 050E	7 090	8 109	8 098[5]	586E	624	1 163	1 229[6]
Church of Jesus Christ of Latter Day Saints (Mormons)	88 000E	79 717	91 032	81 085	3 500E	5 260	7 331	7 200[3]	110E	160	197	200[4]
New Church	3 104	2 533	2 190	1 805	37	35	30	36	47	44	40	40
Church of Scientology	10 000E	20 000E	30 000E	48 000E	200	250	450	450	8E	12	16	19
Spiritualists[1]	44 934	56 766E	52 404E	48 837E	207E	233	290	333	600E	594	578	563
Theosophists[1]	5 588E	5 359	5 122	4 923	–	–	–	1	6E	13	13	13
Unification	50E	150	570	350	5E	15E	35E	53	2E	10	28	30
Unitarian & Free Christian Churches	15 000E	15 000E	11 000	10 000	138	129	155	106	272	257	247	248
The Way Worldwide	100E	400E	1 000E	1 500	1E	1E	5	10	2E	20[2]	50[2]	75[2]
Church of God	1 500E	1 880	2 159	2 374	15E	21	16	47	42E	46	48	50

Notes:
1. A composite figure comprising several associations or groups.
2. Estimated communities not buildings.
3. Includes lay ministers. Residing officials number 398 in 1985.
4. But 353 congregations in 1985.
5. This figure relates to elders; 7,000 ministerial servants are not included.
6. This figure includes about 800 Kingdom Halls. The rest are public hired halls.
Source: UK Christian Handbook, 1978, 1982, 1984, 1986; MARC Europe.

Table 13.21 Non-Christian religions, 1970–85

Religion	Members[1]				Ministers				Buildings			
	1970	1975	1980	1985	1970	1975	1980	1985	1970	1975	1980	1985
Buddhists	6 000	13 000	17 000	23 000	38	150	210	290	8	36	50	86
Hindus	50 000	100 000	120 000	130 000	80	100	120	140E	60	120	125	130E
International Society for Krishna Consciousness	500	10 000	35 000	40 000E	50E	100	250	300E	1E	2	5	8E
Muslims	250 000	400 000	600 000	852 900	400E	1 000	1 540	2 077	75E	150	193	314
Ahmadiyya Movement	5 000E	8 000	10 000	12 000E	3E	5	7	8	3E	5	7	8
Satanists	1 500E	3 200E	7 000E	15 000E	6E	11E	19E	32E	4E	8E	16E	33E
Sikhs	75 000E	115 000E	150 000E	180 000E	100E	120E	140E	150E	40E	75E	105E	150E
School of Meditation	2 821	3 862	4 820	6 000E	0	0	0	0	2	2	2	2
Others	30 000E	50 000E	80 000E	100 000E	40E	80E	100E	120E	40E	80E	100E	120E
Jews	113 000	111 000	110 915	109 150	400	400	416	432E	345	315	321	330E

Notes:
1. Active membership.
Source: UK Christian Handbook, 1978, 1982, 1984, 1986; MARC Europe.

Table 13.22   Age and sex of church-goers, 1979–84, compared to civilian population

| England | Male (%) | | Female (%) | | Total | |
	A	B	A	B	A	B
<15	13	11	13	10	26	21
15–19	4	4	5	4	9	8
20–29	5	7	6	7	11	14
30–44	7	10	9	9	16	19
45–64	9	11	11	12	20	23
⩾65	7	6	11	9	18	15
All ages	45	49	55	51	100	100

A = Church attenders, 1979.
B = Civilian population, 1978.

| Wales | Male (%) | | Female (%) | | Total | |
	A	B	A	B	A	B
<15	11	11	15	10	26	21
15–19	3	4	4	4	7	8
20–29	3	7	5	7	8	14
30–44	5	10	9	9	14	19
45–64	8	11	14	12	22	23
⩾65	8	6	15	9	23	15
All ages	38	49	62	51	100	100

A = Church attenders, 1982.
B = Civilian population, 1981.

| Scotland | Male (%) | | Female (%) | | Total | |
	A	B	A	B	A	B
<15	11	11	14	10	25	21
15–19	2	5	3	4	5	9
20–29	3	7	6	8	9	15
30–44	5	9	10	10	15	19
45–64	9	11	15	11	24	22
⩾65	7	5	15	9	22	14
All ages	37	48	63	52	100	100

A = Church attenders, 1984.
B = Civilian population, 1981.
Sources: *Prospects* series (see Table 13.12).

Table 13.23   Religious marriages, 1900–84, by denomination, England and Wales

Year	All marriages	Total religious marriages	Church of England & Church in Wales	Roman Catholic	Others	Jewish
1900	257 480	218 009	173 060	10 267	33 013	1 669
1905	260 742	212 974	165 747	10 812	34 435	1 980
1910	267 721	213 043	164 945	11 312	34 975	1 811
1914	294 401	223 521	171 700	13 729	36 119	1 973
1919	369 411	284 081	220 557	19 078	42 585	1 861
1924	296 416	225 812	171 480	16 286	36 074	1 972
1929	313 316	232 841	176 113	18 711	35 929	2 088
1934	342 307	245 187	183 123	22 323	37 508	2 233
1952	349 308	242 531	173 282	33 050	24 323	1 876
1957	346 903	249 814	172 010	39 960	36 136	1 713
1962	347 732	244 630	164 707	42 788	35 586	1 549
1965	371 127	253 034	171 848	43 192	36 590	1 463
1970	415 487	251 368	170 146	43 658	35 882	1 682
1975	380 620	198 796	133 074	32 307	32 050	1 365
1980	370 022	186 627	123 400	28 553	33 615	1 059
1984	349 186	178 680	117 506	25 609	34 530	1 035

Table 13.24   Cremations in Great Britain, 1900–84

Year	Deaths	Cremations	Roman Catholic
1900	670 126	444	
1905	594 567	604	
1910	555 515	840	
1915	643 884	1 410	
1920	534 309	1 796	
1925	538 348	2 701	
1930	519 712	4 533	
1935	542 732	9 614	
1940	654 312	25 199	
1945	550 763	42 963	
1950	574 297	89 557	
1955	580 509	141 353	
1960	588 032	204 019	
1965	612 247	271 130	1 000
1970	638 834	353 981	7 241
1975	645 966	395 032	12 265
1980	644 684	420 717	16 171
1985	654 701	443 687	14 492

Sources: The Cremation Society of Great Britain for
Cremations & Roman Catholic columns.
Office of Population Censuses and Surveys for
total deaths column.

Table 13.25   Religious affiliation of UK prison inmates, 1972–85

Religious affiliation	1972	1975	1978	1981	1984	1985
Church of England	19 301	24 190	24 534	25 680	24 466	26 527
Baptist	*	152	127	109	82	131
Roman Catholic	7 648	9 459	9 403	9 701	9 225	9 821
Methodist	947	992	865	638	578	668
Ethiopian Orthodox	*	*	0	74	83	81
Greek Orthodox	*	*	*	55	47	76
Pentecostal	*	*	*	*	*	63
Church of Scotland/Presby-terian	236	532	574	680	503	532
Salvation Army	134	97	81	60	44	46
Christian Scientist	84	48	48	32	0	47
Mormon	*	39	0	0	99	102
Buddhist	*	*	*	91	87	105
Hindu	*	*	*	92	130	204
Muslim	340	682	837	924	1 398	1 474
Sikh	243	315	229	190	279	291
Jewish	245	304	339	289	270	261
Individual	*	*	*	*	*	94
Corporate bodies	*	*	*	*	*	66
No religion	*	3 578	3 654	4 066	3 560	4 003
Total	29 248	40 409	40 691	42 681	40 878	44 592

Note:
*   No previous figures available.
Source: Home Office.

Table 13.26   UK, Europe and world from World Christian Encyclopaedia, 1900–1980, church affiliated adults, congregations, denominations

Area	Adherents			Members		
	1900	1970	1980	1900	1970	1980
Northern Europe						
United Kingdom	37 125 000	49 298 000	49 964 000	36 116 400	43 410 335	41 705 200
Channel Islands	82 170	115 900	126 350	80 510	103 550	112 920
Denmark	2 439 000	4 763 200	4 896 000	2 435 480	4 710 304	4 809 150
Faroe Islands	15 000	38 960	40 350	15 000	38 250	40 215
Finland	2 713 000	4 439 320	4 425 500	2 676 400	4 408 237	4 095 590
Iceland	77 900	199 940	222 630	77 600	197 964	219 920
Ireland	3 227 000	2 942 000	3 280 700	3 196 500	2 808 812	3 106 100
Isle of Man	37 600	52 030	75 055	36 480	43 900	46 960
Norway	2 207 060	3 830 900	4 044 350	2 199 860	3 802 117	4 012 850
Svalberg & Jan May	480	1 500	1 330	450	1 000	770
Sweden	5 077 000	6 032 000	6 059 000	5 076 500	5 992 305	5 999 200
Western Europe						
Austria	5 827 760	7 220 000	7 366 380	5 818 000	7 159 358	7 079 790
Belgium	6 623 000	8 940 000	9 143 100	6 553 000	8 788 886	8 944 400
France	40 731 100	42 559 900	44 110 800	40 730 100	42 402 510	43 900 800
Germany FRG	29 323 000	57 830 000	57 557 300	29 190 000	57 142 713	55 970 400
Liechtenstein	9 380	20 960	22 870	9 330	20 385	22 150
Luxembourg	234 560	323 000	325 670	231 260	304 473	300 670
Monaco	15 300	23 570	25 540	15 190	23 225	25 160
Netherlands	4 998 700	11 650 600	12 093 700	4 939 380	10 006 555	10 027 700
Switzerland	3 295 000	6 154 000	6 559 000	3 228 000	5 771 460	6 011 900
Southern Europe						
Andorra	4 980	18 930	24 910	4 500	17 940	23 600
Gibraltar	19 480	22 970	24 640	18 880	21 330	22 700
Greece	2 599 000	8 643 000	8 911 400	2 589 000	8 539 292	8 760 600
Holy See/Vatican	2 000	4 950	6 000	2 000	4 950	6 000
Italy	32 903 000	48 657 800	47 104 500	32 902 200	48 572 493	47 006 500
Malta	207 800	324 300	331 510	195 000	317 571	323 220
Portugal	5 420 800	8 421 100	8 536 900	5 412 800	8 362 924	8 458 200
San Marino	8 000	18 230	20 000	8 000	18 000	19 780
Spain	18 797 000	32 851 600	35 932 700	18 797 000	32 810 685	35 884 700
Eastern Europe						
Albania	250 000	171 430	100 154	226 500	171 330	154 000
Bulgaria	3 065 780	5 641 130	5 853 300	2 879 350	5 639 630	5 851 600
Czechoslovakia	11 798 840	11 598 712	10 805 571	11 190 840	11 579 212	10 688 800
Germany GDR	12 210 000	11 876 107	10 998 400	11 599 000	11 824 107	10 943 400
Hungary	6 411 000	8 683 928	8 919 000	6 068 000	8 681 828	8 917 300
Poland	21 989 000	29 626 685	31 935 700	21 383 500	29 603 685	31 908 500
Romania	10 384 000	16 840 000	18 172 600	9 997 000	16 781 000	18 111 600
Yugoslavia	8 254 000	15 296 004	16 254 600	7 786 000	15 289 004	16 245 600
Total Europe	278 383 690	405 132 656	415 600 780	273 685 010	395 371 320	399 757 145
USSR	104 993 000	86 012 300	96 726 500	97 002 000	86 002 300	96 713 500
N. America	78 811 810	206 443 460	219 833 450	58 754 690	162 534 468	170 593 780
S. America	62 002 115	267 383 563	348 658 275	60 021 240	261 183 875	339 601 650
Asia, Oceania	23 927 269	108 644 710	148 376 804	22 417 089	100 957 272	138 183 305
Africa	9 938 448	142 962 732	203 490 710	8 755 572	114 930 124	163 082 045
Total world	558 056 332	1 216 579 421	1 432 686 519	520 635 601	1 120 979 359	1 307 931 425

Notes:
Adherents – The whole *de facto* Christian resident population.
Members – As defined here equals affiliated Christians (church members) with marginal Protestants (followers of para-Christian Western movements, or deviations out of mainline protestantism) subtracted.

Table 13.26   (contd.)

1900	Churchgoers 1970	1980	Congregations 1970	1980	Denominations 1970	1980
30 698 940	28 058 871	25 440 170	63 200	63 600	470	530
72 460	72 488	79 039	116	130	21	23
1 704 840	3 155 908	3 125 950	3 370	3 410	47	56
14 300	34 420	36 195	89	93	6	6
2 408 760	3 438 429	3 112 650	2 060	2 070	34	38
62 080	118 780	131 952	394	415	15	16
3 132 510	2 696 462	2 919 730	2 196	2 205	33	36
32 830	30 730	32 870	114	122	21	21
2 089 865	3 041 694	3 210 300	4 260	4 340	41	45
360	700	540	1	1	1	1
4 568 850	4 793 844	4 199 440	11 050	11 070	98	117
5 236 200	5 369 514	5 026 650	4 350	4 450	58	64
5 897 700	6 767 446	6 529 430	4 740	4 820	77	87
34 620 550	31 801 878	32 047 580	44 600	45 200	274	315
26 271 000	45 142 738	43 097 210	43 100	43 500	243	260
8 860	17 330	18 830	15	16	4	5
219 700	277 070	267 596	330	336	25	29
12 150	13 930	15 100	8	10	4	5
4 445 440	7 805 117	7 621 050	8 660	8 890	230	240
2 905 200	4 790 309	4 869 641	5 620	5 680	141	149
4 270	14 352	18 876	10	12	3	3
15 100	10 670	11 350	13	14	6	6
2 511 330	7 856 152	7 884 500	30 040	30 300	51	56
1 980	4 850	5 760	60	65	1	1
31 257 090	38 857 994	36 665 070	30 800	30 400	220	230
189 000	311 215	316 755	90	94	9	9
4 871 520	5 770 420	5 666 990	5 100	5 200	38	42
7 600	16 203	17 627	13	13	2	2
18 421 060	31 826 362	34 808 160	22 370	23 700	144	152
204 000	51 400	46 200	1 000	800	7	6
2 591 410	3 440 175	3 452 447	4 310	4 390	21	22
10 071 760	8 105 450	8 448 160	8 840	8 820	26	26
10 439 100	7 094 460	6 566 040	8 410	8 300	32	32
5 461 200	6 077 280	6 242 110	6 650	6 670	24	25
19 245 200	27 827 460	29 994 180	9 180	9 280	47	49
9 496 852	15 438 520	16 662 670	18 250	18 750	34	36
7 007 400	11 466 750	12 184 200	7 640	7 720	69	71
246 198 467	311 597 371	310 773 018	351 049	354 886	2 577	2 811
87 301 800	64 501 720	74 469 390	78 200	87 900	140	152
55 816 701	146 274 696	150 116 607	386 747	414 567	2 035	2 465
50 976 606	181 482 930	232 715 401	118 679	161 859	3 030	3 504
20 269 040	81 069 927	110 999 146	255 588	338 448	3 059	3 584
7 819 776	89 954 208	127 692 224	231 580	360 744	7 321	8 265
468 382 390	874 880 852	1 006 765 786	1 421 843	1 718 404	18 162	20 781

Churchgoers – As defined here equals practising Christian (total affiliated) with the pro rata ratio Affiliated:Practising, as applied to marginal Protestants, subtracted.
Source: *World Christian Encyclopaedia*, ed. D. Barrett.

Table 13.27 Missionary society personnel

Missionary Personnel	Protestant Societies[1]						Roman Catholic Societies[2]		
	1972[3]	1976[3]	1980[3]	1982[4]	1984[4]	1986[4]	1982[5]	1984[4]	1986[4]
Number abroad	5 300	5 212	4 416	4 617	4 818	4 666	1 202	1 051	1 153
On furlough/home leave	800	579	492	443	400	445	172	107	27
Secondments	100	70	60	89	101	152	0	0	5
UK executive staff	800	797	476	504	492	461	409	559	403
Sub-total: Serving members	7 000	6 658	5 444	5 653	5 811	5 724	1 783	1 717	1 588
UK office staff	700	688	823	1 022	969	842	40	9	77
Associates	500	327	266	432	346	217	55	53	66
Retired personnel	1 100	1 178	1 427	1 740	1 103	1 204	71	86	133
Total missionary personnel	9 300	8 851	7 960	8 847	8 229	7 987	1 949	1 865	1 864
Number of societies	100	100	99	101	102	107	89	91	92
Response rate	84%	88%	94%	98%	94%	96%	100%	95%	97%

Notes:
1. Including estimates for non-responding societies.
2. Figures for earlier years not available.
3. Figures as at 1 July.
4. Figures as at 1 January.
5. Figures as at 1 April.

Source: *UK Christian Handbook*, 1987/88 edition; MARC Europe.

Table 13.28 Number of languages into which the Bible was translated, 1900–1980

Years	Africa	Asia	Americas	Europe	Indian sub-continent & Middle East
1901–10	8	9	2	1	1
1911–20	5	11	1	0	1
1921–30	11	5	1	2	1
1931–40	6	2	0	1	0
1941–50	3	1	0	2	1
1951–60	22	2	1	1	5
1961–70	22	1	0	0	5
1971–80	16	6	0	0	1

Source: *Scriptures of the World*, Bible Society.

Table 13.29 Number of books published

Year	Total number of titles	Total number of religious titles	Total number of titles on occultism (included within Religious total)
1928	13 981	951	31
1930	15 494	857	57
1935	16 678	846	57
1940	11 053	519	40
1945	6 747	464	40
1950	17 072	971	54
1955	19 962	1 058	48
1960	23 783	1 247	70
1965	26 358	1 227	70
1970	33 489	1 245	165
1975	35 608	1 098	240
1980	48 158	1 725	258
1985	52 994	1 992	239

Source: *Bookseller* magazine, published weekly by Whitaker. Numbers include all titles issued, including reprints and new editions. Figures not collected prior to 1928.

Table 13.30   UK v. Europe and world – 'The Worldwide Anglican Communion'

Continent	Churches, dioceses & councils	Anglicans			Baptised		Dioceses		
		1978 Total	1968 % of pop	1978 % of pop	1965	1975	1900	1967	1977
UK	England	30 601 000	67.0	64.81	27 800 000	27 484 000	31	43	43
	Scotland	156 000	3.5	2.90	94 000	76 300	7	7	7
	Wales	1 260 000	46.0	44.95	1 010 000	990 000	4	6	6
	Ireland	480 000	11.0	10.02	469 000	411 000	14	14	12
EUROPE	Europe	300 000	0.1	0.06	150 000	250 000	1	1	1
NORTH	USA	5 268 000	1.7	1.34	3 464 000	3 039 520	74	103	113
AMERICA	Canada	2 567 100	12.2	10.84	1 158 800	1 185 600	23	28	30
	Bermuda	24 800	45.7	42.76	21 400	23 090	1	1	1
SOUTH	South America	19 800	0.03	0.03	21 750	26 050	1	2	5
AMERICA	Brazil	30 000	0.01	0.03	36 500	53 500	1	3	5
	West Indies	976 750	5.6	5.12	592 000	591 100	8	8	9
	Cuba	7 500	0.1	0.07	11 500	12 500	0	1	1
ASIA &	Burma	24 000	0.04	0.07	23 000	31 000	1	1	4
OCEANIA	Ceylon	48 500	0.4	0.33	42 200	51 000	1	2	2
	East Asia	9 359 300	2.5	5.56	3 050 000	8 344 010	0	50	70
	China	28 100	0.6	0.60	21 200	25 000	4	15	1
	Indian Ocean	80 200	0.8	0.83	51 460	71 370	2	2	5
	Australia	4 228 600	35.4	29.21	3 855 800	3 730 200	14	25	24
	Japan	190 650	0.2	0.17	45 000	53 200	5	11	11
	Jerusalem & Middle East	29 260	0.01	0.01	30 000	37 500	1	5	4
	Melanesia	82 800	18.5	18.84	50 800	69 200	1	1	4
	New Zealand	1 061 800	36.7	24.61	866 800	907 200	7	9	8
	South Pacific	243 670	5.3	5.52	102 800	153 050	0	4	10
	Papua New Guinea	150 100	5.2	5.35	45 000	73 500	1	1	5
AFRICA	South Africa	2 151 900	6.0	5.54	1 384 100	1 513 200	9	15	16
	Kenya	1 021 900	6.5	7.06	410 000	728 800	1	5	7
	Sudan	348 300	1.6	1.76	195 000	383 600	0	1	4
	Tanzania	647 000	3.2	3.86	303 020	494 000	1	8	9
	Uganda, Ruanda Burundi & Zanzibar	3 633 900	6.7	7.72	1 325 000	2 113 800	1	10	23
	West Africa	7 371 500	7.6	7.85	2 720 360	3 496 440	2	12	21
	Central Africa	585 300	2.9	3.19	254 000	389 460	2	4	8
TOTAL		72 977 730			49 604 490	56 808 190	218	398	469
Duplications		−9 478 600			−3 114 300	−8 414 190	0	−49	−73

Notes:
1. Refers to percentage of clergy in the churches, dioceses and councils who are nationals.
2. Number of clergy and lay personnel serving the church in countries other than their own.
Source: Preparatory Information, The Lambeth Conference, 1978.

Table 13.30 (contd.)

Bishops 1967	1977	Clergy (men & women) 1967	1977	Citizens[1] 1967 %	1977 %	Ordinands 1967	1977	Citizens abroad[2] 1965	1975
110	105	18 180	17 123	99	99	1 180	879	2 242	2 448
21	8	290	369	99	98	22	25	30	26
20	7	970	861	100	100	128	61	72	50
14	12	790	712	99	99	48	54	70	93
2	5	70	121	1	1	1	6	0	0
7	146	10 180	12 785	98	98	577	669	290	174
36	36	2 260	1 982	98	98	280	200	60	27
1	1	16	14	6	22	1	1	0	0
1	9	50	123	89	73	10	20	0	0
3	6	77	105	85	97	22	8	0	2
13	13	310	444	47	74	30	35	6	68
1	1	23	15	100	100	1	1	0	0
2	5	48	112	100	100	10	20	0	0
2	2	95	119	94	99	4	7	0	20
47	101	1 100	4 129	64	96	30	290	499	478
1	1	55	68	64	73	1	3	5	23
2	5	84	98	87	95	14	10	0	3
36	38	2 040	2 518	93	96	200	230	489	444
15	11	330	295	93	97	21	10	60	12
5	5	57	65	62	39	3	4	0	2
1	5	110	165	80	98	30	52	4	14
14	12	650	831	99	99	80	116	112	75
4	12	225	320	68	88	43	75	4	15
7	5	80	120	60	81	10	18	0	0
2	25	840	1 091	64	88	115	100	50	110
6	9	200	401	80	89	20	115	3	4
13	4	60	194	95	99	5	15	0	5
11	10	330	455	79	94	20	30	0	0
131	25	580	925	88	97	100	350	6	12
13	22	710	1 142	94	98	100	240	2	12
6	9	260	356	51	87	27	101	0	9
547	655	41 070	48 058			3 133	3 745	4 004	4 126
−44	−105	−1 229	−4 319			−270	−344	−504	−192

Table 13.31   British religious books[1] 1950–86

Topic (Dewey decimal subject)		1950–70	1971–76	1977–86
200	Religion, not included below	445	475	778
210	Natural religion	184	70	100
220	Bible	3 229	1 128	2 358
230	Christian theology	2 822	1 042	1 847
240	Christian moral and devotional theology	2 466	1 009	2 357
250	Local church and religious orders	702	244	385
260	Social and ecclesiastical theology	4 013	1 456	3 042
270	History and geography of the Church	1 900	419	753
280	Christian denominations and sects	2 138	1 003	1 402
290	Other and comparative religions	1 421	741	2 141
Total		19 320	7 587	15 163

Note:
1. The number of books held in the British Library published in the years indicated. The ranges of years are as provided by the British Library records.

Table 13.32   Number of Christian organisations in UK by type[1]

Years	Accommodation	Book shops	Church Assocs	Education	Leadership	Media	Overseas	Service	Total
Before 1800	3	32	22	6	3	4	28	10	108
1800–99	49	18	65	44	54	57	92	81	460
1900–09	7	2	17	9	8	7	16	12	78
1910–19	15	2	14	4	7	8	14	8	72
1920–29	39	6	19	7	11	12	17	11	122
1930–39	22	4	11	1	17	12	13	16	96
1940–49	26	26	19	13	22	14	20	22	162
1950–59	40	27	20	8	19	39	25	43	221
1960–64	39	17	7	9	19	23	11	28	153
1965–69	33	40	19	17	29	36	15	49	238
1970–74	46	57	22	28	25	55	21	65	319
1975–79	50	85	18	34	30	86	18	68	389
1980–84	46	140	12	32	49	133	13	96	521
1985–86	12	22	0	9	8	32	4	22	109
Total	427	478	265	221	301	518	307	531	3 048

Notes:
1. The table reflects those 'para-church' agencies, Christian organisations, missionary societies and other like bodies which were in existence in 1985, by the year of their foundation. Those which began and discontinued before 1985 are not included, unless they merged with a body still present in 1985.
Source: *UK Christian Handbook*, 1987/88 edition.

14 Immigration and Ethnicity

Ceri Peach, Vaughan Robinson, Julia Maxted and Judith Chance

This chapter is divided into three parts. First, the background to immigration and legislation controlling immigration will be reviewed; secondly, the characteristics of the main immigrant groups will be outlined; finally, the prospects for ethnic groups in British society will be discussed.

PART I

Background

The most striking change to occur to the population of Great Britain since the turn of the century has been the growth of its third world ex-colonial population from negligible proportions at the end of the Second World War to the present time when coloured ethnics account for 5 per cent of the total. As a very broad generalisation, one could argue that during the course of the nineteenth century immigration into Britain was predominantly Irish, that at the end of the nineteenth and beginning of the twentieth century it was predominantly Jewish, and that in the middle of the twentieth century it was predominantly West Indian and South Asian.

Despite the striking impact of immigration, the United Kingdom's net migratory balance during the period 1901 to 1984 was negative (Table 14.1). Taking the period as a whole, over 2.3 million more migrants left the country than entered it. Even during the period 1951 to 1984, the net migration losses after 1966 outweighed the net migration gains of the earlier period by nearly half a million.

During the period 1900 to 1986, in common with the rest of western European industrialised nations, Britain's immigration field expanded from local-international labour and refugee movements to a world-wide catchment area. In the first edition of this book, the equivalent chapter, by Juliet Cheetham, was entitled 'Immigration'. It is a measure of the social change which the British population has experienced in the meantime, with the coming to maturity of a large second generation, that this present chapter has been entitled 'Immigration and Ethnicity'. Under this heading we do not intend to deal with the resurgence of ethnic identity in the Celtic periphery but only with the questions of ethnicity provoked by immigration during this century.

Table 14.1   United Kingdom net migration balance, 1901–84

Year	UK Census population at beginning of period (000s)	Balance (000s)
1901–11	38 237	− 820
1911–21	42 082	− 919
1921–31	44 027	− 672
1931–51	46 038	+ 465
1951–61	50 225	+ 12
1961–66	52 709	+ 74
1966–71	53 788	− 141
1972–84	56 079	− 388
1901–84		− 2 389

Note: After 1966 figures have been summed from annual statistics.
The 'Balance' column is calculated as the difference between gross immigration and gross emigration for the period stated.

Sources: 1901–1966: *Annual Abstract of Statistics* (1970) Table 17, p. 19 (London: HMSO)
1966–1979: *Annual Abstract of Statistics* (1981) Table 2.13, p. 26 (London: HMSO)
1979–1984: *Annual Abstract of Statistics* (1986) Table 2.10, p. 20 (London: HMSO)

The period since 1900 may be divided into two parts, 1900–1950 and 1950–85. In the first period immigration was of three kinds:

1. Local European regional labour migration especially from Ireland to Britain.
2. Refugee immigration especially of European Jews, from eastern Europe before the First World War and from Germany before the Second World War, but also of Polish fighting men and other groups displaced by the war and German brides of British servicemen.
3. Returning British from the Empire.

The period after 1950 saw a quiet continuation of some of the movements of the first period but was dominated for the first time by a new type of movement: international labour migration from the West Indies and South Asia and to a smaller extent from Hong Kong. There were, in addition, refugee movements of Asians expelled from East Africa and smaller flows of refugees from Vietnam. It is worth mentioning, parenthetically, that, from the beginning of 1973, Britain became a member of the European Economic

Community (EEC). Membership allowed in principle, the free movement of nationals within the Community, but in effect, had little immediate impact on the ethnic composition of the country apart from diverting some Irish who had previously migrated to Britain, to the continent.

The key difference between immigration before 1951 and after that date is that, while in the first period the main ethnic difference between the native British population and the immigrants was cultural, in the second period there were ethnic differences of race as well as culture. Britain had for the first time a significant, widespread, coloured population.

These two periods of migration need to be located within the context of the flux of the British, European and world economies and also in the context of the urban and regional development of Britain itself. During the period 1900–1950, Britain moved from the position of a dominant industrial and political world power with powerful industrial bases in its coalfields and peripheral industrial regions to a radically reduced position. Britain became a European regional industrial power. Industrially, Britain dropped down the world league table; regionally, there was a collapse of the traditional industries of the coalfield peripheries (coal, steel, shipbuilding, textiles). After the 1970s, even the secondary manufacturing centres, such as the car plants of the Midlands, went into steep decline. The movement into very large cities, which had developed strongly since the eighteenth century, peaked, probably about the 1940s and then set into the process of counter-urbanisation. The urban cores of large British cities collapsed, leaving hollow profiles in the population densities of the inner cities. The post-war migration flow from the West Indies and from South Asia was concentrated on the large but emptying conurbations. The population from the decreasing conurbations was redistributing itself into the smaller, rapidly-growing urban centres. Thus the trends of the ethnic and white population flows were in opposite directions (see the final column of Table 14.2).

Net immigration into Britain in the period 1950–86 needs to be seen in the context of the dissolution of overseas European empires and critical shortages of labour in the metropolitan powers. There were both the return of white colonisers and the influx of what some radical writers have seen as a black underclass. The net movement from the West Indies during the period 1950–74, for which continuous data exists, suggests a very close adjustment of the flow to demand for labour in Britain.[1] Net movement from South Asia shows a similar, but lower correlation.[2]

The influx of coloured labour was not unique to Britain. The whole of the industrialised western world experienced substantial inflows from third world countries during the post-war period (especially up to 1973, when the oil crisis produced a convulsive shock to the whole world economy). Thus the United States received perhaps 15 million immigrants during the period 1945–85, the large majority coming from Latin America and from Asia. Western Europe also received about 15 million international immigrants during this period, the

Table 14.2   Population resident in metropolitan counties by ethnic group, Great Britain, 1984
(000s)

Ethnic group	Metropolitan county of residence						Great Britain	Per cent living in met. counties
	Greater London	Greater Manchester	West Midlands	West Yorkshire	Other met. counties	All met. counties		
White	5 497	2 388	2 264	1 859	3 749	15 758	50 895	31
West Indian or Guyanese	309	21	67	22	11	430	529	81
Indian	318	46	148	38	6	556	807	69
Pakistani	43	25	84	74	22	248	371	67
Bangladeshi	60	6	6	6	0	78	93	85
Chinese	37	2	4	2	11	56	109	51
African	71	4	1	2	7	85	109	78
Mixed	84	15	16	6	13	134	205	65
Other (including Arab)	62	9	2	3	4	81	138	59
Not stated	155	50	28	24	75	332	829	40
All ethnic groups	6 637	2 566	2 622	2 035	3 898	17 758	54 084	33

Source: Office of Population Census Survey (OPCS) (1985) *OPCS Monitor*, Labour Force Survey, 1984: LFS 85/1 and PPI 85/3 (London: HMSO).

most notable, though not necessarily the most numerous groups, being those from the third world. West Germany received over one million Turks; France received over one million North Africans; Britain received over one million New Commonwealth citizens from the West Indies, South Asia and East Africa.

Birthplace and ethnicity

In discussing immigration and ethnicity, it is necessary to indicate that nationality, birthplace and ethnicity are not congruent categories. British official statistics tend to use birthplace and nationality as salient categories, while popular interest focuses upon ethnicity. Thus in the early part of the century, when the main international immigrant movement to Britain was Jewish, migration data referred to Polish- and Russian-born persons, but not to Jews. Measurement of the South Asian immigrant population in the post-war period was complicated by the fact that a substantial British ethnic population of whites born in India under the Raj, were indistinguishable in census terms from the Asian ethnic population born in India.[3] Similarly, Asians born in East Africa who were displaced by political pressure from their countries of birth, appear in the British census as African-born. There are thus three problems in inferring ethnicity from birthplace. Many of the Asian-born are white; many of the African-born are Asian; many of the ethnic minorities are UK-born.

Until 1962 British colonial subjects held identical citizenship with the British-born in Britain. Colonial and Commonwealth citizens, as well as the Irish, had an unrestricted right of entry to the United Kingdom until this date, whereupon the British colonial and Commonwealth citizens seeking work were controlled in their entry, while the officially alien Irish continued to enjoy unrestricted entry.

Controversy surrounded attempts to include an ethnic question in the 1981 Census and the attempt was abandoned. However, from 1979 onward, the sample Labour Force Survey asked respondents to identify their ethnic groups. The first survey produced some ambiguous or doubtful answers. A substantial number of East African Asians seem to have reported themselves as being of African origin, while many West Indians seem to have reported themselves as being of English, Welsh, Scottish or Irish origins.[4] The 1981 Labour Force Survey, which took place a few weeks after the 1981 Census, seems to have been the most successful survey to date of ethnic origins. However, direct comparisons between the 1979 and 1981 surveys must be made with some caution.

Table 14.3 presents a cross tabulation of the population of Great Britain in 1981 by country of birth and ethnic origin. This shows that there is consider-able variation in the degree of correspondence between the two categories. It

Table 14.3   Population by country of birth and ethnic origin, Great Britain, 1981 (000s)

Country of birth	Ethnic origin									
	White	West Indian or Guyanese	Indian, Pakistani, Bangladeshi	Chinese	African	Mixed	Other including Arab	Not stated	All ethnic origins	Per cent White
United Kingdom	49 037	244	342	24	17	177	45	196	50 082	98
Outside UK	1 849	274	710	66	48	56	169	35	3 207	58
NCWP	294	271	692	51	40	39	70	15	1 472	19
East African CW	27	1	155	0	12	3	7	1	206	13
Rest of African CW	16	1	1	0	27	1	3	1	50	31
Caribbean CW	14	268	0	0	1	4	6	2	295	5
India, Bangladesh, Pakistan	80	1	524	0	0	14	3	4	626	13
Far East CW	44	0	4	50	0	5	12	2	117	38
Remainder NCW, including Mediterranean	112	0	8	0	0	12	40	6	179	63
Rest of World	1 556	2	18	16	8	17	99	20	1 735	90
Not stated	28	1	2	0	0	0	0	377	407	7
All birthplaces	50 914	519	1 054	91	65	234	214	608	53 697	95
Per cent born in UK	96	47	32	27	26	76	21	32	93	

Note: NCWP = New Commonwealth and Pakistan.

Source: OPCS (1983) *OPCS Monitor*, Labour Force Survey 1981: LFS 83/1 and PPI 83/1 (London: HMSO).

shows, for example that although 'New Commonwealth and Pakistan' is commonly used as a shorthand term for non-white, 19 per cent of the population born in those areas but living in Britain was white. Of the persons born in the African Commonwealth, only 15 per cent were of African ethnic origin; 80 000 of those born in India, Bangladesh and Pakistan but living in Great Britain were white. Similarly, over 700 000 of those born in the UK were children born to coloured immigrants.

Looking at the bottom row of Table 14.3 it can be seen that nearly half of the West Indian ethnic population living in Great Britain had been born in the UK; nearly one-third of the Indian, Pakistani and Bangladeshi ethnic population had been born here and over three-quarters of the 'mixed' population had been born in the UK. As the immigrant populations age, birthplace will become increasingly unreliable as a guide to ethnicity. Thus, the combination of whites born in New Commonwealth countries, and UK-born children of ethnic minorities living in Great Britain necessitates very careful interpretation of ethnic information from birthplace data. Direct ethnic identification will become increasingly important in censuses if ethnicity remains a salient element in British society.

Table 14.3 reveals other information:

1. 95 per cent of the British population is white.
2. The largest single ethnic grouping is the South Asian combination of Indian, Pakistani and Bangladeshi who number over one million.
3. West Indians number just over half a million.
4. The mixed population of Great Britain numbers just over a quarter of a million.

Control legislation

There have been four main areas of legislation in Britain to regulate immigration and immigrants. First, there have been Acts of Parliament to control aliens. Secondly, there have been Acts to control Commonwealth immigrants. Thirdly, there have been Acts to regulate British nationality. Finally, there have been Acts to harmonise race relations in Britain.

Aliens Acts
Legislation to control aliens was concentrated in the period before and after the First World War. The early legislation aimed to control, in particular, the Jewish refugee movements from Eastern Europe, while later legislation reflected deteriorating relations with Germany. Legislation included the Aliens Act, 1905; Aliens Restriction Act, 1914; Aliens Restriction (Amendment) Act, 1919; Aliens Order, 1920 (renewed annually; last order published in 1953).

Commonwealth Immigrants Acts
Although the movement of Commonwealth immigration into Britain during the 1950s and early 1960s was controlled, *de facto*, by the demand for labour in Britain, public disquiet about immigration led to the introduction of political controls. Four Acts were passed during the 1960s and 1970s: Commonwealth Immigrants Act, 1962; Commonwealth Immigrants Act, 1968; Immigration Appeals Act, 1969; Immigration Act, 1971.

The 1962 Act sought to control immigration by regulating the number of workers able to enter the country. Since the movement was already controlled by labour demand, the legislation had little effect in this direction. Paradoxically, the chief effect was to precipitate immigration as potential migrants accelerated their departure to beat the British ban. The Act was used, however, through the 1965 White Paper on Immigration from the Commonwealth to stifle further labour migration and attention was then turned to controlling the arrival of dependants. In the meantime, however, the process of Africanisation in the former East African colonies led to pressure on Asian settlers in those countries who had retained their British citizenship. Some 6000 East African Asians entered the UK in 1965. As the numbers threatened to increase, legislation was introduced (which became the Commonwealth Immigrants Act, 1968) which removed the right of entry to the UK of British passport holders who did not have a parent or a grandparent born in the UK.

The legislation of the 1960s was rationalised and formalised into a new Immigration Act of 1971. Immigration control was based around the single distinction between patrials and non-patrials. This meant that the distinction between aliens and Commonwealth citizens no longer applied in Britain. The term 'patrial' referred to a number of different categories of people but its main reference was to persons born, adopted, naturalised or registered in the UK or born of parents one of whom had UK citizenship or one of whose grandparents had UK citizenship. These persons had the right to live in the UK. Non-patrials had to obtain permission to enter and settle in the UK. They were put on the same footing as alien workers. They could come on a permit only to do specific jobs in a specific place for an initial period of not longer than twelve months. The immigrant was now legally a migrant. Commonwealth immigrants no longer existed. Those who had come before the Act came into force in 1973 were settlers and those who entered after were simply migrant workers. Immigration legislation had led to the establishment of discriminatory nationality laws.

Nationality Acts
There have been five British Nationality Acts since 1900: British Nationality and Status of Aliens Act, 1914; British Nationality Act, 1948; British Nationality Act, 1964; British Nationality Act (number 2), 1964; British Nationality Act, 1981. Of this legislation, the Acts of 1948 and 1981 are the most notable.

The 1948 Act idealistically reaffirmed the principle of the 1914 Act. It treated all members of the British Commonwealth and British colonies and Protectorates as British citizens, with full rights of access to settlement in Britain. The Act continued the British citizenship of newly-independent countries such as India and Pakistan as well as old Commonwealth countries. Potentially nearly 1000 million people could claim British citizenship. The situation remained until potential claims began being translated into real claims, whereupon panic ensued and controls were imposed. The first of these controls came through the Commonwealth Immigrants Act of 1962 which cut off the right of access of even those who had no citizenship other than that of the UK and Colonies. The racially discriminatory nature of the 1962 legislation was evident in that the alien Irish, by far the largest category of immigrants, remained unaffected by the controls.

The 1981 Nationality Act rationalised earlier legislation, in particular that of the 1971 Immigration Act which created classes of claim to citizenship based on the degree of 'Britishness' of the origin of the person. In particular, the Act removed the right of those born in Britain to have an automatic claim to British citizenship.

Race Relations legislation
As a counterbalance to the control legislation on immigration and nationality, successive governments introduced legislation to outlaw racial discrimination. Thus, the Labour Government's restrictive 1965 White Paper on immigration was accompanied by the 1965 Race Relations Act which set up the Race Relations Board. Their 1968 Commonwealth Immigrants Act came with an extended Race Relations Act which instituted the Community Relations Commission (CRC). The 1971 Commonwealth Immigrants Act, introduced by the Conservatives, was followed by a second Race Relations Act in 1976, when Labour was returned to power.[5] The latter Act amalgamated the Race Relations Board with the CRC to form the Commission for Racial Equality.

Summary

Thus, to conclude the first section of this chapter, the situation may be summed up as follows. From 1901 to 1986 the population of the UK rose from 38 million to 58 million. Over the same period there was a net migration loss of over 2.3 million. However, although there was a net migration loss for the country as a whole, there were significant net migration gains both of refugee populations (Jewish at the beginning and middle of the century, East African Asians in the 1970s and Vietnamese in the late 1970s) and of much larger labour migrations from Ireland, the West Indies and the Indian subcontinent.

Although the UK suffered a relative decline in its world economic position, it suffered from major labour shortages in the post 1945 period. In some of the sectors of most acute shortage direct recruitment of labour in the West Indies and Indian subcontinent was made. These small transplants flowered into the later movements.

Immigration of West Indians and South Asians caused a political backlash which, in turn, caused a reversal in the whole concept of British citizenship. From a situation in which every person born in Britain or any part of its previous Empire could claim British citizenship with the right of free access to Britain, British citizenship was pruned back to a more exclusive and restrictive definition in which the aim of racial exclusion was clearly visible. Political control centred first on the exclusion of potential workers, next on the control of dependants. Political pressure was then aimed at attempts to promote repatriation, and more recently has viewed the higher birthrate of coloured minorities[6] with foreboding. Even those born in Britain can no longer automatically claim British citizenship.

Some legislative attempts have been made to outlaw discrimination. However, the political will for the pursuit of integration and the enforcement of non-discrimination as in the US context, has been lacking.

PART II

The second section of this chapter deals with specific ethnic groups in the United Kingdom. The groups fall into two main categories. The first is the labour migration group, which includes large groups such as the Irish, the Afro-Caribbeans and the South Asians, together with smaller groups such as the Cypriots, the Hong Kong Chinese and the Italians. The second group contains populations that were largely refugee in origin: the Jews, Poles, East African Asians and Vietnamese.

Irish immigration to Britain

In the last 200 years growing population pressure and religious and political persecution[7] led millions of the Irish to leave their country, the two most important destinations being Britain and the United States of America. Between 1845 and 1851 the Irish population fell from 8.5 to 6.5 million, the loss being equally divided between death and migration. The peak emigration in the nineteenth century occurred in the years 1841–61, reflecting the devastating impact on a rapidly-growing population of Whig policies, combined with the malpractices of many landlords and the disaster of four successive years of potato blight from 1845 to 1848.[8]

The Irish in Britain have shown two main periods of increase, the first from 1841 to 1861, and the second from 1931 to 1961, commonly referred to as the first and second waves.[9] Table 14.4 shows the numbers of Irish in Britain in the twentieth century.

Table 14.4   Numbers of Irish-born, from all 32
counties, resident in Britain, 1901–81

Date	Number
1901	631 629
1911	550 040
1921	523 767
1931	505 385
1951	716 028
1961	950 978
1966	948 320
1971	952 760
1981	850 397

Source: *Census Reports*, 1901–1981.

The early twentieth century saw relatively little Irish migration to Britain, since passage to America was fairly cheap and America was seen as offering better opportunities. Many of those who did come to Britain came for seasonal work – for instance, gangs of potato pullers, recruited by an experienced leader who had already established contacts with British farmers.[10]

The 1930s saw an increased flow of migrants to Britain, partly because the introduction of immigration quotas in America blocked access for many would-be migrants. In June 1940, following the outbreak of the Second World War, the British Government restricted the flow from Ireland, but these controls were gradually relaxed, until eventually the Irish were to be found even in such strategically sensitive areas as aircraft and munitions production.

There was enormous demand for labour during the post-war period in Britain, especially in the construction industry, traditionally an Irish preserve. In the decade 1951–61 net emigration from Ireland was 409 000, the equivalent of one in seven of the entire 1961 population. This was a response both to the pull factor of the British demand for labour and to push factors operating in Ireland, for example, the growing mechanisation of agriculture.

During the 1960s rates of Irish migration to Britain fell from 18 555 in 1961 to 10 895 in 1969[11] and the 1970s saw, for the first time in over 200 years, a net flow back to Ireland, especially in the early and mid-1970s, when Ireland was benefiting from a short-lived economic miracle while the British economy was already showing signs of recession. Many families, particularly those who had bought houses in the South-East, were able to sell up and use the capital to fund their return to Ireland, and the establishment of small businesses.

Evidence from the late 1970s, and more especially from the 1980s, suggests that we are now experiencing a third wave of Irish migration to Britain. Indeed, by the mid-1980s the numbers of young migrants have become a cause for concern on both sides of the Irish Sea. Preliminary results from the 1986

Census in Ireland show that net emigration 1981–86 totals 75 300.[12] The great majority of these migrants will have come to Britain, but what cannot yet be estimated is how many will stay in Britain, and how many will return to Ireland, or move on to the European mainland, where Germany and Holland are the preferred destinations.

The 1981 British Census records only 5985 people born in the Republic of Ireland who had arrived in Britain within the previous 12 months.[13] Given the growing problem of homelessness among the Irish in Britain, and especially among the new arrivals, many of whom arrive with little money, and no contacts or prearranged work and accommodation, one can safely assume that the census record understates the actual level of Irish immigration.

Areas of Irish settlement in Britain
Traditionally the Irish who have settled in Britain have been concentrated in the major industrial cities, especially London, and in the west coast ports of Bristol, Liverpool, and Glasgow. Over time the relative numbers in different regions has changed, the tendency being for the Irish to move to those areas with expanding economies. A major reason for this is the long-established tradition of Irish employment in the construction industry. Even in 1981, 28 per cent of the Irish men in Britain were employed in this trade.[14]

The dominant pattern in Table 14.5 is one of absolute loss from every region. The only gain is in the West Midlands conurbation, and even there the 1981 figure of 60 505 is only 4.7 per cent higher than the 1961 figure of 57 636. If one looks at the changes in relative numbers the general picture is one of loss from Scotland, which has fallen from 11.5 per cent in 1961 to only 4.4 per cent in 1981, and gain in England which rose from 89.1 per cent to 93.3 per cent in 1971 and remained at this level in 1981. Within the regions of England, with the exception of the South-East, the Irish population has become relatively more concentrated in the major urban centres, a trend which contrasts with the counterurbanisation of the population as a whole.

One of the most significant trends is the increased concentration in the South-East, which is underestimated in Table 14.5, because of the need to combine several regions to avoid the problems caused by boundary changes. Greater London contains by far the largest number of first-generation Irish in Britain, and its importance relative to the older centres of Liverpool and Glasgow is increasing steadily. Analysis of the distribution of those who had arrived within the year preceding the 1981 Census shows this trend even more clearly: 60 per cent were to be found in the South-East region alone, and 71 per cent of these were in London.[15]

This move southwards has not been a simple one-stage process. In the 1950s and 1960s the Midlands proved a particularly attractive area for Irish settlements, having a number of growth industries and a labour deficit – thus the focus of settlement shifted to the Midlands from the earlier honey-pots of Scotland and the North-West. During the 1970s, as the recession started to be

Table 14.5   Great Britain: Eire-born population by region by year, 1961–81

Area	1961 No.	1961 %	1971 No.	1971 %	1981 No.	1981 %
Great Britain	771 903	100.0	709 235	100.0	607 428	100.0
England	665 623	86.2	661 650	93.3	566 965	93.3
Wales	17 273	2.2	14 220	2.0	13 419	2.2
Scotland	89 007	11.5	33 365	5.5	27 044	4.4
North Region	11 226	1.5	10 010	1.4	8 065	1.3
Tyneside[1]	2 939	26.2	2 425	24.2	2 737	33.9
North-West Region	98 977	12.8	95 830	13.5	79 287	13.0
Manchester[1]	50 064	50.6	51 280	53.5	45 343	57.2
Merseyside[1]	21 633	21.9	17 000	17.7	15 004	18.9
Midlands[2]	92 473	12.0	91 975	13.0	76 886	12.7
West Midlands[1]	57 636	62.3	55 800	60.7	60 505	78.7
South-West Region	28 971	3.7	29 065	4.1	27 530	4.5
South-East[2]	367 410	47.6	368 905	52.0	315 327	51.9
Gr. London[1]	253 962	69.1	241 220	65.4	199 460	63.2
North-East[2]	66 566	8.6	65 565	9.2	59 457	9.8
West Yorks.[1]	19 010	28.6	19 515	29.8	18 079	30.4

Notes:
1. The proportions in the conurbations and metropolitan counties are calculated as percentages of the population of the relevant region(s).
2. The South-East area comprises the South, East, and South-East and London Regions (1961) and the South-East, and East Anglia Regions (1971 and 1981).
    The North-East area comprises the East and West Ridings, and the North Midlands Regions (1961) and the Yorkshire and Humberside, and East Midlands Regions (1971 and 1981).
    The Midland area comprises the Midland Region (1961) and the West Midlands Region (1971 and 1981).

Sources: 1961 – OPCS (1964) *Census 1961: Birthplace and Nationality Tables*, Table 1 (London: HMSO).
1971 – OPCS (1974) *Census 1971: Country of Birth Tables*, Table 3 (London: HMSO).
1981 – OPCS (1983) *Census 1981: Country of Birth Tables*, Table 1 (London: HMSO).

felt in the Midlands, the concentration in the South-East became more marked.

The settlement patterns of those of Irish descent are much less clear. It is obvious that many of the earlier centres have large numbers of second and subsequent generation Irish – for instance, the *Irish Post* provides details of the activities of many local groups such as Irish language courses, ceilidhs and Gaelic Athletic Association matches. However, to reach an accurate quantitative picture of the size and distribution of this population is impossible because the census records as Irish only those born in Ireland. Even the 1971 Census, which included questions on parental birthplace, is of no use since it subsumes Irish-born parents into a British Isles category. An alternative approach is to count all those living in Irish-headed households as Irish but, this leaves out Irish women married to British-born men, and their families. Caulfield and Bhat state that only 28 per cent of second generation Irish come from endogamous marriages[16], and if one assumes that the remaining 72 per cent are split equally between Irish mothers and Irish fathers, the 36 per cent with Irish mothers are likely to be missed, using the head of household approximation.

Age and family structure of the Irish in Britain
The Irish population in Britain is an ageing one (Table 14.6) although the current influx of new young migrants has yet to be recorded in a British census. Table 14.6 covers a decade of high rates of immigration, 1951–61, and 20 years which saw falling rates in the 1960s, followed by a net flow back to Ireland in the 1970s. What is particularly clear is the absolute and relative increase in the numbers aged 45 and over, and this is especially important given the high proportion of Irish who do not marry. In 1951, 36.3 per cent of the men aged 15 or more, and 36.9 per cent of the women, were unmarried.

The second distinctive feature of Irish family structure is the relatively high fertility level. Although this has recently fallen, it is still higher than in the total population of Great Britain, and in the total population of first-generation immigrants from all countries. In 1971 the mean number of live births to women in their first marriage was 2.8 for the Irish-born, 2.7 for all

Table 14.6   Age distribution by sex of the Eire-born population in Britain, 1951–81

Ages	m	1951	f	m	1961	f	m	1981	f
0–4	2 072		2 004	3 013		2 782	953		877
5–14	7 363		7 475	13 118		12 876	4 426		4 327
15–19	6 648		11 858	11 912		15 247	3 033		3 320
20–24	21 381		29 801	27 659		31 525	9 090		11 488
25–29	30 562		33 251	32 825		33 678	16 555		19 645
30–34	30 691		31 843	31 323		31 465	24 481		27 733
35–39	30 244		29 093	30 839		29 393	29 182		32 317
40–44	23 393		21 010	28 152		26 583	31 436		33 574
45–60			47 986			51 482			100 867
45–65	56 745			66 807			122 107		
60+			40 507			33 469			88 262
65+	22 397			15 270			43 755		

Note: The figures for 1951 and 1961 refer to England and Wales, and the figures for 1981 refer to Great Britain.

Sources: 1951 – OPCS (1956) *1951 Census, General Tables*, Table 37 (London: HMSO).
1961 – OPCS (1964) Table 5 (see note 11).
1981 – OPCS (1983) Table 7 (see note 13).

mothers born outside the UK, and 2.3 for all women.[17] In 1981, 8.1 per cent of all private households headed by an Irish adult included three or more children, while the corresponding figure for UK-headed households was 4.6.[18]

Socioeconomic status of the Irish in Britain
Most of the first-wave migrants were unskilled labourers and domestic servants, coming mainly from the poorer western half of Ireland. The same generalisation holds good for the majority of the early twentieth century immigrants, although this group also includes a sizeable number of Irish Protestants who were mainly landowners or professional and clerical town-dwellers. The major employment was in building, dockwork, coal-mining and the iron and steel industry.[19]

The Second World War was very important in the subsequent social mobility of the Irish in Britain. Many of the vacancies which they filled were jobs which would not previously have been available to them, being skilled manual or white-collar posts. At first there was some hostility towards the Irish workers and, especially in the smaller towns, the provision of accommodation proved problematic, but in the absence of any other available labour, they were soon accepted as just another facet of wartime Britain.

The demand for labour in the 1950s and 1960s was such that the Irish, far from being a reserve pool of temporary labour, could no longer meet the demand, and were able to move into manufacturing rather than unskilled and heavy labouring, which increasingly became the preserve of the newly-arriving Commonwealth immigrants.[20] Many of those Irish who have been in Britain since the 1940s and 1950s openly acknowledge that the arrival of the New Commonwealth immigrants, and their subsequent racialisation, were the best things to happen to the Irish, reducing the pressures of prejudice and intolerance. It is, however, clear that, especially in the aftermath of any Irish terrorist activity in Britain, the old prejudices survive.

Irish occupations were not recorded in a British census until 1951, so that any analysis of twentieth century trends must be somewhat unbalanced. One trend is for an increasing number of the Irish in the construction industry to set up as contractors and sub-contractors, rather than just working for British contractors. In other words, there is evidence of upward social mobility within a traditional employment sector and one which is still a major employer. Table 14.7 compares the social class distribution of the Irish born with that of the total non-UK-born population.

Table 14.7 highlights the difference in social class distribution between Irish men and Irish women, with the latter having significantly higher proportions in classes 1, 2, and 3 (non-manual), reflecting the high employment in the direct personal service sector, especially in health care. In 1971, 29 per cent of Irish women were employed in direct professional and scientific services.[21]

One characteristic feature of both male and female employment is that the jobs often include tied accommodation – for instance, many construction sites

Table 14.7   Socioeconomic class of Eire-born and non-UK-born working
population, Great Britain, 1966

Social class	Irish		Non-UK	
	Male (%)	Female (%)	Male (%)	Female (%)
1	3.0	10.8	6.0	1.9
2	9.0	18.7	10.8	22.3
3 Non-manual	6.8	21.1	} 40.7	} 33.3
Manual	34.5	6.9		
4	21.7	28.1	24.0	34.7
5	19.8	9.3	14.4	6.8
Unclassified	5.0	14.7	4.1	0.9
Unemployed	3.8	3.1	3.1	3.8

Note: These figures are calculated as percentages of the economically active population for each sex.

Source: Based on OPCS (1969) *1966 Sample Census of Great Britain. Supplementary Employment Tables, part III*, Table 24 (London: HMSO).

house their workers in local camps, while nurses usually have access to nurses' homes, and domestic and hotel staff frequently live at their place of work. While this may be advantageous for young people, especially on their first arrival in Britain, it becomes much less so for the elderly as they reach retirement age, and lose their home along with their job. Given the age and employment structures of the Irish this is a particularly severe and worrying problem.

West Indian migration to Britain

The roots of West Indian migration to Britain lie in the Second World War. West Indians served in the British armed forces, particularly the RAF, and workers were recruited to work in forestry and in the munition factories.[22] In the post-war period, British Rail, London Transport and the National Health Service recruited workers directly in Jamaica and Barbados. Although these direct recruitment exercises were relatively small scale, they formed the nucleus of the much larger unsponsored labour movements that overlapped and succeeded them.

There was a cycle of West Indian migration to Britain which lasted from 1951 to 1971. Arrivals rose from about 1000 in 1951 to a peak of 75 000 in 1961. Thereafter, with the imposition of controls and deterioration of the economy, both gross and net arrivals decreased. By 1971 there was, for the first time, a negative net migration balance for the year – 1000 more West Indians left Britain than entered the country.

Net migration to Britain from the West Indies seems to have been very

Table 14.8 Average monthly unemployment in Great Britain and net annual West Indian immigration, 1955–74

Year	(1) *Average monthly unemployment (male and female)* (000s)	(2) *Net annual immigration from the West Indies*	(3) *'Expected' net immigration from* r = − 0.770
1955	213.2	27 550	24 964
1956	229.6	29 800	24 146
1957	294.5	23 020	20 907
1958	410.1	15 020	15 139
1959	444.5	16 390	13 423
1960	345.8	49 670	18 348
1961	312.1	66 290	20 029
1962	431.9	35 051	14 052
1963	520.6	7 928	9 626
1964	372.2	14 848	17 030
1965	317.0	13 400	19 785
1966	330.9	9 620	19 091
1967	521.0	10 080	9 606
1968	549.4	4 801	8 189
1969	543.8	688	8 468
1970	582.2	1 749	6 552
1971	758.4	− 1 163	− 2 239
1972	844.1	1 176	− 6 515
1973	597.9	− 2 130	5 769
1974	599.7	5 845	5 679

Correlation of cols (1) and (2) $r = − 0.654$
Correlation of cols (1) and (2)
  omitting 1960 and 1961 $r = − 0.770$
Correlation for 1963–74 $r = − 0.788$

Note: After 1974, net migration figures are no longer available as the Home Office discontinued the publication of embarkation figures.

Sources: Column (1) Dept. of Employment *Gazette* (1974) p. 72 and (1975) p. 68. Column (2) Home Office unofficial statistics, January 1955 to June 1962, Peach (1968) p. 12, Table 3. For subsequent years, Official statistics published annually by the Home Office: Cmds 2379, 2658, 2979, 3258, 3594, 4029, 4327, 4620, 4951, 5285, 5603, 6064, 6883, 7160; Peach (1978–9) (see note 1).

closely attuned to the level of demand for labour in Britain. As a result of statistical difficulties (the Home Office discontinued counting West Indians leaving the country after 1974, so that net migration figures are not available after that date), the correlation of measures of the British economy and net migration are available only for the period 1955 to 1974. This period coincides, however, with the major migration cycle. Table 14.8 demonstrates the strong inverse relationship between British unemployment and West

Indian net immigration. Column 3 uses the regression of net immigration on unemployment to produce predicted values for net migration in each of the years. This column demonstrates the disruptive and paradoxical effects of the first attempts to control immigration in the 1962 Act. In 1960, 1961 and 1962, when the political threat of controls was imminent, actual net immigration was precipitated and was much greater than would have been expected from the economic indicators. In 1968 and later, actual net immigration was generally much lower.

British-born West Indian population

Table 14.9 presents figures for the West Indian population of Great Britain from 1951 to 1981. The population expanded rapidly from 17 000 in 1951 to over half a million in 1981. The population seems to have reached a peak in the mid 1970s. The highest figure for the West-Indian-*born* population was reached in the 1966 sample census; the highest estimate of the West Indian *ethnic* population was reached at 548 000 in 1971 (although, if the National Dwelling and Household Survey (NDHS) figure for England were projected to Great Britain on the basis of England's percentage in the 1981 census, the 1977 estimate of about 555 000 would be the highest). The 1979 LFS figure seems to be anomalously low because of confusion over the ethnic question discussed above. This picture of stability or slight decline in the West Indian population is supported by the migration figures, which suggest net outflow since the early 1970s.

From Table 14.9 it can be seen that by 1984 the Afro-Caribbean population has shifted from being a predominantly immigrant population to one in which just over half of the ethnic population has been born in Britain.

Table 14.10 shows that the West Indian population is notably younger than the white population – 59 per cent were aged 29 or under compared with 42 per cent of the white population; only 2 per cent were of retirement age compared with 18 per cent of the white population. On the other hand, the West Indian population was older than that of the Indians, Pakistanis and Bangladeshis. Similarly, while the West Indian family structure seems broadly convergent on that of the white population, Asian household sizes were markedly skewed towards large families (Table 14.11). In one respect, however, West Indian household structure differed significantly from that of all other ethnic groups. Nearly a quarter of West Indian households contained a lone parent with dependent children (Table 14.12). This is, perhaps, a carry-over of family structures from the Caribbean.

Occupational concentration

The West Indian migration to Britain was, in all senses of the word, a replacement population. West Indians moved both to jobs and to areas of the country and areas of cities which, despite a demand for labour, failed to attract the native population. Table 14.13 shows that West Indian men

Table 14.9 West Indian population of Great Britain, 1951–84

Year	Source	Caribbean birthplace	Persons with parents born in W. Indies	UK-born children of W. Indian parents	Persons in households headed by WI-born person	W. Indian ethnic pop.	Best estimate
1951	Census	17 218	n.a.	n.a.	n.a.	n.a.	17 500
1961	Census	173 659	n.a.	n.a.	n.a.	n.a.	200 000
1966	Census	330 780	n.a.	n.a.	n.a.	n.a.	330 000
1971	Census	304 070	548 000	244 000	n.a.	n.a.	548 000
1977	NDHS[4]	n.a.	n.a.	n.a.	n.a.	518 000[1]	555 000[2]
1979	LFS[5]	n.a.	n.a.	191 000	n.a.	441 000	441 000[3]
1981	Census	295 179	n.a.	n.a.	545 744	n.a.	545 744
1981	LFS[5]	268 000	n.a.	244 000	n.a.	519 000	519 000
1984	LFS[5]	242 000	n.a.	281 000	n.a.	529 000	529 000

Notes:
1. England only.
2. Taking the England figure and applying the same % that England formed of the 1981 GB figure to it.
3. Dubious figures; see text.
4. NDHS = National Dwelling and Household Survey.
5. LFS = Labour Force Survey.

580

Table 14.10   Population by ethnic group and age, Great Britain, 1984

Ethnic group	Age					All persons
	Under 16	16–29	30–44	45–64 (men) 45–59 (women)	65 and over (men) 60 and over (women)	
Numbers (000s)						
White	10 450	10 809	10 239	10 028	9 368	50 894
West Indian or Guyanese	139	177	88	112	12	529
Indian	258	224	184	107	33	807
Pakistani	169	83	61	55	4	371
Bangladeshi	46	21	12	14	0	93
Chinese	31	34	29	13	2	109
African	30	39	23	15	2	109
Arab	10	26	21	6	0	63
Mixed	103	56	23	16	7	205
Other	23	17	23	9	3	75
Not stated	232	200	146	131	120	829
All ethnic groups	11 491	11 686	10 850	10 507	9 550	54 084
Percentages						
White	21	21	20	20	18	100
West Indian or Guyanese	26	33	17	21	2	100
Indian	32	28	23	13	4	100
Pakistani	46	22	16	15	1	100
Bangladeshi	49	22	13	15	0	100
Chinese	29	31	26	12	2	100
African	28	36	21	13	2	100
Arab	16	41	34	9	0	100
Mixed	50	27	11	8	3	100
Other	31	23	31	12	4	100
Not stated	28	24	18	16	15	100
All ethnic groups	21	22	20	19	18	100

Source: OPCS (1985) *OPCS Monitor*, Labour Force Survey, 1984: LFS 85/1 and PPI 85/3 (London: HMSO).

Table 14.11   Household size by ethnic group of head of household, Great Britain, 1984
(percentages)

Ethnic group of head of household	Household size						All households (ooos) = 100%)	Average household size
	1	2	3	4	5	6 and over		
White	24	33	17	18	6	3	19 896	2.6
West Indian or Guyanese	16	28	18	17	12	9	186	3.0
Indian	7	12	17	27	16	21	207	4.0
Pakistani or Bangladeshi	4	8	12	16	17	43	98	5.0
Other	22	24	20	19	8	7	176	2.9
Not stated	20	33	17	20	6	3	246	2.8
All ethnic groups	24	32	17	18	7	3	20 809	2.6

Note: The household sizes given in each row sum to 100 per cent of the number of households given in the row.

Source: OPCS (1985). *OPCS Monitor*, Labour Force Survey, LFS 85/1 and PPI 85/3 (London: HMSO).

showed notable concentrations into the metal goods, engineering and vehicles industry (27.4 per cent in 1981 compared with 16.4 per cent of the white population) and also in the transport and communications sector (18.0 per cent compared with 8.5 per cent). West Indian women, on the other hand, showed a high concentration in the amorphous 'other services' sector which includes nursing and catering (57.7 per cent as against 38.4 per cent of the white population).

As far as socioeconomic class was concerned, West Indian men were underrepresented in the white-collar groups and overrepresented in the skilled manual, semi-skilled and unskilled manual jobs. West Indian women were underrepresented in the white-collar grades, and overrepresented in the semi-skilled manual groups (Table 14.14).

Even more indicative of the marginal, replacement population role of West Indians in the British economy was their unemployment rates. West Indian unemployment rates were double the already high national average in 1981, and for young blacks the rates were higher still. The Labour Force Survey of 1981 showed that for persons aged 16–24, West Indian males had an unemployment rate of 27.9 per cent, Asians 15.8 per cent and whites 15.1 per cent. For women in the same age group, the numbers were 16.0, 11.9 and 10.9 per cent respectively.[23]

Table 14.15, taken from the National Dwelling and Household Survey (NDHS) of England in 1978, gives comparative information for West Indian housing and that of other ethnic groups. Divergences in West Indian, white and Asian housing was already apparent at this date. West Indians show a

Table 14.12 Household structure by ethnic group of head of household, Great Britain, 1984 (percentages)

Household structure	Ethnic group of head of household					All ethnic groups (including not stated) (000s)
	White	West Indian or Guyanese	Indian	Pakistani or Bangladeshi	Other (excluding not stated)	
One person households	24	16	7	4	22	4 908
One family households (with or without other persons)						
Couple with no children	27	14	10	4	14	5 457
Couple with children						
with dependent children[1]	30	30	58	71	42	6 264
with non-dependent children only	8	4	5	2	3	1 652
Lone parent						
with dependent children[1]	4	23	3	3	9	895
with non-dependent children only	4	6	2	1	1	730
Two or more family households						
with children	1	2	10	10	2	162
Other households[2]	3	4	5	4	8	740
All households (000s) = 100%	19 896	186	207	98	176	20 809

Notes:
1. Aged under 19 and in full-time education.
2. Household contains either two or more families with no children or two or more persons not in a family.

Source: OPCS (1985) OPCS Monitor, Labour Force Survey: LFS 85/1 and PPI 85/3 (London: HMSO).

Table 14.13 Persons aged 16 and over in employment by ethnic origin, industry division and sex, Great Britain, 1981 (percentages)

Ethnic origin and sex	Industry divisions											
	(0) Agriculture, forestry and fishing	(1) Energy and water supply	(2) Extraction of minerals and ores	(3) Metal goods, engineering and vehicles	(4) Other manufacturing industries	(5) Construction	(6) Distribution, hotels and catering repairs	(7) Transport and communications	(8) Banking, finance and insurance	(9) Other services	No reply/inadequately described/working outside UK	All industries (000s) = 100%
Men												
White	3.6	4.9	5.3	16.4	10.9	10.7	14.5	8.5	6.8	17.2	1.3	13 325
West Indian or Guyanese	0.0	1.3	5.0	27.4	11.2	10.6	10.9	18.0	3.2	11.3	1.1	120
Indian	0.0	0.8	4.7	24.4	15.4	4.0	21.1	11.3	6.5	10.8	0.9	174
Pakistani or Bangladeshi	0.4	0.0	6.4	15.2	23.3	—	29.7	11.9	4.0	7.3	1.8	69
Chinese, African, Arab, mixed or other	0.4	1.5	3.1	16.8	7.4	4.3	27.0	9.5	7.5	20.1	2.4	114
Not stated	0.9	1.4	1.4	4.1	3.2	2.8	2.7	1.8	1.8	4.7	75.3	161
All ethnic origins	3.4	4.7	5.2	16.5	10.9	10.4	14.6	8.6	6.7	16.9	2.2	13 962
Women												
White	1.1	1.1	2.3	6.6	11.4	1.3	24.6	2.8	8.9	38.4	1.5	8 945
West Indian or Guyanese	0.0	0.5	0.7	7.8	8.4	0.5	10.2	5.7	6.3	57.7	2.2	107
Indian	0.5	0.2	3.2	12.0	28.7	1.0	20.9	4.2	7.7	21.8	0.0	93
Pakistani or Bangladeshi	0.0	2.4	4.4	12.0	29.5	0.0	11.7	0.0	10.7	29.2	0.0	10
Chinese, African, Arab, mixed or other	0.0	1.2	1.5	5.6	11.7	1.3	26.7	2.9	3.7	38.9	1.5	70
Not stated	0.2	0.0	0.7	2.1	1.9	0.0	7.2	0.5	2.5	15.1	69.8	102
All ethnic origins	1.1	1.1	2.3	6.6	11.5	1.2	24.2	2.9	8.8	38.2	2.2	9 328

Source: OPCS (1982) Labour Force Survey, 1981 (London: HMSO) p. 2. Reproduced with the permission of the Controller of Her Majesty's Stationery Office.

Table 14.14   Persons aged 16 and over in employment by socioeconomic group, ethnic origin and sex, Great Britain, 1981 (percentages)

Ethnic origin and sex	Socioeconomic group							
	Professional	Employers, managers	Other non-manual	Skilled manual	Semi-skilled manual	Unskilled manual	Armed forces inadequately described/and not stated	All groups (000s) = 100%
Men								
White	6.1	16.2	17.9	38.0	15.7	4.7	1.4	13 325
Non-white	6.6	10.4	14.6	36.7	24.0	6.7	1.0	476
West Indian or Guyanese	1.7	4.0	7.3	48.6	26.6	10.8	1.1	120
Indian	9.0	10.5	16.9	36.7	21.8	4.8	0.3	174
Pakistani or Bangladeshi	4.2	15.4	7.9	31.7	31.8	8.6	0.4	69
Chinese, African, Arab, mixed or other	9.7	14.0	22.9	27.3	19.7	4.2	2.3	114
Not stated	1.7	3.3	4.9	10.0	3.7	1.4	75.0	161

All ethnic origins	6.0	15.9	17.0	37.7	15.8	4.7	2.2	13 962
Women								
White	1.1	6.6	53.0	7.4	23.4	8.1	0.3	8 945
Non-white	1.7	2.9	47.2	8.4	33.5	5.6	0.6	281
West Indian or Guyanese	0.2	1.9	50.0	4.4	34.5	8.4	0.7	107
Indian	2.9	4.2	41.1	13.0	35.3	3.4	0.0	93
Pakistani or Bangladeshi	6.7	2.3	39.9	14.1	34.3	0.0	2.7	10
Chinese, African, Arab, mixed or other	1.8	2.8	52.2	7.7	29.5	5.1	1.0	70
Not stated	0.3	2.5	16.1	1.7	8.3	2.1	69.1	102
All ethnic origins	1.1	6.5	52.5	7.3	23.6	7.9	1.1	9 328

Source: OPCS (1982) *Labour Force Survey, 1981* (London: HMSO) 22.

Table 14.15 Ethnic group of head of household: analysis by tenure, basic amenities, age of property, bedroom standard, shared dwelling and satisfaction with accommodation (percentages)

	White	West Indian	African	Indian/ Pakistani/ Bangladeshi	Other	All households
Tenure						
Owned outright	23.8	4.5	5.0	17.0	14.8	23.4
Owned with mortgage/loan	30.8	31.4	17.6	52.9	33.5	31.0
Rented from council	30.0	45.2	29.0	10.1	18.0	29.8
Rented from HA	1.3	4.4	5.1	0.4	2.3	1.3
Rented privately unfurnished	11.0	6.9	11.9	6.9	12.0	10.9
Rented privately furnished	3.1	7.5	31.4	12.7	19.4	3.5
Basic amenities						
Sole use of all	91.8	86.8	69.4	75.9	81.3	91.4
Some shared, none lacked	2.4	8.6	28.2	12.6	13.3	2.8
At least one lacked	5.8	4.6	2.4	11.5	5.4	5.8
Sole use of bath/shower	94.7	88.8	71.0	82.3	83.8	94.3
Shared use of bath/shower	2.6	9.8	29.0	13.4	13.7	3.0
No bath/shower	2.7	1.3	—	4.4	2.4	2.7

Ethnic group of head of household

Age of property/building						
Pre 1919	26.6	46.8	58.9	61.7	39.7	27.3
1919–1939	23.8	15.3	16.2	20.1	25.0	23.7
1940–1964	27.0	18.6	12.9	9.6	19.0	26.7
1965 or later	22.6	19.3	12.0	8.5	16.3	22.3
Difference from bedroom standard						
2 or more below	0.5	2.2	2.3	8.3	2.6	0.6
1 below	3.9	16.1	14.0	21.2	9.3	4.3
Equal to standard	32.2	53.9	59.0	39.4	48.3	32.7
1 above	40.1	21.5	17.5	24.3	28.1	39.5
2 or more above	23.4	6.4	7.1	6.9	11.7	22.9
Sharing						
In shared dwelling	2.8	10.2	28.4	14.5	12.5	3.1
Not in shared dwelling	97.2	89.8	71.6	85.5	87.5	96.9
Satisfaction with accommodation						
Very satisfied	37.6	13.6	17.1	21.4	25.2	37.0
Satisfied	45.2	44.2	52.1	59.8	49.7	45.4
Neutral	8.8	15.5	11.0	9.6	10.8	8.9
Dissatisfied	5.8	18.3	10.0	6.0	8.6	6.0
Very dissatisfied	2.5	8.4	9.8	3.2	5.7	2.7
All households = 100% (000s)	16 240	152	29	186	217	16 824

Source: National Dwelling and Household Survey (NDHS), Department of the Environment, 1979. Reproduced with the permission of the Controller of Her Majesty's Stationery Office.

more working-class distribution than the other two groups, with a high concentration in the public rented sector (49.6 per cent, compared with 31.3 per cent for whites and 10.5 per cent for Asians). They showed a correspondingly lower representation in owner-occupation (35.9 per cent, compared with 54.6 per cent for whites and 69.9 per cent for Asians). Like Asians, they show a concentration in older housing, with lower standards. They showed, however, a greater degree of dissatisfaction with accommodation than did either whites or Asians (Table 14.15).

Geographical distribution

Geographically, the Caribbean population was highly concentrated in Greater London and the West Midlands. Table 14.16 shows that 55.4 per cent of the West Indian-born population lived in Greater London with a further 13.3 per cent in the West Midlands Metropolitan County. The comparable figures for the total population were 10.8 and 4.7 respectively. Over 80 per cent of West Indians were living in the Metropolitan counties in 1984 compared to 31 per cent of the white population. The West Indian concentrations in these areas seem to have remained fairly constant since the 1960s. The conurbations, on the other hand, have been losing their white populations since before the Second World War. Table 14.16 shows that over one-third of the total West Indian population was located in Inner London, which contained only 3.1 per cent of the UK-born population, and which lost substantial population in the 1971–81 intercensal period.

Although there has been a considerable shift from privately rented accommodation, in the early days of Afro-Caribbean settlement in London, to owner-occupation and, even more importantly, into council housing, the tenure shifts have not been accompanied by major geographical redistributions within the city.[24] Chain migration and the continuing effects of island identity continue to manifest themselves in settlement patterns[25] and in language.[26]

There is, however, clear evidence of massive alienation of the younger generation against racism in British life.[27] The evidence of racism is seen in the unemployment rates of black youth cited above; the effects of alienation are best seen in the riots of 1980, 1981 and 1985.[28]

The Asian population

Records demonstrate that South Asians have been resident in Britain since at least the seventeenth century when they were renowned theatrical performers. In the next century it became fashionable among the upper classes to employ Indian servants. We also know that beyond these isolated individuals significant communities of Indian seamen (Lascars) existed within certain British seaports over 200 years ago. In London, for example, the East India Company contracted to house and feed over 1000 Lascars as early as 1814.

Table 14.16 Population by country of birth, ethnic origin and birthplace of head of household, for selected areas, Great Britain, 1981
(percentages)

	Great Britain	Inner London	Outer London	Outer Metropolitan area of South-East	West Yorkshire	West Midlands Metropolitan County	Greater Manchester	Leicester
Country of birth								
UK	100	3.5	7.3	9.7	3.7	4.7	4.9	0.4
Caribbean CW	100	36.8	18.6	6.0	3.7	13.3	3.2	0.8
India, Pakistan and Bangladesh	100	9.6	21.6	9.2	7.5	15.8	6.3	3.3
Ethnic origin								
White	100	3.5	7.4	9.9	3.6	4.5	4.9	0.4
West Indian or Guyanese	100	38.1	18.5	5.3	4.3	15.1	3.4	1.1
Indian, Pakistani or Bangladeshi	100	9.4	24.6	7.6	7.7	18.2	6.1	4.8
Birthplace of head of household								
UK	100	3.1	7.0	9.8	3.7	4.4	4.8	0.4
Caribbean CW	100	36.3	18.0	5.8	3.9	14.8	2.8	1.3
India, Pakistan and Bangladesh	100	8.4	19.9	9.4	7.9	18.4	6.3	3.4
All persons	100	4.4	8.1	9.8	3.7	4.9	4.9	0.5

Source: OPCS (1983) *OPCS Monitor*, Labour Force Survey, 1981: LFS 83/1 and PPI 83/1 (London: HMSO).

Seamen and adventurers continued to migrate from the subcontinent to Britain until the end of the Second World War, and it was they who laid the foundations of the later settlement and mass migration. Collins describes the housing and lifestyle of Pakistanis in a 'Tyneside port' in the late 1940s, and comments how similar communities could be found in ports throughout the country.[29] Even so, as late as 1949 there were fewer than 100 Indians in the whole of Birmingham.

The reasons why sporadic migration gave way to mass migration have been covered in detail elsewhere[30] and are complex and specific to groups within the Asian population. Underlying the specifics, which include localised factors such as the construction of the Mangla Dam in Pakistan, was the strong attraction of economic conditions in the UK relative to the sending societies. Analysis has shown that mass labour migration of Asians can be correlated with the availability of economic opportunities in Britain,[31] and while the resulting correlation coefficient is neither as large nor as significant as that for net West Indian immigration, it does, nevertheless, underline the primarily economic motives behind the movement. The fact that Indian and Pakistani arrivals tended to be young males travelling without their wives and children and with a pronounced belief in return migration also emphasised the same point.

These early arrivals who began to enter Britain, at a rate of between 8000 and 10 000 per year from 1955 onwards, were part of a chain migration in which the pioneers sent back information on economic opportunities to their friends and relatives. Migrants were thus drawn from quite restricted parts of the subcontinent (most of the Sikhs, for example, came from the Doaba district, south east of Jullundur in the Punjab) and on their arrival in the UK were guaranteed free accommodation and assistance in finding work. Most of the new migrants made their way to areas where labour was in short supply either because the local population was leaving due to the type of work on offer, or because the rapid expansion of certain industrial sectors created a demand for labour which exceeded the local supply. By the 1961 Census, the pattern of South Asian settlement across the country was therefore already formed, with major concentrations of Indians in Greater London, the Home Counties and the West and East Midlands; major Pakistani nuclei were found in the West Midlands, West Yorkshire, Bedfordshire and Greater London (see Table 14.15).[32] Mass labour migration into these areas continued until the 1962 Act which reduced net Asian immigration from a peak of 47 000 in 1962 to 26 000 in the years 1964, 1965 and 1966.

Since Britain was still suffering from the post-war housing crisis in the late 1950s, Asian workers had very restricted housing options and were consequently relegated to certain parts of the cities within which they settled. Council housing was not made available to them because of the lengthy waiting lists which already existed and owner-occupation could not be contemplated because of a lack of collateral and the relative insecurity of employment.

Asians therefore entered the privately rented sector where they occupied rooms in lodging houses, which had often been blighted by planned redevelopment or the limited life of their leases. Such accommodation was often at high density, and tenants had access only to poor facilities despite the exorbitant rents. Rex and Moore's[33] account of life in Sparkbrook in Birmingham tells us much about conditions during this period. Other work does however, indicate that many South Asians at this time had priorities different from those of their British neighbours and that remittances,[34] frugality[35] and a desire for community cohesion also contributed to the housing characteristics and segregation patterns of the day.

The period since the 1960s has seen significant changes for the Asian population, although these have come at different times for the various subgroups within the population. Attempts have been made to develop typologies of actual and potential change[36] for the different subgroups but, as yet, these are only locally applicable. They do indicate that Sikhs and Gujurati Hindus are the most dynamic groups, while Muslim Pakistanis and Bengalis appear to be more conservative. The main motive for change for all these groups has been family reunion. Encouraged by the tightening restrictions on immigration, many male labour migrants have sent for their wives and children and the demographic and social character of the population has undergone a profound change as a result.

Indeed, most South Asian groups are now well into a phase of demographic maturity. This has been manifested in several ways. All groups now record more balanced sex ratios: between 1971 and 1981 the number of men per 100 women fell from 120 to 105 for Indians and from 210 to 121 for Pakistanis and Bangladeshis. All groups have a more diversified age structure: between 1971 and 1981 the proportions of the Indian and Pakistani population beyond retirement age rose from 11 to 17 per cent and from 9 to 13 per cent respectively. Lastly, the groups increasingly have population dynamics which depend upon fertility rather than immigration. Even here, the total period fertility rates are falling to levels nearer those of the West Indian and white populations, and only the increasing number of Indian mothers has prevented there being a fall in the total number of births to Indians in Britain. The impact of both fertility and the migration which brought about family reunion is seen clearly in the fact that the Asian minority (including East African Asians) has grown from 546 000 in 1971 to 1 054 000 in 1981. Asians formed 40 per cent of Britain's coloured population in 1971 but 49 per cent in 1981.

Housing needs were one of the first enforced changes to result from family reunion, and the period 1961–81 has seen significant changes although their net effect is somewhat ambiguous. There has been a progressive shift out of the rented sector into cheap owner-occupied properties (Table 14.15) within the inner city. By 1981, approximately 75 per cent of Asian households owned the houses in which they lived compared to less than 60 per cent of the total population. Recent evidence also indicates a parallel movement into council housing, but this has only gained momentum in the early 1980s.[37]

Despite these trends, the Asian population is still poorly housed on most criteria compared with the white population. Whereas 54 per cent of the white population live in detached or semi-detached houses, only 26 per cent of Asians do so. The proportion of Asians living in pre-1945 dwellings is almost 50 per cent higher than for whites and over one-third of Asians are living at densities which exceed one person per room compared with only 3 per cent of whites.

Moreover, whilst for some, the change in tenure has allowed suburbanisation, there is little sign of decreasing levels of segregation overall. Asians still remain tightly residentially clustered in cities such as Bradford[38] Blackburn[39] and Leicester,[40] and where systematic diachronic analysis has been undertaken, results indicate rising levels of segregation in the early and mid-1970s,[41] and only slightly reduced levels since.[42] Clustering serves not only a defensive function against racial harassment,[43] but also provides a market for community services such as Mosques and Gurdwaras, ethnic food stores and other specialist retailers. It also allows the re-creation of dense traditional social networks with all the implications this has for quality of life and transmission of culture. It is hardly surprising that attempts to disperse the Asian population have not been successful.

The evidence on changes in employment is also open to conflicting interpretation. Those Asians who have jobs seem to be enjoying a degree of social mobility. Asian males have an occupational profile which is superior to that of West Indian males and the 1981 Labour Force Survey indicated that a larger proportion of Indian males are professionals than is the case for whites. Overall, 36.7 per cent were in white-collar jobs (Table 14.14). Even within manual jobs, Indian and Pakistani males have made progress with only 4.8 per cent of the former and 8.6 per cent of the latter in unskilled jobs, compared with 4.7 per cent for whites and 10.8 per cent for West Indians.

Asian women also appear to be making progress. In 1981, 9 per cent of Pakistanis and 7.1 per cent of Indians were professionals, employers or managers whilst 3.4 and 0 per cent respectively were unskilled manual workers. These figures compare very favourably with those for West Indians and whites. Furthermore, Colin Brown's 1982 data show that average incomes for Indian men are the highest of all coloured groups, although still somewhat below white levels. Finally, a growing literature points to the explosion of Asian self-employment, particularly in the retail trade[44] but increasingly also in the wholesaling and manufacturing sectors[45] (see also Table 14.13).

Set against these signs of apparent success are the extremely high levels of Asian unemployment. The 1982 Policy Studies Institute [46] study noted that over 20 per cent of South Asian males were unemployed at a time when comparable figures for the white population were 'only' 13 per cent. For those aged 16–24 years the proportion of unemployed rose to 25 per cent of Asian men and 34 per cent of Asian married women.[47] Even in the 'booming' self-employed category, initial impressions are somewhat misleading: some authors argue that more and more Asian retailers are chasing a static number of consumers, that unemployment is merely disguised not eradicated when unemployed family members serve in the shop rather than register for benefits, that Asian shops are often in poor physical condition and are under-capitalised and that real returns on labour inputs are marginal.[48]

The ambiguities thrown up by the Asian population undoubtedly stem from the diversity of the group, stretching as it does from uneducated rural peasants to highly skilled professionals. Two ambiguities, education and employment, are of particular importance. In comparison with the white population, a larger percentage of Asian men have higher qualifications: yet 43 per cent of Asian men either cannot speak English at all or can speak it only slightly. In employment too, the group evidences both success and failure with above-average self-employment and above-average unemployment. What is clear, however, is that sections of the Asian population are gaining relatively rapid upward social mobility through hard work, entrepreneurial flair, and an increasing emphasis upon education. For these individuals, labour migration to Britain has been a success and they are now reaping the rewards. For others, migration has served only to transfer them from poverty in one country to poverty in another, whilst the colour of their skin has ensured that they are subjected to institutionalised differential treatment, racial harassment and abuse, and attacks upon their property and person.

The Chinese in Britain

Chinese migration to Britain has followed the classic pattern of labour migration to this country. The very earliest settlement took place in Britain's ports. Chinese seamen were employed on British ships from the time of the Napoleonic wars onwards,[49] and occasionally individuals would jump ship and find accommodation near the docks. These settlers were also joined by other Chinese awaiting a suitable ship on which to work their passage home. Even so, contemporary accounts which describe 'China towns' in ports such as London, Liverpool and Cardiff prior to the 1880s are guilty of exaggeration. It was only after 1885 that the first Chinese quarter developed, this being on Limehouse Causeway adjacent to the West India Dock in London. After the turn of the century this centre was joined by a second near Pitt Street in Liverpool. Both, however, contained a population of only 600 Chinese in 1911. These communities, and the similar one which grew up in Cardiff, were geared solely to the needs of seafarers, containing boarding houses, cafes and laundries.

The depression following the First World War, the 1914 and 1919 Aliens Restrictions Acts, and the 1906 Merchant Shipping Act, together, brought this first 'wave' of immigration to an end, leaving the Chinese population with all the characteristic features of pioneer labour migrants. They were young (78 per cent below 35 years old in 1911), single men living in rented lodgings with few creature comforts, in restricted parts of the docklands.[50] Demographic imbalance (a men to women ratio of 8:1) and urban redevelopment ensured that the Chinese were a population in decline in the inter-war period.

The resurgence in demand for foreign seamen in the Second World War provided a temporary fillip for the Chinese population. Over 10 000 Chinese seamen were held in Liverpool for the North Atlantic convoys,[51] but at the end of the war all but 500 were repatriated.[52] The only permanent additions to the population between 1920 and 1950 were therefore the professionals and nurses who came to Britain for training and career advancement.[53]

The second wave of Chinese who came to Britain was of a very different type and developed in the 1950s. Britain was, at the time, undergoing a period of economic prosperity, and one manifestation of this was a desire to dine out and to sample international cuisine. Ethnic demand had ensured that Chop Suey Houses had been founded in most areas of Chinese settlement by the 1950s (50 existed in 1957) and this meant that the community was well placed to take advantage of this new market trend. Coupled with this economic 'pull' factor was a simultaneous 'push' factor encouraging emigration from Hong Kong. After the victory of the Communists in 1949, there was a sizeable flow of refugees to Hong Kong. Many of these were innovative farmers whose new practices made them more competitive than the traditional farming clans of the New Territories. The latter turned to emigration in the face of this new competition, and their movement was later facilitated by the introduction in 1964 of cheap flights direct from Hong Kong.[54] This not only increased the *number* of people who could emigrate but broadened the *range* away from the young, single men who had been able to work their passage on cargo boats. The movement continued unhindered until the legislation of 1962, but even after that Hong Kong Chinese were able to gain access relatively easily to the UK since they had jobs and sponsors awaiting them in the catering trade.

As a result, the population rose from 5000 in 1951 to between 30 000 and 50 000 by the mid-1950s. An unintended consequence of the 1962 Act was that it encouraged chain migration of relatives and friends and it is this which explains the fact that 80 per cent of Britain's Chinese are from a small number of villages in the New Territories north of Kowloon. Fear of further legislation also encouraged early family reunion and this demographic rebalancing contributed towards the growth of the community to a size of 109 000 by 1984 (see Table 14.2).

Contained within this total are different religious groups, and three main linguistic groups: Cantonese, Hakka and Mandarin accounting for respectively 75 per cent, 20 per cent and 5 per cent of all Chinese children in British schools. As a result of their employment niche, the Chinese are distributed widely throughout the country and are not as concentrated in the metropolitan counties as the West Indians and South Asians. Table 14.2 shows that only 51 per cent of the Chinese lived in these areas compared with 81 per cent of West Indians, 85 per cent of Bangladeshis, 69 per cent of Indians and 67 per cent of Pakistanis. However, important nuclei do exist in London, Manchester, Liverpool, Birmingham, Glasgow and Cardiff.

Initially demand for ethnic food produced a rapid growth in the number of Chinese restaurants. Whereas there had been only 50 in the whole of the UK in 1957, the number had risen to over 1400 in England alone by 1963. This necessitated the diffusion of Chinese into progressively smaller towns and even villages across the country. However, with the imposition of Value Added Tax (VAT) and Selective Employment Tax (SET), restaurants became increasingly less competitive and food was largely served instead through take-aways. These too have spread across the country and they are now so numerous that nearly 90 per cent of all the UK Chinese are employed in the catering trade. Limited diversification has taken place recently but this has been mainly into kindred sectors such as wholesaling, importing, farming, shopfitting and signwriting. Some Chinese have opted for other occupations and there has also been limited penetration into the professions.[55]

The concentration of the community into one main economic niche has had profound social implications: 70 per cent of first generation immigrants can speak no English because they do not need to do so in their work. This restricts knowledge of British welfare rights and law and reduces the ability to mix of those individuals who wish to do so. Spatial dispersal in search of 'open points' in the catering business ensures that the Chinese are rarely given priority by local authorities because they are not as numerous in any one locality as other more concentrated ethnic groups as, for example, the Bengalis. Lastly, the long unsocial hours in the catering trade put a further barrier of social isolation around Chinese adults, as well as handicapping Chinese children who are expected to help in the take-away after school. All of this leaves the Chinese an introverted, and often invisible, minority whose needs are poorly understood. Recent trends suggest greater organisation and mobilisation but it is too early to know whether these are permanent trends.[56]

Cypriot migration to Britain

Cypriots formed part of the wave of New Commonwealth migration during the expansion period in the British economy in the 1950s and 1960s. The bulk of the migration took place from 1955 until the implementation of the 1962 Immigrants Act when approximately 25 000 Cypriots had come to Great Britain.[57] By 1962 net arrivals had dropped to a level of less than 4000 per annum and continued to decline. This decrease was more the result of contracting economic opportunities in Britain than of the operation of the Act itself. As with other Commonwealth migrations, this movement was economically motivated, as shown by Oakley's detailed study.[58]

Following the independence of Cyprus in 1960, opportunities outside farming were noticeably lacking. 64 per cent of the island's population at this time were villagers, and population growth had increasingly outstripped the development of the economy. Significantly, however, it was not the farmers or workers on the land who tended to emigrate but the white-collar and service workers from rural areas with at least a primary education.[59]

The economic and political situation in Britain at the time of the mass of this migration constrained choices for the Cypriots on the one hand and presented opportunities on the other. The migrants were drawn to areas where the demand for unskilled labour was greatest, namely the larger conurbations.

Greek Cypriots showed a greater propensity to settle outside London than Turkish Cypriots, but although some Cypriots did move to Birmingham, Manchester and the Home counties, over three-quarters of the estimated population of 160 000 Cypriots live in the Greater London area. This number includes second generation Cypriots and roughly doubles the figure of 84 327 born in Cyprus living in the United Kingdom. The ratio nationally of Greek to Turkish Cypriots is 5:1 as on the island itself, but in London the ratio falls to 3:1 reflecting the greater concentration of Turkish Cypriots on the capital.

The newly-arrived immigrants in the 1950s clustered in a fairly concentrated area of north London around Islington, Camden and Hackney, with smaller numbers moving south of the river. In 1971, the Cypriots were the most highly segregated immigrant group in London and in 1981 their degree of segregation was exceeded only by that of the Bangladeshis. This degree of self-segregation and self-containment as a community parallels that of other Greek settlements abroad. In the peak years of 1961 and 1962 over 80 per cent of the newcomers settled in a small cluster near the West End. Today, Haringey and Islington are the two London boroughs with the largest number of Cypriots. Turkish Cypriots are less concentrated than Greek but show significant clusters in Haringey, Newington Green and Stoke Newington in north London and around the Elephant and Castle, New Cross and Peckham in south london.[60] The Greek Cypriots have tended to settle to the west of the Turkish in north London although there is considerable overlap. The 1971 and 1981 Censuses reveal that both populations were moving north out of inner London in a trajectory similar to that pioneered by the Jewish population. The Greek population was moving at a more rapid speed than the Turkish so that a kind of shear-fault was developing between the two populations. The movement was to the more desirable residential districts of Brent, Barnet, Enfield and Waltham Forest, and shows a high degree of owner-occupation. Very few live in council housing and older buildings in the inner city are being retained and rented to fellow ethnics.

The economic pattern of Cypriot men differs from the majority of New

Commonwealth migrants in that rather than acting as a replacement labour force for jobs vacated by the indigenous population they have tended to move into occupations vacated by other minorities, such as Jews in the clothing industry and Italians in the catering industry. They have tended to form an ethnic economy that contains certain elements of an informal economy, namely cultural visibility, low language and occupational skills, low educational qualifications and involvement to a high degree in entrepreneurial activity in the backwaters of capitalist production.[61] The 1971 Census showed the high degree to which Cypriot men were self-employed – 22.9 per cent, twice the national average and significantly higher than other New Commonwealth migrants. Their lowest representation was in professional employment, where they were lower than New Commonwealth migrants in general. The second important characteristic of Cypriot male employment is in the high proportion in service work – 22.6 per cent, in such areas as catering, hotels, retailing and small businesses.

Cypriot women, on the other hand, have taken on jobs that indigenous women have abandoned for more stable and desirable work in clerical sectors. Cypriot women show an official economic activity rate that is lower than New Commonwealth women in general, but much of their work is unregistered. They are significantly more clustered in unskilled and manual categories than other New Commonwealth women with 16.9 per cent in skilled work compared with 8.8 per cent, and 32.5 per cent in semi-unskilled work compared with 29 per cent. They are underrepresented in both intermediate and professional categories. A typical environment for a Cypriot woman is either in a restaurant or in a small clothing factory, working as a machinist or finisher. Some are engaged in homework for the clothing industry.

Rents for cafes and small businesses were cheap in the area of London where migrants originally settled, and the increase of indigenous worker expectations in the 1950s and 1960s left openings for migrant labour in the clothing industry with its poor pay and conditions. Cypriot men who had migrated alone, working for a year or so as waiters or tailors, having saved a small amount of capital, took over ailing clothes businesses from the Jewish population and sent for their families to join them. They are heavily concentrated as subcontractors for larger concerns in women's outerwear, a market noted for its seasonal changes and instability. The small size of the firms, from 10 to 30 people, and a network of recruitment through kinship, has enabled these firms to survive in a highly-competitive environment. Working from vacated factories and old residential buildings they have remained concentrated in Inner London when other industries have had to move to expand. Those who live closer to the industrial fringe on the outskirts of Inner London are more likely to be employed on the open labour market in light industry than those who live in the inner city where clothing and catering have provided greater employment.

Settlement patterns are significant for accounting for the concentration of

Cypriot businesses such as restaurants, cafes, greengrocers, dry-cleaners, minicabs, laundries, garages, travel and real estate firms. Proximity of residence creates a demand for ethnic services and provides the labour for businesses to meet this demand. Those Cypriots who are not self-employed are likely to work for Cypriot-owned firms, and the two communities are closely interlinked in most economic areas. In general, Greek Cypriot women have been quicker to move out of the ethnic economy and into secretarial and clerical work than Turkish women[62] and likewise, Turkish men are more concentrated as employees in the clothing and catering firms than Greek Cypriot men.

The Cypriot population in Great Britain appears to be settled economically and socially and one out of every six Cypriots resides in this country. They have a youthful age structure in which only 8 per cent of males and 7 per cent of females were 45 years or older.[63] Movement from the island to Britain has remained low since the 1971 Immigration Act which placed Cypriots on the same basis as foreign migrant labour, and subjected it to a higher degree of political and economic control.

Italian imigration to Great Britain

An Italian community has been in existence in Britain for several centuries but only in the last decade of the nineteenth century did significant numbers come to the country. Coming primarily from northern Italy, this group included itinerant organ-grinders and knife-sharpners, ice-cream sellers and others in the catering trade. They were concentrated in the major urban areas, notably London, Manchester and Glasgow.

This population grew from 4500 in 1861 to 10 000 in 1891 and then doubled to 20 000 by 1901.[64] The 1911 census lists some 1600 waiters, 900 chefs, 1000 labourers in hotels, 1200 domestic servants and 1400 bakers of Italian birth in Britain, with a further 500 owning cafes or restaurants.[65] Before the passing of the Aliens Act in 1905, the immigration of Italians was not impeded by any legislation, but after this Act, and its reinforcement in the 1919 Act, immigration was significantly reduced, and the size of the community remained about 20 000 for several decades.

The Depression, the Italian Fascist policy of discouraging working-class emigration, and the Second World War, caused the community to shrink. Following the end of the war, however, it grew rapidly as prisoners of war remained in the country, and various official recruiting schemes were organised by the British and Italian governments. One such scheme was the European Volunteer Workers, which sought to alleviate the labour shortage in post-war Britain. In this scheme workers were bound to a specific job chosen by the Ministry of Labour and could be expelled at any time for misconduct or illness.[66] Only 4000 dependants were admitted with this work force, which was largely male, and restrictions on them were so great that complaints were made at the 1949 General Assembly of the UN. The sectors in which they were put to work – farming, coal-mining, brickyards, steel and tinplate manufacture, were widely spread, and considerable numbers settled in Lancashire, Yorkshire, Bedfordshire, South Wales and the Midlands. Hotels and restaurants continued to be important sources of employment for the Italians.

Unlike the previous migration, three-quarters of the post-war migrants came from southern Italy. A 1956 survey of the Italian community in London revealed three main socioeconomic groupings. The highest status group consisted of the heads of official organisations, lawyers, doctors and businessmen; these were overwhelmingly concentrated in London. The second consisted of small-scale businessmen and employers owning restaurants and shops. The third, of lower status, were skilled and unskilled non-professionals, factory personnel, labourers, domestics and service sector employees. Whereas the first two groups were mostly Italians of northern descent, the latter consisted mainly of peasants from the south.[67]

In 1971 there were 108 930 persons of Italian birth listed in the British Census, but in 1981 this number had fallen to 97 848. Due to the nature of the bulk of this migration from 1951–61 when the population increased from 33 159 to 81 327, Italians are less concentrated in London and the South-East, with only a third of the total population residing in Greater London in 1981. Almost half of the Italian-born population (47 267) are now in the 45 years and older age group, and may follow the pattern of return migration of those Italians who migrated to the United States, namely return after half a lifetime abroad to retire.[68] The length of residence of Italians in Great Britain is longer than in any other European country, and the community is fairly stable, with a high percentage of women and children, compared to other countries, such as Germany or Switzerland. Furthermore, the Italian community in Britain is more heterogeneous, economically and socially, than other Italian diaspora groups.

Thus, despite Britain's entry into the EEC, Italian migration has waned since 1967 and repatriation since then has greatly exceeded immigration, representing a loss of over 5000 per annum since 1972.[69] In the hotel and catering trade they have been replaced by Turks, Latin Americans and Filipinos, though they have retained a high proportion of small business, restaurant and cafe ownership. Conditions for entrepreneurial success in Britain, however, diminished rapidly in the 1970s, and as aliens they had to obtain work permits. As the chance to become economically self-sufficient has evaporated for migrant workers in contemporary Britain, conditions in southern Italy in the past 20 years have vastly improved.

Indeed it appears that Italy as a whole is now concluding its long cycle as a labour-exporting country to various European and non-European countries, and is at the same time becoming a country of in-migration from less developed Mediterranean countries.[70] Emigration from the underdeveloped south was encouraged by the Italian government during the 1950s and 60s as the only possibility for solving an unemployment problem that was dramatic, not just in the south, but in the countryside in general. It felt that migration could serve to transfer large quantities of surplus rural population and through remittances bring in valuable foreign currency to finance imports. However, the past two decades have seen the growth of a modern industrial economy in the north and central Italian regions, an almost complete exhaustion of rural labour reserves even in the south, the build-up of a subsidised economy in the southern region, and a net improvement in education and living conditions throughout the country. Within Europe there has also taken place the substitution of migrants with fewer rights in almost all of the main European countries previously the target of Italian emigration, noticeably France, Belgium, Germany, and the UK, by Yugoslavs, Greeks, Turks, Portuguese, North Africans and Spaniards. The structural conditions leading to this situation have been the increase in education of Italian workers, the expansion of unionisation to all industrial sectors, and the increasing unwillingness of young Italians to take unpleasant menial and manual jobs.

Opportunities to hire cheap labour through legal and illegal channels have presented themselves, and hence Italy has now passed through a post-Second World War transition period to a more advanced Western European labour market situation. In 1981, 61 993 Italians returned after staying in Europe, and the mass emigrations out of the rural south are a memory of the 1960s. Those returning do so mainly to retire, and thus while property development has boomed in the south, few private resources have found their way into rural industrial or infrastructural development. Those Italians who came to Britain to work in the brickyards and steelmills in the post-war period and are now returning to Italy, are witnessing a similar migration of other southern Europeans to fill exactly the same types of jobs in their native country. However, given the universally repressive immigration controls that now exist throughout Europe, the history of these workers will not include the possibility of settlement.

Refugee groups

Before discussing any groups in detail, it is important to point out some of the reasons why refugee groups deserve separate categorisation, and why their subsequent life in the receiving country will differ from that of labour migrants.

Since refugees are rarely given warning of impending persecution or expulsion, they have little time to plan their flight. This is particularly true of 'acute' rather than 'anticipatory' refugees.[71] This has two major consequences: first, that refugees will leave with few resources with which to facilitate their own resettlement and re-establishment; and secondly, they will tend to leave *en masse* over a short period of time. Recipient countries are forced to respond rapidly, and immigration can rarely be phased. This point is of some significance given the known relationship between the speed and scale of immigration and the degree of prejudice engendered in the receiving population.[72]

Refugee movements are usually non-selective in the demographic sense, and will therefore form communities with balanced age and sex structures. The circumstances of flight may, perhaps, leave permanent scars upon refugees, particularly where the movement has involved great mental anguish and physical hardship. Yet, in a sense, this may also have unexpected benefits in that the circumstances of departure may create a tide of goodwill and compassion among the recipient population which can be harnessed by voluntary agencies for the good of the refugees and which might, temporarily, allow positive discrimination in the allocation of scarce resources.

Finally, refugees rarely choose the country in which they will finally settle since they are more likely to be allocated by agencies or by default. This means that refugees may have no commitment to the receiving society or knowledge of its language or customs. It is also possible that there will be no pre-existing ethnic community to assist them in the early and critical period of adaptation.

The Jewish population
The Jews are the longest established of the refugee groups discussed in this chapter. Their earliest known migration to the UK took place immediately after 1066, when Jewish merchants from northern France came to England as financiers and merchants to the Norman settlers. Since then there have been three main periods of immigration, each differing in its characteristics. In 1664 Cromwell readmitted Sephardic Jewish merchants to Britain after their expulsion in 1290. These families established the base upon which Anglo-Jewry has been subsequently built. Migration of pedlars and craftsmen continued throughout the eighteenth and nineteenth centuries, but it swelled rapidly between 1881 and 1914 as a result of political persecution in Russia and Poland. There, the Jews had been forcibly segregated into the Pale of Settlement, and from the 1870s onwards suffered an increasingly repressive regime.

For many, these personal privations could be tolerated, but the outbreak of violently anti-semitic pogroms in the Pale towards the end of the decade was sufficient to drive over a million Jews from Russia alone in the next 30 years. Many paid guides to lead them to the Baltic ports or to Kiev, Minsk and Pinsk where they brought tickets for the journey either to the UK or to the USA.[73] They crossed the North Sea in merchantmen for ports such as London, Grimsby and Hull and from there either made their way across Britain to catch the Atlantic steamers or, wearied and exhausted, decided to put down roots into the booming urban centres of the north and London.

Communities rapidly developed in the East End of London, in Leeds,

Manchester, Glasgow, Birmingham and Liverpool. These soon overshadowed
the established nuclei in old market towns such as Canterbury, Norwich,
Exeter and Bristol.[74]

Subsequently a third set of migrants has joined these early arrivals, and
these too have been refugees. Between 1930 and 1939 persecution of Jews in
Germany, Austria and elsewhere in German-controlled Europe forced many
families to flee. Over 30 000 individuals found their way to London.

The Jewish population seems to have reached its numerical peak in the
1950s. Contemporary accounts suggest a community of some 450 000 people
at this time (Table 14.17) although recent research suggests that 430 000 is a
more accurate estimate. Although there are now worries that the community is
in numerical decline[75] (down to 330 000 by 1985), in all other respects it has
made astounding progress. The refugees from the pogroms were unskilled and
semi-skilled peasants and craftsmen who arrived in the UK with few resources
and little education. A combination of limited resources, sporadic overt anti-
semitism, and a strong sense of identity encouraged very tight concentration in
areas such as Chapeltown in Leeds and West Barr in Sheffield.[76] Most found
employment in the rag trade where women seamstresses might earn as little as
12.5 pence for a 54-hour week. Hard work, frugality, and entrepreneurial flair
converted many operatives into employers, and in due course the post-war
emphasis on education for the second generation has ensured their rapid
social mobility into white-collar employment. They are now statistically
overrepresented in sectors such as the medical profession, education, the

Table 14.17   Numbers of Jews in the United Kingdom,
1891–1985

Year	Number	Actual increase or decrease	% increase or decrease
1891	101 189	—	—
1901	160 000	+ 58 811	+ 58.1
1905	227 166	+ 67 166	+ 41.9
1911	237 760	+ 10 594	+ 4.6
1916	257 000	+ 19 240	+ 8.1
1921	300 000	+ 43 000	+ 16.7
1926	297 000	− 3 000	− 1.0
1931	297 000	—	0.0
1936	333 000	+ 36 000	+ 12.1
1946	385 000	+ 52 000	+ 15.6
1951	450 000	+ 65 000	+ 16.9
1961	450 000	—	0.0
1966	450 000	—	0.0
1970	450 000	—	0.0
1977	354 000	− 96 000	− 21.3
1985	330 000	− 24 000	− 7.3

Source: *Jewish Year Book*, selected years.

judiciary, estate agency and accountancy, and underrepresented in the manual and unskilled categories.[77]

The diminution of numbers since the 1950s may have led to some reconcentration and regrouping of the population into more viable communities. The inter-communal violence in Northern Ireland, however, is probably more responsible for the decrease of the Jewish population of Belfast. Northern Ireland is the only part of the UK for which a religious question is included in the census. From 1961 to 1971 the Jewish population decreased slightly from 1191 to 975. By 1981, however, in the wake of an IRA murder of a Jewish businessman, the population had almost halved to 517. The population had reportedly moved to Manchester.

With social mobility has come suburbanisation. The period since the 1930s has seen widespread movement out of, for example, the East End of London north into Hackney, north-west into Barnet, Brent and Harrow and north-east into Redbridge.[78] Suburbanisation has not meant deconcentration, and the Jewish population remains spatially concentrated between boroughs and within boroughs.[79] Maintenance of spatial concentration has also allowed the retention of a dense social network of communal organisations and institutions, not least of which are the 295 synagogues found throughout Britain, the kosher shops, Jewish day and supplementary schools and the voluntary welfare organisations. Despite these ties there are fears for the future of the community as a religious body (Table 13.21) and this has encouraged the growth of ultra-orthodox groups who are attempting to stem the fall in numbers by relatively high birth rates.[80] Community leaders remain concerned about the progressive ageing of the population[81] and about the loss of young Jewish people through emigration, outmarriage and assimilation.

The Polish population

Unlike the Jewish population, Britain's non-Jewish Polish population is almost entirely a product of the twentieth century. Polish Jews had been involved in the nineteenth century flight from the Pale, but as late as 1931 there were less than 5000 Christian Poles in the whole of the UK. These were concentrated in three main areas – London, Lanarkshire and Manchester and neighbouring districts of Lancashire and Cheshire. In the Whitechapel and Beckton areas of London, Poles were engaged in the clothing trade and personal services. In Lanarkshire they were miners and labourers in the steel industry. In Cheshire, Poles were employed in the salt works.[82]

The major period of growth for Britain's Polish population was the Second World War. With the fall of Poland to the USSR and Germany in 1939, the Polish government left Poland and re-established itself in London. Its arrival introduced a population of some 3000 migrants, many of whom were the families of servicemen. Shortly afterwards, with the fall of France, these early arrivals were joined by over 27 000 members of the Polish armed forces who retreated to Britain to regroup and re-form. Elsewhere in Europe, Russian forces had taken 1.5 million prisoners during their invasion of east Poland, but when the USSR entered the war in late 1941, they were released to fight for the Allies. Over 100 000 volunteered to fight and the Polish Second Corps was raised in Russia under General Anders. They subsequently fought in Palestine and Italy and retained a high degree of autonomy in their operations. As a result of the Yalta Conference which allocated Poland to the communist bloc, the Corps was repatriated to Britain at the end of the war where they were eventually resettled by the Polish Refugee Corps from temporary camps throughout Britain. In the immediate post war period, a further 21 000 ex-prisoners of war, 2000 political prisoners, 33 000 members of Polish military families and 14 000 European Volunteer Workers joined the military nucleus already established in the UK.[83]

The critical feature of Polish settlement in the UK is that the community is in exile, built around a core of disciplined military personnel who had experienced shared suffering and comradeship, and who felt that they had been betrayed by the Allies in the post-war political bargaining. The nature of the community has clear corollaries in its demographic, social and organisational structure. Few migrant groups, for example, start life in a new country with their own government (in exile), religious hierachy, military organisations, party political network, clubs, press and welfare bodies.

Data on the Poles are by no means plentiful, but estimates of the total size of the group suggest that whereas it was 130 000–135 000 in 1960, this had fallen to less than 100 000 by the beginning of the 1980s.[84] This figure includes ethnic Poles born in the UK. Interestingly, the war-time Poles were not a cross-section of Polish society, but were heavily biased towards the professions. Almost 600 writers, artists and journalists arrived in Britain during the war, and one in ten of the refugees had experienced higher education. The relatively homogeneous age structure of the group on arrival means that the Polish population is now an ageing and declining one: 88 per cent of all Poles in south-east Wales in 1985 were over 55 years old, whilst 19 per cent of all females in 1971 were of, or beyond, retirement age. Similarly, the military focus of the group has ensured an imbalanced sex structure with a ratio of women to men of 3:8. Whilst this has stimulated significant outmarriage, natural demographic trends have corrected the imbalance among British-born Poles.

Many Poles suffered loss of status on arrival in the UK, but there are now signs that this may have been partially overcome. Poles are well represented in the medical profession, judiciary and educational sector, and there has also been a movement from unskilled jobs into self-employment and white-collar industrial positions. Others have channelled their obvious talents into a dense network of community associations such as the Polish press, the excombatants association (SPK), the Polish Social and Cultural Association (POSK), and the Federation of Poles in Great Britain. The community now possesses a cultural centre in west London, the last part of which was opened in 1982.

Also important within the community life is the Catholic Church, which in 1985 had 74 independent parishes employing 111 perpipatetic priests.

Data from the 1981 Census on the 93 000 Polish-born persons, indicates a regional concentration in Greater London, West Yorkshire, Greater Manchester and both the East and West Midlands. Within these areas the Poles are residentially dispersed and have moved through the lodging house era and privately-rented accommodation, into owner-occupation. Their spatial distribution is now ossified and with the progressive ageing of the population, the reorientation taking place among the second generation and the increasing realisation that temporary exile has become permanent settlement, the Poles seem set on a route towards integration and symbolic ethnicity.

East African Asians

South Asians have been active members of East African societies since as early as the thirteenth century. Even then they were 'the masters of finance, the bankers and money changers and money lenders'.[85] They retained this position throughout successive centuries of Arab hegemony over the eastern coastal waters, and even the replacement of Arab rule by British colonial administration failed to dislodge the Indians from their economic and social niche. Indeed, British rule served only to enhance the position of Gujurati entrepreneurs and dukawallas, whilst also introducing a sizeable but largely temporary population of Punjabi labourers. In the period since the Second World War, the descendants of these nineteenth century migrants and settlers further strengthened their social and economic position by great emphasis upon education and penetration of white-collar jobs in the public sector.[86]

In retrospect, it is clear that the privileged and relatively affluent position of East African Asians was doomed as soon as the three East African colonies were granted independence. Keen to emphasise their social and economic, as well as political independence, it was almost certain that their Asian populations would be required either to demonstrate their allegiance to the new regimes or to withdraw in favour of their nationals. It did not take long for this to happen – in Kenya, Africans were encouraged to gain entry to the Civil Service at the expense of incumbent Asians until, in 1967, all non-citizens were removed from public employment. Further restrictive legislation followed in the same year, and in 1969 Milton Obote followed Kenyatta's lead and Ugandanisation began to parallel Kenyanisation.

The reaction on the part of the Kenyan and Ugandan Asians was to emigrate, having first transferred as much as possible of their wealth abroad. Between 1965 and February 1968, 35 000 Kenyan Asians fled to Britain, whilst over 24 000 Ugandan Asians left the country between 1969 and 1971. As has been described elsewhere in this chapter, it was the immigration of Kenyan Asians to Britain which led to the summary introduction of the 1968 Immigration Act.

These early anticipatory refugees were, to begin with, young, single men sent to assess economic opportunities in Britain on behalf of the whole family. They were also drawn from the wealthiest Asian families in East Africa. As Africanisation policies began to take effect in the late 1960s, these pioneers were joined by other anticipatory refugees who had been forced out of their jobs. These clerks, shopkeepers and teachers were of intermediate economic position and migrated as family units. By the close of the anticipatory stage of migration, they numbered approximately 68 000 in the UK, or 12.5 per cent of the UK Asian population.[87]

In 1972 the migration of the East African Asians to Britain took another turn when General Amin ordered all Asians out of Uganda within 90 days. Despite the 1968 Act, the British government agreed to receive and resettle the majority of the refugees. Eventually 28 609 were airlifted to the UK. Since they were acute refugees, the Ugandan Asians were drawn from a variety of social classes and age groups and arrived in extended family units with few resources.

The government reacted by establishing the Uganda Resettlement Board and transit camps where the refugees were housed prior to planned resettlement.[88] The latter was designed around the notion of dispersal, although in practice the failure to requisition accommodation forced 62 per cent of those refugees processed by the URB to find their own accommodation in areas which the government had declared as 'no go' areas. These included Leicester and Greater London, two centres which now dominate the group's spatial distribution.[89] At a national level, the Ugandan Asian crisis contributed to the rapid growth of the East African Asian population in Britain. By 1981[90] they numbered 155 000.

Despite a very unpromising start to their lives in Britain, the East African Asians represent a considerable success story. As early as 1974 the group had made rapid strides towards good housing and had already overhauled the established Indian and Pakistani groups on many criteria. By 1982 this trend had become more pronounced; they had gained greater access to council housing as well as to semi-detached and detached properties; they had above-average percentages of households with gardens, central heating and telephones; and they lived in newer properties than any other coloured group.

Their economic profile had improved to become one of the most advanced in the black population. By 1982[91] their average incomes exceeded those of the Pakistani and West Indian populations and were on a par with the more established Indians; 43 per cent of males were employed in non-manual occupations (against 15 per cent of West Indians, 24 per cent of Indians and 18 per cent of Pakistanis); and almost one in four were self-employed. They are particularly strongly represented in the distributive trade where they are both competitive and more adventurous than some of their Asian peers.[92]

The future for East African Asians in Britain is not yet clear. They are showing signs of economic success and social mobility, and many are from an English-speaking, middle-class background. Education will continue to be one of the strategies through which they seek advancement. On the other hand, white Britons rarely differentiate between East African Asians and other Asians such as rural peasants who have migrated from Bangladesh. All groups are treated in a similar manner, and although East African Asians seem set to become economically successful, they will be denied the social acceptance which they so clearly deserve. In short, they will become a marginal middle-man group as they were in East Africa.[93]

The Vietnamese population

The Vietnamese are the most recent arrivals of the groups discussed since they have not yet been in Britain ten years. Until 1978 Britain had no Vietnamese community to speak of, and had remained resolutely detached from the plight of the refugees leaving Vietnam for countries such as the USA and France. Only late in 1978 was Britain involuntarily involved, when a British registered ship which had rescued 350 Vietnamese was refused entry to Hong Kong until such time as another country offered the refugees a permanent home.[94] Britain complied, but it was not until the Prime Minister accepted a quota of 1500 Vietnamese direct from Hong Kong that the country could really be said to be involved in the resettlement of the 'Boat People'. Later in the same year Britain accepted a further quota of 10 000 refugees, most of whom were airlifted out of Hong Kong by June 1981. With additional refugees seeking asylum since that date, the Vietnamese population is thought to number around 19 000, with little likelihood of further growth through immigration.[95] Only the USA, Canada, France, Australia and West Germany have accepted more Vietnamese and Britain was unusual in not insisting that its quota had occupational skills. Most other countries accepted only qualified individuals who could be readily resettled.

Unusually, most of Britain's Vietnamese are ethnically Chinese and originate in the northern part of the country rather than the previously capitalist south. From 1977 onwards ethnic Chinese had their freedom progressively curtailed in the North as relations between Vietnam and the Peoples Republic of China gradually deteriorated. When China eventually invaded Vietnam in February 1979, many Chinese Vietnamese fled rather than face the inevitable retribution. Most were acute refugees and had less than a fortnight to plan their escape.[96] They arrived penniless in Hong Kong after a dangerous and frequently harrowing sea voyage. There they were processed and placed in either 'open' (up to July 1982) or 'closed' (July 1982 onwards) camps to await offers of resettlement.

Most of Britain's Vietnamese are young (70 per cent less than 29 years old) and many were children or adolescent on arrival. 76 per cent were educated to less than secondary standard and almost 80 per cent had been manual workers in Vietnam. Less than 7 per cent had held professional posts. Furthermore, only 12 per cent had chosen to be settled in the UK, the remainder having been allocated to Britain because other countries had refused to take them. All these features make the British Vietnamese population relatively unique and certainly very different from their counterparts in the USA who have been characterised as a modern, well-educated élite.[97]

The government's response to the arrival of the Vietnamese was to establish reception camps and resettle them as quickly as possible, using voluntary agencies wherever possible. Resettlement involved deliberate dispersal of the Vietnamese in small clusters or 4 to 10 families per town throughout the country. This programme has not been a success.[98] The government allowed its resettlement policy to be shaped by the availability of voluntary offers of accommodation. Vietnamese were sent to areas which the local population was abandoning because of lack of economic opportunities. With few transferable skills, and in many cases no English, the Vietnamese were unlikely to succeed where British people had failed. As a consequence, unemployment levels in the community were as high as 80 per cent in 1982 and there has been little significant reduction since then.

Many Vietnamese are frustrated and isolated and some commentators suggest that this will manifest itself in mental disorders.[99] Many have reacted to their plight by moving from their dispersed locations into the major cities. London's Vietnamese population has risen from 3700 in 1982 to 5400 in 1984 for example.

Whilst this secondary migration has produced problems of overcrowding and squatting,[100] it is ensuring that the Vietnamese community in London is sufficiently large to support a range of services and institutions. These include a Buddhist temple in Peckham,[101] local support groups, interpreters and a luncheon club for the elderly.[102] The exact form that secondary migration continues to take is a crucial and as yet unresearched issue which will shape the future of the Vietnamese community in Britain for the remainder of the century. Concentration in London and increasing ties with the Hong Kong Chinese there could lead to the disappearance of the Vietnamese as a separate ethnic group. Alternatively, a more diffuse pattern of secondary migration might allow the creation of distinctively Vietnamese communities with their own separate resources, in cities such as Leeds, Birmingham and Manchester.

PART III

The final section of this chapter deals with the prospects of Britain and its ethnic populations. It is inescapable that since the middle of the twentieth century there have been highly significant changes in the ethnic mix of British society. Although Britain's black and brown population constitutes less than 5 per cent of the total, its rate of growth since 1951 has been dramatic and the potential for a continued increase, albeit at a lower rate, is considerable. The marginal economic character of much of the employment into which the ethnic population has been concentrated, together with the structural as well as cyclical shedding of labour in the British economy since 1973 has had a devastating impact on the life chances of the immigrants and even more on those of their children. The geographical concentration of the immigrant population into the largest cities and often into the decaying parts of those declining centres has added to the concentration and visibility of their problems. It has proved a short step for some politicians to represent effect as cause.

The disaffection of the younger generation has been highlighted in the riots and urban unrest of the 1980s. In 1980 the Bristol riot marked a turning point in British race relations. Up to that time, race riots in Britain had been against blacks.[103] After 1980 blacks were the subjects rather than the objects of riots. In 1981 there were at least 35 cases of serious urban disorder including major riots in Brixton, Southall, Liverpool 8, and Moss Side in Manchester. Scarman[104] reported, and some changes to policing were suggested, but after a four-year lull, major riots broke out in Brixton, Hackney and Handsworth in 1985.

The riots were not race riots in the sense of black against white. The majority of the nearly 4000 persons arrested in the summer of 1981 in riot-related incidents were white. About 30 per cent of those arrested, however, were black and if the less serious events which inflated the arrest total to 4000 were removed from the statistics, the black percentage of the arrests would be higher. Unemployment, poor housing conditions and so on all contribute to the conditioning factors encouraging protest, but the ecological correlations between these conditions and rioting are very low. The correlation is with the distribution of the black population. The riots seem to have more to do with the racism of British society[105] expressed through the policing strategies of some forces than with the conventional measures of social well-being.[106]

Scrutiny of the arrest statistics indicate the Asians and Afro-Caribbeans were very unequally involved in the unrest. Although there are twice as many Asians as Afro-Caribbeans in Britain, over 80 per cent of those the police defined as 'non-white' were Afro-Caribbean.[107]

In a broad, but telling generalisation, John Rex argued that West Indians faced an Irish future in Britain and Asians faced a Jewish future. The analysis could be faulted: there is not one but many Asian populations. East African Asians are very different, for example, from rural Pakistanis or Bengalis. Barbadians differ from, say St Vincentians and so on. However, the phrase captures much of the significant differences between the culturally secure, entrepreneurially successful and educationally attaining and socially encapsulated societies of the Jewish and Asian groups as against the more working-class, council-housing orientation of the West Indians.

If one defines assimilation as the process by which, through entropy, the minority becomes dispersed throughout society so that its distribution becomes indistinguishable from that of the rest of the population, then, for many of the groups which have been discussed, there is a considerable gap still present.

Some of the minorities whose migrations have taken place in several waves and over long periods of time, such as the Italians and Irish, show geographic changes in their distributions which mirror the changes of fortune of the British regional economies. The nineteenth century Irish and Italians showed distributions which favoured the industrial peripheries in Wales, the North-West and Scotland. As the peripheral economies have declined, so the ethnic populations have shifted also towards the South and East.

Spatial regrouping is found among many other groups for different reasons. The Jewish group, small in total and with declining numbers, seems to be regrouping in more viable concentrations in the larger centres. East African Asians and Vietnamese have overcome government attempts to disperse them throughout the country and have produced secondary reconcentrations in Leicester and London respectively. The Chinese, on the other hand, with their niche economy in restaurants and the take-away trade have been forced to progressively disperse in order to reach their clientele.

For the West Indians and Cypriots, there seems to have been macro-scale geographical stability. The proportions of their numbers living in different cities and regions seem to have remained stable since the 1960s; change has taken place only in shifts within these areas.

For West Indians and some Asian groups, such as the Bangladeshis and Pakistanis, prospects seem bleak. Their concentration as replacement populations in areas of decline have led some politicians to treat effect as cause. For differing reasons, these marginalised populations are victims of both the structural and cyclical swings of the British economy. Jobs are ebbing from the older conurbations for both cyclical and structural reasons, but even when the economy recovers, the structural shifts indicate that these areas will not be the main beneficiaries. These populations are stranded on an ebbing economic tide. While Bangladeshis seem to be becoming butts of increasing personal violence, West Indian youth seems to be the victim of progressive criminalisation by British police forces. The radical left, in the meantime, is striving to make academic analysis of ethnic differentiation appear as racist attack and the discussion of ethnicity taboo.

Notes

Introduction
1. C. Peach (1978–9) 'British Unemployment Cycles and West Indian Immigration – 1955–1974', *New Community*, 7: 40–43.
2. V. Robinson (1980) 'Correlates of Asian Immigration to Britain', *New Community*, 8: 115–23.
3. see, for example, E. J. B. Rose *et al.* (1969) *Colour and Citizenship: A Report on British Race Relations* (Oxford University Press, for Institute of Race Relations) 95–9, 774–9; D. Eversley and F. Sukdeo (1969) *The Dependants of the Coloured*

Commonwealth Population of England and Wales (Institute of Race Relations) 10; G. C. K. Peach and S. W. C. Winchester (1974) 'Birthplace, Ethnicity and the Enumeration of West Indians, Indians and Pakistanis', *New Community*, 3: 386–93.

4. Office of Population Censuses and Surveys (1983) *OPCS Monitor*, Labour Force Survey, 1981: LFS 83/1, p. 4.
5. J. G. Reitz (1986) 'The International Structure of Immigration as a Determinant of Inter-racial Competition', unpublished paper, XI World Congress of Sociology, New Delhi, August (Centre for Industrial Relations and Department of Sociology; University of Toronto) 5.
6. See, for example, J. H. Thompson (1982) 'Differential Fertility among Ethnic Minorities', in D. A. Coleman (ed) *Demography of Immigrant and Minority Groups in the United Kingdom* (Academic Press) 71–81; W. Brass (1982) 'The Future Population of New Commonwealth Descent: Numbers and Demographic Implications', in D. A. Coleman ibid., 105–18.

Irish
7. D. Thompson (1976) *Woodbrook* (Harmondsworth: Penguin).
8. E. R. Green (1967) *The Great Famine*, in T. W. Moody and F. X. Martin (eds) *The Course of Irish History* (Cork: Mercier Press).
9. B. Walter (1984) 'Tradition and Ethnic Interaction', in C. Clarke, D. Ley and G. C. K. Peach (eds) *Geography and Ethnic Pluralism* (London: Allen & Unwin); J. A. Jackson (1964) 'The Irish', in R. Glass et al. *London: Aspects of Change* (University College London: Centre of Urban Studies) Report no. 3; K. O'Shea (1985) *The Irish Emigrant Chaplaincy Scheme in Britain 1957–1982* (Naas: IECS); M. J. Chance (1987, 142–60) 'The Irish in London: an Exploration of Ethnic Boundary Maintenance', in P. Jackson (ed.) *Race and Racism* (Allen & Unwin); K. O'Connor (1974) *The Irish in Britain* (Dublin: Torc Books).
10. J. A. Jackson (1963) *The Irish in Britain* (London: Routledge & Kegan Paul); P. MacGill (1914) *Children of the Dead End* (reprinted 1985) (London: Caliban Books); R. E. Kennedy (1973) *The Irish* (Berkeley: University of California Press).
11. OPCS (1974) *Census 1971: Country of Birth Tables* (London: HMSO).
12. Central Statistics Office (1986) *Preliminary Report on the 1986 Census* (Dublin: Central Statistics Office).
13. OPCS (1983) *Census 1981: Country of Birth Tables* (London: HMSO).
14. B. Walter (1986) 'Ethnicity and Irish Residential Distribution', in *Transaction of the Institute of British Geographers*, N.S., II: 131–46; T. Connor (1985) *Irish Youth in London Survey* (London: Action Group for Irish Youth).
15. OPCS (1983).
16. B. Caulfield and A. Bhat (1981) in *New Community*, 9: 73–83.
17. Ibid.
18. OPCS (1983).
19. P. MacGill (1914); J. A. Jackson (1963, 1964); K. O'Shea (1985).
20. B. Walter (1986).
21. OPCS (1974) (see note 11).

West Indians
22. For a discussion of the history of West Indian settlement in Britain, see R. Glass (1960) *Newcomers* (Centre for Urban Studies, and Allen & Unwin); S. Patterson (1963) *Dark Strangers* (Tavistock Publications); R. B. Davison (1962) *West Indian Migrants* (Oxford University Press for Institute of Race Relations); C.

Peach (1968) *West Indian Migration to Britain: A Social Geography* (Oxford University Press for Institute of Race Relations). A recent addition to the literature, taking a broad European perspective is C. Brock (ed) (1986) *The Caribbean in Europe: Aspects of the West Indian Experience in Britain, France and the Netherlands* (Frank Cass).

23. Department of Employment (1983) *Gazette*, October, 426.
24. See, for example, T. R. Lee (1977) *Race and Residence: The Concentration and Dispersal of Immigrants in London* (Clarendon Press); C. Peach and S. Shah, (1980) 'The Contribution of Council House Allocation to West Indian Desegregation in London, 1961–1971', *Urban Studies*, 17: 333–41.
25. See, for example, S. Philpott (1977) 'The Montserratians: Migration, Dependency and the Maintenance of Island Ties', in J. Watson (ed) *Between Two Cultures* (Blackwell); C. Peach, 'The Force of West Indian Identity in Britain', in C. Clarke, D. Ley and C. Peach (eds) *Geography and Ethnic Pluralism* (Allen & Unwin) 214–30.
26. D. Sutcliffe (1982) *British Black English* (Blackwell).
27. There have been a series of damning indictments of racial discrimination beginning with the Political and Economic Planning (PEP) *Report on Racial Discrimination* (1967, but undated) and continuing with D. Smith (1977) *Racial Disadvantage in Britain* (Penguin) and The Centre for Contemporary Cultural Studies (1982) *The Empire Strikes Back: Race and Racism in 70s Britain* (Hutchinson).
28. See, for example, Scarman (1981) *The Brixton Disorders of 10–12 April, 1981: Report on an Enquiry by the Rt. Hon. the Lord Scarman OBE*, Cmnd 8427 (HMSO); C. Peach (1986) 'A Geographical Perspective on the 1981 Urban Riots in England', Ethnic and Racial Studies, 9(3): 396–411.

Asians
29. S. Collins (1957) *Coloured Minorities in Britain* (Lutterworth).
30. R. Ballard and C. Ballard (1977) 'The Sikhs – The Development of South Asian Settlement in Britain', in J. L. Watson (ed.) *Between Two Cultures* (Blackwell); V. Robinson (1980) 'The Development of South Asian Settlement in Britain and the Myth of Return', in C. Peach *et al.* (eds) *Ethnic Segregation in Cities* (Croom Helm).
31. V. Robinson (1980) 'Correlates of Asian Migration to Britain', *New Community*, 8: 115–23.
32. V. Robinson (1986) *Transients, Settlers and Refugees* (Clarendon Press).
33. J. Rex and R. Moore (1967) *Race Community and Conflict* (Oxford University Press for Institute of Race Relations).
34. V. Robinson (1984) 'Asians in Britain: A Study in Encapsulation and Marginality', in C. G. Clarke *et al.* (eds) *Geography and Ethnic Pluralism* (Allen & Unwin).
35. B. Dahya (1974) 'The Nature of Pakistani Ethnicity', in A. Cohen (ed.) *Urban Ethnicity* (Tavistock).
36. V. Robinson (1982) 'The Assimilation of South and East African Asian Immigrants in Britain', in D. Coleman (ed.) *The Demography of Immigrants and Minority Groups in the UK* (Academic Press); V. Robinson (1986).
37. V. Robinson (1980) 'Asians and Council Housing', *Urban Studies*, 17.
38. J. Cater and T. P. Jones (1979) 'Ethnic Residential Space: The Case of Asians in Bradford', *Tijdschrift voor economische en sociale Geografie*, 70.
39. V. Robinson (1979) *The Segregation of Asians in a British City* (Oxford School of Geography).
40. D. Phillips (1981) 'The Social and Spatial Segregation of Asians in Leicester', in P. A. Jackson and S. J. Smith (eds) *Social Interaction and Ethnic Segregation* (Academic Press).

41. V. Robinson (1980) 'Lieberson's P* Index: A Case Study Evaluation', *Area*, 12.
42. V. Robinson (1986).
43. P. Gordon (1986) *Racial Violence and Harassment* (Runnymede Trust).
44. V. Robinson and I. Flintoff (1982) 'Asian Retailing in Coventry', *New Community*, 10.
45. P. Werbner (1980) 'From Rags to Riches: Manchester Pakistanis in the Textile Trade', *New Community*, 8.
46. C. Brown (1984) *Black and White Britain* (Heinemann).
47. Department of Employment (1984) 'Unemployment and Ethnic Origin', *Gazette*.
48. H. E. Aldrich *et al.* (1980) 'Business Development and Self Segregation', in C. Peach *et al* (eds) *Ethnic Segregation in Cities* (Croom Helm).

Chinese
49. D. Jones (1979) 'The Chinese in Britain', *New Community*, 7.
50. M. Broady (1958) 'The Chinese in Great Britain', in M. H. Fried (ed.) *Colloquium on Overseas Chinese* (Institute of Race Relations).
51. S. Collins (1957) *Coloured Minorities in Britain* (Lutterworth).
52. M. Freeberne (1981) 'Chinese Succeed in the UK', *Geographical Magazine*, LIII.
53. House of Commons Home Affairs Committee (1985) *Report on the Chinese Community in Britain* (HMSO).
54. D. Jones (1979).
55. J. L. Watson (1977) 'The Chinese: Hong Kong Villagers in the British Catering Trade', in J. L. Watson (ed.) *Between Two Cultures* (Blackwell).
56. D. Campbell (1985) 'Trouble in Chinatown', *City Limits*.

Cypriots
57. R. Oakley (1971) *Cypriot Migration and Settlement in Britain*, unpublished DPhil thesis (University of Oxford) 241ff.
58. R. Oakley, *ibid.*, 24, 44.
59. *Ibid.*, 79.
60. S. Ladbury (1984) 'Choice, Chance or No Alternative? Turkish Cypriots in Business in London', in R. Ward and R. Jenkins (eds) *Ethnic Communities in Business* (Cambridge University Press) 107.
61 F. Anthias (1983) 'Sexual Division and Ethnic Adaptation: the Case of Greek Cypriot Women', in A. Phizacklea (ed.), *One Way Ticket: Migration and Female Labour* (Routledge & Kegan Paul) 73ff.
62. S. Ladbury (1984) 109.
63. Commission for Racial Equality (1979) *Ethnic Minorities in Britain* (Commission for Racial Equality).

Italians
64. U. Marin (1975) *Italiani in Gran Bretagna* (Rome: Centro Studi Emigrazione).
65. R. Palmer (1977) 'The Italians: Patterns of Migration to London', in J. L. Watson (ed.) *Between Two Cultures* (Basil Blackwell). 246.
66. S. Castles and G. Kosack (1973) *Immigrant Workers and the Class Structure in Western Europe* (Oxford University Press for the Institute of Race Relations) 30.
67. P. Garigue and R. W. Firth (1956) 'Kinship and Organization of Italians in London', in R. W. Firth (ed.) *Two Studies of Kinship in London* (Athlone Press) 65–93.
68. R. King (1977) 'Problems of Return Migration': A Case Study of Italians Returning from Britain', *Tijdschrift voor economische en sociale Geografie*, 68(4): 244.
69. U. Marin (1975).

614 British Social Trends since 1900

70. U. Ascoli (1985) 'Migration of Workers and the Labor Market', in R. Rogers (ed.) *Guests Come to Stay – The Effect of European Labor Migration on Sending and Receiving Countries* (Westview Press) Chapter 9.
71 E. F. Kunz (1973) 'The Refugee in Flight: Kinetic Models and Forms of Displacement', *International Migration Review*, 7.
72. G. W. Allport (1954) *The Nature of Prejudice* (Addison Wesley).

Jews
73. I. Bild (1984) *The Jews in Britain* (Batsford).
74. D. Newman (1985) 'Integration and Ethnic Spatial Concentration: The Changing Distribution of the Anglo-Jewish Community', *Transactions, Institute of British Geographers*, 10.
75. S. Waterman and B. Komsin (1986a) 'The Distribution of Jews in the United Kingdom', *Geography*, 71.
76. B. Kosmin, M. Bauer and N. Grizzard (1976) *Steel City Jews* (Board of Deputies of British Jews).
77. S. Waterman and B. Kosmin (1986b) *British Jewry in the Eighties* (Board of Deputies of British Jews).
78. S. Waterman and B. Kosmin (1986c) 'The Jews of London', *Geographical Magazine*, LVIII.
79. D. Newman (1985), and S. Waterman and B. Kosmin (1986b).
80. A. Caudrey (1986) 'Keepers of the Faith', *New Society*.
81. B. Kosmin and N. Grizzard (1975) *Jews in an Inner London Borough* (Board of Deputies of British Jews).

Poles
82. J. Zubrzycki (1956) *Polish Immigrants in Britain* (Martinus Nijhoff).
83. S. Patterson (1961) 'The Polish Exile Community in Britain', *Polish Review*, 6.
84. S. Patterson (1977) 'The Poles: An Exile Community in Britain', in J. L. Watson (ed.) *Between Two Cultures* (Blackwell).

East African Asians
85. G. Delf (1963) *Asians in East Africa* (Oxford University Press).
86. D. P. Ghai and Y. P. Ghai (1970) *Portrait of a Minority: Asians in East Africa* (Oxford University Press).
87. OPCS Immigrant Statistics Unit (1975) 'Country of Birth and Colour', *Population Trends*, 2.
88. E. N. Swinerton et al. (1975) *Ugandan Asians in Great Britain* (Croom Helm).
89. V. Robinson (1986) *Transients, Settlers and Refugees* (Clarendon Press).
90. Labour Force Survey, 1981 (1983) (HMSO).
91. C. Brown (1984) *Black and White Britain* (Heinemann).
92. V. Robinson and I. Flintoff (1982) 'Asian Retailing in Coventry', *New Community*, 10.
93. V. Robinson (1986).

Vietnamese
94. P. R. Jones (1982) *Vietnamese Refugees* (Home Office).
95. House of Commons Home Affairs Committee (1985) *Refugees and Asylum with Special Reference to the Vietnamese*, vol. 1 (HMSO).
96. P. Edholm et al. (1983) *Vietnamese Refugees in Britain* (Commission for Racial Equality).

97. See G. P. Kelly (1977) *From Vietnam to America* (West View Press); D. Montero (1979) *Vietnamese Americans* (Westview Press); B. N. Stein (1980) *Refugee Resettlement Programs and Techniques* (Michigan State University).
98. House of Commons Home Affairs Committee (1985) vol. 1; V. Robinson (1985) 'The Vietnamese Reception and Resettlement Programme in the UK: Rhetoric and Reality', *Ethnic Groups*, 6.
99. F. Somerset (1983) 'Vietnamese Refugees in Britain: Resettlement Experience', *New Community*, 10.
100. A. Caudrey (1986) 'Britain's Boat People', *New Society*, 3(1).
101. J. Watts, 'When the Boat comes to Shore', *The Observer*, 3 March 1985.
102. House of Commons Home Affairs Committee (1985) vol. 2.

Part III
103. For an account of the early riots, see K. Little (1947) *Negroes in Britain* (Kegan Paul, Trench Trubner & Co.) 61.
104. Scarman, Lord (1981) *The Brixton Disorders of 10–12 April, 1981: Report on an Enquiry by the Rt. Hon. the Lord Scarman OBE*, Cmnd 8427 (HMSO).
105. Centre for Contemporary Cultural Studies (1982) *The Empire Strikes Back: Race and Racism in 70s Britain* (Hutchinson).
106. C. Peach (1986) 'A Geographical Perspective on the 1981 Urban Riots in England', *Ethnic and Racial Studies*, 9(3): 396–411.
107. *Ibid.*

15 Crime and Penal Measures

Nigel Walker

This chapter deals with national trends in:

(a) **Judicial statistics of criminal proceedings** – that is, appearances in criminal courts and the ways in which those found guilty there were dealt with. The relevant tables are 15.1 to 15.2.

(b) **Police cautions** – that is, warnings given to identified offenders instead of prosecution. The relevant table is 15.5.

(c) **Clear-up rates** – that is, the percentages of offences known to the police which were traced to identified offenders, whether or not this led to prosecution, caution or no action. The relevant table is 15.6.

(d) **Prison statistics** – that is, numbers of receptions into prisons and their juvenile equivalents, and average daily populations of such establishments, whether under sentence or awaiting trial or sentence. The relevant table is 15.3.

(e) **Conviction-rates** – that is, the percentages of different birth cohorts who have convictions by certain ages. The relevant table is 15.7.

(f) **Criminal statistics** – that is, numbers of certain types of offence which have been recorded as known to the police. The relevant table is 15.8.

(g) **Police manpower statistics** – that is, numbers of police officers employed by police authorities, and the hours they worked. The relevant table is 15.9.

(h) **Probation manpower statistics** – that is, numbers of probation officers employed full-time or part-time. The relevant table is 15.10.

The figures in each table are confined, perforce, to England and Wales, and – with minor exceptions – are collected and published annually by the Home Office (see Part A of the References). Separate statistics of a similar kind are published by the Scottish Office and the Northern Ireland Office for their countries, but with differences which make amalgamation fallacious. The years selected to demonstrate trends are 1900, 1910, 1920, 1930 (not 1940 because wartime statistics are unreliable and not indicative of long-term trends), 1950, 1960, 1970 and 1980, although here and there other years have been taken because better information is available for them (for example 1952 instead of 1950 in Table 15.2, dealing with traffic offences).

There have been two major overhauls of the criminal and judicial statistics since they began to be collected and published in the middle of the nineteenth century. One took place in the 1890s, and so was completed before the period with which we are concerned; the other took place in the 1970s as the result of the Reports of the two Departmental Committees on Criminal Statistics.[1] For the first seven decades of this century, however, the main criminal and judicial statistics have been compiled on much the same basis, although with minor changes in definition and accuracy, of which the most important examples are

1. **Age of criminal liability:** the minimum age at which a child could be charged with any kind of offence was raised from the 7th to the 8th birthday from 1934; and in England and Wales from the 8th to the 10th birthday from February 1964.[2]
2. **Age of juvenile court jurisdiction:** the maximum age at which a young person could be dealt with by a juvenile court was raised from 16 to 17 from 1934.[3]
3. **Murder:** the creation of the new offence of 'infanticide' in 1922 excluded substantial numbers of homicides by women from both the recorded murders and the convicted murderers from 1925.

   The creation of the new defence of 'diminished responsibility' in March 1957 excluded substantial numbers of homicides by men and women from both the criminal and judicial statistics for 'murder'; these homicides were henceforth shown as 'manslaughter', although separately from other homicides in this category.
4. **Manslaughter:** in addition to the change just mentioned, the creation of the new offence of 'causing death by dangerous (later 'reckless') driving' from 1956 excluded substantial numbers from the judicial and criminal statistics for manslaughter.
5. **Homosexual offences:** these were redefined in 1967 so as to exclude (with minor exceptions) sexual acts in private between consenting men aged 21 or older.
6. **Acquisitive offences:** the Theft Act, 1967, revised the definitions of most acquisitive offences from 1968.

Again, in interpreting changes in courts' choices of sentence, it is important to be sure of the extent to which choices were freely available. Thus the apparent caution with which courts began to use detention centre orders in the 1950s is explained by the slow increase in detention centre vacancies: it was many years before every court could make use of this measure.

Nor should it be assumed that every penal statute came into operation as soon as it received the Royal Assent. Some do: but if a provision involves administrative changes it is likely that the statute will provide that it should not come into operation until such a date as the Home Secretary (or other Minister) may appoint by order (such orders being statutory instruments).

Thus, for example, the sections of the Criminal Justice Act of 1967 which created the suspended prison sentence were brought into operation on 1 January 1968; but the parole provisions, which called for much preparation, were not brought into operation until three months later.

JUDICIAL STATISTICS OF CRIMINAL PROCEEDINGS

Statistics of trials and sentences (that is, 'Criminal Judicial Statistics') have been published annually as parliamentary or departmental papers since 1834. At first they were confined to trials on indictment (that is, before a jury at Assizes or Quarter Sessions), but in 1857 they were extended to summary trials in magistrates' courts. Judicial statistics are based on reports from local police forces, who send the Home Office's Statistical Branch a form for every person brought to trial. Being based, therefore, on reports of easily observed events by persons who are trained to understand what they are observing, they are not subject to large-scale inaccuracies of the kind which vitiate some other forms of statistics. It is important, however, to note their limitations. They do not count persons, but *appearances in criminal courts* by persons who, in some cases, appear more than once a year (for example, for offences of drunkenness). They do not show all the offences of which a person was accused at his appearance, nor all the sentences which he received: only the most serious. Thus a person imprisoned for taking and driving away a motor-car, and fined for careless driving at the same time, would be shown only as imprisoned for the first of these offences.

In their modern published form the judicial statistics distinguish summary trials in magistrates' courts from trials on indictment before juries at the Crown Court (formerly 'Assizes and Quarter Sessions'). Within each category they distinguish certain age-groups, so that, for example, separate tables deal with persons tried in juvenile courts. The statistics for magistrates' courts also subdivide offences into three main groups: indictable (that is, liable in certain circumstances to be tried at higher courts, with the possibility of more severe penalties), non-indictable (that is, triable only by summary courts) and motoring (all but the most serious of these being non-indictable). The centuries-old distinction between 'felonies' and 'misdemeanours' is obsolete, and was replaced in 1967 by the distinction between offences for which suspects may or may not be arrested without a warrant: a distinction not reflected in most of the published statistics.

Table 15.1 shows the numbers of persons dealt with in higher and summary courts in selected years of this century, together with the percentages who were found guilty (unfortunately the statistics do not make it possible to subdivide these into persons who pleaded guilty and persons who pleaded not guilty). It also shows the numbers of those found guilty who were sentenced in the various ways open to the courts.

Table 15.1   Judicial statistics for selected years, 1900–1980, England and Wales
(i) Assizes[1] and Quarter Sessions: all ages

| | No. for trial | | | | Sentences as percentage of those found guilty | | | | | | | |
Year	Total	Male	Female	Nos found guilty[2,15]	Death[12]	Custodial measures[3]	Probation	Fine	Community service order	Nominal penalties[4]	Suspended prison sentences	Otherwise dealt with[5]
1900	10 149	8 928	1 219	7 975	0.3	90.5	–	1.1	–	8.1	–	2(n)
1910	13 680	12 522	1 157	11 337	0.2	83.6	5.2	0.6	–	10.2	–	0.2
1920	9 130	8 141	989	7 225	0.5	76.5	8.1	0.8	–	13.4	–	0.7
1930	8 384	7 781	601	6 921	0.2	71.4	11.3	1.6	–	15.0	–	0.5
1950	18 935	17 990	945	17 149	0.2	62.6	17.2	6.6	–	13.2	–	0.2
1960	30 591	29 462	1 129	27 830	8.0[14]	53.8	22.5	13.8	–	9.3	–	0.6
1970[18]	44 134	41 691	2 443	37 519	–	53.2	12.0	13.7	–	4.6	14.9	1.6
1980[18]	73 830	66 348	7 482	73 256	–	50.5	6.4	12.4	6.5	4.3	16.3	3.6

(ii) *Summary Courts: indictable offences: adults*[6,7]

Year	Nos proceeded against			Nos found guilty or charge proved[2,15]	Sentences as a percentage of those found guilty							
	Total	Male	Female		Custodial measures[3]	Suspended prison sentences	Probation	Fine	Whipping[11]	Community service	Nominal penalties[4]	Otherwise dealt with[5]
1900	43 789[8]	Not distinguished		30 736	47.1	–	14.0	26.7	9.0	–	2.9	0.3
1910	40 434			36 094	47.5	–	11.3	22.1	0.2	–	18.1	0.8
1920	37 107			32 942	31.7	–	11.3	38.6	0.1	–	17.3	1.0
1930	43 464			38 709	25.6	–	21.1	28.3	1.0[14]	–	23.4	1.6
1950	61 701	49 980	11 721	57 102	18.5	–	11.9	48.8	–	–	16.7	4.1
1960	84 527	70 103	14 424	79 538	13.4	–	12.5	56.1	–	–	13.7	4.3
1970[18]	227 072	191 786	35 286	201 017	8.2	9.9	9.5	60.1	–	–	8.1	4.2
1980[18]	311 607	254 592	57 015	306 183	7.0	6.3	8.4	58.3	–	4.8	11.0	4.2

(iii) *Summary Courts[9]: indictable offences: juveniles*

Year	Nos proceeded against			Nos found guilty or charge proved[2,15]	Sentences as a percentage of those found guilty							
	Total	Male	Female		Custodial measures[3]	Probation	Fine	Whipping[11]	Nominal penalties[4]	Fit person order[16]	Attendance centre[13]	Otherwise dealt with[5]
1910	12 275	Not distinguished		10 786	16.1	25.7	7.8	14.4	35.7	–	–	0.3
1920	14 380			12 919	10.9	31.3	17.2	9.9	30.1	–	–	0.6
1930	12 198			11 137	10.0	55.3	3.8	1.2	29.3	–	–	0.4
1950	43 823	40 434	3 389	41 910	10.6	40.8	16.3	–	30.0	1.4	–	0.9
1960	58 350	53 253	5 097	56 114	8.4	33.6	19.3	–	32.0	1.6	4.1	0.6
1970	63 531	56 833	6 698	71 860	8.4	24.8	32.0	–	23.5	2.1	8.2	1.0
1980	98 082	87 506	10 576	89 192	5.1	18.1	32.1	–	21.1	9.2	13.7	0.7

(iv) *Summary Courts: non-indictable offences other than highway offences[10]: adults[6,7]*

Year	Nos proceeded against			Nos found guilty or charge proved[2,15]	Sentences as a percentage of those found guilty						
	Total	Male	Female		Custodial measures[3]	Probation	Fine	Nominal penalties[4]	Suspended prison sentences	Community service	Otherwise dealt with[5]
1900	672 989[8]	Not		557 489	9.5	0.1	86.8	1.4	–	–	2.2
1910	551 395	distin-		483 111	12.9	0.4	77.1	9.2	–	–	0.4
1920	427 556	guished		374 565	4.0	0.5	87.1	8.2	–	–	0.2
1930	317 231			287 691	4.1	0.7	81.5	13.1	–	–	0.6
1950	220 188	181 458	38 730	202 286	3.0	1.0	86.7	9.1	–	–	0.2
1960	247 133	221 703	25 430	232 992	2.5	0.9	90.1	6.2	–	–	0.3
1970	394 540	350 415	44 125	357 043	1.6	1.2	90.7	5.1	1.2	–	0.2
1980	467 825	399 294	68 531	432 368	0.8	1.0	90.5	5.5	0.8	0.5	0.9

(v) *Summary Courts[9]: non-indictable offences other than highway offences[10]: juveniles*

Year	Nos proceeded against			Nos found guilty or charge proved[2,15]	Sentences as a percentage of those found guilty						
	Total	Male	Female		Custodial measures[3]	Probation[17]	Fine	Nominal penalties[4]	Fit person order[16]	Attendance centre[13]	Otherwise dealt with[5]
1910	18 059	Not		14 694	3.9	5.3	51.6	38.9	–	–	0.3
1920	16 953	distin-		14 956	1.6	4.3	67.4	26.4	–	–	0.3
1930	8 842	guished		7 577	1.2	11.4	38.2	49.0	1.0[14]	–	0.2
1950	19 810	18 868	942	18 410	0.9	6.4	56.9	35.4	13.0[14]	–	0.4
1960	28 025	26 521	1 504	26 337	0.8	4.8	67.8	24.3	0.1	0.7	1.5
1970	25 184	23 234	1 950	22 102	1.8	8.8	65.2	20.3	0.6	3.0	0.3
1980	26 561	24 415	2 146	23 408	0.8	6.3	62.8	23.6	0.9	5.3	0.3

Source: Criminal Statistics, England and Wales.

622

Source: Criminal Statistics, England and Wales.

Notes:

1. Including the Central Criminal Court (the Old Bailey). By 1970 Assizes, Quarter Sessions and the Central Criminal Court had been combined into what is called 'The Crown Court', but consists of higher courts in a larger number of cities, presided over by judges of varying status, with juries.

2. Excluding persons found guilty but insane or (after 1964) not guilty by reason of insanity, persons found unfit for trial and, in the case of summary courts, persons committed for trial by higher courts.

3. Including imprisonment, penal servitude (abolished in 1948), preventive detention and corrective training (replaced in 1967 by extended sentences), committal to an industrial school or reformatory (replaced in 1933 by approved schools), remand homes (abolished in 1963), borstals and detention centres.

4. Includes absolute and conditional discharges, recognisances and bind-overs.

5. Includes cases not finally disposed of, committals to institutions for the mentally disordered (for which see Table 15.3) and other miscellaneous and numerically unimportant disposals.

6. Until 1932 persons aged 16 were tried as adults, although in some cases sent to institutions for juveniles.

7. Includes a few juveniles tried jointly with adults, for example, as their accomplices.

8. The published tables for 1900 do not distinguish juveniles from adults, although one table shows that those found guilty included 9450 persons under 16. Most of the 3218 persons whipped in 1900 were probably boys.

9. From 1908 these were in effect 'juvenile courts', although lacking in features which were introduced later (such as the exclusion of the public).

10. For which see Table 15.2.

11. Abolished by statute in 1948, but by then very infrequently used.

12. The death penalty was confined in practice to murder throughout this period (except for wartime executions for treason and espionage). 'Infanticides' (see the text) were exempt from the death penalty from 1922, and from 1957 to 1965 certain categories of murder were 'non-capital'. The death penalty for all kinds of murder was suspended in 1965, and the suspension was made permanent in 1969. Even when it was in force some murderers' death sentences were commuted to imprisonment or detention in institutions for the mentally disordered.

13. Attendance centres (and detention centres) were introduced by the Criminal Justice Act 1948, although it was several years before the first was opened.

14. These are not percentages but numbers too small for conversion.

15. Not all of these were sentenced in the same year.

16. Now 'care order'.

17. From 1970 probation for children under 14 took the form of 'supervision orders', the supervision being the responsibility of social workers.

18. Between 1960 and 1980 summary courts were empowered to deal with several kinds of indictable offence which had higherto been triable only by higher courts.

INDICTABLE OFFENCES

Most of the indictable offences tried, whether by higher or by summary courts, are acquisitive offences of one sort or another, ranging from minor thefts to large-scale robberies or frauds. A substantial number of the minor thefts which reach the courts are by juveniles, especially boys in their mid-teens (girls nowadays show much the same peak age, although the peak itself is much lower).

Less numerous, but causing more concern, are offences involving personal violence, sexual molestation or both. The peak age for personal violence seems to be the late teens and early twenties, at least so far as official statistics are concerned: but a great deal of schoolboy violence is unreported. Sexual molesters are more widely distributed in age.

It is important to realise that over the last hundred years there has been a tendency to 'demote' whole categories of offences which used to be triable on indictment at higher courts so that they could be tried summarily by magistrates. The chief reason has been the increasing demands on the time of the higher courts. The result of such demotions is that the great majority of indictable offences – that is, those which could be tried at higher courts if the accused or prosecution so requested or the magistrates thought fit – are now tried summarily; and in most of these cases the accused pleads guilty. The research worker who is following trends in judicial statistics must be on the alert for administrative changes of this sort. For example, the number of shopbreaking cases dealt with by higher courts fell from 8848 in 1962 to 2803 in 1963; but in magistrates' courts the corresponding number rose from 5805 to 12 460: all that had happened was that the Criminal Justice Administration Act, 1962, had made it possible for most shopbreaking cases to be tried summarily.

NON-INDICTABLE OFFENCES

These are very miscellaneous. Some are acquisitive or dishonest: for example, the evasion of revenue payments, or travelling on public transport without buying a ticket. Others are merely disorderly: minor assaults which do not involve injuries, obstructing pavements by street trading, being drunk and 'incapable' or drunk and 'disorderly' in a public place. Others consist of behaviour which offends people's sensibilities, such as soliciting (or in the case of men 'importuning'). Others – sometimes called 'regulatory' – are breaches of laws, by-laws or regulations designed to protect the public against dishonest trading, dangers to health or damage to the environment. So far as adults are concerned, the numbers of successful prosecutions of non-indictable offences outnumbers those of indictable ones; but because most defendants in such cases plead guilty they take up less of the summary courts' time.

TRAFFIC OFFENCES

Table 15.1 does not deal with traffic offences, which are the subject of Table 15.2. The striking growth in their numbers after the passing of the Motor Cars Act 1903 emphasises the extent to which, as Barbara Wootton once put it, 'the internal combustion engine has revolutionised the business of our criminal courts'. No attempt has ever been made to estimate the annual number of infringements of traffic laws and regulations which take place. The most that can be done is to count the number of prosecutions, the number of fixed penalties imposed without prosecution, and the number of written warnings issued instead of prosecution. Even so, it is only since 1952 that figures for written warnings have been published.

Table 15.2   Offences involving motor vehicles, 1900–1980, England and Wales

Year	Convictions		Written warnings	Fixed penalties
1900	562[1]		No	See
1910	11 048[2]	(15 522)	figures	text,
1920	62 663[2]	(27 083)	published	page
1930	170 963[2]	(26 037)	until 1952	[922]
1952	375 329[3]		170 025[3]	
1960	765 365[3]		245 105[3]	
1970	1 419 670[3]		238 172[3]	1 519 076[3]
1980	2 238 000[4]		304 000[4]	3 622 000[4]

Source: Criminal Statistics, England and Wales.

Notes:
1. Although the Locomotives Act 1896 placed restrictions on the use of 'light locomotives' on the highways (including a speed limit of 14 mph) it was the Motor Cars Act 1903 which introduced the twentieth-century system of control, with licences for drivers and new offences of driving recklessly, negligently and dangerously. The Criminal Statistics for 1900 shows only 562 offences by 'locomotives', without stating their nature.
2. These seem to be offences by motor vehicles in the modern sense. Also shown (in brackets in this table) are offences of obstructing the highways, an increasing number of which were probably what would nowadays be called 'parking offences'.
3. The source for these figures is the Home Office's post-war series of *Offences relating to Motor Vehicles*, which for the first time showed figures for written warnings (the equivalent of cautions for other types of offences), as well as more detailed subdivisions of offences leading to convictions. Later the series showed figures for fixed penalties.
4. The series *Offences relating to Motor Vehicles* has by now been replaced by special issues in the series of *Home Office Statistical Bulletins*, from which these figures are taken.

It was the sheer volume of prosecutions, threatening to swamp the time of the summary courts, which led to the procedure for pleading guilty by post in the 1950s, and in the 1960s to the system of fixed penalties, which are in effect administrative fines, although it is possible to elect for an appearance in court instead of paying the fixed penalty, with the risk of being fined a larger sum by the magistrates. In 1961 the system was introduced to deal with illegal parking in London, and later to deal with the same problem in other cities, as well as other minor violations of traffic regulations. Country-wide statistics of its use were first published in 1970. In 1986 the system was extended to somewhat more serious offences, such as infringements of speed-limits. Eventually it seems likely to be extended to a number of non-indictable offences unconnected with traffic, in order to ease the burden on summary courts. During the 1970s and early 1980s the enforcement of fixed penalty payments presented a considerable problem, and in some areas many offenders refused to pay with virtual impunity; but arrangements for enforcement were improved in 1986, with results that cannot yet be assessed.

More important is the fact that deaths and serious injuries from traffic accidents now far exceed the numbers of intentional homicides and serious woundings which appear in Table 15.8 as indictable offences. For serious traffic offences – such as drunken driving – disqualification is now obligatory; but courts are allowed to refrain from this step for 'special reasons', and only about 1 in 3 disqualifications lasts for more than 12 months.

TRENDS IN SENTENCING

Table 15.1 distinguishes five main types of 'sentence' (although some are strictly speaking not 'sentences'). Capital punishment apart (and now abolished in practice), the main ones are custodial, financial, supervisory and 'nominal', and will be discussed in that order.

Custodial

These consist for the most part of sentences to prison, whether under that name or in special forms such as 'penal servitude', 'preventive detention', 'corrective training' or 'extended sentences'. They also include borstal training – now 'youth custody' – and detention centre orders, as well as committals to industrial or reformatory schools, or remand homes, for teenagers. 'Approved schools' replaced industrial and reformatory schools in the 1930s, but were replaced in turn by 'community homes' in the 1960s.

So far as adult offenders are concerned, the decline in the percentages receiving custodial sentences has been very marked: from 90 per cent to 50 per cent, although at 50 per cent the judiciary seem to feel that the lower limit has been reached. Considerations which prompted a more sparing use of custody were the low crime rates of the early decades of the century, greater awareness of the ill-effects of incarceration on prisoners and their dependants, a decline in optimism about the corrective and deterrent effects of prison sentences, the increasing reputation of the probation service, the possibility of fining (permissible for most offences from 1948), and, most recently, the increasingly overcrowded state of the prisons.

PRISON STATISTICS

Table 15.3 shows that while the daily average population of women's prisons or wings has been almost halved since 1901, the male population has almost trebled, in spite of the decline in the percentages sentenced to prison. The rise in the male population began even during the 1939–45 war, and has continued inexorably since, notwithstanding expedients such as the introduction of suspended sentences and parole in 1967. It has forced the Treasury – for long resistant to proposals for modernising prison buildings – to agree to a large-scale programme for enlarging the capacity of the system. The judges are under pressure from pressure groups to reduce the length of sentences (which they have done for the less serious types of crime) and to make even more use of non-custodial alternatives.

In fact most of the inmates of prisons have been put there by summary courts, either on remand without bail or under the short sentences of 6 months or less which magistrates are allowed to pass. Magistrates too have reduced their 'incarceration rate' for indictable offences from 47 to 20 per cent and for non-indictable offences from 9 to 1 per cent.

Juvenile courts have had less scope for reduction, since their incarceration rates in 1900 were only 16 and 4 per cent for the two groups of offences. Even so, they have been slower to reduce. Belief in the remedial effects of juvenile institutions lasted longer than optimism about the impact of imprisonment; and it was not until the 1960s that the downward trend became marked.

Non-custodial measures

The most favoured alternative to custody so far as summary courts are concerned has always been the fine, and its popularity with magistrates has grown from 27 to 60 per cent for indictable offences. (It has always been over 85 per cent for non-indictable offences.) There are signs that a ceiling has been reached: high unemployment rates have encouraged courts to use other measures in recent years, although many unemployed offenders are still fined small amounts. Higher courts did not have the power to use fines for most of the crimes they tried until 1948; but since then their percentage has climbed from 2 to 12. As for traffic offenders, 99 per cent are fined, although many of them are also disqualified – for short periods.

Table 15.3   Prison sentences and populations in selected years, 1901–1980, England and Wales

Year	Prisoners received under sentence[1]	Daily average prison population[2]		
		Male	Female	Total
1901	149 397	14 459	2 976	17 435
1910	179 951	19 333	2 685	22 018
1914	136 424	15 752	2 484	18 236
1916	58 839	9 244	2 067	16 311
1919	26 050	7 595	1 604	9 199
1920	35 439	8 279	1 404	9 683
1930	38 832	10 561	785	11 346
1938	31 993	10 388	698	11 086
1940	24 870	8 443	934	9 377
1943	32 490	11 430	1 360	12 790
1946	29 998	14 556	1 233	15 789
1948	36 802	18 621	1 144	19 765
1950	33 875	19 367	1 107	20 474
1960	42 810	26 198	901	27 099
1965	56 315	29 580	841	30 421
1970	44 250	38 040	988	39 028
1980	75 896	42 180	1 580	43 760

Notes:
1. This column's figures exclude persons sentenced by courts martial, received under sentence of death (whether or not commuted to imprisonment) or recalled to prison for breach of a licence. They include sentences of penal servitude (abolished in 1948), corrective training and preventive detention (replaced in 1967 by the extended sentence), borstal training (replaced in 1982 by youth custody) and (from 1952) detention centre orders. Persons imprisoned for defaulting in the payment of fines are also included; but not remanded or civil prisoners.
2. That is, the daily average population of all inmates (whether sentenced or not) of prisons, borstals, detention centres and remand centres.

Sources: The annual *Reports of the Prison Commissioners* for England and Wales (from 1963 the Prison Department), or, since 1970, the separately published *Prison Statistics, England and Wales*.

A fine, however, can be no more than a deterrent. Hopes of improving offenders' characters encouraged the use of probation and similar supervisory measures for children. Summary courts had been able to use probation since 1876: higher courts were enabled to do so in 1908. Its use increased markedly after 1920, with the growth in the numbers of probation officers amd the 'professionalisation' of the service (see Table 15.10). Probation has never been much used for traffic or other non-indictable offences, but has been popular for first and even second or third convictions for indictable offences of the less serious kind. Research findings since the late 1950s cast considerable doubt on its effectiveness, but it was the introduction of new non-custodial alternatives rather than research which reduced the percentages.

The first of these alternatives was the suspended prison sentence, made possible by the Criminal Justice Act 1967. Although intended as a substitute for prison sentences of two years or less, it seems to have had more impact on the use of probation, especially in the higher courts, and its contribution to the reduction of the prison population was minimal. A striking feature of this innovation was the decision not to extend it to custodial measures for the young. Detention centres, borstals, and later youth custody centres, were still regarded as more beneficial than prisons, so that it seemed inappropriate to suspend such measures.

The next important innovation, in 1972, was the community service order, which assigned adult offenders to useful unpaid work organised by the probation service. Again this was intended as a substitute for a prison sentence, but seems to have been used as much as an alternative to probation (or in summary courts the suspended sentence). Juveniles were not eligible, but by the 1970s could be placed under a form of supervision by social workers which included periods of 'intermediate treatment'; and this sometimes consisted of interesting or useful activities.

Nominal disposals

Both higher and lower courts have for long had the power to deal with most kinds of offence by 'binding over' the offender, with or without the threat of forfeiture of a sum of money (in effect a suspended fine). As an alternative they may use a 'conditional discharge', of which the only condition is that a further conviction within one, two or three years, as the case may be, will lead to a sentence for the original offence. In cases in which the offender seems only technically guilty, or most unlikely to repeat a trivial offence, he may even receive an 'absolute discharge' with no conditions of any kind, and no liability to a retrospective sentence if he does reoffend. As can be seen from Table 15.1, these were common ways of dealing with juveniles in the early part of the century, but became less popular with juvenile courts as other more attractive alternatives came on offer. Where adults are concerned, however, they were increasingly used until the 1950s, after which courts seem to have resorted more often to fines, and later suspended sentences.

'Otherwise dealt with'

The measures grouped under this head are so miscellaneous and numerically unimportant that there is little that need be said about them. An exception is what can be called '*psychiatric disposals*', to which Table 15.4 is devoted. Although the numbers involved are not large, they demonstrate the efforts of hospitals and courts to deal humanely with a chronic problem, the stage army of the mentally disordered which marches through the criminal courts and into the wings of the hospital services only to reappear again a few months or years later. In the nineteenth century the handful of disordered offenders who were found insane or unfit for trial were committed by higher courts to asylums for long periods: those who were convicted went to the gallows or the prisons. In summary cases the justices could use their civil powers to commit them to asylums. It was not until the Mental Deficiency Act of 1913 that both higher and lower courts were given wider powers of committal, at first limited to what would now be called the 'mentally impaired', later extended to the mentally ill and psychopathic. In 1948 courts were also given the power to make 'psychiatric probation orders', which required the offender to undergo in-patient or out-patient treatment of a psychiatric nature for a limited period,

Table 15.4   Psychiatric disposals[1] by criminal courts in England and Wales, 1914–80

Year	Hospital or guardianship[2] orders	Psychiatric probation orders	
		Residential	*Non-residential*
1914	30[3]	—	—
1920	183[3]	—	—
1930	283[3]	—	—
1950	351[4]	314	393
1960	457	549	376
1970	1 294	515	779
1980	635	314	1 270

Notes:
1. For an explanation see the text.
2. Guardianship orders (which place the offender under the care of a local authority or – in rare cases – a private person) are so uncommon in criminal cases that they can be included without distorting the figures.
3. These were orders under the Mental Deficiency Acts 1913 and 1927.
4. These were orders under the Criminal Justice Act 1948 or the Mental Deficiency Acts 1913 and 1927.

Sources: *Criminal Statistics, England and Wales*, and the Home Office's series of *Probation and After-Care Statistics*.

but as a voluntary patient who could absent himself if he wished (and was willing to take the small risk of being resentenced). As Table 15.4 shows, the use of what are now 'hospital orders' increased steadily until the 1970s. They were being overtaken, however, by psychiatric probation orders, which more and more psychiatrists (and offenders) preferred, because they disliked the element of compulsory detention involved in hospital orders. Another reason for the decline in numbers of hospital orders was the unwillingness of nurses to cope with the more obstreperous, violent and manipulative members of the stage army. Hospitals could, and increasingly did, refuse to accept hospital order cases from courts.

POLICE CAUTIONS

It is particularly important to be aware of the practice known as the 'police caution' or 'warning' (not to be confused with the 'caution' as regards one's right not to make a statement, which the police are required to give to suspects). Until 1986 the decision to initiate a prosecution for most kinds of offence lay with the police; and even the creation of the Crown Prosecution Service in 1986 has not deprived them of the right to decide not to initiate a prosecution, although now it is sometimes the Crown Prosecutor who decides not to proceed.

Decisions to caution offenders are – in theory at least – confined to cases in which the evidence justifies a prosecution, and the offender admits guilt, but prosecution does not seem to be required by 'the public interest'. Minor traffic offences are a common example, although the extension of the 'fixed penalty' procedure seems likely to provide an alternative for many such cases. Children in their early teens, especially girls, are likely to be cautioned instead of being brought to court. Cautions are also used, though more sparingly, for indictable adult offenders who are elderly, or physically or mentally ill, or whose offence, if prosecuted, seems likely to lead only to a 'nominal' disposal.

Figures of police cautions for indictable and non-indictable offences have been published since 1954. As Table 15.5 shows, the numbers have grown steadily from that date so far as indictable offences are concerned. For non-indictable offences, however, the numbers decreased after 1960 but rose again after 1970 to more or less the level of 1960. The explanation is not clear. Some non-indictable offences were prosecuted, not by police, but by other agencies, such as local authorities; but most of these did not report cautions to the Home Office. It is possible that tougher fining policies of courts encouraged police to prosecute for offences for which they would previously have cautioned: it was observable that courts' sentencing policies affected cautioning rates for indictable offences. But so far as non-indictable offences are concerned only speculation is possible.

Table 15.5   Police cautions 1954–80, England and Wales

| Year | Indictable offences | | | | Non-indictable offences | | | |
| | Juveniles | | Adults | | Juveniles | | Adults | |
	M	F	M	F	M	F	M	F
1954	6 672	885	2 023	987	12 425	851	33 608	7 024
1960	15 841	2 548	4 013	1 470	15 517	1 071	21 607	9 636
1970	36 133	8 353	7 387	3 813	8 313	679	14 350	6 424[1]
1980	63 600[1]	21 900[1]	9 800[1]	5 700[1]	17 000[1]	1 900[1]	16 800[1]	9 200[1]

Note:
  1. The published figures are approximated to the nearest 100.

Source: *Criminal Statistics, England and Wales.*

The increasing use of cautions instead of prosecutions for juveniles has not been without critics. One allegation has been that it allows police to 'discriminate' in favour of children whose parents appear respectable, concerned and likely to take their own steps to improve their offspring's conduct, while prosecuting children from less co-operative families. Others argue that this is a rational consideration. Another criticism is that increased cautioning has led to 'net-widening': that is, to official action in cases which previously would have been dealt with by an unofficial telling-off on the spot. A file is opened on the juvenile, and the caution can be mentioned if he or she is later found guilty of another offence by a court. Defenders of cautions argue that it is desirable that courts should be informed of earlier offences, however unimportant.

CLEAR-UP RATES

Since 1918 the annual Criminal Statistics have also shown the numbers of recorded standard list offences which are 'cleared up'. 'Clearing up' usually means 'tracing and arresting (or summoning) the offender' (even if he is in the end acquitted); but it includes other eventualities: an offence is also counted as 'cleared up' if at least one of the perpetrators is identified and then cautioned, or dies, or enters a mental hospital, or cannot be prosecuted for technical reasons, such as the death or recalcitrance of an essential witness (see *Home Office Instructions for the Preparation of Statistics Relating to Crime*, obtainable by research workers from the Statistical Department). The clear-up percentage varies greatly from one type of crime to another. For murder and other serious crimes against the person it is high, partly because police take great trouble over such crimes, partly because the perpetrators are usually close acquaintances of their victims, and are easily identified either by the victims themselves or by their families. Many murderers who have killed spouses, lovers or children either commit suicide, or give themselves up to the police. For minor thefts, on the other hand, the percentage is much lower, partly because the police can spare less time for them, partly because the offences themselves are easy to commit without much risk of detection.

For some kinds of offence the clear-up rates are spuriously high. One example is the dishonest handling of stolen goods, which are usually found only in circumstances which clearly point to the handler. Shoplifting is another example of an offence which is more or less 'cleared up' as soon as it is observed, whereas thefts by staffs of shops are not.

In recent years clear-up rates for burglaries and other forms of theft have become suspect for other reasons. Since they tend to be used as measures of the efficiency of detective officers, there is a temptation to do what is possible to improve the rates on paper. Offenders who have pleaded or been found guilty are allowed to ask the court, when deciding on the proper sentence, to 'take into consideration' offences with which they have not been charged. Since the effect is a small increase in the severity of the sentence, but also a bar on later prosecution for the offence 'taken into consideration', offenders often take advantage of this procedure. Some later claim to have 't.i.c.ed' offences which they have not committed, at the urging of detectives: and there is evidence that the practice is not unheard of. Prisoners serving sentences can also be induced to sign admissions of offences if promised that they will not be prosecuted.

Table 15.6   Clear-up rates for each of the main classes of offences shown for selected years, 1951–80, England and Wales

Class of offence	Crimes cleared up as a percentage of the total recorded in each class						
	1951	*1955*	*1958*	*1961*	*1965*	*1970*	*1980*[1]
OFFENCES AGAINST THE PERSON:							
1. Violence against the person	90.2	90.6	89.2	88.1	84.7	82.2	77
2. Sexual offences	79.9	82.6	81.4	81.7	75.8	76.2	74
OFFENCES AGAINST PROPERTY:							
3. Breaking and entering offences	39.9	38.9	39.3	38.9	33.3	35.0	31
4. Robbery	46.8	52.5	46.6	39.3	36.9	42.0	29
5. Thefts and frauds	44.7	46.1	42.7	42.0	37.1	43.7	[2]
6. Receiving	99.1	99.7	99.5	99.6	99.4	99.9	[2]
7. Malicious damage	69.6	63.5	60.0	56.5	44.2	46.2	[2]

Notes:
1. *Criminal Statistics, England and Wales,* make it clear that these percentages are not strictly comparable with those for earlier years, because of changes in the rules for counting offences. In any case the validity of clear-up rates for many offence-groups is questionable, as the text explains.
2. The 1980 statistics combine different offence-groups from those used by earlier published statistics.

Sources: Based on data obtained from relevant volumes of *Criminal Statistics, England and Wales*; and a table in McClintock and Avison (1968) (see Bibliography).

Consequently, the clear-up rates shown in Table 15.6 should be taken with a large pinch of salt, especially when they show improvement over earlier rates. In any case, the adoption of new 'counting rules' in 1980 meant that the rates for that year are not comparable with earlier percentages. With these reservations, the general trend seems to be downwards. Neither improvements in techniques nor increases in detective manpower seem to have an effect worth mentioning on the probability that an offender will be identified, let alone convicted.

CONVICTION-RATES

Since the same person may be convicted[4] on more than one occasion in the same year, the published annual figures for convictions do not accurately reflect the numbers of individuals involved. A Home Office study,[5] however, of three birth cohorts – for 1953, 1958 and 1963 – has made it possible to compare the young males of the 1950s with those of the 1960s. The comparison is slightly vitiated by two factors. The 1953 cohort became eligible for prosecution at age eight, whereas the two later cohorts did not until age ten. Secondly, the policy of cautioning juvenile offenders – especially on first detection – had become more popular by the time the later cohorts entered their teens. Nevertheless, the comparison of the cohorts in Table 15.7 is interesting. It does not suggest that the later cohorts included larger numbers of standard list offenders.[6] By age 28, however, about 30 per cent of the 1953 cohort had been convicted of a standard list offence at least once, and the percentages for the later cohorts seemed to be marching in step with the earlier

Table 15.7 Conviction-rates[1] for standard list[2] offences by males in the 1953, 1958 and 1963 birth cohorts
(percentages)

| Convictions | Cohorts born in | | |
	1953	1958	1963
Convicted[3] at least once before the 18th birthday (females in brackets)	16.6	17.0	15.9
	(2.6)	(2.9)	(3.1)
Convicted more than once before the 18th birthday (% for females not published)	6.6	7.0	6.2
Males reconvicted[4] within a year of first conviction at age			
10	20	26	29
11	19	28	29
12	22	24	29
13	23	25	27
14	22	25	23
15	18	27	21
16	24	21	21
17	17	18	24

Source: *Home Office Statistical Bulletin* No. 7/85: 'Criminal Careers of those Born in 1953, 1958 and 1963'.

Notes:
1. These are estimates based on a sample of about 8 per cent of each cohort.
2. That is, indictable offences, plus a few other kinds regarded as fairly serious.
3. Strictly speaking, juveniles are not 'convicted' in summary courts: merely 'found guilty'.
4. Of standard list offences – see Note 2.

one. High as the percentages are, it was only a small minority of each cohort – those with six or more convictions – which accounted for 70 per cent of *all* the cohort's standard list convictions.

A difference which does appear in Table 15.7 concerns reconvictions. After a first conviction, members of the later cohorts were more likely to be reconvicted than members of the first cohort.[7] Table 15.7 shows only percentages reconvicted within a year, because only the younger members of the 1963 cohort could be followed up much longer; but the difference was still observable when members of the 1953 and 1958 cohorts were followed up for as long as eight years. A possible explanation is that more members of the later cohorts had been dealt with by cautions for their first offences, so that those convicted were a more persistently delinquent selection. Another possibility is that courts' methods of dealing with offenders from the later cohorts were less effective (or less effectively chosen). A third is simply that juveniles were becoming less corrigible.

CRIMINAL STATISTICS

To be carefully distinguished from the judicial and prison statistics are figures of 'crimes made known to the police', which were first included in the annual volumes for 1857. These are subject to several limitations, some of them inevitable:

(a) They are confined to offences which are regarded as sufficiently important to warrant the work involved in reporting them to the Home Office: these are referred to as 'Standard List Offences'.

(b) Even where standard list offences are concerned they show only what local police forces record and report as 'made known to' them. Thus a member of the public may report that his dog has been stolen, but unless there is evidence to support this the police may, quite reasonably, treat it as a 'lost dog' case and not as a reported crime. In the early 1930s it was found that the Metropolitan Police were recording large numbers of reported thefts merely as 'lost property', and when this was corrected the statistics for recorded thefts rose sharply. More important, until recently the same police force did not record reports of rape – even when they believed them – unless the victim was willing to testify in court.

(c) The police cannot, of course, be expected to record offences which do not come to their notice.

This last difficulty is the major limitation of all criminal statistics, and means that they reflect what actually occurs in a very distorted fashion. (It is not, of course, confined to criminal statistics, but vitiates most other attempts to record social facts, such as mental illness.) The 'dark figure' – that is, the unreported percentage – varies from one sort of crime to another. The reasons why a crime may not be reported are numerous:

1. All those involved may fail to realise that an offence has been committed. Children commit assaults and indecencies without being aware of their criminality.
2. All those involved may be willing participants. This is especially frequent in the case of abortions, homosexual offences, incest and carnal knowledge of girls under 16.
3. Even an unwilling victim may not wish to involve the offender in the consequences of prosecution. This happens not only with sexual offences such as indecent assaults, but also in minor cases of pilfering, embezzlement, or fraud.
4. The victim may himself be antagonistic to the police. Many assaults in certain districts of large cities are not reported because this would be regarded as handing the aggressor over to a common enemy.
5. The victim may regard the offence as too trivial to be worth the trouble of reporting. Many minor thefts are not reported for this reason.
6. The victim may be so pessimistic about the chances of bringing the offender to book that he does not bother to report the offence. This is more likely with minor offences.
7. The victim may be too embarrassed to report the offence. Women – especially the very young – are often inhibited in this way from reporting indecent exposure. Men may keep silent about homosexual importuning in case they are suspected of attracting such advances. Parents of child victims of sexual offences may wish to spare the child the experience of interrogation and appearance in court.
8. The offence may be observed only by someone who disapproves of the law. Poaching is often unreported for this reason.
9. The victim or observer may be intimidated by the offender's threats of violence or by blackmail. Prostitutes' thefts from clients are seldom brought to the notice of the police.
10. The offence may be unknown to anyone but the offender, as must often happen in the case of speeding motorists.

Thanks to the British Crime Surveys of 1982 and 1984, we now know that by far the commonest reason for non-reporting by victims is the triviality of the offence in their eyes. Next in frequency is the belief that the police could do nothing about it, or would not be sufficiently interested to do anything. Next is the view that the offence is not an appropriate matter for police action, and that the victim himself or herself can deal with it. Fear or dislike of the police were reasons offered in a small but not quite negligible number of cases. Fear of reprisals was the least common. The 1983 survey in particular found a very wide difference in the percentages of different sorts of offence which the victims claimed to have reported. For thefts of cars the percentage was 99, and for burglaries 87, for robberies 57. At the other end of the scale the rates for minor damage to cars was only 9 per cent., and for minor sexual offences 10 per cent. Even for major damage to cars (costing more than £20) it was only 30 per cent. For most other kinds of offence the rates were between 30 and 55 per cent.

One of the reasons for the high reporting rates for car thefts and burglaries is almost certainly the terms of insurance policies, which require the offence to be reported to the police if a claim is to be met. Although there are no statistics from which the spread of insurance cover amongst car-owners and house-holders can be followed, it must be a factor which has pushed up the reporting-rates for crimes against property.

With these very important reservations, trends in some kinds of indictable offence are shown in Table 15.8. Most of them have been included because they are of a kind that cause concern; but thefts have been added because they constitute the most numerous group of recorded acquisitive dishonesty. They have almost quadrupled since the turn of the century. Part of the explanation must be the increase in the population; but at least as important must be the increase in affluence. More cash and portable goods are there to be stolen. More cars are standing unattended in the open. More shops have more goods on display on self-service counters.

The enormous increases, however, in robberies and burglaries of homes must point to another factor. Many thefts occur in situations which simply present the opportunistic thief with an opportunity; but robbery and burglary call for more decisive behaviour. The gains are likely to be greater, but so are the risks and the required know-how, even when the robber or burglar – as so often – is a teenager. The crucial question is to what extent the striking growth in this industry is attributable to an increase in the work force – that is, to the involvement of a larger percentage of men and boys – and to what extent it is simply due to greater 'productivity'; that is, to an increase in the average numbers of robberies or burglaries committed by the same individual. The limited findings of the Home Office study of three birth cohorts (discussed in the section on 'Conviction-rates') suggests that increased productivity has made the greater contribution. But this must be a very tentative inference, since those findings were based solely on the convictions of identified offenders.

The steep rise in thefts and burglaries seems to have begun in the 1920s. Robberies, which involve violence or the threat of it, began to multiply during or after the 1939–45 war. Roughly the same seems true of woundings which did not result in deaths. The rise in homicides started much later, as can be seen in Table 15.8. It used to be said, indeed, that in this country homicide differed from other crimes by remaining at the same level; but this has turned out to be too optimistic. Indeed the rise would probably have been a little steeper if it had not been for the increasing skill of doctors, police and

Table 15.8   Recorded numbers of selected types of crime, 1900–1980

Year	Murders, manslaughters, or infanticides[1]	Woundings	Robberies[2]	Burglaries of dwellings[3]	Rapes[2]	Indecent assaults on women or girls[2]	Thefts (excluding robberies and burglaries)
1900	312	1 212	256	3 812	231	727	63 604
1910	291	1 294	198	6 499	146	1 115	76 044
1920	313	791	235	6 863	130	1 372	77 417
1930	300	1 443	217	11 169	89	1 871	110 159
1950	315	5 177	1 021	29 834	314	6 678	334 222
1960	282[1]	14 142	2 014	46 591	515	9 663	537 003
1970	393[1]	38 735	6 273	190 597	884	12 609	952 666
1980	620[1]	95 044	15 006	294 375	1 225	11 498	1 463 469

Source: Criminal Statistics, England and Wales.

Notes:
1. Until 1956 the manslaughters included an unknown number of cases in which death had been caused by the dangerous or reckless driving of a vehicle. In 1956 this was distinguished by law as the offence of 'causing death by dangerous driving', because juries were so unwilling to convict of 'manslaughter' in such cases. In 1960 the recorded number of such homicides was 470, in 1970, 685, but in 1980 only 101. The fluctuations suggest that there have been changes in the policy of charging people with this offence.
2. Not including those involving a homicide, which were recorded as murder.
3. Including the offence of breaking and entering a dwelling by day, which was distinguished from 'burglary' (doing so at night), until the Theft Act 1968 amalgamated them.

ambulance-men in saving lives. Often all that differentiates a wounding from a homicide is the thickness of a blood-vessel or the availability of a blood transfusion. Homicide in Britain is usually committed with a knife or a 'blunt instrument'; only about one in ten killings are by shooting, and the percentage has not increased appreciably in recent years. The reappearance of terrorism – not an entirely new phenomenon even in this country – has contributed only an annual 1 per cent. to the homicide rate.

POLICE MANPOWER STATISTICS

The relationship between policing and crime-rates is a complex subject. The simplest fact is that on the rare occasions on which a police force has been put out of action (as it was, for instance, in Denmark for part of the 1939–45 war, and in cities elsewhere as a result of police strikes) the rates of crimes such as robberies and burglaries have risen, but not the rates of crimes such as frauds and embezzlement (which tend to be traceable to perpetrators without police help). On the other hand mere changes in the sizes of police forces do not seem to have any clear effect on the clear-up rates of any sort of crime. It has to be remembered that dealing with crime is only one of the responsibilities of police forces: coping with traffic and preventing disorder – whether at public gatherings or picket lines – are functions which they are also expected to perform. (The provision of security against robbery, commercial burglaries and industrial pilfering is something usually done by special security staff, such as Transport Police or private security firms; and these employ at least as many men as all the country's police forces).

Nevertheless, it is interesting to study the increase in man- and woman-power of the English and Welsh police forces in this century. By far the best source is the book by Martin and Wilson from which the figures in Table 15.9 have been taken: figures which it has unfortunately not been possible to bring up to date. They show that, while the numbers of men and women employed by police forces more than doubled between 1900 and 1965 (if civilians as well as officers are included) the increase in man-hours actually worked – from some 114 000 to 173 000 per annum – is much less impressive. Moreover, the estimated number of man-hours worked per 1000 of the population by police officers has not increased since 1911: only if civilians hours are included has there been any real increment. No doubt the use of motor-cycles, cars, helicopters, radios, and other mechanical aids, has meant that the time of police is now more effectively used than when police patrolled on foot or bicycle and used whistles to communicate. Most crimes, however, are cleared up – in the genuine sense – not by man-power or man-hours but by information from the public.

Table 15.9   Police service man-hours,[1] 1901–65, England and Wales

Year (1)	Total no. of police officers (2)	No. of police officers (adjusted for sickness) (3)	Hours worked by police officers		Total no. of civilians (6)	No. of civilians (adjusted for sickness) (7)	Hours worked by police service (including civilians)	
			000s (4)	per 1000 population (5)			000s (8)	per 1000 population (9)
1901	43 463	42 138	114 278	3 513	—	—	(as in col. 4)	(as in col. 5)
1911	51 203	50 000	135 200	3 748	—	—	,,	,,
1921	60 709	58 693	140 863	3 718	—	—	,,	,,
1931	60 492	58 577	140 585	3 519	—	—	,,	,,
1938	63 800	62 098	149 035	3 595	—	—	,,	,,
1949	60 418	57 763	133 086	3 040	4 774	4 645	142 934	3 264
1951	62 629	59 690	137 526	3 144	6 023	5 860	149 949	3 428
1961	75 798	73 367	169 038	3 669	12 515	12 177	194 853	4 229
1965	84 425	81 503	163 658	3 426	19 093	18 577	197 394	4 133
(Adjusted for regular overtime in 1965)								
1965	84 425	81 503	173 438	3 631	19 093	18 577	207 174	4 337

Notes:
1. Man-hours in this table include hours worked by women.

Source: Adapted by permission from J. P. Martin and G. Wilson (1969) *Police: a Study of Manpower* (Heinemann). The figures cannot therefore be up-dated.

Table 15.10   The manpower of the probation and after-care service in selected years
1911–198-, England and Wales

Year	Men	Women	Total
1911	730	279	1009

Source: The first *Register of Probation Officers* published by the Home Office.
Probably more than three-quarters of the officers were part-time. The
Register also lists 1002 petty sessional divisions, of which 268 had appointed
no officer.

Year	Men	Women	Total
1923	527	309	836

Source: The Home Office *Register* for 1923 (the series became annual in 1919), which
says that 'about one fourth' were whole-time, and about 650 were paid. 259
were employees of Missions or Societies (155 by the Church of England
Temperance Society, 29 by the Salvation Army, 22 by the Church Army, 19
by Discharged Prisoners Aid Societies, and 11 by the National Society for the
Prevention of Cruelty to Children). There were 1029 petty sessional divisions,
excluding Metropolitan Police and Juvenile Courts: but 189 had not
appointed officers.

Year	Men	Women	Total
1930	480	289	769

Source: The Home Office *Directory of Probation Officers, Probation Hostels and
Homes and Borstal Institutions*, which had replaced the annual Register. Of
the total of 769 officers, 501 were part-time; of the 268 whole-time officers, 82
were women: 226 of the officers were employees of Missions or Societies, in
much the same proportions as in 1923.

Year	Men	Women	Total
1938	612	392	1004

Source: The Home Office's annual *Directory* (see note for 1930), which says that 585
of the 1004 were part-time officers, and that 104 of the full-time officers were
women, but gives no information about the numbers of paid officers or of
those employed by Missions or Societies. By this date there were 1023 petty
sessional divisions, 611 of which were combined into 44 areas, the rest being
independent.

Year	Men	Women	Total
1950	656	350	1006
1955	801	412	1213
1960	1135	498	1633
1965	1687	632	2319

Source: The Home Office report *The Work of the Probation and After-Care Service, 1962–1965*, Cmnd 3107, supplemented by Home Office figures for 1968. By the end of 1965 the process of combining petty sessional divisions had reduced the total of probation areas to 84, of which 5 covered Greater London, and 54 others were combined areas, most of them covering whole counties with all the urban areas in them. In 1968 there were only 57 part-time officers, and by the end of that year 72 per cent of all officers had received a formal professional training in probation.

Year	Men	Women	Total
1970	2447	979	3426
1975	3229	1640	4869
1980	3539	2056	5595

Source: The Home Office series of *Probation and After-Care Statistics*. The numbers do not include the increasing, and nowadays substantial, numbers of ancillary, clerical and other staff employed to assist probation officers. By 1980 the number of probation departments had been reduced by further amalgamations to 56. ('After-Care' was dropped from their titles in 1982).

THE PROBATION SERVICE

A service whose manpower and womanpower has grown remarkably in this century is the Probation Service. Beginning as a small body of Church 'missionaries' in the courts of nineteenth-century London, it has grown into a secular profession of more than 5600 men and women, nearly all with a professional training, organised into 56 local departments, some small but some of more than 100 officers.

The service is responsible not only for the supervision of offenders aged 14 or older whom the courts put on probation (children under that age are nowadays supervised by social workers), but also for providing community service schemes, day centres, welfare officers in prisons, and the supervision of prisoners who are released on licence. It even provides a matrimonial conciliation service for the divorce courts. One of its most important functions, however, has been the provision of 'social inquiry reports' on offenders, to help courts in deciding what to do with them. Some of these responsibilities – such as the submission of social inquiry reports – were acquired in the inter-war years, but prison welfare and the after-care of ex-prisoners were not added until the 1960s. These developments necessitated the manpower increases which can be seen in Table 15.10. (The apparent decline in the 1920s was due to the substitution of full-time for part-time officers). What the table does not show is the increasing numbers of clerical and ancillary staff employed to assist probation officers, for example in operating community service schemes: these now total more than 3000.

Notes

1. That is, the Perks Committee (1967, Cmnd 3448), which was concerned with England and Wales, and the Thompson Committee (1968, Cmnd 3705), which was concerned with Scotland.
2. Scotland did not raise the minimum age, but in 1968 introduced a system whereby most offenders under 16 are dealt with by a 'children's hearing' instead of a criminal court.
3. Separate and roughly equivalent statistics for Scotland are published by the Scottish Home and Health Department. The statistics for England and Wales do not include Northern Ireland, the Isle of Man or the Channel Islands.
4. Strictly speaking, juveniles are not 'convicted' by summary courts, merely 'found guilty'. But 'conviction' is a convenient term, and only technically incorrect.
5. See *Home Office Statistical Bulletin* no. 7/85.
6. The standard list includes all indictable offences, plus a few others regarded as fairly serious.
7. The exception seems to be those first convicted at age 16; but this may well be due to chance in the 8 per cent samples ($p =$ roughly 0.1).

Selective Bibliography

The main sources of periodical criminal judicial and penal statistics (which unless otherwise indicated are compiled annually) are:

A   Published by HM Stationery Office:

The Criminal Statistics for England and Wales (which include judicial statistics for criminal but not civil courts, and statistics for care, protection and control proceedings, criminal appeals, hospital and guardianship orders and the use of the royal prerogative of mercy) (from 1857).

Reports of the Prison Commissioners (or, from 1963, Prison Department of the Home Office. From 1962 the main statistical tables have been published in a separate volume).

Reports of the Parole Board (from 1968).

Offences of Drunkenness (excluding those involving vehicles) (from 1950) now included in the *Home Office Statistical Bulletins* (q.v.).

Offences relating to Motor vehicles (from 1928) now included in the *Home Office Statistical Bulletins* (q.v.).

Statistics relating to Approved Schools, Remand Homes and Attendance Centres in England and Wales (from 1962).

Reports on the Work of the Children's Department (of the Home Office) (nine were published, at irregular intervals, from 1923).

Reports on the Work of the Probation and After-Care Department (of the Home Office) 1962–5, and 1966–8.

Home Office Studies in the Causes of Delinquency and the Treatment of Offenders (at irregular intervals).

Home Office Studies in the Causes of Delinquency and the Treatment of Offenders (for example, *Murder* (1961) by E. Gibson and S. Klein): from 1969 this series continued under the title *Home Office Research Studies* (for example, No. 3 *Murder 1957 to 1968* by E. Gibson and S. Klein).

Home Office Statistical Bulletins (from 1979, at irregular intervals). These provide annual statistics on a number of special aspects of the criminal justice system, devoting a separate bulletin to each (examples are offences relating to motor vehicles, to prohibited drugs and to drunkenness). Other bulletins, at more irregular intervals, provide non-routine statistics on other topics.

Reports of HM Inspectors of Constabulary (from 1945).

B   Other main sources (including local sources):

Reports of the Metropolitan Police Commissioners (HMSO, from 1869).

Reports of local Chief Constables.

Reports of local Probation Committees.

HOUGH, M and MAYHEW, P. (1983) *The British Crime Survey* (Home Office Research Study No. 76: HMSO).

HOUGH, M. and MAYHEW, P. (1985) *Taking Account of Crime: findings from the 1984 British Crime Survey*, Home Office Research Study, no. 85 (HMSO).

McCLINTOCK, F. E. *et al.* (1961) *Robbery in London* (Macmillan).

McCLINTOCK, F. E. *et al* (1963) *Crimes of Violence* (Macmillan).

McCLINTOCK, F. E. (1968) *Crime in England and Wales* (Heinemann).

MARTIN, J. P. and WILSON, G. (1969) *Police: a Study of Manpower* (Heinemann).

ROSE, G. (1960) *The Struggle for Penal Reform* (Stevens) Appendix 1.

WALKER, M. A. (1981) *Crime*: vol. xv in the series *Reviews of United Kingdom Statistical Sources* (Pergamon). This is a guide to sources, not a collection of statistics.

Index

Gross National Product (GNP), 8
  definition of, 135–7, 145, 147
  and social security, 501
Grundy, E., 38
Guttman scaling, 211
Guttsman, W., 316, 317, 319

Hackney, 344–5
Hajnal, J., 70
Hakim, C., 166, 173
Halsey, A. H., xxv, 229, 260
Harrison, A., 142
Hart, J. T., 446
Hart, N., 421
Haskey, J., 75, 81, 129
Hatton, T. J., 86
Hauser, R. M., 205, 218
health, 398–461
  expenditure, 12
  Resource Allocation Working Party (RAWP), 446
health visiting, 477, 500
Heath, A., 202, 213, 219, 229, 260, 314
Hell, R. F., 431
higher education
  binary system, 271
  growth 1900–1963, 269–71
  since 1963, 271–4
Hilton, J., 175
Himsworth, H., 421
Hines, A. G., 175
Hiorns, R. W. 39
Hirst, F. W., 356
Hobcraft, J., 47
Hogben, L., 44
Hole, W. V., 117
holidays, 9, 17
Holmans, A. E., 49, 129
Holmes, M., 141n
Holterman, S., 396
homosexual offenders, 617
Hope, K., 202
Hough, M., 643
hours of work, 9, 177–8
household structure, 116–22
housing
  building rates, 378–85
  costs, 146, 361–2, 389–95
  density of occupation, 364–8
  homelessness, 471
  overcrowding, 12, 364
  owner occupation and tenure, 12, 376–8
  polarisation, 31
  sources on, 357–62
  stock, 157, 362
  structural condition, 368–76
  subsidies, 12, 389
Hunt, A., 166n

Hyman, R., 197

illegitimate births, 19, 56, 62–9
immigration, 11, 102–3, 561–70
  control legislation, 99, 567–9
  and fertility, 56, 95–9
  and mobility, 219
  race relations legislation, 569
income
  definition of National Income, 135–7
  distribution, 8, 28–9, 139–41, 147
  earnings, 3–11, 15, 17
  real disposable, 16–17
Indians
  see Asians
industrial disputes, 193–7
inner city, 11, 32–3, 114, 340–5
  deprivation, 341–5, 386–9
Irish
  age and family structure, 574–5
  immigration to Britain, 570–4
  socio-economic status, 575–6
  sources on, 611
Italians, 598–600
  sources on, 613–14

Jews, 15, 97, 601–3
  sources on, 614
Jones, C., 101
Jones, P. R., 103, 417
Joshi, H., 86
journey to work, 335–7
Jowell, R., 314

Kalton, G., 229
Kay, J., 128
Kelsall, R. K., 229
Kemsley, W. F. F., 141n
Kerr, C., 218
Keynes, J. M., 44
Keynes, M., 430
Kiernan, K. E., 71, 81, 93, 122
Kilroy, B., 397
Kinnear, M., 300
Klein, Y., 166n
Kollman, W., 105
Konig, W., 218
Kruskal, J. B., 211
Kunzel, R., 83

labour force
  occupational composition, 162–5
  participation rates, 167–73
  sex composition, 165–7
Langford, C. M., 57
Laslett, P., 117
Leach, E., 5
Leathard, A., 39